Exploring Careers

- A major career information source for young people

- Revised edition

- 14 major occupational clusters

- Descriptions of over 300 jobs

- Career exploration activities and worksheets

- Separate instructor's guide

Exploring Careers

Revised Edition

Exploring Careers
A Young Person's Guide to Over 300 Jobs

Revised by the editors of JIST Works, Inc.
Based on content provided by the U.S. Department of Labor, Bulletin 2001.
© 1990, by JIST Works, Inc.

Published by JIST Works, Inc.
720 N. Park Avenue
Indianapolis, IN 46202-3490
Phone: 317-264-3720 Fax: 317-264-3709 E-mail: jistworks@aol.com
World Wide Web Address: http://www.jist.com

RELATED MATERIALS FROM THE PUBLISHER:

1. *Exploring Careers, Instructor's Guide*—Over 120 pages including suggested class activities, handouts, discussion questions, projects, and more. It provides enough material for an entire career exploration course or program.

2. *The World of Work and You*—Extra copies of the consumable section of *Exploring Careers*, pages W1 to W32, are available in booklet form.

Contact the publisher for additional information on these materials or for quantity discounts. A free catalog of nearly 500 carefully selected books, videos and software is also available to qualified organizations. Quantity discounts are available.

SEE THE ORDER FORM ON THE LAST PAGE OF THIS BOOK!

Printed in the United States of America

02 01 00 99 98 97   9 8 7

Library of Congress Cataloging-in-Publication Data
Exploring careers. — Rev ed.
     p.   cm.
  ISBN 0-942784-27-8 : $19.95
    1. Vocational guidance—United States. 2. Occupations.
  I. JIST Works, Inc.
  HF5382.5.U5E86   1990   89-19881
331.7'02—dc20   CIP

We have been careful to provide accurate information throughout this book, but it is possible that errors and omissions have been introduced. Please consider this in making any career plans or other important decisions. Trust your own judgment above all else and in all things.

ISBN 1-942784-27-8

How to Use This Book

This book was created to help young people learn about themselves and to explores career alternatives.

The best place to begin is by reading the table of contents. It gives a brief description of the major sections including a listing of the 14 occupational clusters that are covered in this book.

Once you have an overview of the book, the best place for most people to begin is by reading the section titled *The World of Work and You*. This begins on page W1, and its objective is to help you learn more about yourself and which careers most loosely match your needs and interests. This section contains many interesting checklists and activities to help you identify your values, skills, preferred working conditions, willingness to get additional training, school subjects you enjoyed, and other factors. All of this information is then used to help you identify one or more occupational clusters for further exploration. If you already have an idea of the sort of career that interests you, this section will give you even more information to use in career planning.

Once you identify one or more of the career clusters that seem to fit you best, use the table of contents to find the cluster's section in *Exploring Careers*. You can then find specific information about the many jobs available in that cluster in the *Job Facts* section. Or, you can read about how various workers spend a typical day.

We hope that the information in this book is helpful to you in learning about various careers and in making plans for your future. ***Good luck!***

The Editors at JIST

Table of Contents

The World of Work and You

This specially written section will help you understand more about your interests, skills, life-style preferences and other things to be considered in career planning.

The Occupational Clusters

Details are provided on over 300 jobs, organized into 14 occupational clusters. Each cluster includes stories about people in representative jobs. There are also descriptions of all the major jobs within each cluster (listed under *"Job Facts"*) that include information on training, advancement opportunities, working conditions, and many other details.

The World of Work and You

The first step towards a successful career is to have a solid educational foundation.

Who Cares?

You may be thinking, "It's going to be a long time before I have to go to work. Why do I have to spend so much time thinking about jobs now?"

Well, your job will likely be one of your most important life activities. Many years will be spent in one job or another, or in the training you need for a job. So much time will be demanded by your job that the rest of your life may revolve around it—much the way your life revolves around school now. The kind of job you have will affect how much time you have for other activities, the types of people you meet, the friends you make, and the kind of life-style you can afford.

The amount of time you will spend working is a good reason to give careful thought to your career. A person who works full time for 40 years, averaging 40 hours a week for 50 weeks a year, will spend 80,000 hours of his or her life at work. Compare that with the 17,000 hours you will have spent in school by the time you graduate from high school!

How should you go about finding the career that is right for you? The key is YOU: your interests, abilities, and goals. You have a better chance of making a satisfying career choice if you find a match between the things that you like and want to do and the things that a job requires.

That is what career exploration is all about: finding the jobs that give you an opportunity to be happy and successful—and identifying those that don't suit you so that you can avoid them. And that's where *The World of Work and You* comes in. This book will help you think about yourself and the things that are important to you. It will also help you learn how to explore careers that might suit you.

The World of Work and You

Who Am I?

Exploring careers means exploring yourself. It means looking at yourself and identifying your talents, your strengths, and your weaknesses. It means asking yourself some questions:

- What am I really like?
- What am I good at?
- What do I want to do with my life?

To get started, write your answers to the questions that follow in the space provided.

Things I Like To Do	**I'd Describe Myself As:**
Things I'm Good At:	**Other People Describe Me As:**

Exploring careers means finding out as much as you can about different types of work. Exploring careers also means thinking about what is important to you and how you want to live. What kinds of things are vital? What kinds of things would you like to have but could live without? Make a list below of some of the things that are important to you. List at least five things in the spaces below—more if you can think of them.

Things That Are Important to Me

1. _____
2. _____
3. _____
4. _____
5. _____
6. _____
7. _____
8. _____
9. _____
10. _____

 Exploring Careers—Student Guide

Exploring Careers

Sometimes it's not possible to have everything. We have to give up something in order to have something else. We have to compromise. Suppose that you couldn't have all of the things on your list. Which would you be willing to give up? From your list select the three things that are MOST important to you.

1. _____

2. _____

3. _____

You have just prioritized your list! The items that you listed above are your top priorities—the things that are most important to you. The other things on your list are the ones that would be nice to have but aren't as important. As you explore careers, you will prioritize a lot of factors. This will help you find careers that offer the best chance for meeting most of your needs.

These boys are learning the ability to socialize during play. Getting along with others is important in the workplace.

Work Satisfaction Factors

For many people, work is a way to earn a living and nothing more. There's nothing wrong with that. But there are other satisfactions that come from working. Let's examine some of the more important ones.

Other People

The company of other people might seem like an odd reason to choose a job. But stop to think about all the things that school life means. At school you make friends and meet new people. You learn new ideas and new ways of doing things. You socialize. To many people, these things are just as important as what they learn in a classroom.

Work is a lot like that. The people you spend your work day with can be an important part of your life. You will learn from them and socialize with them on the job; you may often socialize with them after work as well. Some of your coworkers may become close friends. Others may try your patience and test your ability to get along with people who are different from you.

Contact with other people is one of the things to think about when you start exploring careers. How important is it to you to do things with other people? Do you like group projects, or do you prefer to do things by yourself? Are you at ease with other people? Are you a leader? Do you enjoy helping others?

You will find questions like these at the end of each chapter in *Exploring Careers*. The questions are meant to help you consider how well you match certain kinds of jobs.

The World of Work and You

A Sense of Satisfaction

Another reason people work is to get a sense of satisfaction. Can you guess what a carpenter has in common with a jeweler, machinist, or chef? All of them create something you can see, touch, or taste. Many people get satisfaction and a sense of pride from using their hands and working with things. As you examine your own interests and abilities, try to think about how important that is to you.

Many people want to put their efforts into something that helps others or promotes the common good. Police officers, teachers, public health officials, and wildlife conservation officers are just a few of the people who work to make society better.

Other people look for ways to express themselves creatively. Some of them may find a place in the world of music, theater, art, dance, fashion, or writing. These careers can be glamorous for a few people, insecure for many. Some people feel such a strong need to express their creative nature that they are willing to sacrifice stability and financial security.

Work Environment

Some people like to work outdoors or look for jobs that let them be physically active all day. Construction workers, loggers, dockworkers, miners, and foundry workers all have jobs that require endurance and stamina. They take pride in being able to withstand the physical demands of their jobs.

Others prefer to work inside in an office or store. Still others prefer jobs where they get to travel, enjoy nature, or work with plants or animals.

There are all sorts of work environments, and your willingness to work in one over another is an important factor in selecting a job.

An office located downtown has a different work environment than an office located in a rural area.

Recognition and Self-Esteem

Self-esteem is another important reason why people work. Exactly what does that mean? Let's look at your school experiences for a comparison. You know the feeling you get when a team you're on beats a rival. The recognition and acclaim give you a lift. It makes you proud of winning and glad you worked so hard.

It's much the same in a job. If you're good at what you do, and other people respect and appreciate your work, you'll probably feel good about yourself. That's because your job and the way you handle it is tied up with your view of yourself as a person. It can make you feel terrific if you believe that your job is worthwhile and that you do it well.

Maybe you can't imagine a job being that important to you. Well, you're not alone. Many people look elsewhere for the feeling that their lives are worthwhile. They find those feelings in their families or friends, hobbies or leisure activities, or involvement in civic affairs. Your job can count a lot—or just a little—in your own view of yourself.

 Exploring Careers—Student Guide

Exploring Careers

Think about your own preferences. Which of the reasons just mentioned above seem important to you?

_____

_____

_____

_____

_____

Can you think of other reasons for working?

_____

_____

_____

_____

The career you choose can influence what you like to do during leisure time.

Keep these reasons in mind as you explore careers and consider which ones could meet your goals. For example, you may have decided that creativity, independence, and a flexible schedule are important. What kind of situation might this describe? One where you could become lost in a project without worrying about a strict schedule? One where you would make things from beginning to end in your own way, not according to someone else's instructions? Can you think of any careers that might match this description? You may find some as you read about workers who tell their stories in _Exploring Careers_.

Your Values

The career you choose will probably affect many parts of your life. It may influence the type of home you live in, the interests and hobbies you pursue, even your political attitudes.

But it works both ways. Your personal values influence your career decision. When you choose a career, you are making decisions about the types of people you would like to associate with, the amount of leisure time you want, and the importance of money. These decisions depend on your personal values.

The work values exercise that follows will help you clarify your feelings about work.

The World of Work and You

Work Values Exercise[1]

Directions: This activity presents 33 common "satisfactions" that people get from their jobs. Begin by reading the entire list. Think about how important each of these things are to you. Then go over the list again and rate each item, using the scale below.

1 = Not important at all
2 = Not very important
3 = Important
4 = Very important

1. ____ *Help society:* Contribute to the betterment of the world I live in.

2. ____ *Help others:* Help other people directly, either individually or in small groups.

3. ____ *Public contact:* Have a lot of day-to-day contact with people.

4. ____ *Work with others:* Have close working relationships with a group; work as a team toward common goals.

5. ____ *Affiliation:* Be recognized as a member of an organizaiton whose type of work or status is important to me.

6. ____ *Friendship:* Develop close personal relationships with the people I work with.

7. ____ *Competition:* Pit my abilities against others where there are clear outcomes.

8. ____ *Make decisions:* Have the power to set policy and determine a course of action.

9. ____ *Work under pressure:* Work in a situation where deadlines and high quality work are required by my supervisor.

10. ____ *Power and authority:* Control other people's work activities.

11. ____ *Influence people:* Be in a position to change other people's attitudes and opinions.

12. ____ *Work alone:* Do things by myself, without much contact with others.

13. ____ *Knowledge:* Seek knowledge, truth, and understanding.

14. ____ *Intellectual status:* Be regarded by others as a person of intellectual achievement or an expert.

15. ____ *Artistic creativity:* Do creative work in any of several art forms.

16. ____ *Creativity (general):* Create new ideas, programs, organizational structures, or anything else that has not been developed by others.

17. ____ *Aesthetics:* Have a job that involves sensitivity to beauty.

18. ____ *Supervision:* Have a job in which I guide other people in their work.

19. ____ *Change and variety:* Have job duties that often change or are done in different settings.

20. ____ *Precision work:* Do work that allows little tolerance for error.

21. ____ *Stability:* Have job duties that are largely predictable and not likely to change over a long period of time.

22. ____ *Security:* Be assured of keeping my job and a reasonable financial reward.

23. ____ *Fast pace:* Work quickly; keep up with a fast pace.

24. ____ *Recognition:* Be recognized for the quality of my work in some visible or public way.

25. ____ *Excitement:* Do work that is very exciting or that often is exciting.

26. ____ *Adventure:* Do work that requires me to take risks.

27. ____ *Profit, gain:* Expect to earn large amounts of money or other material possessions.

28. ____ *Independence:* Decide for myself what kind of work I'll do and how I'll go about it; not have to do what others tell me to.

[1] This excercise was developed by Howard E. Figler, Director of Career Services of the University of Texas, Austin. It originally appeared in PATH: A career Workbook for Liberal Arts Students, published by The Carroll Press.

Exploring Careers—Student Guide

29. _____ *Moral fulfillment:* Feel that my work is contributing to a set of moral standards that I feel are very important.

30. _____ *Location:* Find a place to live (town, geographic area) that matches my lifestyle and allows me to do the things I enjoy most.

31. _____ *Community:* Live in a town or city where I can get involved in community affairs.

32. _____ *Physical challenge:* Have a job whose physical demands are challenging and rewarding.

33. _____ *Time freedom:* Handle my job according to my own time schedule; no specific working hours required.

Location and lifestyle are factors in a career choice.

Others

_____

_____

_____

_____

_____

_____

_____

Look over the list you have just completed. Add any other values that were not included on the list. Then select the values that are most important to you, and list them in order of importance beginning with your most important value in the space provided below.

1. _____

2. _____

3. _____

4. _____

5. _____

6. _____

7. _____

These are the values that you should consider when selecting a career and when making other decisions about your life. The book *Exploring Careers* will help you identify various jobs that support these values.

The World of Work and You

The hobbies you have can give clues about jobs you could be good at.

Personal Characteristics

Suppose that the ability to motivate people is one of your strong points. Perhaps you're a class officer. Or you may be good at selling things. Maybe you're one of the people who ends up in charge of a group project. Or perhaps you're able to get everyone in a group or team to do their fair share of the work. These abilities mean that you would probably be good at a job that involves persuading, instructing, leading, or directing. Some possibilities are:

- Advertising worker
- Supervisor
- Bank officer
- Insurance agent
- Health services administrator
- Counselor

- Police officer
- Coach
- Lawyer
- Automobile sales worker
- Teacher

You might be handy with tools. Perhaps you enjoy gardening. Maybe you recently built a bookcase or repaired an old car. Perhaps you're working on a needlepoint project right now or fixing a bike. Many occupations require this kind of talent. You might want to explore jobs that require working with tools, such as:

- Auto mechanic
- Carpenter
- Surveyor
- Jeweler
- Dental laboratory technician

- Machinist
- Machine operator
- Business machine operator
- Drafter

Exploring Careers—Student Guide

Job Characteristics

There are many jobs that you might do well in. One way to find the best ones for you is to compare job characteristics to the characteristics that you want.

The following is a list of 19 characteristics. Read each one carefully. As you do, think about whether you would like to include that characteristic in a job. If so, put a check next to that characteristic.

1. _____ *Problem-solving ability*—the ability to identify a problem and then to decide what should be done to correct it. Auto mechanics, who spend much of their time fixing cars, need problem-solving ability.

2. _____ *Uses tools, machinery*—takes a talent for working with your hands. Often, knowing how machines work is necessary, too. Tool-and-die makers, who use machine tools and precision measuring instruments to produce other tools and metal forms, need skill in this area.

3. _____ *Instructs others*—the quality of helping others learn how to do or understand something. Receptionists and hotel clerks help others in this way.

4. _____ *Repetitious*—work in which the same thing is done over and over again. An assembler who works on a production line does repetitious work.

5. _____ *Hazardous*—involves the use of dangerous equipment or materials or work in dangerous surroundings. Elevator constructors, who work at great heights, have hazardous jobs.

6. _____ *Outdoors*—refers to occupations in which a major portion of time is spent outdoors, frequently without regard to weather conditions. Roofers, who apply roofing materials to the tops of buildings, work outdoors.

7. _____ *Physical stamina required*—able to lift heavy weights, walk along distances, stand for long periods, or stoop frequently. Bricklayers, police officers, and chefs all need physical stamina.

8. _____ *Generally confined*—workers have to stay in one place most of the time. Truckdrivers who sit behind the wheel for many hours and statistical clerks who do their work at a desk for most of the day are examples.

9. _____ *Precision*—work involves high standards of accuracy. Accountants, air traffic controllers, and machinists are examples.

10. _____ *Works with detail*—refers to technical data, numbers, or written materials. Machinists who consult blueprints or written specifications before making each machined product and programmers who write instructions for the computer are examples.

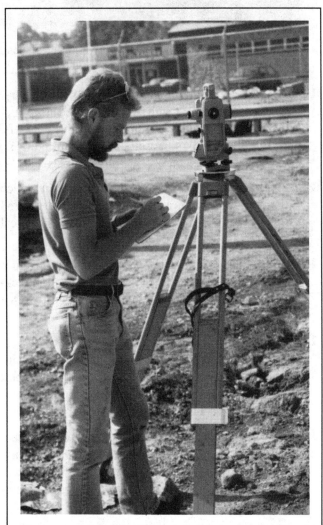

There are many job characteristics to consider if you want to be a surveyor.

The World of Work and You

Each job has its own unique set of job characteristics.

11. _____ *Frequent public contact*—work involves day-to-day contact with people who need information or service. Automobile service advisers, receptionists, hotel clerks, bank tellers, waiters, and barbers are all examples.

12. _____ *Part time*—refers to occupations in which many workers are employed for fewer than 35 hours a week. Waiters and waitresses and real estate agents are examples.

13. _____ *Able to see results*—refers to jobs that produce an actual product or accomplishment. Bricklayers, chefs, and choreographers all see results.

14. _____ *Creativity*—work involves new ideas, programs, designs, or products. Writers, industrial designers, and engineers are examples of the many different kinds of workers whose jobs require creativity.

15. _____ *Influence others*—the ability to stimulate others to think or act in a certain way. Automobile sales workers who influence customers to buy and teachers who inspire students to learn are examples.

16. _____ *Competition on the job*—refers to occupations in which competition with co-workers for recognition or advancement is an integral part of the job. College teachers who compete for tenure, securities sales workers who compete for assignments are all examples.

17. _____ *Works as part of a team*—refers to occupations in which cooperation with co-workers is an integral part of the job. Instrument makers, who work closely with scientists and engineers to translate designs into models, and school counselors, who work closely with other staff members, are examples.

18. _____ *Jobs widely scattered*—occupations that are found in most parts of the country. Occupations that do not have a dot in this space tend to be highly concentrated in one or a few geographic locations. For example, secretaries work throughout the country while petroleum engineers work mostly in the oil-producing states of Texas, Oklahoma, Louisiana, and California.

19. _____ *Initiative*—jobs that demand the ability to determine on one's own what should be done, as well as the motivation to do it without close supervision. Lawyers and newspaper reporters need initiative.

©1990, JIST Works, Inc., Indianapolis, Indiana
Exploring Careers—Student Guide

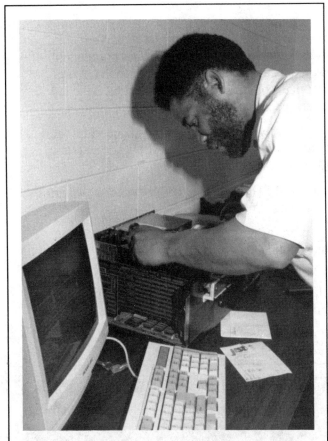

Some jobs require continuous education in order to keep up with advances in technology.

Make a list of at least three characteristics that you would like to include in your career. List as many as you want.

_____   _____

_____   _____

_____   _____

_____   _____

_____   _____

_____   _____

_____   _____

_____   _____

Now select the three characteristics from your list that are most important to you and that you would like to include in your career.

1. _____   _____

2. _____   _____

3. _____   _____

The Job Matching Chart

On pages W12 to W20 is a list of over 200 jobs. These are the most popular jobs in this country and about 80 percent of all people work in one of them.

On this chart, the world of work has been divided into 14 clusters of occupations. Each cluster lists several occupations. The 19 characteristics you just reviewed are listed across the top of the chart. This will help you identify the jobs that best match your needs.

Later, you can obtain more information for each job in *Exploring Careers*. All the occupations on the chart are described in the Job Facts section at the end of each chapter of *Exploring Careers*. The occupations with a check mark in front of them are "featured" in *Exploring Careers*. Featured occupations have a longer story about a typical worker; they also have questions to help you relate to that occupation. Your teacher can provide additional activities to explore these occupations further.

Volunteer work in your areas of interest is a good way to explore different careers.

The World of Work and You

Directions for Using the Job Matching Chart

Step 1: First, look over the chart beginning on page W13 to see how it is organized. The work characteristics you just learned about are listed across the top of the chart. Various occupations are listed in the left column. When one of the work characteristics is likely to be found or used in an occupation, the chart has a dot in the appropriate column. Notice also that jobs in the left column are listed under major occupational clusters listed in capital letters.

Step 2: Once you are familiar with how the Job Matching Chart works, go through it and underline one or more occupational clusters that seem particularly interesting to you. Also underline any specific jobs within these clusters that you are interested in.

Step 3: Review the top three job values from your list on page W7. Return to the Job Matching Chart and circle your top three job characteristics on each page of the chart.

Carefully review each job that requires one or more of the characteristics that you circled. Underline the jobs that you find of particular interest. If a job is already underlined, put a circle around it.

Although this will take some time, it will help you find some jobs that you may not have considered. And one of them just might be the job you really want!

Step 4: When you have completed steps 1, 2, and 3, turn to page W21 and continue reading.

A tool and dye maker has to be imaginative and creative as well as mechanically minded in order to bring a designer's blueprints to life.

 Exploring Careers—Student Guide

Exploring Careers

The Job Matching Chart

	Problem-solving ability	Uses tools, machinery	Instructs others	Repetitious	Hazardous	Outdoors	Physical stamina required	Generally confined	Precision	Works with detail	Frequent public contact	Part time	Able to see results	Creativity	Influences others	Competition on the job	Works as part of a team	Jobs widely scattered	Initiative
	1	2	3	4	5	6	7	8	9	10	11	12	13	14	15	16	17	18	19
INDUSTRIAL PRODUCTION OCCUPATIONS																			
Foundry occupations																			
Patternmarkers		•					•	•	•				•					•	
Molders		•		•	•		•	•					•					•	
Coremakers		•		•			•	•		•			•					•	
Machining occupations																			
√ All-round machinists	•	•			•		•	•	•				•					•	
Instrument makers (mechanical)	•	•						•	•	•			•	•			•		•
Machine tool operators	•	•		•	•		•	•	•				•					•	
Setup workers (machine tools)	•	•			•		•	•	•				•					•	
Tool-and-die makers	•	•					•	•	•				•					•	
Printing occupations																			
√ Compositors		•						•	•				•					•	
Lithographers		•						•	•				•	•				•	
Photoengravers		•						•	•				•					•	
Electrotypers and stereotypers		•			•		•	•					•					•	
Printing press operators		•		•	•		•	•					•						
Bookbinders and bindery workers		•		•	•		•	•											
Other industrial production and related occupations																			
√ Assemblers		•		•				•									•		
Automobile painters		•						•										•	
Blacksmiths		•		•	•		•				•	•	•					•	
Blue-collar worker supervisors	•		•							•					•		•	•	•
Boilermaking occupations	•	•		•	•		•						•					•	
Boiler tenders		•			•		•											•	
Electroplaters		•		•	•			•	•				•					•	
Forge shop occupations		•		•	•		•	•					•	•				•	
Furniture upholsterers		•		•			•	•					•					•	
Inspectors (manufacturing)	•	•		•				•	•	•			•					•	
Millwrights	•	•			•		•	•	•				•					•	
Motion picture projectionists		•		•				•						•				•	
Ophthalmic laboratory technicians		•		•				•										•	
Photographic laboratory occupations		•		•				•										•	
Power truck operators		•		•	•	•	•	•										•	
Production painters		•		•	•		•	•					•					•	
Stationary engineers	•	•			•		•											•	
Wastewater treatment plant operators		•				•	•		•	•								•	
Welders		•		•	•		•	•					•					•	
OFFICE OCCUPATIONS																			
Clerical occupations																			
Bookkeeping workers				•				•	•	•		•	•				•	•	
Cashiers				•				•	•	•	•	•				•		•	
Collection workers				•				•		•	•					•	•	•	•
File clerks				•						•	•						•	•	
Office machine operators	•			•			•	•	•	•							•	•	
Postal clerks		•		•			•		•	•							•	•	
Receptionists			•	•				•	•	•	•	•					•	•	
Secretaries and stenographers				•				•	•	•	•		•				•	•	

The World of Work and You

The Job Matching Chart

	Problem-solving ability	Uses tools, machinery	Instructs others	Repetitious	Hazardous	Outdoors	Physical stamina required	Generally confined	Precision	Works with detail	Frequent public contact	Part time	Able to see results	Creativity	Influences others	Competition on the job	Works as part of a team	Jobs widely scattered	Initiative
	1	2	3	4	5	6	7	8	9	10	11	12	13	14	15	16	17	18	19
Shipping and receiving clerks		●		●			●			●							●	●	
Statistical clerks				●				●	●	●							●	●	
Stock clerks		●		●			●			●							●	●	
Typists				●					●	●		●	●					●	
Computer occupations																			
Computer operating personnel	●	●		●				●	●	●							●	●	
√ Programmers	●							●	●	●							●	●	
Systems analysts	●		●							●									●
Banking occupations																			
Bank clerks				●				●	●	●							●	●	
√ Bank officers	●							●	●	●	●				●		●	●	●
Bank tellers				●				●	●	●	●		●					●	
Insurance occupations																			
Actuaries	●																	●	
Claim representatives	●		●				●			●	●						●	●	
Underwriters	●								●	●							●	●	
Administrative occupations																			
Accountants	●		●					●		●			●					●	
Advertising workers	●									●	●		●	●	●	●	●	●	
Buyers	●									●					●	●	●	●	
City managers	●		●							●	●			●	●		●	●	
Credit managers	●		●					●		●	●				●		●	●	
Industrial traffic managers	●									●							●	●	
Lawyers	●									●	●			●	●	●	●	●	
Market research workers	●								●	●			●	●			●	●	●
Personnel and labor relations workers	●									●	●				●		●	●	
√ Planners	●									●	●		●	●	●		●	●	●
Public relations workers	●									●	●		●	●	●	●	●	●	
Purchasing agents	●									●					●		●	●	
SERVICE OCCUPATIONS																			
Cleaning occupations																			
√ Building service workers		●	●				●						●					●	
Pest controllers		●				●	●											●	
Food service occupations																			
Bartenders								●	●		●						●	●	
√ Chefs		●						●	●				●	●	●		●		
Dining room attendants and dishwashers				●				●			●						●	●	
Food counter workers				●				●	●		●						●	●	
Meatcutters		●		●	●			●					●				●	●	
Waiters and waitresses				●				●			●		●				●	●	
Hotel occupations																			
Bellhops and bell captains				●			●				●	●					●	●	
√ Hotel clerks	●		●					●		●	●	●					●	●	
Hotel housekeepers and assistants										●	●							●	
Hotel managers and assistants	●		●							●	●				●		●	●	
Personal service occupations																			
Barbers		●	●					●	●		●	●	●					●	
Cosmetologists		●	●					●	●		●	●	●					●	
Funeral directors and embalmers	●						●				●		●				●	●	

Exploring Careers—Student Guide

The Job Matching Chart

	1 Problem-solving ability	2 Uses tools, machinery	3 Instructs others	4 Repetitious	5 Hazardous	6 Outdoors	7 Physical stamina required	8 Generally confined	9 Precision	10 Works with detail	11 Frequent public contact	12 Part time	13 Able to see results	14 Creativity	15 Influences others	16 Competition on the job	17 Works as part of a team	18 Jobs widely scattered	19 Initiative
Private household occupations																			
Private household workers		•		•			•					•						•	
Protective service occupations																			
Correction officers			•	•	•		•	•		•					•		•	•	
FBI special agents	•		•		•		•			•	•						•	•	•
Firefighters	•		•		•		•				•						•	•	•
Guards				•	•		•			•							•	•	
√ Police officers	•		•		•	•	•			•	•				•		•	•	•
State police officers	•		•	•	•		•			•	•						•	•	•
Construction inspectors	•		•		•	•			•	•							•	•	•
Health and regulatory inspectors	•		•	•					•	•							•	•	•
Occupational safety and health workers	•		•	•			•			•							•	•	•
Other service occupations																			
Mail carriers				•			•				•							•	•
Telephone operators		•	•	•				•			•								
EDUCATION OCCUPATIONS																			
School occupations																			
Kindergarten and elementary school teachers	•		•							•	•			•			•	•	•
Teacher aides			•							•	•	•		•			•	•	
√ Secondary school teachers	•		•							•	•			•	•		•	•	•
√ School counselors	•		•							•	•			•	•		•	•	•
College occupations																			
College and university teachers	•		•							•	•			•	•	•	•	•	
College student personnel workers	•		•							•	•				•		•	•	•
College career planning and placement counselors	•		•							•	•				•		•	•	•
Library occupations																			
√ Librarians	•		•							•	•			•	•		•	•	•
Library technicians and clerks			•							•	•	•					•	•	
SALES OCCUPATIONS																			
√ Automobile parts counter workers		•		•					•		•							•	
Automobile sales workers		•									•	•			•	•		•	•
Automobile service advisers	•		•								•						•	•	
√ Gasoline service station attendants		•		•	•	•	•		•		•	•							
Insurance agents and brokers	•		•							•	•				•		•	•	•
Manufacturers' sales workers	•		•								•				•	•	•	•	
Models				•							•				•		•	•	•
Real estate agents and brokers	•					•				•	•				•		•	•	•
Retail trade sales workers					•					•	•		•		•		•	•	
Route drivers					•	•				•	•				•		•	•	
√ Securities sales workers	•		•						•	•	•	•			•		•	•	•
Travel agents	•		•							•	•				•		•	•	•
Wholesale trade sales workers	•									•	•				•		•	•	•
CONSTRUCTION OCCUPATIONS																			
√ Bricklayers	•	•			•	•	•						•	•				•	
√ Carpenters	•	•			•	•	•						•	•				•	
Cement masons and terrazzo workers		•			•	•	•						•				•	•	
Construction laborers		•			•	•	•						•				•	•	
Drywall installers and finishers		•		•	•	•	•						•					•	
Electricians	•	•			•	•	•						•					•	
Elevator constructors	•	•			•				•				•					•	

The World of Work and You

The Job Matching Chart

	Problem-solving ability	Uses tools, machinery	Instructs others	Repetitious	Hazardous	Outdoors	Physical stamina required	Generally confined	Precision	Works with detail	Frequent public contact	Part time	Able to see results	Creativity	Influences others	Competition on the job	Works as part of a team	Jobs widely scattered	Initiative
	1	2	3	4	5	6	7	8	9	10	11	12	13	14	15	16	17	18	19
Floor covering installers		•		•			•				•		•					•	
Glaziers	•	•		•	•	•	•						•					•	
Insulation workers		•		•	•		•						•				•	•	
Ironworkers		•		•	•		•						•				•	•	
Lathers		•		•	•		•						•					•	
Operating engineers		•		•	•	•	•						•					•	
Painters and paperhangers		•		•	•		•				•		•					•	
Plasterers		•		•	•		•						•					•	
√ Plumbers	•	•		•	•		•		•				•					•	
Roofers		•		•	•	•	•						•				•	•	
Sheet-metal workers	•	•		•									•					•	
Tilesetters		•											•					•	
TRANSPORTATION OCCUPATIONS																			
Air transportation occupations																			
√ Air traffic controllers	•		•					•		•							•	•	•
Airplane mechanics	•			•					•				•				•	•	•
Airplane pilots	•	•							•								•	•	•
Flight attendants			•	•							•						•	•	
Reservation, ticket, and passenger agents	•		•	•		•			•		•	•					•	•	
Merchant marine occupations																			
Merchant marine officers	•	•	•		•	•	•										•	•	
Merchant marine sailors		•		•	•	•	•										•	•	
Railroad occupations																			
Brake operators		•		•	•	•	•										•	•	
√ Conductors	•		•	•													•	•	•
Locomotive engineers	•	•		•					•								•	•	•
Shop trades	•	•			•		•										•	•	
Signal department workers	•	•		•													•	•	
Station agents	•		•						•	•			•		•		•	•	
Telegraphers, telephoners, and tower operators				•		•			•									•	
Track workers		•		•	•	•	•						•				•	•	
Driving occupations																			
Intercity busdrivers		•		•		•			•		•						•	•	
√ Local transit busdrivers		•		•					•		•							•	
Local truckdrivers		•		•		•			•									•	
Long-distance truckdrivers		•		•		•			•									•	
Parking attendants		•		•							•	•						•	
Taxicab drivers		•		•							•							•	
SCIENTIFIC AND TECHNICAL OCCUPATIONS																			
Life science occupations																			
√ Biochemists	•	•							•	•				•				•	•
Life scientists	•	•							•	•				•				•	•
Physical scientists																			
Astronomers	•	•							•	•				•				•	•
Chemists	•	•							•	•				•				•	•
Food scientists	•	•							•	•				•				•	•
Physicists	•	•							•	•				•				•	•
Environmental scientists																			
Geologists	•	•				•			•	•				•		•		•	•

Exploring Careers—Student Guide

The Job Matching Chart

	Problem-solving ability	Uses tools, machinery	Instructs others	Repetitious	Hazardous	Outdoors	Physical stamina required	Generally confined	Precision	Works with detail	Frequent public contact	Part time	Able to see results	Creativity	Influences others	Competition on the job	Works as part of a team	Jobs widely scattered	Initiative
	1	2	3	4	5	6	7	8	9	10	11	12	13	14	15	16	17	18	19
Geophysicists	●	●				●			●	●				●				●	●
Meteorologists	●	●							●	●				●				●	●
Oceanographers	●	●				●			●	●				●			●	●	●
Mathematics occupations																			
Mathematicians	●								●	●								●	●
Statisticians	●								●	●								●	●
Engineers																			
Aerospace	●								●	●				●				●	●
Agricultural	●								●	●				●				●	●
Biomedical	●								●	●				●				●	●
Ceramic	●								●	●				●				●	●
Chemical	●								●	●				●				●	●
Civil	●								●	●				●				●	●
√ Electrical	●								●	●				●				●	●
Industrial	●								●	●				●				●	●
Mechanical	●								●	●				●				●	●
Metallurgical	●								●	●				●				●	●
Mining	●								●	●				●				●	●
Petroleum	●								●	●				●				●	●
Technicians																			
√ Broadcast technicians	●	●						●	●									●	●
Drafters		●		●				●	●	●		●						●	
Engineering and science technicians	●	●							●	●								●	
Surveyors		●				●	●		●								●	●	
MECHANICS AND REPAIRERS																			
Air-conditioning, refrigeration, and heating mechanics	●	●			●								●					●	
Airplane mechanics	●	●			●	●			●				●				●	●	
Appliance repairers	●	●			●						●		●					●	
Automobile body repairers	●	●			●		●						●					●	
√ Automobile mechanics	●	●			●		●	●					●					●	
Boat-engine mechanics	●	●			●			●					●					●	
Bowling-pin-machine mechanics	●	●		●	●		●						●					●	
Business machine repairers	●	●			●						●		●					●	
√ Computer service technicians	●	●			●						●		●					●	
Diesel mechanics	●	●			●		●	●					●					●	
Electric sign repairers	●	●			●	●					●		●					●	
Farm equipment mechanics	●	●			●	●							●					●	
Industrial machinery repairers	●	●			●								●					●	
Instrument repairers	●	●			●								●					●	
√ Jewelers	●	●							●	●			●	●				●	●
Locksmiths	●	●							●	●			●					●	
Maintenance electricians	●	●			●					●			●					●	
Motorcycle mechanics	●	●			●			●					●					●	
Piano and organ tuners and repairers	●	●							●			●	●					●	
Shoe repairers	●	●		●	●			●		●			●					●	●
Television and radio service technicians	●	●			●					●			●					●	●
Truck mechanics and bus mechanics	●	●			●		●			●			●					●	●
Vending machine mechanics	●	●			●	●				●			●					●	●
Watch repairers	●	●							●	●			●					●	●
Telephone craft occupations																			
Central office craft occupations	●	●			●				●	●			●					●	

The World of Work and You

The Job Matching Chart

	Problem-solving ability	Uses tools, machinery	Instructs others	Repetitious	Hazardous	Outdoors	Physical stamina required	Generally confined	Precision	Works with detail	Frequent public contact	Part time	Able to see results	Creativity	Influences others	Competition on the job	Works as part of a team	Jobs widely scattered	Initiative
	1	2	3	4	5	6	7	8	9	10	11	12	13	14	15	16	17	18	19
Central office equipment installers	•	•			•		•		•				•					•	
Line installers and cable splicers	•	•			•	•	•		•									•	
Telephone and PBX installers and repairers	•	•			•		•				•							•	
HEALTH OCCUPATIONS																			
Medical practitioners																			
Chiropractors	•	•	•						•	•	•	•	•				•	•	•
Optometrists	•	•	•						•	•	•	•	•				•	•	•
Osteopathic physicians	•	•	•		•		•		•	•	•		•				•	•	•
Physicians	•	•			•		•		•	•	•		•				•	•	•
Podiatrists	•	•	•						•	•	•		•				•	•	•
Veterinarians	•	•			•		•		•	•	•		•				•	•	•
Dental occupations																			
Dentists	•	•	•						•		•		•				•	•	•
Dental assistants		•	•	•						•	•		•				•	•	•
Dental hygienists		•	•	•				•			•						•	•	•
Dental laboratory technicians	•		•	•				•	•								•	•	•
Nursing occupations																			
√ Registered nurses	•	•	•		•		•		•	•	•		•				•	•	•
Licensed practical nurses		•	•		•		•			•	•				•		•	•	•
Nursing aides, orderlies, and attendants		•	•	•			•			•	•						•	•	
Therapy and rehabilitation occupations																			
Occupational therapists	•	•								•	•		•	•	•		•	•	•
Occupational therapy assistants and aides		•								•	•		•	•	•		•	•	•
√ Physical therapists	•	•	•				•			•	•		•		•		•	•	•
Physical therapist assistants and aides	•	•					•			•	•		•		•		•	•	•
Speech pathologists and audiologists	•	•	•							•	•		•		•		•	•	•
Medical technologist, technician, and assistant occupations																			
Electrocardiograph technicians		•	•	•						•	•						•	•	
Electroencephalographic technologists and technicians		•	•	•						•	•						•	•	
Emergency medical technicians	•	•	•		•	•	•			•	•						•	•	
√ Medical laboratory technologists		•			•			•	•	•	•						•	•	
Medical record technicians and clerks					•					•	•							•	
Operating room technicians		•	•		•					•	•						•	•	
Optometric assistants		•	•							•	•							•	
Radiologic (X-ray) technologists		•	•							•	•						•	•	
Respiratory therapy workers		•	•							•							•	•	
Other health occupations																			
Dietitians	•								•	•	•		•		•		•	•	•
Dispensing opticians	•	•							•	•	•						•	•	
Health services administrators	•									•			•		•		•	•	•
Medical record administrators	•									•	•				•		•	•	•
Pharmacists	•		•					•	•		•							•	•
SOCIAL SCIENTISTS																			
Anthropologists	•		(1)							•	(1)			•				•	•
Economists	•		(1)							•	(1)			•				•	•
Geographers	•	•	(1)							•	(1)			•				•	•
√ Historians	•		(1)							•	(1)			•				•	•
√ Political scientists	•		(1)							•	(1)			•				•	•

¹ Teachers only.

The Job Matching Chart

	Problem-solving ability	Uses tools, machinery	Instructs others	Repetitious	Hazardous	Outdoors	Physical stamina required	Generally confined	Precision	Works with detail	Frequent public contact	Part time	Able to see results	Creativity	Influences others	Competition on the job	Works as part of a team	Jobs widely scattered	Initiative
	1	2	3	4	5	6	7	8	9	10	11	12	13	14	15	16	17	18	19
Psychologists	●		(1)							●	●			●				●	●
Sociologists	●		(1)							●				●				●	●
SOCIAL SERVICE OCCUPATIONS																			
Counseling occupations																			
School counselors	●									●				●			●	●	●
College career planning and placement counselors	●		●							●	●			●			●	●	●
Employment counselors	●		●					●		●	●		●						●
Rehabilitation counselors	●		●							●	●								●
Clergy																			
√ Protestant ministers	●		●								●			●	●	●	●	●	●
Rabbis	●		●								●			●			●	●	●
Roman Catholic priests	●		●								●			●			●	●	●
Other social service occupations																			
Cooperative extension service workers	●		●								●		●				●	●	●
Home economists	●		●								●							●	●
Homemaker-home health aides			●								●							●	●
Park, recreation, and leisure service workers	●		●			●				●	●	●		●			●	●	●
Social service aides	●		●	●							●	●					●		●
√ Social workers	●		●										●	●		●	●		●
PERFORMING ARTS, DESIGN, AND COMMUNICATIONS OCCUPATIONS																			
Performing artists																			
Actors and actresses			(1)				●				●	●		●			●	●	●
Dancers			(1)				●				●			●			●	●	●
√ Musicians			(1)				●		●		●	●		●			●	●	●
Singers			(1)				●				●			●			●	●	●
Design occupations																			
√ Architects	●	●								●			●	●		●	●	●	●
Commercial artists		●								●			●	●		●	●		●
Display workers		●											●	●	●		●		●
Floral designers								●			●			●					●
Industrial designers										●			●	●		●	●		●
Interior designers										●			●	●			●		●
Landscape architects	●									●			●	●			●		●
Photographers	●									●			●	●		●			●
Planners	●									●				●			●		●
Communications occupations																			
Advertising workers	●									●	●		●	●	●	●	●		●
Interpreters			●							●	●								●
√ Newspaper reporters	●		●							●	●		●	●	●	●		●	●
Public relations workers	●										●			●	●	●	●	●	●
Radio and television announcers								●		●	●					●			●
Technical writers	●							●		●		●							●
AGRICULTURE, FORESTRY, AND FISHERY OCCUPATIONS																			
Agricultural production occupations																			
√ Farmers	●	●				●	●						●					●	●
Farm managers	●		●			●	●						●					●	●
Farm laborers	●			●	●	●	●						●					●	●
Farm labor supervisors	●		●			●	●						●				●		●
Agricultural support occupations																			

¹ Teachers only.

The Job Matching Chart

	Problem-solving ability	Uses tools, machinery	Instructs others	Repetitious	Hazardous	Outdoors	Physical stamina required	Generally confined	Precision	Works with detail	Frequent public contact	Part time	Able to see results	Creativity	Influences others	Competition on the job	Works as part of a team	Jobs widely scattered	Initiative
	1	2	3	4	5	6	7	8	9	10	11	12	13	14	15	16	17	18	19
√ Cooperative extension service workers	●	●									●		●		●			●	●
Soil conservationists	●	●				●							●					●	●
Soil scientists	●								●	●								●	●
Range managers	●				●	●	●											●	●
Agricultural engineers	●								●	●				●				●	●
Food scientists	●								●	●				●				●	●
Farm equipment mechanics		●			●				●				●					●	●
Buyers and shippers, farm products	●										●					●		●	●
Veterinarians	●	●								●	●				●			●	●
Forestry occupations																			
√ Foresters	●					●												●	●
Forestry technicians		●			●	●												●	
Loggers		●		●	●	●							●					●	
Fishery occupations																			
Fishers		●			●	●	●	●								●		●	
Fish farmers	●	●				●							●					●	●

¹ Teachers only.

Some people look for a career with excitement and adventure.

Exploring Careers

Occupations Worth Exploring

Using your completed Job Matching Chart as a guide, complete the Possible Occupations Worksheet that follows. Here is how:

Step 1: Begin by putting an asterick (∗) next to the three job characteristics, located at the top of the "Possible Occupations Worksheet," you feel are most important to you.

Step 2: Next, list all the jobs that you underlined or circled on your "Job Matching Chart" under the "Occupation" column of the "Possible Occupations Worksheet." Put a checkmark in the appropriate column for each characteristics that applies. Look back over your choices. If an occupation has one of your three top job characteristics checked, put a checkmark in the " Level of Interest" column under "Somewhat Interested." If the occupation has two of your three top job characteristics checked, put a checkmark under "Interested." If the occupation has all three of your top job characteristics checked, put a checkmark under "Very Interested."

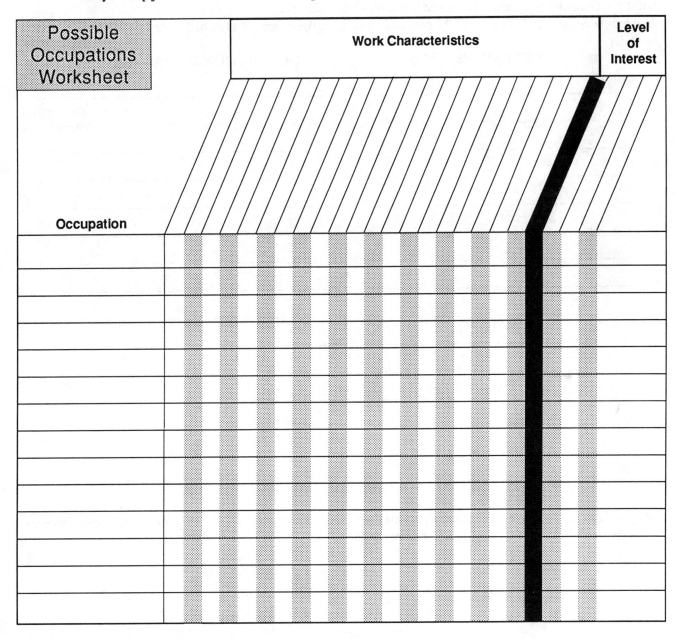

The World of Work and You

Step 3: Now it is time to select the occupations that are most interesting to you. Go over the "Possible Occupations Worksheet" you have just completed and decide how interested you still are in each one. Compared to the other occupations that you listed, are you:

- Very interested?
- Interested?
- Somewhat interested?

Occupations of Greatest Interest

Look over your "Possible Occupations Worksheet" on page W21 and select the occupations that interest you the most. List the one that you have the greatest interest in on the first line. Then list your next choice until you have listed all of the occupations that most interest you in the space provided below.

In the right column, list the name of the occupational cluster the occupation is listed under.

OCCUPATION	OCCUPATIONAL CLUSTER

Congratulations! You have just created a personalized list of job possibilities that fit your unique combination of characteristics! This is your starting point for career exploration.

Exploring Careers

What Else Should I Consider?

The next few pages explain other ways to identify careers that suit you. They may help you narrow your exploration list further or consider other occupations you may have overlooked.

School and Work

Let's look at another way of exploring careers: your school subjects. What subjects do you enjoy the most? Which subjects are easy for you to understand and do well in? List them below.

FAVORITE SUBJECTS   **BEST SUBJECTS**

_____   _____

_____   _____

_____   _____

_____   _____

_____   _____

_____   _____

_____   _____

Do one or more subjects appear in both columns? If you like a subject and do well in it, it's worth investigating occupations that involve that subject.

Taking a printing class in an industrial arts program can give hands on experience.

The World of Work and You

Let's use math as an example. (The same ideas can be applied to any subject you choose.) Some of the occupations in which you would use math are described in *Exploring Careers*: carpenter, air traffic controller, biochemist, electrical engineer, architect, computer programmer, securities sales worker, forester, and others. There are stories about each of these in Exploring Careers. And these are just a few of the occupations that require either practical or theoretical ability in mathematics. Your teacher or counselor can help you identify others.

But what if you are confused and frustrated in math class and don't like the subject at all? Does that mean you have to rule out a career in construction, or health, or forestry? Not necessarily. But it does require some more digging on your part.

You need to be honest with yourself. Is it the subject matter you dislike? Or does something else influence your attitude about math? Could it be a particular teacher or a certain textbook that you dislike? Perhaps you don't see any connection between math class and when you will ever use that information. Would you like math better or work harder at it if you understood how it would help you in a career that interests you?

Office equipment has expanded in recent years.

A secretarial career relies heavily on school subjects like mathematics and English.

It's up to you to determine with the help of your teacher or counselor how much ability you really have in math or any other subject. It's also important how math is used in the kinds of jobs that interest you. A carpenter, for example, doesn't need the same level of math ability as a bank loan officer. Machinists need to be good at arithmetic to calculate quickly and make precise measurements. Systems analysts use calculus and must be able to apply mathematical theory to practical problems. Accountants need both arithmetic skills and algebra. Talking to people about how they use math in their jobs could help you decide whether you should seriously consider work that involves math or rule it out.

You can also use your school subjects to test some of your career ideas in more detail. Suppose that you're good at science and like to build things and work with your hands. Through your exploration activities, you've probably discovered that engineering and drafting are possible career choices. Now is the time to test your interest in these and related fields. Use class assignments, projects, and science fairs to learn about the kind of work drafters and engineers actually do. Find out what engineering and scientific technicians do. How does their work fit in with that of engineers and scientists?

The Suggested Activities sheets that your teacher can provide will give you some other ideas about things you

 Exploring Careers—Student Guide

Exploring Careers

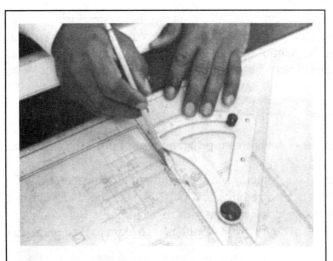

These tools are being replaced by computers.

can do to test out your interests and abilities for scientific and technical careers. While you're at it, investigate the other chapters of *Exploring Careers* and the Suggested Activities for each of them. You'll find other careers that require scientific interests and abilities.

Maybe you're interested in consumer issues but don't know where that might lead you. Try taking a home economics course. That would give you an opportunity to find out about careers in consumer economics, food and nutrition, or clothing and textiles.

The chart below lists subjects taught in most high schools. This chart will help you identify the *Exploring Careers* chapters that are related to each subject. Are some of the chapters that relate to your best subjects the same as the ones you identified on your Possible Occupations Worksheet?

School Subjects and Related Occupations

EXPLORING CAREERS CHAPTERS

SCHOOL SUBJECTS	INDUSTRIAL PRODUCTION	OFFICE	SERVICE	EDUCATION	SALES	CONSTRUCTION	TRANSPORTATION	SCIENTIFIC & TECHNICAL	MECHANICS & REPAIRERS	HEALTH	SOCIAL SCIENTISTS	SOCIAL SERVICE	PERFORMING ARTS, DESIGN, & COMMUNICATION	AGRICULTURE, FORESTRY, & FISHERY
AGRICULTURE														•
ART			•											•
BUSINESS EDUCATION		•	•	•										•
DISTRIBUTIVE EDUCATION					•									
DRIVER EDUCATION							•							
HEALTH								•		•				
HOME ECONOMICS			•	•								•		•
INDUSTRIAL ARTS	•		•			•	•	•	•				•	•
LANGUAGE ARTS		•	•	•	•							•		
MATHEMATICS	•	•				•		•			•	•	•	•
MUSIC				•									•	
PHYSICAL EDUCATION			•	•		•						•		
SCIENCE	•	•						•	•		•	•		•
SOCIAL STUDIES		•	•	•							•	•	•	

Do the occupations on your personalized list of job possibilities on page W21 relate to the occupational clusters listed with your best or favorite subjects? If you enjoy the subjects that are related to that occupation and are good at them, circle the subjects in the School Subjects column of the School Subjects and Related Occupations chart. If you're not certain, or if you are good in some related subjects but not others, put a question mark next to that subject.

Training

Do you have any idea how to become a carpenter? A secretary? A computer programmer or pilot? The first thing you have to do for any job is learn a set of skills.

To become a carpenter, you would have to learn how to use tools properly and work without wasting materials. To work as a secretary, you would have to learn to type, handle office procedures, and possibly take shorthand or use a computer. To qualify as a computer programmer, you would need to learn how to translate ideas into computer language and how to spot and correct errors. To become a pilot, of course, you would have to learn to fly a plane and use charts and maps.

How Much Training and Education Is Required?

Like a hobby or sport, every job involves knowledge and skills that you must learn. An important part of career exploration is deciding how much time and effort you're willing to spend in training. For example, it doesn't make sense to aim for a career as a veterinarian unless you do well in school, are interested in science, and are willing to put in seven years or more of hard work after high school.

Think about your attitude toward school. How long are you willing to stay in school? Would you be willing to take training that might last six months? What about training that lasts two to four years? Are you planning to go to college? Are you willing to study after college for one or more years? Some occupations, such as veterinarian, require that much formal education.

The Cost of Education and Training

The cost of education or training after high school is something else to consider. In addition to the amount of training you would like to obtain, you have to think about how much training you and your family can afford. The training to become a veterinarian is much more expensive than that for a medical technologist, yet both are health occupations. Within most of the career clusters, you will find occupations with different levels of required training.

Remember that there are many sources of financial aid or scholarships. Your counselor can help you investigate the possibilities. If you have the ability and desire to pursue education or training after high school, don't be discouraged if your family can't afford the expense. Schools, educational foundations, businesses, religious groups, unions, community organizations, government, and professional organizations are all sources of scholarships, grants, loans, and other financial aid. But the question of how to finance your education will become important later. For now, let's look at some of the different ways to prepare for the world of work.

Finish High School First

The best way to prepare for a successful career is to complete high school. High school courses give you a foundation in basic skills that help you function as a worker, consumer, and citizen.

A high school diploma is necessary if you want to go to college. It's also required for admission to most training programs including trade schools, technical institutes, or apprenticeship programs. Many training programs in the military require a high school diploma, and graduates are given preference in the selection process. In addition, many employers require persons who are at least high school graduates.

Your job for now is to do as well as you can in school. Later, doing well in high school will be worth more than anything else you could do with your time before graduation.

Your Training and Educational Options

You may sometimes get the feeling that everybody goes to college these days. That's not quite true. While over half of the people who graduate from high school do take additional schooling of some kind, it is not always in a traditional four-year college.

More and more high school graduates obtain job-related training in technical schools, community colleges, government training programs, and other settings. They may work several years after graduating from high school before returning to school full or part time.

Our economy has created many new jobs. Most of them require training or education beyond high school. Many employers who used to hire applicants with just a high school diploma, or sometimes even without a diploma, may now require additional training. As technology advances, you will probably need to update your education and training at various times throughout your life. So even if you plan on going to work right after high school, you need to know about the various training and education options available. It is likely that you will use one or more of them at some time.

The following illustration shows the choices that are available to you after high school. As you can see, there are a variety of ways to get the education and training needed for a job.

- You can learn a trade while you work.
- You can enroll in an apprenticeship program that combines on- the-job training with classroom instruction.
- You can attend a vocational or technical school to learn job skills like cutting hair or mechanics.
- You can get training and work experience in the armed forces.
- You can prepare for a career by going to college.

The path you choose depends on the particular kind of career that you want and the amount of time, effort, and money that you're willing to invest in preparation.

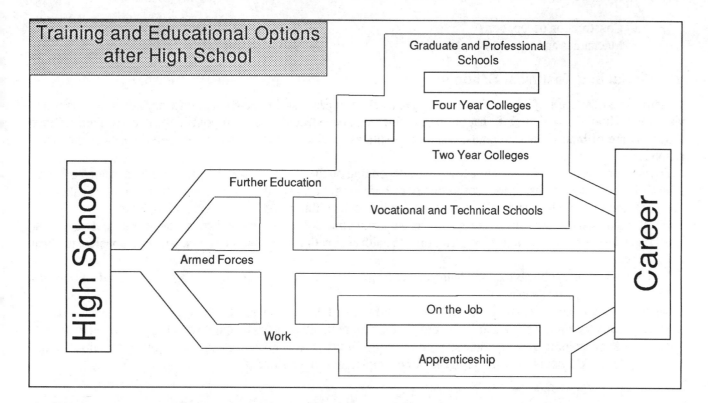

The World of Work and You

On-the-Job Training

Almost every job requires some "learning by doing." Employers make sure that new workers have a chance to learn their jobs. The training can last from just a few days to a year or more.

Assemblers, for example, learn by helping and observing more experienced workers and working under their supervision, and it may take only a few hours to learn their job. Power truck operators, however, require more formal training that includes classroom instruction. They take courses in safe driving that last several days. For some occupations, on-the-job training continues for several years. Air traffic controllers take a 16-week course and must complete independent study courses. They must work for two or three years under the supervision of an experienced controller before being considered fully qualified.

There are many occupations in which you can learn while you work. Some possibilities are in the following clusters:

- Agriculture, forestry, and fishery occupations
- Industrial production occupations
- Office occupations
- Transportation occupations
- Construction occupations
- Mechanics and repairers
- Service occupations

Apprenticeship Programs

Apprenticeship is a way of learning a trade that combines on-the-job training with classroom instruction. Most programs are sponsored by employers, government programs, and labor unions. When you have completed an apprenticeship program (from one to six years), you are formally recognized as being fully qualified in your trade.

As an apprentice, you are taught by experienced workers. You learn by helping them and working under their supervision. Your training covers all aspects of the trade. For example, apprentice mechanics learn not only how to repair engines but also how to diagnose engine problems and how to take care of their tools. They also attend classes or sometimes complete home-study assignments on topics like shop safety practices and customer relations.

People learn to become auto mechanics, carpenters, bricklayers, electricians, and other trade professionals through apprenticeship programs. The following clusters include occupations learned through apprenticeships:

- Construction occupations
- Mechanics and repairers
- Industrial production occupations
- Service occupations

Vocational and Technical Schools

Many types of schools offer vocational training to teach the types of skills you will use on a job. You may be familiar with your school district's vocational program, which can be selected as part of your high school training. Other programs are offered at trade schools, technical institutes, business schools, and correspondence or home-study schools.

Courses may last several weeks or a few years, depending on the program. Some of the programs offered by these schools include electronics, flying, cosmetology or barbering, business and office procedures, computer operating and programming, medical technology, auto mechanics, locksmithing, and truck driving, among others.

Usually, you will practice in the classroom before using your skills in an actual job. In business school you might type, file, take shorthand, or transcribe dictation. In health occupations training programs, you might operate medical equipment.

You will also study subjects that will help you on the job. For example, mechanics and repairers would take classes in blueprint reading and shop math.

When you complete a vocational or technical program, you often receive a certificate of achievement. You are generally ready to begin work when you complete the program, although some employers may want you to receive some on-the-job training as well. Some states may require you to take a licensing exam for some occupations before beginning to work. Pilots and cosmetologists, for example, must have a license.

 ©1990, JIST Works, Inc., Indianapolis, Indiana *Exploring Careers—Student Guide*

Exploring Careers

The ability to solve problems is important in many jobs.

Vocational and technical schools offer the necessary training for some jobs in these career clusters:

- Agriculture, forestry, and fishery occupations
- Health occupations
- Industrial production occupations
- Office occupations
- Service Occupations
- Health occupations
- Mechanics and repairers
- Sales occupations
- Transportation occupations
- Performing arts, design, and communications occupations

When thinking about a technical training program, consider whether the school is accredited by a legitimate accrediting agency. Private business and technical schools are often accredited by national organizations, such as NATTS (National Association of Trade and Technical Schools) or AICS (Association of Independent Colleges and Schools) as well as state agencies. Also ask about the experiences of former graduates in finding jobs in the occupations they were trained for.

Community and Junior Colleges

You can prepare for a specific occupation in some junior or community colleges. Most programs in these schools take about two years and result in an associate's degree. Some programs take a little longer, and others may be completed within one year. Depending on the curriculum, you may be able to begin work for a four-year bachelor's degree by starting at a community or junior college before transferring to another college or university to continue your education.

Some programs at a community or junior college would prepare you for a career as a computer technician, drafter, surveyor, nurse, emergency medical technician, recreation leader, or secretary, among others.

Similar to the offerings in vocational and technical schools, these courses usually qualify you to begin a job when you complete the program. Community and junior colleges offer programs that prepare you for occupations in the following clusters:

- Agriculture, forestry, and fishery occupations
- Health occupations
- Science occupations
- Performing arts, design, and communications occupations

- Education occupations
- Office occupations
- Scientific and technical occupations
- Service occupations

The World of Work and You

Four Year Colleges and Universities — and Beyond

Many students go directly from high school to a four year college or university. Many others return to college when they are older. These schools require classes in a variety of subjects such as English, Psychology, History and Math to help you become a well rounded person. Graduates of these schools earn a bachelor's degree.

You can select a "major" and take many courses in a particular subject such as art, music, chemistry, engineering or business. Some of these majors help prepare you work in a particular profession such as teaching or accounting while others provide you with a general education that will help you in a variety of careers.

Certain occupations require additional education beyond a four year bachelor's degree. A master's degree requires between one and two additional years of schooling and a doctorate or "Ph.D." requires several years beyond a master's degree. Graduates of these programs are in most occupational areas:

- Agriculture, forestry, and fishery occupations
- Education occupations
- Health occupations
- Office occupations
- Science occupations
- Sales occupations
- Scientific and technical occupations
- Social service occupations
- Service occupations
- Performing arts, design, and communications occupations

The Armed Forces

The various branches of the armed forces provide many opportunities for long-term careers.

People train within the military for many of the same occupations that civilians work in—cooks, clerks, secretaries, nurses, carpenters, mechanics, newspaper reporters, photographers, meteorologists, air traffic controllers, and many others.

While in the service, you can learn job skills and gain work experience. When you complete your tour of duty, these skills and experiences can be used to qualify for civilian jobs. The Military Career Guide (published by the U.S. Government) and many other books provide details about the careers for which training is available and which branches of service provide that training.

You can also plan to participate in various armed forces scholarship or tuition aid programs that pay for college or technical training after you finish active duty. Some college students finance their education by participating in the Reserve Officer Training Corps (ROTC) while they go to college. After they graduate, they then serve in the armed forces for several years.

A carpenter needs knowledge in business administration to run a successful construction company.

 Exploring Careers—Student Guide

The Occupational Training, Education, Income, and Growth Worksheet

Look up each of the occupations listed on your personalized list of job possibilities on page W21. List them in the Occupational Training, Education, Income, and Growth Worksheet on page W32. Can you guess how much training or education is required for each of these occupations? If you are not sure, ask your teacher or counselor, or you can look up how much is required in *Exploring Careers* or the *Occupational Outlook Handbook*.

Estimating Training and Education

Use the column titled "Training or Education" to list the training or education you think that occupation requires. Here are the options:

- High school diploma
- On-the-job training
- Apprenticeship
- Vocational school
- Junior college
- College
- Graduate school

Are you willing to participate in that type of training or educational program? If so, give these careers serious consideration.

Estimating Income

Income is another important consideration. Occupations with higher income potential usually require more training or education. As you explore each of your potential occupations, think about the average income in that field. Once again, it may require some research to determine what an occupation will pay. Your teacher or the *Occupational Outlook Handbook* are good sources of information on the salary for various occupations.

Refer again to the Occupational Training, Education, Income, and Growth Worksheet on page W32. Select one of the income ranges listed below, and complete the "Income" column of the worksheet for each of your top occupations.

- Very high
- Average
- Above average
- Below average

There is plenty of on-the-job training for heavy equipment operators.

The World of Work and You

Estimating Growth

Some fields, such as those in computer programming and medical technology, are growing very fast and will offer many opportunities. Others, such as factory assembling and farming, are declining in the number of people they employ, and opportunities will be more limited.

Many of the occupations that are declining are those that do not require training beyond high school. At the same time, the occupations that are growing most rapidly often require education or training beyond a high school degree.

You can obtain information on the projected growth for most occupations in a current edition of the *Occupational Outlook Handbook*.

Occupational Training, Education, Income, and Growth Worksheet			
OCCUPATION	**TRAINING OR EDUCATION**	**INCOME**	**GROWTH**

Continuing to Explore

You've probably learned new things about yourself from the ideas and activities in this book. The occupational information in *Exploring Careers* is designed to help you go on from here. It will help you learn new things about yourself as you expand your awareness of the world of work. Now is the time to let your imagination soar, to test your dreams, to try all kinds of new things. Try to explore the world of work with a truly open mind. Don't limit yourself by examining only a few occupations.

Learning about yourself is a process that will continue throughout your life. Career exploration isn't something you do just once and finish. Some studies now indicate that you will change careers as many as five to seven times during your working years. Many people change jobs because they decide it's time for a change. Changing jobs, training for a new career, or going back to school to keep up with the latest developments in a field are all things to expect once you have entered the world of work.

Exploring careers is especially important right now—as you begin getting ready to enter the world of work. It will be just as important to repeat the process later in your life. Whenever the time seems right, stand back and take another look at yourself. Test your career interests. Are you where you want to be? If not, remember all those other possibilities that you identified once upon a time.

 ©1990, JIST Works, Inc., Indianapolis, Indiana *Exploring Careers—Student Guide*

Exploring Careers

Industrial Production Occupations

Industrial production workers deal with things more than they do with people or ideas.

Exploring Careers

Annie Bergdahl walked down the corridor, wide-eyed. From the moment she first walked through the massive brass doors of the main entrance, the Museum of Science and Industry held her in a spell. The old airplanes hanging from the ceiling, the mummies, the space capsules—everywhere she turned, Annie found wonderful things to explore. She wanted to see it all, read every word, push every button. But the museum was so big!

Most of the other youngsters on the field trip also wanted to run off and spend more time at some exhibit they had spotted. But Mr. Borden, their teacher at Middlesex Junior High, kept them together in a group. There were certain exhibits he wanted them to see, exhibits that should liven up the unit they were doing right now in his social studies class.

The unit on industry had begun last week, and Mr. Borden was teaching the class how factories produce goods. Some of the students were obviously bored. But not all of them ... and certainly not Annie. Annie had enjoyed the film about an automobile assembly line. It fascinated her to watch the metal frames grow, almost magically, into complete cars as they moved along. And she couldn't believe how many workers—*assemblers*, Mr. Borden had called them—it took to build a car. Each assembler performed a single task over and over while the seemingly endless parade of unfinished automobiles marched on. As the engines glided down from above, two or three workers would bolt each one to a frame. Others attached the seats; still others added doors or side panels or wheels or a hood, over and over. Mr. Borden had said that not all assemblers work on an assembly line. Many work at benches or on shop floors and set their own pace. Nevertheless, Annie had decided that assembly work wasn't her cup of tea.

Now, at the museum, she walked with the group toward a tall archway crowned with a large sign in shiny brass letters: HALL OF INDUSTRY. Mr. Borden led the students through the archway into a large room. All

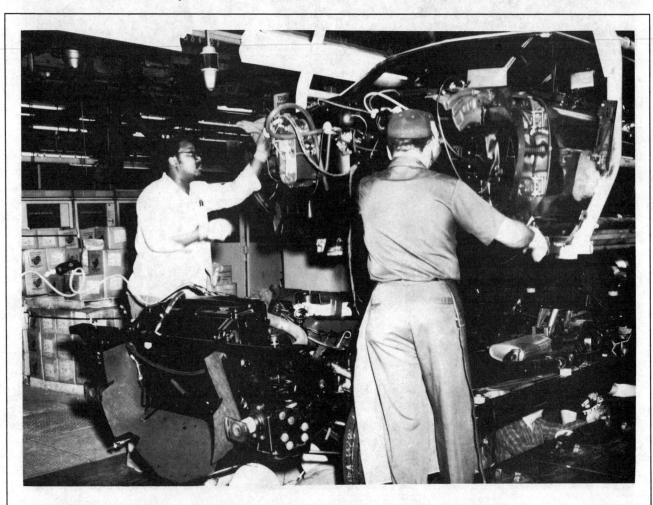

It takes many assemblers, each performing a different task, to produce an automobile.

Industrial Production Occupations

America's industrial plants produce everything from paper clips to rocket ships.

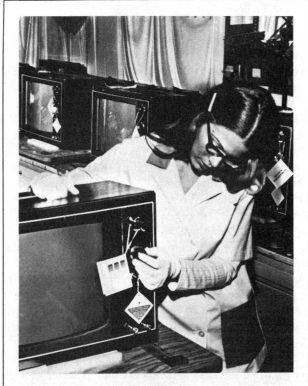

This inspector looks carefully at every television set.

around them they saw exhibits and more doorways. Ushering the group to one side of the room, Mr. Borden sat them on the carpet and introduced them to a casually dressed young man who awaited them there.

"This is Mr. Novacello, class. He works here at the museum, and he's going to tell us about the exhibits in this hall. Now, what are we studying in class these days?"

"Industrial production!" shouted half the group in unison.

"Right!" said Mr. Borden. "And who can tell me what that means?" A sudden attack of shyness paralyzed the group. There was silence until Annie raised her hand.

"Production means making things. Industrial production means making things in factories and plants."

"Very good, Annie," said Mr. Borden, smiling. "Now, let's let Mr. Novacello tell us more about it and demonstrate how some things are made."

Mr. Novacello flashed a smile and greeted the group. After telling them a bit about the museum and himself, he returned to the subject at hand. "Who can tell me why it's important to learn about industrial production?" he asked.

Silence.

"Well, then, who can name some industrial products?"

One by one, the children began to name things made in factories: Cars and trucks, trains and airplanes, books and newspapers, pencils and pens, refrigerators and radios, television sets and telephones, window glass and wallpaper, lampshades and lightbulbs, canned soups and candybars.

"The list is quite long, as you can see," said Mr. Novacello. "Industrial plants produce everything from paper clips to rocket ships. And they produce these things much more quickly, efficiently, and cheaply than was possible years ago. Today, most American families have a car and T.V. Many also have stereos, VCRs, microwave ovens, and other modern conveniences. Without modern industrial production, all these things would have to be built by hand, and most of us could never afford them. Modern industry makes our lifestyles possible, and so we should know something about it.

"There's another reason, too. All those products didn't appear by magic. They were made by millions of workers in a great variety of jobs. When you start thinking about the kind of job you might like when you grow up, it'll help to know about these.

"We have exhibits here that illustrate a dozen different kinds of industrial processes. I want to show you four or five that I think will interest you, and tell you a little about the work and the workers in each. Come with me to the first exhibit and we'll have a look."

Exploring Careers

Foundry Occupations

The youngsters followed Mr. Novacello over to the far wall and gathered around him before a large darkened window. Curious to know what was about to happen, they listened to him closely.

"This exhibit shows an industrial plant called a foundry. The workers there make metal parts for many different things." As he spoke, Mr. Novacello pushed a button on the wall near the glass panel. Spotlights suddenly illuminated the scene behind the glass, in which a dozen mechanical people came to life. All dressed in overalls and hard shoes, they acted out the different kinds of foundry work. At the same time, a clear, deep voice spoke from a wall speaker.

"The process used to make metal parts in a foundry is called casting," began the voice, "and it resembles the way you would mold a ring or some other shape out of gelatin in your kitchen. Workers heat the metal until it liquifies, then pour it into a mold. When it has cooled and hardened, the metal has the desired shape and is taken from the mold.

"Casting is used to make metal objects that must be very strong, such as engine blocks and axles for cars. In order to cast the desired shape, foundry workers create the molds themselves. First, the *patternmaker* creates an exact model, or pattern, of the part out of metal, wood, or perhaps plaster. Patternmakers are highly skilled workers. They make a model from a set of drawings called blueprints that give the exact measurements of the part. And since the quality of the product depends upon the quality of the pattern, patternmakers work very carefully and deliberately.

"When the pattern is finished, the *molder* uses it to make a mold. Molders pack special sand around the pattern in a box called a flask. After pressing the sand very tightly with mallets or powered rammers, they carefully remove the pattern, leaving a space in the sand exactly the shape of the final piece. This is the mold.

"Some castings have hollow sections," continued the voice. "They are formed when the liquid metal flows around a "core" that the *coremaker* creates. Coremakers start with a wood or metal block with a space hollowed out in the proper shape. After packing sand into the hollow, they bake it or dry it by some other method. Once dry, the sand core is hard enough to remove and use in casting."

Fascinated by the mechanical figures, the children stared for another minute or so while the voice described other aspects of a foundry. Then the display went dark and the speaker silent. Mr. Novacello's voice broke the trance.

Steel workers may have to wear special clothing for protection.

Foundry workers make metal objects that must be very strong. Here the worker is pouring liquified metal into a mold.

Industrial Production Occupations

"Today, some foundries use industrial robots and CAD/CAM systems to perform some of these jobs. CAD/CAM means "computer aided design and computer assisted manufacturing." With these systems, a pattern can be created by machinery which is controlled directly from the computer in which the design is stored. Robots can also be used to perform some of the *molder's* and *coremaker's* operations, which are sometimes dangerous for people.

"In the near future we'll have a new exhibit that shows how industrial robots work. You'll have to visit us again when that exhibit is ready. For now, follow me to another display where we'll see other workers who make things out of metal."

Other Metalworking Occupations

Leading the children to a large floor-to-ceiling display case, he pointed to the first of several life-sized figures posing behind the glass. "Now," he began, "who can tell me the occupation of this man standing at the anvil with a big hammer in his hand?"

"Blacksmith," answered the class in unison.

"Right!" said Mr. Novacello. "And what do blacksmiths do?"

"They put shoes on horses," answered a few voices.

The guide smiled. "That's partly correct. Many blacksmiths specialize in shoeing horses and are called *farriers*. But blacksmiths also make or mend metal objects for many other purposes. The process they use is called forging. First, they soften a piece of metal, usually iron, by heating it in a fireplace called a forge. Next, holding it on the anvil with a pair of tongs, they strengthen and shape the metal by hammering and chiseling it. Then they cool it in water.

"This blacksmith is forging metal in essentially the same way that his predecessor did a hundred years ago. Even his tools are similar. In a modern *forge shop*, you would find workers who look like these next figures in the case. They heat the metal in a furnace and use large power hammers and presses to pound and squeeze it into the desired shape. With their equipment they can produce objects such as keys, wrenches, drill bits, or huge parts for heavy machinery. And they do it much faster than a blacksmith.

"Now this occupation," continued Mr. Novacello, indicating the next figure, "may be harder to figure out. As you can see, this woman is placing a metal object in a vat of liquid. An electrical wire is connected to the object, and another runs into the liquid. Can anyone tell me what she's doing?"

Mr. Novacello looked out across a sea of blank faces. "Do you all give up? This woman is an *electroplater*. She puts a metal layer, or plating, on an object. She does this by passing an electric current between the plating material which can be silver, chromium, or some other metal, and the object. She covers those parts of the object that aren't to be plated, and she carefully controls the strength and duration of the current. Then she checks the plating to make sure it was applied evenly and in the right thickness. In this display she is putting chrome plating on an automobile bumper, but she could be plating any of the shiny, silvery parts of a car.

"The next occupation might be a bit easier. Two people wearing face masks are standing over a metal object, while one holds a torch to it. What do you think they're doing?"

Silence.

This welder is using heat from an acetylene torch to join pieces of metal.

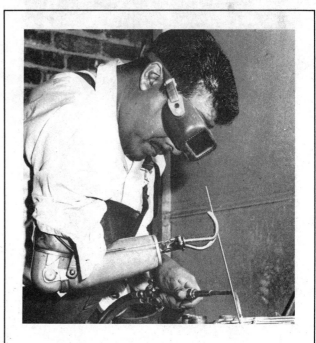

An artificial limb doesn't prevent this worker from pursuing his trade as a welder.

"I thought you'd guess this one," said the guide. "These are *welders*. They use heat from gas or electric torches to join pieces of metal together. These two work in a plant where bulldozers are made. They're joining two pieces of a bulldozer frame together. Welders also work in factories that make trucks, boilers, and all kinds of heavy machinery. But you see welders at work just about everywhere, not just in factories. They work on bridges, roads, pipelines, and construction sites, joining the metal beams and steel reinforcing rods that make those structures so strong. And they work on ships. Ship welders have to be highly skilled and they have to do their jobs very carefully indeed, to be sure that the ship doesn't break apart in rough seas. But that's enough for today about welders.

"Now let's look at these last workers in the display. They are demonstrating three different steps in *boilermaking*. The first worker measures and cuts all the pieces from metal, according to the blueprints. These measurements must be precise, because it may be impossible to correct a bad cut. The next worker joins the pieces together temporarily to see if they fit properly. It may be necessary to grind or cut in places to make a good fit. Then the last worker assembles the boiler by welding or riveting the pieces together. Small boilers, like the one shown here, may be assembled in the shop, but large ones, such as those that supply steam to drive turbines in electric power plants and in ships, must be put together in place. Any questions?"

Annie remembered some of Mr. Novacello's earlier comments and asked, "Couldn't robots do some of these jobs, too?"

"That's an excellent question," Mr. Novacello replied. "Welding is one of the most common uses for robots. In companies that do use robots, human welders are often used for less routine welding jobs and to set up the welding robots. Robots are also used for some forging, electroplating, and boilermaking jobs since the hot metal isn't as dangerous to the robots as it is to people," Mr. Novacello explained.

"So far we've seen occupations related to metal products. Now let's look at workers who make something entirely differently, something you all use every day in school — books."

Printing Occupations

"Most people in this country read and own books," continued Mr. Novacello. "But hundreds of years ago books were handwritten, and only the very rich could afford them. And of course in those days, ordinary people didn't know how to read. With the invention of the printing press and movable type, books became much easier and cheaper to print. More people bought them and learned to read them. So those of you who love reading can be grateful to the people who invented the processes we're about to see!"

Following their guide through a wide doorway, the children found themselves on a long balcony overlooking a huge factory in miniature. When they had spread themselves out along the railing to get a better view, Mr. Novacello continued his talk.

"If you could remove the roof of a printing plant and look inside, this is what you might see. The printing process begins in that far room, called the composing room. There the *compositors* set a written text, or manuscript, in type.

"In the old days, they had to choose type by hand from a large case, one letter at a time. And since all the letters were backwards, it was easy to make mistakes—especially with letters that look alike. Compositors had to take a good look at each letter to be sure they had the right one. That's where the saying 'Mind your ps and qs' comes from. Today, setting type by hand in this traditional way is done only for very special printing jobs.

"These days, compositors use machines with keyboards on which they type the text. These machines set type much faster than is possible by hand. Until the mid 1970s, Monotype and Linotype machines were the most

Boilermakers need mechanical aptitude and manual dexterity.

common typesetting machines—both of which force hot molten metal into rows of type. "Hot metal" typesetting is seldom used anymore. Most typesetting is now done by *photocompositors* who set type on a special kind of computer which uses light to create images of the letters on special photographic paper.

"These pages of text are then cut up and arranged into pages which are attached to mounting boards by paste-up or layout artists. The completed boards, or "flats," look like the pages of a finished book and are used for the printing process.

"Now there are even newer computer systems which combine the tasks of a *compositor* and a *layout artist*. In desktop publishing, one person uses a microcomputer to set type and form it into the columns which create a page. These systems then produce completed pages on a laser printer which are immediately ready for the printing process."

Mr. Novacello pointed to another room in the model. "Lithography is one of the most common types of commercial printing. You can see the lithographic process over here. *Lithographers* photograph the boards with large cameras and make negatives. They lay the negatives over metal plates that have been treated with a special light-sensitive chemical. When a plate is exposed to light, the chemical eats into the metal only in the places where the negative lets the light through until

... Presto! The plate has the image from the negative etched into it. And so a printing plate is created. Have I confused you all yet?"

Annie raised here hand. "How do the compositors make type for the pictures in a book?" she said.

"Good question!" answered Mr. Novacello, smiling. "The answer is that they don't. When they paste up a board, they leave blank spaces where the pictures will appear. Meanwhile, other workers enlarge or reduce each picture to the desired size and insert it in its intended space. Then the lithographer makes a plate of the entire page, pictures as well as words.

"When all the plates are ready, they go to the pressroom, this large area nearest us. There, the *press operators* set up the printing presses. They insert and adjust the plates, check the supplies of paper and ink, and run the presses. These presses print on both sides of paper that comes from a large roll, and then cut the paper into sheets of several book-pages each.

"These sheets go to the *bookbinders*, who fold them and assemble them into books. Using stitching and glue, they bind the books and attach the covers. After some final touches, the books are ready to be sold. And, if you have no questions, we are ready to move on."

Mr. Novacello led the group back through the main hall and into an adjoining room. The major exhibit was

Many printing press operators learn their trade through apprenticeship programs.

hall and into an adjoining room. The major exhibit was a large scale model, similar to that of the printing plant. Scattered around the edge of the room were life-sized figures standing at various machines. The children's curious gazes wandered every which way until the guide began to speak.

"I want to show you a few more metalworking occupations," he began, "but first I have a question. Who can tell me what a tool is?"

After a conspicuous silence, one brave boy raised his hand. "A tool is something you use to help you do something."

"Excellent," said Mr. Novacello. "And what are some examples of tools?"

Hammer, saw, screwdriver, pliers, chisel, all were mentioned in turn.

"Very good," commented the guide. "You have all given examples of handtools. What you see in this room are examples of *machine* tools. Some are about the size of a person; others, as you can see in the scale model, fill an entire room. Some perform only one kind of operation; others carry out a whole sequence of tasks automatically. But they all use power to cut, grind, drill or shape metal.

"Machine tools are an important part of industry because they can produce metal parts quickly with a high degree of precision. They make it possible to build complex machines, like automobiles, in large numbers. And those machines have interchangeable parts. For example, if your family's car has a worn-out gear, you can buy a new gear that will be virtually identical to the original one. If the gears were made with machine tools, we can mass produce automobiles, electric motors, airplanes, and hundreds of other everyday products.

"The people who work with machine tools have different kinds of jobs. *Machine tool operators* have the least complicated jobs and need the least training. They run a machine and watch for problems after *set-up workers* have performed the more demanding job of adjusting the machine and preparing it for use. Set-up workers and operators usually stick to one kind of tool, such as a drill press or a grinder. This type of job is often being done by computers and robots also, freeing human workers for the more complex jobs, like set-up work.

"*All-round machinists* have much more training and skill than machine-tool operators. They can operate many different kinds of machine tools, instead of just one kind. With their knowledge of materials and tools, they can do everything necessary to turn a block of metal into an intricate part."

Mr. Novacello walked over to one of the machines. "Take a close look at a machine tool," he said. "On each one you'll find a jig or fixture to hold the metal. You'll also see the "tool" portion of the machine that actually cuts, drills, grinds, or presses the metal. Very often, in order to make a particular part, a special jig or tool is needed. If so, a *tool-and-die maker* produces it. Tool-and-die makers are not only skilled machinists, but creative workers, too.

"And speaking of creativity, the most creative machine work of all is that of *instrument makers*. They are a bit like inventors—they take someone's else and translate it into a piece of experimental or custom-built equipment. And instrument makers work without the benefit of a detailed set of blueprints. Often there's only a rough sketch or idea to work from. They use their skill and imagination to fill in the details of the design and then carry it out.

"The CAD/CAM systems that I mentioned earlier can be very helpful here. Instrument makers can design

Tool-and-die makers need mechanical ability.

experimental equipment and test them in the computer with special model-making programs or produce test parts with machines that are controlled by the design computer. The computer can also control machinery to help tool-and-die makers produce very precise jigs and fixtures."

After pausing to take a breath, Mr. Novacello called for questions. Annie, who was fascinated by the size of some of the machines, raised her hand. "How do they put these machines in the factories?" she inquired.

Industrial Production Occupations

"Installing industrial equipment is the job of *millwrights*. They may have to dismantle the old machinery, lay a foundation, move the new equipment in, and assemble it. All of this takes a great degree of skill. Any other questions?"

There were no further questions.

"Well then," announced the guide, glancing at his

Millwrights use ropes and other rigging devices to help them move machinery.

watch, "so much for machining occupations. I'm going to take you now to another part of the museum. There we will closely examine the nature of one last production occupation. Follow me, if you will, as we set off to explore the production of hot dog lunches by the cafeteria cooks!"

Personal Characteristics

The day after the field trip, Mr. Borden had his social studies class review what they had learned at the museum. Walking up to the chalkboard and picking up a piece of chalk, he said, "Let's start by brainstorming for a few minutes. We learned a lot yesterday about the different kinds of jobs there are in industry. What can we say about these jobs? What are they like? What do

they have in common? And what sort of person would be good at this work?"

There were a few moments of silence. Then Dave raised his hand and answered, "Making things is what their jobs are all about. So you could say that industrial production workers deal with *things*. They have a lot more to do with things than they do with people or ideas."

"They *work with things*," Mr. Borden wrote on the board. "Very good. Is there anything to add to that?"

Dave continued, "Well, yes. The things these workers deal with could be raw materials ... machines ... tools ... equipment ... the final product itself. But whatever it is, it's an object of some kind. Something you can touch or feel or handle."

"Fine," said Mr. Borden. "Now, does everyone agree with what Dave has said?"

Phil spoke up. "I agree that all industrial production workers deal mainly with things, but beyond that, their jobs aren't the same at all. Just think about the different levels of skill they need. You have the set-up worker who gets a drill press ready to use, makes all those calculations and adjustments and so forth... And then you have the drill press operator who just runs the machine! That operator's job seems pretty straightforward to me. It's just a matter of starting and stopping the machine and watching it while it's running.

"And don't forget the machinist," Phil continued, warming to his subject. "The machinists do highly skilled work. They have to know a lot to be able to set up and operate a lathe to make a part for a motor, for example. So even though industrial production workers' jobs have some similarities, they aren't all alike. They range from routine and simple to very complex."

"Industrial production work involves *varying degrees of skill*," wrote Mr. Borden. "Thanks, Phil. Now, what else?

"These workers work mostly with their hands," suggests Barbara.

"That's right," said the teacher. "They do *manual work*. They have to be good at doing things with their hands in order to work with handtools or operate machines. It takes coordination and dexterity ... the same kind involved in making a model or repairing a lawn mower, for example. Anything more?"

Annie had something to say. "These workers have to use their heads. They read blueprints, measure things, and make calculations."

"You're right," answered Mr. Borden. "Some of the industrial production workers we've learned about need what's called *spatial ability* to work from diagrams and blueprints. Spatial ability means they can look at a flat drawing of a three-dimensional object and picture the object in their mind. They also have to have good *form*

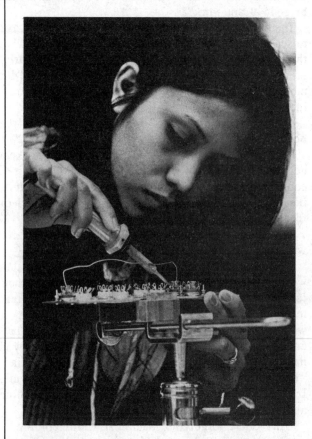

Working with handtools takes concentration.

"*Mechanical interest* is important," Mr. Borden wrote. "And...?"

There was silence.

"Well, I can think of several things," continued the teacher. "Industrial workplaces can be noisy and dirty. Industrial workers have to be able to do their jobs in places that may be *uncomfortable* or *unpleasant*. Some of the jobs are strenuous, and require both *strength* and *stamina*. Not all industrial production workers have to lift and carry heavy things, of course, but some do. And workers like assemblers and machine-tool operators may be on their feel all day long. That's tiring, too."

Mr. Borden glanced around the room. "Does anyone have anything to add? No? Well, then, let's go on. The other day we saw a film about an automobile factory..."

Training

A week after the museum trip, Annie gave an oral report in Mr. Borden's social studies class.

"If you wanted to be a lawyer," she began, "you would go to law school. To become a dentist, you'd attend a

This automobile worker enjoys his job.

perception to notice details and detect slight flaws in shapes and surfaces. And, like just about all workers, they have to be able to understand instructions, reason, and use common sense. As Phil has just told us, reasoning ability is much more important for some industrial production workers than for others. I think we were all impressed with the problem-solving skills it takes to be an instrument maker.

Pat spoke up. "Some of the jobs seem boring to me. Workers like assemblers do the same thing over and over again.

"Yes, that's right," agreed Mr. Borden. "Some industrial production jobs involve repetitive tasks. Jobs like that are just right, though, for people who like *repetitive*, *concrete*, *organized* activities. Now, what else can we say about these workers and their jobs?"

Emily raised her hand. "It seems to me that people who have what it takes to learn a skilled trade are people with some sort of *mechanical interest*. So many of the jobs we learned about at the museum involved machines and mechanical principles. The workers were applying mechanical principles to practical situations."

Industrial Production Occupations

school of dentistry. But where would you go to learn an industrial trade? For less difficult occupations, such as machine tool operator or assembler, you could train right on the job. But how would you break into a skilled occupation? Would you enroll at the State College of Boilermaking? Tool-and-Die Graduate School? Welding University? That would be one way.

"Trade schools and technical institutes offer programs in the skilled trades—welding, printing, and tool-and-die making, for example. These programs provide theoretical instruction and the practical skills

you'd need right away on the job. Vocational training is given in both public and private schools. You're probably familiar with the vocational education courses given here in our school system. There are, in addition, thousands of private schools that teach the skills you'd need for a job in industry.

"There are other ways to train for industrial production occupations, too. Often, the best route is through an apprenticeship. Consisting of planned classroom and on-the-job instruction, apprenticeships normally last about 4 years, although they range from 1 to 6 years. It

This woman is training for a job as an electric power plant operator.

all depends on the occupation. Apprenticeships are arranged by unions and employers.

"Here's how they work. Let's say you are an apprentice machinist with the Wonderful Widget Company. As an apprentice, you train for 4 years on the job, learning every aspect of a machinist's work. You also go to class to learn blueprint reading, shop mathematics, and other subjects. After completing all the requirements for the program, you receive a certificate that proves you have all the skills of a journeyworker machinist.

"Many workers do learn their skills without apprenticing. Quite a few get their training on the job by watching experienced workers, asking questions, and having someone guide them as they try the job themselves. While some of these workers have attended a vocational high school or a trade school, others begin with no previous exposure to the occupation. And then there are workers who "pick up the trade" on their own by watching, imitating, and experimenting whenever they can."

Employers generally prefer to hire people who have finished high school.

Many workers learn their skills on the job.

More About Training

The Job Facts at the end of this chapter summarize the training requirements for each of 33 industrial production occupations. If one interests you, you can begin preparing in high school. Math, science, drafting, shop, and other industrial arts courses will help. You can join a chapter of VICA (Vocational Industrial Clubs of America), if your school has one. VICA chapters plan projects, take field trips, and hold competitions in such skill areas as welding, machining, and printing.

One final tip: Plan to finish high school. Employers do hire people who haven't finished high school, but they prefer those who have. They know that high school gives you basic skills you'll need for the job. And the diploma shows them that you're willing to finish something once you've started it. The increasing use of technology, like computers, robots and CAD/CAM systems, also demands a higher level of education from people who will work with this expensive and sophisticated equipment. You may need to get additional training or education beyond high school to qualify for some of these jobs.

Assembler

Karen says, "You don't need a great deal of education and experience to do what I do, but you have to be good with your hands."

Exploring Careers

The traditional Fourth of July picnic in Elks Gap last weekend had been a big affair; everyone in town had been there. Under the trees the fire department had set up grills to barbeque the chickens that would be eaten long before the fireworks began. There, Karen ran into her new neighbor, Sarah Green. Sarah and her husband had moved to Elks Gap just a few weeks before, and she and Karen had quickly gotten to be friends.

Over barbequed chicken, Sarah had told Karen that she was thinking about looking for a job. Karen told her about Astro Electronics, the plant where she worked.

"Why don't you come out and apply for a job like mine?" she had suggested. "You don't need a great deal of education or experience to do what I do. But you do need to be good with your hands. You need patience, too, and have to be able to concentrate on very small tasks."

Karen is a bench assembler. She assembles circuit boards for television sets and other electronic equipment, and works at a bench rather than on a moving assembly line. Putting together complete circuit boards means installing all the components: Capacitors, resistors, diodes, transistors, and meds. It means soldering these components into place, and installing connecting wires where necessary. Karen usually works from a diagram or blueprint that shows her where to insert each component. Sometimes, however, Karen uses a "sample board"—an exact model of the board she is constructing.

Karen's job as a bench assembler is more complex and involved than that of an assembly line worker. Karen assembles the circuit boards from start to finish, instead of just inserting one or two components, which is what she might be doing if she were working on an assembly line. On an assembly line she would repeat the same task

Assembling electronic components is very delicate, detailed work that requires concentration.

Industrial Production Occupations

over and over again, rather than complete all the steps of the circuit board assembly process herself.

Karen didn't need any special training to get her job at Astro Electronics. The company put her through a training course the first day she went to work there, and since then she's been learning and gaining speed through practice.

"It's a bit like putting together a puzzle or a model airplane," she had told Sarah. "It's very delicate, detailed work that requires a lot of concentration. I have to use a magnifying glass sometimes, when I'm working on very tiny boards. It can be hard on the eyes. But I enjoy the work. It's not boring at all, because I put together

Karen uses a magnifying glass to put together very small parts.

many different kinds of circuit boards, and the variety makes it interesting."

Karen had been excited and enthusiastic when she talked to Sarah about her job. But now the holiday is over and Karen is back at work. She has to make an effort to concentrate on the work in front of her.

Tools are scattered around Karen's workbench—wire strippers, wire cutters, pliers, lacing cord, a soldering iron. There's cleaning fluid on the workbench, and several trays of electrical components, too. Karen picks up an electrical component and plugs it into some holes in the circuit board. She turns the board over and uses her wire cutters to clip the wire that is sticking out of the circuit board in the back. Then she picks up her soldering iron and solders some metal onto the bottom of the component that's sticking through the circuit board. The melted metal, as it dries, holds the component securely in place. Karen picks up another electrical component and repeats the process.

The "bench" that Karen is sitting at is actually a row of long tables, like the kind used in a school cafeteria. There are lots of benches—row after row. The benches fill up the large warehouse-like building where Karen works. The work area is clean and the temperature is comfortable. Karen likes being able to sit down all day rather than stand, as she'd probably have to do on an assembly line. Sometimes her neck and back get sore from bending over her bench, but it's better than standing all day, in her opinion.

All of the people working at Karen's bench are assembling the same kind of circuit board that Karen is. They work quietly, each concentrating on the work at hand. It's easy to become involved in the work when there's so much detail.

"How's everything down on this end?" The question startles Karen, but she recognizes the voice. It's her supervisor, Betty.

Karen smiles and replies, "All right, I guess, but I'm going to need some more resistors soon."

Betty nods. "I'll go bring some over. Does anyone else need anything?" The man next to Karen asks for some more wire. Betty nods again and then hurries off.

"She's always rushing around," Karen thinks to herself. "But then I guess supervising 30 workers is a pretty demanding job."

Before long Betty is back with the materials. "Oh, Karen," she says, "we have a new worker. She'll be coming out of training after lunch. I thought I'd place her next to you, so that you can help her if she has any problems."

"All right," Karen replies quietly.

"By the way," says Betty, "it's your friend Sarah." Karen looks up with a surprised smile.

Exploring

Assemblers need to be good at working with their hands.
- Are you good at fixing things?
- Are you handy with tools?
- Can you repair your bicycle?
- Do you enjoy leisure activities that involve working with your hands, such as sewing, macrame, stringing beads, model building, or furniture refinishing?

Assembly work usually involves a lot of repetition. Assemblers must be willing to perform repetitious tasks.

- Do you enjoy needlework such as knitting, crocheting, or quilting?
- Can you put up with the repetition involved in mowing grass, shoveling snow, painting a house, or putting down tile?

Speed can be important in assembly work.

- Are you good at activities that require finger dexterity such as slapjack, jacks, or shuffling and dealing cards?

Assembly work requires attention to detail and the ability to follow diagrams and written directions.

- Are you good at following a recipe, sewing or doing needlepoint from a pattern, building a model from written instructions, assembling a radio from a kit, or painting by numbers?
- Are you good at reading maps?
- Do you understand football plays when they're written out?

Assemblers work indoors. They stay in a small work area while they do their jobs.

- Can you sit still through your classes?
- Can you concentrate without feeling the need to move around all the time?

Factory workers relaxing in the products they make.

Machinist

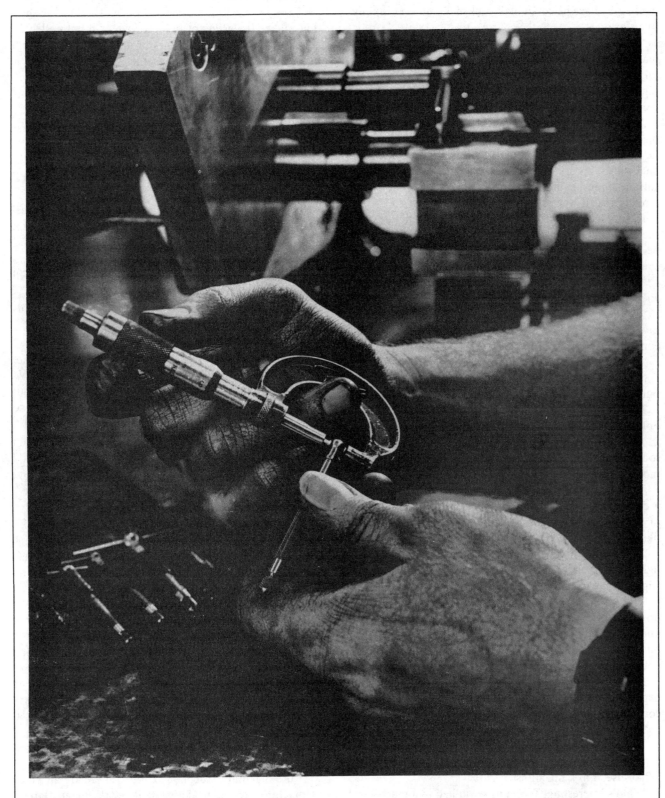

Machinists do very precise work.

Joe rolled over and opened his eyes. Through the dense grey haze he could make out small lights twinkling like stars.

"Strange, it wasn't foggy out," he thought, trying to make some sense of the haze that had swallowed him up. Images swirled through his mind: A quiet summer night, the street leading to his house, unfamiliar lights behind a hedge, a blinding flash, and. . . .

Joe realized with a start that he was no longer outside his house. In fact he had no idea where he was. Alarmed, he jumped to his feet, but lost his footing and fell backwards. As Joe struggled to his feet, he saw that the surface underneath him was as clear as glass. He knew already that it was as slick as ice.

Joe made an effort to focus on his surroundings despite the grey haze that made it difficult to see. He seemed to be in the middle of a large round room. He stood and cautiously took a step toward the lights.

"Who are you?" boomed a loud, authoritative voice. Joe froze.

"Who are you?" repeated the voice impatiently. Joe saw the spheres of light blink as the voice spoke. He felt compelled to answer.

"I'm Joe Von Braun. Where am I?"

No answer. Joe thought about making a break for it, but remembered how slippery the floor was.

"I must be dreaming," he thought. "Of course, this is only a dream. I'll wake up any minute."

"Please, don't run," said another voice, a soft and soothing one this time. The sound frightened him even more, because this voice was closer and undeniably real.

As Joe turned in the direction of the voice, the haze grew lighter. Only a few yards in front of him a sphere of light was suspended in midair. In the haze it looked like the sun on a cloudy day.

"Please, sir, don't run," repeated the gentle voice. The light blinked as the words were spoken. Joe still was too frightened to speak.

"We know our first voice disturbed you, but we mean no harm. We are visitors to your world and we wish to know more about you. We have talked to many of you, but there is still so much to learn. Please tell us about yourself."

The voice was calm and reassuring. Encouraged, Joe began to speak. He spoke haltingly at first, then more confidently.

"I don't know where to begin. . . ."

"Tell us anything."

"Well, my name is Von Braun. I'm 35. Have a wife. What else? I'm a machinist. . . ."

"That's interesting. We've never talked to a machinist before. What is it?"

"A machinist is. . .that is. . .I make things."

"What things?" asked the voice, quietly.

"Parts for machines, usually. I work in a machine shop that makes replacement parts for water pumps, electric generators, sometimes cars. . .well, anything, really. We'll make almost anything from metal."

"What is metal?"

"What is metal?" repeated Joe, puzzled. "Everyone knows what metal is."

"We're sorry, but we don't," replied the voice. "Please explain metal to us."

"Metal is a. . .well, it's steel, iron, brass. . .I don't know the scientific definition. How can I explain? Wait, I'll show you."

Joe searched his pockets and found the 6-inch steel ruler he used at work. He held the ruler in front of him and said, "This is metal. This is steel. . . ."

A white light streaked from above, touched Joe's hand and instantly disappeared. The ruler was gone. Joe fell to his knees. He was almost in tears.

"We do know metal. We have seen it before. Tell us more about how you work with metal."

"Please don't hurt me," cried Joe.

"Don't be afraid," responded the voice, as the sphere of light blinked rapidly. "We would never hurt you. We only want to understand. We have seen metal before, but we have nothing like it where we live. We are eager to learn about it. How do you make things from metal?"

Joe hesitated, then began talking again. He did not know what else to do.

"Usually I work from a blueprint the boss gives me. I start. . . ."

"What is a blueprint?" interrupted the voice.

"A blueprint is a drawing of the part I have to make. By looking at it I know what the final product will look like. The blueprint also has the specifications. They tell me how long and wide to make the part and what kind of metal to use. Usually the specifications also give an estimate of how much time I have to make the part."

"Thank you, we understand what a blueprint is. Please continue," said the voice, as the sphere blinked.

"First I gather the metal stock. I'd better explain that. "Metal stock" is a term for all the different pieces of metal I'll be working with: Steel rods, brass tubing, bars of aluminum, whatever. Then I do the layout. I mark the metal to show where I should cut it, put holes in it, or shape it."

"How do you cut it or shape it? Isn't metal too hard?"

"I use machines," explained Joe. "There are all kinds of machines specially designed to work metal—lathes, milling machines, drill presses, planers, and grinders, for example.

Industrial Production Occupations

"I use saws to cut metal to the right length; drills to put holes in it; planers to shape it; and grinders to smooth its surface. The milling machine and the lathe are the most versatile of all. They can do almost any job."

"So these machines do all your work," said the voice.

"No, no, no," Joe said hastily. "The machines are useless without me. I have to set them up, so they run properly."

"Oh, excuse us. Please go on."

"After I've done the layout, I start using the machines. The first thing I do is decide which machines to use. Usually that depends on what I'm doing. For some jobs I have to use a certain size lathe or a milling machine. For others I can choose how I do the job. Take drilling a hole. I can use a drill press or a milling machine. The drill is a little faster, but the milling machine is more accurate.

"The next step is to set up the machine. The part of the machine that actually cuts the metal I'm working on is called the tool. Tools come in all shapes and sizes. Some are round with teeth like a circular saw. Others look like chisels. Tools are made from different types of metal, usually very hard steel. Before I can cut the metal workpiece, I have to select the tool that's the right shape, size, and hardness to make the cut I need.

"Then I mount the tool on the machine and set the speed that determines how fast the tool will cut the metal. The speed is very important. If I make the cut too fast, the tool will wear out quickly or break. This could ruin the workpiece. Sometimes I set up a hose that sprays liquid on the tool and the metal. The liquid keeps them cool as the cutting is done.

"All of this may be hard to understand. Let me give you some examples. Say I had a bar of metal an inch in diameter and I wanted to make it thinner—just half an inch in diameter. I would put the bar on a lathe. The bar lies in the machine horizontally and spins very fast. A tool that looks like a chisel would be held in a clamp on the side of the machine. By moving handles and gears at the base of the lathe I can position the tool against the spinning bar, to cut it to the right size.

"If I wanted to put a hole in the same bar, I would use the milling machine. The bar would be clamped on a flat table that moves up and down and sideways. The tool—in this case a drill—is held in an arm above the table. The tool spins and the bar is positioned under it.

Machinists are among the most highly skilled manual workers.

I make the hole in the bar by moving the table up until the tool cuts through the metal.

"I hope that's clear. I wish I could explain it better."

"You're doing fine," said the voice. The lights blinked several times. "What do you do after you have cut the metal with the machines?"

"Well, after I've cut the metal, I measure it to make sure it meets the specifications. Sometimes I can do it with a ruler, that thing I showed you before. Most jobs require more precision. A workpiece may have to be between 5.999 and 6.001 inches long. I use a micrometer to make really precise measurements. The precision is necessary because the part I make usually goes into a larger machine. I have to make it just the right size, so it fits.

"When I'm sure all the pieces are acceptable, I can assemble the part. That means a lot of hand work with files, hammers, and screwdrivers—more measuring. And that's it," concluded Joe.

"Do all machinists do the same things you do?" asked the voice.

"No, not at all. It depends on where you work. Some machinists make the same part over and over again. In some modern machine shops, industrial robots now do that kind of repetitive job. Other machinists make many different kinds of parts; that's what I do. And some machinists work in factories repairing production machinery. Well, is there anything else you want to know?" sighed Joe.

Machining requires concentration.

"Are you tired? You have been very helpful."

"No, I feel fine. I like talking about my job. Not everyone could do what I do. You have to like machines and tools. It's dirty, hard work a lot of the time. You're on your feet most of the day, and it's not just physical work. You have to be able to plan. You have to be good at math to calculate the measurements, machine speeds, and such. You have to be able to concentrate and have the patience to do really precise work. Besides all that you need a bit of imagination. Not everyone can make a three- dimensional object from a flat drawing."

"You are very proud of your skills."

"I always have been—ever since my apprenticeship. There's something special about taking a piece of metal and turning it into something useful."

"What is an apprenticeship?"

"It's a traditional way of learning a craft or trade. You learn by working with experienced workers. And by studying. After I graduated from high school I was accepted in an apprenticeship program at the Navy Yard. I learned to run the machines on the job and studied math blueprint reading, and the characteristics of metals in evening classes."

"You have been most helpful," said the voice. "But if we don't return you now, you will be missed."

"Wait a minute," shouted Joe. "Who are you? Don't you think you owe me some explanations?"

"Whatever we tell you, you would forget in a short time. Goodbye and thank you." The sphere vanished.

"Wait! Wait!"

As Joe shouted the grey haze grew more dense. Soon he could not see anything. He felt very warm and the haze was so thick he had trouble breathing. He thrashed wildly with his arms.

A hand firmly gripped his shoulder. "Joe, wake up! Wake up!"

Joe jumped up. He was in his bed and his wife was shaking him.

"That must have been some dream," she said.

"Was it ever!"

"It's over now. Go to sleep."

The next day Joe could not recall any of the details of his dream nor could be find his steel ruler.

Industrial Production Occupations

Most machinists learn their skills on the job.

Exploring

Machinists make parts for factory machinery, cars, and other metal products.

- Do you like to build things?
- Do you like to work with your hands?
- Do you build models or make jewelry?
- Do you repair bicycles or customize automobiles?
- Do you enjoy woodworking?

Machinists use handtools and such machines as lathes and drill presses.

- Do you use tools or machines for a hobby, for work around the house, for gardening, for farming, or for repairing cars, vans, or trucks?
- Do you like to learn how machines work?
- Do you like to learn how to use tools?
- Is it easy for you to learn how to use a tool you've never used before?

Machinists follow blueprints and diagrams. They use mathematics to make measurements and set up their machines.

- Can you read and understand graphs, diagrams, and charts?
- Can you read road maps?
- Can you look at a drawing and picture the three-dimensional object in your mind?
- Do you like to work with numbers?
- Do you like to solve written math problems?

Machinists must do accurate work.

- If you are fixing or building something, do you try to do it just right?
- Have you ever done any detailed work?
- Do you build complicated models or embroider?
- Can you work on something for a long time without becoming bored or careless?

Machinists usually work with little direct supervision. They must be responsible.

- Do you usually get your school assignments done on time?
- Can you work along successfully?
- Do you have hobbies in which you work alone?

Photocompositor

Bernard Petrocelli has seen the changes made in the printing industry by the advancement in the fields of electronics and computer science. Hobbies and courses in these areas can help provide a good background for a career in the printing inindustry.

Industrial Production Occupations

Bernard Petrocelli pulled into the parking lot of Broadview Elementary School. Before getting out of his car, he glanced in the rear-view mirror to make sure that his tie was on straight. "I'm glad I don't have to put on a suit and tie every morning," he thought to himself.

He checked in at the office, where Ms. Kawasaki, his daughter's sixth grade teacher, was waiting to greet him.

"It certainly is nice to meet you, Mr. Petrocelli. We've all been learning so much from the parents who come and speak to the class about the work they do. I'm sure the children will be fascinated to hear about your job."

"Thank you very much," replied Mr. Petrocelli as the two walked down the hall.

Ms. Kawasaki continued, "I've been doing a bit of research and I'm amazed at the changes that have taken place in the printing industry in the last 20 years. Phototypesetting, laser printing, desktop publishing... It's hard to believe all of the changes that have developed in such a short time!"

"Yes, there have been some astounding changes in printing technology. And, with the use of computers, things are changing more rapidly than ever. My work in the composing room has come a long way from the days behind a noisy Linotype machine casting hot metal."

The two adults entered Ms. Kawasaki's classroom and took seats in the back of the room, waiting quietly for the music teacher to finish his lesson.

After music was over, Ms. Kawasaki went to the front of the room to speak to the class. "As you all know, we have a guest speaker today who is here to help us learn more about the world of work. He is Maria's father, Mr. Petrocelli, and he is going to tell us about his job as a photocompositor in a print shop. We already have discussed how important printing is, as a means of both communication and learning, so I think you will all be interested in finding out more about the process. Now, without further delay, I'd like to introduce Mr. Petrocelli."

"Good morning, boys and girls," Mr. Petrocelli began. "It's a pleasure to be here. As your teacher told you, I'm a photocompositor and I work for the Atlas Printing Company—a large shop downtown. We print everything that's fit to be published, including magazines, brochures, advertisements, envelopes, and even labels for cans of food. This morning I'm going to talk to you briefly about the history of printing and then I'll tell you about my job and what I do. Please feel free to ask questions at any time."

A boy who was sitting on the edge of his seat raised his hand and burst out, "Do you print money, too?"

Mr. Petrocelli smiled and replied, "Paper money is printed, but that's one job we don't handle at Atlas. It's illegal for anyone but the Federal Government to print its paper currency. That's done at the U.S. Bureau of Engraving and Printing in Washington, D.C.

"Printing was first practiced by the Chinese over a thousand years ago," Maria's father continued. "They used carved wooden blocks to print. I imagine you've done pretty much the same thing yourselves in art class. Those early Chinese printers carved pictures or words on wooden blocks, inked or painted the blocks, then pressed them against another surface to make a print.

"The wood block method of printing developed by the Chinese was slow and painstaking. Most books and manuscripts were handwritten until the 1400's. About this time, people began experimenting, looking for a way to produce books more quickly and cheaply. Around 1450, a German named Johann Gutenberg invented a process for making movable type out of metal. The process allowed him to use the same type over and over again to print different pages. He also invented the printing press, which he probably adapted from a wine or cheese press, and developed sticky ink to be used with the metal type."

A girl in the front row raised her hand. "We learned that Johann Gutenberg is called the Father of Printing."

Mr. Petrocelli replied, "Yes, he is often referred to as the Father of Printing because his invention of movable type revolutionized the printing process. Printing spread rapidly in Western Europe, and by the early 1500's more than a thousand print shops were operating."

"What has happened since then?" asked a small boy in the back of the room.

"Our story continues," said Mr. Petrocelli. "The first book printed in America less than 20 years after the Pilgrims landed at Plymouth Rock. The writings of two early printers, Benjamin Franklin and Thomas Paine, strengthened the spirit of unrest in the 1700's that eventually brought about the American Revolution. Their influence kept up the will of the Colonies to win the war.

"Over the years, printers gradually introduced improvements in the typesetting and design of books. Eventually, the job of printing became specialized. That means the printer—who in the days of Benjamin Franklin was also the publisher, editor, type designer, and book seller—no longer performed all those other duties."

"Are you a printer?" a girl in the third row wanted to know.

"Well, not exactly...I was just getting to the part where I fit in," answered Mr. Petrocelli. "The 20th century has witnessed many changes in printing. Jobs have become much more specialized as the industry has grown. And the printing industry has grown tremendously! Well over a billion books are bought each year in the United States alone. Furthermore, technology has changed the way we do our jobs. Today's world is one of automation. Machines perform much of the work that used to be done by hand. I think my job in the composing room illustrates some important changes that have taken place in the printing industry over the last 25 years.

"In the composing room, we set type. We take the "copy"—the material that is to be printed—and from that we prepare pages of type. When I first started as a compositor 27 years ago, I operated a machine called a Linotype. I learned the work right on the job, as an apprentice. To make a line of type, I punched the letters from the keyboard. The machine then made words from a hot metal mixture it had pressed into molds of these letters. This cooled into a solid metal strip—or 'lineo'type'." He reached into his pocket and pulled out a silver colored bar. "To give you a better idea, I brought along a line of type."

"Can we pass it around the room? I can't see it," came a voice from the back of the room. "We'll handle it very carefully."

Mr. Petrocelli smiled. "That's a good idea, because the metal is a misture of lead, tin, and antimony, and it will bend or scratch rather easily. It's not hard like steel or copper."

He continued, "Operating the Linotype was hard work. The machines were hot and noisy and my clothes often got splashed with hot lead."

"Then why did you stay in the job?" a girl asked.

"There were lots of good things about the job," Mr. Petrocelli replied, "For one thing, I've always been proud to work in the printing industry because it's so important to all of us. And a job like mine takes skill. When I was operating the Linotype, I had to space all the words

Mr. Petrocelli is setting type on a phototypesetter. "This is like using a typewriter," he explains, "but there is a lot more to know than just being able to type on a keyboard.

properly to fit the column size and decide where to break words at the end of a line when necessary—all those things require judgment.

"After I had been there about 10 years, the company I was working for adopted a new method of setting type. Instead of the machine casting of molten metal, type is set by a photographic process that uses paper and chemicals. Because photography is such an important part of this process, it's called phototypesetting. Sometimes it's called photocomposition.

"To make the change, I had to go through a training program. I wasn't at all pleased about changing over to cold type at first, and complained about it to the union representative. I figured that I had mastered the Linotype and I didn't want to start from the beginning with a new machine. I was pretty upset for a while. But eventually I realized that the Linotype machine really was on the way out, and that I had no choice but to pick up new skills."

"Wasn't it hard to "relearn" your job after all those years?" asked a boy sitting near the windows.

"Becoming a photocompositor did take some getting used to," Mr. Petrocelli replied. "I had to learn to work a whole new machine. The keyboard was completely different, so I had to block the old one from my mind. Also, this machine produced paper prints or film negatives instead of strips of metal."

"Why did the company change from hot metal to phototype?" a girl asked.

"Phototypesetting offers many advantages over casting type from hot metal," answered Maria's father. "It's a fast, flexible, relatively inexpensive method of setting type.

"For example, in phototypesetting, the print will always be clear and perfect, no matter how many copies must be produced. That's because it's photographed. When metal type is used—the kind you're passing around the class right now—the metal letters must be inked to make print. However, the pressure of the metal type against the paper causes "ink squeeze", which tends to make the edges of the printed letters irregular. Also, phototype is very convenient when different type sizes are needed for one job. A simple magnifying lens allows the machine to photograph correctly sized type."

Mr. Petrocelli went on. "My career took one more major twist when I went to work for Atlas about 4 years ago. Being a large company, they had the most modern equipment. Once again I needed more training. . .because Atlas uses computers in their typesetting system."

An enthusiastic student burst out, "Wow, another "new career" for you!"

"In a way, yes," Mr. Petrocelli responded. "In this typesetting operation, I type on a special keyboard just like I did in the other phototype process. The keyboard has many extra keys, however, and I had to learn them all. There are keys, for example, that indicate the size and style of type and the space between letters. There also are keys that give the machine directions such as "delete" or "store in memory". A screen that looks like a television screen has been added to the keyboard so now I can see the characters as I set the manuscript. The screen is called a Visual Display Terminal.

"After the copy has been typed onto the keyboard, my machine produces a tape that later is fed into a computer. The computer's job, basically, is to decide when to hyphenate words and how to space them properly so that the margins will be even. The computer has been programmed with a set of rules so that it knows, for example, that *hearing* should be hyphenated *hear-ing*. It also is instructed that *ring* should not be hyphenated *r-ing*, as that's a one-syllable word. When I handled the Linotype, I made all those decisions myself. The computer produces a tape that "drives" our phototypesetting machine and prints out material much faster than any person could do it. Our system, for example, can print a page of type every 3 or 4 seconds!"

The students clearly were impressed. Maria beamed. Her father then asked for more questions.

One boy hesitated, then asked, "In the beginning, you said you learned your trade by apprenticeship. I'm not sure what that means."

"That's a good question," Mr. Petrocelli replied. "In the apprenticeship training program, I learned my trade on the job—at first by watching others and then picking up skills on my own. At the same time I had classroom instruction in related subjects, such as typography, printing, and English. The program was run jointly by the union I belong to and the company. It lasted 4 years; I gradually gained more responsibility and earned more money."

Another pupil asked Mr. Petrocelli what advice he'd give to students interested in printing.

"First of all, I would recommend that you finish high school. There are courses you can take in school that will give you a good background—typing and English, for example. Don't underestimate English! Grammar is a "must." And learn all you can about electronics, computers, and photography—for that is where the future lies in the printing industry. Desktop publishing is really revolutionizing the printing industry. It allows people to use micro computers, similar to the ones that you may have here at school, to set type, design the page layout, and produce completed pages that are already to be printed."

Ms. Kawasaki walked up the aisle and joined the speaker at the front of the room. "I'm afraid our time is up, but I'd like you to know how much we enjoyed your talk today."

"It was my pleasure to be here," replied Mr. Petrocelli.

Just then the class broke out in loud and enthusiastic applause.

Mr. Petrocelli helps an assistant with layout work.

Exploring

Photocompositors need finger and manual dexterity in order to type copy on the keyboard of a composing machine.

- Do you knit, do needlework, or do macrame?
- Can you thread a needle quickly?
- Can you type?
- Are you good at games like slapjack and jacks?
- Can you shuffle and deal a hand of cards quickly?
- Do you enjoy leisure activities that involve working with your hands, such as making jewelry, building models, or refinishing furniture?

Photocompositors must have an eye for detail. They must follow the copy exactly and detect every single mark on material that comes back for correction.

- Can you read road maps easily? Can you find a place on a road map quickly?
- Do you like to do word-finds and other games where you must find hidden objects in pictures?
- Are you good at following a recipe, sewing or doing needlework from a pattern, building a model from written instructions, assembling a radio from a kit, or painting by numbers?

The work of photocompositors can be repetitious.

- Do you enjoy needlework that involves a lot of repetition, such as knitting, crocheting, or quilting?
- Can you put up with the repetition involved in mowing grass, shoveling snow, painting a house, or putting down tile?

Photocompositors work indoors. They are confined to their work areas for long periods of time.

- Can you sit still in the car during long trips?
- Can you sit still through your classes or an assembly program?

Industrial Production Occupations

Job Facts

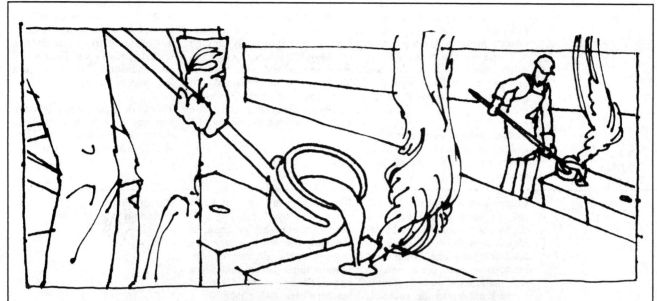

There isn't room in this book for a story about every industrial production occupation. However, you'll find some important facts about 32 of these occupations in the following section. If you want additional information about any of them, you might begin by consulting the Department of Labor's *Occupational Outlook Handbook*, which should be available in your school or public library.

Occupation	Nature and Places of Work	Training and Qualifications	Other Information

FOUNDRY OCCUPATIONS

Occupation	Nature and Places of Work	Training and Qualifications	Other Information
Patternmakers	Foundry patternmakers are highly skilled craftworkers. They make the metal or wood patterns that are used in producing industrial and household goods from metal castings. Most patternmakers work in shops that make and sell castings. The rest work in plants that make castings to use in their final products, such as plants operated by manufacturers of automobiles or machinery.	Precision, accuracy, and manual dexterity are very important. Patternmakers work from blueprints and check dimensions with instruments such as micrometers and calipers. To read blueprints, they must be able to visualize objects in three dimensions. Apprenticeship, usually lasting 5 years, is the best way of learning to be a patternmaker. A few apprenticeships last only 3 or 4 years. Although it is difficult to learn the trade on the job, some skilled machinists transfer to metal patternmaking with additional on-the-job training and experience. Employers almost always require apprentices to have a high school education. Vocational and technical school training in patternmaking, metalworking, and machining may be credited toward completion of the apprenticeship.	Patternmakers work indoors in well-lighted, well-ventilated areas and are not exposed to the heat and noise of the foundry floor. Although not strenuous, patternmaking requires considerable standing and moving about. Because patternmakers learn either basic metalworking or woodworking, they are qualified for related jobs—as machinists or cabinetmakers, for example.

Occupation	Nature and Places of Work	Training and Qualifications	Other Information
Molders	Molders make sand molds for use in producing metal castings. Most are machine molders; they operate molding machines that pack and ram the sand mechanically. Others are hand molders, and use manual methods and power tools to construct sand molds. Molders work in shops that make and sell castings, or in plants that make castings to use in their final products.	People become skilled hand molders by completing a 4-year apprenticeship program or learning the work informally through on-the-job training. Less hand molding jobs and most machine molding jobs can be learned with 2 to 6 months on-the-job training, but employers prefer those with apprenticeship training.	Working conditions vary. In older foundries, work is performed in a dusty, noisy, dirty, hot atmosphere. In foundries with improved ventilation and air-conditioning, there is much less heat and dust. The work is physically demanding and may be hazardous at times. Molders must be careful to avoid burns from hot metal.
Coremakers	Coremakers prepare the "cores" that are placed in molds to form the hollow sections in metal castings. Cores are made either by hand or by machine. When hand methods are used, the coremaker uses mallets and other handtools to pack sand into the corebox. Machine coremakers operate machines that pack the sand. Coremakers work in shops that make and sell castings or in plants that make castings to use in their final products.	People become skilled hand coremakers by completing a 4-year apprenticeship program, or learning the work informally through on-the-job training. Apprenticeships also are sometimes required for more difficult machine coremaking jobs. Apprenticeships in coremaking and molding often are combined.	Coremaking is one of the least hazardous foundry jobs.

Industrial Production Occupations

Occupation	Nature and Places of Work	Training and Qualifications	Other Information

MACHINING OCCUPATIONS

All-round Machinists

Machinists are skilled metalworkers. They use metalworking machines of various kinds to make and repair metal parts, tools, and machines.

Most machinists work in factories that produce metal products such as automobiles and machinery. Almost every factory using substantial amounts of machinery employs all-round machinists to maintain its mechanical equipment. The Federal Government employs machinists in Navy Yards and other places.

Leading areas of employment are Los Angeles, Chicago, New York, Philadelphia, Boston, San Francisco, and Houston.

Precision and accuracy are very important. Machinists consult blueprints before beginning to make a machined product, and check the results with precision instruments such as micrometers.

A 4-year formal apprenticeship is the best training, although many machinists learn this trade on the job. A high school or vocational school education is desirable.

All-round machinists can operate most types of machine tools, whereas machine tool operators generally work with one kind only.

Machinists must follow strict safety regulations when working around high-speed machine tools. Short-sleeved shirts, safety glasses, and other devices are required to reduce accidents.

Opportunities for advancement are good. With additional training, machinists can become tool-and-die makers. Skilled machinists can open their own shops.

Many machinists are members of unions.

Instrument Makers (Mechanical)

Instrument makers work with scientists and engineers to translate designs and ideas into experimental or custom-built mechanical equipment. Most of them work for firms that manufacture instruments or for research and development laboratories that make special devices for scientific research. The Federal Government also employs instrument makers.

The main centers of instrument making are in and around New York, Chicago, Los Angeles, Boston, Philadelphia, Washington, Detroit, Buffalo, and Cleveland.

Precision and accuracy are important, for instrument makers often work to very fine tolerances. They need spatial and reasoning ability, plus imagination and resourcefulness, for they often work from rough sketches or ideas rather than detailed blueprints.

Some instrument makers advance from the ranks of machinists or skilled machine tool operators by completing 1 or 2 years or more of instrument shop experience. Others learn their trade through 4-year apprenticeships.

Employers generally prefer high school graduates for apprenticeship programs, and additional technical school training is desirable.

Instrument assembly rooms are sometimes known as "white rooms" because almost sterile conditions are maintained.

Serious work accidents are not common, but safety rules require the wearing of certain apparatus and clothing.

Many instrument makers are union members.

Exploring Careers

Occupation	Nature and Places of Work	Training and Qualifications	Other Information
Machine Tool Operators	These workers use machine tools such as lathes, drill presses, milling machines, grinding machines, and punch presses to shape metal. Most work in factories that produce metal products, transportation equipment, and machinery. Skilled machine tool operators also work in production departments, maintenance departments, and toolrooms. Employment is concentrated in major industrial areas including the Great Lakes region, Los Angeles, Philadelphia, St. Louis, and Indianapolis.	Machine tool operators usually learn their skills on the job. Most are semiskilled operators; they perform simple repetitive operations that can be learned in just a few months. Becoming a skilled operator often requires 1 to 2 years of experience and on-the-job training. Some companies have formal training programs for new employees. Although no special education is required, courses in mathematics and blueprint reading are helpful.	Most operators stand a great deal of the time and work in a relatively small space. Machine tool operators have job titles that refer to the machine they operate: Drill press operator, milling machine operator, and the like. Skilled machine tool operators may become all-round machinists, tool-and-die makers, or advance to machine maintenance jobs. Most machine tool operators belong to unions.
Setup Workers (Machine Tools)	These skilled workers, often called machine tool job setters, prepare large complex tools such as a drill press or lathe for use. They consult blueprints, written specifications, or job layouts; select and install proper cutting or other tools; and adjust guides, stops, and other controls. They explain to semiskilled operators how to run the machine. They work in factories that manufacture fabricated metal products, transportation equipment, and machinery. Employment is concentrated in major industrial areas including Los Angeles, Philadelphia, New York, Chicago, Detroit, and Cleveland.	They must meet the same qualifications as all-round machinists. Good judgment is needed to select the sequence of operations so that metal parts will be made according to specifications. The ability to communicate clearly is important in explaining the machinery operations to semiskilled workers. Setup workers may advance to shop supervisor or transfer to other jobs such as parts programmer.	Because they work with high-speed machine tools that have sharp cutting edges, setup workers must follow certain safety practices. Many setup workers are members of unions.

30

Industrial Production Occupations

Occupation	Nature and Places of Work	Training and Qualifications	Other Information
Tool-and-Die Makers	These highly skilled, creative workers produce tools, dies, and special guiding and holding devices used by other machining workers to mass-produce metal parts. They have a broad knowledge of machining operations, mathematics, and blueprint reading; use almost every type of machine tool and precision measuring instrument; and do repair work. Most work in plants that produce manufacturing, construction, and farm machinery. Others work in automobile, aircraft, and other transportation equipment industries, small tool-and-die shops, and electrical machinery and fabricated metal industries. About one-fifth work in the Detroit and Flint, Chicago, and Los Angeles areas. Employment also is concentrated in Cleveland, New York, Newark, Dayton, and Buffalo.	Mechanical ability, finger dexterity, an aptitude for precise work, and a good working knowledge of mathematics and physics are important. They obtain their skills in a variety of ways including formal apprenticeship, vocational school, and on-the-job training. A 4-year apprenticeship probably is the best way to learn the trade. Most employers prefer persons with high school or trade school education for apprenticeships. Several years of experience after apprenticeship often are necessary to qualify for more difficult work. Some advance to supervisory and administrative positions in industry; many become tool designers; others open their own shops.	Because of their extensive skills and knowledge, tool-and-die makers are able to change jobs within machining occupations more easily than less skilled workers. As with other machining workers, they wear protective glasses when working around metal-cutting machines. Tool-and-die shops usually are safer than similar operations in production plants. Many are members of unions.

PRINTING OCCUPATIONS

Compositors	Compositors set type. Nearly all compositors use machines and press keys similar to a typewriter's. Type is set by hand only for very special printing jobs. Most compositors work for newspaper plants, or for commercial printing plants, book and magazine printers, and printing plants. Some work for banks, insurance companies, advertising agencies, manufacturers, and other firms that do their own printing.	Skilled compositors usually learn their trade through a 6-year apprenticeship. This period may be less for apprentices who have already worked in the printing industry. Shorter apprenticeships also are customary for people who have had courses in printing technology. Newer computer technology makes it possible for some people to become compositors with a high school diploma and good typing skills. They receive on-the-job training to apply their skills in this specialized setting. Applicants for apprenticeship generally must be high school graduates. Courses in mathematics and English, especially spelling, are important, and a background in electronics and photography is increasingly useful.	Working conditions vary from plant to plant. Some are hot and noisy. In general, new plants are well-lighted and clean. Many compositors are union members.

Exploring Careers

Occupation	Nature and Places of Work	Training and Qualifications	Other Information
Lithographers	Lithography, also known as off-set printing, is a printing process in which the material to be printed is either drawn or reproduced photographically on a flat metal plate. Then the plate is treated chemically so that the printing areas will attract ink while the nonprinting areas repel it and stay blank. Lithographic workers specialize in different steps of the printing process. Some are camera operators; others are artists, strippers, or platemakers. Lithographers work for commercial printing plants, newspapers, and book and magazine printers. Some work for the U.S. Government Printing Office.	Lithographic craft workers usually must complete a 4- or 5-year apprenticeship program. Apprenticeship applicants usually must be high school graduates and at least 18 years old. Some lithographers learn the craft by taking a 2-year program in printing technology at a vocational school, technical institute, junior college or college. High school courses in printing, photography, mathematics, chemistry, physics, and art are helpful.	Although the work is not strenuous, lithographers are on their feet much of the time. They sometimes are under pressure to meet publication deadlines. Many lithographers are union members.
Photoengravers	Photoengravers make metal printing plates of drawings, photographs, and other copy that cannot be set in type. These plates are then printed in the letterpress process. Over half work in shops that make photoengravings for other printing firms. Other employers include newspapers, photoengraver shops, book and magazine printers, and the Federal Government. Some photoengravers have their own shops.	Most learn through a 5-year apprenticeship program. Apprenticeship applicants must be at least 18 years old and generally must have a high school or vocational school education. Advances in technology make an understanding of computers increasingly important.	Although the work is not strenuous, photoengravers stand up much of the time. Good eyesight is particularly important because of the close work and color discrimination involved. Most photogravers are union members.
Electrotypers and Stereotypers	These workers make duplicate press plates of metal, rubber, and plastic for letterpress printing. Duplicate plates are used when there is a large volume of printing to be done. Electrotypers work mostly in plants that print books and magazines. Most stereotypers work for newspaper plants. Electrotypers and stereotypers also are employed in shops that provide this service for printing firms.	Nearly all complete 5- to 6-year apprenticeships. Electrotyping and stereotyping are separate crafts and relatively few transfers take place between the two. Apprenticeship applicants must be at least 18 years old.	Although operations are highly mechanized, some lifting of heavy press plates occasionally is required. Nearly all electrotypers and stereotypers are union members.

Industrial Production Occupations

Occupation	Nature and Places of Work	Training and Qualifications	Other Information
Printing Press Operators	These workers set up, adjust, and operate offset, letterpress, and gravure printing presses. Over half work in commercial printing plants or in the printshops of book, newspaper, and magazine publishers. Others work for banks, insurance companies, manufacturers, and other organizations that do their own printing.	Most press operators learn through apprenticeship, while some learn as helpers or press assistants. Others obtain their skills through a combination of work experience and vocational or technical school training. The length of apprenticeship and the content of training depend largely upon the kind of press used in the plant. Apprenticeships in commercial shops generally last 2 years for press assistants and 4 to 5 years for press operators. Mechanical aptitude is important in making press adjustments and repairs. The ability to visualize color is essential for work on color presses. Physical strength and endurance are needed for work on some kinds of presses, where operators lift heavy plates and stand for long periods.	Pressrooms are noisy and workers in some areas wear ear protectors. Press operators are subject to hazards when working near machinery. They sometimes work under pressure to meet deadlines. Many pressroom workers are union members.
Bookbinders and Bindery Workers	Bookbinders glue, sew, or staple the pages and the covers together to produce a book. They operate machines and do some of the work by hand. Many work in shops that specialize in bookbinding. Others work in bindery departments of book publishing firms, commercial printing plants, and large libraries. Some skilled bookbinders work in hand binderies. They design original bindings for a limited number of copies of a large edition, or restore and rebind rare books.	A 4- or 5-year apprenticeship generally is required to qualify as a skilled bookbinder. Apprenticeship applicants usually must have a high school education and be at least 18 years old. Although most bindery workers learn their tasks through on-the-job training lasting from several months to 2 years, many learn through formal apprenticeship. Accuracy, patience, neatness, and good eyesight are qualities needed by bookbinders. Good finger dexterity is necessary for workers who count, insert, paste, and fold.	Bookbinding shops are noisy when machinery is operating. Long periods of standing and constant use of the arms can be tiring. Many bindery workers are union members.

Exploring Careers

OTHER INDUSTRIAL PRODUCTION AND RELATED OCCUPATIONS

Occupation	Nature and Places of Work	Training and Qualifications	Other Information
Assemblers	Following instructions or diagrams, assemblers put together the parts of manufactured items using hand and machine tools. Many perform a single operation on an assembly line. Others have more complex jobs: Bench assemblers may make steering columns for automobiles, build rifles, or put together the small components used in radios; floor assemblers put together large machinery or equipment on shop floors; highly skilled assemblers may have to wire tubes for a television set or put together and test a calculator. All work in manufacturing plants, almost two-thirds in plants that make machinery and motor vehicles. Over half work in the heavily industrialized States of California, New York, Michigan, Illinois, Ohio, and Pennsylvania.	Speed and accuracy, manual dexterity, patience, good eyesight, and physical fitness may be important. Assemblers often work with very small parts. Floor assemblers may have to lift and fit heavy objects. Skilled assemblers use precision measuring instruments and must know how to read blueprints and other engineering specifications. Inexperienced people can be trained in a few days or weeks. Longer training is required for skilled assembly jobs. Employers prefer applicants with mechanical aptitude and vocational school training.	Assembly jobs tend to be more monotonous than other blue-collar jobs. Working conditions differ depending on the job performed. Some work in clean, well-lighted rooms while others work in noisy, dirty areas. Some are under pressure to keep up with the speed of assembly lines. Work schedules may vary at plants with more than one shift. In very modern factories, some assembly jobs may be done by robots. Assemblers who work in these settings must be very skillful so they don't disrupt the robot's routine. Many assemblers are members of unions.
Automobile Painters	These skilled workers repaint older vehicles that have lost the luster of their original paint and make body repairs almost invisible. They remove old paint by sanding, fill nicks and scratches with body putty, and mix paints when necessary. Almost two-thirds work in shops that specialize in automobile repairs. Most others work for automobile and truck dealers. Some work for organizations that maintain and repair their own fleets of vehicles, such as trucking companies and buslines. Many experienced painters open their own shops.	Good health, keen eyesight, and a good color sense are very important. Agility also is vital as they often bend and stoop to reach all parts of the car. Most auto painters start as helpers and gain skills by working with experienced painters. Becoming highly skilled requires 3 to 4 years of on-the-job training. A few learn by completing 3-year apprenticeship programs. Experienced painters may advance to shop supervisor, while those with the necessary funds open their own shops.	They may wear protective equipment because of fumes. Many painters belong to unions.

34

Industrial Production Occupations

Occupation	Nature and Places of Work	Training and Qualifications	Other Information
Blacksmiths	Blacksmiths make and repair equipment and other items made of metal. Those who specialize in shoeing horses are called farriers. Almost two-thirds work in factories, railroads, and mines. The remainder work in small shops, and most are self-employed. Most farriers are self-employed and contract their services to horse trainers at racetrack stables and to owners of horses used for private or public recreation.	Good physical conditioning is important because pounding metal and handling heavy tools and parts require strength and stamina. Farriers must have the patience to handle horses. Many beginners enter the occupation by working as helpers. Others complete 3- or 4-year apprenticeship programs that teach blueprint reading, proper use of tools and equipment, heat-treatment of metal, and forging methods. Many farriers learn by assisting experienced workers. Some take courses in horseshoeing at a college or private horseshoeing school. At least 3 to 5 years of experience are required to obtain skills necessary to shoe racehorses. Farriers who wish to work at racetracks must pass a licensing exam.	A blacksmith's job may be hazardous. Blacksmiths are subject to burns from forges and heated metals and cuts and bruises from handling tools. They often wear protective devices. Some farrier jobs are seasonal and may involve long hours, weekend work, and much travel. Many blacksmiths belong to unions.
Blue-Collar Worker Supervisors	These workers train new employees, maintain employee and production records, plan and schedule work, and prepare reports on production, cost, personnel, and safety. Over half work in manufacturing, supervising the production of cars, washing machines, or any of thousands of other products. Most of the remainder work in the construction industry, in wholesale and retail trade, and in public utilities.	Most supervisors are promoted through the ranks. Experience, skill, and leadership qualities are vital. Employers place special emphasis on the ability to motivate employees, maintain high morale, command respect, and get along with people. Completion of high school is the minimum educational requirement. A college or technical school background can be helpful, particularly in industries with highly technical production processes.	Supervisors generally work more than 40 hours a week and sometimes do paperwork at home. They may receive overtime pay. Working conditions vary and some are subjected to noisy, dirty conditions. On the other hand, they have more challenging and prestigious jobs than most blue-collar workers.

Exploring Careers

Occupation	Nature and Places of Work	Training and Qualifications	Other Information
Boilermaking Occupations	Boilermakers assemble, erect, dismantle, and repair boilers and other pressure vessels. They use power tools and devices such as oxyacetylene torches, welding equipment, power shears, and rigging equipment. Layout workers follow blueprints in marking off lines on metal plates and tubes. Fitters see that boiler parts fit together properly before assembly. Boilermakers work in the construction industry, in iron and steel plants, petroleum refineries, railroads, shipyards, and electric powerplants. Some work in Navy shipyards and Federal powerplants. Layout workers and fitters work mainly in plants that make fire-tube and water-tube boilers, heat exchangers, heavy tanks, and similar products.	Physical strength and stamina are required to do the heavy work, and manual dexterity and mechanical aptitude are needed to handle tools. Many people have become boilermakers by working for several years as helpers to experienced boilermakers, but a 4-year apprenticeship is considered the best way to learn this trade. Most layout workers and fitters are hired as helpers to experienced workers, and they take about 2 years to become highly skilled. Employers prefer high school or vocational school graduates as apprentices or helpers.	The work may be hazardous. Boilermakers often work in damp, poorly ventilated, cramped quarters and sometimes at great heights. Workers often wear protective equipment. Most workers belong to unions.
Boiler Tenders	Boiler tenders operate and maintain the steam boilers that power industrial machinery and heat factories, offices, and other buildings. They also may operate waste heat boilers that burn trash and other solid waste. About half work in factories. Plants that manufacture lumber, iron and steel, paper, chemicals, and stone, clay, and glass products are among leading employers. Others work for public utilities and in hospitals, schools, and Federal, State, and local government.	Persons learn through on-the-job training as a helper in a boiler room. Some high school courses are helpful. Applicants for helper jobs should be in good physical condition and have mechanical aptitude and manual dexterity. Some large cities and a few States require boiler tenders to be licensed. Two types of licenses exist—for low pressure and high pressure boilers. Because of regional differences in licensing requirements, one who moves to another city or State may have to pass an exam for a new license.	They have to work in awkward positions and may be exposed to noise, heat, grease, fumes, and smoke. They also are subject to burns, falls, and injury from defective boilers or moving parts. Modern equipment and safety procedures, however, have reduced accidents. Some boiler tenders are union members.

Industrial Production Occupations

Occupation	Nature and Places of Work	Training and Qualifications	Other Information
Electroplaters	Electroplaters use an electro-chemical process to give metal articles such as silverware, jewelry, and jet engine parts a protective surface or an attractive appearance. About half work in shops that specialize in metal plating and polishing. Other platers work in plants that make plumbing fixtures, cooking utensils, household appliances, electronic components, motor vehicles, and metal products.	An eye for detail, patience, manual dexterity, and good eye-hand-arm coordination are important. They must carefully study job specifications for each item to be plated and must examine their work for defects. In addition, good physical condition is important as workers may have to lift and carry heavy objects at times. Most learn by helping experienced workers, and it usually takes at least 3 years to become an all-round plater. A small proportion work for 3 or 4 years as apprentices. Some high school or vocational school courses are helpful, and a few people take a 1- or 2-year electroplating course in a junior college, technical institute, or vocational high school.	The work may be hazardous. They are subject to burns from splashing acids and inhalation of toxic fumes. Humidity and odors also are problems. Workers may wear protective clothing. Some platers are members of unions.
Furniture Upholsterers	Furniture upholsterers repair or replace fabrics, springs, padding, and other parts of furniture that are worn or damaged. They use tack and staple removers, pliers, hammers, hand or power shears, webbing stretchers, upholstery needles, and sewing machines. Over three-fourths own and operate or work in small upholstery shops. Some work in furniture stores and for businesses, such as hotels, that maintain their own furniture.	Manual dexterity, coordination, an eye for detail, good color sense, patience, and a flair for creative work are helpful. Occasional heavy lifting may be required. Most people complete about 3 years of on-the-job training before becoming fully skilled. Vocational or high school courses in upholstery are helpful.	Working conditions vary. Some shops are large and clean while others are small and dusty. Workers stand while they work and do stooping, bending, and some heavy lifting. Some upholsterers are union members.

Exploring Careers

Occupation	Nature and Places of Work	Training and Qualifications	Other Information
Forge Shop Occupations	Before metal can be shaped, it must be heated in intensely hot furnaces (forges) until it is soft. Forge shop workers place the heated metal between two metal dies that are attached to power-presses or hammers. The hammers or presses pound or squeeze the metal into the desired shape. Hammersmiths direct the operation of open die power hammers; hammer operators manipulate impression die power hammers; press operators control huge presses equipped with dies; upsetters operate machines that shape hot metal; heaters control furnace temperatures; inspectors examine forged pieces for accuracy, size, and quality; die sinkers make impression dies for forging hammers and presses; trimmers, grinders, sandblasters or shotblasters, picklers, and heat treaters are involved in cleaning and finishing operations.

About three-fourths work in shops that make and sell forgings. The remainder work in plants that use forgings in their final products, such as plants operated by manufacturers of automobiles, farm equipment, and handtools.

Employment is concentrated in and around Detroit, Chicago, Cleveland, Los Angeles, and Pittsburgh. | Forge shop workers must be strong enough to lift and move heavy forgings and dies. They need the stamina and endurance to work in the heat and noise of a forge shop.

Most learn their skills on the job. They generally join hammer or press crews as helpers or heaters, and progress to other jobs as they gain experience. Some forge shops offer 4-year apprenticeship programs for skilled jobs such as die-sinker, heat treater, hammer operator, hammersmith, and press operator. Training requirements for inspectors range from a few weeks to several months of on-the-job training.

Employers usually do not require a high school diploma, but graduates may be preferred. | The work is more hazardous than most manufacturing occupations. Workers are subject to noise, vibration, heat, and smoke. Workers may wear protective eqiupment. Because of these hazards, some forging jobs are being done by robots in newer factories. Therefore, fewer opportunities exist for these jobs.

Most workers are union members. |

Industrial Production Occupations

Occupation	Nature and Places of Work	Training and Qualifications	Other Information
Inspectors (Manufacturing)	Inspectors make certain that products meet specifications. For example, they may taste-test soft drinks, use tools such as gauges and magnifying glasses to make sure airplanes are assembled properly, or examine a jacket for flaws. Two-thirds work in plants that produce durable goods such as machinery, transportation equipment, electronics equipment, and furniture. Others work in plants that produce goods such as textiles, apparel, and leather products. Almost two-thirds work in Ohio, New York, Michigan, Illinois, Pennsylvania, California, New Jersey, North Carolina, and Indiana.	Inspectors generally are trained on the job for a brief period—from a few hours or days to several months, depending on the skill requirements. Preferences of employers vary widely with respect to education, experience, and qualifying aptitudes. Good health and eyesight, accuracy, and the ability to pay attention to detail, work with numbers, and get along with people may be important. Some may use computers, lasers, or X-ray equipment.	Working conditions vary considerably. Some have well-lighted, air-conditioned workplaces while others are exposed to high temperature, oil, grease, and noise. Many inspectors are members of unions.
Millwrights	Millwrights prepare machinery for use in a plant. This may involve constructing concrete foundations or wooden platforms, dismantling existing equipment, and moving, assembling, and maintaining machinery. Most work for manufacturing companies. The majority are in transportation equipment, metal, paper, lumber, and chemical products industries. Others work for contractors in the construction industry; machinery manufacturers employ a small number. Employment is concentrated in Detroit, Pittsburgh, Cleveland, Buffalo, and the Chicago-Gary area.	Mechanical aptitude is vital because millwrights work with various tools while putting together and taking apart complex machinery. Strength and agility also are important because millwrights do much lifting and climbing. The ability to give and carry out instructions accurately and analyze and solve problems also is important. Some spend 6 to 8 years learning the trade informally on the job as helpers to skilled workers. Others complete 4-year formal apprenticeship programs. Specialized millwrights may install industrial robots or computerized manufacturing equipment. They may need additional training in electronics and advanced technology.	The work may be hazardous, and workers wear protective devices. In addition to the dangers of being struck by falling objects or machinery or falling from high places, millwrights are subject to the usual hazards of cuts and bruises. Millwrights employed by factories generally work year round. Those employed by some construction companies may experience periods of unemployment. However, they usually earn higher wages. Frequently these millwrights travel. Most millwrights belong to unions.

Exploring Careers

Occupation	Nature and Places of Work	Training and Qualifications	Other Information
Motion Picture Projectionists	Motion picture projectionists operate and maintain movie projectors and sound equipment. They may inspect film, load and start the machine, adjust light and sound, make the changeover to a second machine at the end of a reel, rewind film, splice film when required, and make repairs. Many of these functions are automated in modern theaters. The majority work for indoor theaters. Most of the remainder work for drive-ins, while some work for large manufacturing companies, colleges, television studios, and Federal, State, and local governments.	Good eyesight and normal color perception, good hearing, manual dexterity, mechanical aptitude, and a temperament for performing routine work alone are important. Most theaters are unionized, and union membership requirements vary considerably among the locals. Applicants often must work for trial periods lasting several weeks or complete union training programs without compensation. They may have to pass a written exam before becoming a union member. Unions prefer high school graduates. In a few cities and States, projectionists must be licensed, often before applying for union membership.	Most work evenings on weekdays, generally 4 to 6 hours, and 10 hours or more on Saturdays or Sundays. Some work at several theaters. In small towns, they usually work only part time because of the small number of shows. Those at drive-ins, particularly in northern States, may be laid off during the winter. The work is not strenuous and is relatively safe, but there is the danger of electrical shock and acid burns from the projector's lamp.
Ophthalmic Laboratory Technicians	Ophthalmic laboratory technicians (also called optical mechanics) make eyeglasses. The two types of technicians are surfacer (lens grinder) and bench technician (finisher). In small laboratories, one person may perform both functions; in large laboratories, these duties may be performed by several people. Most work in ophthalmic laboratories but some work for retail optical dispensaries or other stores that sell prescription lenses. A few work for eye physicians or optometrists who dispense glasses directly to patients.	Because they work with machines and small handtools, finger dexterity, some mechanical ability, patience, and a liking for precision work are important. The vast majority learn their skills on the job, usually taking 3 years to become all-round mechanics. High school graduates may learn by completing 3- to 4-year apprenticeship programs, and most authorities agree that this training leads to more opportunities. Some technicians receive training in the Armed Forces or complete 9-month vocational school programs and then receive on-the-job training. Employers prefer high school graduates. Some States require licenses.	Work surroundings are noisy because of power grinding and polishing machines. Some technicians are members of unions.

Industrial Production Occupations

Occupation	Nature and Places of Work	Training and Qualifications	Other Information
Photographic Laboratory Occupations	Photographic laboratory workers develop film, make prints and slides, and perform related tasks such as enlarging and retouching photographs. All-round darkroom technicians can perform all the tasks necessary to develop and print film. Color technicians specialize in processing color film. Darkroom technicians are assisted by specialized workers such as developers, printers, and retouchers. Other workers include film numberers, who sort film according to the type of processing needed; film strippers, who unwind rolls of film and place them in developing machines; printer operators, who operate machines that expose rolls of photographic paper to negatives; machine print developers, who operate machines that develop these rolls; chemical mixers, who combine chemicals that make up developing solutions; slide mounters, who operate machines that cut, insert, and seal slides in mounts; and photocheckers and assemblers, who inspect finished slides and prints and package them for customers.

Most semiskilled workers are employed by large photofinishing labs that specialize in processing film for amateur photographers. A large proportion of darkroom technicians work in labs operated by portrait and commercial studios, manufacturers, newspaper and magazine publishers, advertising agencies, and other organizations. Some work in commercial labs specializing in processing work of professional photographers. | For many photography laboratory jobs, manual dexterity, good vision, including normal color perception, and good hand-eye coordination are important.

Most darkroom technicians learn their skills on the job, taking about 3 years to become fully qualified. Employers prefer high school graduates. Training is offered in high schools, trade schools, and the Armed Forces. A few colleges offer 2-year programs in photographic technology.

Semiskilled photolab workers train on the job for a few weeks to several months.

Many darkroom technicians eventually become professional photographers. | In some labs, employees may work much overtime during the summer and other peak periods, and temporary workers may be employed during these peaks.

In many semiskilled occupations, the work is repetitious and the pace is rapid. Some workers are subject to eye fatigue. |

Exploring Careers

Occupation	Nature and Places of Work	Training and Qualifications	Other Information
Power Truck Operators	Power truck operators drive trucks with lifting mechanisms to move heavy materials. Operators must follow special procedures when using a truck at a plant, warehouse, or construction site. They may manually load and unload, keep records of materials moved, and maintain trucks in good working condition. About three-fourths work in manufacturing industries. Many work in plants that make automobiles, machinery, fabricated metal products, paper, building materials, and iron and steel. Many also work in warehouses, depots, freight and marine terminals, and mines.	Operators need manual dexterity, strength, and stamina to drive the truck and to load and unload goods. They need good eyesight, including good depth perception, to pick up, move, and deposit loads. They often need mechanical ability to perform minor maintenance. Large firms generally require applicants to pass a physical examination. They train on the job for several days, but it usually takes several weeks to reach maximum efficiency.	Work may be hazardous, and operators may be exposed to all kinds of weather. Operators are subject to collisions and falling objects; some transport dirty material. However, working conditions are being improved.
Production Painters	Production painters apply varnish, lacquer, paint, and other finishes to the surface of manufactured items. Most painters use sprayguns while others use automatic equipment such as spraying machines, dipping tanks, and tumbling barrels. They may use masking tape to prevent colors from overlapping, mix paint, and clean equipment. As production lines become more automated, painters must learn to use modern machinery such as electrostatic applicators and powder-type painting systems. About two-thirds work in plants that make automobiles, machinery, furniture and other wood products, or manufactured metal products such as cans, tinware, and handtools.	Production painters need good eyesight to distinguish colors and check for even application of paint. The job also demands a tolerance for repetitious work and good physical condition since painters stand for long periods of time and often work in awkward and cramped positions. No formal apprenticeship or training exists. Workers may spend from a few days to several months acquiring their skills on the job. High school graduation may be needed for advancement. A few painters become supervisors.	The job may be hazardous as painters are exposed to fumes and noises. Workers may wear protective clothing and apparatus. Routine painting jobs are being done by robots in many modern plants. Opportunities are decreasing in this type of work except for very advanced or specialized workers.

Industrial Production Occupations

Occupation	Nature and Places of Work	Training and Qualifications	Other Information
Stationary Engineers	Stationary engineers operate boilers, generators, turbines, condensers, and other equipment that provide power, heat, air-conditioning, and light. They regularly inspect equipment, check meters and gauges, and make minor repairs. They may supervise others. Places of employment include power stations, factories, sewage and water treatment plants, offices and apartment buildings, hotels, hospitals, and Federal, State, and local governments.	Good physical condition is important because these workers may crawl inside boilers and work in crouching or kneeling positions. Mechanical aptitude, manual dexterity, and accuracy also are important. Many start as helpers or oilers and acquire their skills on the job. A good background can be obtained in the Navy or Merchant Marine. However, most training authorities recommend a formal 4-year apprenticeship. High school or trade school graduates are preferred for apprenticeship. Many States and localities have licensing requirements. Although licensing requirements differ from place to place, applicants usually must be 18 years old, reside for a specified period in the area in which the exam is given, meet experience requirements, and pass a written exam. One who moves to another area may have to obtain a new license.	Workers may be assigned to any one of three shifts around the clock, and to weekend and holiday work. In many plants, only one engineer works on each shift. The work may be hazardous as workers may be exposed to heat, dust, dirt, oil and grease, and fumes or smoke. They also are subject to burns, electric shock, and injury from moving machinery. Some stationary engineers are union members.
Wastewater Treatment Plant Operators	Wastwater treatment plant operators control and maintain pumps, pipes, and valves that send harmful domestic and industrial waste to treatment facilities. They may read and interpret meters and gauges to check plant equipment; operate chemical feeding devices to remove pollutants; take samples of water for laboratory analysis; and test and adjust the level of chlorine in the water. They keep records and may make minor repairs using a variety of tools. Most work in municipal plants and private industry while some work in Federal installations.	Mechanical aptitude and competence in basic mathematics are important. Operators also must be agile as they must climb ladders and move easily around heavy machinery. Trainees start as helpers and learn their skills on the job. Employers prefer high school graduates and in some States this is a minimum requirement. Some 2-year associate degree programs in wastewater technology are available. In many States, supervisors and certain operators must pass an exam to certify that they are capable of overseeing plant operations. There are different classes of certification for different sizes of plants. These also may entail education and experience requirements.	Many operators in small towns work part time. They work different shifts and may have to work overtime in an emergency. They may be exposed to odors, as well as noise from the operation of electrical motors and pumps.

Exploring Careers

Occupation	Nature and Places of Work	Training and Qualifications	Other Information
Welders	Welders join two or more pieces of metal by applying intense heat and adding filler materials when necessary. These permanently connected metal parts are then used in the construction of cars, ships, household appliances, and thousands of other products. Jobs vary from those of highly skilled manual welders who can use welding equipment in more than one position and who can plan their work from drawings and other specifications to those of unskilled welding machine tenders who simply press a button to start a machine. Almost two-thirds help manufacture durable goods such as boilers, bulldozers, trucks, ships, and heavy machinery. Most of the remainder repair metal products or help construct bridges, large buildings, and pipelines.	Manual dexterity, good eyesight, and good eye-hand coordination are important. Workers should be able to concentrate on detailed work for long periods, and should be in good physical condition since welders bend, stoop, and work in awkward positions. It takes several years of training to become a skilled welder. Some of the less skilled jobs can be learned in a few months or less, although these routine welding operations are being done by robots more and more. A few companies offer apprenticeship programs. Employers prefer applicants with high school or vocational school training in welding. Some welders may be required to pass certification exams. Welding machine operators may learn skilled welding jobs; skilled welders may be promoted to inspectors, technicians, or supervisors. Experienced workers with college training may become welding engineers, while a few open their own shops.	Welders work in the presence of toxic gases, fumes, rust, grease, and dirt. They wear protective clothing and devices. Many welders are union members.

Office
Occupations

Until the middle of the 19th century, clerical work almost always was done by men.

Danny owns a lunch truck. "Not just any old lunch wagon, but the best rolling cafeteria in the whole city!" he says. Danny sells sandwiches downtown, in the heart of the steel and glass jungle inhabited by the city's office workers. Every Monday through Friday at 11 o'clock in the morning, Danny parks his truck in front of the Benton Building. After loading his special cart with food, he pushes it through the building, selling sandwiches and drinks to the workers there.

Does Danny ever get tired of his job? "No way! You see, people fascinate me. I like talking to them, learning their names, finding out what they do, how many kids they have, everything. Even though I sometimes have to rush to finish my run on schedule, I always manage to find a few minutes to chat. I've been making this run for a couple of years, and I've gotten to know some of these people very well.

"It amazes me how many different kinds of work people do. Now you take this building, for instance. Just 4 floors, no more than 5 or 6 big companies altogether. But I'll bet if you made a list you'd count over 50 different jobs in the Benton Building. All office jobs, but each one different. Some of them I wouldn't mind having myself; some I wouldn't take if they paid me twice as much as I earn now. But even if I wouldn't want their jobs, I never get tired of talking to people and finding out what they do. Why don't you come with me on my run and see what I mean!"

The Commerce National Bank

Danny loads his cart with sandwiches, sodas, pastries, and fruit until it appears ready to spill over. Pushing it towards the double glass doors, he parks it in the lobby next to the Commerce National Bank.

"I've got lots of good customers in this bank," explains Danny as workers leave their desks and crowd around his cart. "Take these two, Burt Lansing and Paula Robinson. They're *tellers*. They act as the bank's cashiers. They take money from people who want to deposit it here. They cash checks and give money to customers who want to withdraw it from their accounts. They handle a lot of money every day, so they've got to be very careful not to make mistakes and not to leave their stations unguarded. If money is missing they might be held responsible.

"Paula used to work in a smaller bank than this one. She and the other tellers handled everything—making deposits and withdrawals, selling traveler's checks, writing money orders, taking Christmas club payments. In this big bank, each teller specializes. Paula misses the variety, but her chances of getting ahead are better here. She and Burt both take courses in the evenings to become *loan officers*.

"Burt says the best part of the job is dealing with the public. He likes people. But sometimes it's quite a challenge to be courteous to an angry, unreasonable customer. Believe me, I know! Burt has unlimited patience, though, and he makes a good teller.

"Most of the people who work in the bank are tellers, like Burt and Paula, or *officers*, or *clerks*. See that fellow in the grey suit? His name's Manuel Ortez. He's a *commercial loan officer*. When business people want to borrow money to build a new store, to buy equipment, or for some other project, he investigates to see whether they'll be able to pay the loan back. If their loan is approved, he discusses with them any problems they might have paying it back. While Manuel handles business loans, other officers specialize in loans to farmers, to people who want to buy land, or to people who want to improve their homes. Manuel is lucky, though, because he has customers all over the country, so he gets to travel more than the others.

"Over there is the woman who hired Manuel, Catherine Wallace. She's a *personnel officer*, and she's been with the bank a long time. She interviews people when there are openings, and hires them if she thinks they'd do a good job at Commerce National. Occasionally she gives an applicant a typing or math skills test. She knows the organization and the personnel policies of this bank backwards and forwards. She knows the laws against discrimination in hiring and promotion. And she knows how to deal with people. That's very important in her work.

"You know, when you walk into a bank like this one, you never see most of the people who make it tick, the *clerks*. They work behind the scenes, processing thou-

The never-ending flow of paperwork in business creates clerical jobs—like this one in a bank.

sands of little pieces of paper every day. Each of those pieces of paper represents money somebody paid to somebody else, and the bank has to record every one of those payments correctly. Some of the clerks have fancy electronic machines to help them. This fellow, Andy Hayes, for example, is a *reading-sorting clerk*. He operates a machine that prints codes on checks in a special ink so that another machine can read them. Then Andy's machine sorts the checks by the bank they came from. The woman next to him, Christy Ross, is an *interest clerk*. She uses the bank's computer to keep track of how much interest people owe the bank for loans. There are so many other clerks in this bank, it boggles the mind!"

All the time he talks, Danny takes coins and bills and gives change. When everyone has paid, Danny rolls the cart to an elevator and punches the button. "Next stop, the second floor!" he exclaims as he pushes the cart into the open elevator car. Arriving at the next floor, he rolls his cart down the paneled, carpeted hallway toward a large door labeled "All-Risk Insurance."

The All-Risk Insurance Company

"Have you ever visited an insurance office?" asks Danny as he rolls his cart through the doorway into a room with a desk and a leather couch. "Well, step right into the reception area, where you will be greeted by my friend, the *receptionist*! His name is Jim Rodgers," he explains, indicating the man behind the desk. "When visitors come to the office, Jim greets them, asks them whom they came to see, and sends them to the right room. He also answers the phone and switches calls to the proper people. Now and then he helps with typing, too. You find a receptionist in just about every office you walk into. But none of them is as friendly and helpful as Jim!"

Danny smiles as Jim announces his arrival over the intercom. Soon, men and women wander out of the rear of the office and gather around Danny's cart. Once again he takes money and makes change, talking all the while.

"I've already told you about some of the clerical workers who keep things moving at Commerce National. Well, an insurance company needs clerical workers, too. In fact, you'll find clerks wherever you find paperwork or number work, which is just about everywhere! Let me tell you what the clerical workers here at All-Risk do. Those folks standing over there in a group are good examples. The tall fellow, Jeff Graham, is a *word processing clerk*. He spends most of his time at a com-

puter terminal, typing forms from insurance policies or claims. Jeff's work used to be done mostly on an electric typewriter. But with computers they can make changes and corrections a lot quicker. That guy can really type up a storm. I hear he does more than 75 words a minute! And he never gets distracted by all the hubbub around him. He just types away.

"The other guy, McCoy Johnson is a *file clerk*. Now you may think filing is easy, but not in a place like this. They keep information on thousands of people. To organize all that information so it can be found easily, they have a special system. McCoy works like a librarian, and he has to know that system. When someone needs a file, he finds it. He keeps track of who is using it, and puts it back when they're done. And he has to make sure he puts it back in the right place, because otherwise a lot of time could be lost looking for it the next time it's needed. I hear they're thinking about putting in an electronic filing system using computers. McCoy would still have to file some papers, like things with signatures, but basic customer records, like policy numbers and things, would be in a computerized system called a data base. Then people who need information could get it on the computer screens at their own desks. Sounds like it would make McCoy's job a lot easier.

"That lady talking with Jeff and McCoy is Linda Inouma. She's a *secretary*, and a hard worker, from what I hear. She answers her boss' phone calls, transcribes her dictation tapes, types letters and reports that her boss creates, and keeps special files that relate to their projects. She used to use an electric typewriter or a word processor for most of her typing. But a few months ago Linda got a desktop publishing system. Now, Linda and her boss can create really neat looking reports with charts and illustrations and everything. Linda says it saves a lot of time waiting for things to come back from the typesetter and she can make things look just the way her boss wants them.

"The woman with the cheese sandwich in her hand is Donna Murphy. Donna is a *statistical clerk*. "Statistical" means working with numbers—in this case numbers about people. You see, Donna assists that woman in the white blouse, Betty Fong. Betty is one of All-Risk's *actuaries*. She helps figure out what All-Risk's rates should be.

"It works this way: I want insurance for my truck in case I have an accident. All-Risk decides to insure me, for a price. The greater my chances of having an accident, the higher the price. Right? Right!

"But how do they know my chances of having a wreck? They don't. But they can come up with a pretty

Precise and orderly work habits are a "must" for bookkeepers.

The profession of legal assistant, or paralegal, is quite new.

good estimate by looking at the accident record of lunch truckdrivers as a group. Putting together that information is Betty's job.

"The person who actually decides whether I'm a good risk—which is a short way of saying I'm worth insuring—is the *underwriter.* All-Risk has many underwriters, including that man in the pin-striped suit, Pat Wash. Pat specializes in automobile insurance, while others handle life or health insurance. They all act a bit like private investigators, finding out whether a person or a business is a good risk.

"My neighbor, Judy Schwarz, is a *claim adjuster* for All-Risk. If something happens to you and you want to collect money on your policy, she's the one to see. Let's say you have a policy that protects your home from damage from natural causes. A big windstorm comes and blows your tree over. The tree falls on the roof of your back porch and puts a hole in it. After you call the company, Judy comes out and looks at the damage. First she sees whether the damage is covered under your policy. If so, she estimates the cost of fixing the hole and writes you a check, or maybe arranges to have it fixed.

"Judy doesn't work in this office. She works in one of the many adjustment centers throughout the city. But she actually spends most of her time out checking on claims.

"Of course, not all claims are so simple to adjust. Two years ago, a car hit my truck down on Main Street. The other guy said I ran the red light, but that wasn't true. Since we couldn't agree on who should pay for repairs, the case went to court. My claim adjuster gave the case to the company's legal department, where it was handled by their *lawyers.*

"These two getting coffee, Elisabeth Kahl and Ed Novak, are lawyers. They buy lunch from me when they're too busy to eat out. I guess they have a lot of cases these days. They've been buying my sandwiches for the last 3 weeks! Elisabeth took care of my claim against the so-and-so who hit me 2 years ago. She handled all the court procedures, collected evidence, and argued my case in the courtroom. And I finally got my money!

"Ed and Elisabeth tell me that some lawyers work for large corporations, because big businesses have enough legal matters to keep a lawyer busy full time. But most lawyers work for law firms. Some practice alone, others have partners and assistants. And those lawyers handle lots of matters besides insurance claims. They handle problems concerning divorces, wills, contracts, patents, taxes, and government regulations. And we can't forget criminal cases. Some lawyers never see the courtroom; others seem to live there."

Danny glances at his watch. "Omigosh! I've got to

stop babbling so much and move on. I'm late!" Packing up the cart again, he wheels it back to the elevator and takes it to the third floor. The hallway is identical to that of the floor below, except that now Danny enters a door labeled "A. J. Marx Garment Company." The receptionist announces his arrival.

The Marx Garment Company

"This office," Danny begins, "is the headquarters for a large company that manufactures women's and children's clothing. They actually make the clothes in a factory just outside town. But they handle all their business here.

"There are people here with jobs like those we saw downstairs. The first person we met was the receptionist. There are secretaries, typists, file clerks, maybe even a lawyer lurking around here somewhere. But you'll find some new occupations here, too.

"This woman with the corduroy suit is Lois Terlizzi, *chief purchasing agent.* She's in charge of the purchasing department, which is especially busy these days. The company is getting ready to produce its new fashions for spring. The designers have finished drawing patterns and choosing fabrics. Now the purchasing agents must buy the fabrics.

"Lois' staff has frantically phoned and visited fabric suppliers, inspected their fabrics, and written reports. With all that "legwork" completed, Lois knows what's available. Now she and her staff will decide what and how much to buy. To do that, they have to know how much fabric is used for each garment and how many garments will be produced. Then, in another flurry of phone calls and visits to suppliers, they hunt down bargains and buy, buy, buy!

"Now, this man in the tan three-piece suit is the advertising manager. He never buys my food, but I know all about him. Name's John Vorhes. John and his staff plan the advertising campaign for the spring fashions. They decide how much to spend on ads and how to spend it. Then they create the ads. Sometimes they do the writing and artwork themselves. But for a big campaign like this, they'll call in an advertising agency.

"John's people depend heavily on the work of this woman in the green skirt, Ann Karras. She's a *market researcher.* It's her job to find out who buys Marx clothes and why. Her staff conducts surveys to find out what the

Purchasing agents work under pressure almost all the time.

Lawyers complete 3 years of law school after graduating from college.

Advances come so rapidly in the computer field that it's essential to take courses to keep your skills up to date.

how to spend money and expand the company."

Danny continues chatting until it's time to move on, then packs up and rolls the cart to the elevator again. On the fourth floor, the final stop, he enters the offices of Computer Resources, Inc., otherwise known as CRI.

Computer Resources, Inc.

Danny parks his cart again and begins to talk as people gather around him.

"The work in this office all revolves around one machine, the computer. CRI has fantastic computers that can store billions of little bits of information and do thousands of calculations at lightning speed. These computers are used to do work for other businesses. The bank we visited uses CRI's computers to keep track of savings accounts, while the insurance company uses them to store and process statistics.

"Not all computers are alike. There are many kinds, designed to handle different kinds and amounts of work. CRI has a variety of equipment to choose from. So when a company wants to use CRI's services, the first step is to design a system. This woman in the brown sweater, Leila Kermani, handles that responsibility. She's a *systems analyst*. She knows which computers can do what, and she finds out all she can about the work to be done. In this way she can design the best system for the job.

"After Leila has designed the system, a *programmer* takes over. Vince Scaglia, the man in the plaid tie, is one. He knows the languages, or special number codes, that

public wants. Their information helps John's advertising workers aim their ads at the consumers most likely to buy from Marx. Ann's work also helps the designers know what designs will be most popular.

"Of course, you may be offering the best clothes in the world, and have the customers lined up at the store with their money in hand. But you won't sell a stitch if you can't move it from the factory to the store. That's the job of this lanky lad with the pencil on his ear, Ray Clark, the Marx Company's *industrial traffic manager*. Ray knows the shipping regulations and rates. He figures out the cheapest, most efficient way to ship clothes all over the country.

"And you can't run a business unless you can keep track of your money, believe me. That job goes to the accounting department. Maria Fernandez, the lady with the wire-rimmed glasses, is one of their *accountants*. She manages Marx's taxes. She keeps records of how much the company spends and each year she fills out its tax return. Others in her department make decisions about

Computer programmers need imagination to find new ways to solve problems.

are used to tell a computer what to do. He writes the program, a detailed, step-by-step set of instructions in the appropriate language. Maybe you know that a computer can't actually think the way a human brain can. So when it finds an error in the program, it can't figure out what the programmer meant. Vince takes great care in writing programs, and even so he expects to spend lots of time working out the "bugs."

"Once Vince has written the program, it has to be fed into the computer. Now, a computer can't read handwriting from a piece of paper the way we can. But it can "read" holes punched in a card or information recorded on magnetic disks or tape. So the program and the numbers it will operate on—known as data—must be put onto cards, disks, or tape. In the old days, people called "keypunch operators" would type data on a keyboard connected to machines that punched little holes in special cards. The computer would "read" its instructions from the number of holes and their locations on the cards. All of that information is now put on magnetic disks or tape by people like Tony Klein, that redheaded fellow over there. Tony and his co-workers are called data entry, or sometimes key entry, operators. They're a lot like typists or other clerks who use typewriter style keyboards.

"There are other people who actually run the computer. Mary Mitchell, that woman with the green jacket, is a *console operator*. She feeds in the program and data, runs the equipment, and tries to find the source of any problem that occurs. The man next to her, Matt Janicki, is a *high-speed printer operator*. He runs a machine that prints out the results of the program so fast

This inventory clerk is using a desk-top terminal linked to a computer several miles away.

it takes your breath away.

"You know, this office has over 50 workers. It always amazes me that it takes so many trained, intelligent people to operate a machine. But of course, this is a computer company and they use really sophisticated computers to create lots of different kinds of programs for other companies to use. Some people just follow directions to use programs on their computer terminals that were created here."

When the last wave of hungry workers has passed by, Danny packs up the cart once more. A short elevator ride later, he is back on the street. "Now you see what I mean," he reflects. "You find so many different occupations in these offices. I pointed out a couple of dozen, but there are many more in this building, not to mention the other high-rises all along the street.

"All these people work in clean, well-lighted offices. Most of them have desks. And most of them work a normal 9-to-5, Monday-through-Friday week. But the similarity ends there. Some office occupations require creativity, while others are routine. Some are for high school students, others for Ph.D's. Some work with numbers, others deal in words. Some involve nonstop contact with the public, others involve none at all. There's so much variety...take your pick!"

Danny pauses for a moment, scratches his head, then reaches into his cart and pulls out two square items

Keeping track of all the tapes at a university computer center is this tape librarian's job.

Exploring Careers

Employers prefer high school or business school graduates for jobs as office machine operators.

Cashier training is offered in many high school distributive education programs.

wrapped in paper. "All that talking made me forget how hungry I am! Here, have a cheese sandwich, on the house!"

Training

There's a lot of variety in office occupations, as Danny says. And the training you would need for these occupations varies almost as much. If you want to be a bank teller, for example, high school is all the preparation you really need before you begin. The bank will train you to do what tellers do. But to become a lawyer, to take another example, you must do much more. After finishing high school, you attend college for 4 years, then spend 3 years in law school. And when you graduate from law school, you face another hurdle. Before you may practice law, you must pass a long, difficult test call a bar examination. Not every office occupation, of course, requires so much preparation. The training requirements for each are given in the Job Facts at the end of this chapter.

You don't have to go to college to enter the world of office work. Many high schools have business education courses. These courses teach you skills that are use-ful in office occupations, including typing, shorthand, bookkeeping, accounting, business economics, and office procedures. Some high schools or vocational schools have special courses in how to use computers, word processors, dictating machines, transcribers, and other office equipment.

Many high schools allow you to work part-time at a related job while you study. The job gives you a chance to practice your training and gain experience in the working world. In addition, many schools have a chapter of Future Business Leaders of America or Junior Achievement. These organizations work with the schools and the business community to sponsor local and national activities that are both fun and educational for students in business education. The activities include contests, community service projects, and model or actual businesses. A high school counselor or business education teacher can give you information about activities in your area.

52

Office Occupations

Bank Officer

Bill Hooker is an assistant cashier for the Commerce National Bank.

Exploring Careers

The telephone on the desk rang twice. A tall man in a three-piece suit punched the lighted button and pickup up the receiver before the third ring escaped.

"Good morning, Commerce National Bank, William Hooker speaking."

"Hi, Bill. How's the bank's busiest assistant cashier?" asked a voice at the other end of the line.

"Fine Liz, but you're right, I'm awfully busy. Can we meet for lunch at noon? I should eat at my desk today, but I can't stand Danny's lunchwagon specials 3 days in a row."

"No problem," answered Liz. "We'll get a quick bite down the street. I'll come by at 12. See you then."

Bill put the receiver down and sighed as he looked at the pile of work before him. Sometimes it was too much for him—and Bill certainly wasn't afraid of hard work! Thinking back over the 3 years he had spent with the Commerce National Bank, Bill could remember quite a few times when he had worked long into the night. He had joined the bank right after receiving his bachelor's degree in economics. During his first year at the bank, he was a trainee. He became familiar with the many different kinds of business that Commerce National handled by spending a few months "learning the ropes" in each of the bank's divisions. He worked in commercial lending first and then transferred to checking. After that he worked in the international division. After a year he knew the bank as well as some of the more experience officers.

During the time he worked as a trainee, Bill decided that consumer lending interested him most. A job was available in that division, and Bill spent the next 9 months lending people money for new cars, home improvements, vacations, college tuition, and other personal needs. Then he was promoted to the job of assistant cashier. He was expected to handle any problems or business the customers brought to him. If he couldn't take care of them himself, he had to know

"I joined the bank right after receiving my bachelor's degree in economics."

Office Occupations

Bill is expected to handle any financial problems that the bank's customers may have.

who could. His performance never slackened, but still there were days like this one, when the mountain of work just continued to grow.

As he was about to dig into that mountain, Bill noticed a middle-aged couple approaching his desk. "May I help you?" he asked, smiling.

"I think so," answered the man. "My name is Joseph Lupovich, and this my wife Margaret. We'd like to borrow some money to buy a new car."

"Well, I can certainly help you with that. Please have a seat, Mr. and Mrs. Lupovich," said Bill, indicating the chairs next to his desk. "Now, how much did you want to borrow?"

"We found a car that costs 5,500. We have $2,000 in savings that we can spare, and the dealer will give us $500 for our old car. So we need $3,000 more, said Mrs. Lupovich.

"Does the $5,500 include State and local taxes, license, and extra insurance costs?" asked Bill.

"No, we'd forgotten about those."

"Well, they will bring the cost of the car to around $6,000. So you'll need about $3,500. No problem so far," said Bill, "Now, if you'll fill out this two-page loan application form, we'll be able to evaluate your request."

Bill handed Mrs. Lupovich the standard form used at Commerce. Together, the couple began filling it out. They wrote down their names and address, where each one worked and how much they earned. They also gave information about their savings, checking, and charge accounts, as well as precious loans they had received. When they were finished, they handed the form back to Bill, who looked it over.

"Now, let's see. Together, you earn about $30,000 a year. You have one child. The mortgage, taxes, and insurance on your house cost you about $350 a month, and you don't owe very much on your charge account.

"On our new car loans we charge interest at an annual rate of 9 percent and the loan must be repaid in 3 years. So besides the original $3,500, you'll owe us another $512 for interest. That's the "cost" of the loan. If you take the entire 3 years to pay us back, you'll pay about $111 a month. I should think you'd have no trouble with that."

Exploring Careers

"So what do we do now, Mr. Hooker?" asked Mrs. Lupovich.

"Nothing, until we call you back. We'll simply check to see that everything you wrote here is in order, and then you'll receive your loan. Since you have a checking account with us, I can look at our records my self to make sure you maintain the account properly. Your savings and charge accounts and your mortgage are all with other banks, however. To check on those, I'll give your application to our credit investigator. She will call the central credit bureau for your credit history. She'll also call your employer to verify your income. This will all take a few days; then you can come in to sign the papers and receive your money.

"There's one other thing. On most consumer loans, your signatures are the only assurance we need that you will pay us back. These are called "unsecured loans." For a new car, however, we ask that you sign an agreement called a "chattel mortgage." It says that if you fail to pay us, we can take the car as payment. Now, we have faith that you will pay us on time, of course. This is just a precaution."

"I understand," replied Mr. Lupovich. Mrs. Lupovich nodded in agreement. "Then we'll hear from you shortly?"

"Right, and thank you for coming it!" said Bill, wishing them a pleasant day.

"Back to the mountain of paperwork," he muttered to himself after the couple left. "And now it's even higher!" But he really didn't mind. He spent almost half of each workday talking with customers and enjoyed that part of the job very much. In fact, now that he thought about it, helping people like Joseph and Margaret Lupovich gave him more pleasure than any other aspect of his work. Bill hoped their credit history was in order. They seemed nice, and Bill wanted them to have their new car. Usually everything checked out properly, but not always...

Bill picked up some papers from his desk and looked through them. Here's a request I'll have to turn down, he thought. A man wanted to buy a boat for $20,000. He had $3,900 and wanted to borrow the rest. Normally the bank would ask him to pay at least $5,000 himself, but he had a checking account and another loan with them. So Bill thought he could bend the rules. But he found that several of the man's checks had "bounced" (had been returned because he had too little in the account to cover them). And some of his loan payments were late.

"Helping customers gives me more pleasure than any other aspect of my work."

Office Occupations

Bill knew he couldn't lend the man more money; he was unreliable. Bill disliked this part of his job—telling someone he couldn't approve a loan they wanted—but it had to be done. The whole purpose of investigating a person's credit history was to weed out these "bad risks."

Much of the work on Bill's desk involved consumer loans: Evaluating an application for approval or rejection; looking at the bank's records; having the credit investigator check someone's credit history; calling the customer and saying the loan was approved; or having the secretary type up papers for the customer to sign. For loans of more than $3,500, he also had to consult his supervisor. (As he gained experience with the bank, his "assigned lending authority"—the amount he could lend on his own judgment—would increase).

He did other things, too, and some of them had nothing to do with loans. Yesterday, a man who was not a Commerce customer wanted to cash a check from a different bank. The teller asked Bill to approve the check. The day before, a woman who had just moved to town came in to open a savings account. Bill filled out a form, deposited her money, and gave her a passbook.

A regular customer, planning a long vacation in France, came in first thing this morning to ask how he should carry his spending money. Bill advised him that travelers' checks were much safer than cash. "You sign the checks once now and again when you spend them," he explained. "If they get lost or stolen, they are no good to anyone else, so the bank can pay you back for them. But if your cash is lost or stolen, it's next to impossible to recover it."

As Bill was examining a loan application, the mail clerk dropped a batch of letters in his "In" box. He immediately noticed the letter on top of the pile. It was on thin airmail stationery and had Japanese postage stamps. The letter came from Russell Anderson, an American businessman who had been sent to Tokyo for 6 months. In his letter, he asked Bill to transfer $500 from his Commerce account to a Toyko bank. Bill laid the letter aside and made a mental note to take care of it as soon as he finished reading this loan application.

Exploring

Bank officers must show their best side to customers.

- Do you like meeting and talking with people?
- Do you enjoy getting to know strangers?
- Are you comfortable talking with strangers on the telephone?
- Can you remain friendly and courteous, even with irritating people or when something is troubling you?

Bank officers must know how to "read" people as well as financial records when judging a request for a loan.

- Are you a good judge of character?
- Can you tell when a friend has made up a supposedly "true" story?
- Do you question things you read or hear that don't seem right?

Bank officers deal with large sums of money and with information about people's private lives. They must be honest and trustworthy.

- Are you careful with another person's belongings and with valuables?
- Are you careful with money?
- If you receive an allowance, do you spend it wisely?
- Do people trust you?
- Can you keep a secret even though you want to tell someone?

Bank officers are part of a team. They must be able to get along with their co-workers.

- Do you enjoy working with others in group projects?
- Do you like team sports?
- Are you willing to follow another person's instructions?

Bank officers work with detailed financial statements, which they must read and write very carefully.

- Do you enjoy working with numbers?
- Are you good at math?
- Do you check your homework before handing it in?
- Are you an organized person?

Bank officers often have to refuse loans, even to customers they would like to help.

- Do you know how to say no?
- Do you keep people from taking advantage of you?
- Can you stand firm with your younger brothers and sisters, even if they beg or cry?

Exploring Careers

Planner

As a planner, Lyn wears many hats. "In one day I may talk with a transportation engineer, a lawyer, and an architect."

Office Occupations

A community is a living thing. It wakes and sleeps, uses energy and produces waste, just as you do. Its "nerves" carry information while its "arteries" carry traffic through its system. The people who live and work in a community are its blood. Without them, it cannot live.

Like other living things, communities grow and change. Farmland gives way to towns. Towns push outward and become cities. Forests are cleared for new homes. Old brick buildings make way for steel and glass skyscrapers.

But not all parts of a community change in the same way or at the same speed. At the edge of a city, for example, you might see a rapidly growing neighborhood with wide, well-paved streets and clean, modern buildings. Closer in, you might pass through an older part of town. The trees are bigger, the buildings look a little more run down than they did 10 years ago. But nothing else has changed. And at the heart of the city, you might see a different kind of picture. The broken windows and burned-out buildings, the garbage on the sidewalks and graffiti on the walls tell you that this neighborhood is dying.

Communities grow up and grow old, just as people do. And just like people, they need care. Think of what happens to people who don't take care of themselves. They get sick or hurt more often. And they may die sooner. So, too, with a community. Without proper care it becomes run down. Eventually it turns into an unhealthy, ugly, even dangerous place to live.

Who takes care of a community? Many people do in different ways. The police and fire departments protect it from crime and fire. A council makes laws. The mayor guides the community on its day-to-day course. But who sits in the lookout tower? Who keeps track of how the community is changing? Who watches to see that in 10 years it will be the kind of home its residents want?

That job belongs to the planners.

Planners help a community make decisions that will affect its future health. For example:

- Should a factory be built to provide jobs for local residents, even if it will pollute the water they drink?

- Should a county keep its farmland or allow houses to be built on it?

- Should a city tear down houses to make room for a new highway or office building?

- Should the electric company clear a forest to build a new power plant?

Citizens and government bodies face such decisions all the time. But they can't decide what's best for everyone without information. They must know all the effects—good and bad—that each choice would cause. Planners provide that information.

What is it like being a planner? "It's a balancing act," says Lyn Coleman. "On one side, private citizens want to use their land as they please. On the other side, the public wants the land used in a way that will benefit the whole community. The planner has to balance these two sides."

Lyn knows this as well as anyone. As a planner for Montgomery County, Maryland, she performs this balancing act every working day. Right now, for example, she is working on a new "master plan" for the area around the town of Olney. A master plan is a blueprint for the future. It shows how each piece of land should be used, whether for heavy industry, commercial business, single-family homes, farms, recreation, or some other purpose. In this way, a plan guides the growth of the community.

"A master plan is only good for 5 to 10 years," explains Lyn. "Then it becomes outdated." The last Olney plan was written in 1986. Now, like a child outgrowing clothes, Olney has outgrown its old plan and needs a new one.

Lyn and an urban designer, John Carter, are given the job, which will take about a year. They could finish it pretty quickly if they stayed in the office all day long. But if they did that—using just their own ideas and not getting anyone else's—they'd be taking a big chance. Like a person selling refrigerators at the North Pole, they'd soon find that nobody wanted their product. It would simply gather dust on a shelf.

Lyn knows how important it is to be in touch with local citizens from the start. At a public meeting in Olney one evening, she talks to citizens and sets up an advisory committee. The committee will see to it that the people of Olney understand how the master plan will affect their everyday lives. The committee also will advise Lyn and tell her what the citizens want.

After setting up the committee, Lyn returns to research. She must have the answers to a long list of questions about the Olney area before she can begin writing the plan. Part of her list looks like this.

Questions about the natural features of the area:

- What types of soils are found in the area, and where?
- Where are the hills and valleys?
- Where are the waterways? How clean are they?
- In which directions does rainwater run off the land?

Questions about people:

- How many people live there? Where do they live?

- How many children are there? How many older people?
- What about income? Is there a mixture of people with different income levels?
- What kind of business is there?
- How has the population grown over the years?

Questions about land use:

- How is each piece of land used today?
- For what use did the old plan intend it?
- Where are the important historical sites?

Questions about transportation:

- Where are the roads and railroads?
- How much traffic travels on them?
- Where do traffic jams take place?

"Planning is an art, not a science."

The answers to these questions come from many places. To find out how the land is being used, Lyn and John study aerial pictures. Then they drive and walk around the neighborhoods to get a closer look. To answer other questions, Lyn relies on studies done by other divisions of the planning staff, other county agencies, and the Federal Government. She also gets useful tips from citizens.

And speaking of the citizens, Lyn's next step takes her back to them. In a series of public meetings, she again tries to get a sense of what the people want for their community. How would they like to see it grow? What kinds of changes are important to them? What things do they *not* want to change? Lyn knows there are almost as many answers to these questions as there are people in Olney. That's why the planners hold several meetings. They talk to farmers at one, land developers at a second, citizens of the town at a third.

And this is just the beginning. During the whole time the plan is being written (and even after that) there will be public meetings. Every time a Chamber of Commerce or a PTA, neighborhood association, or other civic group asks a planner to come and speak, Lyn (or one of her co-workers) will take the colored maps and go. She tells citizen groups what the planning staff has in mind for Olney. She also listens to suggestions and complaints.

Once she has a good idea of what the people want, Lyn starts writing. "As a planner, you must know how to write well. The citizens will read your plan, so you have to keep it clear and simple."

And with the writing begins the balancing act. Lyn brings together all she knows about what the citizens want, what the community as a whole needs and wants, what has already been done, and what makes good sense.

Bit by bit, piece by piece, she figures out how to use the land in a way that is best for everyone.

If that seems easy, think again. "Planning is an art, not a science," Lyn points out. "There's no formula you can use to answer a question or solve a problem, because every one is different. There are only basic principles of good planning. The rest is creativity, hard work, and common sense. But that's what makes the job challenging and fun."

Lyn draws on the knowledge and expertise of other people on the county planning staff. There are several divisions, and each specializes in something different. One division puts together information on soil, terrain, water, air quality, and other environmental matters. Another covers architectural and engineering problems. There are divisions for parks and recreation, for housing, and for transportation. And a research division gives advice on population characteristics and market trends. The experts in these other divisions help Lyn solve the many problems that come up as she writes the plan. "The Olney plan is a team effort," she explains, "and I'm the team leader. I put it all together."

Working with people in so many different fields gives Lyn's job a lot of variety. "A planner wears many hats," she says. "In one day I may talk with a transportation engineer, a lawyer, and an architect. To speak each one's language, I must know a little about engineering, law, and architecture. Planning is an occupation for someone with many different interests."

Lyn has her own specialty: Rural and agricultural planning. "Most people think of planning as only for cities," she explains. "And it's true that planning started there. But the cities have grown so quickly that the farms and small towns are disappearing. Now planners are trying to preserve them, too."

Office Occupations

Lyn's own interest in planning also started with cities. As the daughter of an Air Force officer, she traveled widely in the United States and Europe when she was growing up. "I saw many cities," she recalls, "and I noticed some were nicer than others. I began to wonder why."

Lyn learned more about cities in college. Majoring in political science, she studied urban politics. With her bachelor's degree she got a job as a research assistant in a planning office. "I thought I could work my way up. But I just couldn't pick up what I needed to know."

So Lyn went back to college for 2 more years to earn a master's degree in urban planning. Taking courses in many different departments, she learned a little about everything. "Because planning is so broad, there wasn't time to specialize in school. For me, specialization came in my job. The main thing we learned in school was how to think about and solve problems."

The Olney master plan promises to be a major step for Lyn in developing a specialty as a planner. Olney is a small suburban community surrounded by farms. The town has grown very quickly in the last few years, eating up the farmland. With the new plan, Lyn hopes to slow the town's growth and save the rural area.

One way this might be done is with a rule requiring every new home to have at least 5 acres of land. In most neighborhoods in a city or town, each home has half an acre of land or less. With a 5-acre rule, there would still be lots of open space.

But every rule makes someone unhappy. In this case it might be a couple who bought 20 acres of that land years ago. They expected the town to expand and they hoped the land would become very valuable. They hoped to sell it for a great deal of money to a developer who would build 40 or 50 new homes on it. But the 5-acre rule would allow only four new homes, making the land much less valuable. The couple could lose thousands of dollars.

When Lyn has to face that couple, the balancing act becomes really tough. "They're almost in tears because this part of the plan will ruin them. And I have to explain why it's necessary. This is the hardest part of my job."

It is also a large part of her job. Many people come in to ask about the new plan (though not all of them are as upset as that couple). Others call or write for information. Lyn talks or writes to each one of them, which takes a great deal of time.

The phone calls, letters, and visits continue while Lyn writes the Olney plan. Do they stop when she has finished? Not at all! In fact, they increase, because the plan she has produced is not a final version. It is only a "sketch plan." After it is published, the people of Olney

"Most people think of planning as only for cities. But cities have grown so quickly that farms and small towns are disappearing. Now planners try to preserve them, too."

have a chance to read it and react to it. For Lyn, this means more phone calls, letters, and visits. It also means more public meetings with the colored maps.

Lyn points out how important this part of her work is. "You have to be quick on your feet. Public speaking ability is essential! After all, as a planner, you're telling people how to use their land. You have to expect opposition. But you also have to convince people that your plan makes good sense. It won't sell itself."

Lyn enjoys dealing with the public. "Average citizens have become aware of the need for long-range planning. I'm glad to see that, and I like working with them."

Based on the public's reactions, the staff members make changes in the sketch plan. Then they give the new version to the five-person planning board. After the planning board approves the plan, it goes to the County Council, which makes laws for the county, for adoption as official county policy.

And still Lyn's work is not finished! After all, what good is a master plan that stays on paper? It must be put into effect. How? Through zoning regulations. Each piece of land in the county belongs to a zone. And in each kind of zone, only certain types of buildings may be legally built. Let's say you wanted to build a shopping center on land that was zoned for single-family homes. Before you could build, you would have to get the County Council to "rezone" the land (change its zoning) for commercial business.

To put the new plan into effect, much of the Olney area must be rezoned. That means many County Council sessions and public meetings. And as the plan's author, Lyn must be there to explain it. The meetings continue until rezoning is finished and the new plan takes effect.

And where does that leave Lyn?

With other projects to do. With more letters to answer. With more phone calls to return. With more people to speak to.

And with the satisfaction of knowing she's helped improve her environment.

"And that," she says, "is the best part."

Exploring

Planners figure out the long-range effects of building something new—a highway or housing project, for example. To do so, they must think ahead.

- Do you save money for things you can't buy right away?
- Do you enjoy games of strategy, such as checkers, chess, or bridge?
- Do you plan your weekends and vacations in advance?
- Do you daydream about your future?

Planners must have a talent for design and for arranging space.

- Do you like to design and sketch airplanes, buildings, clothes, or automobiles?
- Have you built a model railroad layout or a miniature town?
- Do you sometimes rearrange the furniture in your bedroom?
- Have you ever designed a garden?
- Can you give directions by drawing a map?
- If asked to clean a cluttered closet or garage, do you reorganize the things in it?

Because they deal with many different aspects of community life, planners must know about and be interested in many subjects.

- Do you read books on many different subjects?
- Do you watch a variety of TV programs?
- Do you have more than one hobby, or play several sports?

Planners are concerned about the environment around them.

- Do you react to changes in your neighborhood, such as a new street or building?
- Does it bother you to find garbage in a park or lake?
- Do you participate in local recycling drives?

Planners deal with many different people, including professionals in other fields and the general public.

- Do you enjoy working on group projects?
- Do you get along with most of your classmates?
- Do you like playing team sports?
- Can you listen with interest to another person's point of view?
- Can you convince a group to go along with your ideas?

Planners make plans that take a long time to fulfill and sometimes never take effect.

- Do you enjoy projects that take a long time to complete, such as growing vegetables or putting on a play?
- If you are taking music or dance lessons, do you practice faithfully?
- Do you keep trying if things don't turn out just the way you wanted?

Office Occupations

Computer Programmer/Systems Analyst

Joe sometimes works odd hours, because computer systems sometimes work at odd hours and problems can arise at anytime.

Exploring Careers

Joe worked his way up in the computer field. He had several years experience as a Programmer before being promoted to Systems Analyst.

Joe Jaramillo yawned and stretched his arms just as the TV announcer was introducing the half-time entertainers. His friend and neighbor, Harry Barns, looked at him in surprise and exclaimed, "Hey, Joe, you can't possibly be bored. That touchdown at the buzzer was a great play!"

"No, I'm not bored at all. It *is* a great game. I'm just tired. I got called into work at 4:15 this morning and didn't have time to catch a nap before the game started."

"4:15 on a Sunday morning?" Harry asked in amazement. "I thought only doctors and police officers got those kinds of calls. Did your computer turn human and get lonely?" he asked, teasingly.

"I wish it was that simple. Then I could have just talked to it and gone back to sleep!" Joe said, in the same joking manner. "Most people don't realize that Computer Systems Analysts have to be "on call" in case of an emergency. If there's a major problem and the computer shuts down, that means that dozens of people can't continue with their work, and it could even prevent business from starting up the next day. That costs the company a lot of money, wastes a lot of time, and can be a real inconvenience for lots of customers. So, if the computer operators or technicians can't find and correct the problem, they call me. That's what happened this morning."

"What was so important?" Harry asked.

"The system that I've been working on for the last 9 months is supposed to go into operation when the bank opens tomorrow. It's a quicker, more efficient way to process checks. Everything was in place except to switch over from the old system to the new one. That had to be done over the weekend, while the bank was closed, so that it wouldn't disrupt business. I thought that the technicians could handle it, but they ran into some problems. And since I designed the system..."

Harry looked impressed. "You designed the system? That sounds sort of like being an inventor. I thought you just wrote the programs to make the computers do what other people want them to."

"It is like being an inventor, sometimes," Joe agreed. "...and a magician, as well as a *programmer*, trouble shooter, *forms designer*, *cost accountant*..."

"Wait a minute," Harry interrupted. "I'm confused. You do all of that?"

"And more," Joe said. "See, I started out as a *programmer*. Other people told me exactly what kind of program they needed, what it had to do, etc. I worked at the computer most of the time, either writing the program instructions or "debugging" to find the errors that could cause problems when people tried to use the program. But I only saw my little slice of the bank—the part that used the programs I was writing. And I didn't get phone calls at 4 a.m.!

"Then I was promoted to *Systems Analyst*. Now I work with people from consumer lending, internal operations, auditing—all of the bank departments. I get to see the big picture and try to help people understand what the computer can do for them—how it can help them do their work better. It lets me be a lot more creative. I find out exactly what people need, then think things through and design a new system. I seldom touch the computer anymore. That's mostly done by the two programmers who work under me. Now *I'm* the one telling *them* what kind of program to write, and what it has to do. Then I install the system and test it. If I worked in a smaller bank or company, I'd probably do more of my own programming, but I have too many other responsibilities."

"How do you know what people need and how to make things work for so many different jobs?" Harry was so fascinated, he didn't even notice the half-time show on the TV set across the room.

"It's a real challenge," Joe acknowledged. "Take this latest assignment, for example. Tom Arnold, head of the check processing department, wanted a new system for processing checks. So I went over to meet with him. I had to ask a lot of questions to find out what Tom wanted. He explained to me that his check processing system depended too much on people and not enough on machinery. It was working O.K. for the moment, but he was afraid that, as the volume of checks grew, the present system wouldn't be able to keep pace. So, I gave Tom some ideas about the possibilities and he told me more about other things he'd like to be able to do—like tracking down errors faster. He also wanted the system to identify who the bank's largest customers were, how much money they maintained on deposit, and how long they kept it there. That first meeting was over nine months ago.

"The next step was for Tom to show me how his department processed checks every day. If I understand how things are done manually, it's easier to figure out how to make the computer do them more efficiently. Tom showed me that the checks and deposit slips arrive in bundles. The first step was proofing and encoding. Tom had 30 clerks operating proof encoding machines that printed the amount of each check in a special ink that other machines could "read." As the checks were encoded, the operator and machine made sure that the amounts were the same as the teller's tally. That's called "proving." Then another machine, called a reader-sorter, read the specially printed number on each check and tallied the amounts from all 30 proof encoders. It also sorted the checks by the city they came from so they could be sent back to other banks and exchanged for credit. The faster this is done, the more money the bank has available for its customers. Finally the checks are photographed on microfilm for future reference.

"The system had been good at first. But Tom was right; it would soon be overburdened. I knew what kind of equipment was available. So, once I understood Tom's current system and his needs, I started putting together the combination of equipment that would do the job better, faster, and easier. But I also had to think about how reliable each machine would be, not just how fast. Every time something breaks down and the system stops running, it costs the bank money—and increases the possibility that I'll get called in the middle of the night!

"The cost of the equipment was an important consideration, too. Whenever I design a system, I have to calculate the cost of doing things the new way versus the old way and be sure that we can do things economically, as well as efficiently.

"Anyway, I finally came up with the right combination of things to do the job. With the new system, the checks will be proofed, encoded, and automatically sorted into several categories. With the new proof machine, Tom will be able to get the information he wanted about certain accounts whenever he wants it. The checks will be microfilmed while they're sorted on a high speed reader- sorter, so we'll have a film record of them as the bank received them. That will make it easier to track them down and find errors. And the new equipment will sort checks faster and allow the bank to

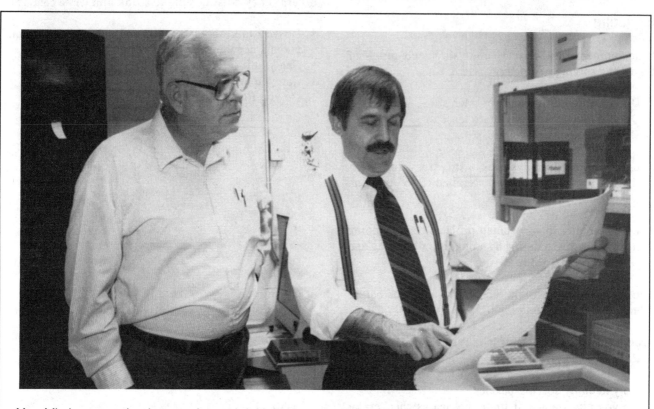

After I find out exactly what people need, I think things through and design a new computer system," says Joe.

forward them to other banks sooner than we can now.

"So, once I had a new system designed, and all of the equipment identified, I had to get the *programmers* working on writing the software that would control the machines and link them to the bank's main computer. Since the two systems use different coded languages, we had to design an interface so that they could communicate with each other. My programmers did a great job with that one!

"Meanwhile, I also had to develop some new forms for people to collect information and develop reports that would provide the kind of information Tom wanted in an easy to understand format. Then I tested the system as it was being installed. And, as of 11:00 this morning, everything is on line and running fine!" Joe finished.

"Whew. I'm almost worn out just listening to you describe everything!" Harry said. "Well, at least it's done."

"Right," agreed Joe. "And at 9:30 tomorrow morning I'm meeting with Anita in consumer loans to start working on..."

"Hey, second half is starting," noticed Harry.

"Great. Enough shop talk anyway," Joe announced. "As satisfying as it is, let's get back to the really important stuff: beating the Packers!"

Exploring

Programmers and systems analysts spend much of their time solving problems.

- Do you enjoy doing math problems?
- Do you like puzzles and brain teasers?
- Do you read mystery stories?

Programmers and systems analysts work with problems that are long and detailed. Solving them takes a great deal of patience.

- Do you enjoy long, detailed projects such as doing jigsaw puzzles, painting by numbers, or building and rigging a model ship?
- Do you like to read long books?
- Do you check over your homework and tests before handing them in?

Programmers and analysts look for creative solutions to the problems given them.

- Do you enjoy solving puzzles?
- Do you play games of strategy, such as checkers or chess?

- Do you like to think of new ways of doing things around the house?
- Do you occasionally rearrange your bedroom furniture?

Programmers and systems analysts often run into very stubborn problems. If at first they don't succeed in solving a problem, they must try, try again.

- Do you keep trying when you can't solve a problem right away?
- If you play a sport or musical instrument, do you practice faithfully?

Programmers and systems analysts work with information, called data, that usually is in the form of lists of numbers.

- Are you good at remembering historical dates, batting averages, telephone numbers, bus schedules, or other numerical information?
- Do you like to memorize the amounts of ingredients in a recipe?
- Do you find it easy to use a phonebook or dictionary?

Programmers and systems analysts work closely with others. They must be able to speak and write clearly.

- Do you talk about complicated subjects with your parents, teachers, or friends?
- Can you listen to or give a detailed explanation?
- Can you give clear instructions to do a task?
- Do you find it easy to say what you mean?

Office Occupations

Job Facts

There isn't room in this book for a story about every office occupation. However, you'll find some important facts about 33 of these occupations in the following section. If you want additional information about any of them you might begin by consulting the Department of Labor's *Occupational Outlook Handbook*, which should be available in your school or public library.

Occupation	Nature and Places of Work	Training and Qualifications	Other Information
CLERICAL OCCUPATIONS			
Bookkeeping Workers	All kinds of firms employ bookkeeping workers. About a third of the jobs are in wholesale and retail trade.	Employers generally hire high school graduates who have taken business arithmetic, bookkeeping, and principles of accounting. Some high school students learn bookkeeping on the job through work-study programs. College courses are necessary for some jobs.	An increasing amount of bookkeeping is done by machine and computers rather than by hand.
Cashiers	Cashiers work in all kinds of business establishments. Supermarkets and food stores employ more cashiers than any other kind of store.	Employers prefer high school graduates. Courses in bookkeeping, business arithmetic, and typing are good preparation. Many schools offer cashier training as part of distributive education programs. But cashiers generally train on the job.	More and more stores and supermarkets are using computerized checkout systems. Many cashiers work part time.

Exploring Careers

Occupation	Nature and Places of Work	Training and Qualifications	Other Information
Collection Workers	Most collectors work for banks, loan companies, and collection agencies. Others work for wholesale and retail businesses.	High school graduation is necessary for most beginning jobs. Experience in person-to-person contact is helpful, because collectors have to be able to persuade people to pay their bills. Most training takes place on the job.	Collectors do most of their work over the phone.
File Clerks	File clerks work for all kinds of businesses. About half work in banks, insurance companies, factories, or government agencies.	Employers prefer to hire high school graduates who can read quickly and accurately, spell well, and type. Beginning workers learn their employer's filing system on the job.	Filing often is a job for beginning office workers. After working a while, file clerks may be promoted to jobs as typists, secretaries, or office machine operators.
Office Machine Operators	Manufacturing companies, banks, insurance companies, and wholesale and retail stores all employ office machine operators. Some operators work for businesses that specialize in providing word-processing, copying, and other clerical services.	Employers prefer to hire high school graduates who can type and operate an adding machine or calculator. Workers are trained on the job for the particular machines they are to operate.	There are many kinds of office machine operators. Their job titles depend on the machine they use, such as: switchboard operators and duplicating machine operators. Workers may operate only one machine or a variety of machines, depending on their job and experience.
Postal Clerks	Many clerks are employed at local post offices, but most work at one of the more than 300 mail processing centers across the country.	High school graduates 16 and older as well as anyone 18 and older may apply. They must pass several tests that measure their clerical and physical ability. Postal clerks are trained on the job.	The Postal Service classifies clerks into four categories. *Casual* employees help with usually large volumes of mail during Christmas and other peak mailing periods. *Part-time flexible* employees work regularly, but not according to a set schedule, as *part-time regular* employees do. Most clerks begin as part-time flexible workers while waiting for an opening as a *full-time* clerk.
Receptionists	Almost every kind of organization employs receptionists, but about half work in the health field, for doctors, dentists, and hospitals.	Employers usually hire high school graduates. Courses in English, typing, and basic bookkeeping are helpful. A neat appearance and pleasant manner are very important.	Receptionist is a job for beginning office workers. In a large office, however, a receptionist with clerical skills may be promoted to typist, secretary, or administrative assistant.
Secretaries and Stenographers	Two out of three secretaries and stenographers work in banks, insurance companies, real estate firms, government agencies, and other organizations. Medical secretaries work for doctors, and legal secretaries work for lawyers. Executive secretaries work for top officials in business and government.	Employers generally hire high school graduates and may prefer people with additional business or secretarial training. Some secretarial jobs involve a great deal of responsibility, judgment, and skill. For these, secretarial school or college is often a must.	Secretaries do clerical work and handle many of the business and administrative details that need to be taken care of in offices of all kinds. Many use computers or word processors. Some may work temporarily or part-time. Experienced secretaries may be promoted to jobs as administrative assistants, office managers, or executive secretaries.

Office Occupations

Occupation	Nature and Places of Work	Training and Qualifications	Other Information
Shipping and Receiving Clerks	Factories employ more than half of all clerks. Large numbers also work for wholesale houses and retail stores.	Employers prefer high school graduates who have taken some business courses. Legible handwriting is important. Training generally takes place on the job.	Clerks often must perform strenuous work in cold, drafty, dirty warehouses. Occasionally they may have to work overtime to unload a late shipment.
Statistical Clerks	Although nearly every industry employs statistical clerks, most work in finance, insurance, and real estate companies, in manufacturing firms, and in government.	Employers prefer high school graduates who have had math courses and can do detailed work. Training in data processing, bookkeeping, and typing is helpful.	Many clerks work closely with computers.
Stock Clerks	Factories, wholesale firms, and retail stores employ most stock clerks. Others work for airlines, government agencies, and hospitals.	Employers prefer high school graduates with basic reading, writing, and math skills. Training usually occurs on the job.	Clerks spend much of their day on their feet. They often work in damp, drafty stockrooms and may have to do considerable bending and lifting. With experience, clerks may move to higher positions in stock handling or to sales positions.
Typists/word processors	Almost every kind of organization employs typists, though most work in factories, banks, insurance companies, real estate firms, and government agencies.	Most employers require high school graduates with good English skills who can type at least 50 to 60 words per minute. Many work at computer or word processing terminals. The ability to operate dictating equipment, calculators, and copy machines is also helpful.	A typist's job is often a beginning job; from there it is possible to move into a job as a secretary, office machine operator, or computer operator. One typist in four works part time.

COMPUTER OCCUPATIONS

Occupation	Nature and Places of Work	Training and Qualifications	Other Information
Computer Operating Personnel	Most operating personnel work for manufacturers, banks, wholesale and retail businesses, government agencies, and data processing firms. There are several different kinds of operating personnel, including data entry operators and highspeed printer operators.	Employers usually hire high school graduates, and prefer people with college training in data processing. Beginners are trained on the job.	Because large computers must be operated at carefully controlled temperatures, some operators work in air-conditioned rooms. Some computer operators work in typical office environments. Some may work on night shifts since many companies want to make use of their computers as much as possible.
Programmers	Most programmers work for large firms that have big computer systems. This includes manufacturers, banks, insurance companies, data processing firms, and government agencies. Many also work for software publishers who develop the computer programs that people buy for home use or in small businesses.	College training generally is necessary for a job as a programmer. Firms that use computers to handle scientific and engineering problems usually require their programmers also have a degree in science or engineering. Some positions may require an advanced degree.	Programmers occasionally must work nights and weekends, in order to use the computer when it is available or to solve a problem.

Exploring Careers

Occupation	Nature and Places of Work	Training and Qualifications	Other Information
Systems Analysts	Most systems analysts work for manufacturers, banks, insurance companies, and data processing firms. Many also work for data processing service firms or consulting firms that are hired by other companies on a contract to create or customize their computer system. Systems analysts work throughout the country but a large percentage are in the Northeast and West due to the concentration of computer firms in those areas.	Employers prefer college graduates with a degree in a field related to the kind of work the company does, and with training in computer techniques, concepts, and programming. Prior experience with computers is important; many systems analysts start out as programmers.	Systems analysts normally do not work the odd hours that other computer workers do, though occasionally they must work evenings or weekends to finish a project or remedy an important problem.

BANKING OCCUPATIONS

Occupation	Nature and Places of Work	Training and Qualifications	Other Information
Bank Clerks	Although clerks work in every branch bank, the larger branches and main offices employ most of the more specialized workers.	A high school diploma is usually sufficient. Courses in typing, bookkeeping, and other clerical areas are helpful. Clerks receive their training on the job.	The work of bank clerks is often very detailed and repetitious. Many use computer terminals and other office machines.
Bank Officers	Every branch bank employs officers, but the greatest variety and specialization are found in the large branches and central offices.	Banks prefer college graduates for management training. A degree in business, accounting, or economics is excellent preparation, though graduates in other fields are in demand, too. Occasionally, banks promote outstanding tellers and clerks to jobs as officers.	Officers can specialize in a wide range of areas, such as lending, trust management, or correspondence banking.
Bank Tellers	Specialized tellers generally work in large and main branch banks, while smaller branches usually employ all-purpose tellers.	Employers prefer high school graduates. Basic qualities such as clerical skill, friendliness, neatness, courtesy, and attentiveness are important.	A teller's job is repetitive and demands great attention to detail. They must be very accurate in counting and working with numbers. Most bank tellers work with computer terminals and encoding machines.

INSURANCE OCCUPATIONS

Occupation	Nature and Places of Work	Training and Qualifications	Other Information
Actuaries	Two out of three actuaries work for insurance companies, mostly those that handle life insurance.	Actuaries generally need a bachleor's degree in math, statistics, or actuarial science. They have to pass a series of difficult exams given by one of the professional societies of actuaries.	Most actuaries specialize in life and health insurance, property insurance, or pension plans.
Claim Representatives	While a handful of claim representatives work for banks, finance companies, and other business firms, the majority work for insurance companies.	Many employers prefer college graduates in almost any field, though specialized work experience will often be an adequate substitute for a degree. In some states, claim representatives must have a license.	Many claim settlements involve a great deal of travel.

Office Occupations

Occupation	Nature and Places of Work	Training and Qualifications	Other Information
Underwriters	Most work for property and liability insurance companies. The rest work for life or health insurance companies.	A bachelor's degree in almost any field is preferred for beginning positions. However, to get ahead, further study is necessary.	The work of underwriters is very detailed and carries a great deal of responsibility.

ADMINISTRATIVE OCCUPATIONS

Occupation	Nature and Places of Work	Training and Qualifications	Other Information
Accountants	There are three main kinds of accountants. *Management accountants* are the most numerous. They handle the records of the companies they work for. *Public accountants* analyze and prepare financial reports for individuals and businesses. They work for, or own, independent accounting firms. *Government accountants* examine the records of government agencies and audit private businesses and individuals whose financial affairs are subject to government regulations.	Most large employers prefer college graduates with a bachelor's degree in accounting or a closely related field. A master's degree may help in some cases, as would computer training. In order to move up, public accountants sooner or later must get their certification, by passing a State exam.	Accountants often specialize in one phase of accounting, such as auditing, tax matters, or management consulting.
Advertising Workers	Advertising workers have jobs with many different kinds of firms. First and foremost, they work for advertising agencies. But they also work in the advertising departments of manufacturing firms, retail stores, and banks, or for printers, art studios, letter shops, and similar businesses.	Most employers prefer college graduates, but work experience may be more important than educational background.	People in this occupation work under great pressure to do the best job in the shortest period of time. Often they work long or odd hours to meet deadlines.
Buyers	Buyers work for retail businesses of every size and variety all across the country. Most, however, work in large cities.	A college degree in almost any field is sufficient for beginning positions. Training takes place on the job.	Buyers regulate their own schedules and often work long or odd hours. They may spend some time traveling, depending on the kind of merchandise they buy.
City Managers	Three out of four city managers work for cities of fewer than 25,000 inhabitants, though many larger cities employ managers, too.	A master's degree in public or business administration is almost essential for a career in city management.	Managers often work long, difficult hours, especially during times of emergency.
Credit Managers	Wholesale and retail business employ about half of all credit managers, while a third work for manufacturers and financial institutions.	Employers prefer college graduates who have majored in business administration, economics, or accounting.	Highly qualified credit managers can advance to top-level executive positions.
Industrial Traffic Managers	Most industrial traffic managers work for manufacturing firms. Some work for wholesale and retail establishments.	Employers prefer, and in some cases require, college graduates for this job.	Industrial traffic managers analyze cost and efficiency of various ways of transporting goods. They need to know the government regulations that affect that transport.

Exploring Careers

Occupation	Nature and Places of Work	Training and Qualifications	Other Information
Lawyers	Three out of four lawyers work in law firms. The remainder work for businesses, private organizations, or government.	A bachelor's degree and 3 years of law school are required for a law degree. Degree holders must pass a bar exam to practice law.	Many lawyers specialize in a particular legal field, such as tax, patent, divorce, or criminal law.
Market Research Workers	Manufacturers, advertising agencies, and independent research organizations employ most market research workers. However, some work for retail stores, broadcasting companies, and newspapers.	A bachelor's degree in a field such as marketing, business, psychology, or statistics is necessary for a beginning job. However, to get ahead, graduate training is almost essential.	Market research activity goes through ups and downs that depend on the general health of our economy.
Personnel and Labor Relations Workers	Three out of four workers in this occupation are employed in private industry, including manufacturers, banks, and insurance companies. Government agencies also employ large numbers of these workers.	A bachelor's degree in personnel administration, industrial and labor relations, business, or liberal arts is desirable, depending upon the employer. For labor relations work, graduate study is often necessary.	Getting along with people is an essential part of this occupation.
Planners	Most planners work for city, county, or regional planning agencies. Some work for government agencies that deal with housing, transportation, or environmental protection. Still other planners work for public interest organizations or consulting firms.	Employers prefer applicants with graduate training in urban or regional planning. However people with bachelor's degrees in city planning, architecture, landscape architecture, or engineering also qualify.	In large organizations, planners specialize in areas such as housing or economics, while in small offices they must work in several different areas.
Public Relations Workers	Public relations workers present their employer's image to the public. They work for organizations of all kinds: Manufacturers, insurance companies, public utilities, transportation companies, hospitals, colleges and universities, and government agencies.	A college education with public relations experience is excellent preparation. The appropriate field of study depends on the employer's needs.	Public relations workers often have to work overtime to finish a project. They occasionally travel on business. An ability to get along with people and to understand their needs is essential.
Purchasing Agents	About half of the purchasing agents work for manufacturing firms, government agencies, construction firms, hospitals, schools, and other places that buy in very large quantities.	Large firms usually hire college graduates and prefer applicants with a master's degree in business administration. Small firms hire people with fewer years of college.	In large organizations, agents usually specialize in one or more specific items, such as steel or lumber.

Police officers must be able to give an accurate, detailed account of an event.

The late bell was ringing as Laura Meehan rushed into the classroom. Most of the students were already inside, chatting noisily with one another. At the sound of the bell, they quieted down and took their places.

"That was lucky," thought Laura. "I just made the bell." Laura was never *really* late, but she never arrived early, either. She always managed to slip in at the last minute. Even today, when she had an oral report to give.

Ms. Nazarian was getting things underway. "Good afternoon, class," the teacher said quietly. "Today we are going to begin the final phase of our unit on the history of occupations. For the last 6 weeks, you all have been working in small groups collecting facts about jobs that interest you. We will start the reports with a presentation by the committee chaired by Laura Meehan. They will tell us about the service occupations."

Five students came forward and seated themselves at a rectangular table facing the class. With her note cards in hand, Laura began.

"Six weeks ago, when this project was assigned, our group got together and decided that the first thing we had to do was agree on the topic we were going to study. Choosing a topic turned out to be harder than any of us expected and we were pretty confused for a while.

"We didn't have any trouble at first. Someone suggested researching circus occupations and we liked that idea. We thought it would be fun to find out about clowns, animal trainers, trapeze artists, and all the others. Then, as we talked, Craig started telling us about the job he had just started that week at Beefy's Inn. He's a short order cook there and most of the time he cooks hamburgers and steaks on the grill.

"Well, that started a discussion of the jobs that all of us have had at one time or another," Laura continued. "Joel Girdie, for example, has had a newspaper route for years. He puts in at least an hour every single day— more if it's raining and he has to bag the papers, and on days when he has to put in advertising supplements, comics, and other inserts. It's not always convenient to be up delivering papers at 5 a.m. But after several years, Joel has developed a routine. And he makes about $100 a month at it.

"Renee Harris is an assistant at a day camp. She's in charge of the younger children. She sees to it that they get their milk and crackers on time and that they take their naps. Of course, they're awake and raring to go most of the time and Renee directs them in games and activities. She really has her hands full.

"As for myself, I'm a lifeguard at the YWCA pool. I love being around water—I guess most of you know how much swimming I do—but being a lifeguard takes more than a love of the water. It takes a sense of responsibility and good judgment. You have to know when to stop

Working in a restaurant kitchen is one way of finding out whether this field appeals to you.

youngsters from horsing around in the pool, for one thing. That takes firmness, but a sense of humor certainly helps! Giving water safety lessons is one of the things I like best about my job at the Y. When I teach other people the basics of swimming and water safety, I feel as though I'm passing on a skill that adds a lot to my own life.

"Because it was a logical starting point, our committee decided to take a closer look at the kinds of jobs we were already familiar with—those we had been working at ourselves. And that's when things started to get complicated. First of all, we learned that three of the jobs I've mentioned—short order cook, child care aide, and life-

Service Occupations

Being a mail carrier may appeal to people who enjoy working outdoors.

Food and Lodging Occupations

Somewhat nervous about giving his report, Craig cleared his throat and began. "Having recently been hired at Beefy's Inn, I naturally chose to do my research on the food and lodging occupations."

After a bit of friendly laughter from his classmates, Craig was reassured and continued.

"The need for temporary lodging has been with us since ancient times, ever since people traveled more than a day's journey from home. At first, travelers were well received and cared for by strangers. If a traveler happened to knock on your door, you were honored to invite the person in·to spend the night. Often these evenings were spent swapping yarns, or tales of adventure.

"However, by the Middle Ages, so many people were traveling that something more was needed. Inns were established where paying guests could find a bed to sleep in and food to eat. And, importantly, these were places where you could feed and water your horse. In those days, you didn't expect to have a room to yourself. There might be two or three rooms altogether, each with several beds. If there were lots of travelers, you might find yourself sharing not only your room but your bed! If any of you have visited restored communities like Colonial Williamsburg, in Virginia, you've seen the sort of lodgings that were available to travelers in this country in the past.

"Things have changed a lot since then," continued Craig. "The lodging industry has grown tremendously. What was once a small number of local inns has become a network of hotels and motels. And the number of people it takes to run them has grown as well.

"These days, when guests enter a hotel or motel, they are greeted by the *desk clerk*. Desk clerks register guests, assign rooms, and hand out keys. *Bellhops* carry the guests' luggage and escort them to their rooms. They may run errands and answer questions for the guests. Hotels and motels need a large housekeeping staff to keep rooms and lobbies neat and clean. *Cleaning workers* make beds and provide fresh linens and towels; *linen room attendants* and *laundry room workers* mark and inspect the linens and operate the washing and pressing machines in the laundry. Keeping track of all these workers, and of the supplies needed to keep the hotel clean and attractive, is the job of the *executive housekeeper*. In every hotel, someone must make sure that everything is running smoothly and that the guests are satisfied. *Hotel managers and assistants* are in charge of every aspect of a hotel's operation. They oversee room reservations, banquet arrangements, safeguarding of guests' property, hiring and training of staff—anything at all connected with the way the hotel runs. But they

guard—are service occupations. In these jobs, we are concerned with the care, comfort, well-being, or safety of others. The common thread is that we are performing a service for other people.

"But we were surprised to learn that newspaper carrier is not considered a service occupation. Joel complained and said the rest of us were wrong. After all, he said, he does something for people: He brings them the paper so they won't have to go out and buy it at the store. And he has to please his customers. Why, he wanted to know, wasn't *his* job a service occupation, too? Well, we ended up in an argument as to just what a service occupation really is, but fortunately Ms. Nazarian was able to straighten us out. She explained to us that Joel's job is a sales occupation. She went on to say that we had hit upon a very important point: Personal traits and job duties in the different occupational clusters *do* overlap. Dealing with people is an essential part of the job not just for service workers, but for sales workers as well. That's why it's important for workers in both clusters to be outgoing and good at getting along with people.

"Well, by that time, we had gotten so wrapped up in the issue that we decided to drop the circus occupations and concentrate on service occupations instead. And now we'll share the results of our research. Craig will present our committee's first report."

pay particular attention to the business end of the operation, for it is up to them to be sure that the hotel is run efficiently and profitably. They depend on the *business staff* to help them handle the bookkeeping and accounting.

"And, of course, just about every hotel and motel has a *dining room and kitchen staff*. Food service workers have jobs in many places besides hotels. They prepare food wherever it is served away from home. They work in restaurants; in cafeterias; in schools and colleges; in hospitals and nursing homes; in prisons; in private clubs; at camps and resorts. They work at the food stands at sports events and county fairs. They even work for the catering firms that prepare the dinners we eat on airplanes and the sandwiches we get from vending machines. Food service workers make up one of the largest and fastest growing occupational groups in the country.

"Let's take a look at some of the occupations in this field," continued Craig. "We can start with my job. As Laura explained, I'm a short order cook. In my job, I cook the same sort of thing all the time—hamburgers and steaks, mostly. It didn't take very long to learn how to work with the grill correctly. What *is* important in a job like mine is the ability to work quickly under pressure. No matter what kind of food service operation you have in mind—from a gourmet restaurant to a school cafeteria—preparing the food correctly is the key to keeping customers happy. And that takes skill on the part of the *cooks and chefs*. The dishes that come from the kitchen reflect their creativity and skill, and often are the basis for a restaurant's reputation.

"But other things are important too. Atmosphere is one. Service is another. Those of you who are working as *waiters* and *waitresses* know how important good service is. You take customers' orders, serve their food, and give them personal attention to help them enjoy their meal. A pleasant manner is very important in this job. A good waiter or waitress can make all the difference between a delightful experience in a restaurant and an uncomfortable one.

"You'll find other food service workers in particular kinds of eating establishments. *Food counter workers* take food orders and collect payments in fast food restaurants and cafeterias. *Bartenders* mix drinks in bars, cocktail lounges, and restaurants that serve alcoholic beverages."

Craig paused, then asked for questions. Katie Maggs spoke up. "What's the difference between a cook and a chef?"

"The distinction isn't always clear cut," replied Craig. "Chefs usually are highly experienced cooks, but in fact a restaurant can give the title of chef to anyone at all.

"Still," he went on, "the way it usually works is this.

Waiters and waitresses often make more money in tips than in salary.

The chef is the person who's in charge of the kitchen. He or she may not even do much cooking. The chef's job is to see to it that everyone else in the kitchen does things properly.

"You see, the work of a restaurant cook depends very much on the size of the restaurant. In a small restaurant, as in your own home, one person usually handles every part of the job. However, in a large restaurant, there usually are several cooks. A saute cook might take care of all the food requiring quick-frying. A fry cook might make the deep-fried foods like French fries and fried chicken. There might be other cooks as well: A broiler cook, a soup cook, a sauce cook, and a pastry chef. Now, in a kitchen as large as that, the person in charge would be a chef. Chefs have the skill and experience to oversee the operations of an entire kitchen. Their jobs often are administrative, while the cooks are the people who prepare the food we eat."

Craig looked around for more questions from the class. Greg Morisse raised his hand. "I'd like to know

Service Occupations

Many waiters and waitresses are students who work part-time.

what kinds of kitchen jobs there are in a fast-food restaurant."

"Well," began Craig, "you have to remember that the kind of cooking done in these kitchens is far from the traditional image of a cook preparing an elaborate meal from scratch. Fast-food kitchens are geared toward efficiency and speed. Kitchen jobs are clearly designated. In a typical fast-food kitchen, you might see grill cooks fixing already-prepared meat patties; a bun cook toasting the buns; fry cooks handling French fries and fried chicken or fried fish; and "dressers" adding condiments such as lettuce, pickles, or dressing."

"Thanks, Craig," said Laura. "Now we'll hear from Alan."

Personal Service Occupations

"Personal service workers do things for individual customers," began Alan Oberstein. "And personal services are just that. Personal. They can include just about anything—shining customers' shoes, shampooing their

hair, giving them a massage or a beauty treatment, helping them use exercise equipment in a health studio or gym, checking their coats at a theater, bringing them an umbrella at the beach. For all of these workers, pleasing the customer is an important part of the job."

He added, "Being a lawn care worker myself, I know how important a satisfied customer is. Mowing lawns is a real business for me during the summer, when the grass grows so fast. I handle four or five lawns on a regular basis. So I know that a satisfied customer is a steady customer!

"Throughout history," he continued, "people have paid attention to their appearance. They've used cosmetics and perfumes and cared about the way their hair looked since ancient times. Likenesses of barbers' razors have been found dating all the way back to the Bronze Age. And Egyptian women of 8,000 years ago, especially those of wealth and nobility, took great pains with their hair.

"In early times, *barbers* were known as barber-surgeons. As the name suggests, they performed surgery as well as barbering services. A barber-surgeon might have pulled your tooth, treated you for indigestion, cut your hair, or trimmed your beard. It was not until the late 1700's, a period of advances in medical science, that the two trades began to separate. Today, the red and white striped pole we see in front of a barber shop is a reminder of the barber-surgeon. The red symbolizes the patient's blood and the white stands for the bandages that were used.

"The portraits of our founding fathers that we've all seen countless times show us how popular wigs were during the colonial period in America. Both men and women wore high-fashion powdered wigs. There were wigmakers in those days, but beauty salons as we know them didn't exist. Until the early 1900's, beauty services were almost always provided to customers in their own homes. And the "unisex" salon is an even more recent development, having come into its own in the 1970's.

"There are certain specialties in the field that you might want to know about. Cosmetologists shampoo, cut, style, and color hair. Also known as beauticians or beauty operators, they may straighten hair or make it curly, depending on the customer's wishes; give scalp treatments; and shape or color eyebrows and eyelashes. Hair stylists specialize in arranging and shaping customer's hair according to the latest fashion. Wig dressers do the same sort of things for wigs and hair pieces. Manicurists clean, shape, and polish customers' fingernails and toenails. Makeup artists apply cosmetics and makeup materials such as wigs, beards, rouge, powder, and grease paint. They generally work with actors and actresses who are appearing on state or in film or television productions. Electrologists remove unwanted hair from their customers' skin using a method called electrolysis that involves a needle and use of electricity.

"Now I'm going to finish up with a few words about a special occupation. Funeral directors help make arrangements for burial. Few occupations call for the compassion and tact required of these workers, who deal with others in their time of deepest sorrow."

Alan put his notes down on the table. The class was suddenly subdued, and there were no questions. Laura's own report was next.

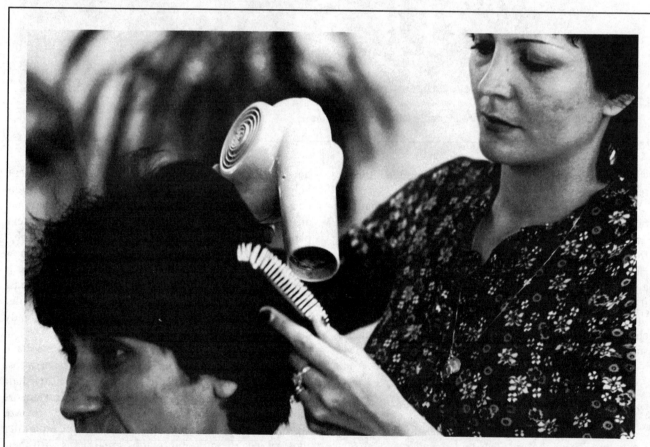

Hair stylists need a sense of artistry.

Exploring Careers

Private Household Occupations

"More people than you might think work in private households," Laura began. "They clean and maintain the house and yard, help care for children, and cook and serve meals. In fact, many of you have been private household workers yourselves—for a few hours, anyway. Babysitting is one of the many occupations in this category. And nearly all of us have done babysitting at one time or another.

"The occupation of household worker was more prominent in ancient times than it is today. For many centuries, the size of a family's household staff was a measure of its wealth and position in society. This is not the case today. Changes in our values and in our way of life have caused us to cut down on the use of servants and household help. Then, too, labor-saving machinery of all kinds is available today. Just think of all the household and garden appliances we have today: Power mowers, electric hedge clippers, vacuum cleaners, washing machines, dishwashers, food processors, microwave ovens. Machines like these make us less dependent on the manual labor provided in the past by a large staff of servants."

"Don't forget electric ice cream makers," exclaimed Jason Reynolds.

"You're right," agreed Laura.

"But still," she continued, "many families need help with chores or child care. Or they may need help caring for an elderly relative. Nearly 1 million people have jobs in private households in America. Most are day workers who clean. They usually make the beds, dust, vacuum,

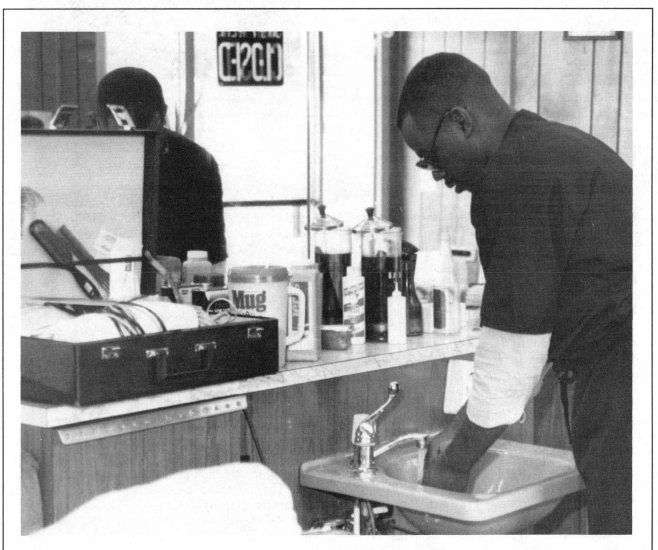

Barber school training usually takes 9 to 12 months, and includes instruction in equipment hygiene.

wash windows, and wax floors. They may also do the laundry and ironing, help with the cooking, and care for children. Some families hire full-time *child care workers* to help with the youngsters—to supervise their activities, prepare their meals, and bathe them and get them ready for bed.

"Arrangements vary, of course. Sometimes, families offer room and board in exchange for babysitting services or companionship for an elderly person. No money changes hands. If a family needs full-time cleaning or child care, however, they pay a wage and may provide room and board as well. Usually, though, the household workers live "out" rather than in the employer's household.

"Most households in America that employ household workers hire day workers to clean or child care workers to watch children. But there are other kinds of private household workers. *Companions* are hired to provide company for elderly or handicapped people, and sometimes, for children. Some families employ *cooks, launderers,* or *gardeners. Caretakers* do heavy household tasks and take care of such things as yard maintenance, window washing, and minor repairs. If the household staff is large, the family may employ a *housekeeper* or *butler* to supervise the other servants."

Having finished her report, Laura went ahead and introduced Joel.

These men wearing the traditional costume of Victorian chimney sweeps have started their own business—cleaning chimneys and fireplaces.

Cleaning Occupations

"Laura has just told you about workers who keep private households clean and in good repair," began Joel. "My report is about workers who clean buildings like this school.

"Every building needs to be kept clean and in good condition for the comfort and safety of those who live or work there," Joel went on. "This involves not only sweeping or mopping the floors, but washing the windows, polishing furniture, vacuuming, emptying trash, cleaning the bathrooms, and getting rid of insects and rodents, too.

"In the past, when businesses and buildings were much smaller, innkeepers or shopkeepers might clean their establishments themselves. Or, more likely, they'd have a servant, a member of the family, or an employee do the job. After the Industrial Revolution, large plants and factories were built. Then large apartments and huge office buildings sprang up to provide a place for all the people in the rapidly growing cities. A way had to be found to keep such large buildings clean and safe. In time, cleaning services became specialized and they eventually became a business in their own right. Today, commercial cleaning firms handle this important task for

the owners of many large buildings.

"But let's take a closer look at these workers. Craig has already told you about some of them. The cleaning staff in a hotel or motel is very important. Guests get annoyed quickly if there's no fresh linen or if no one comes in to clean their rooms. Craig mentioned the *housekeeper* who supervises the hotel's entire housekeeping department. That's an administrative job, as a rule. It takes organizational ability and skill in supervising others. The housekeeper may be in charge of dozens of workers who actually handle the fresh linens and clean the rooms. Housekeepers do similar kinds of work in hospitals and nursing homes, in boarding schools and colleges, and in prisons. They work anywhere, really, where large numbers of people stay overnight.

"*Porters, cleaners,* and *janitors* are responsible for the upkeep of offices, apartments, hospitals, industrial plants, and other buildings. They sweep, dust, mop, polish floors, clean walls and fixtures, and dispose of trash. They may take care of minor painting, plumbing, and carpentry repairs and tend furnaces or boilers. There often are other duties, too: Shoveling snow, cutting and trimming grass, setting up tables and chairs in auditoriums and halls.

"*Pest controllers* are the people we want to see when

Service Occupations

This window washer has a remarkable view of the St. Patrick's Day parade.

we can't get rid of bugs ourselves. *Fumigators* release poisonous gas and set traps to kill termites, beetles, cockroaches, rats, and other pests. *Exterminators* treat buildings that already have been infested by termites.

"I don't think I need to explain what *window washers* do," said Joel with a smile, "but I think I should explain what a *sexton* is. This is the term used for a janitor at a church. Sextons keep the church buildings and furnishings clean and in good condition and keep the church-yard and cemetery looking neat. They also ring the church bells to announce services, care for clothing worn by clergy, and help out in other ways."

Bob finished reading from the last of his note cards. Laura took over once more. "And now," she said, "unless there are questions about Bob's report, we'll finish up with Renee."

Protective Service Occupations

"At the time of the American Revolution," Renee began, "there were no police departments and fire departments as we know them today. Instead, night watchmen were hired to patrol the streets of the cities and towns. Walking the dark streets carrying a lantern, they were on the lookout for fires, crimes, or trouble of any kind. If they saw something, they'd call out and warn the citizens who would come rushing from their homes to deal with the threat.

"The first modern police forces were established in America in the mid-1800's as cities like Philadelphia, Boston, and New York grew large and crowded. Conditions then were disorderly and violent; riots and fires took place so frequently that people decided they needed a better way of keeping order. By 1850, most of the major cities in the East had a police force that patrolled the city regularly to maintain order and discourage crime.

"Today, well trained and equipped *police officers* and *State police officers* uphold the law and maintain order in our communities and on the highways. *FBI special agents* investigate violations of Federal law and are concerned mostly with bank robberies, kidnappings, espionage, sabotage, and white-collar crimes such as embezzlement and dishonest land deals. *Correction officers* work in jails and prisons where they keep order and enforce rules and regulations. *Private detectives* are hired by people who want information about the actions of others. More often than not, they investigate business or domestic matters.

"Now I'd like to tell you about private guards," continued Renee. "Private guard services date back to the mid-1800's too. They first appeared outside the cities, in areas where new factories were being built or where mining operations were beginning. The guards in those days were hired to protect industrial property from riots, sabotage, and robbery. Today, *guards* still are needed in manufacturing plants, construction sites, and transportation terminals. But private security guards also work in museums, libraries, schools, hotels, supermarkets, department stores, apartment buildings, and offices.

"Modern fire departments also are fairly new. In the 1700's, at about the time fire insurance was being introduced, the insurance companies hired their own firefighters to take care of the properties they insured. When the alarm was sounded, all the companies in the city would rush to the fire. But only one company would fight to save the burning building—the company that recognized its own sign on the building. That system turned out to be impractical, and today all communities of any size have trained, professional *firefighters*.

Many firefighters are on duty for 24 hours, then off for 48 hours.

These officers have been trained to handle emergency calls.

"There are other kinds of workers who protect the public," said Renee. "They're less familiar than the police officers and firefighters who keep our neighborhoods safe. But they, too, have an important job to do in protecting our well-being.

"*Construction inspectors* make sure that our homes and schools—and our highways and tunnels and bridges—are built safely. *Health inspectors* help us in many ways. They make sure that the food we buy in grocery stores and restaurants is clean and won't make us sick. They also make sure that the water we drink is pure, and that the water we swim in is safe. Health inspectors warn us when the air becomes so polluted that we should be careful, and perhaps stay inside. *Occupational safety and health workers* inspect mines, factories, farms, and business establishments to make sure that it isn't dangerous or unhealthy for the workers in those places. *Compliance officers* check to be sure that employers are obeying the laws that say that workers must be paid properly for the hours they work.

"As you can see," Renee continued, "the people in these jobs do very technical work. They need formal training in science or engineering, plus a great deal of experience in the field, to be able to tell whether a borderline situation is safe. After all, if they shut down a business unfairly, they create a hardship for the employer and all the workers there. Inspectors—like other people in the protective service occupations—must do their jobs thoroughly, fairly, and conscientiously."

Ms. Nazarian joined the group at the front of the room. "I'd like to congratulate each of you," she said, smiling. "Your committee did a fine job. You studied the topic thoroughly and presented the information in a very original way."

Turning to the class just as the bell began to ring, Ms. Nazarian continued, "And tomorrow we'll hear a report from Jennifer's committee."

What Makes a Good Service Worker?

The jobs of service workers differ a great deal. Yet, if they're good at what they do, all service workers have certain traits in common.

Doing things for other people is what the service occupations are all about. For this reason, *the ability to deal effectively with people* is a "must". This takes sensitivity, flexibility, and communication skills. Service workers must be good at adapting to different kinds of people in every imaginable situation. Police officers, for example, must be equally good at handling a lost child, a robbery suspect, or a crime victim. Child care workers must be good at supervising children and getting along with their parents. Hotel managers deal with people

Service Occupations

constantly. They must be firm in firing a dishonest employee, then turn around and greet a very important guest with just the right tone of welcome and respect.

Bear in mind that it is important for service workers to pay close personal attention to their customers. People who are dissatisfied aren't likely to return. That's the reason for the saying, "The customer is always right." *A pleasant, outgoing personality* helps a great deal in jobs that involve pleasing a paying customer.

There are times when a great deal of *patience and understanding* are called for. After all, in a business where you're dealing with people most of the time, you're bound to run into people who are cranky, unreasonable, or just mean. Having an easygoing manner and a winning way with people can be a great asset, and is the key to building a steady flow of customers.

Many service workers need *the ability to keep calm and perform under pressure.* This is obvious in the case of firefighters, FBI special agents, and police officers. However, emergency situations crop up for other service workers too, and they must always be prepared for the unexpected. A cook may have to salvage the situation when the power goes off in the middle of a busy dinner

hour. A hotel manager may have to contend with an angry guest complaining about a reservation mixup when the hotel is completely filled. A building service worker needs to know what steps to take when the air-conditioning system in a luxury apartment building breaks down during a heat wave. A cosmetologist may have to think fast when he or she discovers that something has gone wrong with a permanent or a color job. To cope with situations such as these, service workers must be levelheaded and unflappable. Imagination and resourcefulness help, too.

Many of the service occupations require *good health and physical stamina.* Bellhops carry baggage for hotel and motel guests and may run errands for them as well. Mail carriers, waiters and waitresses, cosmetologists, barbers, and private household workers are on their feet all day long. So are kitchen workers. Cooks, chefs, dishwashers, and others sometimes work in extremely uncomfortable temperatures, and always handle large, heavy pots and pans. Police officers and firefighters must be in good physical condition to handle the rigors of their jobs.

The ability to plan and organize the work is important.

Firefighting requires organization and teamwork.

A chef must organize things so that the appetizers, main courses, salads, and desserts for 100 people or more are all ready at the proper time. Mail carriers must plan their routes so that everything is delivered on schedule. Building service workers and private household workers, like mail carriers, work independently and can set their own pace. But they have to be sure that everything gets done.

Business and managerial ability is important in some of these occupations. Funeral directors, for example, arrange both the personal and business aspects of a burial. Barbers, cosmetologists, and restaurant owners often operate their own businesses. This takes energy, drive, and the business sense to handle budgets, finances, suppliers, and staff. And business owners must also find the time to maintain a good relationship with their customers.

Flexibility about working hours can be very important. Long or unusual hours are commonplace for workers in food, lodging, and personal service occupations. Police and fire protection must be available around the clock, 7 days a week. Emergencies must be dealt with immediately, no matter how many hours you may already have worked. The standard 9-to-5 workday is often the exception rather than the rule in these occupations.

Training for Service Occupations

Like the members of Laura's committee, you may already know something about the service occupations through hobbies, jobs, or school activities. You may have done some babysitting or helped with younger children at a day care center or summer recreation program. You may have been a school safety aide or playground aide. It's likely that mowing the grass, shoveling snow, washing the dishes, or cleaning your room are among your household chores. Maybe you like to bake for your family or fix your friends' hair. Perhaps you have held a part-time job at a fast-food restaurant. All of these are good ways to try out the service occupations and to begin to develop useful skills and attitudes.

Formal training for service occupations varies a great deal. For a job as a dishwasher, for example, you don't need to complete high school. All the skills you'll need can be picked up on the job. But suppose you wanted to work as an industrial hygienist. Industrial hygienists do very technical work; they protect workers' health by studying the hazards created by noise, dust, and vapors. To get this sort of job, you would need a graduate degree in industrial hygiene, safety engineering, or a similar field. Those are the extremes. The training required for each of 27 service occupations is described in the Job Facts at the end of this chapter.

There are a number of different ways to prepare for a career in the food or lodging industries. They range all the way from vocational high school courses in cooking to 4-year college programs in food service or hotel administration. Training for high school graduates is offered at public and private vocational-technical schools and in 2-year community and junior colleges. Several highly specialized and well-respected programs in culinary arts—cooking and related food service skills—are in existence. Home study programs—correspondence courses—offer another way of learning about hotel and restaurant management. The hotel industry itself sponsors a home study program.

Large hotel and restaurant chains offer their own training programs for new workers. And the Armed Forces offer food service programs that provide training for executive chef, chef, cook, food and sanitation inspector, bread baker, pastry baker, and cafeteria manager.

Barbers and cosmetologists must be licensed to practice their trade. Licensing is meant to protect the public. By establishing minimum requirements as to age, character, health, education, and knowledge of the trade, authorities in each State try to make sure that the people who work with your hair or give you beauty treatments know what they're doing. People can learn cosmetology or barbering in vocational high school programs or through apprenticeship. Or they can attend one of the many public and private schools that teach barbering or cosmetology. Training usually takes 6 months to 1 year.

As Renee pointed out, people like construction inspectors, health inspectors, and safety engineers need to know their fields thoroughly. This usually means a college degree in science or engineering, plus experience on the job. Construction inspectors, for example, benefit from having worked as building contractors or construction superintendents.

The kind of training needed to become a police officer or firefighter varies, for local departments all set their own requirements. Bear in mind, though, that almost all departments demand a high school diploma and some insist on several years of college, or a college degree. Even more training is needed to apply for a job as an FBI special agent. Special agents usually must be college graduates with a degree in accounting or law.

Regardless of the service occupation that interests you, plan to get your high school diploma. Not all jobs require it, of course, but promotion to higher paying and more responsible jobs usually comes faster if you have finished high school. Courses in English, home economics, and industrial arts would help you in some of these occupations. For others, courses in science and mathematics are very important.

Service Occupations

Chef

"I plan menus well in advance," says Chef Nan Bogarty, "so that I have time to test the recipes."

Exploring Careers

Nan glanced at the clock as she finished her work on next week's schedule for the kitchen staff. "Is it 9:30 already?" she thought. "I'd better get back to the kitchen and see how things are going. Lunch is not very far away."

Wednesday morning is the time that Nan Bogarty, the chef at the Beef Eaters Restaurant, ordinarily reserves for paperwork. She always starts by preparing the weekly schedule for the kitchen staff.

She needs some peace and quiet to juggle the schedules of the pastry chef, the line cooks, the pantry people, and the dishwashers—14 people altogether. Of course, only 4 or 5 of them are at work in the kitchen at any one time. But Nan has to plan work assignments so that the kitchen is covered 2 shifts a day, 7 days a week. That's not as easy as it sounds, for some of the kitchen staff work full time and others work part time. Some prefer to work nights so that they can go to school during the day; others like to work days so they can be with their families at night. Yes, it takes a bit of concentration to keep everything straight.

She also uses her paperwork time to work on the food budget and make notes about problems she wants to bring to the restaurant manager's attention. This month, for example, the price of romaine lettuce is astronomical. They can't stop using it in the Caesar salad, of course, but Nan plans to suggest that they hold down their food cost by substituting other kinds of lettuce in the greens they use for the salad bar.

Nan won't have any more time for paperwork this morning, though. She wants to spend a little extra time in the kitchen because there's been a last-minute change in staff. Ellen Radner, her most experienced line cook, had called in sick early this morning.

"There's always something," thought Nan as she straightened out her papers. "Last week it was Frank. But that was worse," she reminded herself. Frank had burned himself with fat from the deep fryer. It still bothered Nan to think about the accident, for kitchen safety was one of her responsibilities and she had called not one but several staff meetings to point out the hazards of a busy kitchen. Frank obviously hadn't paid any attention. Well, this week he was back at his station and it was Ellen—experienced, dependable Ellen—who was out.

"Lucky for me that Phil was able to come in and lend a hand." The thought restored Nan's good spirits. After all, it had been easy enough to get a substitute. Phil Olsen, one of the line cooks, had been home when Nan called at 8 o'clock and he had agreed to come right in. Sometimes Nan had to call three or four people before she succeeded in rounding up a substitute. Nonetheless, Phil was new here. He had worked at Beef Eaters for only a few weeks and Nan wasn't sure how well he had mastered their kitchen routine. Well, this morning she'd find out. He would be running the line and she would have a chance to observe. Phil had good support, though, with Sam Spirdone on the broiler and fryer.

Nan arranged her files and clipboard in a neat pile. All that would have to wait for a quiet moment later in the day. Right now, her top priority was making sure the kitchen was ready when Beef Eaters opened for lunch at 11:30 sharp.

As she entered the kitchen, she flinched. It was hot in there, drippingly, uncomfortably hot. "Summer is murder in this kitchen," she thought as she slipped on her white tennis headband. Her paper hat just wouldn't do in this weather. Some restaurant kitchens are air-conditioned. But Beef Eaters, a small business just beginning to establish a name for itself, operates on a shoestring. Air-conditioning had been out of the question when the kitchen equipment had been installed, and summertime was indeed murderously hot. The temperature in front of the range could climb as high as 130 degrees.

Nan walked briskly toward the range, where Phil was now in charge. An outburst near the salad station made her change course; something clearly was wrong over there. Jim Petras was staring in dismay at a carton that had just been delivered by Apex Produce.

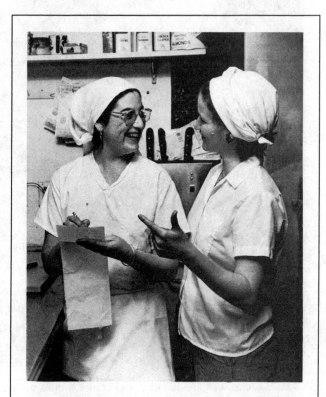

Nan confers with one of the line cooks.

Service Occupations

"Just look at the fruit that Apex sent over!" Jim exploded. "That's the second time this month it has been overripe. These bananas are much too soft for the flaming glazed bananas. We'll have to drop that from the menu today, and you know it's one of our best-selling desserts. And look at these strawberries! They're better suited to jam than my fresh strawberry tart."

It wasn't the first time Jim had raised the roof about the condition of the fruit. Jim Petras was one of the best dessert and pastry chefs in town, and the restaurant critics invariably praised his creations when they reviewed Beef Eaters. Jim took understandable pride in his efforts and insisted on working with only the finest ingredients.

Nan looked more closely at the fruit and agreed with Jim that the flaming glazed bananas would have to be dropped from the menu that day. Nan made a mental note to let the waiters and waitresses know and to inform the manager, too. The manager wouldn't be happy. That dessert was one of the restaurant's specialties, and a big seller. Then Nan took up the subject of the strawberry tarts. Jim, calmer now, agreed that he could probably make do. He'd salvage what he could of the strawberries and go ahead with his tarts. As she left him, Nan made another mental note: A strong complaint to Apex Produce was a "must."

Finally, Nan walked over to Phil, who was checking a beef roast in the oven. "Sam and I are doing okay, Nan," he said. "I think the new Hungarian goulash is good. Do you want to taste it?"

Nan complimented Phil on the way he was handling the job as she picked up a spoon to test the goulash.

The kitchen crew.

"Excellent," she said warmly. "I'm glad you noticed the change on the recipe card. Increasing the grated lemon rind certainly adds to the flavor," she added, putting down the spoon.

Nan looked as though she was about to walk away. Phil said hurriedly, "By the way, Nan, when I was slicing the meat for Swiss steak, I had a rough time. I don't understand it—I followed the procedures you showed us last week."

That had been at Nan's demonstration of ways to carve and slice meat. Her training sessions for the kitchen staff had started out as a series of useful tips and soon evolved into lessons in professional technique. Nan kept these lessons as informal as possible. But she covered her subjects in a crisp, professional manner. She explained kitchen safety and sanitation procedures; demonstrated food preparation and cooking techniques; and showed her staff how different garnishes—decorations—could make a dish look more appealing. She was getting a good response from the staff, few of whom had any formal training in food service. Because of their enthusiasm and willingness to learn, Nan found herself sharing many of the "trade secrets" she herself had learned over the years.

Nan had decided during her second year of college, where she had been studying oceanography, that college wasn't right for her. She had dropped out and taken the first job she could find—as a salad maker in a restaurant. Although she soon got tired of washing lettuce and chopping vegetables, she was fascinated by the restaurant business and decided to get the training she'd need to run a kitchen. She completed a 2-year program in culinary arts, taking such courses as food chemistry, equipment technology, and accounting and management. Nan then worked as an assistant chef in a hotel kitchen. After several years there, she accepted the top job in the kitchen here at Beef Eaters.

Nan looked up at the clock and noticed that it was 10 o'clock, time to fix lunch for the staff. Since Phil was new, she decided to take care of that for him while he finished his "prep" work. The staff took their lunch break at 10:45 ... too early for some but better than a chorus of growling stomachs until 3 o'clock!

She checked to see if the pantry and dish stations were ready for service, made sure the morning bread was delivered, and that the dining room attendants had filled the coffee machine and put out the garnish trays. Phil really appreciated her help.

By 11:45 the first food orders had come in to the kitchen, where they were pinned to the line spindle. As noon approached, the restaurant became much busier, and the tempo of the work increased. Nan helped out wherever it was necessary. She garnished the plates Phil put up and slipped in comments and advice whenever he had a moment to listen. The height of the lunch service, from 12:00 to 2:00, passed quickly. This time always seemed to fly by, for everyone was so busy there was hardly time to stop and take a breath.

As the dining room thinned out, the pace of work in the kitchen slowed. Nan split up the kitchen staff so that half of them could take a break while the others covered for them. When the first half came back to their stations, the others could sit down and cool off for a few minutes. They would all start preparation for dinner in the time left before the night crew arrived.

Nan fixed a plate of food for herself, picked up her clipboard, and went to a table in the back of the empty dining room to finish writing up her comments on the food budget. The rest of the paperwork would have to be squeezed in another time. She was pleased with Phil's first attempt at running the line. They had served 100 "covers" without a hitch.

"It certainly feels good to sit down," she thought.

Soon Nan was totally immersed in her estimate of food costs. She was startled to realize it was already 3:30 when Jim joined her at the table.

"About those bananas," he began abruptly. "I suppose I could use them for a Brazilian banana cake."

"Sounds like a good idea, Jim," said Nan, smiling.

As the temperamental pastry chef walked away, Nan remembered something. "One more thing to take care of," she said to herself. She went to the phone and dialed the Apex Produce Market.

"Hello, Mr. Yankelovich? This is Nan Bogarty at Beef Eaters and we seem to have a problem . . . . "

Exploring

Chefs must know a great deal about food. They need this expertise to plan menus, develop recipes, order food-stuffs, and supervise the preparation of meats, sauces, soups, vegetables, desserts, and other foods.

- Can you select fresh fruits and vegetables?
- Can you pick out good cuts of meat?
- Can you select fresh fish?

"No matter what, I'm responsible for what comes out of the kitchen."

Service Occupations

Chefs must be knowledgeable about nutrition. They must be able to plan meals and menus that are appetizing and nutritionally sound.

- Do you know the four food groups?
- Do you know what carbohydrates, fats, and proteins are and how the body uses them?
- Can you tell whether a meal is balanced?

Chefs must have an aesthetic sense where food is concerned. They must have an eye for attractive and original ways of presenting food.

- Do you like to decorate cakes or fix trays of appetizers? Do you like to decorate holiday cookies?
- Do you make an effort to plan meals that are balanced in color and texture as well as being nutritionally sound?
- Do you take the trouble to garnish sandwiches or hamburgers?
- Do you enjoy planning the table decorations for a party or a holiday?

Chefs must be well organized and be able to handle several things at once. It takes careful planning and good timing to prepare hundreds of meals during a single luncheon or dinner "turn."

- Are you good at estimating how long it will take to do your homework or a school project?
- Do you organize your time on tests so that you have enough time for each part?
- Are you good at keeping up with all the activities you're involved in? Do you get everything done without panicking?

Chefs must have leadership and communication skills. They supervise cooks and other kitchen workers and must be able to deal effectively with management, suppliers, and dining room staff.

- Are you a good leader? Do other people go along with your ideas when you're in charge? Do they follow your suggestions?
- Do you enjoy organizing trips, parties, sports events, picnics, and dances?
- Are you good at coordinating cookie sales, calendar sales, or other fund-raising projects?
- Do you enjoy working with other people on class projects?

Chefs must be able to think quickly and make decisions under pressure. Emergencies are not uncommon in restaurant kitchens.

- Are you levelheaded in an emergency?
- Could you keep calm and get help right away if the kitchen caught fire?
- Would you know what to do if an infant got hurt or stopped breathing while you were babysitting?
- Would you act sensibly if your brother or sister swallowed poison?

Chefs are responsible for keeping their kitchens clean and safe. They must know the local health and sanitation regulations and see to it that they are respected.

- Do you obey traffic regulations when you cross a street or ride your bicycle?
- Do you follow common safety precautions?
- Do you follow the instructions on the label when you use electric appliances?

Chefs need physical stamina. They spend hours on their feet, may have to lift heavy pots and pans, and sometimes work in very hot kitchens.

- Do you enjoy strenuous activities such as dancing, hiking, climbing, backpacking, running, jogging, swimming, and skiing?
- Do you like being active?

Building Service Worker

Harry Rand is head of the maintenance crew at Broadview Elementary School.

Service Occupations

Harry stretched his arms and sighed as he entered his office. "It's 11:30 already, and this is the first chance I've had to stop!" he thought, as he fell into his chair. "I'm glad every day isn't this hectic."

Harry Rand, the head building service worker for Broadview Elementary School, had been on the job since 7 o'clock that morning—a full 30 minutes ahead of schedule. He often arrived early when he planned to cut the grass. That way he could mow completely around the building before the children arrived. Once school was in progress, he did the lawn by the basketball courts and softball field so he wouldn't disturb classes. Cutting the grass was quite a chore. Harry was glad it was mid-October; this probably was the last time he'd have to mow until next spring.

When it came to mowing the lawn, Harry was not willing to rush. He paid a lot of attention to trimming the edges, for he felt the lawn's appearance "said something" about himself. In fact, come to think of it, that's why he made such a point of keeping the inside of the school in good repair and as neat and clean as possible.

As he returned to the building after putting the mowing equipment away, Harry had run into Brian "Smitty" Smith, another member of the building service staff.

"Morning, Harry," said Smitty. "Looks like you've been hard at work."

Smitty had been working at Broadview Elementary for just a few months. Unlike Harry, who was assigned to this school full time, Smitty was a member of the "roving crew." He helped out wherever he was needed, generally working for a few days at one school and then going to another. Besides working part-time with the building service crew, Smitty took courses at night towards his high school diploma. Harry admired Smitty's ambition and sometimes thought about signing up for a couple of college courses himself.

Together they headed for the boiler room. Checking the equipment in this room was a daily ritual for Harry, usually the first thing he did each morning. This week, however, he had waited for Smitty each day. The first few days, Harry did most of the work, explaining as he went along. Today, Smitty was going to try it on his own, with Harry there to observe and guide. This on-

Harry trouble shoots the the equipment in the boiler room every day. He practices preventive maintenance in order to keep machine down time to a minimum.

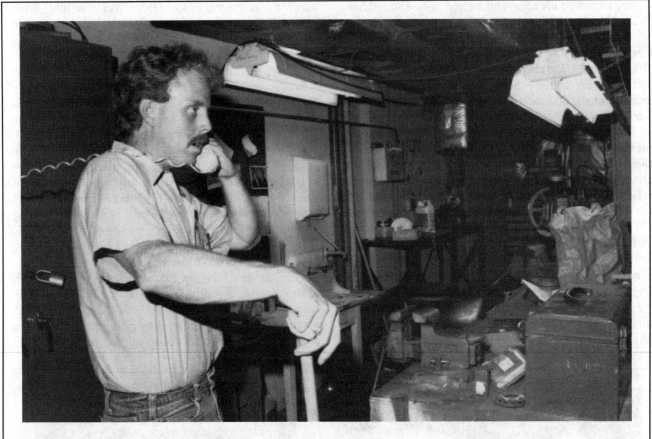

Harry gets calls about potential maintenance problems from members of the school's staff who work in other parts of the building.

the-job training was part of the course on boiler operations that Smitty had to pass in order to meet the County Board of Education's requirements for its building service workers.

The two men unlocked the door marked, "Danger—Boiler Room," and faced an arrangement of pipes, valves, gauges, and machinery. Smitty began by checking the gauge attached to the steam boiler. This was just a matter of reading the water level.

"Looks okay to me," he commented. Harry nodded in agreement.

Then Smitty checked the boiler for anything that might be wrong. He looked to see if smoke was coming out where it shouldn't, or to see if any of the tubes were leaking. Next he cleaned the oil filter. Then he finished his inspection of the boiler room by checking the motor and belts on the pump and air compressor.

"Too bad, no major problems for you today," joked Harry.

You never knew when something would go wrong; machinery generally broke down at the worst possible moment. Harry tried to keep a close eye on the equip-

ment so that he could spot trouble early. Harry didn't fix the machinery himself, though. Instead, he called the county maintenance workers to come over and make repairs or replace parts.

Harry glance at his watch and realized that he was running late. He hurried toward the school cafeteria.

"Fine morning, isn't it, Harry?" said Audrey Wayne, the cafeteria manager. "The milk is already on trays. It's in the last refrigerator on the right."

Harry nodded walked across the large room to the refrigerators. Delivering milk every morning to the younger children at Broadview was one of Harry's favorite tasks. This "Eight ounces of energy to boost your day" program had been started a few years ago for the first, second, and third graders. It was part of a countywide nutrition program for youngsters.

One of the things Harry like about the program was the opportunity to get to know the teachers better. Even more important, to his way of thinking, was the contact with the children. He enjoyed getting to know them, and was pleased that some many of the younger children treated him as a special friend. Previously, most of his contact had been with the older children at Broadview, when he umpired for their softball games.

He loaded up a cart and delivered the milk to the 12 classrooms as scheduled. Just as he finished, two soft tones were heard over the intercom system. This was Harry's signal to check with Judy Howell, the school secretary, to see what he was wanted for.

"What's up?" Harry asked as he entered the office.

"Two things, Harry. First there's a cracked window in Room 16. A familiar story—kids in Physical Education class were playing softball. Also, Tom Hansen reported that someone jammed a crayon into his pencil sharpener. That's room 7," explained Judy.

"Consider everything taken care of," Harry replied.

On his way to Room 16, Harry stopped at the supply closet and picked up a piece of heavy cardboard to cover the window. Ordinarily, cardboard is not considered a "supply" but Harry found it handy to have some around for occasions like this. He grabbed a broom and dust pan in case of any shattered glass.

After covering up the cracked window. Harry called the county maintenance service and arranged for someone to replace the window the next morning. Then he picked up a screwdriver from his tool box and headed for Tom Hansen's classroom.

"Perfect timing, Harry," said Tom. "You can try to fix the pencil sharpener while the children are at lunch."

"I'll see what I can do for you," Harry replied. He removed the pencil sharpener from the wall and then took it apart. Next, he pushed the jammed crayon through the sharpener with the tip of the screwdriver. Harry took a few paper towels from his pocket and wiped the sharpener clean. After fastening it back to the wall, Harry commented. "Should work like new now."

"Thanks for the quick service, Harry. I'll try to keep the crayons out," Tom replied.

Harry smiled and left the room. He made his way back to his desk determined to take a short rest. After all, it was 11:30 already, and with lunch period over in the next 45 minutes, he'd soon have to get out the mop and bucket to prepare for the daily cleaning of the cafeteria.

Exploring

Building service workers have to be "jacks of all trades." They need a working knowledge of many different kinds of tools and machinery.

- Are you good at fixing things?
- Are you handy with tools?
- Is it easy for you to learn how to use a tool you've never used before?

- Are you good at using and maintaining household appliances such as toasters, rug shampooers, vacuum cleaners, fans, and garden machinery?
- Do you like to take care of home repairs?
- Have you ever fixed a leaky faucet, unstopped a toilet, or replaced a fuse?
- Have you ever helped repair a bicycle, mini-bike, lawn mower, or car?

Building Service workers need stamina to do such chores as mopping, sweeping, waxing, and mowing. They work both indoors and outdoors.

- Do you enjoy strenuous activities such as dancing, hiking, climbing, and skiing?
- Do you participate in sports at school?
- Do you like to be active most of the time?

Building service workers generally set their own schedules and work on their own. They must be able to organize their time and get the job done without close supervision.

- Do you do your homework without being told to?
- Do you complete projects and book reports on time?
- Do you like to spend time by yourself?

Building service workers do many of the same chores day after day. Checking the boiler room equipment, sweeping and mopping floors, and emptying trash are all repetitive.

- Do you have a daily schedule?
- Can you put up with the repetition involved in mowing grass, shoveling snow, painting a house, or putting down tile?
- Have you ever undertaken routine tasks such as delivering newspapers or collecting from door to door?

Hotel Clerk

Cheryl Smith likes her job as hotel clerk. "My ambition is to manage a hotel someday."

Service Occupations

Cheryl Smith spotted the man as soon as he walked through the door into the crowded lobby. He looked confused and excited and clearly was impressed by so much activity. Cheryl knew by the way he kept staring, his face showing his amazement, that he had never stepped inside a large hotel before. Perhaps this was the first time he had visited a city as large as Boston.

The man was heading toward the counter where Cheryl stood. "Good morning, sir," she said to catch his attention, "and welcome to the Pilgrim Inn. May I help you"

"Oh ... of course, thanks a lot!" answered the man, as if awakened from a dream. "I'm with the convention."

"Which convention is that, sir?" asked Cheryl.

"The American Bolt Manufacturers Association," he replied. "Say, young lady, how do you clean those chandeliers way up there?"

Cheryl smiled in spite of herself. "We have a man who stands on a tall ladder and dusts them once a week. Now, what is your name, sir?"

"Hanks. Neal Hanks. Tell me, how many rooms are there in this hotel?"

"We have 800 rooms, Mr. Hanks," replied Cheryl. She typed his name into the computer terminal and waited for his reservation to appear on the screen. "According to our list, Mr. Hanks, you requested a single room. Is that correct?"

"Eight hundred rooms! That many! Oh yes, that's right," answered Mr. Hanks.

Cheryl turned back to the computer terminal and pressed a few keys to request information about how many single rooms were vacant and made up. The screen information told her that 17 single rooms were ready for guests and displayed the first group of available room numbers. She selected room 235 and pressed another key to indicate that the room had been assigned.

"You'll be in room 235, Mr. Hanks. Please check to see that this information is correct and sign here," she said, handing him the computer-printed registration form. "How will you be paying for your stay?"

"With a check," Mr. Hanks replied as he signed the registration.

"Fine," said Diem. "Please fill in your bank information at the bottom there.

"The room is reserved for tonight and tomorrow night. If you wish to stay longer, please let us know as soon as possible. Your convention will be meeting in Conference Suite 3, one floor below the lobby. Just take the stalls there on the left or the elevator on the right. Registration began about 30 minutes ago. Around the corner here you'll find our Mayflower restaurant, open for breakfast, lunch, and dinner, as well as the Pilgrim cocktail lounge. The bellhop will show you your room. If you need anything at all, please call us. We hope you'll enjoy your stay!"

With that, Cheryl signaled the red-uniformed bellhop standing near the desk and handed him the room key. Picking up Mr. Hanks' suitcase, he led the way to the elevator.

Cheryl watched a moment as Mr. Hanks followed the bellhop, still looking excitedly in every direction. He's a rare guest, thought Cheryl. So easy to please. Few customers showed as much enthusiasm over the hotel as Mr. Hanks.

Cheryl double checked the registration form with the computer information. She pressed a few more keys to complete Mr. Hanks' registration and entered his bank information so that his check would be authorized when he was ready to check out. She filed his signed registration form in a alphabetical file and waited for the next guest to arrive.

A young couple and two small children had appeared at the counter. "Good morning, may I help you?" asked Cheryl pleasantly.

"We have a reservation under the name of Stavros," answered the young man.

"One moment, please, Mr. Stavros," said Cheryl. She pressed a few keys on the computer and waited for information to appear on the screen. "George Stavros, a room with two queen-sized beds, for 3 nights. Is that correct?"

"Right. Could we have a room with a good view of the city?"

"Well, Mr. Stavros, to be honest, the best view is from the front of the hotel, and even from there you can't see much. The front rooms tend to be noisier because of street traffic. I think you might be happier with a quieter room facing the inner courtyard."

"Okay, fine," answered Mr. Stavros.

"How will you be paying for this, sir" asked Cheryl.

"Can I use my National Bank Card?"

"Certainly. If you'll let me have the card, I can make up the voucher slip right now and avoid delay when you check out. Meanwhile, if you would check this registration information and sign..."

While Mr. Stavros verified his address and other information, Cheryl pulled a credit card form from the drawer and placed it in the imprinter over his National Bank Card. She rolled the press over the card and form to imprint his credit account number. Later, she would enter his charge account information into the computer so that an accounting clerk could check to be sure his credit was good.

When Cheryl had finished, she handed back the credit card and explained to the Stavros family where the restaurants were. "If you need anything else, please ask," she added.

"We would like to take a bus tour of the city," said

Exploring Careers

Mrs. Stavros.

"Why certainly," replied Cheryl, handing her two pamphlets. "This pamphlet has sightseeing information and a map. I'll be happy to answer any questions you have." She then wished them a pleasant stay, signaled the bellhop, and handed him the key to room 714. Wheeling their luggage on a cart, he led the family to the elevator.

No sooner had Cheryl filed the Stavros' registration and credit card form than a tall man appeared at the counter. "I'd like a room," he said abruptly, before Cheryl had a chance to speak.

"Do you have a reservation?"

"No."

"Well, I'm very sorry, sir, but all our rooms are booked."

"Don't you have anything, just for one night?" he said in an argumentative tone of voice.

"I'm afraid not. This is a very busy time for us. We have two conventions that begin today and another that is still going on. The remaining rooms were reserved in advance."

Cheryl could tell that the frustration on the man's face was about to turn to anger. She added quickly, "But I might be to arrange for a room in another hotel."

The man looked surprised. "That would be nice."

Cheryl glanced down at the large box under the counter. The box was one of a system of terminals connecting the major hotels downtown. Each window on the face of the box had the name, address, and phone number of another hotel in the system. The lighted windows showed which hotels had vacant rooms. Today only one window lit—the one for the Park Hotel.

Cheryl called the Park. Yes, they had a room for one person for one night. The man thanked her with a smile and left.

"I've always enjoyed meeting and helping people," says Cheryl.

Service Occupations

A smile like that, thought Cheryl, was what really made the job fun. She didn't like everything about her work. She wished she could sit down and relax once in a while instead of having to stand 8 hours a day. Sometimes the work became repetitious. And when she was working the day shift, which started at 7 a.m., she couldn't possibly sleep late. Still, the day shift was better than either of the other two. The night shift in particular got pretty boring.

Nonetheless, Cheryl like the job because she loved meeting and helping people.

Cheryl was about to run a check on George Stavros' credit account when the telephone buzzed. Both her coworkers were talking to customers, so Cheryl picked up the phone and punched the lighted button.

"Front desk. Cheryl Smith speaking."

"Cheryl, this is Leslie. Could you come to my office for a moment?"

"I'll be right there," answered Cheryl, hanging up the receiver. Then, turning to the clerk next to her, she said, "The manager wants to see me. I'll be back in a minute."

The manager has some exciting news for Cheryl. She had been accepted into the management training program. United International Hotels, the company that owned the Pilgrim and other hotels across the United States and Europe, had an 18-month program in hotel management and only a few desk clerks were selected for it.

Cheryl knew she had been lucky to get a job at the Pilgrim. She had worked at the front desk for well over

Cheryl can tell at a glance which hotel rooms are available.

Exploring Careers

a year, and with management training she felt her career could really take off. The competition for management positions was stiff, but Cheryl would try hard. She knew that hard work was the key. She also knew that her ability to speak French would help. With a chance like this to move into a management position with an international corporation, Cheryl's future was looking very bright indeed.

Exploring

Room clerks deal with the public all day.

- Do you like meeting people?
- Do you start conversations with people you don't know?
- When you see people having trouble carrying a package or finding their way, do you offer to help before they ask.

Room clerks must look nice and act pleasant all the time they are working.

- Do you care about how you look?
- Do you like to wear clean, neat clothes to school?
- Are you polite and cheerful to others, even when you aren't feeling completely happy or well?

Rooms clerks must remain calm and helpful with angry guests.

- Can you let someone else have the last word in a argument?
- Can you accept blame for something you didn't do?
- Can you play a game by someone else's rules?

The activities of a room clerk change very little from hour to hour and day to day.

- Are you comfortable with routine activities?
- Do you have a daily schedule?
- Have you ever worked at routine jobs, such as delivering newspapers, selling candy, or collecting for charity door to door?

Room clerks must be able to remember and give directions and other detailed information.

- Can you relay messages correctly?
- Do you remember names of people and places?
- Can you give street directions clearly?

Room clerks must keep track of many things at once. They must be able to work quickly without making mistakes.

- Do you keep track of your homework assignments?
- Do you generally finish tests on time?
- Do you enjoy card games that require a good memory, such as fish, hearts, poker, or bridge?

Service Occupations

Police Officer

Earl Hayes likes investigative work.

"Car 331. A silent burglar alarm has gone off at the Foxhall Inn. That's at 3200 Braddock Road. Over."

Before the last few words had come across the radio, Earl Hayes had his squad car's flashers and siren working, and was halfway down the street. At the same time, he picked up the microphone from the police radio and relayed, "Car 331. Over," to let the dispatcher know that he had received the call and was on his way. As he pulled up to the red light at the intersection, Earl quickly looked in all directions for oncoming traffic and then turned onto Westchester Boulevard.

A few miles down Westchester, Earl put out the flashing lights and turned off the siren. The next corner was Braddock and he didn't want to give the prowler any clues of his arrival. As he approached the Foxhall Inn, Earl saw four young men crowded around the front door, trying to peer through the curtains of the window. Even though he didn't think he'd need it, Earl grabbed his nightstick before leaving the squad car.

"Evening, gentlemen. Are you looking for someone?"

"Good evening, officer," the tallest one said. "This must look strange, but there's really a simple explanation. We are part of the Starfire Band, and we're playing here tonight. We were supposed to meet the owner here at 7:30 so that we could set up our gear and warm up. Well, we've been here over 15 minutes now, and no sign of the owner. We thought he might have arrived early and gone inside so we decided to bang on the door and see if we could get him to open up for us. But so far, no luck."

"I see, fellows," Earl replied. "Do you have any identification?"

Once again the tallest one responded. "As a matter of fact, sir, I happen to have a copy of the contract in my pocket. Here, let me show it to you."

Earl accepted the piece of paper and looked it over carefully. The contract listed the names of all the band members. Earl asked for identification from each of them to double check. Each name and address matched that on the contract. Satisfied that it was all an honest mistake, Earl explained to the group that they had set off a silent burglar alarm when they had jiggled the door. He suggested that they sit out front in their van to wait for the owner.

Earl got into the squad car and made some notes. He would need them later tonight when he wrote up his report. As he started down the street, Earl picked up the microphone from the police radio and called in to the station to "clear himself." This meant that he was ready to accept any new calls.

As he continued slowly down Braddock Road, Earl noticed a shiny red sedan that looked like it had been freshly painted. He pulled up and saw that it had out-of-state license tags. His intuition told him that this might be a stolen car and should be checked out. Earl picked up the microphone once again.

"Car 331. Please check for a 10-23 on a red sedan, Florida tags. The plate reads Adam-Frank-Zebra-seven-one-nine. Over."

The voice from the radio recited, "Car 331—that's Adam-Frank-Zebra-seven-one-nine. Over."

Earl had learned to be alert to suspicious circumstances—cars that looked out of place or vacant buildings with a light on. And he enjoyed the challenge of following up on his suspicions. His intuition was sharpened by the skills he had acquired in a criminal investigation course he had taken recently. Earl hoped to become a detective one day, and realized that the ability to conduct a thorough investigation was a "must."

Earl continued on his way, knowing that the dispatcher handling the radio calls would now feed that license tag number into a national computer network. Anytime he wanted to find out if an item was stolen or if a person was wanted by authorities elsewhere, he relayed a message to the computer, and in a matter of minutes he got a reply.

He passed through the business district and decided to check the alley behind the Oakview apartment complex, a spot where abandoned cars often were left. Tonight Earl was searching for a green 1970 station wagon, license number EWE722, that had been reported missing earlier that afternoon. Earl had found out about the missing car by reading Officer Rejonis' report. She was the officer who had been patrolling the same beat earlier that day. Earl made it a habit to skim through the reports directly after roll call.

"No luck tonight," Earl thought as he drove through the alley. He spotted some children playing catch. As he approached them, he smiled and waved. "Nice evening to be outside, isn't it?" he said as he drove slowly by.

Earl knew how important it was for a patrol officer to talk to the people on his beat—especially the children. This practice established a friendly and helpful image of police officers in the minds of the public. Being a naturally outgoing person, Earl handled this aspect of the job quite well. Also, he had taken courses in speech and psychology at the university. Earl had known then that he wanted to be a police officer; he had majored in law enforcement.

When he first joined the force, about 4 years ago, Earl had learned even more about communicating effectively. He had been taught how to phrase a question or command, how to calm a lost child, and how to get information from a badly frightened crime victim. Along with the other "rookies", Earl had taken courses on communications and public relations at the police academy. In those 6 months of full-time study, they also covered

Service Occupations

criminal law, civil law, accident investigation, self-defense, patrol techniques and safe driving, first aid, handling of firearms, and how to deal with emergencies.

Earl turned back onto the main street and heard a voice crackle over the radio, "Car 331. That's a negative on the 10–23 for the red sedan, Adam-Frank-Zebra-seven-one-nine. Over."

"331. Over," Earl replied. He glanced at his watch, noticed it was almost 8:30 p.m., and decided to head over to the Big T Diner and pick up a cup of coffee and a hamburger.

As he pulled into the parking lot of the Big T Diner, Earl spotted a car parked in the fire lane, blocking a row of legally parked cars. "Giving out traffic tickets is not my favorite job, but when it comes to glaring violations I have no choice," muttered Earl as he wrote out the ticket. Then he picked up his walkie-talkie, placed it in his belt, and walked over to the fire lane. Earl always carried his walkie-talkie with him when he left the squad car. That way, he could communicate with the station and listen for incoming calls wherever he went. He

secured the ticket to the windshield of the car, then headed up the front steps of the Big T. Before he had opened the door, however, another call came in.

"Car 331. There's been a complaint by the neighbors about some noise and loud music at 9820 Britton Avenue. Over."

"Guess that coffee will have to wait," Earl thought. He picked up the walkie-talkie and replied, "331. Over."

Earl drove quickly but carefully to Britton Avenue. He didn't use his lights or siren. The sound of rock-and-roll music guided him to the correct house. In the backyard were two boys and a girl, about 14 or 15 years old, on skateboards. They had set up a large ramp and were skateboarding across the lawn and over the ramp.

"Hi. Anything wrong?" one of the boys said.

The other boy quickly broke in. "I bet it's that grouchy Mr. Benson complaining again."

Earl smiled and answered, "You're right. There was a call about the noise and the music."

With a sullen look, the boy continued, "I don't understand why Mr. Benson always ruins our good time."

"In my line of work, you need all the friends you can get."

"The problem is that Mr. Benson's idea of a good time is a quiet summer evening," Earl lightheartedly replied. "He probably feels that you are ruining his good time." Earl thought for a moment and then continued, "Why don't you set the radio outside on the porch? That way, you can still listen to the music, but you won't have to turn it up so loud."

"Okay, but I just don't think it's fair ..." the boy complained.

"It's not that bad, Kevin," the girl interrupted. "We can still have a good time. By the way, would you like to try a run on my skateboard, officer? It's really not as hard as it looks."

"I don't think so," Earl chuckled. As he turned to leave, he said, "Have fun, kids, but try to keep it down a bit. Even though you may think Mr. Benson is a sourpuss, he has a right to his peace and quiet."

Back in the patrol car, Earl radioed to the station to clear himself. He stretched and thought, "With a little luck, I'll be able to grab that coffee and hamburger now."

Exploring

Police officers uphold and enforce the law. They must have a deeply ingrained respect for law and order.

- Do you think it's important to obey the law even though you don't agree with it?
- Do you think it's important to be honest?
- Do you disapprove of cheating on exams or homework?
- Are you comfortable with the idea of people looking to you as an example?
- Are you conscious of your public responsibility when you are elected to the student council, chosen to be yearbook or newspaper editor, or asked to chair a club or committee?

"Most people don't intentionally violate traffic laws," says Earl. "They are just careless."

Service Occupations

Police officers spend much of their time educating the public about safety precautions.

- Do you obey traffic regulations when you cross a street or ride your bicycle?
- Do you have reflectors on your bicycle for riding at night?
- Do you check for oncoming traffic when you cross the street?
- Are you careful not to swim alone?
- Do you follow the instructions on the label when you use electric appliances?

Police officers must be able to think quickly and make decisions under pressure. They need excellent judgment to deal with such emergencies as a family quarrel, a highway accident, or a bank robbery.

- Could you keep calm and get help right away if your kitchen caught fire?
- Would you know what to do if an infant got hurt or stopped breathing while you were babysitting?
- Would you act sensibly if your brother or sister swallowed poison?
- Would you know what to do if a friend injured himself or herself on the playground?

Police officers must be observant in order to recount details about people and events later on.

- When you are introduced to strangers, do you remember their names?
- Can you recall identifying characteristics about your friends—birthmarks, scars, eye color, hair color, height, and weight?
- Can you tell when a car needs a tune-up?
- Do you notice minor changes in television, radio, or stereo reception?
- Do you notice it when a movie reel is changed?
- Do you enjoy identifying trees, leaves, or birds?
- Are you a collector? Do you like to collect stamps, coins, or sea shells, for example?
- Can you tell if something is missing from your room?
- Can you find a place on a road map quickly?

Police officers must be good at communicating effectively in different kinds of situations.

- Can you strike up a conversation easily?
- Can you talk to a child without talking down to him or her?
- After listening to a friend, are you good at putting his or her situation into words?
- Do you usually express yourself clearly?

- Are you good at speaking in front of a group?

Police officers must be good at giving orders, but they must be able to take orders as well.

- Are you good at supervising younger children?
- Have you ever been a camp counselor?
- Do you do what your parents or teachers ask without getting angry?
- Can you judge how far you can go when arguing with a teacher over a grade or with a class adviser over a yearbook picture?

Police officers must keep accurate records.

- Do you keep good records when you're a club treasurer or secretary?
- Do people ask you to keep score in bowling or other activities?
- Are you good at taking the minutes at a meeting?
- Are you conscientious when you take notes in class?

Police officers must be in top physical condition and have stamina to handle both emergencies and the ordinary demands of the job.

- Do you enjoy strenuous activities such as dancing, hiking, climbing, backpacking, running, jogging, swimming, and skiing?
- Do you participate in sports at school?
- Do you like being active?

Job Facts

There isn't room in this book for a story about every service occupation. However, you'll find some important facts about 26 of these occupations in the following section. If you want additional information about any of them, you might begin by consulting the Department of Labor's *Occupational Outlook Handbook*, which should be available in your school or public library.

Occupation	Nature and Places of Work	Training and Qualifications	Other Information
CLEANING OCCUPATIONS			
Building Service Workers	These workers keep office buildings, factories, schools, hospitals, apartment buildings, and stores clean and in good condition.	Most are trained on the job. A high school diploma is not required as a rule, but workers should know simple arithmetic and read well enough to follow written instructions. High school shop courses are helpful because minor plumbing or carpentry work may be a part of the job.	Because most buildings are cleaned while they are empty, these workers often work evening hours. They spend most of their time on their feet.

Service Occupations

Occupation	Nature and Places of Work	Training and Qualifications	Other Information
Pest Controllers	Professional pest controllers protect our health and property by exterminating rats, mice, and insects. Most work in major metropolitan areas for firms that specialize in this service. Jobs also are available with the government, Armed Forces, and food processors.	Beginners are trained on the job by watching and helping experienced workers. Many large firms provide classroom training too. Employers prefer trainees who are high school graduates, have safe driving records, and are in good health. Because these workers deal with customers, employers look for applicants who are courteous and well-groomed. High school courses in chemistry and business arithmetic provide a good background. Almost all States require pest controllers to pass a written test demonstrating their knowledge of pesticides.	Pest controllers work both indoors and outdoors in all kinds of weather. They often have to carry equipment and materials.

FOOD SERVICE OCCUPATIONS

Occupation	Nature and Places of Work	Training and Qualifications	Other Information
Bartenders	Bartenders serve cocktails, wine, beer, and nonalcoholic drinks. They often are asked to mix drinks to suit a customer's taste. They work in bars, restaurants, resorts, cocktail lounges, hotel and motel dining rooms, and private clubs.	Bartenders should be pleasant and look neat because they deal with the public. Generally, bartenders must be at least 21 years old. Most learn their trade on the job. Experience as a bartender's helper, dining room attendant, waiter or waitress is good training. Some private schools offer short courses in bartending that include instruction on local regulations, cocktail recipes, attire and conduct, and stocking a bar.	Bartenders often work nights or weekends. There are many part-time bartending opportunities. Some bartenders are union members.

Exploring Careers

Occupation	Nature and Places of Work	Training and Qualifications	Other Information
Cooks and Chefs	A cook's job depends partly on the establishment he or she works in. A small restaurant, for example, usually has a limited menu and one cook prepares all of the food. Larger restaurants usually have a variety of foods on the menu, and the cooks usually specialize in one or a few dishes. Head cooks or chefs coordinate the work of the kitchen staff and direct food preparation. They often plan menus and buy food supplies. Cooks work in restaurants, cafeterias, hotel and motel dining rooms, private clubs, schools, hospitals, department stores, government agencies, and private homes.	Cooks and chefs work with people in a team relationship, and must be able to work under pressure in busy periods and in close quarters. Although a high school diploma is not required for most entry level jobs, it is recommended for those hoping for advancement or planning a career in this field. High school courses in business arithmetic and business administration are very helpful. Many cooks acquire their skills on the job while employed as kitchen helpers. However, many high schools and vocational schools offer courses in commercial food preparation. Apprenticeship and training programs are also offered by some professional associations and trade unions. Workers who have had these courses may be able to obtain jobs as cooks and chefs without spending time in lower skilled kitchen jobs. They also have an advantage in securing jobs at larger hotels and finer restaurants. Some large restaurant or hotel chains conduct their own training programs.	Cooks and chefs may work over 40 hours per week. They often work nights, weekends, and holidays. While on the job, cooks and chefs must stand most of the time, and may have to lift heavy pots and pans. Many cooks and chefs are union members.
Dining Room Attendants and Dishwashers	Dining room attendants clear and reset tables, carry dirty dishes from the dining area to the kitchen, and clean up spilled food and broken dishes. Dishwashers pick up where the attendants leave off—with the dirty dishes. They operate machines that clean silverware and dishes. They may scrub large pots and pans by hand. Dining room attendants and dishwashers work in restaurants, cafeterias, hotel and motel dining rooms, private clubs, schools, hospitals, and department stores.	A high school education is not needed to qualify for jobs as dining room attendants and dishwashers. Many employers will hire applicants who do not speak English. These workers should have stamina because they stand most of the time, lift and carry trays, and work at a fast pace during busy periods.	Dining room attendants and dishwashers may have to work nights, weekends, and holidays. Many part-time opportunities are available. Some of these workers belong to unions.

Service Occupations

Occupation	Nature and Places of Work	Training and Qualifications	Other Information
Food Counter Workers	Food counter workers take customers' orders, serve food and beverages, write out checks, and take payments. They work in coffee shops, sandwich shops, restaurants (especially carryout or fast-food restaurants), cafeterias, and schools.	Because counter workers deal with the public, a pleasant personality and neat appearance are important. Physical stamina also is needed, as these workers stand most of the time and must work fast during busy periods. There are no set educational requirements for food counter workers. Employers often hire high school students for these jobs. Most counter workers learn their skills on the job by observing and working with those more experienced.	Many part-time opportunities are available. Flexible schedules often allow students to fit their working hours around their classes. Weekend and holiday work often is required.
Meatcutters	Meatcutters prepare meat, fish, and poultry. Their primary duty is to divide animal quarters and carcasses into steaks, roasts, chops, and other serving-sized portions. They work in food stores, meat markets, meatpacking plants, wholesale food outlets, and in large hotels and restaurants.	Manual dexterity, good depth perception, color discrimination, and good eye-hand coordination are important in cutting meat. Better-than-average strength is needed to lift heavy pieces of meat. Meatcutters usually learn their skills on the job. Some learn informally, but most are trained through apprenticeship programs. Apprenticeship generally takes 2–3 years, and consists of on-the-job training plus classroom work. After this time, apprentices must pass a test to demonstrate their expertise. A few meatcutters learn their skills by attending private schools specializing in this trade.	Meatcutters work in coldrooms designed to keep meat from spoiling. They must be careful when working with sharp tools. Most meatcutters are union members.

Exploring Careers

Occupation	Nature and Places of Work	Training and Qualifications	Other Information
Waiters and Waitresses	Waiters and waitresses take customers' orders, serve food and beverages, write out checks, and sometimes take payments. They also may set up and clear tables and carry dirty dishes to the kitchen. They work in restaurants, cafeterias, hotel and motel dining rooms, private clubs, schools, hospitals, department stores, government agencies, and private homes.	Because waiters and waitresses are in close and constant contact with the public, a neat appearance and an even disposition are important. Physical stamina also is important, as these workers are on their feet most of the time. Most waiters and waitresses pick up their skills on the job. Some may attend special training courses offered by some public and private schools, restaurant associations, and some restaurant chains. Business arithmetic provides a helpful background, and knowledge of a foreign language may be useful in some restaurants.	Many part-time opportunities are available for waiters and waitresses. They may have to work evenings, weekends, or holidays. It is essential that waiters and waitresses be pleasant and friendly. Many earn very low hourly wages and depend on "tips" for a large part of their income. Some waiters and waitresses belong to unions.

HOTEL OCCUPATIONS

Occupation	Nature and Places of Work	Training and Qualifications	Other Information
Bellhops and Bell Captains	Bellhops carry baggage for hotel and motel guests and escort them to their rooms on arrival. They also may offer information or run errands for guests. Bell captains supervise bellhops. They plan work assignments, record the hours each bellhop is on duty, and train new employees. Bellhops and bell captains work in hotels and motels throughout the country.	Because bellhops have frequent contact with guests, they must be neat, tactful, and courteous. A knowledge of the local area is an asset because guests often ask about local tourist attractions, restaurants, and transportation services. Bellhops must be able to stand for long periods, carry heavy baggage, and work independently. No specific educational requirements exist for bellhops, although high school graduation improves the chances for promotion. They usually are trained on the job.	Bellhops may have to work nights, weekends, or holidays. Some bellhops are union members.
Hotel Clerks	Hotels and motels employ clerks to handle room reservations, greet guests, issue keys, and collect payments. Every hotel and motel, from the smallest out-of-the-way motor inn to the largest, fanciest red-carpet establishment, employs clerks at its front desk.	Neatness, a courteous and friendly manner, and a desire to help people are all important for clerks. In large hotels with many foreign guests, the ability to speak a foreign language may be helpful. Workers usually are trained on the job. Employers prefer high school graduates with some clerical aptitude. Often a knowledge of bookkeeping is desirable.	Large hotels usually have several clerks to perform different jobs, such as assigning rooms, keeping records, or making reservations. In small hotels and in many motels, a single clerk may do all these jobs. Some clerks are union members.

Service Occupations

Occupation	Nature and Places of Work	Training and Qualifications	Other Information
Hotel Housekeepers and Assistants	Hotel housekeepers are responsible for keeping hotels and motels clean and attractive and providing guests with the necessary furnishings and supplies. They hire, train, and supervise the housekeeping staff. Hotel housekeepers work in hotels and motels across the country. In small or medium-sized hotels, they not only supervise the staff, but do some of the housekeeping themselves. In large hotels, their jobs are primarily administrative.	Executive housekeepers should be good at planning and organizing work, and must be able to get along well with people—especially those they supervise. Housekeepers also should like to work independently and be able to keep records. Although there are no set educational requirements, high school education usually is preferred. Experience or training in housekeeping is helpful in getting a job. Courses in housekeeping are offered by colleges with programs in hotel administration, trade schools and technical institutes, and home study (or correspondence) schools.	Many temporary positions exist in resort hotels and motels that are only open for part of the year. Hotel housekeepers may have to work shifts, including nights and weekends. Some housekeepers belong to unions.
Hotel Managers and Assistants	Hotel managers are responsible for operating their establishments profitably and for satisfying guests. They determine room rates, direct the operation of the kitchen and dining rooms, and manage the housekeeping, accounting, and maintenance departments of the hotel. These managers work in hotels and motels across the country. Over a third of all hotel and motel managers are self-employed.	Managers should have initiative, self-discipline, and the ability to organize work and direct others. They must be able to concentrate on details and solve problems. Although employers increasingly prefer college graduates, especially of hotel management programs, an applicant's work experience is the most important consideration in getting a job. Courses in hotel management are available at a number of 4-year universities, as well as many junior colleges and technical institutes throughout the country. Some large hotels have special on-the-job management trainee programs.	In small hotels and many motels, a manager's work is less specialized and may include clerical and front desk work. Some managers are union members.

Exploring Careers

Occupation	Nature and Places of Work	Training and Qualifications	Other Information
Hairstylists (Barbers and Cosmetologists, Beauticians)	Barbers and cosmetologists cut and style hair to suit each customer's taste. They may give permanents and color or straighten hair. Some may fit hairpieces, offer hair and scalp treatments, give facial massages, shaves, or make-up applications. The specific job title usually depends on the type of shop where a person is employed, or on personal preference. Usually barbers work in barbershops which specialize in male customers and cosmetologists or beauticians in beauty salons which cater to females. Those who work in "unisex" shops are usually called hairstylists. Some may work in department stores, hospitals, nursing homes, hotels, or air and railroad terminals.	Dealing with customers takes patience and a good disposition. They should enjoy working with the public and be able to follow customers' instructions. Workers should have finger dexterity, a sense of form and artistry, and the physical stamina to stand for long periods of time. All states require barbers and cosmetologists to be licensed. Requirements vary from state to state, but minimum standards usually include a physical exam, graduation from a state-approved school, age 16 or older, and passing a licensing exam. Most states require a high school diploma. Instruction is offered in public and private vocational and trade schools. Programs usually include classroom study, demonstrations, and practical work.	Earnings often include tips. Most work over 40 hours per week, though part time positions are also available. Lunch hours and Saturdays are usually very busy times. Many are union members.

Service Occupations

Occupation	Nature and Places of Work	Training and Qualifications	Other Information
Funeral Directors and Embalmers	Funeral directors help make the personal and business arrangements necessary for the service and burial of the deceased. Embalmers prepare the body for viewing and burial. Funeral directors and embalmers work in funeral homes, morgues, hospitals, and mortuary schools.	Important personal traits for funeral directors are composure, tact, and the ability to communicate easily with the public. They also should have the desire and ability to comfort people in their time of sorrow. A license is needed to practice embalming. Although licensing standards vary by State, an embalmer generally must be 21 years old, have a high school diploma, graduate from a mortuary science school, serve an apprenticeship, and pass the State board exam. Most States also require funeral directors to be licensed. Requirements are similar to embalmers, but directors have special apprenticeship training and board exams. Most people obtain both licenses. High school courses in biology, chemistry, and speech provide a good background for a career in this field.	In large funeral homes, employees usually have a regular schedule. Occasionally overtime or evening work may be necessary.

PRIVATE HOUSEHOLD OCCUPATIONS

Occupation	Nature and Places of Work	Training and Qualifications	Other Information
Private Household Workers	Private household workers may help care for children, clean and maintain the house and yard, and cook and serve meals. They work in private homes throughout the country.	Private household workers must have physical stamina because they are on their feet most of the time. The desire to do a job carefully and thoroughly is important. Household workers should be able to get along well with people and be able to work independently. For most household jobs, no formal education is required. Instead, the abilities to cook, sew, wash and iron, clean house, and care for children are important. Home economics courses are helpful.	Sometimes these workers live in the home of their employer. Many household workers use their skills and experience to transfer to jobs in child care or day care facilities, or take jobs as kitchen workers or building service workers.

Exploring Careers

Occupation	Nature and Places of Work	Training and Qualifications	Other Information
Correction Officers	Correction officers are responsible for the safekeeping of persons who have been arrested, are awaiting trial, or who have been tried and convicted of a crime and sentenced to serve time in a correctional institution. Their work involves maintaining order and enforcing rules in the institution, and often counseling inmates. Most of these officers work for state and local governments, often in correctional institutions in or near metropolitan areas.	Correction officers should be in good health. Most penal systems require officers to be U.S. citizens who are at least 21 years old and have a high school education. In addition, many states have height, weight, vision, and hearing standards. Strength, good judgment, and the ability to think and act quickly are important. The Federal Government as well as almost every state, provides training programs. They are generally informal and include classroom instruction as well as on-the-job experience.	Correction officers usually work a 40-hour week. Since security must be provided around the clock, some officers must work nights, weekends, and holidays.
FBI Special Agents	FBI special agents investigate violations of Federal laws in connection with bank robberies, kidnapings, white-collar crimes, thefts of government property, organized crime, espionage, and sabotage. Most agents are assigned to the FBI's 59 field offices located throughout the United States and Puerto Rico. Some work at headquarters—in Washington, D.C.	To be considered for appointment as an FBI special agent, applicants usually must be law school graduates or college graduates with a degree in accounting, engineering, or computer science. They must be a U.S. citizen between 23 and 35 years old and be fluent in a foreign language. Also, they must pass a rigid physical exam, as well as oral and written exams testing their aptitudes for meeting the public and conducting investigations.	Agents are subject to call 24 hours a day and must be available for assignment at all times. Some travel is necessary. They often work more than 40 hours per week.

Service Occupations

Occupation	Nature and Places of Work	Training and Qualifications	Other Information
Firefighters	Firefighters put out fires. They also educate the public about fire prevention and check buildings for hazards. They also clean up chemical spills or gas leaks which present a fire hazard. They work in municipal fire departments all over the country. Some may work in the private fire departments of very large corporations.	Firefighters need mental alertness, courage, endurance, mechanical aptitude, and a sense of public service. Initiative and good judgment are extremely important because firefighters often make quick decisions in emergencies. Members of crews should be dependable and able to get along well with each other. Applicants for firefighting jobs must pass a written test, a medical exam, and tests of strength, physical stamina, and agility, as specified by local regulations. They must be at least 18 years old, meet certain height and weight requirements, and have a high school education. Experience as a volunteer firefighter or training in the Armed Forces is helpful. Many also have training in first aid or emergency medical treatment. Many fire departments have training programs for new workers. These include classroom study and practice drills.	Usually firefighters work shifts often more than 40 hours per week. They may have to work overtime when fighting fires. Most firefighters are union members.
Guards	Guards patrol and inspect property to protect it against fire, theft, vandalism, and illegal entry. Most guards work in office buildings, government installations and buildings, stores, hotels, banks, schools, and manufacturing plants. Most jobs are located in cities and industrial areas.	Applicants should be in good health, have good character references, and good personal habits such as neatness and dependability. They should be mentally alert and emotionally stable. Most employers prefer high school graduates. Experience in the military police or in the local police department is helpful. Many employers provide on-the-job training in areas such as the use of firearms, first aid, and how to handle emergencies.	About two-thirds of all guards work at night. Often guards work alone.

Exploring Careers

Occupation	Nature and Places of Work	Training and Qualifications	Other Information
Police Officers	Police officers enforce laws to protect citizens and property. The job can include a variety of duties including controlling traffic, investigating crime, and public relations. Officers work for local police departments in cities and towns throughout the country.	Personal characteristics such as honesty, good judgment, and a sense of responsibility are especially important for police officers. They should enjoy working with people and serving the public. Candidates for police officers must be 21 years old, be U.S. citizens, and meet certain height and weight standards. They may have to pass a physical exam, including tests of strength and agility. Usually high school graduation is required; some areas prefer college graduates. Most police departments provide training for new workers. This includes classroom study as well as supervised work experience.	The scheduled workweek for officers usually is 40 hours and may include nights, weekends, or holidays. Officers are subject to call anytime their services are needed.
State Police Officers	State police officers patrol the highways and enforce the laws and regulations of our roads. They also provide assistance to motorists when necessary. They work for State police forces in every State except Hawaii.	Honesty, good judgment, and a sense of responsibility are all important for these officers. Often, tests of strength and agility are required. Those who want to be State police officers should be able to work independently and willing to serve the public. All officers must be U.S. citizens. Most States require applicants to be at least 21 and have a high school education. Officers must meet physical requirements, such as height, weight, and eyesight. All recruits enter a formal on-the-job training program which lasts several months.	Usually State police officers work shifts, with some on duty nights, weekends, and holidays. They are subject to emergency calls at any time.
Construction Inspectors	Federal, State, and local construction inspectors insure that recognized standards are met in all types of construction. The structures they inspect include buildings, bridges, dams, sewer systems, and streets. Over three-fourths work for municipal or county building departments.	Applicants should have a high school diploma. In addition, several years of experience as a construction contractor, supervisor, or craft worker generally are required because these workers need a thorough knowledge of construction materials and practices. Newcomers are trained on the job by working with experienced inspectors. High school courses in drafting, math, and English are helpful.	Construction inspectors often spend a large portion of time traveling between worksites. Usually an automobile is furnished for their use. They are exposed to all types of weather.

Service Occupations

Occupation	Nature and Places of Work	Training and Qualifications	Other Information
Health and Regulatory Inspectors	Health and regulatory inspectors help protect the public from health and safety hazards, and help stop unfair trade and employment practices. Nearly two-thirds work for the Federal Government, although State and local governments employ many of these inspectors.	People who want to become health and regulatory inspectors should be able to accept responsibility and like detailed work. They should be neat and be able to express themselves well orally and in writing. Because inspectors perform such a wide range of duties, the qualifications vary. Most inspectors must have experience in a field related to the area in which they will work. Often a bachelor's degree may be substituted for the experience. Specialized knowledge and skills are learned on the job in many cases.	Many inspectors travel frequently and are usually furnished with an automobile. At times working conditions may be unfavorable and hours may be long and irregular.
Occupational Safety and Health Workers	Occupational safety and health workers in a number of different occupations strive to control occupational accidents and diseases, property losses, and injuries from unsafe products. They work at a variety of jobsites, including industrial, manufacturing, and commercial plants; mines; in laboratories; for property and liability insurance companies, and for goverment agencies.	Occupational safety and health workers must be able to communicate well and motivate others. They should be able to adapt quickly to different situations. In this field, a bachelor's degree in science or engineering is the minimum requirement for beginning professionals. A graduate degree in occupational safety or health is an asset. Employers attach great importance to prior work experience in the field. For jobs at the technician level, completion of a 2-year associate degree in an appropriate curriculum plus relevant work experience provide a good background.	Depending on the specific job and geographic location, travel may be required. For example, a plant safety engineer may travel only to conferences, while an insurance consultant may spend about half the time traveling between worksites.

OTHER SERVICE OCCUPATIONS

Mail Carriers	Mail carriers travel planned routes delivering and collecting mail. They often spend a few hours at the post office each day, arranging their mail for delivery and taking care of other details. Their route may be a single office building or many miles of country roads.	Mail carriers much be at least 18 years old and pass a written exam that tests clerical accuracy, the ability to read, do simple arithmetic, and memorize mail distribution systems. They also may have to pass a driver's test, if the job involves driving. Applicants also must pass a physical exam, and may be asked to show that they can lift and handle heavy mail sacks. Carriers are trained on the job. They may begin as part-time workers, and get regular positons as openings occur.	Most carriers begin work early in the morning. They spend most of their time outdoors, in all kinds of weather. Generally, they are free to work at their own pace as long as they get the job done. Many of these workers are union members.

115

Exploring Careers

Occupation	Nature and Places of Work	Training and Qualifications	Other Information
Telephone Operators	Providing service to those who need it when making phone calls is the job of telephone operators. This includes those operators who work in telephone company central offices, as well as those who work for private businesses and run private branch exchange (PBX) switchboards. More than half of all operators are employed as PBX operators in manufacturing plants, hospitals, department stores, and businesses. The remainder work for telephone companies.	Those interested in becoming telephone operators should have a clear and pleasing voice, good hearing, and not mind sitting at a switchboard for long periods. Most operators receive on-the-job training to become familiar with equipment, records, and work activities. After about 1 to 3 weeks of instruction, they are assigned to regular operator jobs. High school courses in speech, office practices, and business math provide a good background.	Operators sometimes work shifts that include evenings, weekends, or holidays. The pace may be hectic during peak periods in the late morning and late afternoons. Many telephone operators are union members.

Elementary school teachers help awaken their students' desire to learn.

One morning in late August or early September not so long ago you began a great adventure.

It probably started in a room that was crowded with children and adults. You might have been a bit scared. After all, you were only 5 years old and the place and the people were new to you. Still, your mother or father was with you, and you were fairly certain you could handle this new experience called school.

Your parents had told you school would be exciting. They said you would make new friends, play games, paint pictures, and learn about letters and numbers. That sounded nice. But they also said you would stay in school all morning. That did not sound nice. And they had not told you about all these strangers. So with a mixture of fear and anticipation you entered what is called the educational system.

The educational system is the world of schools and libraries, of books, films, records, and many other things to help you learn. More important, it is a world of people—teachers, counselors, administrators, and librarians—people who help others learn, explore, and grow.

You have come a long way in the educational system since that first morning. You have studied reading, writing, grammar, mathematics, science, history, art, and music. Do you think your parents were right? Is learning exciting for you? Is it exciting enough to make you want to help others learn? Have you ever thought there might be a place in education for you? Let's explore some of the possibilities.

Teachers

Who helps people learn? Teachers, of course. You may think there's nothing we can tell you about teachers that you don't already know. After all, you've seen teachers "on the job" for years. You've taken part in the class discussions and demonstrations, gone on the field trips, and taken the tests. But there's more to teaching than the things that go on in the classroom.

Have you ever considered how much work teachers do "behind the scenes?" First of all, they need to know the subjects they teach. To learn enough about their subject—whether it's fingerpainting or engineering—teachers need 4 years or more of college training. Even after this, they need to keep up with their subject and with current teaching methods. They keep up by studying on their own and by taking courses and going to conferences and workshops from time to time throughout their careers.

Knowing their subjects is just the beginning. Next, teachers have to decide how to present information to a class. What ideas and facts should be emphasized? How quickly should different topics be covered? How should the students' learning be tested? As teachers plan their classes, they must consider school policy and the abilities and needs of the students.

Teachers spend time at night and during weekends preparing their class presentations and correcting exams, papers, and homework. But beyond these similarities,

All educators need a love of the world of learning

Many teachers attend summer school to study the subjects they teach.

Education Occupations

Teachers of exceptional children need special training.

teachers' jobs vary with the age and needs of their students.

Preschool and kindergarten: Getting ready to learn. Starting school is a big step for young children. They have to get used to the daily routine. They have to learn to get along with other children. They have to develop a desire to learn. *Preschool and kindergarten teachers* help children make these adjustments.

These teachers plan and supervise activities that will help children grow socially, physically, and mentally. Singing and dancing aren't just fun. They're taught to help children get accustomed to groups and encourage them to exercise their bodies. Fingerpainting, story readings, and field trips all stimulate curiosity—a very important part of learning.

Preschool and kindergarten teachers try to keep in touch with parents and talk to them frequently. They let the parents know how their children are doing in school and on the playground.

Elementary school: Learning the basics. In the elementary grades, children start learning basic skills they will use and build on throughout their school years. Reading, writing, and arithmetic get the most attention at first.

Then children start spending more of their time in school learning about the world they live in; they study science, social studies, and literature. Stimulating students' desire to learn and helping them develop good study habits also are high priorities in the elementary grades.

Elementary school teachers usually specialize in a particular age group. They plan and conduct all the classes for a certain grade, and come to know all the ins and outs of dealing with first graders, for example. Art, music, reading, and some other elementary school teachers specialize in a subject rather than an age group.

Elementary school teachers are very much interested in the personal and social growth of their students. They watch for emotional and health problems. They also try to maintain close contact with parents.

Junior high and high school: Learning in more detail. Junior high and high school students are ready for more intensive study of the subjects they take, so *secondary school teachers* are subject specialists. They teach a single subject, such as literature, industrial arts, mathematics, or business, to students on several grade levels.

Secondary school teachers are actively concerned with students' personal development. They are expected to enforce school rules in the classroom, the cafeteria, and

119

the halls. Secondary school teachers also have opportunities to work with students outside the classroom as advisers to school activities and clubs. These teachers, too, meet with parents to discuss students' problems and achievements.

Special teachers for special students. Some students need help in learning because they have physical handicaps or emotional problems. Special education teachers provide such help.

Some students have handicaps that prevent them from studying in regular classes. They must learn skills that will enable them to communicate more effectively. *Teachers of the deaf* show their students how to communicate through lip reading, finger spelling, and other methods. *Teachers of the visually handicapped* teach students to read and write in braille. Using these skills, deaf students and blind students can study regular elementary and secondary school subjects. These teachers also may teach subjects such as English, mathematics, or social studies.

Some special education teachers work with students who suffer from mental or emotional problems. *Teachers of the mentally retarded* help students learn basic academic and living skills. They teach subjects such as reading, writing, and arithmetic and also teach personal and job skills. *Education therapists* work with students who have nervous or emotional disorders. Besides teaching academic subjects, they watch the students for signs of problem behavior.

College: 2 years, 4 years, or more. College is where subjects are explored in depth. Students expect to learn a great deal about the subjects they study, and *college teachers* provide that in-depth analysis. Whether they are in a small junior college or a large university, college teachers must give a complete and detailed presentation

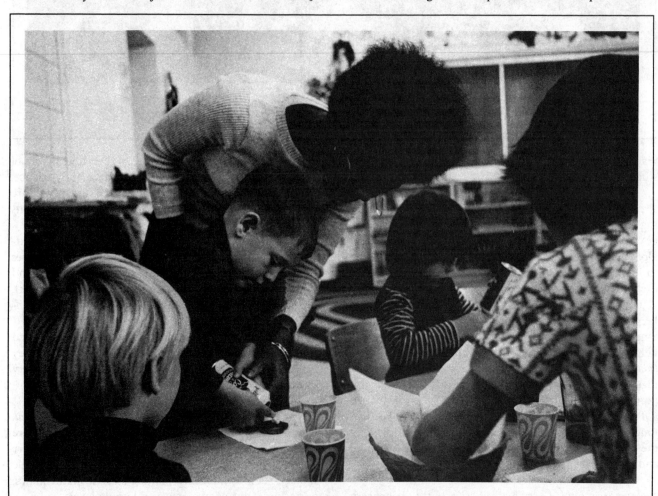

Arts and crafts stimulate curiosity—an important part of learning.

of a subject in their classes. Like high school teachers, college teachers are subject specialists, usually teaching several classes in one subject. Because college teachers are expected to be experts in their subjects, they often spend more time preparing for classes, doing research, and writing than they do teaching in a classroom or laboratory.

College teachers have many nonteaching duties. They work on faculty committees and with student organizations. They may advise students about planning their courses. However, college teachers usually do not concern themselves with their students' personal development.

Learning throughout your life. You may think that your education will end when you graduate from high school or college. However, learning is a lifelong endeavor. You're likely to go on picking up new information, mastering new skills, and broadening your horizons throughout your life. All this activity will create work for teachers.

You might, for example, decide to learn a job skill at a trade school or technical institute. Teachers in these schools instruct students in such areas as automobile mechanics, truckdriving, locksmithing, bookkeeping, cosmetology, or flying.

Or you might take courses to update or upgrade your skills after you've been working for a while. Many companies hire instructors to teach their employees to use equipment properly, to do their work safely, to manage their time more effectively, or to prepare for new responsibilities.

You might take courses for pleasure or recreation or personal fulfillment. Teachers conduct classes in art, music, religion, sports, dancing, yoga . . . just about every subject imaginable.

The reasons people want to learn are almost endless, and teachers of all kinds help them learn.

Teacher Aides

In many elementary schools, *teacher aides* help teachers with their work. Some high schools use teacher aides, too. Although the duties of teacher aides vary from school to school, their purpose is always the same: To give teachers more time to prepare for classes and work with students.

Some teacher aides do routine or clerical tasks, such as grading papers, taking attendance, or monitoring halls, lunchrooms, or school yards. In some schools, aides help by making maps, charts, or diagrams and by operating audiovisual equipment. Some aides work directly with the students. Under the supervision of a teacher, an

College professors are experts in the subjects they teach.

Dance teachers help students develop coordination and self-confidence.

aide might help a group of children do research for a class report or help a student who has missed school catch up with homework.

Counselors

One of the toughest tasks facing students during their school years is learning about themselves. Unless students recognize and understand their own abilities, needs, and desires, they may have difficulty planning their education or finding a job. Understanding themselves also helps students deal with personal problems such as family disputes. *Counselors* in all types of schools help students learn about themselves.

Counselors use many methods to learn about students. They talk with the students individually and in groups. They meet with parents, teachers, and other school officials. They administer aptitude and other self-evaluation tests.

Using their knowledge of students, counselors can help

This school counselor is helping a student use a computer to explore careers.

them plan for further education, pick a career, or solve personal problems. Counselors work as part of a team. An elementary school counselor, for example, might send an emotionally troubled student to a school psychologist.

Administrators

In many ways, schools are like businesses. Supplies must be ordered and distributed. The building and its furnishings have to be kept in good repair. Insurance policies have to be renewed. The people who work there—teachers, secretaries, janitors, and cooks—have to be hired, supervised, and paid. Schools also have some special needs. Courses have to be selected. Rules of conduct for students and faculty have to be set and enforced. The people who handle all these things so that teachers can teach, counselors can counsel, and students can learn are the school administrators.

Elementary and secondary school administration. Most elementary and secondary schools are governed by local school boards that are elected by the people of a city, town, or county. The school board delegates the day-to-day job of running the schools to a school superintendent, several supervisors and consultants, and school principals and their assistants. The *school superintendent* is the chief administrator for a school district. Superintendents are responsible for everything about the schools in their district. Superintendents prepare the budget for the school district. They plan for the construction of new schools and the closing of old schools. They make recommendations to the school board and they enforce the policies of the board. In short, superintendents run the whole show.

School districts also employ people called *supervisors* or *consultants* who are in charge of a specific subject or program for the entire school district. There might be an English supervisor, a vocational education supervisor, a career education consultant, and many others in one school district. Supervisors and consultants have many duties. They develop curriculums, visit classrooms, and set up conferences and training sessions for teachers, for example.

School principals control all the education and administrative business of a school. As a result principals have many duties. They supervise the teachers and other school employees. They must maintain good relations with the community. They must enforce the policies of the school board and the school superintendent.

To help them, principals in large schools have assistants. *Assistant principals* usually have authority in one or

Education Occupations

more areas of school administration. An assistant principal, for example, may be in charge of student discipline.

College and university administration. Colleges and universities are administered in different ways. The highest authority in many institutions of higher education is the board of trustees. This board delegates day-to-day administration of the school to the *college president* or *chancellor.* Like school district superintendents, college presidents are responsible for all aspects of the school's operation. As a result, they have many duties. Presidents oversee the preparation of the college budget. They also enforce the regulations of the school's board of trustees and recommend policies to the board. Naturally, college presidents can't do all this alone. They have the help of several other adminstrators.

The *academic dean* administers the academic policies and programs of the college. In cooperation with the faculty, the dean decides what courses the college should offer and what the academic standards for students and faculty members should be. The academic dean also coordinates the work of the *department chairpersons.* These are faculty members who administer a single department, such as English, mathematics, or chemistry.

The *dean of students* is in charge of student programs and policies. Deans formulate and enforce rules for student conduct. They also may advise students and groups about personal problems, social activities, and financial assistance.

There are a number of other administrators on college and university campuses. The *registrar* directs the college's registration activities and keeps records of students' grades. The *director of admissions* recruits students and sees that applicants meet the school's standards. The *financial aid officer* helps students obtain scholarships, grants, and loans. The *director of student affairs* plans and coordinates social and recreational activities for students.

No matter how busy he is with other things, this school principal finds time for students.

Exploring Careers

Librarians work with people—not just with books.

Librarians

Much of the information that people use to learn is contained in books, magazines, newspapers, films, tapes, and many other types of published material. Acquiring this material, organizing it, and helping other people use it is the job of librarians and their assistants.

Some librarians work behind the scenes. They handle jobs such as preparing the library budget, acquiring books and other materials, and organizing and processing them for use by readers. Three such librarians are the acquisitions librarian, the classifier, and the cataloger.

Acquisitions librarians review book catalogs and advertisements to learn what materials are available. Then they order or "acquire" them. To do their jobs well, they must know the books, magazines, or technical informa-

tion that library users want.

After they have examined a new book, *classifiers* select the classification numbers and descriptive headings for it. To do this, classifiers must know the different systems used to organize library material—the Dewey Decimal system, for example. Classifiers also write out a sample card that shows the author, title, and classification number of the new acquisition.

This sample card is put to use by the *cataloger*. Catalogers prepare the cards in the card catalog that identify all the books, records, and other material in the library's collection. Catalogers also keep the cards in the catalog up to date by adding new information from time to time.

The librarians we know best work directly with the public, helping people use the library. These librarians usually are identified by the kind of library they work in or the group of people they work with.

Education Occupations

Librarians generally need a master's degree.

School librarians help students and teachers use school libraries or media centers. These librarians, who sometimes are called *media specialists,* select and order the books, magazines, records, films, tapes, maps, and kits in libraries just like the one in your school. They must know the needs of the teachers and the students in the school. They let teachers and students know what materials are available. Sometimes they set up programs to encourage students and teachers to use the library. Or they conduct tours of the library and show students how to unlock some of its "secrets" by learning to use references such as the *Reader's Guide to Periodical Literature* and the card catalog.

Academic librarians work in college and university libraries. Research and reference collections are very important in these libraries, where students and professors are engaged in serious scholarship. The emphasis on research is so great that in large academic libraries even the acquisitions librarians and catalogers specialize, and handle only certain collections—Slavic books, for example.

Public librarians often specialize in helping a particular group of people. *Children's librarians,* for example, select books and have story hours for youngsters. *Young adult* and *adult librarians* provide services tailored to the interests of their readers. *Extension* or *outreach librarians* work out of bookmobiles and find other ways of bringing library services to people who cannot come to the library. *Reference librarians* help people use the many reference sources in a library. They spend a great deal of time answering questions or showing people where to find answers. In small public libraries, a librarian may handle several of these jobs. It is not unusual for a children's librarian to double as a young adult librarian, for example.

Many law firms, medical schools, government agencies, business firms, and research laboratories have their own libraries. So do historical societies, newspapers, labor unions, music publishers, movie studios, and many other kinds of organizations. The librarians who maintain and run these "special" collections are called *special librarians.* These librarians need a good background in the area that they work in. A librarian who works for a telecommunications firm, for example, may have a college degree in engineering as well as a degree in library science.

Library Clerks and Technicians

All types of librarians are helped in their work by clerks and technicians. *Clerks* do many of the routine and clerical jobs in the library, shelving books, checking in returns, and collecting fines. *Library technicians,* sometimes called library technical assistants, are more skilled than clerks and handle more responsible jobs. They may keep the card catalog up to date, operate audiovisual equipment, and answer readers' questions.

Personal Characteristics

Do you have what it takes for a career in education? What does it take, anyway? There are so many traits that are helpful that it is impossible to list them all. These are some of them.

You should have a *desire to help others* and a *sensitivity to their needs.* As an elementary school teacher you will have to spot the students who have problems with their lessons and personal development and identify the cause of the trouble. In all the teaching occupations you may spend extra time with students who have difficulty with their studies.

Patience helps. If you teach seventh grade algebra and the class cannot understand factoring after your fourth explanation, you can't give up. You simply have to try again.

You will find *tact* useful. As a school counselor, you may need to talk to parents whose child is a troublemaker in school. Unless you are tactful, the parents may not want to cooperate and everyone—the school, the student, and the parents—will suffer.

It is important to be *outgoing*. If you become a teacher, you will be on stage during every class. As a librarian, your job will be to offer assistance to frustrated researchers and confused patrons.

You should *enjoy learning* if you want a career in education. As a high school teacher much of your free time will be spent studying the subject you teach.

You should be a *good organizer*. People in teaching and library occupations often work on several projects at the same time. A high school teacher might have to keep track of five English classes plus two school clubs and serve as class adviser to boot.

A *good memory* is very valuable. As a librarian, you will read hundreds of books and then have to recall the best one for a reader who wants to learn about sailing.

Imagination is an important tool for educators. You might have to think of ways to excite students about high school physics, to lure children away from Saturday morning cartoons to come to the library, or to help high school dropouts prepare for the future.

Training

To prepare for a career in education you will spend many years as a student. For most of the occupations in this field you will need some college training. The number of years that you attend college and the subjects that you study depend on the career that you choose.

Teachers' aides and library technicians generally do not need a college education. However, the education requirements for aides and technicians vary with the amount of responsibility that their job involves. In many school districts and libraries you could be hired as an aide or library clerk directly from high school. You would learn your duties on the job. Some school districts and libraries prefer to hire teacher aides and library

Teaching often continues after the class ends.

Many college professors do research.

Education Occupations

technicians who have attended college. Formal training for these occupations is offered by some community and junior colleges.

You would need a State teaching certificate—a license—to become a kindergarten, elementary, or secondary school teacher in any public school, and in a private school in many States. To qualify for the teaching certificate, you'd need a bachelor's degree from a college with a State-approved teacher education program. In college you learn about the subjects that you'll be teaching later on. You also learn methods of teaching and ways of handling students. Student teaching—teaching classes under the supervision of an experienced teacher—is a very important part of the training.

To become a school counselor or administrator you would need teaching experience and additional training. Most States require school counselors to have a teaching certificate and a counseling certificate. Depending on the State, a master's degree in counseling and up to 5 years of teaching experience are required for a counseling certificate. School administrators generally must have many years of teaching experience plus graduate study in education.

To become a librarian you would need a master's degree in library science. Where you go to library school and what you study there depend on the type of library that you wish to work in. To become a school librarian, you have to train as a librarian and also as a teacher. If you want to be a special librarian, you generally need a college degree in the subject that you intend to specialize in—chemistry or music, to give just two examples. There are special programs to train you as a law librarian or medical librarian, if that is where your interest lies.

Because college teachers must have an in-depth knowledge of their subjects, you would need at least a master's degree to enter this occupation. It usually takes 5 years or more after high school for the master's degree, then 3 or 4 more years of study for a Ph. D. Even then your study of your subject would continue. You would do research and publish books and articles.

Regardless of the occupation that you choose, you will find that your training never really ends. There always will be something new to learn. Your career in education will require a lifetime commitment to your own education.

Teacher aides encourage students to participate in class activities.

Children's Librarian

"When you've worked with children long enough, you get to know what they want," says Librarian Maggie Thompson (left).

Education Occupations

Linda paused at the foot of the steps to the Baldwin Public Library.

"Why am I doing this?" she thought.

Linda took a deep breath and marched up the steps, through the door, and to the circulation desk.

"Excuse me," she said to the woman behind the desk. "My name is Linda Sherin. I'm from West End High School and I'm supposed to talk to Ms. Martin about working here as a volunteer aide."

At that, a tall woman walked across the room, smiled, and said, "I'm Gail Martin. I'm glad to meet you, Linda. Ms. Matthey recommended you very highly. Let's go into my office so we can talk."

The office was a small room just behind the circulation desk. After they were seated Ms. Martin said, "As you know, this interview is supposed to give you a chance to decide whether you want to work here as a volunteer page. Let me begin by telling you about the library and the job. We're not a big library, but we're very busy. There always is a lot to do. Since the staff is small, we depend on volunteers like you. You ..."

"Excuse me," interrupted a young man from the doorway. "Gail, I'm filling out the requisition for the new film series. I need the catalog that has the ordering information."

"Sure, I have it right here," replied Ms. Martin. The man took the catalog and left.

"We show films every Wednesday night," explained Ms. Martin. "That was Tomas Reno. He's one of our library technicians. He's really marvelous. Handles all our audiovisual equipment and half a dozen other jobs.

"As I was saying, there's always a lot to do. As a page, you would shelve books, check in returns, check out books, and any one of a dozen other jobs that come up.

"According to our arrangement with your school, members of your Community Action class work from 1 o'clock to 3 o'clock on Monday, Wednesday, and Thursday afternoons. We expect you to be here on time. Actually I hope you'll like it here so much that you'll look forward to coming here. Maybe even decide to work more than 6 hours a week.

"Well, Linda, what do you say? Do you want to give us a try?"

"I guess so," said Linda hesitantly.

"But you're not sure?" asked Ms. Martin. "Linda, it's important to us that our volunteers like their work. Is something bothering you?"

"No ... well, I'm not sure I want to work here. I signed up for Community Action to get a chance to work as an aide in the hospital, or in a day care center, or even as a tutor in school. I only came here because Ms. Matthey said I should. She said you needed the most help right now. What I really want to do is work with people. You know, help them somehow."

"I see," said Ms. Martin. "And you don't think you can help people in a library."

"I guess you can, a little."

"Linda, I know we were only supposed to talk today but I'll make a deal with you. You work in the children's section for a couple of hours with Ms. Thompson. If you still don't want the job, I'll talk to Ms. Matthey. Fair enough?"

"I suppose so," Linda said uncertainly.

Ms. Martin led Linda downstairs to the children's room. It was a large room with low bookshelves lining all the walls. On top of the shelves stood large books with bright covers. The walls above the shelves were decorated with colorful posters. In the center of the room were several low tables surrounded by small chairs. On the right side of the room was a low wooden counter, piled high with stacks of books. Seated behind the counter was a woman with long red hair, intent on the piece of furry white cloth she was sewing. She was so engrossed that she didn't look up as Ms. Martin and Linda walked toward her.

"Sewing in a library? What's going on here?" thought Linda to herself, her doubts returning. She was beginning to be sorry that she had agreed to spend the afternoon here.

"Maggie," said Ms. Martin, breaking the woman's concentration, "this is Linda Sherin, a new volunteer aide. She'll work with you until 3 o'clock this afternoon."

"Fantastic," replied the woman. She smiled warmly and hurried from behind the counter, dropping her sewing in her rush.

"I'm Maggie Thompson and am I glad to see you! I have a group of first graders coming in a few minutes, so I won't even have time to give you a quick tour, but you can ..."

"Hold on, Maggie. We don't want to scare her away on the first day," said Ms. Martin.

"Okay, Gail. I'll go easy."

"I know you will," said Ms. Martin and she went upstairs.

"As I was saying, a class of first graders is coming for a tour," continued Ms. Thompson. "I like to get them in here early in their school careers. Anyway, while I handle the children, you can help me catch up with these returns."

She pointed at the books on the counter. "I wanted to take care of these this morning, but I got tied up with something else. There's always so much to do. I'm talking too much, aren't I? I do that now and again! Well, let's get you started."

Linda was a bit overwhelmed, but she dutifully followed Ms. Thompson to the counter.

Maggie shows Linda how to check in books.

Ms. Thompson showed Linda how to check in the books. The job was simple and Linda soon was working by herself. Ms. Thompson started sewing again.

With only the two of them in the room, it was very quiet. Linda soon lost interest in what she was doing.

"Boring," she thought. "I'll be glad to get out of this place."

Suddenly she heard the clatter of feet and the sound of children's voices from the stairway. In a moment a group of wide-eyed children swept into the room.

It took several minutes for their teacher to get them seated at the tables in the center of the room. During that time Ms. Thompson put down her sewing and stepped from behind the counter. She greeted the teacher and then turned to the children.

"Hello, girls and boys. How are you? My name is Maggie Thompson and I'm a librarian. Your teacher has told me how well you all read, so today I'm going to tell you about a very naughty monkey. You can read more about him in class next week. After that I'll help each of you find a book to take home."

After reading from a large, colorful picture book, Ms. Thompson took some books from the shelves and described them. She acted out scenes from the books and joked with the children. Linda marvelled at the way Ms. Thompson handled the group. She immediately got along with the children and their teacher. She was a real ham and the children loved it.

Ms. Thompson then gave a brief explanation of how to use the children's encyclopedia and the card catalog. Finally she gave the children library cards that already were filled out and showed them how to check out books. After that the children were allowed to look for books on their own. The result was bedlam, or so it seemed to Linda.

Ms. Thompson was swamped with questions. "Where can I find a book about dinosaurs?" "I want a book about space." "Can I read *The Wizard of Oz?*" "Do you have any comic books?" The librarian and the teacher helped each child select a book and check it out.

As the teacher got the children together again at the tables, Ms. Thompson went to the counter and picked

Education Occupations

"Every time I help a child find a book, I help him or her grow a little."

up the furry cloth she had been sewing. She held it behind her back. When the children were all seated quietly, Ms. Thompson spoke to them again.

"Girls and boys, it was a pleasure to have you here. I hope you enjoy your books. Please remember to take good care of them and return them here or to your teacher in 2 weeks.

"By the way, every Saturday morning at 10 o'clock we have a story hour and I'd be happy to have you come. This Saturday is very special, because our story will be told by puppets. Right, Mr. Bird?"

From behind her back Ms. Thompson pulled a white furry hand puppet that looked like a bird.

"That's right, Ms. Thompson, and I want all these children to come and meet my friends," mouthed Ms. Thompson.

Linda was impressed by Ms. Thompson's ventriloquism. The children loved it. The children left as noisily as they had come. There was a long chorus of good-bye's and thank you's as Ms. Thompson walked them to the stairway.

"Well, that was fun," she said, returning to the counter. "How are you doing?"

"Pretty well," replied Linda, "I'll be finished soon."

"Good. I'll show you how to shelve the books when you're ready."

"Ms. Thompson, do you give tours like this often?"

"Yes, during the school year. Even though most schools have good libraries, I like to have the children come here. That way they know we have something to offer them."

"How do you know so much about the books? There are so many of them."

"I selected a lot of them," replied Ms. Thompson. "I read book reviews and browse through book stores. My husband says I spend as much time looking for books as I do with him."

"Do you read them all?"

"I try to. That way I can match books and children."

"How do you do that?"

"A little witchcraft."

"What?"

"I'm only teasing. When you've worked with children long enough, you get to know what they want. Even if the children themselves can't explain it very clearly."

"How long have you been a librarian?"

"About 4 years. Before that, I was a budget analyst for the county government. It was a good job, but I decided I wanted a change of scene. I have a friend who is a librarian, and his work always sounded interesting. So I took a year off and went back to college for a master's degree in library science.

"I had planned to become an acquisitions librarian. That's a behind-the-scenes job. You work in an office downtown, and select books, films, magazines—whatever—for the libraries in this system. It's interesting work, but before long I realized that it would be a lot like my old job. And I wanted a big change. So I switched my specialty to children's librarianship. I'm glad I did. I've always wanted a job where I could help people. Now I have it."

"Do you really think you help people here?" Linda asked.

"Certainly," replied Ms. Thompson, astonished. "That's what the library is all about. Every time I help a child find a book I help him or her grow a little. The other day I showed a little girl how to use the encyclopedia. Now that may not seem like much to me or you, but it was tremendously exciting for her. It was as though I had given her the key to a whole new world. She sat here all morning long, just looking things up. It may seem silly, but I was excited too."

"But what's it like when the children aren't here? Don't you get bored?"

"Bored!" said Ms. Thompson, smiling. "Let me tell you what I have to try to do between now and 3 o'clock, when the children start arriving from school. I have to finish working on these puppets. Make some scenery. Set up a new display of books. Talk to Ms. Martin about my budget. Read as many book reviews as I can. Bored? There's no time for it. But we have work to do. Let me know when you're ready to shelve books."

"Um ..." Linda hesitated a moment, then asked, "Will you need any help on Saturday? With the show?"

"I can always use an extra hand, but are you sure you want to give up your Saturday morning?"

Linda thought a moment. "Yes, now I'm sure."

Exploring

Children's librarians help children use the library.

- Are you outgoing?
- Do you like to help people?
- Do you enjoy group activities such as team sports?

- Do you like to babysit or take care of your younger brothers or sisters?

Children's librarians organize story hours and other kinds of programs to interest children in reading and the library.

- Are you good at organizing parties, picnics, or school activities?
- Are you good at thinking up activities on a rainy day?
- Can you keep young children occupied when you are babysitting?
- Are you at ease leading a group?

Children's librarians answer all kinds of questions. They need to be familiar with many subjects.

- Are you curious?
- Do you have many interests in school?
- Do you have several hobbies?
- Do you have a good memory?
- Do you enjoy games that require knowledge of trivia?

Children's librarians select books, films, records, maps, and other material for the library.

- Do you like to read?
- Do you like to do book reports for your school classes?
- Do you read reviews of movies or television shows? Do you ever compare the reviewer's opinion with your own?
- Can you explain why you like or dislike a book, a movie, or a television show?
- Do you ever recommend books, movies, or records to your friends? Do they usually like your recommendations?

Children's librarians often have administrative duties such as supervising clerks and preparing a budget.

- Are you a good organizer?
- Can you handle several jobs at the same time?
- Can you give directions to other people?

Education Occupations

Secondary School Teacher

When discussion dies down in his English class, Mr. Flannery has to get things moving again.

"Todd? . . . Todd? . . . Does anyone know if Michelle Todd is in school today?"

The clamor of voices in the classroom came to a halt. A girl called out from the back of the room, "Michelle went to see the nurse. She didn't feel well."

"Michelle never seems to feel well," thought Mr. Flannery, as he made a note beside her name. The students were beginning to talk loudly again by the time he finished taking attendance.

"They're louder than usual today," he thought. "I suppose it's the anticipation of the 4-day weekend. I'll be glad to get a few days' rest myself, even if I have to spend at least 2 days grading papers and preparing exams."

Mr. Flannery shook his head and said, "Okay, let's get down to business."

The class chatter gradually died down.

"Today we will summarize the lessons about the short story. Are there any questions about the parts of the short story?"

A room of blank faces stared up at the English teacher.

"Do you have any questions about theme . . . plot . . . characterization . . . or what they contribute to the story?"

The class remained quiet.

"Today it will be like pulling teeth," thought Mr. Flannery.

"Well, since there are no questions, I have a little surprise for you." He took a stack of papers from his briefcase.

A groan rose from the class. Several students rustled through their notebooks to find questions.

"Don't worry. I'm not giving a quiz," he said. Instantly the students relaxed.

"This sheet has some questions about the themes, plots, and characters of the stories that we read this week. We'll discuss the answers today. Pay attention because there will be a test with similar questions next Tuesday."

"Next Tuesday," groaned several students.

"Mr. Flannery, if the test is Tuesday we'll have to study over the weekend," said Earl Pickett from the front of the class. "Couldn't you postpone it? Please?"

Several students joined in the plea.

"Sorry, but the test will be Tuesday. We've fallen too far behind the other 9th grade literature class. By the way, I also want the topics for your book reports by the end of next week."

It took several minutes for the grumbling to die down. By then Mr. Flannery had finished handing out the papers.

"Okay, read the first question and write the answer. You can use your notes and books."

As the class worked, Mr. Flannery walked around the room and glanced at the students' papers. Occasionally he commented on a student's answer or gave hints to those who were stuck.

After a few minutes Mr. Flannery said, "Let's get started. Earl, what do you have for an answer?"

"Um . . . I didn't write anything. I couldn't think of an answer."

"Not a good start," thought Mr. Flannery.

"Would you read the question, Earl?"

"What is the theme of *The Cask of Amontillado* by Poe? List sections in the story to support your answer."

"Do you know what a theme is, Earl?"

"Yes, it's what the story is about."

"Right, it's the central idea in a story," said Mr. Flannery. "What happens in this story?"

"Well, this man, Montressor, leads another man, um . . . Fortunato, into a wine cellar, chains him to a wall and buries him in with stone," replied Earl.

"Very good. Why did Montressor do this?"

"Because Fortunato insulted him and Montressor wanted to get even."

"In other words Montressor wanted revenge."

"Right," replied Earl.

"Not bad," thought Mr. Flannery. "Earl usually doesn't read the assignments that carefully. I'd better involve some of the others before they fall asleep."

"Betty, what did you think the theme of the story was?"

"I said the story was about revenge."

"What about revenge?" Mr. Flannery asked the class. "Is the author saying something about revenge? Ron, what do you think?"

"I think the story says you can't really get revenge."

"Very good. Why do . . . "

"I don't understand," interrupted Earl. "Montressor got revenge. He killed Fortunato."

"Amazing," thought Mr. Flannery. "This is the first time Earl's been interested in a class discussion."

"Okay, Earl. Montressor does kill Fortunato, but does he really get the revenge that he wants?"

"Sure he does."

"Let's take a closer look," said Mr. Flannery. "In the first paragraph in the story, Montressor says there are two conditions for successful revenge. What are they?"

The students leafed through their books.

"This is great," thought Mr. Flannery. "They're really interested."

"He says the person has to know that he's being punished," called out Jim Riley.

"Very good. What else?"

"Montressor says that he has to punish with impunity," volunteered Steve Muir.

"What does that mean?" asked Mr. Flannery.

"He doesn't want to get caught," said Earl.

"Good. Does Montressor's revenge meet the conditions that he sets?"

"Sure," replied Earl. "Fortunato knows he's being punished and Montressor isn't caught."

"Isn't he?" quizzed Mr. Flannery.

Earl said hesitantly, "It says the body lay undisturbed for 50 years."

"True," said Mr. Flannery. "But doesn't it seem odd that after 50 years Montressor still remembers so many details of his crime? The last line is "In pace requiescat." What does that mean?" continued Mr. Flannery.

"May he rest in peace," replied Earl.

"Right. Why would Montressor wish that for his enemy?"

"Maybe he didn't think Fortunato was resting in peace," replied Jim.

"Yes, maybe Fortunato's ghost was haunting him," said Ron.

"They're getting it," thought Mr. Flannery. "Very good. What else does Montressor say after Fortunato's death that makes you think he was punished?"

The class was silent for a few moments, then Betty said, "He said his heart grew sick."

"Right. Now let's examine what we have said. Montressor wants revenge. Moreover, he wants it with impunity—that is, without being punished himself. At the end of the story Montressor says he is sick at heart, and indicates that the crime and the memory of Fortunato still bother him after 50 years."

"Okay, Earl," Mr. Flannery thought to himself. "I know you have it. Don't let me down." The teacher stepped right next to Earl and looked directly at him.

"Earl, now can you explain the story's theme—that it is impossible to get revenge?"

"No."

Mr. Flannery almost staggered back a step. He felt crushed by Earl's answer. "Oh, Earl, I was sure you had it," he thought.

"I wish I had more time to help each student."

After a moment Mr. Flannery said slowly, "Okay, I'll explain. Montressor doesn't get the revenge that he wants because he feels guilty. Even though he's not caught, he's punished by his conscience."

"Oh, I see," said Earl quickly. Mr. Flannery wasn't sure that Earl really understood.

"Try the next question," he said.

As the class worked on the second question, Mr. Flannery leaned against his desk. He noticed some students talking instead of working. As he was about to correct them, the classroom door swung open and Michelle Todd walked in.

"Mr. Flannery, the nurse said I can go home, but you have to sign this note," said Michelle very loudly. Several students looked up from their work.

"Michelle, please be quiet. You're disturbing the class," said Mr. Flannery. "What's the matter?"

"I don't know," the girl replied. "I just don't feel well."

"Michelle, this is the third time that you've left early this month. You know your grades...."

"I can't help it if I'm sick," said Michelle even more loudly. Several students giggled.

"I guess not," said Mr. Flannery. "Here's the note." Michelle left the room and slammed the door behind her. The class looked up, startled.

"Back to work," snapped Mr. Flannery.

"Calm down, Flannery. You're not a miracle worker. You can't work with some kids," he thought.

Mr. Flannery kept the discussion going, but the class had lost its enthusiasm. Most of the students closed their books and were ready to leave long before the bell rang.

When it did ring, the students rushed out the door. Mr. Flannery dropped into his chair. He was ready for a break. After a few minutes Mr. Flannery took a small notebook from his briefcase and checked his schedule for the day.

9:20—9th grade literature, first section
10:05—Work on term papers.
10:50—10th grade literature, third section.
11:35—Lunch patrol.

"I don't need that today," he thought. "I'd really prefer to eat with adults today or better yet alone."

12:30—9th grade literature, second section.
1:45—10th grade literature, first section.
2:30—12th grade writing course.
3:15—Talk to principal about cheerleader uniforms.
5:00—Pictures of basketball game for yearbook.

"And then I get to go to my class at night school. Maybe I shouldn't have taken a course this semester. Monitoring the cheerleaders and the yearbook take up

"Teaching has its headaches, but I can't see myself in any other line of work."

enough of my free time. But Professor Walton's class on classical themes in modern drama was too tempting to pass up. Besides, going to school at night is no tougher now than it was 5 years ago when I was taking the graduate courses I needed for my permanent certification.

"Five years of teaching," he mused. "With all the headaches it sometimes feels like 50. But I can't see myself in any other line of work. I wonder why."

"Mr. Flannery," Earl stood in the doorway.

"Earl, what's up?"

"I wanted to know if I could do my book report on another one of Poe's stories," said Earl. "I really liked *The Cask* and your explanation of it. I'd like to read some other stuff of Poe's."

"That will be fine," said Mr. Flannery. Earl left the room.

"Well, I guess that's one reason why."

Education Occupations

Exploring

Secondary school teachers help students learn.

- Do you like to help other people learn?
- Do you help your classmates with their school work?
- Do you like to help young children learn their letters and numbers?

Secondary school teachers learn as well as teach. They must know a great deal about their subjects and keep up with new information and ideas.

- Do you enjoy learning?
- When you are curious about something, do you go to an encyclopedia or library to learn more about it?
- Can you learn on your own? Can you read a book and pick out the important ideas?
- Is there a subject that you especially enjoy studying?

Secondary school teachers must be able to command the attention of a group.

- Are you good at making class presentations?
- Is it easy for you to speak up at meetings or in groups?
- Do friends ever ask you to be the spokesperson for a group?

Secondary school teachers work with people—students, parents, faculty, and school administrators.

- Do you like to work with people?
- Are you active in school clubs or committees?
- Do you enjoy working with others on class projects?
- Do you like team sports?
- Are you patient?
- Are you tactful?
- Are you diplomatic when people don't go along with your ideas?

Secondary school teachers often have nonteaching duties. They monitor lunchrooms and serve as advisers for student activities.

- Are you a good organizer?
- Can you handle several jobs at one time?
- Do you participate in extracurricular activities in school?
- Are you good at directing the work of other people?

Secondary school teachers often work in the evenings and during weekends.

- Do you think you would be willing to work at night or on weekends?

Exploring Careers

School Counselor

Jean Matthey feels that the best part of her job is helping students understand themselves.

Education Occupations

Jean Matthey took one last sip of coffee before leaving the faculty lounge.

"I hope no one bothers me this first hour," she thought as she opened the door to her office. "I need some time to catch up on my paperwork."

"No such luck," she said out loud as she spotted the note on her desk. It was from Ms. Thornton, the school principal: "Jean, please see me as soon as possible."

Ms. Thornton was looking over some budget figures for the school board when Jean entered the office.

"You wanted to see me?" asked Jean.

"Oh, yes. Won't keep you a minute," replied Ms. Thornton. "It's about Michelle Todd. She's been out of school a lot recently, as you know."

"Yes," agreed Jean. "Doesn't she have tonsilitis?"

"We thought so. But yesterday, while Mr. Flannery was at the mall arranging exhibition space for the cheerleader tryouts, he saw Michelle. And in the middle of the morning!"

"Have you notified the truant officer?" Jean inquired.

"No, not yet. I think you'd be well advised to have a talk with Mrs. Todd before we contact the truant officer. A little straight talk from the school counselor might be sufficient."

"Have you made an appointment with Mrs. Todd?" Jean asked.

"Yes, she's coming today at 1:30, during your free hour. Do you think you can handle this problem for me? The situation is rather delicate since Mrs. Todd continually writes notes to excuse her absences."

"I see what you mean," said Jean hesitantly. "I'll try to be diplomatic. I'm certainly glad to have this chance to get to the root of the problem without involving the truant officer. I'll keep you posted."

"Thank you, Jean."

As she headed for her office, Jean suddenly remembered her morning appointment with Julie Cauldwell. Her step quickened.

"Hi, Jean." It was Mr. Flannery.

"Oh, hello, Jim. Say, why do you suppose Michelle Todd is missing so much school lately?"

"I don't really know, Jean. It's all the more surprising when you consider she was one of my best students a month ago. Now I can't even get her to sit through an entire class period. I've tried talking to her but she seems very uptight. Some kids . . . you know how hard it can be to get through to . . . ."

"Thanks for the information, Jim," said Jean, interrupting the English teacher in mid-sentence. "I'm late for an appointment so I've got to go," she apologized.

"Sure, Jean. See you later."

"Jim really is a good teacher," she thought to herself. "He tries to reach out to all of his students, but he doesn't always have the time to get to the root of their problems. But that's why I'm here, after all."

She had a fleeting thought of herself as a teacher 3 years ago. She had been spending so much time helping her students with their courses and concerns that she decided to train to become a counselor. Two years back at the university in a master's program in counseling and then—Middlesex Junior High. "I'm really glad I made the change," thought Jean proudly. "This is more for me . . ."

"Good morning, Julie," the counselor said to the youngster quietly waiting in her office. "Did you look over the list of organizations that are cooperating in our work-study program?"

"No, ma'am. I lost my copy. But I already know where I want to work. Would you sign me up for The Crazy Horse Boutique?"

"Gladly, Julie. I didn't realize that you were interested in fashion retailing," said Jean cheerfully.

"I'm not. I mean, I'm sort of interested in it. But mostly I want to work there because Mary Simmons is."

"Oh," said Jean softly. "Listen, Julie, why don't we go over the list once more. Perhaps we'll come across something you are particularly interested in and . . . ."

"No, thanks, Ms. Matthey. Just sign me up for The Crazy Horse. I've got to be going since I have to meet Mary . . . ."

"O.K., Julie. The Crazy Horse it is."

As Jean watched the girl leave, she suddenly began thinking about herself at 14. Pamela Glenn had been her best friend in ninth grade. Inseparable! Or so everyone had said . . . . The phone rang as Jean was trying with some difficulty to remember the last time she and Pam had seen each other. The call jarred her from her thoughts.

"Hello, Jean? Jean, are you there?"

"Liz, you sound panicked. What can I do for you?"

"I am in a panic," replied Liz emphatically. Liz Swoyer taught drama at Middlesex Junior High. "Rudy Kowalski, my student stage manager, is moving with his family to Cincinnati," she continued in an agitated voice. "We were about to begin rehearsing for our second production, My Fair Lady, but without a stage manager, we are at a standstill. Do you know a hard-working student with leadership ability and organizational skills? I only have a few days to train him or her so we must find someone quickly!"

"Let me think about it," said Jean. "Can I get back to you tomorrow morning?"

"Sure, Jean. I'll be waiting to hear from you. Goodbye."

After hanging up the phone, Jean began flipping through her student activity card file.

"Hmm . . . Let's see, Mark Feingold? No, he's too busy with football. Susan Vetter? No. she has soccer practice every day after school. Hmm . . . Maybe Barbara Shapley. No, her grades are slipping as it is now. Maybe Phil Caron . . . ."

After lunch Jean walked to her office to meet Mrs. Todd. The woman's face showed her concern. She was nervously flipping through a magazine. As Jean approached, she felt a surge of compassion.

"Hello, Mrs. Todd. I'm Jean Matthey, the school counselor. I'd like to talk to you about Michelle. Lately she hasn't . . ."

"I know," interrupted Mrs. Todd. "She hasn't been coming to school. I'm partly to blame, you know, because I allow her to stay home. She has not wanted to come to school this past month. And she has been so sad lately I haven't had the heart to force her to go."

"She's been sad?" inquired Jean softly.

"Well, yes. You see, for months she practiced her speech for the debate team tryouts. I used to find her 3x5 cards all over the house. She's never worked so hard for anything in her life!"

"And did she make the team, Mrs. Todd?"

"No, she was rejected in the first round." Mrs. Todd's eyes misted over. "It broke my heart to see it. This age is difficult enough without this kind of rejection. I don't see why everyone can't be accepted. Do you? Can you do anything to help, Ms. Matthey?"

Jean was deep in thought. "Actually, Mrs. Todd, I do think I can help Michelle recover from her disappointment. Is she home now?"

"Why yes, I suppose so. What do you have in mind?"

"I would prefer talking to Michelle about it first, if you don't mind."

"Oh, not at all, Ms. Matthey. If you could do anything to help boost her spirits, I'd appreciate it very much."

"I'll do what I can, Mrs. Todd. I'll give you a call after I've talked to Michelle."

"Fine. Thank you so much, Ms. Matthey."

Jean felt exhilarated. Every now and then things seemed to click.

She dialed the Todds' number.

"Hello?"

"Hello, Michelle. This is Ms. Matthey. I was wondering if you would come to school an hour early tomorrow morning to meet with Ms. Swoyer, the drama teacher . . ."

Jean likes talking with parents. "They help make counseling work."

Education Occupations

Exploring

School counselors help students talk about their personal and social concerns. They must have an understanding of human emotions and behavior.

- Are you interested in knowing what causes people to respond as they do to an advertisement, a public appearance by a rock star, or a disaster?
- Are you able to forget about your problems in order to concentrate on those of a friend?
- Do you respond compassionately when a friend is upset, even though you feel he or she is overreacting?
- Are you able to comfort a younger brother or sister when his or her feelings have been hurt?
- Can you comfort a parent when he or she is upset?
- Can you tell when someone's feelings have been hurt even though he or she is trying to conceal it?

School counselors must be able to establish warm relationships with others. This encourages people to express their true feelings and, ultimately, to grow.

- Are you able to make guests feel welcome?
- Are you good at introducing people to one another at a party?
- Are you friendly with newcomers in your school or neighborhood?
- Do your friends confide in you?
- Are you able to criticize others in a way that doesn't hurt their feelings?
- Are you good at dealing with someone who constantly interrupts or never gets to the point?
- Are you patient in listening to someone else's troubles even though you hear the same thing over and over again?
- Do you become annoyed if a friend doesn't follow your advice even though he or she asked for it?

"I often see myself in the teenagers I counsel. I had many of the same problems."

School counselors must believe that a person can succeed if he or she really tries. They must remain supportive during trying times in the lives of individuals.

- Are you an optimistic, up-beat sort of person?
- Do friends come to you when they are sad?
- Can you talk someone into a good mood?
- Do you get excited about little things?
- Are you good at boosting a friend's confidence when he or she is nervous about an exam, a tryout, or asking someone for a date?
- Would you be good at coaching a team?

School counselors don't always see the results of their work right away. They must remain supportive and hopeful even though progress is slow.

- Do you appreciate small gains or progress?
- Do you have the patience to grow a garden?
- Are you able to stick with a diet or exercise program?

School counselors assist students with education and career planning.

- Are you good at planning ahead for things?
- Are you aware of the curriculum choices that you'll be asked to make in high school?
- Do you know which high school courses you'd need to be accepted for college, vocational school, or apprenticeship training?

School counselors must administer the school guidance program. They must be good at organizing work and getting along with people.

- Are you able to organize your time?
- Are you able to carry out a study plan?
- Are you a good leader? Do other people go along with your ideas when you're in charge of a group?
- Do you like to coordinate cookie sales, calendar sales, greeting card sales, or other fund-raising projects?
- Do you like to organize trips or parties?

School counselors must "sell" the guidance program to school faculty as well as students.

- Are you good at making presentations to the class?
- Are you able to command the attention of others while speaking?

- Are you successful at getting your point across in an argument?
- Are you able to convince your parents of the merits of a particular activity that you wish to pursue when they are against it?

School counselors must be able to identify students in need of special assistance.

- Can you tell which of your friends need help with schoolwork?
- Can you tell when a friend is upset about something?
- Do you know whether there's a drug problem in your school?
- Do you know if any of your classmates have been in trouble with the police?

Education Occupations

Teachers need patience to go over the same point again and again.

Job Facts

There isn't room in this book for a story about every education occupation. However, you'll find some important facts about nine of these occupations in the following section. If you want additional information about any of them, you might begin by consulting the Department of Labor's *Occupational Outlook Handbook*, which should be available in your school or public library.

Occupation	Nature and places of work	Training and qualifications	Other information

SCHOOL OCCUPATIONS

Kindergarten and Elementary School Teachers	Most elementary school teachers work in public schools in grades 1 through 6. Some work in private schools or in middle schools.	A bachelor's degree from a State-approved teacher education program is required for most beginning jobs. In some States graduate study is necessary to get permanent teaching certification. States and local school systems may have other requirements, such as U.S. citizenship. Elementary school teachers should have a strong desire to work with young children. They need to be warm, creative, and patient.	Elementary school teachers often work evenings and weekends. They prepare lessons, grade papers, attend meetings, and supervise student activities.

Education Occupations

Occupation	Nature and places of work	Training and qualifications	Other information
Teacher Aides	Most teacher aides work in elementary schools. Schools with many students are more likely than small schools to employ teacher aides.	The training of teacher aides varies among school districts. Many teacher aides train on the job or in classes conducted by their school district. Some aides train at 2-year colleges, where they receive an associate degree. Teacher aides must have a desire to help children and a willingness to follow a teacher's directions.	Many teacher aides are part-time workers. Some are unpaid volunteers.
Secondary School Teachers	Most secondary school teachers work in public schools. Over half teach in senior high schools; about one-third teach in junior high schools.	A bachelor's degree from a State-approved teacher education program is required for most beginning jobs. In some States graduate study is necessary to get permanent teaching certification. State and local school systems may have other requirements, such as U.S. citizenship. Secondary school teachers need a keen interest in their subject as well as a desire to work with young people.	Secondary school teachers often spend evenings and weekends preparing lessons, grading papers, attending meetings, and supervising student activities.
School Counselors	School counselors help students understand themselves and resolve their problems. They give aptitude, interest, and ability tests. They hold individual and group sessions so that students can "talk through" their concerns. They may teach classes in occupations and careers or other special subjects. Most counselors work in elementary, middle, or high schools.	A master's degree in counseling and some teaching experience usually are necessary. Most States require school counselors to have counseling and teaching certificates. The education and experience requirements for these certificates vary among States. School counselors must be able to deal with all types of people. They work with students, parents, teachers, school administrators, and community leaders.	Some counselors work part time as consultants for private or public counseling centers, government agencies, or private businesses.

COLLEGE OCCUPATIONS

College and University Teachers	Most college and university teachers work for public colleges and universities. Over half teach in universities and 4-year colleges and about one-fifth teach in 2-year colleges.	Graduate study is necessary. In most subjects at least a master's degree is required for a beginning job as an instructor. Additional graduate study, teaching experience, and research and publication of books and papers are needed to advance to the higher faculty ranks—assistant professor, associate professor, and full professor.	Although college and university teachers seldom teach more than 14 or 15 hours a week, they often spend about 55 hours a week on school-related activities, such as research and meetings with students. College and university teachers need a keen interest in their subject. They must study constantly to learn more about their field.

Exploring Careers

Occupation	Nature and places of work	Training and qualifications	Other information
College Student Personnel Workers	These workers develop and administer services for college students. The field includes people with a number of different job titles: Admissions officer, dean of students, registrar, student housing officer, residence hall director, college placement officer, financial aid officer, student activities adviser, foreign student adviser, and counselor. These workers are employed in colleges and universities throughout the country.	Educational requirements vary for the different jobs in this field. A bachelor's or master's degree in personnel administration or in one of the social sciences often is preferred. For work as a counselor, a master's degree in clinical or counseling psychology usually is required. These workers must be interested in people and good at dealing with them. They must be able to handle unexpected and unusual situations.	Unlike college teachers, college student personnel workers usually work all 12 months of the year. Irregular hours and overtime work often are necessary.
College Career Planning and Placement Counselors	These workers help college students and alumni examine their career goals and find jobs. Sometimes they arrange for job recruiters to visit the campus and set up interviews with students. They work for colleges and universities and for community and junior colleges.	A bachelor's degree in psychology or sociology is customary for a job in this field. A master's degree in clinical or counseling psychology is helpful. People in this field should be energetic and able to work under pressure because they must organize and administer a wide variety of activities. They must have an interest in people and be able to get along with them easily.	These workers also are known as college placement officers. These workers frequently work more than 40 hours a week. The workload is especially heavy during the recruiting season.

LIBRARY OCCUPATIONS

| Librarians | Most librarians work in school libraries or media centers, public libraries, and college or university libraries. Some work for organizations that have their own library, such as government agencies, law firms, research organizations, and business firms. | Librarians usually need a master's degree in library science.

School librarians may be hired with a bachelor's degree in library science plus appropriate courses in education. School librarians in most States must be trained and certified as teachers as well as librarians.

Special librarians may need a master's degree or a Ph.D. in their subject field—law, chemistry, or fine arts, for example—as well as a master's degree in library science. | Librarians may work evenings and weekends. |

Education Occupations

Occupation	Nature and places of work	Training and qualifications	Other information
Library Technicians and Clerks	These workers do many of the routine and clerical jobs in libraries: They check out books, collect fines, sort and shelve books, order and process new materials, answer routine information requests, and operate the library audiovisual equipment. Library technicians—also called library technical assistants—have more training and greater responsibility than library clerks. Clerks work in all types of libraries. Technicians work mostly in large libraries.	A high school diploma usually is required. Most library technicians and clerks learn their skills on the job. Some technicians take courses in library technology at community and junior colleges; such programs generally lead to an associate of arts degree.	Job titles vary. People doing this kind of work may also be called library assistants, library aides, or pages. Library technicians and clerks may work evenings and weekends.

Kindergarten teachers initiate children into the school system. They must be patient and highly motivated.

This sales worker is pointing out the features of a trail bike to a prospective buyer.

Exploring Careers

"Hi. I'm Bryce Winters, your man on the street for WKRX. Today I'm interviewing Bill Morgan, a local automobile sales manager. Bill is a success at his job. He likes his work, likes his fellow workers, and earns a substantial income. However, success didn't come overnight or easily. Indeed, Bill has a long and interesting work history and has had all sorts of jobs. There is a common thread, though, that runs through almost all of the jobs Bill has ever held. Almost all involved selling. Let's see if we can get Bill to talk about some of the things he has done and tell us how he feels about his work. Mr. Morgan, tell me about your very first sales job."

Mr. Morgan: That was a long time ago. I started selling newspapers on the street in my home town in Oklahoma when I was 14. The early edition of the Sunday paper came off the press at about 6 p.m. on Saturday. A lot of farmers and oil field workers were in town on Saturday night for shopping and entertainment, and many liked to buy the paper then instead of getting home delivery on Sunday morning. On a good night I could sell 50 papers, which gave me a good supply of pocket money for the following week.

Interviewer: Did you have a particular corner or location where you sold papers?

Mr. Morgan: No, it didn't work like that. The kids who had been with the newspaper company for a long time were given the choice locations. The other kids just had to walk the streets, asking people to buy.

Interviewer: Did that seem unfair to you?

Mr. Morgan: I don't remember; probably not. Those who had been with the newspaper the longest got a better deal. Most businesses do that in one way or another. Anyway, I discovered ways of selling. For example, I would find out what times a movie was going to let out and be waiting in front. Also, I knew the schedule for buses arriving at the local bus station. Some of the drivers would let me board their buses to sell papers. One kid got permission from bartenders to walk through their places a couple of times a night. People in bars tend to be generous tippers.

Interviewer: Was that kid you?

Mr. Morgan: How did you guess?

Interviewer: What was your next sales job?

Mr. Morgan: A newspaper route.

Interviewer: I wouldn't have thought of that as a sales job.

Mr. Morgan: Well, it's true that I spent most of my time delivering the papers house to house and collecting money at the end of the week. But the job also involved sales. I wanted to make more money, which meant persuading more of the people who lived along my route to subscribe to the paper. The same is true for the route drivers who deliver bread, milk, soft drinks, and the like. To be successful, these people must build up their routes.

Interviewer: Were you successful at building up your paper route?

Mr. Morgan: Well, yes, I found new customers. I remember being a little frightened at first at the thought of knocking on doors and asking strangers to take the paper. This was very different from approaching customers on the street. I guess I was afraid that knocking on doors would disturb and annoy people. And I was right. Some got angry and showed it by slamming the door in my face. It didn't take long, however, to realize that those people didn't have anything against me personally. I can't say the same for some of the dogs along the route! Anyway, most people were pretty nice, and I did find a lot of new customers.

Interviewer: What did you do with the money you earned?

Mr. Morgan: I was saving some to buy a car, but I blew most of the money. I spent a lot on fishing gear. That's how I got to know Mr. Andrews, the owner of the local sporting goods store. He needed part-time sales help, so I quit the paper route to work after school and Saturdays in his store.

Interviewer: Did he hire you because of your knowledge of fishing equipment?

Mr. Morgan: Yes, I'm sure that was one of the reasons. Product knowledge was important in that kind of store. Some of Mr. Andrews' customers knew exactly what they wanted, but others needed information before deciding. I was flattered at being recognized as a good source of information on fishing. Being able to help customers with my knowledge made me feel important. I think many people get into sales work through their hobbies. It makes sense to take advantage of your natural interests. My 16-year-old daughter is working this summer in a pet shop. One of her hobbies is raising tropical fish.

Interviewer: And that's how she got the job?

Mr. Morgan: Yes, but it wasn't quite that easy. The pet shop owner wasn't looking for help, as far as we know. Linda just took the initiative, walked into the pet shop, and asked for a job. The owner said he was sorry, but he didn't need more help. Linda was very disappointed because that was her first choice for a summer job. I advised her to go back and tell the man that she would work for a week without pay to prove herself. Linda did, and he must have been impressed because he hired her with pay.

Interviewer: Getting back to your job at the sporting goods store, was there anything you didn't like about it?

Sales Occupations

"A sales manager is like a coach," says Bill Morgan (center). "I have good players, and it's up to me to get the best out of them."

Mr. Morgan: No, I liked it and I worked there until I left home for college. Well, I'll take that back. I didn't like sweeping the floor. And taking inventory was a nuisance, but we only did that once a year.

Interviewer: Did you plan on a sales career when you entered college?

Mr. Morgan: No, I was going to major in engineering. That's not to say that engineering and sales don't go together. Many industrial products are so complex that it takes people with engineering backgrounds to sell them. But I didn't know that at the time. Looking back, my plan to study engineering wasn't really well thought out. Engineers were in demand at the time, and all the smartest kids were majoring in it. I was just following the crowd.

Interviewer: I would like to ask you more about that later, but let's talk about the jobs you had in college.

Mr. Morgan: At first, I worked at a soda fountain, but that's not really a sales job. True, you take money from people and you give them ice cream and sodas in exchange. You don't need to persuade the customer, though. Just take the order. Anyway, I left the soda fountain after a few months to take a job in a clothing store near the campus. A friend of mine who worked there recommended me to the manager when a job opened up.

Interviewer: Did you have any experience selling clothes?

Mr. Morgan: No, and the manager was a bit hesitant about hiring me for that reason. But I did have the 3 years of retailing experience in the sporting goods store.

Interviewer: How long did it take to learn the job?

Mr. Morgan: After a couple of months I felt pretty confident. The manager was a patient instructor and the other sales people also gave me advice. In selling menswear you try to help the customer select something to make him look good. Of course, the same holds true for women. But anyway, you learn certain rules. A dark suit, for example, is more flattering to a heavy person than a light-colored suit. Fit is also very important. Fitting a customer can be frustrating. Clothing comes in standard sizes; people do not. It's better to lose a sale than try to get the customer to take something that doesn't fit well or can't be satisfactorily altered.

Interviewer: Why is it better to lose the sale?

Mr. Morgan: Because clothing stores, like many other businesses, need steady customers. Sooner or later the customer will discover that the suit, or whatever, fits poorly. Perhaps his wife or girlfriend will let him know. As a result, he probably will take his business elsewhere.

Interviewer: You mentioned suggesting clothes that look best on the customer. How did you handle people who disagreed with your recommendations?

Mr. Morgan: Well, sometimes they were right. And sometimes customers made selections that obviously weren't right for them. You felt like saying, "Gee, the coat looks terrible on you." Sometimes there was the temptation to ask the customer if he was colorblind. I always tried to be as tactful as possible and steer the customer to something better. But I didn't argue. I'm sure you have heard the old saying, "Win an argument, lose a customer."

Interviewer: Did you work in the clothing store through college?

Mr. Morgan: As long as I stayed in college. I dropped out the second semester of my sophomore year. The math for engineering was not easy, and I just wasn't that interested in working at it. There I was, feeling like a failure at age 20.

Interviewer: What was next?

Mr. Morgan: Well, I stayed on at the men's store for a while, but the manager made it clear that he felt obligated to employ students. I knew some people who had left school to work in an aircraft plant in Texas that paid high wages. So I drove down there and was hired for a job in the incoming inspection department. All of the materials and parts that the aircraft company ordered from other companies came through that department. My job was to inspect these items to make sure the company was getting what had been ordered.

Interviewer: That certainly seems different from sales work.

Mr. Morgan: Yes, it was. I enjoyed the job for a while. It seemed like a very responsible position, and I was learning many new things. However, it did not involve contact with the public, which I missed. In fact, I began to feel isolated.

Interviewer: Was this your first experience with a job that didn't involve contact with the public?

Mr. Morgan: The summer following my first year in college, I got a truckdriving job with a freight company. I delivered incoming freight to stores and factories, and picked up outgoing freight. It didn't last long. I got fired after a couple of weeks. I was driving the truck up a steep hill, and several cartons fell out the back. I didn't realize what had happened, so I kept driving. If I had loaded the truck properly to begin with, it never would have happened.

Interviewer: Still, that seems like a minor thing to be fired for.

Mr. Morgan: My boss had no sense of humor.

Interviewer: What did you do then?

Mr. Morgan: You mean for the rest of the summer?

Interviewer: Yes.

Mr. Morgan: I went to work in a bakery. That place was hot and the work was physically hard, but I knew it was temporary. You can tolerate a job you dislike if you know it will be over at the end of summer.

Interviewer: Getting back to the aircraft plant, did you look upon that as something to do until you found another sales job?

Mr. Morgan: Well, no, I didn't go into it with that in mind. After being there for several months, though, I realized that I much preferred sales work. It finally dawned on me that I was cut out for sales.

Interviewer: What was your next step?

Mr. Morgan: Selling cars. I had been considering car sales for some time. I was especially interested in sports cars, having recently bought a used British roadster. So I figured out reasons why sports car dealers in the Dallas-Fort Worth area should hire me. First, I had sales experience from the men's store and the sporting goods store. Second, I had a keen interest in sports cars and knew all about them. Third, I believed sports cars were catching on with the public, and this was a good opportunity for me to get in on the ground floor.

Interviewer: Were you successful in selling yourself?

Mr. Morgan: It took a while. The sales managers' reactions were, "Well, that's fine, but we don't need anyone right now." I got the brushoff. You know— "Don't call us, we'll call you." I followed up by writing letters to them, giving them even more reasons why they should hire me. That worked. After just a few days, I had a positive reply. A sales person at one of the dealerships was leaving, and the manager was willing to give me a chance. I was delighted.

Interviewer: Was selling cars like selling clothes?

Mr. Morgan: In many ways. For a lot of people, cars are a form of dress. Clothes make an impression; cars make an impression. People think, "This car says something about what I am." You, for example. I believe you are a very practical-minded person. Do you have a small economy car?

Interviewer: Yes, as a matter of fact I do. But I think that was a lucky guess.

Mr. Morgan: No, I was looking out the window when you drove up.

Interviewer: Can sales people really judge what customers are like?

Mr. Morgan: To a certain extent, yes. People give impressions by the way they dress, talk, and act. A professional sales person is good at observing people. You have to be a good observer in order to "qualify" a prospective customer.

Interviewer: What does "qualifying" customers mean?

Mr. Morgan: Finding out if the person has the ability to buy a car, and if this person really is interested in buying. Many people like to visit a dealer's showroom just to look at the new models. Perhaps they are curious or like to dream about having their favorite car. Some can't afford to buy, and others aren't ready to. Usually, a good sales person can quickly find out by asking

Sales Occupations

questions. If the person doesn't seem like a buyer, you might say something like, "Look around all you like and then let me know if I may be of help," and then politely excuse yourself. Most people who sell cars are paid a commission on each car they sell. The more you sell, the more you make. Obviously, you can't afford to spend much time with someone who isn't going to buy. Nevertheless, it's important to be polite and leave the nonbuyers with a favorable impression. This person is going to buy someday—hopefully from you.

Interviewer: Suppose the prospective customer does want to buy, but isn't convinced that he or she should get one of your cars?

Mr. Morgan: I would find out what appealed to that individual. What are his or her needs? I would then point out how one of my cars could meet those needs. Actually, a professional will sell the entire car dealership, not just the car.

Interviewer: I don't understand.

Mr. Morgan: I'll give an example. The dealer I was with in Texas had one of the best service departments for imported cars in the entire area. People would drive 50 miles to have their cars serviced there. I always emphasized the excellence of our service department when talking with customers. That helped sell a lot of cars.

Interviewer: I can appreciate what you are saying. I've had problems getting the dealer to fix my car. You mentioned being paid a commission on each one you sold. Did a week ever go by when you didn't sell a car?

Mr. Morgan: The first 2 weeks on that job I didn't sell anything. Luckily, I had saved some money to tide me over. My first sale was to an elderly man who taught history in high school. And I almost blew it because I couldn't see him driving a sports car. So I tried to sell the man a compact sedan. He was a bit shy about admitting what he wanted and I had trouble picking that up. It was like having to read between the lines. That experience taught me not to judge a book by its cover.

Interviewer: Was that first sale a big event for you?

Mr. Morgan: Wow—was it ever. I had never sold anything that expensive in my life. I felt like jumping and shouting with joy. I had begun to have some doubts about my ability and needed that boost to restore some confidence. I still get a good feeling from making a sale. But back then things seemed much more challenging, so each sale was a personal victory. Within a few months, I was averaging about three cars a week and trying hard to become the leading seller in the company. The manager talked the owners into having a contest for us. First prize was a 2-week vacation in Mexico. Second prize was a week's vacation in New Orleans. The owner had two dealerships, so about a dozen sales people were in the contest. Winners would be the two who sold the most

"Whenever you try to persuade a person to do something, you are using sales skills."

cars during a 4-month period.

Interviewer: You won?

Mr. Morgan: I came in a close third. But that was good. With less than a year's experience, I was one of the three top people. And I met my wife Eve during that contest.

Interviewer: You met your wife by selling her a car?

Mr. Morgan: Yes, and it wasn't easy. Eve wanted a particular model that came only with a 4-speed transmission. The problem was she didn't know how to use a stick shift. I was determined to win the contest so I promised to give lessons if she bought. She ordered a car but called the next morning to cancel out because she was having second thoughts about her ability to learn. Back then, she didn't seem to have the self-confidence that she has now. Well, I didn't want to lose the sale so I had to think of an alternative. I suggested we start the lessons with my car that afternoon and assured her that she could still cancel if things didn't work out. That's how our relationship started. We still have a copy of that sales contract. We got married about 2 years later. The wedding was a week after she graduated from college.

Interviewer: What did Eve major in?

Mr. Morgan: Education. She taught in high school for several years and then returned to college full time to get a master's in school administration. She's a high school principal now.

Interviewer: How long did you stay with the car dealer in Texas?

Mr. Morgan: Eve had an offer to teach in California. The West Coast appealed to us, and I figured it would be easy to find a job selling cars out there. One of the advantages of a sales career is the freedom to move about. You can sell anywhere, except maybe in the smallest towns. I went to work for a dealer in the Los Angeles area. The place was practically within walking distance of Eve's school and a short drive to the beach. It was a nice setup.

Interviewer: Why did you leave?

Mr. Morgan: Uncle Sam's orders. I got a letter directing me to report to the Army at Fort Ord, California. After basic training, they transferred me to Fort Myer, Virginia.

Interviewer: And you never returned to live in California?

Mr. Morgan: No, Eve joined me in Virginia and found a teaching job nearby. We got to like this area and saw no reason to leave.

Interviewer: What kind of job did you have in the Army?

Mr. Morgan: Would you believe I drove a truck?

Interviewer: That's a far cry from sales work.

Mr. Morgan: Well, any activity involves selling in some way. Anytime you persuade or induce a person to do something that you want, you are using sales skills. For example, you appealed to my ego in inducing me to do this interview.

Interviewer: While in the Army, did you have part-time sales jobs?

Mr. Morgan: Yes, a few. I worked briefly for a car dealer, but we couldn't agree on a satisfactory part-time schedule, so I gave the job up. I sold appliances in a department store for a while. I also dabbled in life insurance, but with little success.

Interviewer: What was the problem with life insurance?

Mr. Morgan: I just couldn't get interested. I'm not sure why. Perhaps because I had always sold products that people actively shop for—cars, clothes, sports equipment. Things they get enthusiastic about. People generally don't get enthusiastic about life insurance but buy it to protect their families. They must be convinced of the need for this protection. Therefore, selling life insurance successfully seems to require much more perseverance than selling cars successfully. Finding customers is such an important part of the job. Any type of selling requires perseverance, though, and I know several very successful insurance sales people who used to sell cars. I just feel more at ease with customers coming to me.

Interviewer: So you returned to selling cars after getting out of the Army?

Mr. Morgan: Yes, I went with a local import dealer first, and then switched to a larger dealer that handled domestic cars—the organization I'm with now.

Interviewer: Why did you switch dealers?

Mr. Morgan: Better opportunities. This organization had a reputation for being a good place to work. They treated the sales staff right, and the morale showed it. Within a year, I doubled my earnings.

Interviewer: How long have you been the sales manager?

Mr. Morgan: About 4 years. I was an assistant manager for 3 years before being promoted.

Interviewer: Do you ever miss being a sales worker?

Mr. Morgan: I still am—but I know what you mean. At times, I do miss selling. But managing a sales staff is another kind of challenge for me and I thrive on challenges. I'm quite a competitive person. I keep pushing myself to see what else I can handle, how much more I can accomplish. In my job as sales manager, the challenge lies in getting a bunch of aggressive sales workers to pull together as a team. At the risk of sounding corny, I see myself as coaching a sales team. I have good players, and it's up to me to try to get the best out of them. It's especially satisfying to see the young people develop their potential.

Interviewer: Thank you very much. I appreciate your

Sales Occupations

taking time out for this interview.

Mr. Morgan: It's been my pleasure.

Interviewer: Well, that's it for today, listeners. Tune in tomorrow when I talk with skydiver Laurie Stapleton. This is Bryce Winters, your man on the street, saying goodbye from WKRX.

What Makes a Good Sales Worker?

This section discusses personality traits that contribute to success in sales work. Personality often is the key factor in enjoying sales work and doing well at it, and such traits as self-confidence, enthusiasm, and drive usually are evident in people who make a career of sales.

In his interview by radio station WKRX, Bill Morgan revealed some of the personal characteristics and attitudes common to successful sales workers. See if you can remember things Bill said in the interview that clarify or support the points being made.

Sales workers constantly deal with other people on a one-to-one basis. Insurance agents, for example, are always on the lookout for potential customers, or prospects. They must like people and enjoy striking up conversations with strangers to handle this aspect of the job well. Because contact with other people is so important, an *outgoing personality* is a plus. This is not to say that one must be a "gladhander" or a "backslapper" to be successful. In fact, some people are put off by too much friendliness. Genuine warmth and a pleasant personality, however, often make customers more receptive to a sales worker's ideas.

Contacting prospects and keeping in touch with customers are important parts of the job. Real estate agents who handle commercial or industrial property, for example, may take a long time putting together a big deal because of its intricate legal, financial, and political aspects. To keep the prospect of a sale "alive," they must keep in touch with all the parties to the deal—over a period of months or even years—and keep their interest from flagging. In situations such as these, *drive and motivation,* or the ability to be a "self-starter," are absolute "musts."

Enthusiasm and a positive outlook are also valuable traits. A sales worker's enthusiasm can be infectious, and often plays a big part in overcoming a customer's hesitancy to buy. Even enthusiastic sales workers have bad days or experience slow sales periods, however. An upbeat, positive attitude helps sales workers make it through discouraging times.

The sales worker's *product knowledge* has a lot to do with the attention we give to his or her "pitch." Sales

An outgoing personality is a "must" for people who sell "big ticket" items.

workers' familiarity with the products they sell often makes the difference in overcoming our hesitancy to buy. Imagine, for example, that you are in a stereo store, shopping for a new component stereo system. Would you buy from a clerk who didn't know the differences between the various systems available and couldn't suggest even one that would match your particular needs and pocketbook?

Because sales work is highly competitive, such traits as *aggressiveness and self-confidence* are important for people in this line of work. A manufacturer's representative trying to convince a customer to buy the company's multimillion-dollar computer system, for example, may have to beat out a number of competitors. He or she must be firm and convincing in the sales presentation to company officials and must not hesitate to call back

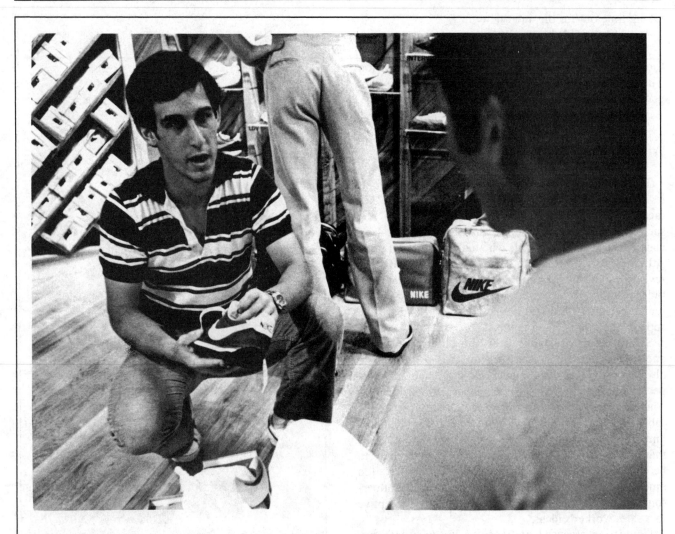

A job selling athletes' footwear may require learning about all the major brands of running shoes.

again and again to explain how the system he or she is selling is superior to what competitors have to offer.

Aggressiveness alone won't make many sales, however. Sales workers also need a keen *understanding of people and human nature.* Sensitivity to people's behavior and to the things that motivate them is quite important. Successful sales workers use this sensitivity to judge when a sales approach is "working" and when it should be changed. This quality is especially helpful in dealing with people buying very expensive items that reflect their self-image as well as affect their pocketbook, such as cars or houses. Real estate agents, for example, must be able to select the kind of properties that will appeal to their clients. Otherwise they won't be able to satisfy their customers' needs, and won't make many sales.

Closely related to understanding people is the *ability to inspire trust and confidence.* Imagine, for example, that you are in the market for insurance to protect your home and family. Would you buy from an agent who didn't seem to know the business and whom you weren't sure you could trust?

Persistence is another characteristic of successful sales workers. A securities sales worker, for example, may call a client many times over a period of months without getting a single order to buy or sell stock. The client may be short of cash, have tax problems, or just not think the time is right to make a move. Eventually, however, conditions usually change, and that client may then become a good customer.

Because of the competitive nature of sales work, people in this field must be *able to work under pressure.* The way many sales workers are paid is one of the reasons the

Sales Occupations

This street vendor has turned her knowledge of plants into a profitable business.

A college degree helped this woman land a job in insurance sales.

field is so competitive. Many firms set quotas, or a minimum number of sales, for their sales workers. Other firms pay neither an hourly wage nor a straight salary to their sales workers; they pay commissions instead. That is, they pay a percentage of the value of the goods that are actually sold. Or, in some cases, many sales workers may be trying to sell the same product, such as a house in the case of real estate agents.

Sales workers often work independently, with little guidance or supervision. This requires the *ability to plan and organize.* Insurance agents, for example, often schedule appointments in the evenings and on weekends, when prospective customers are usually free. It's up to the agent to organize his or her time efficiently—to see clients and take care of paperwork, too.

The ability to plan and organize is nowhere more important than in the sales worker's own financial situation. Sales workers who live on commissions, for example, may have very irregular earnings. A real estate agent may earn $5,000 in 1 week and then nothing at all

during the next several months. Sales workers such as these have to be able to withstand slow sales periods. This means saving during times when earnings are high. The following exercise on setting goals illustrates the kind of planning involved.

Setting goals. Commissions are the only source of income for many sales workers. As a result they often must plan carefully and set sales goals for themselves to be financially secure. If you were in the situation below, what sales goal would you set?

1. The company you work for pays you a commission of 5 percent of the total cost of the items you sell. If you sell $1,000 worth of goods, you make $50; if $2,000, you make $100; and so on. The cost of each item you sell is $500.

2. Your fixed monthly living expenses are as follows:

Rent and utilities $600
Car payment and upkeep 350
Food 300
$1250

Given the above, how many items must you sell each month just to meet your expenses? How many additional items must you sell to pay for the other things you would like to have such as savings, entertainment, eating out, and furniture? Add those two numbers together and you have your monthly sales goal.

Training

Sales work covers a very wide range of occupations—from department store clerk to insurance agent, from people who sell one piece of bubble gum at a time to those who sell $10 million of stock at a time. Training requirements, too, vary a great deal.

In some sales occupations, skills can be obtained relatively quickly right on the job. Gas station attendants, for example, must be able to pump gas, make change, and keep the station clean. These are things they generally learn their first day on the job.

Other sales occupations require advanced degrees in technical fields. Manufacturers' representatives who sell helicopters for aerospace firms, for example, need degrees in aeronautical engineering in order to fully understand the products they sell and to be able to communicate effectively with their customers. In addition to their academic training, sales workers in firms such as these usually receive a thorough orientation in the kinds of aircraft the company makes.

These are the extremes. More information on the training needed for specific sales occupations appears in the Job Facts at the end of this chapter.

Many high schools offer programs in distributive education that provide an excellent background for a wide variety of jobs in sales and merchandising. Students in these programs generally spend half their time in school and the other half working in jobs that provide practical sales experience. They take such courses as an introduction to marketing occupations, general merchandising, fashion merchandising, hotel and motel management, marketing, creative selling, advertising, and food distribution. Practical sales experience comes from working in local businesses, including department stores, grocery stores, and restaurants.

There are college programs that lead to associate, bachelor's, and advanced degrees in such fields as business, marketing, real estate, and insurance. The courses given at community and junior colleges and in 4-year colleges and universities provide a background for selling jobs and also for management jobs in marketing and merchandising.

Business and trade schools offer programs that last from a few months to several years in such fields as marketing, merchandising, and real estate.

In some sales occupations, employers or industry associations offer formal training for beginning and experienced workers alike. Training programs for people who sell securities, insurance, real estate, or automobiles provide a thorough coverage of these fields. Continuing education is important because the regulations affecting sales work in these industries are numerous and complex and because the products or services being offered to the public change, too. Even experienced sales workers must refresh and update their knowledge of the field.

Some sales workers, such as insurance agents and real estate agents, must be licensed by the State in which they work. Others, such as securities sales workers, must be registered with the firm they work for. To qualify for licensing or registration, workers must pass an examination that tests their knowledge of the field they work in. These measures are designed to ensure that sales workers who handle our property or large amounts of our money are properly trained to do so.

Demonstrating a new product is an effective sales technique.

Sales Occupations

Security Sales Worker

Janet Woods sells stocks and bonds for a large brokerage firm.

"Why did I stay up for the late movie?" thought Janet Woods as she turned off her alarm clock and rolled sleepily out of bed at 6:30 a.m. "I've got a busy day ahead, and I'm going to have to be as alert as possible. A lot of people will be asking my advice today, and I also have to teach that class at noon."

An hour and three cups of coffee later, she was in her car on the way to another day at the brokerage house where she had been a securities sales worker for the past 4 years. Janet had joined the firm immediately after receiving her master's degree in finance. The first 2 years were hard, as she struggled to get customers in this very competitive field. But by now she was beginning to achieve real success, and thought she had a good chance of being promoted to office manager someday.

When Janet arrived at her office, a copy of *The Wall Street Journal* was already on her desk. Although the stock market doesn't open till 10 a.m., Janet always arrives at work well before the market opens to read various financial publications and keep up with current developments in the world of business. She also finds this a good time to catch up on her paperwork.

As she was finishing the newspaper, a phone call came through from Jack Martin, a student at Middlesex Junior High, where Janet had given a talk the week before. Jack explained that he had saved about $400 from his paper route over the past year and was interested in investing this money in the stock market. He asked Janet if she would recommend a stock.

"That's hard to do, Jack," Janet said, "unless I have some idea of your investment goals. Are you willing to take a chance on a stock with good potential for capital gain? Or are you interested in a stock that is less sensitive to the ups and downs of the market, but that pays a good dividend?"

"I'm not quite sure what you mean by capital gain," Jack responded. "Is that just the profit you make when you sell a stock?"

"Yes, a capital gain is the profit you make when you sell your stock for more than you paid for it," replied Janet. "And a dividend is the money paid to shareholders out of a company's earnings."

Jack seemed puzzled. "Why can't I buy something that both has a good chance of going up and pays a high dividend? Wouldn't I make much more money that way?"

"That's true, Jack, you probably would if we could pick out such a stock. But we would really have to be lucky. You see, stocks are usually thought of as belonging to one of two broad categories: Growth stocks and income-producing stocks. Many growth stocks do pay some dividends, but the companies usually use most of their profits to help the company expand, rather than pay this money out to shareholders in the form of dividends. Then, because the total worth of the company increases, the company's stock also increases in value. Income-producing stocks, such as utility company stocks, on the other hand, generally are better for people who want a good yield on their money but aren't so concerned with quick capital gains."

"I see that picking a stock is more complicated than I thought," said Jack. "I guess I should learn some more about the stock market before I actually invest. How should I start?"

"I think I can help you with that," replied Janet. "My company has prepared a pamphlet that explains the basics of investing. We also put out a monthly list of recommended stocks, both for capital gain and yield. I'll mail these to you today. By the way, I'd like to commend you on the way you are going about investing your money. You certainly seem to have a good head on your shoulders."

"Thanks—and thank you for your time," Jack said. "I'll call back after I've learned some more."

Janet smiled as she put down the phone. She enjoyed helping young people, especially those as ambitious and eager to learn as Jack. He might be a good customer one day . . . .

Janet knows the importance of having steady customers. In her 4 years as a securities sales worker, she has built a following of investors who have confidence in her judgment. They return time and again to buy and sell stock, and each time Janet earns a commission. In

Janet must keep up with what is happening in the business world.

Sales Occupations

addition, the fact that people trust Janet with large amounts of money makes her feel important.

Around 9:15 Janet received a call from Ellen Swanson, one of her clients. As usual, Ellen got straight to the point.

"Janet, I've just finished that article in this morning's paper on the proposed merger between Carbon Industries and United Copper Company. What is that going to do to the value of my shares in Carbon Industries? Should I sell?"

Janet replied firmly, "I believe the merger will have a favorable effect on your Carbon Industries shares, and I certainly don't think that now is the time to sell." She went on to explain her reasoning, presenting a picture of the industry and its financial workings in a direct, easily understood manner.

"What you're saying makes sense to me," said Ellen. She asked Janet to contact her if there were any further developments and then said good-bye.

"Well, the telephone calls have begun," thought Janet. "I might as well make that call to Mr. Johnson right now." Mr. Johnson had opened an account just the week before.

"Good morning, Mr. Johnson," said Janet a few moments later. "I think that now would be a good time for you to buy AC&C. The price is a little depressed right now due to the downturn in the market, but the stock has an excellent history of earnings and dividend increases and prospects for the future look good. In addition, at its current price the company has a dividend yielding over 7 percent. I believe this is important to you as I know you are looking for income as well as possible capital gain."

"The stock sounds like a good investment," said Mr. Johnson, "but is there any chance of my losing money?"

Janet replied, "Over the next few weeks the stock may go down a little more, of course, but over the long run

Janet has built up a following of customers who want to invest their money.

prospects are excellent for capital gain. In the meantime, you will be receiving good income from dividends, which I believe the company will continue to pay. It has been paying dividends since 1880 and the prospects seem as bright as ever. Of course, not all of your money should be invested in any one company, but I believe AC&C is safe."

"It does seem like good stock to have and I could use the income from dividends," said Mr. Johnson. "Why don't we buy about 300 shares?"

"Good, then, I'll put in an order for 300 shares of AC&C at the market," said Janet.

After hanging up, Janet placed a buy order through the computer for Mr. Johnson's 300 shares of AC&C with the firm's trading department at the stock exchange in New York. There the order would be sent to a trader on the floor of the exchange who would execute the transaction.

When the market opened at 10 o'clock, Janet watched the ticker tape and soon saw a trade for 300 shares of AC&C go by on the tape. Within a few minutes, she received confirmation of the purchase from the New York office of the firm's trading department. Then she called Mr. Johnson to tell him that the trade had been executed.

Janet was very busy for the rest of the morning. She spent much of the time on the phone—talking to customers, confirming buy and sell orders, providing information.

Around noon, two of her co-workers stopped by to ask if she would like to go out to lunch.

"No, thanks," said Janet. "I'm giving the course at the library this week for beginning investors." About once a month, Janet's firm sponsors a 1-week course on investing in stocks and bonds. These courses, conducted by the brokers, provide the public with useful information and enable brokers to speak to a number of people at one time. Often brokers gain additional customers through these seminars.

When Janet returned to her office after the seminar, she found that a number of messages had already piled up on her desk.

"It looks like a busy afternoon ahead," thought Janet as she picked up the phone and began returning her customers' calls.

For the rest of the afternoon, until the market closed at 4, Janet was indeed very busy calling and being called by her clients, placing buy and sell orders and giving her opinion on specific stocks.

After the market closed, things slowed down. Janet stayed at the office for about 45 minutes taking a few buy and sell orders for the next day and exchanging ideas on stocks with some of the other brokers.

Then she checked her calendar to be sure she didn't have any appointments with clients or prospects that evening. Tonight she would catch up on her sleep.

Janet says, "I like knowing that people trust me with their investments."

Sales Occupations

Exploring

Securities sales workers must be articulate and persuasive. Persuading people to buy or sell securities is one of the most important parts of the job.

- Are you a good listener?
- Do you remember what people tell you about themselves?
- Can you tell how people feel about things by talking to them?
- Do you like to campaign for a school office?
- Are you often chosen for group activities?
- Do you like to debate?
- Do you like to speak in front of your class?

Because they often work for commissions, securities sales workers must have initiative and be self-starters.

- Do you get up in the morning by yourself?
- Do you do your homework and household chores without being prodded by your parents?
- Do you stick with projects until they are finished?

Securities sales workers must perform well in a highly competitive situation.

- Do you like being best at the things you do?
- Do you like entering contests and playing competitive games?
- Do you want to be at the top of your class?

Securities sales workers must be optimistic in order to face slow sales periods and downturns in the stock market.

- Are you persistent?
- Do you always assume things will get better?
- When your team loses, do you still look forward to the next game?
- Are you good at cheering up your friends when they are depressed?
- Does failure make you want to try harder?

Unlike many other jobs, success in sales work can be measured directly by the amount of money one makes.

- Is making money important to you?
- Do you like having your performance measured?
- Do you like to be recognized when you do something well?

Exploring Careers

Auto Parts Counter Worker

Norman Edwards is an expert on auto parts. His store stocks over 20,000 different items.

Sales Occupations

Norman Edwards stood behind the counter of Southeast Auto Parts Store. In front of him, he could look out the window past the battery and tool displays at the people and cars passing on the busy street. Behind him, there were about 20 metal shelves, each 7 feet high and about 30 feet long. These shelves contained over 20,000 automobile parts. Norman had memorized the number, use, and price of hundreds of these parts.

It was only 8:30 a.m. and the telephone was ringing again for at least the tenth time since the store had opened at 8:00. "Southeast Auto Parts, may I help you?" said Norman calmly as he pulled a note pad closer to the phone.

"I hope so," answered the caller. "This is Jerry over at Collin's Exxon. Do you have any brake shoes for a 1987 Plymouth Reliant?"

"Just a second, Jerry, let me check," said Norman as he quickly thumbed through his parts catalog to find the proper number for the part. The parts catalog was actually a loosely bound collection of various manufacturers' catalogs. The catalog rested on top of the counter and extended over 4 feet along the counter. Norman quickly found the desired part and checked the number, ST5329. Once he had found the part's number, he knew from memory that he had the part in stock and that the

price was $12.25. If he hadn't known the price, though, he could have checked the current price list that accompanies each manufacturer's catalog.

"We have the part in stock, Jerry. I'll have Susan deliver it in just a few minutes. Do you need anything else?"

"Not right now, thanks," said Jerry.

Norman then turned to the young woman who was stocking shelves behind the counter and said, "Susan, would you get some brake shoes, number ST5329, and deliver them to Collin's Exxon?"

"Sure," said Susan. "Anything else you want while I'm out?" Susan is a driver. It is her job to deliver parts to customers, pick up parts at the warehouse, and help stock parts on the shelves. Sometimes she helps wait on customers when Norman is very busy. Norman himself started out as a driver and in fact learned the trade that way. When he became familiar enough with the business he was promoted to parts counter worker.

Norman then handed Susan a list of numbers of parts that were not in stock but that customers had ordered that morning.

"While you're out, pick these up at the warehouse. I promised we would have them by noon," he said.

Just after Susan left, three customers walked into the

"If you treat people right, they come back again and again. I know a lot of them by name."

store at the same. time "That's how this business is," thought Norman, "it comes in spurts." Norman then waited on the customers at a steady pace. The first wanted a bypass hose for a 1987 Chevrolet Camaro which Norman quickly found was part number CH476. He then got the part off the shelf, wrote out a receipt, and took payment.

Norman's next customer had a problem. His 1985 Chevrolet Van was burning too much oil and he wanted to know if Norman had any ideas for improving this situation.

"What kind of oil are you using in your car now?" Norman asked.

"I believe it's 10–W–30, but I'm not absolutely sure," the customer responded.

"That could be the problem, then," Norman said. "10–W–30 is a fairly thin oil. Why don't you try this 10–W–50? It just might solve your problem. It is much thicker and as a result is not so likely to burn."

The customer said that sounded reasonable and bought 5 quarts of 10–W–50, enough to change the oil in his car.

Norman's next customer was not so easy to please. He wanted a part that independent parts stores, such as the one Norman works in, do not stock. Automobile dealers do, however. Norman politely explained this to the customer and said he was sorry he couldn't be of help this time but to check with him if the customer needed any other parts in the future. He then referred the customer to a local Ford dealer who Norman knew would have the part.

During the time Norman was waiting on the walk-in customers he was also helping customers over the phone. As he spoke, he took orders on a note pad which he always kept beside him.

About 10:30, Jane Bregan walked into the store, greeted Norman, and went to the shelves behind the counter. Jane was a manufacturer's representative and was in the store to be sure that there was an adequate stock of all her company's parts. She would be in the store for another couple of hours, taking inventory on her line of parts and ordering those the store needed.

While Jane was in the back of the store, Norman continued waiting on customers. He knew many of the customers by name and, when business slowed, he would sometimes stop and talk for awhile with them. But lulls didn't occur very often, and never lasted long.

A little after noon, Susan returned, bringing sandwiches from a local carryout for them both. Norman always ate in the store, grabbing a bite when he could. Norman was just about to eat his sandwich when a customer walked into the store.

"May I help you?" Norman asked.

"Yes, I need a new clutch plate for my car. Do you have any in stock?"

"We sure do," said Norman. "What kind of car do you have?"

"It's a 1986 Chevrolet Impala."

"What size engine?" asked Norman.

"I don't know," said the customer.

"Sorry," said Norman, "but I can't get the part unless I know what size engine your car has. General Motors made both 10-inch and 11-inch clutch plates for 1986 Impalas, depending on the number of cubic inches in the engine. I could sell you a clutch plate right now, but there is no way of being sure it would fit without knowing the size of your car's engine."

"Well, I can take both clutch plates and return the one that doesn't fit," replied the customer.

"Sure," said Norman, "but I'll have to charge you now for both of them and give you a refund when you return the one that doesn't work."

"It sounds like you don't trust me," said the customer angrily. "I'll just take my business elsewhere," he added, slamming the door as he stomped out of the store.

Norman was sorry to lose the sale but relieved that the customer had left. When he had first started in the business, Norman had gotten an ulcer from dealing with customers like this one. But by now he was more philosophical. He regarded unreasonable customers as an unavoidable part of dealing with the public. Norman was always polite and tried to help, but it no longer bothered him if a difficult customer went away angry. In fact, thinking of the customer's next encounter with a parts counter worker brought a smile to Norman's face.

Exploring

Parts counter workers deal with the public.

- Do you enjoy talking with people?
- Is it easy for you to talk with people you don't know?
- Do you like giving directions to strangers?
- Can you keep your temper even when people are rude to you?
- Are you good at remembering people's names?

Parts stores, like any other business, require a great deal of organization and recordkeeping in order to run smoothly.

- Do you make lists of things to do?
- Do you finish your homework on time?

Sales Occupations

- Do you like to keep your room neat and orderly?
- Can you find your possessions quickly?

Parts counter workers often work under pressure. They have to work quickly and accurately. They need good memories to keep track of thousands of parts.

- Can you do good work even when you are rushed?
- Do you like playing chess or checkers against a time clock?
- Are you good at remembering your friends' phone numbers, addresses, and birthdays?

Parts counter workers must have a good knowledge of cars and how they work.

- Do you like to read car magazines?
- Are you interested in how things work?
- Do you know what a carburetor is and what it does? A clutch? A shock absorber? How many other auto parts can you name?
- Do you repair your bicycle when it breaks down?
- Do you take things such as old clocks and toasters apart to see how they work? Can you put them back together?

To serve customers faster, Norman has memorized the location of most parts in the store. ''Our customers don't want to waste a lot of time waiting for me to find something.''

Gas Station Attendant

Al Dietrich likes the variety in his job.

Sales Occupations

Al Dietrich had worked the 3-to-11 shift 6 days a week at Simm's Service Station since he had entered the University of Oregon 2 years ago. He was studying to be an accountant and needed a job to help pay his school expenses. Al had jumped at the chance when he heard about the opening at the gas station. He had worked around cars even before he could drive. The hours of his shift were just right since all his classes were in the morning.

Al arrived at Simm's just before 3 p.m. As he entered the office area, he ran into Brian, whose shift was just ending.

"How's it going, Brian? Been busy today?"

"No, I guess the rain is keeping people home," Brian replied. "In fact, I even had time to clean the service bays. I thought you might want to do some studying tonight."

Cleaning the bays was one of Al's jobs and he appreciated Brian's taking on the job himself.

"Thanks a lot. I don't suppose you had time to clean the restrooms, too?" Al said with a grin. That was another of Al's jobs, since he was on the late shift which generally was less busy.

"No, I didn't, but they shouldn't be too bad. See you tomorrow."

Soon after Brian left, Al's first customer of the day pulled into the station in a red Ford pickup. "Fill it up with regular, please," said the customer when Al walked over to the driver's window.

Al turned on the pump, inserted the nozzle, and set the handle at a moderate flow of gas. He walked over to the driver again and asked, "Shall I check under the hood?"

"Thanks, I checked it before I left home, but would you check the tires? I think the left rear one may be a bit low."

"Sure thing," said Al as he began checking the tire pressure with his gauge.

"The front two look okay, 28 pounds each," he said as he walked to the rear of the car. When he checked the left rear tire, though, the gauge read only 24 pounds. Al used the air hose to bring it up to the proper pressure.

Just as he finished recoiling the air hose, the gas pump clicked off. Al finished filling the truck's tank without spilling a drop.

"That will be $18.50," he said. He made change for the $20 bill he was handed and said, "Thanks."

By 6 p.m. in the 3 hours since Al's shift had started, it had gotten very dark. It was quiet; only about a dozen customers had pulled into the station in all that time. Deciding that this would be a good time to clean the restrooms, Al got the cleaning materials out of the storeroom and tackled the job. He had almost finished one of the restrooms when the bell rang to indicate that a customer was out front.

It was a man in a white Pacer with out-of-State plates.

"May I help you?" Al asked.

"Yes," the man replied, "can you tell me how to get to the main highway?"

Al gave him the directions and then asked if he needed any gas.

"No, thanks," said the man as the white Pacer pulled away.

Al headed back toward the restrooms. "If I finish quickly, maybe I can get a little studying done tonight," he thought.

But it was not to be.

"I was tinkering with cars even before I could drive, so in a way this job was made for me."

169

Exploring Careers

Just as Al finished mopping the second restroom, the station's bell rang again. The Dodge did not stop at the pumps, but instead parked in front of one of the service bays.

"Can I help you?" Al asked the driver who had gotten out of her car and was walking towards him.

"I hope so," the customer replied. "I've got a flat tire that needs fixing and I have to drive another 100 miles tonight. And I don't think the spare I have on would make it."

Al glanced at the car's left back tire and noticed that it was worn slick. "I wouldn't trust that spare either," said Al. "Let's take a look at the flat."

The customer opened the trunk of the Dodge and Al took the flat tire into the service bay. He filled it with air and slowly let the water trickle over the tire until he came to a spot where he could see bubbles coming off the tire. "Here's the leak," said Al, as he marked the spot with a piece of chalk. Then he took the tire over to a machine that would help him strip the tire from its rim so it could be patched. After patching the tire, Al used the same machine to put the tire back on the rim. He filled it with air and again checked the tire with a trickle of water to be sure it wasn't leaking air.

"I had better put this tire back on your car now," said Al. He was worried about the customer driving on the worn spare. "Do you want to buy a new tire now to replace that spare?"

Al likes dealing with people. "They make life more interesting."

"Perhaps I should," she replied. "How much would that cost?"

"$54.00 plus tax," said Al.

"Okay, I'll take one," said the customer.

Al put the customer's car on the lift in the service bay. Then he removed the worn spare from the car and replaced it with the tire he had repaired. He took a new tire of the same size down from the rack and put it on the rim of the worn spare. This required repeating much the same procedure as he had used to fix the flat. Finally, he put the new tire in the customer's trunk.

"That should just about do it," said Al.

"Great," said the customer. "How much do I owe you?"

Al wrote up the bill which included $6 for fixing the flat, $4 for changing the tires around, $54 for the new tire, and $3.20 in tax. "That comes to $67.20," said Al. "Will that be cash or charge?"

"Cash," she replied, as she gave Al three twenties and a ten.

Al gave the customer her change, thanked her, and wished her a good trip. Even though he had missed studying, Al was glad to have helped the woman because he would receive a commission on the sale of the tire. In addition, he got a sense of satisfaction from making the woman's trip safer on this cold, rainy night.

Just as the Dodge was pulling out of the station, a late model Cadillac drove up to the pumps. As Al approached, the driver lowered her window and said, "Would you fill it up with premium, please?"

"Sure thing," said Al. "Shall I also check under your hood?"

"The car seems to be running well, thank you. But maybe you could check just to be sure."

Al opened the hood and proceeded to check the water levels in the radiator and battery, the transmission fluid level, and the oil level on the dipstick. He saw that there was plenty of oil in the car, but it seemed very dark in color. He rubbed his fingers around the oil on the dipstick and noticed that it felt gritty.

"It looks like you need to have the oil changed," Al said. "It really seems dirty and that could harm your engine."

"Are you sure you're not just trying to sell me some oil, young man? After all, I've had this car less than a year."

"Oh no, ma'am, the oil is dirty," Al assured her. "How many miles do you have on the car?"

"Well, it had about 25,000 miles when I bought it, and I've put on another 10,000 miles," the woman replied. "Are you sure the oil is dirty?"

"Yes, ma'am," said Al. "And it should be dirty after

10,000 miles. You should have it changed every 6,000 miles or so."

The woman looked skeptical, so Al just closed the hood and finished filling the car with gas. Before she left, however, she told Al that she was taking the car to a dealer next week to get the air-conditioning fixed and would see what they had to say about the oil change.

As the woman drove away, Al smiled to himself because he was pretty sure that once the mechanics at the dealership explained about changing the oil, the woman would remember him and trust him in the future. In fact, she might well become a steady customer at Simm's.

By this time, Al's shift was almost over and he soon saw his replacement, Chet, pull into the station. He spoke to Chet for a few minutes and then went home to study for his cost accounting class which would begin at a very early 9:10 the next morning.

Exploring

Gasoline service station attendants constantly deal with the public.

- Do you like helping people?
- Do you enjoy speaking with strangers?
- Can you give directions to someone who is lost?
- Can you keep your temper even when people are rude to you?

Attendants must make change and fill out credit card slips rapidly and accurately.

- Are you careful when you do your homework or take a test?
- Are you good at adding and subtracting in your head?
- Is your handwriting easy for other people to read?
- Can you do good work even when you are rushed?
- Do you count your change?

Gasoline service station attendants work outdoors and often get greasy and dirty.

- Do you like outdoor sports and recreational activities?
- Do you prefer outdoor chores such as mowing the lawn to indoor ones?
- Are you willing to get your hands dirty?
- Even though you get dirty, can you keep your work area neat and clean?

- Do you like to put gas in the family car at a self-service gas station?

Gas station attendants make minor automobile repairs.

- Are you handy with tools?
- Do you work on your own bicycle?
- Are you interested in automobiles and how they work?
- Before you start working on something, do you think about how you will go about it?

Job Facts

There isn't room in this book for a story about every sales occupation. However, you'll find some important facts about 13 of these occupations in the following section. If you want additional information about any of them, you might begin by consulting the *Occupational Outlook Handbook,* a publication of the Department of Labor which should be available in your school or public library.

Occupation	Nature and Places of Work	Training and Qualifications	Other Information
Automobile Parts Counter Workers	These workers sell replacement parts and accessories for cars, vans, trucks, and other motor vehicles. They also keep parts catalogs and price lists up to date, unpack incoming shipments, and take care of the paperwork. Most work for automobile dealers and parts wholesalers. Others work for truck dealers, retail automobile parts stores, and warehouse distributors of automotive parts. Trucking companies and bus lines employ counter workers to dispense parts to their mechanics.	Counter workers must know the different types and functions of motor vehicle parts and be able to work with numbers. Because they must identify and locate parts quickly, a good memory and the ability to concentrate on details are desirable. Most learn the trade on the job. Beginners usually start as parts deliverers or trainees. Generally it takes about 2 years to become fully qualified. Employers generally look for high school graduates. Courses in automobile mechanics, math, merchandising, and bookkeeping are helpful.	The work is not physically strenuous, but counter workers spend much time on their feet. At busy times, they may be under some pressure waiting on customers and answering the phone at the same time. Many counter workers have to work on Saturdays as well as weekdays, and sometimes Sundays. Some counter workers are members of unions.

Sales Occupations

Occupation	Nature and Places of Work	Training and Qualifications	Other Information
Automobile Sales Workers	These workers sell new and used automobiles and trucks. They contact prospects, appraise the trade-in value of the old vehicles, and arrange for financing, servicing, and delivery of the new one. New car dealers employ most automobile sales workers. The rest work for used car dealers.	Most beginners are trained on the job. Many dealers also provide several days of classroom training on the basics of the job. Automobile manufacturers also offer some training programs and may furnish manuals and other materials. A high school diploma usually is required, and some college may be preferred. Previous sales or public contact experience is helpful. High school courses in public speaking, business arithmetic, merchandising, and business law provide a good background. Sales ability, initiative, and self-confidence are essential. The ability to express oneself well is also important.	Sales workers frequently work evenings and Saturdays because customers find shopping after work convenient. Some also work Sundays and take a day off later in the week. Both employment and earnings of automobile sales workers vary from year to year because new car sales are sensitive to changing business conditions.
Automobile Service Advisers	These workers are the link between customers and mechanics in many large repair shops. When customers bring their cars into the service department, service advisers find out what has to be done and arrange for mechanics to do the work. Most work for large automobile dealers that employ from 1 to 4 advisers. Some work for large independent automobile repair shops.	Service advisers are trained on the job and many work their way into adviser positions after starting as auto mechanics or helping the service department dispatcher. Beginners usually can become qualified in 1 to 2 years, but learning to estimate body repairs may take longer. Employers prefer high school graduates over 21 with experience in auto repair. Courses in auto mechanics, commercial arithmetic, sales, public speaking, and English are helpful. Tact is an important quality for service advisers because they sometimes must deal with unhappy customers.	Service advisers are busiest early in the morning when customers bring their cars and late in the afternoon when they return. Many service advisers are members of unions.
Gasoline Service Station Attendants	These workers sell gas and accessories to motorists. They may also check tire pressure, wash automobile windows, and check crankcase oil level. Service station attendants work in gasoline service stations throughout the country.	Applicants should have a driver's license, an understanding of how automobiles work, and some sales ability. They should know simple arithmetic to make change quickly and help keep business records. They receive most of their training on the job. It can take up to a year to become fully qualified. Many high schools offer formal training programs for students in their last 2 years of high school.	Many service stations stay open 24 hours a day, 7 days a week. As a result, work may include evenings, weekends, and holidays. There are numerous opportunities for part-time work, which makes the occupation attractive for students working their way through school and other workers who want to add to their incomes.

Exploring Careers

Occupation	Nature and Places of Work	Training and Qualifications	Other Information
Insurance Agents and Brokers	These workers sell policies that protect individuals and businesses against future losses and financial pressures. They also help policyholders obtain settlements of insurance claims. About half of the agents and brokers specialize in life insurance while the rest sell liability insurance. A growing number sell both types of insurance.	Most employers prefer college graduates. Courses in sales, accounting, economics, finance, business law, and insurance are helpful. Appropriate personal qualities such as aggressiveness and self-confidence are important. Newly hired workers usually receive training at the agencies where they will work and frequently also at the insurance company's home office. All agents and most brokers must be licensed in the State where they work. Most must pass an examination.	Due to the competitive nature of this field, many workers transfer to other occupations when they are unable to get enough clients to earn a good living. As a result, there are usually numerous openings for individuals with the appropriate personal characteristics.
Manufacturers' Sales Workers	These workers represent companies that manufacture products ranging from computers to can openers. They sell these products mainly to other businesses and to institutions, such as hospitals and schools. Most work out of branch offices, usually in big cities near potential customers. Almost all industries employ manufacturers' sales workers.	Employers generally prefer college graduates. The recommended course of study depends on the product sold. For example, those who work for drug manufacturers usually have studied pharmacy in college. A pleasant personality and appearance and the ability to meet and get along well with people are important. Newly hired workers generally receive formal training from the company before starting the job.	Some manufacturers' sales workers have large territories and do considerable traveling, sometimes on nights and weekends. When on business trips, sales workers are reimbursed for expenses such as transportation and hotels.
Models	Most of these workers model the latest fashion designs and cosmetics. Others pose for a wide variety of products, including cars, soft drinks, and perfume. Clothing manufacturers, designers, and wholesalers employ the largest number of models. Modeling jobs are available in most urban areas, but most are in New York City because it is the center of the fashion industry.	There are no educational requirements for models. Courses in drama, art, and fashion design may be helpful. A model's most important asset is a distinctive and attractive physical appearance. Some models attend modeling schools and a few promising beginners receive training from agencies. Female models must be at least 5 feet 7 inches tall and weigh no more than 120 pounds. Male models must be 6 feet tall and wear a size 40 suit. Most agencies require that models obtain a portfolio of photographs of themselves.	Models sometimes must work under uncomfortable conditions—posing in a swimsuit in midwinter, for example. Competition for modeling jobs is very keen.

Sales Occupations

Occupation	Nature and Places of Work	Training and Qualifications	Other Information
Real Estate Agents and Brokers	Real estate agents and brokers represent property owners in selling or renting their property. Most work for small real estate firms, but a few work for builders to sell homes in a particular development. Real estate is sold in all areas, but employment is concentrated in urban areas and smaller, but rapidly growing, communities.	High school graduation is generally the minimum requirement. Many employers prefer college graduates. Courses in math, business law, real estate, and finance are helpful. Many colleges and universities offer degrees in real estate. Personality traits are fully as important as academic background. Real estate firms look for applicants who have a pleasant personality and neat appearance. Maturity, tact, and enthusiasm for the job also are important. Many firms offer formal training programs for real estate sales workers. All States and the District of Columbia require sales workers and brokers to pass a written examination and to be licensed.	Agents and brokers often work evenings and weekends to suit the convenience of customers.
Retail Trade Sales Workers	In addition to selling, these workers make out sales or charge slips, receive cash payments, and give change and receipts. They also handle returns and exchanges of merchandise and keep their work areas neat. Most work in retail stores ranging in size from small drug stores to huge department stores. They also work for door-to-door sales companies and for mail-order houses. Jobs are available in almost every community but most sales workers are employed in large cities and nearby suburban areas.	Employers prefer high school graduates. Some high schools have programs that teach the principles of retail selling. Most sales workers learn their skills on the job. In large stores, training programs for newly hired workers usually begin with several days of classroom instruction followed by on-the-job training under the supervision of an experienced worker.	Because Saturday is a busy day for stores, employees usually work that day and have a weekday off. Sales workers may work very long hours before Christmas and during other peak periods. There are many opportunities for part-time employment during peak periods.

Exploring Careers

Occupation	Nature and Places of Work	Training and Qualifications	Other Information
Travel Agents	Travel agents help their customers plan trips. They suggest itineraries and points of interest, make hotel reservations, arrange for transportation, and handle other details. In making arrangements, they consult fare schedules and fact sheets for hotel ratings and other tourist information. About one-half of all travel agencies are located in large cities, one-third are in suburban areas, and one-fifth are in small towns and rural areas.	Most agencies provide either formal or informal on-the-job training programs for their agents. Working part time or during summers as a reservation clerk or receptionist in a travel agency provides useful experience. Several home study courses also provide a basic understanding of the travel industry. Since the ability to speak of personal experiences frequently helps influence customers' travel plans, broad travel experience is an important qualification. Travel agents should have pleasant personalities and patience. Agents should be efficient and responsible. High school courses in geography, foreign languages, and history are helpful.	One travel agent in four is self-employed. However, agents going into business for themselves should be prepared for low earnings for the first few years they are in the business. Travel agents frequently travel at substantially reduced rates. Sometimes a hotel or resort will offer a travel agent a free holiday. Many agents, especially those who are self-employed, frequently work overtime.
Wholesale Trade Sales Workers	These workers sell for wholesale houses that distribute goods to retail stores and consumers. Many are employed by wholesalers or distributors who handle machinery, building materials, food products, drugs, drygoods, motor vehicle parts, or electrical appliances. Wholesale houses usually are located in big cities, but sales workers may be assigned territories in any part of the country.	High school graduation is the usual requirement although some sales jobs require college training. Courses such as commercial arithmetic and merchandising are helpful. Selling certain products requires more specialized training. Those who work for drug wholesalers, for example, would find courses in biology, chemistry, and pharmacy helpful. Workers usually begin as trainees and are trained in non-selling jobs before being assigned to sales. Trainee programs usually involve classroom instruction as well as rotations to non-selling jobs. Generally 2 years or longer are required before trainees are ready for their own territories.	Sales workers often have long, irregular work hours and frequently have to travel in their work. Most companies provide cars for their sales workers or reimburse them for their expenses while on the road.

Sales Occupations

Occupation	Nature and Places of Work	Training and Qualifications	Other Information
Route Drivers	These workers sell and deliver goods and services such as dairy products and drycleaning directly to customers. Most work for small companies that distribute food products or provide personal services, for example, dairies, bakeries, food and beverage distribution firms, and drycleaning plants. Jobs are available in small towns as well as in large cities.	Most States require that route drivers have a chauffeur's license. Most employers prefer applicants who are high school graduates and over 25 years of age. Courses in sales techniques, public speaking, driver training, and bookkeeping are helpful. Some large companies have classes in sales techniques, but training is mostly on the job.	Route drivers have to make deliveries in all kinds of weather and do considerable lifting, carrying, and walking. Many start work very early in the morning. For many route drivers, the fact that they do not work under close supervision is an attractive part of the job.
Securities Sales Workers	These workers buy and sell stocks and bonds for individuals. They also give market advice, and keep records on customer accounts. Securities sales workers are employed by brokerage firms, investment banks, and mutual funds in all parts of the country. Most, however, work for large firms with offices in big cities.	Employers prefer college graduates with degrees in business administration, economics, finance, or liberal arts. Successful sales or managerial experience helps because many employers look for specific personality traits and signs of sales ability. Most States require persons who sell securities to be licensed and registered. Examinations and character investigations are required for registration. Most employers provide training to help sales workers meet the requirements for registration.	Securities sales workers work fairly regular hours although they may meet with customers on evenings and weekends.

When you have your own shop, your duties are many, including product inventory.

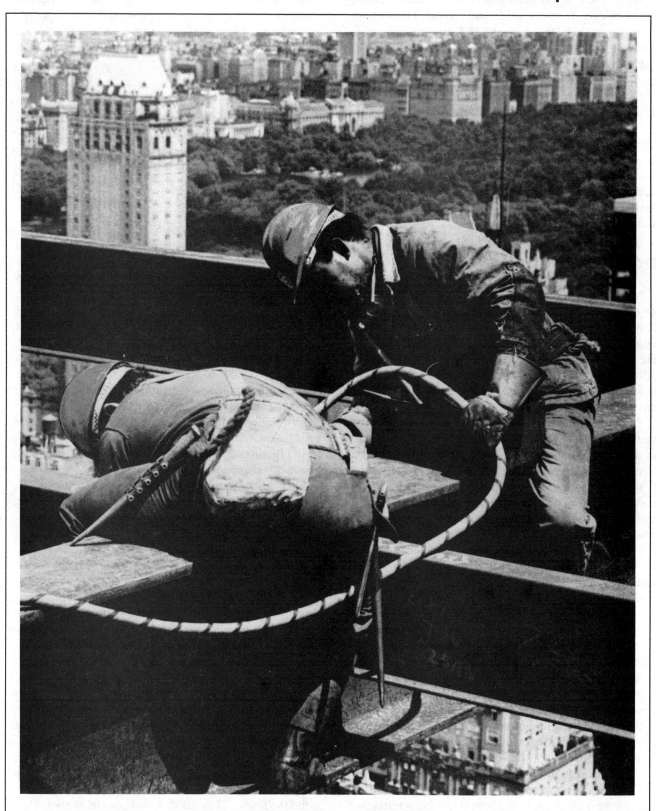

Ironworkers high above the city are protected by a system of belts and ties.

Exploring Careers

We live in a world of structures of all kinds: Houses, stores, bridges, factories, roads, and schools. Think about your community for a moment and see how many different structures you can name.

Putting up a building requires the effort of people with many different skills. At every stage, from clearing the site to putting on such finishing touches as signs or door knockers, construction means a team effort. Although the members of this "team" aren't all on the site at the same time, they depend on each other. To get an idea of how this works, let's see what's involved in building a house. We'll follow the progress of the Wright family's house, which you'll read more about in the story about the architect in the chapter on Performing Arts, Design, and Communications Occupations.

Before the Framework Goes Up

A lot had to be done before the house could begin to go up. First, the Wrights' *architect,* Jack Myers, had to design the house and draw up blueprints for the construction workers to follow. Blueprints are plans that show the general layout of the building and give such detailed information as the exact measurements of rooms, windows, and doors and the places where pipes, wires, and ducts should be placed.

Then the builder, or *contractor,* had to obtain all the materials, equipment, and labor. It's the contractor's job to make sure that every phase of the work is done on schedule, so that the house will be finished when the Wrights are ready to move in. This means checking to make sure that the job is being done properly and maintaining an inventory of supplies so that workers don't waste precious time waiting for materials to be delivered. The contractor already has obtained the building permit, a legal document that is required before construction can begin. The permit shows that the Wright house meets county zoning regulations for the site where they plan to build. Several months ago, after obtaining the building permit for the Wrights' house, the contractor hired a *surveyor.* The surveyor measured the land and drew maps that showed boundary lines and such features as roads and underground utility lines.

What else has to be done? The land must be prepared. That will happen soon, for the *operating engineers* are scheduled to arrive tomorrow with their bulldozers and other earth-moving equipment. A hill will have to be leveled and, in spite of the Wrights' desire to save them, several trees will have to be cut down.

The operating engineers are among the first construction workers on the site. Helping them are *construction laborers,* or "helpers", who have work to do during nearly every stage of the building. Once the operating engineers have prepared the ground, the surveyor will come back and use stakes and lines to lay out the exact location of the house on the property.

The Structure Rises

Once the land is ready, it will be time for the foundation to be laid. A building as heavy as a house rests on a foundation buried in the ground. This is done so that the weight of the building will rest on the hard, solidly packed ground below the frost line. Otherwise it might develop structural damage, such as cracks and doors and windows that won't open.

The foundation starts with "footings"—large blocks of concrete that are completely sunk into the ground. Footings are placed under the edges of the house and at certain points inside where there will be extra weight—under a fireplace or porch, for example. The first step in laying the foundation is digging trenches for the footings. An excavation crew of operating engineers will dig out, or excavate, the earth to make room for the footings. Then *cement masons* will pour wet concrete into the trenches. Pouring concrete is hard work that requires strength and stamina. Sometimes this job is done by a crew of construction laborers rather than by the more highly skilled cement masons. Once the concrete is set, bricklayers will come in and place cinder blocks on top of the footings and build the foundation wall to slightly above the ground surface.

Then it's time for utilities to be brought in from the street. Such utilities as water, sewerage, and gas are brought to individual houses by means of undergound pipes called mains that run beneath the streets. The floor of a new house cannot be laid until these water, sewer, and gas mains are tapped and connecting pipes attached that will lead into the house.

After the utility pipes have been brought up through the ground inside the outer boundary of the house, cement masons will pour a slab floor. They will pour the concrete carefully, making sure it is level, and smooth it down as it hardens to give it an even finish. They'll keep the concrete moist while it's "curing" to make sure it will be hard and strong when it dries. It's not unusual for cement masons to work overtime, because once the concrete is poured they must stay on the job until it is completed.

With the foundation and slab floor in place, *carpenters* can begin work on the wooden frame of the house. Carpenters follow the architect's blueprints when they build the frame. They use different sizes of lumber: Studs for the walls, joists for the attic floors, and rafters for the

Construction Occupations

Laying concrete is a team effort.

roof. They will begin by building the wall framework, nailing pieces of lumber together and securing them to the foundation with metal bolts. The carpenters must be sure to place the studs a certain number of inches apart, as called for in the building code. They must be sure to leave spaces for windows and doors.

As soon as the wall frame is up, the carpenters will build the attic floor frame and the roof frame. On top of the roof frame they'll place sheets of plywood called roof decking. Then *roofers* will come in and put roofing felt or tar paper on the roof deck. Since the architect decided long ago that asphalt shingles would be best for the Wrights' house, that's what the contractor has bought. When the time comes, the roofers will put them on. The roofers will also add gutters, downspouts, and flashing around the chimney and edges of the roof to prevent water from running down the sides of the house when it rains.

Once the roofers have finished, it will be time to put up the outside walls of the house. As the first step,

carpenters will nail sheathing boards across the outside of the wall frame. They also will install windows at this stage. When the windows and sheathing board are in place, the outside walls can go up. The Wrights' house will have brick on the front and sides, and aluminum siding on the rear.

Bricklayers will lay the brick. They will have to be sure that the walls are straight and level and that they intersect at right angles. The bricklayers must follow the architect's blueprints very carefully. They have to pay attention to every detail, making sure that the rows of brick line up with doors and windows, for example. Helping them will be *hod carriers* or *mason tenders* who mix the mortar and make sure the bricklayers don't run out of materials.

The aluminum siding for the rear of the house is made at the factory, but the carpenters who install it measure and cut it at the job site. They nail the panels in place and add molding at corners and along windows and doors to give a neat finish.

181

Carpenters work quickly and accurately with hand tools or power tools.

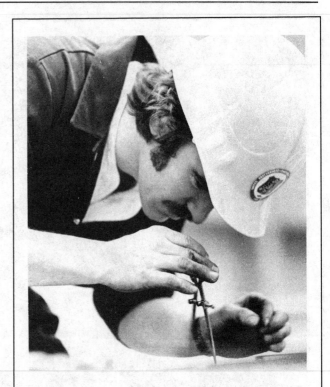

Precision measuring instruments are required in some construction trades.

A mask protects this plumber's eyes when she is welding.

Construction offers good opportunities for young people who are willing to spend several years learning a trade.

Construction Occupations

Moving Indoors

All the workers you've read about so far have outdoor jobs. Working together, they'll build the "shell" of the Wrights' house. But there still will be a lot to do before the family can move in.

You've seen how the water, sewer, and gas mains will be tapped before the slab floor is laid down. Until more work is done, the ends of pipes will simply stick out of the floor in the utility room, kitchen, and bathroom. When the time comes, *plumbers* will come in and install the fresh water pipes and the drainage system within the house. They will put pipes inside the walls before closing them up on the inside so that the pipes aren't visible when the house is finished.

Plumbers will install heating and air-conditioning units, too. The Wrights will use electricity to heat their house. Warm air will be sent throughout the building by means of a system of thin-walled rectangular pipes called ducts. *Sheet-metal workers* have already made the ducts at the shop; later they'll bring them to the construction site to install them. The sheet-metal workers will install ductwork inside the walls and ceiling, making sure that there are outlets or registers in each room. They also will install return air ducts so that the air will circulate back to the air conditioner or furnace.

Since both the plumbing and the ductwork are installed inside the walls or ceiling, they're hard to get at once the house is finished. For this reason, the plumbers and sheet-metal workers will have to be very careful to install the pipes and ducts correctly in the first place. They may have to work in awkward or cramped positions to do this.

Another important utility that will be installed is electricity. To do this, *electricians* will connect a cable from the street to the house. They'll bring the cable to the house and attach it to a meter, which measures the flow of electricity, and then to a distribution panel. From this panel the electricians will connect more wires that lead to electrical outlets and switches all over the house. The electricians run these circuit wires inside the walls and ceiling and floors, being careful not to let them interfere with the metal ductwork or plumbing system.

To save energy and keep the house warmer in winter and cooler in summer, insulation will be applied to the insides of the outer walls and to the attic floor. Insulation also helps absorb noise and prevents water vapor from passing through the walls. *Insulation workers* will cut strips of fiberglass or other insulating material to the right length, and then staple each strip into place inside the wood framework. They also will cover the ducts and pipes that carry hot air or water.

Like many construction workers, this painter has his own contracting business.

After the utilities have been roughed in and the insulating materials installed, the finishing work can begin. There will be a lot for the finishing workers to do, for the inside of the house will be no more than a wooden skeleton.

Drywall installers will close up the walls and ceilings by nailing wallboard panels to the wooden framework inside the house. They will cover all joints and nail holes with tape and joint compound, and make sure the surface of the wallboard is smooth and ready for painting.

Years of experience enable this floor installer to work quickly.

Once the wallboard has been installed, *painters* will arrive on the scene. The painters will paint the walls and ceilings, using brushes, rollers, or spray guns. They need to know the characteristics of different paints, and how to mix different colors. Since Mr. and Mrs. Wright want wallpaper on the bedroom walls, *paperhangers* will be needed too. Both the painters and the paperhangers must be skilled at what they do so that they can work rapidly but neatly.

Floor covering installers will be on the job then also. These workers will finish the floors by putting hardwood, resilient tile, or carpeting on top of the concrete slab floor. *Tilesetters* will come in to lay ceramic tile on the floors and walls of the bathrooms.

Finishing carpenters will install the interior wooden trim: Casings around windows and doors and base and shoe moldings where the walls meet the floor. The finishing carpenters also will hang the doors, being careful to make sure each door is the right size and that it hangs straight.

Fixtures and accessories will have to be installed. The plumber will return to put in sinks and bathroom fixtures such as bathtubs and toilets. Finishing carpenters will install kitchen cabinets and counter tops. The electrician will come back to install overhead lights and light switches. The painter will return to finish the hardwood floors, the trim, and any marred or damaged areas.

Various finishing jobs often overlap, so cooperation is essential. The different craftworkers will have to be careful not to get in each other's way or spoil the work that others have done. All of the finishing work affects the final look of the house, and therefore requires careful attention to detail.

As the inside of the house nears completion, cement masons will return to lay the sidewalks and driveway. A *landscaper* will come in to plant grass, shrubs, or small trees. And then one last step is necessary. A crew of construction laborers will clean up the inside of the house and the work site, and carry away debris left by the finishing workers. Finally, the house will be ready for the Wrights.

Other Jobs in the Building Trades

A large project such as a high-rise apartment or an office building requires many more workers than a house. Furthermore, it requires some very specialized workers. On construction projects as large as these, there are jobs for *elevator constructors,* workers who install elevators in high-rise buildings. And jobs for *glaziers,* who install glass on wall surfaces or put in windows. *Ironworkers* erect the steel framework and other metal parts in big buildings, bridges, and other structures. Plaster, rather than drywall, is used to cover walls and ceilings in many commercial buildings. Before any plastering is done, *lathers* install supports such as metal lath or gypsum lath board to hold the plaster, stucco, or concrete materials. *Plasterers* then finish interior walls and ceilings with plaster coatings and apply durable cement plaster or stucco to exterior surfaces. *Marble setters* install marble facing on walls, columns, and floors. *Terrazzo workers* apply terrazzo to floors in buildings such as stores, offices, and hospitals. Terrazzo is tinted concrete with which marble chips are mixed.

What it Takes to be a Construction Worker

As you have just seen, construction takes a team effort. Much of the work takes place one step at a time, and almost every step depends on another having been completed. Cement masons cannot pour concrete footings, for example, until the land has been cleared and trenches have been dug. Carpenters cannot begin nailing up the wall framework until the foundation has been laid. Walls cannot be finished until utilities are installed. Each worker depends on others doing their jobs well and without delay. Since it takes the skills of many different

Construction Occupations

Glaziers install all types of building glass.

Many people like the physical activity of construction jobs.

people to put up a building, *construction workers must be able to work well with others.* They must be willing to take orders from those in charge, do their share of the work, and cooperate so that no one gets in anyone else's way.

What other traits are important for people in the building trades? For plumbers, painters, electricians, carpenters, bricklayers, and others whose work requires a high degree of skill, a talent for *working with one's hands* is important. It takes manual dexterity to work quickly and accurately with handtools such as the trowels, hammers, mallets, and chisels that bricklayers use. Or to cut and shape wood with portable power saws and drills as a carpenter does. Do you like working with your hands? Are you good at working with tools or machinery? Are you mechanically inclined? These qualities are essential in the building trades.

Skilled construction workers often are called upon to *solve mechanical or structural problems.* A tilesetter might be asked, for example, to create an intricate design in tile for an outdoor patio. With general guidelines from the architect, a plumber might have to plan the layout of a plumbing system for a specific room to make the best use of limited materials and space. Coming up with a workable solution requires that the worker know a great

deal about his or her craft. It takes expert knowledge of both the theoretical and practical aspects of a craft or trade to figure out the best way of handling a particular problem.

Much construction work requires *precision.* Workers such as electricians and plumbers must meet strict standards of accuracy in their work; they need to be able to take measurements and calculate dimensions quickly and accurately. This is such an important aspect of construction work that apprenticeship programs generally include one or more courses in applied mathematics.

Many construction workers need to be able to *picture objects from blueprints* and read scale drawings. Also important is an *eye for detail*—the ability to see slight differences and detect flaws in shapes or surfaces. Painters in particular require good *color discrimination* in order to match colors and shades, and to select those that go well together.

Many people prefer construction work because it so often is *outdoor work.* Working outside is enjoyable when the weather is nice, of course. But construction workers have to be prepared to work outside on days when the weather is terrible. Do you spend a lot of time outdoors right now? Would you be willing to work outside in cold or very hot weather?

A 4-year apprenticeship program is the best way to become an electrician.

Finally, every aspect of construction work involves *physical activity*. If you like exercise, one of the construction trades may be just right for you. A willingness to be physically active on the job certainly is a "must" for anyone interested in entering the field, for people in the building trades do a lot of standing, stooping, bending, squatting, stretching, or kneeling. Some construction workers do a great deal of heavy lifting. Moreover, they don't get much time to rest. They must keep moving all the time, working steadily. Depending on the job, construction work can take a lot of strength and stamina.

What the Job Offers You

You've just read about personal traits that are important for construction work. There are other things to consider as well. What about wages? Chances for promotion? Steadiness of the job? Opportunities to go into business for yourself?

The building trades generally offer high hourly pay. Being paid by the hour means that the total earnings of construction workers are affected by how many hours they work. During good times, there's lots of work for everyone. Since construction workers receive extra pay for overtime work, they sometimes can make a lot of money by working overtime to finish a project by a certain deadline.

On the other hand, in construction there's no promise of steady employment. Some construction workers are employed for years by a single contractor, but others must seek a new job after each project is completed. And even if you work for a single contractor, you can't always be sure how many hours you'll work. Construction activity often swings from highs to lows. Building generally is curtailed in the winter when it's very cold, snowy, or rainy. Fewer new homes are built when the economy is in a slump. Work on a big project may stop altogether because of a business failure. A delay in obtaining building materials can lead to temporary layoffs. In these cases being paid by the hour means not getting paid at all for time you don't work. If you're considering construction work, you should be prepared for periods when your income would be uncertain.

Construction Occupations

The building trades offer an opportunity to work your way up to a supervisory position, particularly for workers who are ambitious, and good at what they do. Experience also improves chances for promotion. An experienced worker might be promoted to a position supervising other workers of that craft. After several years he or she might become a construction superintendent, and then perhaps a project manager. Many people in the building trades eventually begin businesses of their own. This is especially true of carpenters, floor covering installers, painters and paperhangers, plasterers, and tilesetters. As their businesses expand, they may employ other workers and become contractors. Sometimes construction workers move into office positions as estimators.

Training

How do people enter the building trades? What do you need to know to get a job? Most construction workers are skilled craftworkers. They learn their trade through several years of on-the-job training—or by completing an apprenticeship or other training program that may take as long as 4 years. Individual training requirements for each of the construction occupations are listed in the Job Facts at the end of the chapter.

Apprenticeship programs, offered by local union and employer groups working together, are a good way of learning one of the construction trades. These programs combine actual work experience with classroom instruction, and may last anywhere from 2 years (cement masons, drywall installers, lathers) to 4 years (carpenters, electricians, glaziers, insulation workers, plumbers, and sheet-metal workers). "Apprenticeship" comes from a French word meaning "to learn", and if you choose this way of training for a trade, you'll need to be serious about learning.

Not everyone trains for construction work in an apprenticeship program, however. Many people learn the construction trades on the job, by working with experienced construction workers in their community. A summer construction job while you're still in high school can be a good way to find out if you're suited for this work.

Construction offers good opportunities for young people who are willing to spend several years learning a trade. Most high schools offer classes in mathematics, mechanical drawing, drafting and design, and shop. Many have programs in the building trades, and offer courses in bricklaying, carpentry, electricity, plumbing, heating and air conditioning, and general maintenance mechanics. These classes provide good experience, because you work with the same kinds of machines and tools in class that you'd use on the job. Such high school

Many people choose construction work because of the high hourly pay.

courses may give you the skills to land your first job or open the way for further training. Some programs give building trades students an opportunity to participate in the construction or renovation of houses through actual on-the-job work experience.

Bricklayer

Andy considers himself lucky to get into the apprenticeship program. "I'm being paid good money to learn a highly skilled trade."

Andy walked onto the site and saw Joe, the bricklayer supervisor, examining some blueprints. "Hi," he said, yawning as he approached. "What time is it? This site *would* have to be way on the other side of town. I had to get up an hour and a half earlier than usual this morning to allow enough time to get here."

The supervisor look up, glanced at his watch and said, "It's 7:15. I'm glad you got here a little early today. You can help me lay out these walls."

Andy was an apprentice bricklayer. At the age of 23 he was more than halfway through his 3-year apprenticeship program. The program had two parts: On-the-job training every day and classroom instruction 2 nights a week.

Andy considered himself lucky to have been accepted for apprenticeship. First there had been the aptitude test, and then the oral interview with the union apprenticeship committee. The committee had asked him about his school record, his interests, his hobbies. The last question had been the hardest: What makes you think you'd be a good bricklayer? Andy had passed the interview with flying colors, but even then he had to wait nearly a year before there was an opening. The apprenticeship committee accepts people into the program only a few at a time—it all depends on the amount of construction activity in the area, and the need to train more bricklayers. The committee tries to train only as many bricklayers as there are jobs.

Andy was pleased with the way things were going for him. He was learning a skill and getting paid while learning. Every 6 months since he had started, the apprenticeship committee had examined his progress, and each time they'd promoted him and raised his pay. When he had first started the program he had been paid only about half the usual hourly wage for experienced bricklayers, but the amount had been increasing steadily. Soon he'd be making as much as any experienced bricklayer. Andy knew that with the apprenticeship committee constantly reviewing his progress he couldn't afford to waste time on the job, or skip classes, or be late for work. So there he was even though he'd rather have been home in bed.

That morning Andy and the other bricklayers in the crew were to begin laying the exterior walls of a high-rise apartment building. Andy had learned long ago that there's more to being a bricklayer than just slapping bricks together in a haphazard fashion. Bricklaying, he had discovered, is a precise activity, and there is a lot of measuring to do before the first brick is laid.

The bricklayer supervisor must study the architect's blueprints and compare the dimensions indicated there to the actual surface on which they're working. The blueprints tell the length and width and height of the walls to be built and the kinds of materials to be used. They show the size and locations of doors and windows, the pattern in which the bricks or blocks are to be placed (known as the pattern bond), the number of units needed for a row or "course" of brick or block, and the size of the joints between units. The bricklayers need all of this information before they can begin laying any bricks or blocks.

Andy walked over to look at the architect's blueprints with Joe. Right away, he saw that the wall they were about to build was a composite wall. This meant that the wall was to be made of row upon row of cement block faced with rows of brick. The parallel rows are called wythes. The brick facing and block backing would be bonded with metal wall ties at regular intervals for added strength. The architect had specified exactly what types of brick and block and wall ties to use.

The first step in laying out such walls as these is marking the dimensions on the foundation. Andy and Joe began measuring in from one of the corners of the foundation. They checked the dimensions of the foundation against the dimensions given in the blueprints.

"Let's start laying the bricks out dry," Joe said.

The two bricklayers laid a course of bricks without mortar in order to space them correctly. Then Joe marked the spaces where there were to be doors and windows to make sure that the units would be placed properly around those openings to allow for a strong bond.

Andy got up from his kneeling position and looked at the layout. "It looks pretty good," he said. Joe nodded.

By now the other bricklayers had arrived. In addition to Andy and Joe there were six bricklayers and eight helpers, called mason tenders or hod carriers.

"You'll be working with Fred," Joe told Andy. "He's been doing this for a long time, and he'll be able to help you out if you have any problems." Joe made sure that all of the other bricklayers saw the markings for the doors and windows.

A mason tender brought a batch of freshly mixed mortar, and the bricklayers picked up their trowels. Fred moved to one of the corners. He cut into a pan of wet mortar with his trowel, spread the mortar thickly on the foundation surface, and then pressed a brick into place. He picked up another brick, "buttered" one end of it with mortar, and pressed it into place next to the first brick. After placing each brick in place, he used his trowel to cut off the excess mortar that had been squeezed out from the brick joints.

Andy watched Fred for a while, admiring the single flowing motion with which he loaded the trowel and spread the mortar. Then he stepped up and began helping the other man. Together, they built the outside corner

"There's a lot of more to being a bricklayer than just slapping bricks together. It's very precise work."

to talk and let your mind wander while you're working," thought Andy as he listened to some of the other bricklayers joking with each other. The other people on the job really helped make the work enjoyable.

When they finished the sixth course of the brick wall, Andy stopped and examined the work he and Fred had done so far. His arms and back were tired from stooping over and lifting the bricks, but he was pleased with the wall. The sight of the finished brick work made him feel good. The mortar joints between courses still needed to be finished, so Andy picked up a tool called a jointer and ran it along the edge of each joint. The jointer left an indentation in the mortar that made the joints look much neater than before.

The sun was very strong now. Andy could feel it burning his face and arms. His shirt was soaked with perspiration. There wasn't much shade around, nowhere to escape from the heat. "Isn't it lunchtime yet?" Andy wondered.

Minutes later, Joe called out, "Let's break for lunch now. You have half an hour." Then he walked over to Andy and Fred and examined the work they had just completed.

"When we get back," he said, "we'll lay the block backing inside the brickwork."

Andy nodded. Then he looked over at Fred, who grinned and said, "Let's find some shade to sit in so we can cool off. I've got to get out of the sun for a while. And the way you've been working, you must be pretty hot and tired yourself. You're not so bad, you know."

"Thanks," Andy replied, flashing a broad smile. Then the two bricklayers walked off to pick up their lunch bags.

Exploring

Bricklayers work with their hands. They use handtools such as trowels, hammers, and chisels. Sometimes they use power tools.

- Do you enjoy activities that involve working with your hands, such as building ships or airplane models, building or refinishing furniture, making ceramics, weaving, doing macrame, making stained glass, or making candles?
- Are you accustomed to using tools for work around the house or garden, or for repairing bicycles or lawn mowers?
- Do you help put up shelving, install screens or storm windows, replace loose shingles, or fix loose boards or stair railings?
- Do you enjoy learning how to use a tool you've never used before?

of brick, and inside it another one of block. The other bricklayers had split up into smaller groups and had moved to other sections of the building. There they were building corners just as Fred and Andy were doing.

It didn't take long for the crew of bricklayers to build the corners to the desired height. Then they began to lay the brick wall between the corners. First they stretched a line betwen the corner units at the top of the first course. The line was a guide for keeping the bricks all at an even height, as well as for keeping the row straight. Then they began laying the first course of bricks. On top of the first course they laid a second, then a third, and so on until the wall was six courses high.

The motions involved in laying brick are repetitive, and soon Andy was moving at a quick pace. Andy and Fred talked for a while about the upcoming World Series, but then lapsed into silence. "It's nice to be able

Construction Occupations

"Talking and joking with the other bricklayers is one of the best parts of this job."

Bricklayers follow blueprints and diagrams.

- Can you read and understand graphs, diagrams, and charts?
- Can you read roadmaps?
- Can you look at a drawing and picture the three-dimensional object in your mind?
- Do you understand football or basketball plays when they're written out?
- Can you follow the diagrams in the service booklet for a refrigerator, air-conditioner, or dishwasher?

Bricklayers need a working knowledge of mathematics.

- Do you know how to take measurements and calculate fractions, proportions, and percentages?

Bricklayers do strenuous outdoor work. The job involves
a lot of lifting, standing, and stooping.

- Are you in good physical condition?
- Do you enjoy outdoor sports and recreational activities, such as football, baseball, softball, track and field, hunting, fishing, climbing, hiking, or camping?
- Do you prefer mowing the lawn or working in the garden to working indoors?

Carpenter

Brenda has always liked building things. ''In high school, I built the props for plays.''

Construction Occupations

"Hey, get that other clamp over there, will you?" Brenda says. She guides a panel of wood into place as the crane swings it towards her. Steve wedges another panel into place while Pete brings the metal clamp, places it on the form, and tightens it. The column form they are building consists of four wooden panels clamped together at opposite corners. They work in silence for a few minutes, placing the clamps about a foot apart all the way to the top. At last, the form stands secure—a tall, boxlike structure about 16 feet high and 4 feet square.

Brenda and Steve are carpenters. Pete is a carpenter's helper. The work they're doing—building concrete forms—is called "rough carpentry". The forms are molds into which wet concrete can be poured to create the large concrete columns that will support the ceiling of a parking garage. Next year there will be a large office building here, and the parking garage will occupy the first two underground levels. High buildings require a lot of concrete, and wherever there's concrete to be poured, carpenters are on the job—building the forms that provide the shape for the concrete.

Brenda and her co-workers are working outside, in the center of the second level of the parking garage. Since there aren't any columns up yet in the area where they're working, there's no concrete slab above to serve as a

Brenda feels that being a carpenter helps her stay in good physical condition.

roof. Luckily, the sun is out and it's a beautiful spring day.

Today Brenda, Steve, and Pete will spend most of the day putting up column forms. Tomorrow, they're likely to be doing something different. The parking garage is in many different stages of construction, most of which require some kind of rough carpentry.

At one end of the parking garage, the second level is just being started. There a crew of carpenters is laying down the plywood decking onto which the wet concrete will be poured to form the second-level slab floor.

At the other end, things are further along. The slab floor for the second level has been laid and columns already are in place. There another crew of carpenters is busy putting up the lumber that will support or brace the plywood decking onto which the concrete slab above will be poured. To do this, the carpenters nail or brace pieces of lumber called jacks, ribs, and stringers to form an overhead frame on which they can nail the sheets of plywood.

"Maybe we'll be working over there by the end of the week," Brenda thinks to herself. She's not looking forward to it. Putting up the ribs and stringers can be dangerous work. To put up the ribs, for example, the carpenters often balance on one rib (a long piece of lumber only 4 inches wide and 4 inches thick) while they're spreading down the one next to it. Just last week one of the carpenters fell backwards off a rib and landed on his back 15 feet below. He's in the hospital now and will be out of work for some time. The carpenters have to be especially careful to avoid that kind of accident.

Brenda will probably spend most of tomorrow stripping column forms. She'll remove the forms from columns in which the concrete has begun to set. That can be a rough job, because the wooden forms stick very tightly to the concrete that has hardened against them, and the carpenters must use a combination of leverage and strength to get them off. Once the carpenters have stripped the forms, they'll coat the insides with form oil to help the forms separate more easily from the hardened concrete next time they're used. When this fluid dries overnight, the forms will be ready to be used again the next day.

As soon as they finish one form, Brenda moves on and begins constructing the next one. You never know when a supervisor's going to be watching you, she figures, and those who don't do their share of the work are most likely to be laid off when things get slow.

"Hey, you don't get tired very easily, do you? Where'd you learn carpentry, anyway? You're good!"

Brenda smiles at the compliment, so different from the treatment she's gotten at other jobs. Why, just a few years ago, people always seemed to be asking why she

Brenda has lunch with her co-workers.

wanted to do "a man's job." Brenda never thought of carpentry as "man's work." It's something she's always been good at and enjoyed doing. Suddenly she realizes that Steve is waiting for an answer.

"Well, I just picked it up, I guess," she begins. "The way you did, probably. I was always building things as a kid. Then, in high school, I got interested in the theater and built the props for plays. The more carpentry work I did, the more I found myself enjoying it.

"That was all there was to it until I found out how much carpenters get paid around here! The chance to make a lot of money convinced me to try to make a career of carpentry. Right after high school I applied for a job with a small construction company that needed carpenters pretty badly. Since then I've gained experience and picked up new skills by working on different kinds of construction jobs.

"Now," she says, changing the subject, "why don't we get this last form built and then move over to the other side?"

There are plenty of people working on the site today. Construction jobs haven't been so easy to come by lately, and so most of these workers feel lucky to be out here working. At least Brenda doesn't have to drive too far to get to work each day. Some of the other carpenters live in another State, and have to commute over 3 hours each way to get to and from work. "When you have to be at work at 7 a.m., that makes for a very long day," she thinks.

Besides the carpenters, the workers on the construction site are mostly cement masons or rodbusters. The rod-busters work with the form carpenters, preparing for the pouring of the concrete. Their job is to install the steel rods that will give added strength to each column. The rodbusters attach the steel rods with wire to other steel rods, called dowels, that are sticking up out of the concrete slab. Once this is done the spot is ready for the carpenters to come and build the form around the rods.

Carpenters have been on the site almost since construction began. When the form work runs out, most of the form carpenters will move on to another site to begin the same type of work on another project. However, Brenda will try to stay on at this site and do some of the other carpentry jobs that will need to be done, installing dry-wall, for example. In times like these, when construction isn't exactly booming, Brenda knows that to stay employed year-round it helps to be versatile. She's made it a point to learn to handle as many different kinds of carpentry work as possible. During the 5 years she's worked as a carpenter she's learned how to install acoustical tile and drywall, and how to hang doors. These skills, she believes, give her an advantage over some of the other carpenters.

"So, do you think you're going to stay on in construction?" Steve asks as they move over to another column location.

"Sure," Brenda replies quickly. "Maybe someday I'll have a contracting business of my own."

"Great idea," says Steve. "Well, you know what you're doing, that's for sure."

As he walks away, she thinks to herself, "Doing a good job is what counts, after all." Brenda takes pride in

Construction Occupations

doing work of high quality and knows that she's earned the respect of most of her fellow workers. She's looking forward to many more years in carpentry.

Exploring

Carpenters work with their hands. They use both hand and power tools and must handle their tools quickly and skillfully.

- Do you like working with your hands?
- Are you handy with repairs around the house?
- Are you good at working with tools?
- Do you enjoy such activities as building ship or airplane models, building or refinishing furniture, framing pictures, making ceramics, weaving, or doing macrame?
- Are you accustomed to using tools for work around the house or garden, or for repairing bicycles or lawn mowers?
- Have you ever helped put up shelving, install screens or storm windows, replace loose shingles, paint, or fix loose boards or stair railings?
- Do you enjoy learning how to use a tool you've never used before?

Carpenters follow blueprints and diagrams.

- Can you read and understand graphs, diagrams, and charts?
- Can you read road maps?
- Can you look at a drawing and picture the three-dimensional object in your mind?
- Do you understand football or basketball plays when they're written out?
- Can you follow the diagrams in the service booklet for a refrigerator, air-conditioner, or dishwasher?

Carpenters need a working knowledge of mathematics.

- Do you know how to take measurements and calculate fractions, proportions, and percentages?

Carpenters do strenuous outdoor work. The job sometimes involves prolonged standing, climbing, and squatting.

- Are you in good physical condition?
- Do you enjoy outdoor sports and recreational activities, such as football, baseball or softball, track and field, hunting, fishing, climbing, hiking or camping?
- Do you prefer mowing the lawn or working in the garden to working indoors?

"Someday I hope to have a contracting business of my own," says Brenda.

Plumber

Bob looks over plans for the school's plumbing system.

Construction Occupations

Bob makes his way down the main hall of what soon will be a brand new high school. Painters are on the job now, and Bob has to step carefully around their equipment—ladders, paintbrushes, rollers, cans of paint, and dropcloths.

Bob's in charge of a crew of plumbers. He's been around this site almost since construction began and knows the layout of this building backwards and forwards. Not only does he know the blueprints, he helped design the plumbing system that runs through every part of the building much like the blood vessels in our own bodies. Installing the plumbing for this school was a big job. Bob guided the other plumbers through the entire process, relying on the basic knowledge he gained during his apprenticeship, and the 8 years of experience he's had since then.

The plumbing crew arrived at the site over a year ago, right after the excavation crew left. One of their first jobs was tapping the water and gas mains that lie beneath the city streets. This involved drilling a hole in each of the mains running under Market Street, where the school is located, and installing pipe to run from the main to the school. The plumbers installed underground piping systems for the fresh water that would be brought to the school, as well as for the natural gas that would fuel the school's heating system.

At the same time, the plumbing crew installed the underground clay pipes that carry water waste away from the school. This job involved installing two separate systems of pipes—a sanitary sewer system and a storm sewer system. The school's sanitary sewer system feeds into the city system, which in turn carries waste to the local sewage treatment plant. A separate piping system was installed to handle water runoff. The school's storm sewer system drains water from the athletic fields, from the school parking lot, and from the yard right around the building. Not all of the storm runoff can be thrown together immediately, however. The water from the parking lot, for example, will have oil deposits mixed in it which must be filtered out before this water can be mixed with other runoff and emptied into a lake or river. The plumbers therefore had to lead pipes from the parking lot to a separate chamber where the rainwater runoff could be cleaned up before being channelled into the city's storm sewer system. Installing all that underground pipe took quite some time.

Through the windows that line one side of the hall, Bob sees that it's still gloomy and overcast outside. The weather reminds him of the rainy spring they had while they were putting in those sewer pipes. The plumbers lost more work time than usual because of the heavy rains. And when the rain let up, they found themselves ankle-deep in mud. It wasn't exactly a picnic, working outside in a fine rain, slipping and sliding in the mud. But how quickly a sunny day restored everyone's spirits! On those beautiful days in May, Bob and his crew forgot all their gripes about the weather. In fact, they had had quite a few laughs about all those people with indoor jobs who couldn't enjoy the great weather . . .

After the underground piping systems were installed, the plumbers left the site while the shell of the building was put up. Then the plumbers returned to install pipes inside the walls, ceilings and floors. Although the architect had shown in his floor plans where the fixtures would be placed and how the pipes would run, his diagram actually left much to the plumbers' ingenuity. Using the architect's plans as a guide, Bob and Ted Jones, the plumbing contractor Bob works for, drew up detailed plans for the plumbing system. These plans showed the other plumbers exactly where to lay the pipes, what angles to use at each turn, what size pipes, and what kinds of supports to use.

The plumbers had to design and install several different piping systems for use inside the school. There were the hot and cold water lines that led to the bathroom sinks and to the sinks in the home economics room. Other cold water lines led to sinks in the art rooms and the science laboratories, and to the water fountains in the halls. Cold water lines also led into the fire extinguisher system. In addition, drainage pipes had to be led away from each of the fixtures, and venting pipes had to be installed to allow air into the drain system.

Bob turns a corner in the hall and heads toward the locker rooms at the back of the school to check on the plumbers' progress there. On the way he passes Jack, one of the young plumber apprentices, who is installing metal registers in the hallway. These registers are the last part of the school's heating system to be installed. Earlier, the plumbers had installed the furnace that will burn the gas to heat the air.

"How's it going, Jack?" Bob calls out.

"Just fine," answers Jack, looking up quickly.

Jack's a good worker. He takes his job seriously and never hesitates to ask questions if there's something he's not sure of. Something about Jack's determination to make the most of his apprenticeship reminds Bob of his own start in the trade.

Bob had been accepted in the apprenticeship program right after he graduated from high school. The program lasted 4 years, and during that time Bob was assigned to a variety of projects, from large office buildings to small housing developments. Twice a week he attended classes at night. The combination of classroom instruction and on-the-job training gave him the thorough preparation he needed for becoming skilled and versatile in his trade. After serving his apprenticeship, Bob spent the next 5

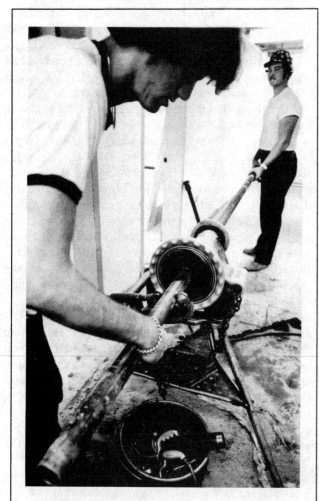

Bob helps Jack cut pipe. Jack is learning the trade through a 4-year apprenticeship.

done, when to do it, and what problems to expect. If he handles jobs like this one as well as he expects to, he may be able to move up to the job of project superintendent before too long. That would mean overseeing an entire construction job and coordinating the work of people in all the building trades, not just the plumbers.

Bob's thoughts are interrupted as he notices Carl walking toward him from the other end of the hall. Carl's a veteran member of his plumbing crew.

"Say, Bob," Carl calls out. "The truck with the sinks and toilets just pulled up, and we're starting to unload. We can start installing the fixtures right away. Do you want us to start with the locker rooms?"

"Right," Bob answers. "I'm going that way right now."

The plumbing crew had put in the piping systems and supports some time ago, before the inside walls were closed up. Heavy fixtures like large sinks and water fountains need plenty of support, so the plumbers had mounted special hangers, screwed into strong supporting braces inside the walls. Now that the walls were finished, there was no sign of any of this plumbing work. Only the fixtures that they were about to install would give evidence of the plumbers' hard work.

Bob makes his way outside now to watch a group of construction laborers unloading some of these fixtures from a large truck.

"Careful, now," he warns as he approaches the truck, where one laborer is pulling at a commode. "That's about 60 pounds of pretty expensive china." The laborer reaches for it more carefully, picks it up and takes it into the school. The plumbers must be strong enough to hold such fixtures in place while bolting them into the wall.

Bob watches while more commodes, some sinks, and some water fountains are unloaded. Things have been running smoothly today, and Bob is feeling good about his job. Bob thrives on his work as a supervisor; he likes organizing the work, supervising the other plumbers, and managing day-to-day problems. And since he likes being on the go all the time, the busy pace is fine with him. He's learning a lot, too. His job gives him a broad view of all the phases of a construction project, and how they fit together. Plumbing is still his favorite construction activity, of course. And in his job as supervisor, Bob has gotten a clearer idea of the variety of tasks that this craft entails. With that thought, Bob turns to go back into the school.

Exploring

Plumbers work with their hands, using handtools such as wrenches, hammers, chisels, and saws. Sometimes they use power tools and gas or acetylene torches.

years working at a number of different jobs. As soon as he heard of a construction project nearby, he'd apply for work and stay with the job until the plumbing installation was finished. Then he'd move on to another construction site. Three years ago, Bob decided that he wanted a more permanent job. That's when he started working for Ted Jones, the plumbing contractor. Ted was impressed with Bob's work and his knowledge of the field, so impressed that after less than 2 years he put Bob in charge of the other plumbers in his crew.

This school is the biggest plumbing project Bob's been responsible for so far. Although he was in charge of the plumbing crews on two other projects last year, they were much smaller jobs. However, the solid training he had as an apprentice and his years of experience as a plumber make him sure of himself, even in a job this big. He's been around construction for more than a dozen years, after all—long enough to know what needs to be

Construction Occupations

Carl is the most experienced plumber on Bob's crew.

- Do you enjoy activities that involve working with your hands, such as building ship or airplane models, building or refinishing furniture, framing pictures, making ceramics, doing macrame, or making candles?
- Are you good at working with tools?
- Do you enjoy learning how to use a tool you've never used before?
- Are you handy with repairs around the house?
- Do you help put up shelving, install screens or storm windows, fix loose boards or stair railings, or fix leaky faucets?
- Do you know how to repair a bicycle or lawn mower?
- Do you enjoy working on motorcycle or automobile engines?

Plumbers often have to search for the cause of a problem. They need to know mechanical principles and understand how things work.

- Are you curious about how things work?
- Would you take something apart—your bicycle or an alarm clock, for example—just to see how it's put together?
- Do you try to solve problems in an orderly and logical way?
- Are you persistent? Will you work on a problem until you solve it?

Plumbers follow blueprints and diagrams.

- Can you read and understand graphs, diagrams, and charts?
- Can you read roadmaps?
- Can you look at a drawing and picture the three-dimensional object in your mind?
- Do you understand football or basketball plays when they're written out?

- Can you follow the diagrams in the service booklet for a refrigerator, air-conditioner, or dishwasher?

Plumbers need a working knowledge of mathematics and science.

- Do you enjoy mathematics and science courses?
- Do you know how to take measurements and calculate fractions, proportions, and percentages?

Each plumbing job is a little different from the rest.

- Do you like variety and change in your daily or weekly schedule?

A plumber's work can be strenuous. It involves a lot of standing, stooping, lifting, and squatting. Much of it is done outdoors.

- Are you in good physical condition?
- Do you like to be active most of the time?
- Do you enjoy outdoor sports and recreational activities, such as football, bicycling, softball, track and field, hunting, fishing, climbing, hiking, or camping?
- Do you prefer mowing the lawn or working in the garden to working indoors?

Construction Occupations

Job Facts

There isn't room in this book for a story about every construction occupation. However, you'll find some important facts about 19 of these occupations in the following section. If you want additional information about any of them, you might begin by consulting the Department of Labor's *Occupational Outlook Handbook*, which should be available in your school or public library.

Exploring Careers

Occupation	Nature and Places of Work	Training and Qualifications	Other Information
Bricklayers, Stonemasons, and Marble Setters	Workers in these crafts build and repair structures such as walls, fireplaces, patios, and walkways using brick, tile, terra cotta, marble, and other materials. Most work for building contractors. Bricklayers work throughout the country, but most stonemasons and marble setters work in metropolitan areas. In cities that are too small to have a demand for full-time masons or setters, bricklayers may install stone or marble as a sideline. Many bricklayers are self-employed and specialize in contracting on small jobs such as patios and fireplaces. Bricklayers work on all kinds of buildings, but because stone and marble are expensive, stonemasons and marble setters work mostly on high cost buildings such as offices, hotels, and churches.	Most bricklayers, stonemasons, and marble setters learn their skills informally by working as helpers or hod carriers. They start with carrying materials, moving scaffolds, and mixing mortar. It takes several months to a year before they are taught to spread mortar and lay brick. Other workers in these crafts learn their skills through apprenticeship, which involves 3 years of on-the-job training plus classroom instruction in such subjects as blueprint reading, mathematics, and sketching. A high school education is important for entry into an apprenticeship program. Manual dexterity is important, because these workers use handtools such as trowels, brick and stone hammers, wood or rubber mallets, and chisels. For exacting cuts of brick, stone, or marble, they use electric saws with special cutting blades. The work can be strenuous because it involves lifting and prolonged stooping and standing. Most of the work is performed outdoors.	Many bricklayers, stone masons, and marble setters are union members.

Construction Occupations

Occupation	Nature and Places of Work	Training and Qualifications	Other Information
Carpenters	Carpenters construct, remodel, and repair wooden structures. They are the most numerous of all building trades workers, and work in almost every kind of construction activity. The work is commonly divided into two categories: "rough" and "finish" carpentry. Rough carpentry involves erecting the wooden framework of a building, making forms for concrete, and putting up scaffolds. Finish carpenters install molding, wood paneling, cabinets, window sash, and so forth. Skilled carpenters can do both kinds of work. Most carpenters work for contractors, but many are self-employed. Some carpenters alternate between working for contractors and doing small jobs on their own. Some carpenters do construction work in factories, government installations, mines, shipyards, and large buildings.	An apprenticeship program is recommended as the best way to learn carpentry. Apprenticeship usually consists of 4 years of on-the-job training plus classroom instruction in drafting and blueprint reading, mathematics, and the use of woodworking machines. Training may also be acquired on the job. A high school education or its equivalent is desirable. Some knowledge of the trade may be obtained through vocational school courses in carpentry and shop. Manual dexterity is important because carpenters use handtools such as hammers, saws, chisels, and planes and power tools such as portable power saws, drills, and rivet guns. Good physical condition, a good sense of balance, and a lack of fear of working at heights also are important attributes for carpenters.	Carpenters have greater opportunities than most other construction workers to become supervisors since they are involved in the entire construction process. Some become contractors and run their own businesses. Many carpenters are union members.
Cement Masons and Terrazzo Workers	Cement masons mix, pour, and finish concrete for projects ranging in size from small patios to large office buildings to huge dams. Terrazzo workers apply a mixture of concrete and marble chips to surfaces to create attractive floors and walkways. Most masons specialize in small jobs, such as driveways, sidewalks, and patios; most terrazzo workers specialize in floors. Cement masons work for general contractors who construct entire projects, and for contractors who only do concrete work. Most terrazzo workers work for special trade contractors who install decorative floors and wall panels.	Cement masons and terrazzo workers learn their trade either through on-the-job training as helpers or through 2- or 3-year apprenticeships. On the job, helpers begin with simple tasks, but usually are doing finishing work within a year. In the apprenticeship program, apprentices learn applied mathematics, blueprint reading, and safety. Three-year apprentices receive special instruction in layout work and estimating. Masonry or terrazzo work is active and strenuous, and requires much stooping, bending, and kneeling. Cement masons and terrazzo workers therefore need physical strength and stamina.	Cement masons often work overtime, because once the concrete has been poured the job must be completed. They generally receive premium pay for overtime work. Many cement masons and terrazzo workers are union members.

Exploring Careers

Occupation	Nature and Places of Work	Training and Qualifications	Other Information
Construction Laborers	Laborers under the direction of other trade workers provide much of the routine physical labor on construction and demolition projects. They erect and dismantle scaffolding and clean up rubble and debris. Laborers also help unload and deliver materials, machinery, and equipment to other construction workers. Construction laborers work on all types of construction projects. They work for construction contractors, for State and city public works and highway departments, and for public utility companies.	Little formal training is required for work as a construction laborer. Generally, applicants must be at least 18 years old and in good physical condition.	Construction laborers are usually the first workers to arrive on a construction project—assisting in site preparation—and the last to leave. After several years of experience and training, many laborers advance to craft jobs, such as carpenter, bricklayer, or cement mason. Some construction laborers are union members.
Drywall Installers and Finishers	Drywall installers create inside walls by fastening drywall panels to the framework inside houses and other buildings. Finishers do touchup work to get the panels in shape for painting. Most drywall installers and finishers work for contractors that specialize in drywall construction; others work for contractors that do all kinds of construction. In many small towns, carpenters install drywall and painters finish it.	Drywall installers and finishers usually start as helpers and learn most of their skills on the job. Some employers, in cooperation with unions, offer classroom instruction to supplement on-the-job training. Apprenticeship programs last about 2 years. Drywall installers must have the stamina to spend most of the day on their feet, standing, bending, stooping, or squatting. They must be able to lift and maneuver heavy panels.	Some drywall installers and finishers are union members.

Construction Occupations

Occupation	Nature and Places of Work	Training and Qualifications	Other Information
Electricians	Construction electricians install electrical systems that operate heating, lighting, power, air-conditioning, and refrigeration components. These workers also install electrical machinery, electronic equipment and controls, and signal and communications systems. Most construction electricians work for electrical contractors. Many others are self-employed contractors.	Most training authorities recommend the completion of a 4-year apprenticeship program as the best way to learn the electrical trade. However, some people learn the trade informally by working for many years as electricians' helpers. Many helpers gain additional knowledge through trade school or correspondence courses, or through special training in the Armed Forces. Electricians must be able to work in cramped places and in awkward positions, to stand for long periods of time, and to climb ladders and balance themselves while working. Finger dexterity is important for working rapidly and accurately with small handtools such as pliers, screwdrivers, and knives. Normal color vision is important because workers frequently must identify wires by color. A license is necessary for employment as an electrician in some cities.	The seasonal nature of construction work affects electricians less than workers in most building trades, because so much of their work is indoors. Many electricians are union members.
Elevator Constructors	Elevator constructors assemble and install elevators, escalators, and similar equipment. After it is in service, they maintain and repair it. Most elevator constructors are employed by elevator manufacturers. Others are employed by small, local contractors who specialize in elevator maintenance and repair. Still others work for government agencies or business establishments that do their own elevator maintenance and repair.	Almost all elevator constructors learn their job primarily through on-the-job training supplemented by classroom instruction. A trainee usually can become a fully qualified constructor within 4 years. A high school education is required. Some States and cities require elevator constructors to pass a licensing examination. To install and repair modern elevators, elevator constructors must have a working knowledge of electricity, electronics, and hydraulics. They also must be able to repair electric motors, control systems, and signal systems. Because of the variety of their work, they use many different handtools, power tools, and testing meters and gauges. The ability to work at great heights without fear is important.	Unlike most other construction trades people, elevator constructors usually work year round. When construction of new buildings declines, the construction of new elevators and escalators does also, but the demand for the repair and maintenance of older elevators and escalators remains constant. Most elevator constructors are union members.

Exploring Careers

Occupation	Nature and Places of Work	Training and Qualifications	Other Information
Floor Covering Installers	Floor covering installers install and replace carpet or resilient floor covering materials such as tile, linoleum, and vinyl sheets. Most installers work for flooring contractors. Many others work for retailers of floor covering and home alteration and repair contractors. About four-fifths work primarily with carpet, and the remainder with resilient flooring. About 1 out of 4 floor covering installers is self-employed, a higher proportion than the average for all building trades. Installers are employed throughout the Nation, but most are concentrated in urban areas that have high levels of construction activity.	The vast majority of floor covering installers learn their trade informally on the job by working as helpers to experienced installers. Most others learn through formal apprenticeship programs, which include on-the-job training as well as related classroom instruction. Courses in general mathematics and shop may provide a helpful background for floor covering work. High school graduates are preferred. Floor covering installers must be able to stand, bend, and kneel for long periods of time, to work in awkward positions, and to work rapidly and accurately with small handtools.	Floor covering installers generally specialize in either carpet or resilient floor covering installation, although some do both types. Many floor covering installers are union members.
Glaziers	Construction glaziers cut and install all types of building glass, including windows, glass doors, and mirrors, and also install steel sash. Most glaziers work for glazing contractors in new construction, alteration, and repair. Others work for government agencies or businesses that do their own construction work. Glaziers work throughout the country, but jobs are concentrated in metropolitan areas. Glaziers occasionally may travel to work for a day or two in small outlying towns where few people, if any, are equipped and qualified to install glass in commercial buildings such as stores.	Most glaziers learn their trade through a 4-year apprenticeship program. Others learn the trade informally on the job by assisting experienced workers. Learning the trade through on-the-job experience can take considerably longer than through apprenticeship. A high school diploma is generally desired for helpers, and is required for apprenticeship applicants. Courses in general mathematics, blueprint reading or mechanical drawing, general construction, and shop provide a helpful background. Glaziers need manual dexterity and the physical ability to carry plates of glass and climb, reach, and stretch while installing the glass.	Many glaziers are union members.

Construction Occupations

Occupation	Nature and Places of Work	Training and Qualifications	Other Information
Insulation Workers	Insulation workers cover surfaces such as walls, ducts, pipes, and tanks with insulation materials that prevent excessive loss of cool or hot air. Most insulation workers work for insulation contractors. Others are employed to alter and maintain insulated pipework in chemical factories, petroleum refineries, power plants, and similar structures which have extensive steam installations for power, heating, and cooling. Some large firms which have cold-storage facilities also employ these workers for maintenance and repair.	Almost all insulation workers learn their trade through either informal on-the-job training or a formal 4-year "improvership" program similar to apprenticeship. A high school diploma is preferred for entry level jobs, and is required for improvership positions. High school courses in blueprint reading, shop math, and general construction provide a helpful background. Insulation workers must have the physical stamina to spend most of the day on their feet, standing, bending, stooping, or squatting. They should not be afraid to work on ladders or in tight spaces.	Many insulation workers are union members.
Ironworkers	Ironworkers put up the steel framework and other metal parts of buildings, bridges, and other structures. They also deliver heavy machinery to new sites. Most ironworkers work for general contractors, steel erection contractors, or ornamental iron contractors. Many work for large steel companies or their subsidiaries engaged in the construction of bridges, dams, and large buildings. Some work for government agencies, public utilities, or large industrial firms that do their own construction work.	Most training authorities recommend the completion of an apprenticeship as the best way to learn these trades. Some people, however, learn the trades informally by working as helpers to experienced ironworkers. Applicants for the 3-year apprenticeship program generally must have a high school education. Courses in general mathematics and mechanical drawing provide a helpful background. Since materials used in ironworking trades are heavy and bulky, above-average physical strength is necessary. Agility and a good sense of balance also are required in order to work at great heights and on narrow footings.	Ironworkers comprise four related trades—structural ironworkers, riggers and machine movers, ornamental ironworkers, and reinforcing ironworkers. Many ironworkers are skilled in two of these trades or more. Ironwork can involve considerable travel because demand in an area may be insufficient to keep local crews continually employed. Many ironworkers are union members.

Exploring Careers

Occupation	Nature and Places of Work	Training and Qualifications	Other Information
Lathers	Lathers install lath—the base for wet cement—plaster, or stucco on walls and ceilings. Most lathers work for lathing and plastering contractors on new residential, commercial, or industrial construction. They also work on modernization and alteration jobs. A relatively small number of lathers are employed outside the construction industry; for example, some make the lath backing for plaster display materials or scenery.	Although many lathers acquire their skills on the job, apprenticeship is recommended. Apprenticeship programs usually last a minimum of 2 years, and include classroom instruction in applied mathematics, blueprint reading, sketching, estimating, basic welding, and safety. Apprenticeship applicants usually are required to have a high school education or its equivalent. Courses in general mathematics and mechanical drawing can provide a helpful background. Lathers need manual dexterity and mechanical ability. Although a lather's work is not strenuous, it does require standing, squatting, or working overhead for long periods.	Many lathers are union members.
Operating Engineers	Operating engineers run the power construction equipment used to excavate and grade earth, erect structural and reinforcing steel, and pour concrete. Workers are often identified by the type of machine they operate. For example, they may be known as crane operators, bulldozer operators, or derrick operators. Most operating engineers work for contractors in highway, dam, airport, and other large-scale construction projects. Others work for utility companies, manufacturers, and other business firms that do their own construction work, as well as State and local highway and public works departments. Some work in factories and mines to operate cranes, hoists, and other power-driven machinery.	Most training authorities recommend completion of a 3-year apprenticeship as the best way to become an operating engineer. Apprentices learn to operate a variety of machines, and receive classroom instruction in engine operation and repair, cable splicing, hydraulics, welding, and safety and first aid. Less extensive training is available through special heavy-equipment training schools. Courses in driver education and automobile mechanics provide a helpful background. Experience in operating tractors and other farm machinery also is helpful. Operating engineers need stamina to withstand high noise levels and constant shakes and jolts from the machines.	The range of skills for operating engineers may vary widely because they work with many different types of machines. Heavy machines (like large cranes) are usually complex and difficult to operate; medium-sized equipment (like bulldozers) generally requires less skill, and lightweight equipment (such as air compressors) is the easiest to operate. Some operating engineers know how to operate several kinds of machines. Many operating engineers are union members.

Construction Occupations

Occupation	Nature and Places of Work	Training and Qualifications	Other Information
Painters and Paperhangers	Painters apply coats of paint, varnish, stain, enamel, or lacquer to decorate and protect building surfaces. Paperhangers cover walls and ceilings of rooms with decorative wallpaper, fabrics, vinyl, or similar materials. Many painters and paperhangers work for contractors who do new construction, repair, alteration, or modernization work. Many organizations that own or manage extensive property holdings also employ maintenance painters. A high proportion of workers in these trades are in business for themselves.	Most training authorities recommend the completion of a formal apprenticeship as the best way to become a painter or paperhanger. However, because apprenticeship programs are limited, many new workers begin as helpers to experienced painters. Generally, painters only paint. Paperhangers, however, both paint and hang wallpaper. As a result, paperhangers require more training and additional skills, and a larger percentage of paperhangers than painters are trained through apprenticeship. A high school education is preferred for both occupations. Painters and paperhangers must have stamina, because their jobs require a considerable amount of climbing and bending, as well as standing for long periods. Painters in particular should not be afraid of heights. A painter also must have strong arms, because much of the work is done with arms raised overhead. Manual dexterity and good color sense are important.	Many painters and paperhangers are union members.
Plasterers	Plasterers apply coats of plaster to finish interior walls and ceilings. They apply durable cement plaster or stucco to exterior surfaces. Plasterers work mostly on new construction and alteration work, particularly where special architectural and lighting effects are part of the job. Some plasterers repair older buildings.	Most training authorities recommend completion of a 3- or 4-year apprenticeship as the best way to learn plastering. However, many people learn the trade by working as helpers or laborers, observing and being taught by experienced plasterers. Courses in general mathematics, mechanical drawing, and shop provide a useful background. Manual dexterity is important. Strength and stamina are also necessary, because plastering requires considerable standing, stooping, and lifting.	Many plasterers are union members.

Exploring Careers

Occupation	Nature and Places of Work	Training and Qualifications	Other Information
Plumbers and Pipefitters	Plumbers and pipefitters assemble, install, and repair pipe systems that carry water, steam, air, or other liquids and gases. They also install plumbing fixtures, appliances, and heating and refrigeration units. Most plumbers and pipefitters work for plumbing and pipefitting contractors engaged in new construction activity, and work mainly at the construction site. Many plumbers are self-employed or work for plumbing contractors doing repair, alteration, or modernization work. Some plumbers install and maintain pipe systems for government agencies and public utilities, and some work on the construction of ships and aircraft. Others do maintenance work in industrial and commercial buildings. Pipefitters, in particular, are employed as maintenance personnel in the petroleum, chemical, and food-processing industries where manufacturing operations include the processing of liquids and gases through pipes.	A 4-year apprenticeship including related classroom instruction is recommended as the best way to learn all aspects of the plumbing or pipefitting trade. However, many people learn plumbing or pipefitting by working for several years as helpers to experienced plumbers or pipefitters. A high school or vocational school education is recommended. Courses in chemistry, general mathematics, mechanical drawing, physics, and shop are helpful. Some localities require workers to pass a licensing examination. Manual dexterity and mechanical ability are important. Plumbers must also be able to stand for long periods and occasionally must work in cramped or uncomfortable positions.	Some plumbers and pipefitters are union members.
Roofers	Roofers install and repair roofing using such materials as sheet metal, tile, slate, asphalt shingles, composition, felt, tar, and gravel. They may also waterproof walls and floors. Most roofers work for roofing contractors on construction or repair jobs. Some work for businesses and government agencies that do their own construction and repair work. A few roofers are self-employed.	A 3-year apprenticeship including related classroom instruction is recommended. Most roofers, however, acquire their skills informally by working as helpers for experienced roofers. A high school education is helpful for people interested in becoming roofers. Courses in mechanical drawing and basic mathematics are especially helpful. Good physical condition, a good sense of balance, and an ability to work at heights without fear are important assets.	Roofers have to be outdoors in all kinds of weather, and the work can be very hot in the summer months. Many roofers are union members.

Construction Occupations

Occupation	Nature and Places of Work	Training and Qualifications	Other Information
Sheet-Metal Workers	Sheet-metal workers make and install sheet-metal ducts for air-conditioning, heating, and ventilating systems; flat metal for kitchen walls and counters; and stamped metal for roofing and siding. Some workers specialize in onsite installation. Some work primarily in shops doing fabricating and layout work. Others do both. Sheet-metal workers in the construction industry are employed mainly by contractors who specialize in heating, refrigeration, and air-conditioning equipment, and by general contractors engaged in residential, industrial, and commercial building. Additional sheet-metal workers are employed by government agencies or businesses that do their own construction and alteration work. Very few are self-employed.	A 4-year apprenticeship program is recommended, and most sheet-metal workers learn their skills this way. Many others, however, have acquired their skills by working as helpers to experienced workers. A high school education is required for entry to apprenticeship programs, and courses in mathematics, mechanical drawing, and shop provide a helpful background. Sheet-metal workers need to be able to work high above the ground at times. At other times, they must be able to work in cramped and awkward positions. Good physical condition is important.	Many sheet-metal workers are union members.
Tilesetters	Tilesetters apply tile to floors, walls, and ceilings. Tilesetters are employed mainly in nonresidential construction projects, such as schools, hospitals, and public and commercial buildings. A significant proportion of tilesetters—about 1 out of 5—is self-employed.	A 3-year apprenticeship program is recommended as the best way to learn tilesetting. Many tilesetters, however, acquire their skills informally by working as helpers to experienced workers. When hiring apprentices or helpers, employers usually prefer high school or vocational school graduates who have had courses in general mathematics, mechanical drawing, and shop. Good physical condition, manual dexterity, and a good sense of color harmony are important assets.	Since tilesetters work mostly indoors, the annual number of hours they work generally is higher than some of the other construction crafts. Many tilesetters are union members.

Apprenticeship training helped this carpenter
develop a high standard of workmanship.

This flight engineer is checking out her jet before takeoff.

Exploring Careers

Earnings of airline pilots are among the highest in the Nation.

Well-designed cabs reduce the strain of truckdriving.

Coming from the West

The Midwestern plane began a smooth descent as it neared Lambert Field, the St. Louis international airport. Walter Faraday, the pilot on Flight 682, was carrying a full plane of 300 people from Denver. He was surrounded by an assortment of electronic and mechanical buttons and gauges, all of which required special attention. The cockpit was equipped with communications equipment that allowed contact with air traffic controllers along the way. Other instruments showed the plane's speed and position, the amount of fuel, and the condition of the engine. Working alongside him in the cockpit were the co-pilot and the flight engineer, who helped maneuver the plane for a safe flight.

"I was afraid those strong headwinds we ran into over Topeka would really put us behind schedule," he said to Raul Morales, his co-pilot. "But going up to 25,000 feet helped us pick up the speed we needed. We're only 15 minutes behind schedule." As he spoke, his left hand pulled the throttle, slowly decreasing the speed of the plane.

"Yes, looks like we did a fine job," Raul replied. He was busy checking other instruments.

"This is Midwestern 682 to St. Louis tower," Walter said into the microphone. "Request final approach instructions."

Coming from the East

Not quite 200 miles east of the St. Louis airport, on Highway 40, a large grey truck was cruising at a comfortable speed. Seated behind the wheel, Louise Windsor rubbed her tired eyes and glanced down at her watch. "Making pretty good time," she thought. "We should be in St. Louis by dinnertime."

Louise and Frank (her husband and driving partner) had been on the road for 3 full days, with only a few hours' sleep along the way. Arriving in St. Louis meant the end of the line, where they would drop off the load of furniture they were carrying and spend a comfortable night before heading back home to North Carolina.

Her eyes were fixed on the crowded interstate as mile after mile passed. Located high in the cab of the 18-wheeler, it was easy for Louise to watch the road and plan her route to minimize delays. After all, the longer it took to deliver each load, the more time and money it cost.

Louise chatted on the CB radio to find out about weather and road conditions up ahead and to pass the time. Occasionally, she looked down at the instrument panel in front of her to check her speed, fuel, oil pressure, and the temperature of the engine. "We'd better stop for fuel," she said.

"Let's stop at the next exit," Frank replied. "I could use a cup of coffee anyway."

Louise eased onto the exit ramp, downshifting the truck through many gears. She braked to a stop next to the diesel fuel pump and said to the attendant, "Fill it up, please."

Transportation Occupations

Coming from the South

Some 300 miles south of St. Louis, a broad-beamed tugboat was pushing a string of barges carrying fuel oil from the Gulf Coast.

"Head about 10 degrees northeast," Bud Hennison directed his second mate, Rick Proctor. "The radar equipment picks up a barge 8 miles to the north," he added.

The two merchant marine officers stood at the controls of the tugboat *Olympia*. They had been on the river for days and were now on the last leg of their voyage up the Mississippi River to St. Louis. As chief mate and head officer of the deck crew, Bud's job was to navigate the ship. This meant plotting and maintaining the vessel's course. At the moment, they were in a heavy fog that made it impossible to see other river traffic.

"Give a short blast on the whistle," Bud ordered.

As the *Olympia's* whistle sounded through the fog, Bud took the clipboard from its place next to the radar and sonar equipment and began writing. Being responsible for the safe, smooth operation of the ship involved recording or "logging in" all the events of the voyage. Just then there was a distant whistle from the starboard side.

"Looks like they received our signal," said Bud. "Keep an eye out for them. I'm going down to the deck."

You have just spent a few moments with an airplane pilot, a long-distance truckdriver, and the chief mate on a cargo carrier. Let's see if these people have anything in common other than being bound for St. Louis.

All of them work in the transportation industry. Transportation is the business of moving people and goods from one place to another. It includes travel by air, rail, water, on roads and highways, even underground. Someday it may include travel in space.

This man is training to become a riverboat pilot.

The Nation's 200,000 miles of railroad track are an important means of moving people, food and industrial goods.

We all depend on the transportation industry. For example, you may take a bus to get to school each morning. Your parents may travel to work by car, bus, train, or subway. Even if you walk or ride your bicycle most of the places you need to go, the transportation industry serves you in other ways.

It is the means through which energy, raw materials, and finished products are channeled where they are needed. Railroads and trucks carry the food, lumber, automobiles, furniture, clothing, and thousands of other goods that fill our stores. Ships and airplanes carry goods between cities in America and throughout the world. The food we eat may come from farms hundreds or even thousands of miles away. All this is possible because railroad trains, trucks, and planes are constantly on the move. The transportation industry links Americans with each other and with the rest of the world.

Transportation Occupations

The people we usually think of as "transportation workers" are those who operate the vehicles—pilots and busdrivers, for example. However, people with many different skills are needed to keep America on the move. Mechanics and technicians keep the vehicles and equipment in top working condition. Railroad yard clerks and taxicab dispatchers are transportation workers who perform clerical and administrative tasks. Still other transportation workers deal with the public. They may seek new customers, make reservations, help children or handicapped travelers, or take care of complaints.

We can begin to explore transportation careers by looking at each of four groups of transportation occupations: Air transportation, merchant marine, railroad, and driving.

Transportation Occupations

Air transportation occupations. The *pilot* and *flight attendant* may be the first people who come to mind when you think about flying, but many other workers are needed to ensure a safe flight. Helping the captain, or pilot, guide the plane is the *co-pilot*. The co-pilot is the second in command on any flight. Also aboard is the *flight engineer*, who monitors the engine, fuel, and all other systems. Just as important are those who provide airplane services on the ground. These include the *air traffic controllers* who monitor the path of the airplane from start to finish. Generally, the pilot does not make any move without first "okaying" it with the controllers. *Aircraft mechanics* keep airplanes running safely and well. Besides repair work they do maintenance regularly. Many different people are employed to book customers and coordinate flights. *Reservation, ticket, and passenger agents* give customers flight information, sell tickets, assign seats, and check baggage. The personal contact with the public in this job is very important. It can make all the difference between a satisfied customer and a dissatisfied one. *Ramp agents* help guide airplanes into the gates using hand signals to pilots. They also load and unload baggage, freight, or mail. Other jobs in aviation include *flight instructors* who teach people to fly and *crop dusters* who fly over fields and spray them to aid growth of crops.

Flight attendants have to serve people graciously, but quickly.

Commercial aviation offers jobs on the ground and in the air.

Exploring Careers

Merchant marine occupations. The maritime industry offers travel and adventure and many different kinds of work. Work aboard ship is divided among the deck, engine, and steward's departments; sailors in each of these departments do different things. The *captain* or *master* commands the ship and has complete authority over everyone and everything aboard.

The deck department is responsible for regulating the course, position, and speed of the ship; maintaining and repairing the hull and deck equipment; and loading, unloading, and storing cargo. New sailors in the deck department start out as *ordinary seamen.* They do general maintenance, such as scrubbing the decks and painting. *Able seamen*, those who steer the ship and do skilled repair work on deck, are the next rank. The *boatswain*, or bosun, is the top ranking able seaman. The deck officers, or "mates," include the *chief mate*, who is the captain's top assistant in assigning duties to the deck crew, and the *second and third mates.*

The engine department crew works below deck and runs all the engines and machinery. It includes workers at all skill levels. *Wipers* are beginning level sailors who keep machinery clean. Other sailors include *oilers*, who lubricate and maintain equipment, and *fire-watertenders*, who check gauges on the ship's boilers. Other engine crew members include the *electrician* and the *refrigeration engineer.* The *chief engineer* is in charge of the engine department, and has the help of the *first, second, and third assistant engineers.*

The steward's department feeds the crew and maintains the living and recreation areas. Sailors in this department begin as *utility hands*, doing kitchen work such as scouring pots and preparing vegetables, and *mess attendants*, serving meals and taking care of the ship's living quarters. The *chief cook* plans and prepares the meals. The top sailor in this department is the *chief steward*, who is responsible for the meals and upkeep of living quarters. This is the only department head who is not an officer.

Railroad occupations. The Nation's 200,000 miles of railroad track are an important means of moving people, food, and goods among our cities and towns. Over half a million people are employed to operate trains and keep them in top working condition. *Conductors* are in charge of running the train. Their primary concerns are safety and running on time. On passenger trains, conductors collect tickets and fares as well. Conductors are always in communication with *locomotive engineers*, who work all the controls—such as acceleration and brakes—on the train. *Brake operators* work on trains and in railroad yards, making sure that trains are coupled (or linked) and uncoupled properly. They also inspect airhoses and handbrakes on all cars and assist the conductor when

Experience in the Coast Guard or Navy may help get a merchant marine job.

necessary. Other members of the train crew are *hostlers*, who help prepare the locomotives for their run, and *switchtenders*, who throw track switches in railroad yards. But many others are responsible for seeing that trains run efficiently. Shopworkers are the skilled employees who build, maintain, and repair railroad cars and other equipment. Some of these workers are *machinists, electrical workers, car repairers, sheet-metal workers, boilermakers*, and *blacksmiths*. To direct train movement and assure train safety, *railroad signal workers* install, maintain, and repair the communications and signaling systems. *Track workers* inspect and regularly maintain railroad tracks. They also put down new track when it is needed. *Dispatchers* work in stations along the railroad lines, sending messages to train crews by way of *telegraphers, telephoners*, and *tower operators*. These messages contain such things as track conditions and routing instructions. *Station agents* are the railroads' contact with the public. They offer information and try to get new business for the company.

Transportation Occupations

Applicants for truckdriving jobs must have good driving records.

Because of the millions of travelers who depend on them, transportation workers must be *conscientious* in their work and *pay close attention to detail*. The shopworkers who build and repair railroad cars, for example, must do their work carefully so that cars don't break down while they're in use. Air traffic controllers have to pay strict attention to guide planes safely on their proper course. Long-distance truckdrivers must stay wide awake and concentrate on driving for hours at a time. Sailors, drivers, pilots, and railroad engineers all need to be alert while they're on the job.

For many transportation workers, the ability to keep calm and *work under pressure* is important. Meeting schedules—delivering goods or people on time—is very important in the transportation industry. Yet storms, accidents, traffic tie-ups, and other unexpected situations crop up from time to time. Transportation workers have to be able to think quickly and act decisively in order to get things back on schedule as soon as possible.

An *easygoing personality* is an asset for transportation workers who are in direct contact with the public. Local transit bus and taxicab drivers, for example, must have the patience to deal effectively with passengers—the rude ones as well as the pleasant ones—and the steady nerves to drive in all traffic situations. Workers who sell tickets,

Driving occupations. Truck, bus, and taxi drivers move passengers and goods over the Nation's highways and through the streets every day. More people than you might think are *local truckdrivers*. These are the people who drive moving trucks, newspaper trucks, mail trucks, freight delivery trucks, and other kinds of trucks in and around the city. Those who carry goods thousands of miles across the country in large trucks such as "18-wheelers" are known as *long-distance truckdrivers*. There are other kinds of drivers, too. *Taxicab drivers* operate without fixed routes or schedules and offer individualized service to passengers. *Local transit busdrivers* drive city and suburban routes to transport millions of Americans daily. They also collect fares and answer questions. *Intercity busdrivers* follow a route between communities, which may be on city roads or on highways or both. In small towns, these buses may be the only public transportation to other towns. Then there are support workers such as *traffic agents*, who try to get new business for companies, and *dispatchers*, who supply the drivers with scheduling and route information.

Personal Characteristics

Although it takes people with many different skills to keep our planes, ships, railroads, trucks, and buses on the move, transportation workers have certain traits in common.

Taxicab drivers have to work in all kinds of weather.

answer questions, listen to complaints, or try to get new business need to be good at dealing with all kinds of people.

Some transportation workers need the *ability to work as part of a team*. In the merchant marine, for example, cooperation and interaction among the deck, engine, and steward's departments are essential for the "smooth sailing" of the ship. Not only do members of the ship's crew work as a team, but they eat, sleep, and socialize together too.

Others in transportation need to *be able to work independently*. Long-distance truckdrivers may spend days alone on the road. They must organize their time and set a steady speed in order to deliver goods on schedule.

The things that transportation workers do are not necessarily strenuous, but they require *good health and physical stamina*. Baggage attendants, for example, carry and load passengers' luggage on trains, buses, and airplanes. Parking attendants and flight attendants are on their feet and serving customers most of the time. Some jobs may not require much physical activity but demand excellent health just the same. Air traffic controllers, local and long-distance bus and truck drivers, and locomotive engineers are some examples. These jobs all require workers who are levelheaded and have steady nerves. In many cases workers must pass strict physical exams to enter these occupations.

A job in this field is likely to mean *working nights or weekends or on rotating shifts*, because transportation is not just a 9-to-5 operation. Many trucks, buses, planes, ships, and trains run 24 hours a day, 7 days a week.

Training

Through your hobbies or school activities you may already have begun acquiring skills that will lead to a career in transportation. Do you enjoy building and fixing things in your spare time? Mechanical aptitude and analytical ability are important in such occupations as airplane mechanic, able seaman, and locomotive engineer. Perhaps you are a ham radio operator. This hobby can provide a solid foundation for the training you'd need to become an air traffic controller or a railroad tower operator. You may have had the opportunity to sell tickets, collect money, schedule events, or give information to others. Can you think of transportation occupations that require these skills?

Formal training for transportation occupations varies a great deal. Detailed information on training requirements can be found in the Job Facts at the end of this chapter.

In some transportation occupations, the necessary skills are learned right on the job. In railroading and the

In railroading, workers typically learn their skills on the job.

merchant marine, for example, beginners start out as helpers and work their way up, a process that typically takes many years.

Some transportation workers get their training in trade schools or technical institutes. Many airplane mechanics, for example, attend trade schools that provide practical job experience as well as classroom instruction. Long-distance truckdrivers also may train in this way.

If you're interested in a career in aviation, plan on attending college. A college degree—or at least several years of college training—is preferred for most aviation occupations, including pilot, air traffic controller, flight attendant, and reservation, ticket, or passenger agent.

In some transportation occupations, workers must have a license that demonstrates their expertise in the field. This is the case for airplane pilots, who must have a flying license certified by the Federal Aviation Administration, and for truckdrivers, busdrivers, and taxicab drivers, all of whom must have a State chauffeur's license.

Regardless of which transportation occupation you're interested in, you'll find a high school diploma an asset. Even in jobs that don't require it, advancement to more responsible positions often goes to those who have a diploma. High school courses in math and English are helpful for any of the transportation occupations. Other courses, such as machine shop, driver education, and public speaking, may be helpful for certain occupations.

Air Traffic Controller

As a ground controller, Mia Hensen is responsible for directing runway traffic.

"Washington Tower, this is Global Airlines Flight 702. Request permission for takeoff."

Mia Hensen carefully checked the radar screen in front of her. It was filled with lines that represented airspaces, and moving blips, or symbols, that indicated planes. To the untrained eye, this large glowing screen would seem impossible to interpret. But to Mia, a veteran air traffic controller, checking traffic patterns and positions of airplanes from the radar screen was a routine part of every takeoff and landing.

After closely reviewing the radar screen, Mia turned her head slightly to the right where the flight strips were posted. These long strips of paper contained information about each flight that was due for takeoff, such as its destination and scheduled time of takeoff. They helped Mia get the waiting planes off the ground in the safest, most efficient manner.

"Cleared for takeoff, Global 702 . . . Wind is from the southeast at 14 miles per hour," Mia radioed the pilot. At the same time, her fingers were punching out this information on the keyboard in front of her. It would then be relayed to the computer that kept track of all inbound and outbound flights.

Although she made it seem effortless, working her shift as ground controller—directing traffic down the runway and out of Washington National Airport—was a demanding job. Besides checking the pattern from the radar screen and the flight strips, there were dozens of other details running through Mia's mind. Every controller had to know the geography of the area as well as the weather conditions and visibility. Other facts, such as the size, weight, speed, and route of each airplane had to be considered in order to direct the outbound traffic safely and smoothly.

From the glass-enclosed airport tower, Mia watched Flight 702 gain speed down the runway. As the plane gracefully lifted into the air, she phoned downstairs to inform the department controllers. These air traffic controllers were responsible for watching aircraft and guiding them by radar for as much as 30 miles from Washington National Airport.

Mia was interrupted by the voice over the radio. "This is Pacifica Flight 445 ready for takeoff."

"Proceed down the ramp to runway 9, Pacifica 445," Mia radioed to the pilot a few seconds later. She then announced the wind and weather conditions.

The silence on the radio lasted no longer than 20 seconds. "This is Southern Airlines Flight 32 scheduled to leave for Miami at 4:57 p.m. We've had some problems in refueling and won't be finished for at least half an hour. I'm requesting a delay of 30 to 40 minutes."

"Roger, Southern 32 . . . this is ground control. I'll reschedule your departure for approximately 5:40 p.m. Keep me posted if there are any further delays." As Mia spoke, her fingers raced over the keyboard in order to communicate this information to the computer.

Mia had just finished answering some questions about the expected weather conditions for this evening when a soft tap on the shoulder startled her. It was Manny McGinnis, who was waiting to relieve her.

"I like knowing that people trust me to make the right decisions."

Transportation Occupations

"I didn't mean to scare you, Mia," Manny apologized, "but I couldn't get your attention. It's time to stand up and stretch for a few minutes."

The level of Mia's concentration was intense at this time of day, when traffic was at a peak.

"I didn't even hear you come in, Manny," Mia responded. She had been at her post as ground controller for about 2 hours now, but the time had passed very quickly.

Mia stood up and Manny slipped into her chair. She briefed Manny on the traffic situation, and then headed downstairs to relax.

Mia entered the employee's lounge, picked up a doughnut and a cup of coffee from a tray in the far corner of the room, and joined some others at one of the tables. She made an effort to relax her neck and shoulder muscles.

"Hi, Mia, how's it going?" Norman Walton greeted her. Norman was also an air traffic controller, and her tennis partner as well.

"Have you met George Foster? He's just completed training at the Federal Aviation Administration Academy in Oklahoma."

"Pleasure to meet you, George," Mia said as they shook hands. "Welcome aboard."

"Thanks a lot," replied George.

Norman smiled and said. "I was just trying to reassure

"Some people questioned my ability at first, but I was confident that I could do the job."

George. I was telling him that directing air traffic at a metropolitan airport is not as scary as it seems at first."

"I must admit I am a bit nervous," acknowledged George. "I've had some experience in the military as a pilot and navigator, and then the training in Oklahoma. But to think that over 500 planes fly in and out of Washington National daily...!"

"Don't let it bother you, George," Mia responded. "It's not as though you have to direct all those planes yourself! Besides, your military training is excellent background. And the on-the-job training you'll get here at Washington National is outstanding. Especially those "practice problems" that are programmed into the computer."

Norman added, "All you need to build up your confidence is a little time and experience. We all felt the way you do when we started out."

"I'm sure you're right," George replied. He glanced down at his watch "I hate to run, but I'm due in the tower in 5 minutes. Thanks for the pep talk."

As he walked away, Mia recalled *her* first days on the job. She had not had military training, and some people had questioned her ability to handle the job without it. Mia had been sure that she could. That had been 7 years ago in Miami. Since then, she had worked in three different airports.

Mia and Norman chatted for a few minutes more. These short breaks helped to relieve the tension and refresh the controllers for their next 2-hour shifts.

Mia finished the last of her coffee and then headed down the hall. She walked through a set of double doors and entered the approach control room from which incoming aircraft were being directed. A number of voices could be heard throughout the large room.

After a short briefing on the current traffic situation, Mia took her place behind a large radarscope keeping track of planes approaching from the East. Working as an approach controller now, Mia's duties included assigning planes to the proper courses and sending messages to the ground controllers (who directed planes from the runway to the gates) upon their arrival.

"This is Atlantic Airlines Flight 572 to Washington National," a voice said over the radio. "Request final approach instructions."

Mia turned to the circular radar screen and found the symbol that represented Atlantic Airlines 572 from among the flashes of light.

"Washington National approach to Atlantic 572," Mia said into the microphone. "Your position is 30 miles northwest of the airport. Expect approach to runway 9. Wind is from the east at 10 miles per hour."

"Roger, approach control," acknowledged the pilot.

Mia then gave the pilot direction and altitude instructions to bring the airplane close to the airport. When the flight was about 6 miles away, Mia said, "Atlantic 572 ... cleared for approach. Call Washington tower now."

Assured that the plane was safely on the approach, she took a deep breath and then relayed the information to the computer and phoned ahead to ground control. Having finished that, Mia could now answer a call from a Central plane that was waiting. "Go ahead, Central 324."

"This is Central 324," the pilot responded. "I'm in a holding pattern at 8,000 feet. I've been informed that runway 6 has been closed temporarily and would like further instructions for landing."

Mia followed the regular procedures and directed the pilot down runway 9.

She leaned back in her chair for a moment to relieve the tension from her lower back. However, what appeared to be an unmarked symbol flashed on the radar screen. This brought Mia back to the edge of her seat to take a closer look. She watched the symbol fade to the right and disappear off the edge of the screen. Immediately Mia phoned Teressa Williams, the approach controller directing incoming traffic from the south. Teressa had just picked up the flash on her screen.

"I'll try to establish contact with the aircraft and then get back to you," she told Mia.

A few minutes later, Teressa phoned and explained that the "mysterious flash" they had both seen was a small private plane that hadn't bothered to radio in.

"I directed it in safely, though. I also made it clear to the pilot that he should have called and told us where he was!"

"I just don't understand why some pilots don't use their common sense," observed Mia.

The pace of the traffic slowed as the evening rush ended. Mia continued giving directions and answering questions, always alert for the unexpected. Before she knew it, Bert Johnson came by to relieve her.

"Is it that time already?" Mia asked. She looked down at her watch, which read 7:30. Just then her stomach let out a growl. Mia smiled at Bert and said, "Well it looks like my stomach knows what time it is! I guess I'll get some dinner now."

Exploring

Air traffic controllers must have confidence in their judgment as well as the ability to make decisions quickly.
- Can you make decisions on your own? Are you willing to take the responsibility for your decisions?
- Do you trust your own judgment?
- Do friends often confide in you?

Air traffic controllers must be able to see objects on a two-dimensional screen and visualize them in the air.

- Can you read and understand graphs, diagrams, and charts?
- Can you look at a drawing and picture the three dimensional object in your mind?
- Do you ever put together models?
- Are you good at solving geometry problems?

Air traffic controllers are subject to stress and tension when they're on the job. They must be able to keep calm and be able to concentrate under pressure.

- Are you able to organize your thoughts during tests even though you may be nervous beforehand?
- Do you usually perform well at crucial moments—for example, the big play in a ball game?
- Are you good at giving reports in front of the class?

Air traffic controllers must have a good memory for detail. They must remember wind and weather conditions, geography, and the size and speed of planes when giving directions.

- Do you remember people's names easily?
- Can you relate an exact conversation the next day?
- Can you remember what you ate for lunch yesterday?

Air traffic controllers often have to work early in the morning or late at night. To keep up with these demands, they must be in good physical condition and have stamina.

- Do you enjoy jogging, bicycling, hiking, backpacking, climbing, basketball, and other active sports?
- Do you enjoy dancing? Gardening?
- Do you like being active most of the time?

Transportation Occupations

Railroad Passenger Conductor

Together, Charlie and Max have more than 60 years of railroad experience.

Exploring Careers

It was a crisp spring morning, not yet dawn. Charlie Campbell, in his freshly pressed white shirt and dark tie, was on Track B giving the final inspection to train 171, scheduled to leave for Washington in 10 minutes. As conductor of the Baltimore-Washington commuter run, Charlie was responsible for the train. He liked to check the railroad cars to make sure they were in top running condition before the train left the station. To do this, Charlie reported for work promptly at 5:30 a.m. every morning, a full 30 minutes before the train made its first run.

Charlie had a routine he followed daily to prepare the train and its crew for departure. After signing in, Charlie reported to the dispatcher to pick up his copy of the train's orders. Then he headed out to the tracks to check the condition of the train and greet his crew.

"Morning, Jim ... morning, Max. How's everything look?"

Charlie confers with Jim Beall, the locomotive engineer.

"Should be about set," replied Max Spiegel, the brake operator. "She's all fueled and the cars are coupled. Right now I'm going to check the tail markers."

"Good work, Max."

Charlie then turned to Jim Beall, the locomotive engineer, who was up in the cab eyeing the brakes and other controls. "Have you had a chance to look over the orders?"

"Yes, Charlie," Jim responded. "Doesn't look like we should have any delays. Track and weather conditions both are excellent."

"Good," said Charlie. "We should be ready to roll in about 15 minutes." Charlie and Jim synchronized their watches at exactly 5:48 a.m.

Passengers were boarding the train now. Charlie climbed aboard so that he could doublecheck the lights and other equipment. Everything looked fine.

"All aboard!" called Charlie as the last few passengers hurried down the platform.

With everyone safely seated, Charlie pulled the last door shut. Then he gave the engineer the go-ahead.

"Move her out," Charlie said to Jim over a two-way hand radio. They would communicate by radio frequently during the run.

"Have your tickets ready, please," Charlie announced as he began down the aisle of the first car to collect tickets and fares. Most of the faces were familiar ones, as many of the passengers were daily commuters who had been riding the 171 as long as Charlie had been its conductor.

"Excuse me," said a middle-aged man as Charlie made his way down the aisle. "Will the train be on its normal schedule next week on Memorial Day? Or do you have a holiday schedule? I'm new in town and don't know the train schedules around here."

"Well, sir, we do have a holiday schedule and that's what we'll be using on Memorial Day," replied Charlie. "By the way, you can pick up the schedule for all our Baltimore-Washington commuter runs at the station. Just ask any of the ticket agents."

"Thanks a lot, I'll do that."

"Not at all," Charlie said with a slight smile. He got a feeling of satisfaction from helping passengers.

The train rode along smoothly, making stops at Elkridge, Columbia, and St. Dennis. At each stop, Charlie collected tickets and fares, working his way from the first car back to the third.

"Sir ...," Charlie heard a woman calling loudly from the rear of the car. He moved quickly down the aisle.

"Can I help you, ma'am?"

"You certainly can! Would you tell this gentleman to put out that smelly cigar? I've tried to ask politely, but as you can see he has ignored me."

Transportation Occupations

"I'm afraid you're going to have to put your cigar out, sir. If you want to smoke, the next car is the smoking section on this train," Charlie said politely but firmly.

With a sour look on his face, the man said, "Okay, okay, I'll put it out. But if you ask me, her manners are worse than my cigar is!"

Charlie felt that it would be best to separate the two passengers before one or both of them completely lost their temper. "There are a few empty seats up front, sir. You'd probably be more comfortable if you moved to one of those. Then, if you want, you can move to the smoking car at the next stop."

"That suits me just fine," he replied as he picked up his briefcase and headed up the aisle.

"Now that that's cleared up, I hope you can relax and enjoy the rest of the trip, ma'am," Charlie said as he breathed a slight sigh of relief. He then walked up to the man and thanked him for being cooperative.

He had never taken a course in psychology or supervision, but Charlie knew he was good at working with people. He had the tact and judgment to deal with people successfully—the train crew as well as the passengers.

The train chugged on ... Odenton, New Carollton, and Cheverly. Almost every seat was taken now.

The next stop, the last one, was College Park. It was usually one of the more crowded stops along the route to Washington. As the train came to a halt, Charlie opened the door of the first car and lowered the steps. He stepped onto the platform and announced, "Have your tickets ready, please," so he could board the passengers and check their tickets in the most efficient way. Most of the passengers were regular riders. They greeted Charlie, showed him their weekly or monthly passes, and stepped onto the train.

At exactly 6:48 a.m., the 171 pulled into Washington's Union Station. Charlie and Max helped the passengers down the steps and onto the platform.

The train empty now, they both climbed back onto the first car and each sank into a seat. "I'd say we had about 200 paying customers on that run," Charlie offered.

Max calculated out loud and nodded his head. "Let's see ... all the seats filled, that is 65 times 3 cars or 195 ... and about half a dozen standing. Yes, that seems about right to me."

Next, Charlie counted the number of tickets sold and then added up the money collected. He made notations in his notebook which would help in writing his report tonight after the last run.

With a few minutes left before the return journey to Baltimore, Charlie and Max relaxed and began to chat.

"You know, I thought working the commuter line was

Charlie knows many of the commuters by name.

going to be a breeze after 27 years on freight trains," Max said. "It isn't as physically demanding as work on a freight train, I'll say that. But the business of collecting fares, answering questions, and keeping the passengers happy certainly keeps me on the go."

Charlie nodded in agreement. "And keeping the passengers happy is no easy job!" he said. "Two of my passengers got into an argument this morning because one was smoking and it bothered the other one."

After a comfortable silence, Charlie began to reminisce. "You know, I started working for the railroads 36 years ago. I began right after high school as a substitute brake operator in a switching yard. It was tough work, blistering hot summers and winters so cold they'd numb your fingers and toes. After a year and a half, I became a regular, and 4 years after that I got promoted to a passenger brake operator. Like you, I expected the work on a passenger line to be easier."

"Tell me more," Max said.

"Well, after 22 years as a brake operator, 10 years as a freight train conductor, and over 4 years as a passenger conductor, I guess I've learned that things don't get easy. After all those years, I still get to work at 5:30 each morning, make three morning and three evening runs, have a daily layover in Washington, and don't get home until 8:00 each night!

"I must admit, though, that I wouldn't trade this job for anything else in the world. There are so many rewards. I like working with people as well as machinery. I enjoy the responsibility and freedom I get on the job. There's no close supervision. And there's the 5- or 6-hour layover each day in Washington, when I can catch up on my sleep, read a good book, take in a movie, or anything else I want to do." Charlie paused for a moment. "Yes," he said, "Working on the railroad is more than just a job to me, it's a way of life!"

Glancing down at his watch, Charlie noticed it was nearly 8 o'clock. "I could probably go on talking for hours, but we'd better prepare for the next run."

Exploring

Conductors are in charge of running the train. They are responsible for the care and comfort of the passengers, for directing the other members of the train crew, and for making sure the train runs safely and on time.

- Have you ever been responsible for the care of others—babysitting, for example?
- Have you ever organized a school club or been an officer of the student government?

"Working on the railroad is more than just a job to me, it's a way of life," says Charlie.

Transportation Occupations

- Have you ever taken care of pets or plants for your neighbors while they were out of town?

Conductors must be tactful and courteous when dealing with passengers. This can include anything from giving out information to dealing with a passenger who doesn't have enough money for the fare. The conductor is the railroad's representative to the public.

- Have you ever been the spokesperson for your class or school club?
- Are you good at settling arguments among your friends?
- Can you remain calm and courteous, even when people irritate you or something troubles you?

Conductors must have an eye for detail. They must make sure all cars are clean and have been properly coupled. At the end of each run they must report such things as the number of passengers, track conditions, and departure and arrival times.

- Do you enjoy working with numbers?
- Do you like to play games where you must find hidden objects or words?
- Do you like to put together puzzles?
- Can you read maps easily? Can you find a place on a map quickly?

Conductors must be flexible about their work schedules. The job may call for time away from home.

- Have you ever spent a few weeks away from your family—at camp or visiting relatives, for example?
- Do you like to stay overnight with friends?
- Can you find plenty of things to do with free time?

Conductors must understand how the train operates. This takes mechanical ability.

- Do you have any hobbies in which you build or repair things? Have you ever done woodworking, sculpting, carpentry, or put together models?
- Have you ever tried to fix your bicycle or replace a fuse or a light switch?

Bus Driver

In 4 years of driving a bus, Betsy Hanratty has learned how important it is to be calm in dealing with customers.

Transportation Occupations

A pleasant smile appeared on Betsy Hanratty's face as she greeted Dan Martin. Dan was a regular customer on the X-2 bus that ran from Hillside into the city every morning.

"Looks like it's going to clear up this morning ... should be a beautiful weekend," Dan remarked as he dropped two quarters into the coin machine. He took a few steps down the aisle and chose the first empty seat.

Behind Dan, another half dozen passengers followed, most of them also on their way to work. One by one, they deposited their coins and moved back.

Once all the riders were safely on the bus, Betsy grabbed the handle that was connected to the door and pulled it towards her to close the door. Out of habit, she glanced up at the rearview mirror that gave her a full view of the interior of the bus. Next, Betsy checked the sideview mirrors on both sides of the bus and turned her head to take a quick look at the traffic. This allowed a complete view that Betsy felt was necessary before she pulled away from the curb and joined the flow of traffic.

Light chatter could be heard throughout the bus, which was about one-third full now. Many of the passengers, however, settled back and read the morning newspaper or a book.

Betsy continued on her way, stopping every block or two to pick up passengers. The morning rush hour traffic was heavy, as usual, but moved at a steady pace. The early morning fog had lifted, and the sun was beginning to break through the clouds. Betsy reached to the panel on her right and picked up her sunglasses, which had been resting between the buttons marked "Defroster" and "Hi-Beam Lights".

A young woman with two children stepped onto the bus. "Does this bus go to Greenwich?" she asked in a shy voice.

"No, ma'am," Betsy responded. "The X-2 only goes as far as Cedar Crossroads. You can take this bus if you want, but you'll have to transfer at Cedar Crossroads to get to Greenwich. Or, if you want to wait, the X-18 will be by in about 20 minutes. That one goes all the way to Greenwich."

"Are you sure this doesn't go to Greenwich? My sister

"When I first started driving, I figured that being in traffic all day would take the most patience. But hectic traffic is nothing compared to some of the people I meet."

told me to catch the bus at 7:15 at the corner of 35th and Wilson Boulevard. She said that one would take me to Greenwich."

"I'm sorry, ma'am, but I'm only going as far as Cedar Crossroads. You can ride this bus if you'd like; the transfers will cost 10 cents extra apiece."

"But I know my sister can't be wrong. She rides the bus all the time."

"Well, ma'am, you must decide what you want to do now. By the way, next time why don't you telephone for bus information? That way you will be sure to get the correct bus routes and time schedules."

The young woman, still looking bewildered, opened her purse and took out some coins. "How much is children's fare?"

"Thirty-five cents, plus ten cents extra if you want to buy a transfer. That comes to a total of $1.50 for all three of you."

As the coins fell to the bottom of the coin box Betsy tore three transfers from a booklet attached to the box. The women moved to the back of the bus and Betsy breathed a slight sigh of relief. After 4 years of driving a city bus, Betsy had learned to be calm and courteous in dealing with customers. She also had learned to answer all questions and complaints politely, but firmly. "It's funny," she thought, "when I first started driving, I figured that being in traffic all day would take the most patience. But hectic traffic is nothing compared to some of the people I meet!"

In the next few stops, all the seats filled up. The pace of the traffic slowed as the X-2 approached the city. The road became more crowded, and Betsy instinctively became more cautious about her driving. Too many times, Betsy had seen drivers make a last-minute decision to turn—not paying any attention to the fact that they were in the wrong lane or that the traffic light was red. Betsy felt that a good driver must be a defensive one. She took pride in her own fine driving record.

The bell rang frequently between stops, signalling to Betsy that a passenger wanted to get off at the next stop. Occasionally, she glanced at her watch to make sure she stayed on schedule. Along with safety, Betsy considered being on time a very important part of the job.

Up ahead, Betsy saw that a delivery truck was stopped in the right lane with its lights flashing. This meant that the driver was delivering goods nearby and would return shortly. Being able to see "trouble spots" in plenty of time was one of the advantages Betsy enjoyed because, in driving the bus, she sat quite a bit higher off the ground than most of the other drivers in the traffic. Whenever she could, Betsy would plan ahead to minimize her delays.

"Good morning, Mrs. Goddfrey," Betsy greeted the elderly woman who was boarding the bus. Mrs. Goddfrey was one of the few patrons who rode the morning bus regularly on its return from the city out to Hillside. Three times a week, she volunteered at the YWCA.

"Hello, Betsy. Fine morning, isn't it?" the woman replied as she reached into her purse for the bus fare. "Oh, dear, I have forgotten my change purse. What shall I do?"

"Don't worry," Betsy replied kindly. She took some change from her pocket, deposited it in the coin box, and said, "You can bring me the money on Friday."

"You're a real lifesaver! You can trust me not to forget it on Friday." Mrs. Goddfrey made her way to the first empty seat.

The return run from the city to Hillside went quickly, as Betsy passed many of the bus stops along the route without having to stop and pick up passengers.

"Excuse me, ma'am, but does this bus go by St. John's Hospital? It's on the corner of Fourth and Pine Streets," asked a well-dressed man as he stepped onto the bus.

"Yes, it does, sir. If you'd like, I'll call out that stop as we get to it," Betsy replied.

"That would be very helpful, thank you," he said as he dropped some coins in the box. "By the way, what's a pretty little girl like you doing in a job like this?"

"What do you mean? I can handle this bus as well as anyone," she replied good-naturedly.

"In fact," she thought to herself, "I can handle it better than most. After all, when I applied for the job of a busdriver, I had over a year's experience driving a delivery truck for a dry cleaner's. And in the training program the bus company gives, I had the best grades in my class—both on the written exam and in driving skills! Not bad at all."

Meanwhile the man bound for St. John's had found a seat at the back of the bus.

The rest of the trip was smooth, with no major problems or traffic delays. In fact, at one point Betsy had to make an effort to pace her driving so as not to get ahead of her schedule. She didn't want to pass any of the bus stops early and take the chance of leaving a passenger behind.

After this run was finished, Betsy drove about a mile to the garage, where she checked in with the dispatcher. This included reporting the runs she made that morning, counting the fares collected, turning in her booklet of transfer slips, recording the number of transfers given out, and reporting special problems or delays. Since Betsy worked a split shift—from 5:30 to 9:30 a.m. and later from 4:00 to 8:00 p.m.—she did not have to write up her reports until later that evening.

Transportation Occupations

Exploring

Busdrivers must be easygoing and even-tempered to be able to deal with all kinds of passengers, weather conditions, and traffic problems.

- Can you control your emotions when everything seems to go wrong?
- Can you keep your temper when an umpire calls you out and you thought you were safe?
- Can you remain calm and courteous, even when people irritate you or something troubles you?

Betsy feels that a good driver must be a defensive one. She takes pride in her good driving record.

- Can you make your case calmly when a teacher gives you a grade that you think is unfair?

Busdrivers must be safety conscious and follow traffic regulations in delivering passengers safely to their destinations.

- Do you look both ways before you cross the street?
- Do you obey traffic regulations, such as riding your bicycle with the traffic and only crossing at a crosswalk?
- Have you ever been responsible for the care of anyone else—baby-sitting, for example?

Busdrivers are generally free from close supervision while at work. They must be able to drive their routes, stay on schedule, and handle any emergencies on their own.

- Do you do your homework without being told to?
- Do you clean your room or help with chores around the house without being told to?
- Are you generally on time for class or for meetings?
- Do you budget your time?
- Would you know what to do in case of a fire or other emergency at home?

Busdrivers must have good driving ability to maneuver the bus in heavy traffic. This includes good eye-foot-hand coordination, quick reflexes, and good depth perception.

- Can you ice skate, ride a skateboard, or ride a bicycle?
- Are you a good bowler?
- Can you pitch, hit, and catch a softball?

Exploring Careers

Job Facts

There isn't room in this book for a story about every transportation occupation. However, you'll find some important facts about 21 of these occupations in the following section. If you want additional information about any of them, you might begin by consulting the *Occupational Outlook Handbook*, a publication of the Department of Labor which should be available in your school or public library.

Occupation	Nature and Places of Work	Training and Qualifications	Other Information

AIR TRANSPORTATION

Air Traffic Controllers	Controllers keep track of planes on the ground and in the air, and give pilots instructions to keep planes on course and prevent accidents or delays. All civilian air traffic controllers work for the Federal Government as employees of the Federal Aviation Administration (FAA). They work in the control towers at airports and at control centers along air routes throughout the country.	Controllers must be in excellent health and pass a yearly physical exam. They should be articulate, since directions to pilots must be given quickly and clearly, and have a decisive personality. Applicants must have 3 years of work experience or 4 years of college, or both. Civilian or military experience as a controller, pilot, or navigator is an asset. Successful applicants receive both on-the-job and formal training. It usually takes 2 to 3 years to become a fully qualified controller.	Controllers work a basic 40-hour week. Because control towers and centers operate 24 hours a day, 7 days a week, controllers are assigned to night and weekend shifts on a rotating basis. Controllers sometimes work under great stress. They must keep track of several planes at a time and make certain all pilots receive correct instructions.

Transportation Occupations

Occupation	Nature and Places of Work	Training and Qualifications	Other Information
Airplane Mechanics	Mechanics keep planes in top operating condition. They inspect and maintain planes on a regular schedule and make repairs. Over half of all mechanics are employed by the airlines, working near large cities at the airlines' main stops. Others work for the Federal Government, mainly at military bases, or for small repair shops at airports throughout the country.	Most mechanics learn their job in the Armed Forces or in trade schools certified by the FAA. Trade school courses last about 2 years. Most of the mechanics who work on civilian aircraft are licensed by the FAA. Unlicensed mechanics are supervised by those with licenses. Experience in automotive repair or other mechanical work is helpful, as are high school courses in mathematics, physics, chemistry, and mechanical drawing. Mechanics must have strength and agility to lift heavy parts and do climbing and reaching.	Mechanics sometimes must stand or lie in awkward positions when making repairs. Work areas are noisy when engines are being tested. Many mechanics are union members.
Airplane Pilots	Although most pilots fly planes that carry passengers and cargo, some do crop dusting, inspect power lines, or do aerial photography. Most pilots work at major airports. About half work for the airlines, and the rest work for private businesses and the government.	All commercial pilots must be licensed by the FAA. To receive the license, they must pass a written and physical exam and demonstrate flying ability. Flying is taught in military or civilian flying schools. Either kind of training satisfies requirements for licensing, but Armed Forces pilots have the opportunity to gain experience on jet aircraft that is preferred by airlines and many businesses. College graduates are preferred for airline jobs. New airline pilots usually start as flight engineers.	Pilots must be able to make quick decisions and accurate judgments under pressure; the mental stress of being responsible for a safe flight can be tiring. Pilots cannot fly more than 85 hours per month. Most flights involve layovers away from home. Work schedules often are irregular. Most airline pilots are union members.
Flight Attendants	Flight attendants help make the passengers' flight safe, comfortable, and enjoyable. Most flight attendants are stationed in major cities. Large numbers work out of Chicago, Dallas, Los Angeles, Miami, New York, and San Francisco.	Poise, tact, resourcefulness, and a pleasant manner with strangers all are important traits. Applicants must be high school graduates. Those with some college, nurses' training, or experience dealing with the public are preferred. Most large airlines give newly hired flight attendants about 5 weeks of training in their own schools.	Attendants usually fly 80 hours per month or less but may devote up to 35 more hours on the ground to prepare for flights. They may have to work nights, weekends, or holidays. Most are union members.

Exploring Careers

Occupation	Nature and Places of Work	Training and Qualifications	Other Information
Reservation, Ticket, and Passenger Agents	These workers reserve seats, sell tickets, and help passengers board planes. Most agents work in downtown offices or at large metropolitan airports.	Because agents deal directly with the public, airlines seek pleasant, personable, attractive applicants. A good speaking voice is essential. A high school diploma is required and some college is preferred. New employees usually receive about a week of classroom instruction to learn how to use the flight schedule book and the computer. Once they are on the job, at least 3 weeks of close supervision by an experienced worker are needed before they can handle the job alone.	Work schedules may be irregular. During holidays and other busy periods, agents may find the work hectic. Many agents belong to unions.

RAILROAD OCCUPATIONS

Occupation	Nature and Places of Work	Training and Qualifications	Other Information
Brake Operators	Brake operators couple and uncouple cars and operate track switches in railroad yards. They also look for faulty equipment and make minor repairs.	Brake operators need to be in good physical condition and have mechanical aptitude to operate switches and handbrakes and to board moving trains. Employers prefer high school graduates. Skills are learned on the job and it takes about a year to learn them thoroughly. It usually takes several years, however, before brake operators have enough seniority to get regular assignments.	Brake operators may have to work nights, weekends, and holidays. Those who don't have regular assignments may be called to work on short notice. The job often calls for time away from home. Most brake operators are union members.
Conductors	Conductors are in charge of train and yard crews. They must make sure passengers and cargo are delivered safely and on time.	Qualified brake operators are promoted to conductors on a seniority basis. They must pass exams covering signals, timetables, operating rules, and related subjects. Until permanent positions become available, new conductors substitute for experienced conductors who are absent.	Conductors may have to work nights, weekends, and holidays. The job often calls for time away from home. Since most freight trains are unscheduled, freight conductors may be called to work on short notice. Many conductors are union members.

Transportation Occupations

Occupation	Nature and Places of Work	Training and Qualifications	Other Information
Locomotive Engineers	Engineers operate the throttle to start and accelerate the train and use airbrakes to slow and stop it. They also watch gauges and meters that measure speed, fuel, battery charge, and air pressure in the brake lines.	Openings for locomotive engineers are filled by promoting engineers' helpers on a seniority basis. Helpers qualify for promotion by proving their ability to operate locomotives and by passing a written exam. For engineer helper jobs, railroads prefer applicants who are high school graduates and at least 21 years old. They must have good hearing, eyesight, and color vision. Good eye-hand coordination, manual dexterity, and mechanical aptitude also are required. Helpers receive on-the-job training that lasts about 6 weeks.	Locomotive engineers may have to work weekends and holidays. The job often calls for time away from home. Since most freight trains are unscheduled, freight engineers may be called to work on short notice. Most engineers are union members.
Shop Trades	Every railroad employs its own workers to maintain and repair cars and other equipment. These skilled workers include car repairers, machinists, electrical workers, sheet-metal workers, boilermakers, and blacksmiths. They work in railroad yards, terminals, and engine houses, as well as in locomotive repair shops.	Apprenticeship training is the most common way of entering the railroad shop trades, although some workers learn on the job and are upgraded from jobs as helpers and laborers. Applicants who have had shop training in high school or vocational school are preferred. Automobile repair and machining courses are useful for machinists. Courses in electricity and physics will help those who want to be electrical workers.	Shop work is active and strenuous. It involves stooping, lifting, and climbing. Some workers may face noisy shop conditions. Other workers, such as car repairers, must work outdoors in all kinds of weather. Most shop workers are union members.
Signal Department Workers	Railroad signal workers install, repair, and maintain the train control, communication, and signaling systems that direct trains and assure safety. These include gate crossings, signal lights, and switches.	Applicants who are high school or vocational school graduates are preferred. Courses in blueprint reading, electricity, and electronics provide a helpful background. Applicants also should be able to do heavy work. New workers are assigned as helpers to experienced workers. After 60 to 90 days of training, they may advance to assistants. After another 2 to 4 years, qualified assistants may be promoted to signal installers or maintainers.	Since they work over large sections of track, installers usually live away from home during the workweek, frequently in camp cars provided by the company. Maintainers usually live at home and service signals over a limited stretch of track. However, they must make repairs regardless of weather conditions or time of day. Most signal installers and maintainers are union members.

Exploring Careers

Occupation	Nature and Places of Work	Training and Qualifications	Other Information
Station Agents	Station agents are the customers' contact with the railroad. They take customer orders, arrange a delivery schedule, inspect merchandise, and prepare customers' bills. At passenger stations, agents supervise and coordinate selling tickets and checking baggage. Most agents work in railroad freight stations. Some work in passenger stations.	Station agents usually rise through the ranks of other railroad occupations, such as telephoners, telegraphers, tower operators, and clerks.	At major freight and passenger stations, the agents' duties are mainly administrative and supervisory. Most station agents are union members.
Telegraphers, Telephoners, and Tower Operators	Following instructions given by dispatchers and yardmasters, tower operators route train traffic by working controls that activate signals and switches on the tracks. Telegraphers and telephoners receive orders about the train's movement, such as its speed or its route, and pass them on to the train crews. Tower operators work in towers located in railroad yards or at major junctions near cities. Telegraphers and telephoners work in yards and at railroad stations.	Telegraphers, telephoners, and tower operators should be responsible and alert, as they have to make quick decisions. Good hearing and eyesight, including normal color vision, are required. Jobs usually are filled from the ranks of clerical workers by seniority. Newcomers receive on-the-job training that covers operating rules, train orders, and station operations. Trainees must pass exams and demonstrate abilities before they qualify. Until permanent positions become available, newly qualified workers substitute for experienced workers who are absent.	Most telegraphers, telephoners, and tower operators are union members.
Track Workers	Railroads employ these workers to service, repair, and replace sections of track.	Railroads prefer applicants who can read, write, and do heavy work. The job is active and strenuous. A physical examination may be necessary. Most new track workers learn their skills through training on the job, which lasts about 2 years.	Track workers on traveling crews may have to commute long distances to work. Many live in camp cars or trailers provided by the railroads. Most track workers are union members.

Transportation Occupations

Occupation	Nature and Places of Work	Training and Qualifications	Other Information

MERCHANT MARINE OCCUPATIONS

Merchant Marine Officers	In command of every oceangoing vessel is the captain, who has complete authority and responsibility for the ship. A typical crew on a ship is divided into the deck department, the engine department, and the steward's department. Deck officers direct the movement of the ship and the maintenance of the deck and hull. Engine officers are responsible for starting, stopping, and controlling the speed of the main engines, as well as maintaining the machinery and equipment aboard ship. Steward officers supervise the cooking and serving of meals, and the upkeep of living quarters. Officers work aboard dry-cargo ships, tankers, barges, ferries, freighters, passenger liners, and excursion steamers.	No educational requirements have been set for merchant marine officers. However, because of the complex machinery and navigational and electronic equipment on modern ships, formal training usually is needed to pass Coast Guard examinations. Candidates must meet certain legal (age, citizenship) and medical requirements. For example, they must be at least 21 years old, U.S. citizens, and have a health certificate proving good physical condition. They also must have at least 3 years of appropriate sea experience or be a graduate of an approved training program. Formal training for merchant marine officers is available at the U.S. Merchant Marine Academy in Kings Point, N.Y., and in six State merchant marine academies. These 4-year programs in nautical science or marine engineering provide classroom instruction as well as practical experience at sea.	Officers must be able to live and work in close quarters as part of a team. They are away from home for long periods of time. Generally, officers at sea work 7 days a week with two 4-hour shifts every 24 hours and 8 hours off in between. Overtime pay is received for over 40 hours work per week. Vacations range from 90 to 180 days a year. Almost 90 percent of all officers belong to maritime unions.
Merchant Marine Sailors	Sailors may be assigned to either the deck department, the engine department, or the steward's department. Under orders from their officers, they do most of the manual labor in these departments. Sailors work aboard dry-cargo ships, tankers, barges, ferries, freighters, passenger liners, and excursion steamers.	Although not required, sea experience in the Navy or Coast Guard provides a good background for merchant marine jobs. Applicants must get a health certificate from a doctor and then must obtain a letter from a shipping company stating that they will be hired when a job becomes available. In addition, applicants must register with the U.S. Coast Guard and acquire identification papers. All these requirements do not guarantee a job; they merely qualify you. To get a job, you must be present at a hiring hall when an opening becomes available. Hiring halls are located in the chief ports around the country.	Sailors must be able to live and work in close quarters as part of a team. They are away from home for long periods of time. Generally, sailors are required to work 7 days a week, with two 4-hour shifts every 24 hours and 8 hours off in between. Overtime pay is received for over 40 hours per week. Vacations range from 90 to 180 days a year. Most sailors belong to unions.

Exploring Careers

Occupation	Nature and Places of Work	Training and Qualifications	Other Information
DRIVING OCCUPATIONS			
Intercity Busdrivers	These workers drive passengers between communities and cities. They also inspect buses before leaving, collect fares or tickets from passengers, and load and unload baggage. Most work out of large cities.	Since they represent their companies in dealing with passengers, bus drivers must be courteous and tactful. They should have steady nerves and a relaxed personality, as heavy traffic can be a strain. The U.S. Department of Transportation requires that intercity drivers be at least 21 years old and be able to read, write, and speak English. They also must have good hearing and vision and normal use of arms and legs. Applicants must pass a driving test and a written exam that tests their knowledge of State traffic regulations. Most States require drivers to have a chauffeur's license. Many private bus companies prefer applicants to be at least 25 years old; some require bus or truck driving experience. Most companies conduct 2- to 8-week training programs for new drivers that include both classroom and driving instruction. Until permanent positions become available, new drivers substitute for experienced drivers who are absent.	Since intercity buses run at all hours, drivers may have to work nights or weekends. The job may require time away from home. Most of these drivers are union members.

Transportation Occupations

Occupation	Nature and Places of Work	Training and Qualifications	Other Information
Long-Distance Truckdrivers	These workers travel along turnpikes and highways carrying goods between cities that are hundreds or even thousands of miles apart.	The U.S. Department of Transportation requires that long-distance drivers be at least 21 years old and in good physical condition, including good hearing and vision, normal use of arms and legs, and normal blood pressure. Applicants must pass written and driving examinations. Most States require truckdrivers to have a chauffeur's license. Some companies require truckdrivers to be at least 25 years old and have several years of truckdriving experience. New drivers are usually trained on the job under the supervision of an instructor or an experienced driver.	A workweek of more than 40 hours is very common. This may include nights or weekends, and often time away from home. The noise and vibration of the truck, and being on the road for long periods of time, may be physically straining and tiring. Most long-distance drivers are union members.
Parking Attendants	Parking attendants park customers' cars and collect payment. They work in public and private parking lots throughout the country.	Attendants must have a valid driver's license, be able to drive all types of cars, and have good eyesight and peripheral vision. They also must be able to keep records of claim tickets, compute parking charges, and make change. Parking attendants should be neat, tactful, and courteous when they are dealing with the public. Good physical condition is helpful, because attendants may have to stand for long periods of time or move cars in a hurry. Although there are no specific educational requirements for parking attendants, many employers prefer high school graduates. Most attendants are trained on the job, under the supervision of a more experienced worker.	Attendants often work long hours and on nights and weekends. In addition, many attendants spend much time outdoors in all kinds of weather. A number of parking attendants are union members.

Exploring Careers

Occupation	Nature and Places of Work	Training and Qualifications	Other Information
Local Transit Busdrivers	These workers drive passengers over city and suburban streets following specific routes and timetables. They also inspect buses before leaving, collect fares or tickets, and answer passengers' questions. They work in cities and towns throughout the country.	Busdrivers must be courteous and tactful in dealing with passengers. They should have steady nerves and a relaxed personality, as heavy traffic can be a strain. New drivers should be at least 21 years old, be in good health, and have good eyesight. They must pass physical and written exams. Most States require a chauffeur's license. High school graduates may be preferred. Most companies conduct on-the-job training for new drivers that includes classroom and driving instruction. Until permanent positions become available, new drivers substitute for experienced drivers who are absent.	The workweek for regular drivers usually consists of any 5 workdays during the week; Saturday and Sunday are counted as regular workdays. Some drivers work a split shift in which they work in the morning, have the afternoon free, and go back to work in the evenings. Most of these drivers are union members.
Local Truckdrivers	These workers drive around town, moving goods from warehouses and terminals to factories, stores, and homes. They often load and unload goods.	Qualifications for drivers vary, depending on the type of truck and nature of the business. Most States require a chauffeur's license. Applicants should be in good health, including good vision and hearing. Experience in loading and unloading freight or as a truckdriver's helper is useful. Since drivers often deal directly with the company's customers, the ability to get along well with people is important. Training given to new drivers is usually informal and may be only a few hours of instruction from an experienced driver.	Local truckdrivers frequently work over 40 hours per week. Night or early morning work is sometimes necessary. Many truckdrivers are union members.

242

Transportation Occupations

Occupation	Nature and Places of Work	Training and Qualifications	Other Information
Taxicab Drivers	Taxicab drivers pick up passengers at any location and drive them to their destination. Although taxicab drivers are employed in all but the smallest cities, employment is concentrated in large metropolitan areas.	Taxi drivers usually must have a State chauffeur's license and a taxicab operator's license issued by the local police or Public Utilities Commission. In most communities, applicants must pass a written exam on taxicab and traffic regulations. Many companies hire only applicants who are over 21 years old. Although there are no minimum educational requirements, many companies prefer applicants who have at least an eighth grade education. Applicants generally must be in good health and have a good driving record. Tact and courtesy are important in dealing with the public. A relaxed personality is also important.	Drivers may have to work nights or weekends. Many cab driving jobs are available for college students and others who want part-time work. Some cab drivers in large cities belong to unions.

This driver of a paper delivery truck works regular business hours unlike other truckers whose hours may vary.

Once in orbit, the Comstar D-3 satellite will be used for long-distance telephone service.

Exploring Careers

Have you ever gazed at the stars on a clear night and wondered what's out there? Have you asked yourself what causes volcanic eruptions, earthquakes, or tidal waves? Or wondered why some mothers have twins or triplets? Perhaps you've never thought about these particular things. Undoubtedly, though, something in the world around you has made you stop and search for an explanation. This experience of yours is shared by humans throughout history, from the cave dwellers to your parents and friends.

People have always wanted to understand the universe. Out of this desire has grown the work of scientists, engineers, and technicians. The scientist gathers knowledge, which the engineer applies to practical problems in agriculture, health, energy, transportation, communication, and other fields. Technicians assist scientists and engineers in their work. Let's look at each a little more closely.

Scientists Investigate the Unknown

Scientists study the universe around us to learn why it behaves as it does. They investigate every aspect of our natural surroundings, from the center of the earth to the farthest star. They study things as small as the tiniest nuclear particle and as gigantic as a galaxy. Scientists examine bursts of energy lasting a millionth of a second as well as rock patterns formed over millions of years. Plants, animals, the oceans, the atmosphere all fall under the questioning eyes of scientists.

All scientists gather knowledge through *research*. To understand how, let's pretend you are a scientist trying to solve a problem. How would you go about it? That depends on the kind of problem you have. If you are a biochemist seeking a cure for cancer, you might examine the effects of certain drugs on rats or guinea pigs in a laboratory. But if you are a geologist studying the formation of a mountain range, you might spend much of your time outdoors collecting rock specimens.

No matter what problem you set out to solve, your research will follow certain guidelines. The first step is to learn what is already known about your problem. Your work depends on the work of scientists before you just as each brick of a building rests upon those below it. Without background preparation, you would spend all your time "reinventing the wheel" and have none left for new discoveries.

Once you have learned all you can from others' work, you consider how to solve the problem facing you. Often, the solution will involve some sort of *experiment*. You have probably performed some already. If so, you know that experiments must obey certain rules to be considered reliable.

Let's assume that you are the world's leading botanist (plant biologist) and want to determine the best growing conditions for geraniums. If you want to study the effect of water alone, you must keep all other growing conditions—soil, temperature, and light—the same. Otherwise, if a plant grows poorly, how will you know whether it has received too little water or too little of something else? You can use many plants—let's say a hundred of equal size, planted in identical pots and soil. If you grow them in the same place under a fluorescent light, they will all receive the same amount of light and heat. You can group the hundred into tens, giving each group a different daily ration of water. Each geranium in group 1, for example, will receive one tablespoon a day; in group 2, five a day, and so on. Then you watch the plants' progress. As a good scientist, you keep a record of everything you do in the experiment, so that you and others may study it later. You want to measure and record the plants' growth every few days, because you may find the information useful. After several months' growth, you can begin to draw conclusions from your observations. If you find that one group of plants grew fastest during the first weeks, while another group grew fastest during the later weeks, you might conclude that the best amont of water depends upon a plant's size. Perhaps another experiment would tell you more precisely how much water the geranium needs.

You trust your conclusions because you followed rules of experimentation that all good scientists follow:

• Isolating one item to study (in this case, the effect of water on the plant's growth);

• Setting up the experiment to examine only that item;

• Recording your procedure and observations; and, finally,

• Basing your conclusions on evidence from the experiment.

Scientists use the information they gather from experiments to either confirm or deny the *hypothesis* they started out with. A hypothesis is an unproven guess about the results of a particular experiment. A hypothesis that is general enough becomes a theory. Theories are accepted explanations of what is known, but often a new theory will replace an old one as scientists investigate further. Astronomers long believed, for example, that the sun, planets, and stars all revolved around the earth. They constructed elaborate models to explain the movements they saw in the night sky. As new movements were observed, these models became more and more complex. Finally, a Polish astronomer named Copernicus stated a theory that the earth and other planets move around the sun, and the earth turns on its axis. Because it was simpler and more logical, Copernicus' theory

Scientific and Technical Occupations

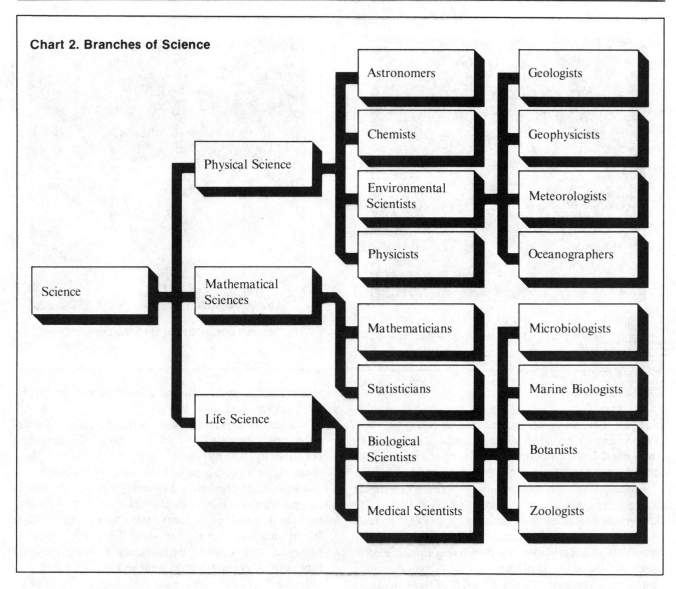

Chart 2. Branches of Science

Science

- Physical Science
  - Astronomers
  - Chemists
  - Environmental Scientists
  - Physicists
  - Geologists
  - Geophysicists
  - Meteorologists
  - Oceanographers
- Mathematical Sciences
  - Mathematicians
  - Statisticians
- Life Science
  - Biological Scientists
  - Medical Scientists
  - Microbiologists
  - Marine Biologists
  - Botanists
  - Zoologists

eventually replaced the old theory as the foundation of astronomy.

What Makes a Good Scientist?

We see that scientists investigate the universe by learning what others already know, performing experiments, and constructing theories that explain the unknown. But what kind of person makes a good scientist? A list of the most important characteristics includes these:

Orderly Thinking. Scientists must be able to analyze problems and information logically in order to draw correct conclusions.

Systematic Work Habits. As we saw, scientists must perform experiments according to certain rules. To do so, they must work carefully and methodically.

The Ability to Work Alone or as Part of a Team. Most scientists work with technicians and other scientists. Cooperation is crucial. At the same time, scientists often work without supervision.

Patience. Some research (such as cancer research) can continue for years without results. A scientist must be able to keep searching for answers, despite occasional frustration.

Above all, *Curiosity.* Scientists have an unquenchable thirst for knowledge, an undying desire to understand the unknown. This intense curiosity inspires them to devote their lives to solving scientific problems, often without the reward of knowing how their discoveries will be used. Many of their achievements do not become important until long after their death. But those scientists continue to explore anyway, driven on by their curiosity.

Exploring Careers

Chemists must have patience and the ability to concentrate on detail. Experiments may take months to complete.

This botanist specializes in studying prehistoric plants.

Careers in Science

If you choose a career in science, what will you study? Take your pick from the whole universe. As you can see from chart 2, the numerous branches of science all grow out of three basic fields. (See previous page.)

People in the *life sciences,* the first field, investigate living things. *Biological scientists*, or biologists, want to know how life on earth began, how plants and animals function, and how they reproduce. Biologists usually specialize in a particular group of living things. *Zoologists*, for example, study the animal kingdom, while botanists investigate the plant world. *Marine biologists* examine the living world of the oceans, while *microbiologists* study bacteria, viruses, and countless other organisms around us that we can see only with a microscope.

What biologists learn about living things, *medical scientists* use to understand and control diseases. Medical scientists differ from doctors (or physicians) who normally come to mind when we think of medicine. Medical scientists seek cures for diseases through research in laboratories, while physicians work directly with sick people. The work of physicians is described in the chapter on health occupations.

The *physical sciences,* the second basic field, cover the rest of our physical universe. Here we find *physicists*, who investigate the behavior of light, heat, electricity, magnetism, and gravity. They see how objects behave at very high speeds or very low temperatures. Past research in physics has provided the knowledge needed for such accomplishments as radio and television, nuclear energy, refrigeration, and space travel.

We also find *chemists,* one of the largest science occupations. Chemists study the 103 known elements (and occasionally discover new ones). They examine how these elements combine to form every substance in the universe, what properties they have, and how they react to one another. For example, chlorine and hydrogen, two gases, combine to form hydrochloric acid, a clear liquid that can burn your skin. The same chlorine, however, will combine with sodium to form ordinary table salt. A chemist would want to know how and why chlorine forms two substances with such different characteristics.

Astronomers, the smallest group of physical scientists, study the heavens with telescopes, cameras, and other devices in order to answer age-old questions about the universe: How large is the universe? How were the stars and planets formed? How do they move? What are they made of? And, perhaps most exciting of all, is there intelligent life elsewhere in the universe?

While astronomers look to the stars, *environmental scientists* examine the earth. *Geologists* study the history and composition of our planet. They also examine movements such as earthquakes and volcanic eruptions. *Geophysicists* turn their attention toward the interior of the earth, the movement of the continents, and the earth's magnetic and gravitational fields. *Oceanographers* focus on the oceans, their movements, and the land beneath the oceans, while the atmosphere and the weather are

Scientific and Technical Occupations

Entomologists develop ways to encourage the spread of helpful insects and the control of harmful insects.

Geologists study the earth's crust. Their research can help locate oil and other valuable minerals.

the domain of *meteorologists*.

Biological and physical scientists could not have achieved as much as they have without discoveries in the third field, the *mathematical sciences*. In addition to being a science in its own right, mathematics is the language of other sciences. *Mathematicians* study this science of ab-stract numbers. Most mathematicians develop their theories to solve a specific problem. Many, however, produce theories that find practical use only much later. *Statisticians* develop and use theories that allow scientists to make generalizations about a group of people or objects without studying every member of the group.

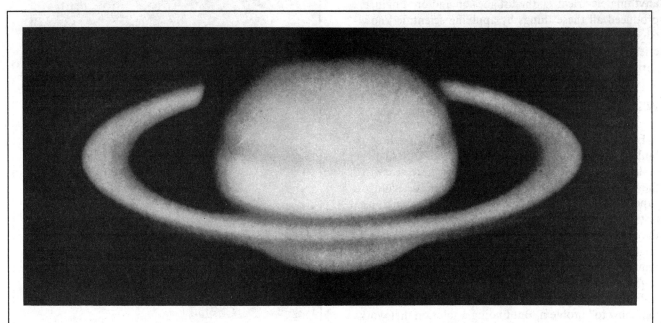

Astronomers took this picture of Saturn through a telescope. Careers in science are for people who like to explore the unknown.

Exploring Careers

We have not named every kind of scientist. There are many more. Some, such as biochemists and astrophysicists, do research in overlapping branches of science. A few scientists move forward in totally new areas of science. . . . This is what an engineer named Karl Jansky did. He discovered that stars give off invisible waves just like the ones carrying music and news to our radios. Other scientists knew about these radio signals from the stars, but nobody paid them much attention. Jansky listened to them with a very sensitive "radio telescope." In this way he began the science of radio astronomy. Progress in science depends upon the pioneers who, like Jansky, break down the old barriers of knowledge and venture forth into unexplored territory.

Engineers Put Science to Work

Did you ever stop to think how many plastic items you use every day? At school you use plastic pens and rulers. You may sit at a desk with a plastic top. In the cafeteria you eat from plastic plates and trays. Perhaps the plates and cups in your kitchen at home are plastic, too. You talk on plastic telephones, listen to plastic records, and use plastic sports equipment. Look around, and see if you can count the number of plastic items in the room you're in right now.

Plastics are just one result of the work of engineers. Others include radio and television, automobiles and airplanes, bridges and skyscrapers, ships and submarines, anything electrical . . . the list goes on and on. Engineers produced all these things by applying scientific knowledge to everyday problems. In fact, most of the discoveries of modern science would have remained laboratory curiosities if not for engineers.

What Do Engineers Do?

Engineers begin with a "how to" problem—how to build a bridge, how to increase the output of a factory, or how to turn sunlight into electricity. Like scientists, they do research to find a solution. In designing a supersonic airplane, for example, aeronautical engineers test different airplane shapes in a wind tunnel to see how they behave at high speeds. Such tests help them decide on the best design before actually building the plane. Similarly, civil engineers make models of various bridges to test each design for strength.

Through research, engineers find scientific answers to the "how to" problem. But finding a solution that works is only the beginning. Engineers also must figure out the cost and difficulty of using that solution. Imagine you are a civil engineer designing a subway tunnel for a large

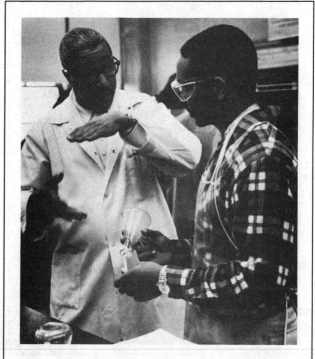

Many chemists teach in universities.

To do their jobs well, engineers must be creative.

Scientific and Technical Occupations

Engineering careers are for people who like to solve problems.

city. You have designed a tunnel that you think would work very well. But you would not have solved the city's problem if your tunnel would cost twice what the city could afford, or if large buildings had to be moved to build it. You have to make sure that your solution to the problem is *economical* and *practical* as well as technically correct.

How do engineers solve problems? They use tools of various kinds, the most important being analytical tools. Analytical tools permit engineers to reshape their problems into manageable forms, and this helps in the search for a solution. Mathematical models are one such analytical tool. The model that an engineer builds is nothing more than a set of equations that describes the problem mathematically. By building a model, an engineer can examine the effects of changes in different parts of the final product.

Engineers also employ equipment of all shapes and sizes for measuring, calculating, and testing. Some devices, such as wind tunnels, serve a very specialized purpose. Others, such as calculators and oscilloscopes, you would find in the laboratories of many kinds of engineers. Some tools remain in the lab; others are used outside, "in the field."

The computer is very important. It can perform calculations that are too long or involved to do by hand. It can handle hundreds of equations at once, so that the engineer can build larger, more complex mathematical models. It can also be used to actually help design whatever the engineer is trying to create.

Engineers rely on one other important tool: Creativity. Unlike math, creativity can't be taught. But good engineers have it and use it to apply science in new, slightly different ways. Although engineers rely heavily on the work of others (such as scientists), they constantly face problems requiring original solutions. They discover, explore, invent, and devise. To do their job well, they must be creative.

Careers in Engineering

If you decide on a career in engineering, you can choose from a wide variety of fields. They are as diverse as the needs of society. Some types of engineers specialize in a particular industry. *Agricultural engineers,* for example, develop ways to produce, process, and distribute food more efficiently. They might design new harvesting equipment or a better canning process. *Chemical engineers* create plastics, synthetic fabrics, and other new materials through chemical processes. *Mining engineers* locate minerals in the ground, design mines, and make sure they operate safely. They also devise ways to transport the minerals to processing plants. *Petroleum engineers* perform a similar role for oil and gas products.

Other engineers specialize in a particular type of technology. *Mechanical engineers,* one of the largest groups, design and develop machines that produce or use power. Every day we rely on such machines—cars and trucks, refrigerators and TV sets, heaters, air conditioners, factory machines, and countless others. Mechanical engineers help create and produce all these machines as well as gasoline engines, steam turbines, jet engines, and nuclear reactors. Some mechanical engineers specialize by concentrating on a single type of machine (such as a jet engine) while others specialize in a single industry (such as the automobile industry).

Electrical engineers, another large group, design and develop electrical and electronic devices. Anything that uses electricity is electrical. Electronic machines—such as radios, TV's, telephones, and computers—convert electricity into sound, radio waves, or some other form of energy. Like mechanical engineers, electrical engineers work in many different industries and usually specialize in a particular area.

Astronaut Guion S. Bluford, Jr., has a doctoral degree in aerospace engineering.

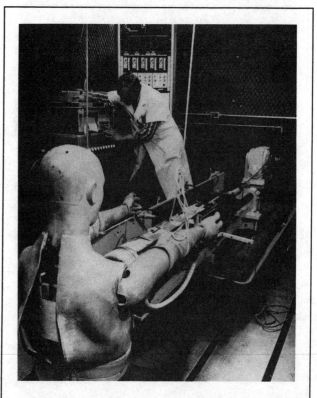

By studying collisions in the lab, engineers and scientists can design safer automobiles.

The world of flight is the world of *aerospace engineers*. They deal with every aspect of aircraft and spacecraft performance, from planning and design to production, testing, and actual use. *Biomedical engineers* use their engineering skills to improve health care in many ways, such as by designing artificial organs or by adapting computers for use in hospitals. *Ceramic engineers* design and develop products from ceramic materials, which are nonmetallic substances processed at high temperatures, such as glass or porcelain. *Metallurgical engineers* cover the broad technology of metals—understanding their properties, extracting them from the earth, refining them, and converting them into finished products.

Other engineers work in construction and a wide variety of industrial activities. *Civil engineers* design large facilities such as highways, railroads, bridges, airports, and water and sewage systems. *Industrial engineers* are "the manager's engineers." They look for ways to make factories and other business operations run more smoothly and efficiently.

We have mentioned only the major categories of engineering. We could not possibly describe each individual specialty. Not only are new ones created all the time, but every engineer's craft is slightly different, depending upon his or her particular training and job. Within the few engineering occupations mentioned there are hundreds of specialties.

Technicians Perform the Practical

We have said that scientists and engineers work as part of a team. Who are the other members of the team? Many are technicians.

But what is a technician? The word (along with the words *technical, technology,* and *technique*) comes from a Greek word meaning *skillful* or *practical*. And there you have the key: Technicians perform the practical aspects of a job, leaving theory to the scientists and design to the engineers. They are the "doers."

Technicians perform the day-to-day tasks necessary in creating a new project or running an operation. They operate testing and measuring equipment in a laboratory. They make drawings of new designs. They build physical models of new projects. They estimate the cost of a project and the amount of materials and labor needed to complete it. They inspect a manufacturing plant to see that the product's quality stays high. They repair machines that break down. They may act as sales repre-

Scientific and Technical Occupations

sentatives, selling products like airplanes or computers.

What Makes a Good Technician?

Every branch of science and engineering has its technicians. Just listing their titles would take several pages. All of them have certain qualities in common:

Basic Background. Technicians have a good foundation in math and the basic sciences—physics, chemistry and/or biology. But they learn more practical problem-solving and much less theory than a scientist or engineer.

A "Head" for the Practical. Many technicians use theoretical knowledge in their work, but most of what they do is of a nuts-and-bolts nature.

Patient, Systematic, Precise Work Habits. Often a technician must repeat a test many times in exactly the same way, or perform a task within very narrow standards. These require reliable work habits.

Ability to Work Under Pressure. In many kinds of work, if something important goes wrong, the technician must think and act quickly without panicking and without making mistakes.

Good Hands. Technicians build, use, and repair equipment and do many other tasks that require them to be good with their hands.

Training for Scientific and Technical Occupations

How would you train for a career as a scientist, engineer, or technician? You may already have begun. If you have hobbies related to science or engineering you already are gaining valuable experience. Using a chemistry set, building radios, fixing bicycles—activities such as these teach skills that could be useful in science or engineering occupations. Do you like to go to museums to learn about the stars, the oceans, or natural history? You may already have begun your science education.

Formal training in science begins in high school. You should take as much math as possible, as well as basic science courses—biology, chemistry, physics, earth science. Your high school probably offers other classes, such as electronics and drafting, that would be useful in some career fields. English courses are important, too, since scientists, engineers, and technicians must be able to communicate clearly with their co-workers, both orally and in writing.

Most of your training, of course, would occur in college. Scientists and engineers generally earn a bachelor's degree after 4 or 5 years' study, and then go on to

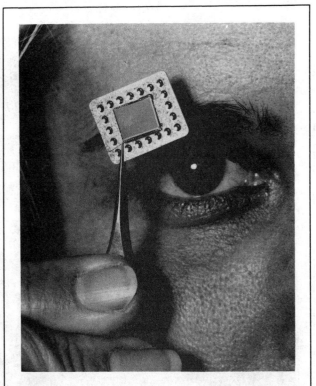

Developed by electronics engineers, this tiny device made possible TV cameras no larger than a deck of cards.

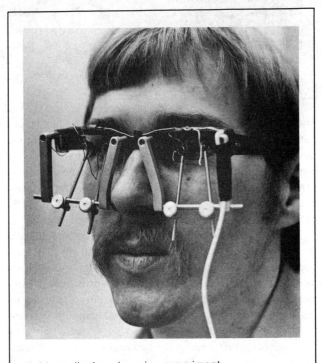

A biomedical engineering experiment.

Drafting can be a career for people who like to draw.

graduate school, if necessary. Today, most science occupations require a Ph.D. Fewer engineers than scientists need a doctorate. Most find work with a bachelor's or master's degree. For teaching or for advanced research, however, the Ph.D. is essential. Technicians usually spend 2 years in special technical training programs after high school, although some have 4-year degrees.

Training does not end when you earn a college degree. New discoveries occur so often that what you learn in college soon will become outdated—though not useless. Just as you can expect to learn new words your whole life, scientists, engineers, and technicians continue to learn new theories and applications their entire lives. They learn by reading books and magazines, going to conferences, and attending occasional seminars. Careers in science are for people who like to learn outside as well as in school.

A Final Word

If you have a strong interest in science or mathematics, don't stop here! Several other chapters of *Exploring Careers* are worth looking into.

There is a chapter on Health Occupations, many of which require a sound grasp of biology and chemistry and the ability to draw on scientific principles in dealing with day-to-day health care.

Students who are good in mathematics or physics might want to learn more about a career in architecture. This field, like engineering, involves an understanding of materials and their properties. A story about an architect appears in the chapter on Performing Arts, Design, and Communications Occupations. A field closely related to both architecture and engineering is urban and

Scientific and Technical Occupations

Technicians assist scientists and engineers. "Technician" comes from a Greek word meaning practical skill.

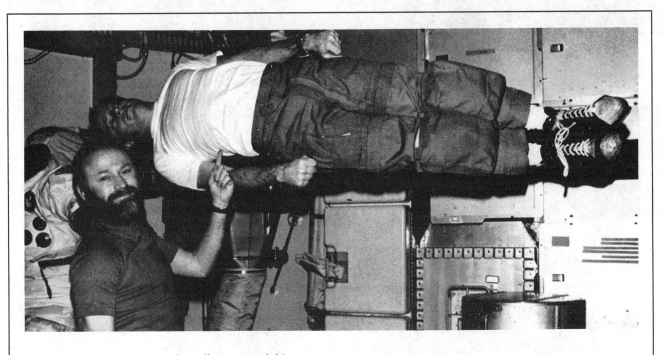

Astronauts demonstrate zeroing effects on weight.

regional planning. A story about a planner appears in the chapter on Office Occupations.

Interested in computers? You may already know of the broad range of scientific and technical jobs in the field of computer science, including programming, systems analysis, and computer design. To learn a little more about this field, read the story about the program-

mer/systems analyst. This, too, is in the chapter on Office Occupations.

Did you know that it takes more than an interest in the environment and the outdoors to become a forester? Scientific training is important, too. A story about a forester appears in the chapter on Agriculture, Forestry, and Fishery Occupations.

Biochemist

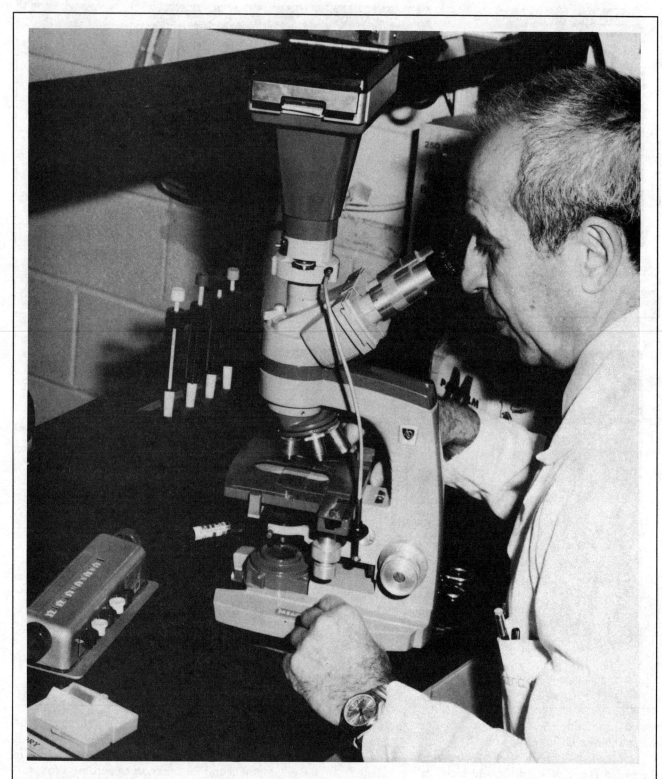

Dr. George Catravas' plans took several twists and turns before he decided on chemistry. "I didn't even like chemistry in high school," he recalls.

Scientific and Technical Occupations

George Catravas works in a special world. He wears a white coat. He walks on concrete floors in large rooms with cluttered counters and cabinets. He works at tables covered with glassware, hardware, and plastic tubes. He handles mice and rats in cages. He uses large machines with long names like "analytical ultracentrifuge" and "recording spectrophotometer."

Most of us never see this world.

At the same time, he works in a world common to all of us. His is the world of the cell, the basic unit of life.

George Catravas is a biochemist.

As chairman of the biochemistry department at the Armed Forces Radiobiology Research Institute in Bethesda, Maryland, Dr. Catravas has many duties. He plans, supervises, and coordinates activities of the whole department. Now and then he teaches at a nearby university, which he enjoys.

But most of all he loves research. "Molecules don't cheat," he points out. "They remain the same, waiting for you to figure them out."

As the Institute's name suggests, Dr. Catravas studies radiation and its effects on humans and other animals. People receive doses of radiation from many sources. Every day we all absorb small amounts of natural radiation from outer space and from radioactive minerals, such as uranium, in the earth. Radiation also comes from X-ray machines, nuclear reactors, and other places where radioactive materials are used. "Radiation" actually means any of a whole variety of energy rays, including visible light, ultraviolet light (the kind made by sunlamps), heat, radio waves, and others. Most of these rays are harmless to living things. Many kinds, however, such as X-rays and gamma rays, can be dangerous. These dangerous rays are the ones studied at the Institute.

Radiation can cause cells to reproduce in a new form and become cancerous. Dr. Catravas and his colleagues want to know exactly how this occurs. The damage depends on the type of cell as well as the type and intensity of radiation. When they understand this process well enough, they will better understand how to protect people from harmful radiation and how to use radiation for beneficial purposes.

Dr. Catravas and his team of workers have several different projects in progress. He himself spends most of his time studying how radiation and certain drugs affect the cells of the brain. He also takes part in projects to answer other questions, such as how radiation affects liver cells, how it can be used to treat cancer, and how we can protect ourselves from it.

Before beginning an experiment, Dr. Catravas, like any good scientist, must plan. He and his assistants decide exactly what they hope to learn and how this experiment will give them their answer. They then discuss what they will need. What kind of animals should be used? How much radiation should they be exposed to and for how long? Must anything be done to the animals beforehand? When and what will they be fed?

Dr. Catravas explains all the details of the experiment to his laboratory technicians so that they can perform the necessary steps, with his help and guidance. He will perform especially delicate experiments first, while his assistants look on. But, being a teacher as well as a researcher, Dr. Catravas gives his helpers as much responsibility as possible so that they may learn by doing.

How does the actual experiment proceed? In studying the cells of the cerebral cortex of the brain, for example, Dr. Catravas may decide he needs only a few milligrams of brain tissue for each of three or four types of analysis he wants to perform. One mouse is enough to provide that amount. The Institute buys rats and mice from companies that breed them especially for laboratory purposes, and has its own veterinarian to keep them free of disease.

Dr. Catravas selects his mice at random for the experiment and feeds them. He places them in small cages that confine their movement, so that they will receive a uniform dose of radiation. He then puts the cages in a large chamber where they will be exposed to X-rays. He may decide to expose them for 90 minutes a day for 7 days, or for some other length of time.

Once he has exposed the mice, he has them dissected and their cerebral cortexes removed so that their cells can be examined. He uses biochemical techniques to separate the cells into their parts, in order to look at each. First he uses chemicals that break the membrane, or outer covering, of each cell. Then he puts the sample in a centrifuge, a machine that spins the sample at very high speeds, the way you might swing a ball in a circle on a length of string. The centrifugal force pulls the heaviest part of the cell, the nucleus, closest to the bottom of the tube, away from the center of the machine. Lighter parts of the cell migrate toward the middle of the tube, while many of the enzymes remain at the top. In this way the centrifuge creates layers in the tube, with each layer containing different parts of the cell. Using this and other sophisticated techniques, Dr. Catravas can separate the cells into their various parts.

Next, he examines the parts by using other instruments. One instrument, the electron microscope, allows him to view parts of the cell too small to be seen through normal microscopes. Another, called an analytical ultracentrifuge, photographs the cell molecules in ultraviolet light as they are spun to see if they are broken. These and other techniques allow Dr. Catravas to study the damage caused by the radiation.

An experiment may require several weeks to complete.

Exploring Careers

After it is finished, Dr. Catravas again meets with his co-workers, this time to discuss the results. Did the experiment run as planned, or should it be repeated? Should it be changed and rerun? Did a new factor appear that requires further study? What new experiments are needed? With each experiment the researchers come closer to the answers they seek.

How does one become a biochemist? Dr. Catravas' own path took several twists and turns. His background includes some training in law, as well as separate degrees in chemistry, biochemistry, and organic chemistry. He studied and taught in Greece, Germany, England, and France before coming to the United States to do further study and research at the University of Chicago. After 7 years there, he left to join a company that makes laboratory instruments. Several years and a few inventions later, he moved to his present position.

You needn't study in as many places nor take as many degrees as Dr. Catravas to find interesting work in biochemistry. Some of his assistants, for example, have bachelor's degrees, while others have master's degrees. They all learn on the job as well as in school. But Dr. Catravas points out that, to reach positions of responsibility in this field, you should have a Ph. D. degree. That may seem like a mountain of work, but it can also be a short beginning step in a long, satisfying career.

Just ask George Catravas.

Exploring

Biochemists are curious about the wonders and mysteries of life.

- Do you enjoy looking at ordinary living things, such as leaves, insects, and flowers, through a magnifying glass or microscope?
- Do you try to learn more about what you see?
- Do you wonder what your body, the earth, or the stars are made of?

Biochemists continue learning all their lives.

- Do you like to read?
- Do you look up words you don't know in a dictionary?
- Do you like to browse in the new book section of your library?
- Do you belong to a science club?

Biochemists must think like detectives to solve the mysteries of science.

- Do you like to solve puzzles, riddles, and brain teasers?
- When you don't understand something, do you try to figure it out before asking for help?

Biochemists work with numbers and advanced mathematics.

- Do you do well in math?
- Do you enjoy working with numbers?
- Do you like to calculate sports statistics or automobile mileage?

Biochemists do experiments that may take weeks, months, even years to finish. They must be very patient.

- Do you enjoy crafts such as paint-by-numbers or needlepoint?
- Do you like to do large jigsaw puzzles?
- Do you like long projects such as growing vegetables or putting on a play?

Biochemists pay attention to detail when they do research.

- Can you follow the instructions correctly when you build a model airplane, assemble a radio from a kit, make a casserole, sew clothes from a pattern, or put together a bicycle from parts?
- Can you give detailed instructions?
- Can you read a road map?

Scientific and Technical Occupations

Electrical Engineer

As vice-president in charge of engineering, Gloria Blue uses her talents to develop new hi-fi products.

Gloria Blue pulled into her parking space and turned off the engine. Climbing out of the car, she noticed how warm the morning was. Although she had moved to Los Angeles from Chicago over 6 years ago and should have been used to the weather by now, spring-like days in November still seemed odd.

Gloria entered the modern brick building with the sign above the double glass doors that read "Auto Fidelity Inc." After greeting the receptionist, she stopped to chat with another co-worker before climbing the stairs to her own office, the one marked "Vice-President of Engineering."

Laying her briefcase on the table, Gloria ran over the day's work in her mind. Normally Friday was the easiest workday, but there'd be plenty to do today before going home for the weekend.

Auto Fidelity Inc., known as AFI, is one of the nation's leading distributors of sound equipment for cars and other vehicles. AFI manufactures radios, tape players, speakers, and other products and distributes them to stores and dealers across the country. As Vice-President of Engineering, Gloria Blue uses her electrical engineering skills to develop new products that meet the needs of customers. She is the bridge between the technical side and the sales side of AFI's business.

Armed with a cup of coffee, she sat down to the first task of the day—completing a technical bulletin she had begun earlier in the week. Since many car owners install two pairs of speakers in their cars instead of just one, Gloria and her staff had designed a new connector plug that allows the customer to connect all four speakers to the radio without splicing wires. But AFI couldn't get its sales campaign underway until the sales staff understood what the new connector could do, and what advantages it offered. Gloria's bulletin would explain all this to the sales people.

She had nearly finished writing it when Bob Cohen, chief design engineer, called. "Come on down to the lab when you have a chance," he said. "I've finished the model of the DAT."

"I'll be right down," answered Gloria, anxious to see Bob's results.

Bob was leaning over a table, changing a few details on a drawing, when Gloria walked into the room. "It's over here," said Bob, turning to one of the metal workbenches littered with electronic devices, handtools, wires, half-dismantled radios, and loose parts. He picked up a small metal box with several knobs on one side and handed it to his boss. Removing the top and examining the box closely, Gloria commented, "I think we have a winner."

The DAT, or digital audio tape, was one of her better ideas. She had followed trends in the home stereo equipment market as well as in the automobile products sold by AFI's competitors. From all she had seen, Gloria felt that the public would buy a recordable digital audio unit. The DAT would increase the fidelity of a radio or tape player and the recording feature would allow listeners to record from the radio while driving down the street. No other company offered such a product for automobiles.

After creating the general concept, Gloria had handed the idea to Bob and his staff, who actually designed the device. They figured out what parts to use, arranged them in a package, and tested it. But they worked under the guidance of Gloria, whose job it was to make sure the product would be attractive, reliable, and inexpensive.

Gloria and Bob, both electrical engineers, performed quite different engineering jobs at AFI. Bob's position was purely technical, while Gloria had moved into a management job. The work was a far cry from what she had dreamed about as a teenager.

When she was in junior high, Gloria was sure she'd be a nurse one day. Her favorite aunt was a head nurse at one of Chicago's largest hospitals, and Gloria enjoyed talking with her about the job. By her senior year in high school, she had changed her mind. A long talk with her guidance counselor encouraged her to think about a career that involved mathematics; Gloria always had made excellent grades in math. So she started college with plans to become a math teacher.

That fall she met her husband-to-be, Larry, who was a junior at the engineering school. They frequently studied together and discussed their courses. Gloria grew more and more interested in Larry's engineering problems, and liked trying her hand at solving them. Before the school year was over, Gloria had decided to switch to electrical engineering. It took all summer to sell her parents on the idea but they finally agreed that the decision was hers to make. Gloria recalls how proud they were when she received her bachelor's degree in engineering.

Gloria started out in the research and development division of a large manufacturer of electrical products in Chicago, and spent the next 10 years there. She developed a solid reputation in the area of product development. At the same time, she was attending evening classes in business and management to earn a master's degree in business administration. This combination of technical and nontechnical skills made her just the right person for the California job advertised by AFI.

Gloria and Bob discussed the DAT for almost an hour. Once the company's designer developed the cosmetics, or outer appearance, for the product, the factory could begin producing it. Then, after testing, it would appear

Scientific and Technical Occupations

in the stores. Gloria looked forward to that day; of all the things she did for AFI, she most enjoyed seeing an idea grow into a successful product.

On her way back to her office, she bumped into Jim Leviton, the company president. "By the way, Jim," said Gloria, "I've looked at that new FFT that we discussed and read the literature on it. A Fast Fourier Transform analyzer would let us test a radio in about 2 seconds, much faster and better than we can now. Even though it costs $40,000, we need it badly for our laboratory."

"Let's get together with Al and decide if we can afford it," answered Jim. "How about this afternoon?"

"Fine," replied Gloria, "as long as we don't talk too long. I'll have that sales bulletin on the connector done before lunch, but I still have some preparing to do for Monday's meeting with Toshiro."

"That meeting will be a long one," thought Gloria. Hero Toshiro is an engineer who works with the manufacturing division of AFI. Gloria gives him her ideas in the form of a drawing or, as with the DAT, a model. He and his staff then complete the design and put it into production. Gloria was encouraging the development of thinner and thinner and thinner radio and cassette mechanisms for the new year. She felt that the latest trends were leading in that direction, and she hoped that Toshiro and his staff could develop them in time for the new product year. At their Monday meeting they would discuss problems and progress of the new design.

After the conversation with Jim, Gloria continued on her way back to her office. "You'd never know how much work I have by looking at my desk," she thought as she sat down. The desk top was large but fairly empty. Between the "In" box on one side and a stack of trade journals on the other lay the bulletin she was working on. Everything else was put away. Gloria felt that you couldn't get ahead unless you were organized. And she was proud of her talent for organization.

Gloria glanced at her watch. It was 11:30, and she had an appointment for lunch at noon. With quick strokes of her pen she continued writing, changing a word here and adding a sentence there, until the bulletin was finished. Then, after checking the diagrams once more, she gave it to her secretary to be typed.

Gloria and Bob discuss plans for a new product. "A career in engineering has given me the opportunity to express myself creatively," says Gloria.

Exploring Careers

Exploring

Electrical engineers must deal with complex devices and understand how they work.

- Do you enjoy taking things apart to see how they work?
- Do you like to repair your bicycle?
- Do you fix your younger brothers' and sisters' toys?
- Are you good at repairing things around the house?
- Do you like to read about new inventions?

Electrical engineers apply what they know to solve practical problems.

- Do you like word problems in math?
- Do you like to solve engineering problems around the house, such as the best way of putting up a shelf?
- Do you wonder what relation your school subjects have to the real world?
- Are you more likely to study if you think a subject has practical value?

Electrical engineers deal with many ideas and objects that cannot be seen or felt. They must be able to think abstractly.

- Can you look at a pattern for a model or for clothing and picture the finished product?
- Can you look at a machine such as an automobile and picture its inner workings?

Electrical engineers look for creative answers to problems.

- Do you play games of strategy such as checkers, chess, or bridge?
- Do you enjoy solving puzzles?
- Do you like to think of new ways of doing things around the house?

Electrical engineers must pay attention to detail.

- Do you enjoy projects that involve precise, detailed handwork?
- Do you enjoy doing needlepoint? Painting by numbers? Building and rigging model ships? Building a radio from a kit?
- Do you go over your homework carefully before you hand it in?

Electrical engineers must continually read and learn, because new discoveries and inventions are made all the time.

- Do you like to read for pleasure?
- When you are curious about something, do you go to an encyclopedia or library to learn more about it?
- Do you like to read any popular scientific or technical magazines?
- Do you look up words you don't know in a dictionary?

Electrical engineers must be able to write clearly.

- Can you write street directions or other instructions?
- Can you write a recipe?
- Do you write your math or science homework clearly enough for others to follow it?

Electrical engineers must be able to discuss technical subjects.

- Can you express yourself well?
- If a teacher doesn't answer your question exactly, do you ask it again in a different way?
- Can you help your brothers, sisters, or friends with their homework?

Scientific and Technical Occupations

Broadcast Technician

Technical school training in electronics led to a career in broadcasting for Edna Tower.

Exploring Careers

Edna Tower held up her right hand, palm forward, like a courtroom witness taking an oath. Punching a lighted button in front of her with her left hand, she heard the tape reels begin to spin. Then she closed her right fist and pointed her index finger forward. The woman on the right side of the double glass began reading in a crisp, pleasant voice from a page in front of her: "Looking for a truly professional dry cleaner? Then come to Top Notch Cleaners at six locations in Springfield …" While the announcer's voice radiated from speakers in the control room, Edna watched the sound meter needles bounce and adjusted a slide control here and there. When the reading was finished, she punched another button to stop the tape. The women left the studio and Edna prepared for her next assignment.

Edna Tower works at radio station WELL as a production technician or engineer. WELL broadcasts classical music on AM and FM, and while located in a major city, the station employs a relatively small staff. This means that an experienced technician like Edna has many different kinds of duties each day. She enjoys this variety. Even though the big operations like rock 'n roll WAIL or news station WHAT could offer her more money, "they have you doing the same thing all day," explains Edna.

Edna had arrived at the station a bit before 9:30, had drunk a quick cup of coffee with one of the announcers, and was now in her control room.

Control room 3 is where Edna spends most of her time. She sits at a control board directly in front of the window facing the studio. The board has dozens of buttons, dials, meters, and slide switches that allow her to set sound levels in the studio, mix sounds from different sources (such as a speaking voice and background music), and operate the turntables, tape recorders, and compact disc players (CDs) in the room. From this board she can even control a live broadcast coming from outside the studio, such as a concert at the local symphony hall. Edna is particularly proud of this equipment, which she installed herself. At a larger station, she might not have been given the opportunity. And she knows those buttons and switches by heart. "When you're in the middle of a performance, you can't take time to look at the board. You have to know where everything is by feel." The control room also contains a turntable for playing records, two CD players, three reel-to-reel tape decks, two machines that play cartridge tapes (known as carts), plus devices for erasing used tape and cabinets containing tapes and tools.

Edna had begun this particular workday with the daily ritual of checking the equipment. First she had cleaned and "demagnetized" the "heads" on the tape decks (the small metal parts that touch the tape as it moves and actually create or erase the recording). Cleaning them requires only a wipe with a cotton swab dipped in alcohol, while a special electrical device, called a demagnetizer, is used to remove any unwanted magnetic interference that might make the recordings noisy. Next she had checked the machines overall to be sure they were running smoothly. (Once a week they would be tested more thoroughly, with electronic tools).

Shortly before 10, Renee Baily, the assistant programming director, had walked into the room with a pencil behind her ear and a clipboard in her hand. "There's a change of schedule," she had said. "The woman from the hospital came in early, so we'll tape her interview right away, then do the commercial spots, and do Lisa's program at 11."

Edna had glanced at the production schedule taped to the wall. The mimeographed sheet showed her workweek in half-hour slots and listed her assignments next to them. At 11 today she was scheduled to tape an interview with Emma Swenson, the special projects coordinator for the city's hospital for children. John Griffin, one of WELL's announcers, would conduct the interview. Since Mrs. Swenson had arrived early, they would do the interview immediately. Lisa Dillich's music appreciation program, which Edna was scheduled to record at 10, would be postponed.

Just then John walked in and introduced Mrs. Swenson. Edna then led them into the studio.

Much of what WELL's listeners hear on the air takes place in this 12- by 14-foot room called Studio 4. Inside the room one finds a carpet-covered table with several chairs, a grand piano, half a dozen large microphones on long stands, and an endless tangle of electrical cords on the floor. Mrs. Swenson commented on the large potted broadleafed palm standing in one corner of the room. "The music makes it grow very well," replied Edna.

John and his guest sat down at the table. After positioning a microphone, or "mike", between them, Edna returned to her control board and adjusted the volume level while the pair chatted. She threaded a reel of tape on one of the decks, reminded Mrs. Swenson to avoid rustling papers, and then signaled to John through the window that she was ready to go. Edna talks to people in the studio over the intercom, except when she is recording. Then, she signals by hand through the window. She held up her hand to ask for silence, started the tape, and pointed at John to tell him to begin. At the same moment she started a timer. "We have a 15-minute slot on Sunday," said Renee, watching over Edna's shoulder. "So let's take about 20 minutes' worth and cut it to size."

Scientific and Technical Occupations

While John and his guest talked, Edna made a few minor sound adjustments. As the 20th minute approached, John wrapped up the interview. Edna anticipated his last words and stopped the tape just after he uttered them. "Great interview!" exclaimed Renee. "We'll air it Sunday." As Renee left the control room to say goodbye to Mrs. Swenson, Edna rewound the tape and returned it to its box. Later she and John would decide which parts to edit out.

Edna checked her watch. "It's 10:30. Tom should be here any minute to do these commercials." And as she was spinning a reel of tape on the bulk eraser to make it as clean as possible, Tom Nardone, another WELL announcer, walked into the studio with a sheaf of papers. He sat down at the table and adjusted the mike to his height. Edna threaded the tape and sat down at the board. "Read to me," she told Tom over the intercom, adjusting the volume. "We have half a dozen ads here," Tom finally said, "so it may take about 20 minutes." "Fine," answered Edna, and as she started the tape, she signaled Tom to begin.

Tom read each commercial in turn. Edna captured them all on reel tape; later she would transfer each ad to an individual cartridge. Then, during a broadcast, it would simply be popped into the cart machine and played at the right moment.

After putting away the tape she had just used, Edna went into the studio to set up the mikes for Lisa Dillich's program. Lisa had a weekly series of 1-hour shows in which she explained music concepts (such as key, chords, and harmony) in a way the average listener could understand. She would play one or two pieces of music at the beginning, then talk about them, playing the piano to clarify her explanation. Lisa's programs were one reason Edna like working at WELL. Though she had never thought much of classical music before, Edna grew to enjoy it as she heard more and more at the station. Listening to Lisa's series taught her something about the theory behind music.

Preparing for Lisa's show posed a new problem: Setting up the mikes to make both voice and piano sound good. While studying mechanical engineering in trade school, Edna learned about acoustics (the science of sound) and tone. So she knew that the studio, like any room, had certain acoustical characteristics. She had recommended that to improve sound quality, special panels be hung on the walls of the studio, some to reflect and some to absorb sound. Changing a room in this way is called "tuning" it. A studio used only for voice would be tuned differently than one used only for music. In this studio, which was used for both, a compromise had to be made. With her experience and technical knowledge, Edna was able to arrange the mikes to achieve a good sound.

Lisa came into the studio and sat down at the piano with her script. After a sound test on Lisa's voice and the piano, Edna signaled her to begin. Lisa read her script, illustrating with the piano where necessary. When she reached the place in the script where two complete musical selections would be played, she paused and then continued reading. Later Edna would take the music from records and mix it with Lisa's voice recording into a master tape.

The session with Lisa lasted until a quarter to 12. Forty-five minutes until lunch, with no other assignment. Just enough time to transfer those commercials to carts and insert the music in Lisa's show.

Edna's schedule after lunch, from 1:30 to 5:30, looked much like the morning—more recording and editing. But not every day was the same. Tomorrow she wouldn't have to arrive at the station until 1:30 p.m. From 6:30 to 9:30 she would operate the controls for WELL's nightly live program.

On Sunday, she'd be pulling the "graveyard" shift at the transmitter.

The transmitter, located on a hill five miles from the studio is the source of WELL's signal, the invisible waves that travel to people's radios carrying music and voices. WELL has four 450-foot towers clustered around a small building.

Edna is proud of the station's equipment, much of which she installed herself. "I have to keep checking it to make sure everything works right."

Exploring Careers

The transmitter was operated by remote control from the station. But every Sunday night, after midnight, one of the technicians was assigned to PM—preventative maintenance. That meant vacuuming out the transmitter and cleaning the contacts to be sure that the station wouldn't have technical problems or go off the air during the week.

Edna wasn't crazy about this part of her job, which usually took four to six hours. But it was better than the old days, before remote control, when someone had to be at the transmitter all the time to be sure things ran smoothly. Those shifts had been boring and lonely. At least these PM sessions were only once a week and Edna shared the duties with a few more people, so she only pulled the duty about once a month. And she couldn't help smiling as she thought of the station manager's favorite saying, "Preventative maintenance eliminates panic maintenance!"

The irregular schedule let Edna organize her time for studying and classes. Although she had attended technical school for two years after high school, she was taking evening classes in electronics. She wants to increase her knowledge of electronics, in order to keep up with new developments and to remain competitive in her occupation. The community college offers a degree in electronics, and Edna hopes to have hers next term.

Generally, Edna Tower is satisfied with her job. She uses knowledge of electronics, acoustics, and music. She installs and repairs the equipment as well as operates it. She does many different things. And she does them all with pride. Anything it takes to improve WELL's sound quality, she's willing to do. Her only complaint is that WELL's listeners don't know about her work. "The better a job technician does the less it's noticed. I'm behind the scenes—the audience may not even know about my part in presenting a show."

Exploring

Technicians must train their ears to pick out imperfections in the recordings they make and in the broadcasts they engineer.

- Do you like to listen closely to music and pick out its different parts?
- Can you tell a good recording from a poor one?
- When listening to the radio, do you adjust the tuning to get the best sound from the station?

Technicians often have odd work schedules.

- Would you mind working nights, early mornings, or weekends?

- Could you adjust to having different working hours each day of the week?

Technicians often must operate controls continually through long broadcasts.

- Can you sit still and pay attention to something for a long period of time?
- Can you be patient during classes that don't really interest you?
- Do you play long games such as Monopoly?
- Do you watch TV programs that run 2 hours or more?

Technicians usually spend most of their workday in a few small studio rooms.

- Would you be satisfied working inside all day long?
- Would it bother you to spend the day in a small room with no outside windows?

Technicians often are given new tasks before they finish their current ones.

- Are you able to handle several projects or homework assignments at the same time?
- Can you finish them all on time?
- Is it easy for you to switch back and forth from one project to another?

Technicians must think and act quickly if something unexpected happens during a broadcast.

- Can you stay calm and act sensibly if a toilet overflows, the lights go out, the roof leaks, or some other emergency occurs at home?
- Do you know whom to call if something goes wrong when your parents are away?
- Are you good at handling crises on the school grounds or playground?

Technicians must keep an eye on several things at once.

- Can you cook a whole meal yourself and have everything ready at the same time?
- Do you enjoy watching sports such as football, basketball, soccer, or hockey in which you have to keep track of many players at once?
- Do you play complex games like chess or bridge?

Technicians work with their hands.

- Do you have any hobbies or crafts that require fine handiwork?
- Are you good with tools?
- Do you play a musical instrument?

Scientific and Technical Occupations

Job Facts

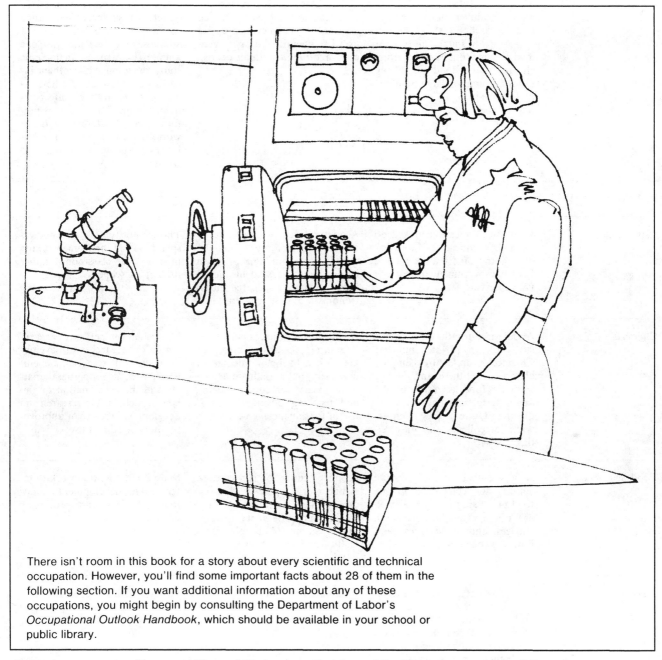

There isn't room in this book for a story about every scientific and technical occupation. However, you'll find some important facts about 28 of them in the following section. If you want additional information about any of these occupations, you might begin by consulting the Department of Labor's *Occupational Outlook Handbook*, which should be available in your school or public library.

Occupation	Nature and Places of Work	Training and Qualifications	Other Information

LIFE SCIENCE OCCUPATIONS

Biochemists	About half of all biochemists work for colleges and universities, while a fourth work for private companies. The rest work for government agencies, private research institutes, or for themselves.	A graduate degree is necessary. A bachelor's degree in biochemistry or chemistry may lead to a job as a research assistant or technician. People with jobs as biochemists, especially in research or teaching, generally have a graduate degree in biochemistry.	The great majority of biochemists hold research positions, rather than managerial or other positions.

Exploring Careers

Occupation	Nature and Places of Work	Training and Qualifications	Other Information
Life Scientists	Most life scientists work for colleges and universities as teachers and researchers. Many do research in hospitals and other medical institutions. The drug, chemical, and food processing industries employ large numbers of life scientists, as do Federal, State, and local government agencies.	A bachelor's degree in biology may lead to a job as a research assistant or technician; a career as a life scientist, however, generally requires a graduate degree.	Life scientists specialize in a wide variety of subjects. They may concentrate on either plants or animals, or even study just one kind of plant or animal. Some study breeding while others investigate diseases. Still others examine drugs and their effects on living things. Life scientists perform many different kinds of work, from research and teaching to advising, managing, and writing.

PHYSICAL SCIENTISTS

Occupation	Nature and Places of Work	Training and Qualifications	Other Information
Astronomers	Most astronomers teach and do research in colleges and universities. Many others work for the Federal Government and for private observatories.	A doctoral degree in astronomy is necessary for most jobs. To qualify for a graduate program in astronomy, a student should have a bachelor's degree in astronomy, physics, or math.	The majority of astronomers spend most of their time working in offices or classrooms, rather than at telescopes.
Chemists	About three-fourths of all chemists work in private industry. Chemical manufacturers employ almost half of these, and the rest work for food, scientific instrument, petroleum, and other industries. Quite a few chemists work for colleges and universities.	A college education is necessary. Beginning jobs are open to people with a bachelor's degree in chemistry, but a graduate degree is necessary for some research and teaching positions, and is useful for advancement.	Most chemists perform basic research or research and development. In basic research, a chemist explores the properties of matter and the combination of elements. A chemist in research and development creates or improves products for direct use.
Food Scientists	Food scientists work all over the country for companies in the food processing industry as well as for Federal and State agencies, colleges and universities, and other organizations.	A college education is necessary. A bachelor's degree in food science, biology, or chemistry is the minimum requirement for beginning positions. Many jobs, especially teaching and research, require a graduate degree.	Many food scientists work in research and development of new food products and processing techniques.
Physicists	Nearly half of all physicists teach or perform research at colleges and universities. Many others work in chemical, electrical equipment, aircraft and missile, and other manufacturing companies.	Graduate study in physics is essential for most beginning positions and for all advanced ones.	Physicists usually specialize in a particular area, such as nuclear physics, optics, or acoustics.

ENVIRONMENTAL SCIENTISTS

Occupation	Nature and Places of Work	Training and Qualifications	Other Information
Geologists	Most geologists work in private industry, for petroleum, mining, quarrying, and other companies. Many work for Federal and State agencies and colleges and universities.	A college education is necessary in this occupation. While a bachelor's degree is enough for some starting jobs, a graduate degree is helpful for promotion.	Geologists may work outdoors much of the time, depending upon their specialty. They often work in offices and laboratories, however.

Scientific and Technical Occupations

Occupation	Nature and Places of Work	Training and Qualifications	Other Information
Geophysicists	Most geophysicists work in private industry, for petroleum, natural gas, mining, and other companies. Most of the others are employed by Federal and State government agencies or by colleges and universities.	A college education is necessary in this occupation. A bachelor's degree in geophysics is sufficient for most beginning jobs. A degree in a related field is also adequate, as long as the student has taken certain courses. For higher positions in research, exploration, and teaching, a graduate degree is desirable.	Many geophysicists work outdoors and travel extensively. Some work at research stations in remote areas or on ships or aircraft.
Meteorologists	The National Oceanic and Atmospheric Administration, private industry, and colleges and universities all employ meteorologists. The Department of Defense employs civilian meteorologists in addition to those in the military services.	A college degree is necessary. A bachelor's degree in meteorology or a related science is the minimum requirement for starting jobs. A graduate degree is important for promotion, and essential for research and college teaching jobs.	Not all meteorologists forecast the daily weather. Some work in climatology, the study of long-term weather trends; others administer programs or teach.
Oceanographers	About half of all oceanographers teach or do research at colleges and universities. A fourth work for Federal agencies. The rest work for other government agencies and for private industry.	A college education is necessary. Most beginning positions require a bachelor's degree in oceanography, biology, earth or physical sciences, mathematics, or engineering. For many advanced positions, however, an advanced degree in oceanography or a basic science is desirable.	Some oceanographers are away from home for weeks or months at a time while on ocean research voyages.

MATHEMATICS OCCUPATIONS

Occupation	Nature and Places of Work	Training and Qualifications	Other Information
Mathematicians	About three-fourths of all mathematicians work in colleges and universities, the majority of them as teachers. Most others are employed in government and private industry.	A graduate degree usually is necessary. While a bachelor's degree may lead to a beginning job, promotional opportunities are limited without graduate study. A person seeking work as an applied mathematician in a field such as physics or economics needs training in that field as well as in mathematics.	Mathematicians can work in theoretical (pure) or applied mathematics. Theoretical mathematicians develop new mathematical techniques and knowledge without necessarily having a practical use in mind. Applied mathematicians use that knowledge to solve everyday problems in physics, engineering, business, economics, and other fields.
Statisticians	Most statisticians work for insurance firms, finance companies, public utilities, manufacturers, and research organizations. Many others work for Federal, State, and local government agencies.	A college education is necessary. Most beginning positions require a bachelor's degree either with a major in math or statistics or with a major in an applied field, such as economics, and a minor in statistics. Graduate training is necessary for teaching positions and helpful for promotion in other areas.	Because the science of statistics is used so widely in other fields, statisticians often work under other titles. A statistician working with information on the economy, for example, may have the title of economist.

Exploring Careers

Occupation	Nature and Places of Work	Training and Qualifications	Other Information
ENGINEERS			
Aerospace Engineers	Most aerospace engineers work for the aircraft and parts industry. Many others are employed by the National Aeronautics and Space Administration and by the Department of Defense.	A bachelor's degree in engineering is required for most beginning jobs. Some engineering jobs are filled by people trained in the appropriate natural science or in mathematics. Graduate study is increasingly important for advancement.	Aerospace engineers often specialize in one area, such as structural design, navigation systems, or production methods. They may also specialize in a particular product line, such as passenger planes, helicopters, or satellites.
Agricultural Engineers	Most agricultural engineers work for manufacturers and distributors of farm equipment and supplies or for electric utility companies serving rural areas. Many do farm consulting work independently or for consulting firms. Others work for the U.S. Department of Agriculture, for colleges and universities, and for State and local government agencies.	A bachelor's degree in engineering is required for most beginning jobs. Some engineering jobs are filled by people trained in the appropriate natural science or in mathematics. Graduate study is increasingly important for advancement.	The work of agricultural engineers covers many different aspects of agriculture: Conserving and managing soil and water resources, designing farm equipment, and improving techniques for producing, processing, and distributing food.
Biomedical Engineers	Most biomedical engineers teach and do research in colleges and universities. Some work for Federal and State agencies or for private industry.	A bachelor's degree in engineering is required for most beginning jobs. Some engineering jobs are filled by people trained in the appropriate natural science or in mathematics. Graduate study is increasingly important for advancement. Biomedical engineers need some background in mechanical, electrical, industrial, or chemical engineering, as well as specialized biomedical training.	The small size of this occupation means that there are relatively few job openings each year.
Ceramic Engineers	Most ceramic engineers work in the stone, clay, and glass industries. Many others work in the iron and steel, electrical equipment, aerospace, chemical, and other industries that produce or use ceramic products.	A bachelor's degree in engineering is required for most beginning jobs. Some engineering jobs are filled by people trained in the appropriate natural science or in mathematics. Graduate study is increasingly important for advancement.	Ceramic engineers generally specialize in particular products, such as heat-resistant material, porcelain, building material, glass, or cement.
Chemical Engineers	Most chemical engineers work for chemical, petroleum, and related manufacturers. Others are employed by colleges and universities and by government agencies.	A bachelor's degree in chemical engineering is required for most beginning jobs. Graduate study is increasingly important for advancement.	Chemical engineering is a broad field with many specialties.

Scientific and Technical Occupations

Occupation	Nature and Places of Work	Training and Qualifications	Other Information
Civil Engineers	Most civil engineers work for government agencies or in the construction industry. Others provide engineering advice for consulting or architectural firms. Still others work for public utilities, railroads, and manufacturers.	A bachelor's degree in engineering is required for most beginning jobs. Some engineering jobs are filled by people trained in the appropriate natural science or in mathematics. Graduate study is increasingly important for advancement.	Civil engineers may specialize in such areas as structural, hydraulic, sanitary, and transportation systems.
Electrical Engineers	Electrical engineers are employed in private industry by manufacturers of many different products, particularly electrical and electronic equipment, aircraft and parts, and business machines. Others work for public utilities, government agencies, and colleges and universities.	A bachelor's degree in engineering is required for most beginning jobs. Some engineering jobs are filled by people trained in the appropriate natural science or in mathematics. Graduate study is increasingly important for advancement.	Electrical engineers generally specialize in a major area such as computers, communications, integrated circuits, or power distribution.
Industrial Engineers	Industrial engineers are employed by a greater variety of industries than any other type of engineer. Most work for manufacturing firms, but many work for hospitals, insurance companies, banks, and consulting firms.	A bachelor's degree in engineering is required for most beginning jobs. Some engineering jobs are filled by people trained in the appropriate natural science or in mathematics. Graduate study is increasingly important for advancement.	Industrial engineers concern themselves more with people, organizations, and business methods than do other kinds of engineers.
Mechanical Engineers	Most mechanical engineers are employed by manufacturers of metals, machinery, transportation and electrical equipment, and other products.	A bachelor's degree in engineering is required for most beginning jobs. Some engineering jobs are filled by people trained in the appropriate natural science or in mathematics. Graduate study is increasingly important for advancement.	Mechanical engineers specialize in such areas as automotive engineering, marine equipment, heating and air-conditioning, and instrumentation.
Metallurgical Engineers	Most metallurgical engineers are employed by the iron and steel and other metalworking industries. Many work in the mining industry or for firms that manufacture electrical equipment, machinery, and aircraft.	A bachelor's degree in engineering is required for most beginning jobs. Some engineering jobs are filled by people trained in the appropriate natural science or in mathematics. Graduate study is increasingly important for advancement.	Most metallurgical engineers specialize in one of three areas: Extracting metals from ore and refining them; studying the properties of metals and developing uses for them; and working and shaping metals into final products.
Mining Engineers	Most mining engineers are employed in the mining industry. Others work for mining equipment manufacturers, colleges and universities, and government.	A bachelor's degree in engineering is required for most beginning jobs. Some engineering jobs are filled by people trained in the appropriate natural science or in mathematics. Graduate study is increasingly important for advancement.	Mining engineers often specialize in the mining of a specific mineral, such as coal.

271

Exploring Careers

Occupation	Nature and Places of Work	Training and Qualifications	Other Information
Petroleum Engineers	Most petroleum engineers are employed by oil companies and by drilling equipment manufacturers. Almost three-fourths work in Texas, Oklahoma, Louisiana, and California, where most of the oil and gas is found.	A bachelor's degree in engineering is required for most beginning jobs. Some engineering jobs are filled by people trained in the appropriate natural science or in mathematics. Graduate study is increasingly important for advancement.	Most petroleum engineers concern themselves with ways of increasing the amount of oil and gas that can be removed from the ground.

TECHNICIANS

Occupation	Nature and Places of Work	Training and Qualifications	Other Information
Broadcast Technicians	Broadcast technicians are employed by radio and television stations. Most technicians work in large metropolitan areas.	A radiotelephone operator permit or license is required by Federal law. The type of equipment a technician will be operating determines whether a permit is sufficient or a license necessary. Knowing how to operate a computer is essential due to the widespread use of computers and microprocessors in the broadcasting industry. High school courses in algebra, trigonometry, physics, electronics, and other sciences provide good background for this occupation. Those who hope for advancement, or positions at large stations and networks, should obtain training in electronics or engineering at a technical school, community college, or university.	A technician's range of duties depends upon the size of the station. Large stations may assign each technician a specific duty, while at small stations a technician may perform any task necessary.
Drafters	Most drafters work in private industry. Almost one-third of these work in engineering and architectural firms. The government also employs many drafters.	Most positions require training in drafting such as is available at technical institutes, junior and community colleges, university extension services, and vocational and technical high schools. Courses in math, physical sciences, mechanical drawing, and drafting are important. Courses in shop practices and shop skills are also helpful to develop a knowledge of manufacturing or construction methods.	Drafters usually specialize in a particular area, such as mechanical, electrical, electronic, aeronautical, or architectural drafting. By the year 2000, most drafters will be using CAD (computer aided design) systems. Therefore, a familiarity with computers and CAD methods is increasingly important.

Scientific and Technical Occupations

Occupation	Nature and Places of Work	Training and Qualifications	Other Information
Engineering and Science Technicians	Most technicians are employed in private industry, though a large number work in government.	Most positions require technical training in a particular speciality. This is available through technical institutes, junior and community colleges, university extension services, and vocational-technical high schools. On-the-job experience apprenticeship programs, and correspondence schools may also provide the necessary training.	More than two-thirds of all technicians work in engineering. Many work in the physical sciences, and the rest work in the life sciences.
Surveyors	The government employs many surveyors. Other employers include construction companies, engineering and architectural firms, and surveying companies.	Post-high school courses in surveying combined with extensive on-the-job training provide enough background for many positions. A degree in surveying from a junior or community college, technical institute, or vocational school is also sufficient. High school courses in mathematics, drafting, and mechanical drawing are helpful.	Surveyors often specialize in surveys for highways, real estate boundaries, maps, or other purposes.

Surveyors require the abilities to measure and record data accurately. Precision must be part of their nature.

Mechanic jobs involve considerable physical activity, but most require only moderate strength.

Exploring Careers

It was Superbowl Sunday. Ed turned on the television set and sat down to watch the game. Even before he could open the bag of potato chips, the picture began to roll ... and then it was gone. Not wanting to miss a minute of the game, Ed ran to the phone to call Kathy. He was sure he could watch it at her house. But when he picked up the phone, there was no dial tone. Annoyed, Ed decided to drive to Kathy's anyway. The car started with a roar. Then there was a loud crack, the roar turned into a weak wheeze, and the engine sputtered into silence. Very upset, Ed jumped out of the car and slammed the door. Too late, he realized that he had locked it. Inside the locked car, dangling from the ignition switch, was the key ring with his house key. As the first drops of rain began to fall, Ed looked into the sky and shouted, "Help!" This certainly wasn't his day. He hoped his team was having better luck than he was.

The help that Ed needed could have come from four people: A television service technician, a telephone repairer, an automobile mechanic, and a locksmith. These skilled workers could have repaired the machines that caused Ed's trouble. Like Ed, we all use machines and, at times, need mechanics to repair and service them. Many businesses and industries rely on these workers every day.

Have you ever thought about working as a mechanic? There are many jobs to choose from—so many that just listing all of them would take several pages. After all, every machine creates work for some type of mechanic. Just think about all the machines you see in a single day. Sooner or later, all of them need to be serviced or repaired.

What Do Mechanics Do?

What comes to mind when you picture a mechanic at work? You may see the feet of an automobile mechanic sticking out from underneath a car. Perhaps you picture an appliance repairer poking around the back of your refrigerator. Maybe you imagine a business machine mechanic repairing a typewriter in the office of your school. Or see a jeweler replacing the diamond in a gold ring.

So many different images come to mind, you might wonder what all these workers have in common. All of them use their minds and hands to fix things—air conditioners, farm equipment, motorcycles, pianos, or some other machine. Mechanics use their minds to find the cause of mechanical problems and their hands to correct the problems. Let's examine their work more closely.

A mechanic needs patience to do the job right.

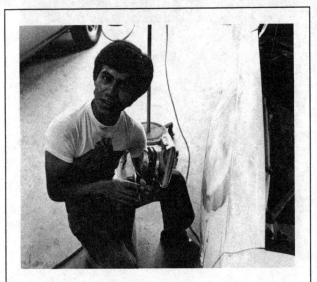

Body repairers take pride in their ability to make damaged cars look like new.

Mechanics and Repairers

Mechanics Solve Mechanical Puzzles

Before mechanics can repair a machine they must find out why it isn't working. Why won't a boat motor start? Why doesn't a soda machine give the correct change? Why are the copies from a photocopier so light? This is just what a doctor has to do before prescribing treatment for someone who is sick. This "diagnostic work" often is very difficult, but many mechanics feel that solving the mechanical puzzle is the most interesting part of the job.

To find out why a machine will not work, mechanics first check the common and obvious causes of trouble. When an electric sign does not light, the mechanic begins by checking the bulb. If that's not the cause of the trouble, the mechanic looks elsewhere.

Mechanics search for clues to the cause of the problem in an orderly way. Their knowledge of how the machine works tells them where to look and what to look for. Mechanics may listen to a motor for a telltale whine. They may test electrical circuits to see if electricity is running through them properly. They may take a machine apart. They do whatever is necessary to check the possible causes of a mechanical problem. Because many machines are complex, mechanics often rely on repair books and technical manuals to guide their search.

Trial and error also plays a role in the search. If adjusting the do-hickey does not make the widget work, maybe the gizmo should be tightened. However, even this is done in an orderly way. Mechanics know what to do if the first repair does not do the trick. Their knowledge shows them how to try, try again.

Finding the cause of a problem in a stereo amplifier is like solving a puzzle.

Mechanics Correct Mechanical Problems

Once mechanics have determined why a machine will not work, they make the necessary repairs. The repair work often involves taking apart a machine and repairing or replacing worn or broken parts. However, it may be possible to fix a machine by simply turning a screw that tightens a rubber belt or scraping the rust off an electric contact. Some machines are harder to repair than others. There's a big difference between repairing a toaster and repairing a diesel engine.

To make repairs, mechanics work with their hands and with tools. They use common hand and power tools such as screwdrivers, pliers, and electric drills. They also use special tools of the trade. Shoe repairers, for example, use skivers—knives that are made especially to split leather.

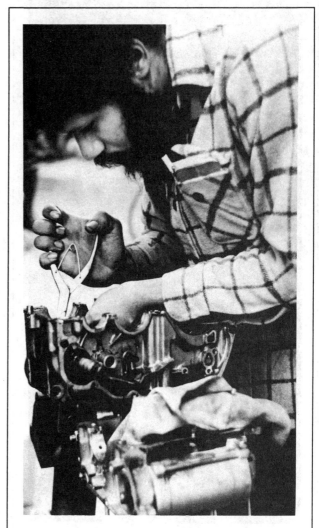

This motorcycle mechanic finds that time passes quickly when he is absorbed in his work.

277

Mechanics Prevent Mechanical Problems

Many mechanics spend much of their time keeping machines in good working order. This is called maintenance work. Most machines need regular maintenance work to keep them in top condition. If the engine in a bus is not tuned regularly, it will run poorly and use more fuel. Eventually it will break down. Maintenance work is especially important with machines that must not fail in use. If an airplane engine has a problem, the mechanic had better spot it while the plane is on the ground!

Mechanics Do Other Things

In addition to repair and maintenance work, mechanics do other things. Some install machines—telephones, for example. Some mechanics do paperwork; they may record the amount of time they spend on a job or accept payment from customers. Experienced mechanics may train new workers. Mechanics who have their own repair shops order supplies, hire and supervise other workers, and keep the records for the business.

Jet engine mechanics help make air travel safe.

This auto mechanic is getting a new car ready for a customer.

Mechanics and Repairers

What Makes a Good Mechanic?

What does it take to be a mechanic? If you asked employers or experienced mechanics that question, you'd probably get several answers.

- "You have to be good with your hands."
- "You have to understand machines."
- "You have to know how to use tools."

All these descriptions refer to something often called "mechanical aptitude." People who have mechanical aptitude have a knack for understanding how machines work and for fixing them. It's a knack that is essential for anyone who wants to work as a mechanic.

The ability to solve problems is an important part of mechanical aptitude. Repairers must be able to understand what makes a machine run. What does each part do? How do the parts work together? What can happen to the parts to cause trouble? Mechanics must be able to use this understanding to answer the questions, "What's wrong with this machine?" and "How do I fix it?"

Another important part of mechanical aptitude is the ability to work with your hands and with tools. This may seem easy. After all, many people work with their hands and use the same tools mechanics do. It would be exaggerating to say that mechanics need the hands of a surgeon, but manual skill is important. You may be able to take a watch apart. And you probably can learn to put it back together so that it works. But do you have enough manual dexterity and eye-hand coordination to fix dozens of watches in a single day? You would need those skills to earn a living as a watch repairer. To put it another way, a lot of people play basketball, but only a few are pros.

In addition to mechanical aptitude, there are other characteristics that are helpful to a mechanic.

Ability to work under pressure. Whether mechanics are repairing a pinsetter in a bowling alley or a generator in a factory, they often must work quickly so that customers are not inconvenienced.

Ability to work without supervision. On most repair jobs it is just the mechanic and the machine, one to one. Mechanics set their own schedule and pace, but they have to get the work done, on time and correctly.

Good eye-hand coordination is needed to install telephone wiring.

Telephone line installers must be agile.

haps you build models, make jewelry, or draw. Many mechanics get their start by doing repairs around their homes. Through activities such as these you learn to work with your hands and to use tools.

High school is the first step to a career as a mechanic. You may have heard that mechanics do not need a high school education. In some occupations this is true. However, all employers prefer to hire high school graduates. And in high school you will learn a lot that will help you later on. In mathematics classes you work with numbers and solve problems—good practice for solving mechanical problems later on. In science classes you study physics and electricity. These subjects help mechanics understand how machines operate.

Many high schools also have classes in woodworking, metalworking, drafting, electronics, and specific types of repair work such as appliance repair, auto mechanics, and television and radio repair. These classes provide good experience, because you work with the same kinds of machines and tools in class that you would use on the job. Such high school courses may give you the skills you need to land your first job or open the way for further training.

After high school, there are several ways to train for a career as a mechanic. You can attend a vocational school or a community or junior college. These schools offer training in almost every type of repair work. Such training programs sometimes are preferred for mechanics who repair complex machines, such as computers, business equipment, robots, and electronic instruments.

In many mechanical occupations you can start work immediately after high school and train on the job. You learn the trade by observing and helping experienced mechanics. You can train for some occupations through apprenticeship. Apprenticeships combine on-the-job training with classroom instruction in job-related subjects, such as blueprint reading, electrical theory, and safety practices. You may have to belong to a union or already work for a company to be eligible for an apprenticeship.

Another possibility is the military, which employs many mechanics. You can train and get valuable experience for many repair occupations in the Armed Forces.

Once you become a mechanic, it won't take long to learn that your training never ends. Every year machines are improved and made more complex. Hundreds of new machines are introduced. To keep up with these changes mechanics must continue to train throughout their careers. You will have to study new repair books and technical manuals. You may have to attend classes run by companies that make machines or even take classes at a high school or a community or junior college. There always will be something new to learn.

Stamina. Some mechanics are very active workers. They may stoop, bend, kneel, and crawl around machines. They may lift, push, and pull machines, tools, and spare parts. They may climb ladders and scaffolds or drive a repair truck many miles during a day.

Patience. Finding and fixing the problem in a machine may take hours or days. If the mechanic rushes through a job, it could cause more trouble later.

Tact and courtesy. Mechanics often have to deal with customers and machine operators who are upset because their machines are not working.

Training for Mechanic and Repair Occupations

Repairing is skilled work. It takes training to learn how a machine runs and how to fix and service it. For most repair occupations there are several ways of getting the training you need. To find out about training requirements in specific mechanic and repair occupations, see the Job Facts at the end of this chapter.

You may be preparing for your career already. Do you read about machines—what they do and how they do it? If so, you are developing a background in basic mechanics that will help you understand more difficult repair books and technical manuals later on. You may have hobbies in which you work with your hands. Per-

Mechanics and Repairers

Auto Mechanic

Mechanic Carlos Romo and mechanic trainee Pamela Dobbins.

The sky was slate grey and the rain had slowed to a fine mist. It was surprisingly chilly for a late May morning. A wave of cold damp air greeted Carlos Romo as he stepped out of the tow truck. A tractor trailer roared by. Carlos shivered a moment. "Glad I wore my Army field jacket," he thought.

This was the first repair call of a day that promised to be a long one. Carlos' partner was on vacation. The man who usually drove the truck was sick. The weather was lousy. And it was only 6 o'clock in the morning! Carlos had been fast asleep when the phone had rung ... a driver on Route 29 needed emergency road service.

"What seems to be the matter?" said Carlos to the man who stood gloomily by the side of the road, leaning against a dark green sedan. "Am I glad to see you!" responded the man. Then he explained that his name was Jack Kelly and the trouble had begun when he had pulled off the road to check the windshield wipers. The wipers had been acting "funny". When Mr. Kelly had tried to start the car again, nothing had happened. So he had called Carlos. Carlos' was the only 24-hour towing service listed in the phone book.

Carlos slipped behind the wheel of the green car, then took a good look at the gas guage and gear selector. No problems there; the car had gas and was in park. From Mr. Kelly's description, Carlos was almost certain that the battery was dead. But it always paid to check everything. Carlos turned on the ignition. The engine would not turn over. Sure enough, the battery was dead. Now the question was, "Why?"

Carlos found the answer as soon as he opened the hood. The fan belt was broken. Without a fan belt, the car's alternator would not work. All the electrical systems—the lights, the radio, and the windshield wipers—had to use power from the battery. So much of the battery's power had been used already that there wasn't enough left to restart the car.

"Your battery is dead," said Carlos to Mr. Kelly.

"That's what I figured," replied Mr. Kelly. "Well, give me a jump and I can be on my way."

"I'm afraid not. The fan belt is broken. I can jump start the car but the battery would just die again. I'll have to tow you into the shop and replace the belt."

Frustration was written all over Mr. Kelly's face.

"Are you sure there's nothing you can do here to get it to run? I have to be in Philadelphia by tonight."

"Sorry," replied Carlos. "I don't have a belt here and the battery should be recharged, if it can be. It may be totally gone. You might need a new one."

"Well ... okay. Let's go."

Carlos hooked the car to his tow truck and drove to his garage.

The garage was a small rectangular building with bare cinder block walls, a cement floor, and steel frame roof. On the left side in the rear was a hydraulic floor jack. Next to the jack were Carlos' workbench and tool chest. The workbench was littered with greasy rags, the parts of a disassembled carburetor, and some papers. In contrast, the tool chest and its contents were in perfect order and spotless. Carlos could work on a messy bench, but not with messy tools. Besides, the handtools had cost over $1,000 and he wanted to protect that investment. Storage shelves lined the back wall of the garage. The shelves were stocked with spare parts. Carlos did not keep a large supply of parts, just enough to handle common repairs and maintenance jobs.

Next to the shelves was a small room with a shower and some lockers. Tom's work area took up the right side of the garage. Tom was Carlos' partner. As usual, Tom's area was neater than Carlos'. Carlos often wondered how Tom could possibly work that way....

Carlos lowered Mr. Kelly's car from the tow truck and pushed it near his work area. Then he returned to the front of the shop to speak to Mr. Kelly.

"This will take a couple of hours. There's a cafe down the block, if you want breakfast."

"I think I'll just hang around here," said Mr. Kelly.

"Suit yourself. I'll be making some coffee, if you want any."

Carlos could tell that Mr. Kelly's frustration was turning to impatience. Sometimes I wish I were back at the Service Center, he thought. No contact with the customers, just get the cars from the service manager and do the work.

As Carlos made the coffee, he remembered how excited he had been when Tom had first suggested that they start their own business. All they had to begin with was a tow truck and an ad in the yellow pages.

Business had been slow at first, but as time went on they had earned a reputation for honesty and good work. Their customers had begun asking them to service their cars. So Tom and Carlos had rented a service station and garage, hired a part-time truckdriver, and begun doing tune-ups, lube jobs, and minor repairs.

Now they had a small group of regular customers and all the work they could handle. In fact, business was so good that Tom and Carlos were thinking of dropping the towing service. "That might not be a bad idea at all," thought Carlos as he suddenly noticed Mr. Kelly glaring at him from across the garage. Carlos sighed and started to work.

Carlos used a hydrometer to check the battery's cells. The battery was not completely dead, which meant it could be recharged. Carlos disconnected the cables, removed the battery, and placed it in the recharger.

"How much longer?" demanded Mr. Kelly.

Mechanics and Repairers

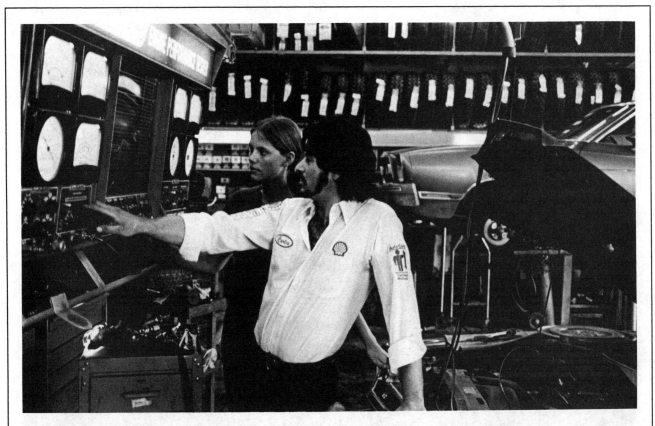

Carlos shows Pam how to use an engine tester. "You can learn a lot by helping friends fix cars," advises Carlos.

"About an hour," replied Carlos.

"Well, I guess that will have to do," replied Mr. Kelly.

"What's up, Carlos?" called a voice from the rear of the shop.

Carlos turned and saw a teenage girl walking toward him. It was Pam, his trainee.

"Nothing much, I'll be busy with this job for an hour or so. That station wagon out front needs to be tuned. Points, plugs, condenser, timing, the whole bit. If you have any trouble, just yell. The keys are on my bench somewhere."

"I could spend all morning looking for them in that mess," Pam said in mock horror.

"Very funny. Get to work," answered Carlos with a smile.

Pam went to the locker room to change.

Pam was a senior at Central High. Her auto repair teacher, a friend of Carlos', had asked him to give her a part-time job so that she could get some experience.

Carlos had hesitated at first. He was not sure he wanted to take the time to supervise an inexperienced worker. After all, his income depended on the amount of work he did. But then Carlos remembered how hard

it had been to get his first job. He always had liked working on his car, or helping friends and neighbors with theirs. When Carlos had graduated from high school, he had tried to get a job as a mechanic. But there weren't many jobs for people without experience or training. It wasn't until Carlos got out of the Army—where he had taken training in automotive mechanics—that a shop owner was willing to give him a job. Now, with Pam, he had a chance to give someone else a start.

Carlos went to the storage area to get the belt that he would need. He checked a parts supply book to get the number of the belt that fit the car. He also noticed the supply of oil filters was low. When he returned to his bench, he wrote a note to himself to call the parts distributor and order some filters.

By the time Carlos returned to Mr. Kelly's car, Pam was working on the station wagon. Mr. Kelly was pacing back and forth.

It didn't take long to install the new belt. When Carlos had finished, he walked over to Pam.

"How are you doing?" he asked.

"Fine," she replied, looking up from her work. "But this car is a mess. Look at these spark plugs. I didn't

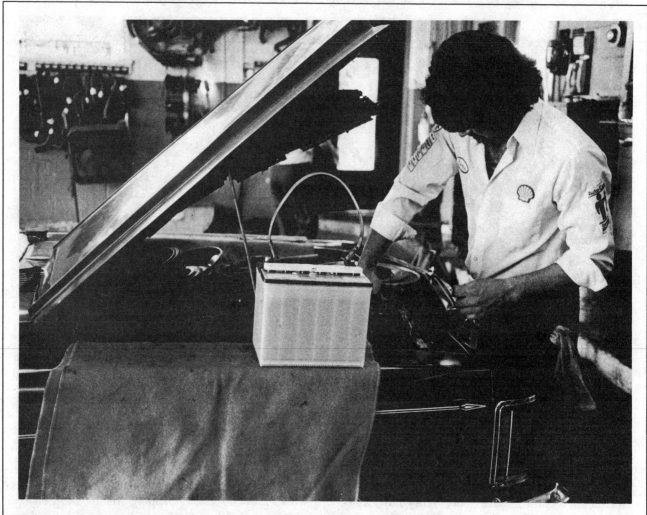

"Being a mechanic has given me the opportunity to have my own business," says Carlos. "I prefer working for myself."

think a car could run with plugs that old. I think this thing needs more than a tune-up. The belts and hoses look worn. The oil is filthy. I bet the transmission fluid should be changed. I'd feel guilty sending it out with just a tune-up."

"Well," said Carlos as he glanced at the engine. "I'll take a look at it later. Then I'll call Mr. Howard and tell him what should be done. He'll probably want the work done. I'd better finish over there before that guy paces a rut in the floor."

Carlos went to the battery recharger; the battery was ready. Carlos replaced it as quickly as he could. All the time Mr. Kelly kept fidgeting.

When Carlos had finished, he tried to start the car. The engine coughed, sputtered, wheezed, and made sev-

eral noises Carlos had never heard an engine make. But it started.

"It's fixed," shouted Mr. Kelly. "Sounds great."

"He's got to be kidding," thought Carlos. He suspected that something was seriously wrong with the engine.

"The car is running and it should get you to Philly, but the engine sounds like it needs more work," Carlos explained, "I can do it next. . . ."

"So long as it lasts through the trip, I'll be satisfied," interrupted Mr. Kelly. "I'll dump it soon anyway. It's always been a lemon."

"Okay. I'll get your bill," said Carlos as he walked back to his bench.

After Mr. Kelly had paid, he rushed to the car and called, "Thanks a lot, see you. . . ."

"Maybe sooner than you think," thought Carlos.

Mechanics and Repairers

Exploring

Automobile mechanics repair and service cars.

- Are you interested in machines and the way they work?
- Do you like to read about cars, motorcycles, and other motor vehicles?
- Have you ever wondered how cars run?
- Have you ever wondered why cars break down?

Automobile mechanics work with their hands. They use tools and must do their work quickly and skillfully.

- Do you like to work with your hands?
- Do you like to build models or repair things around your home?
- Do you ever help repair bicycles, mini-bikes, lawn-mowers, or cars?
- Do you enjoy fixing things? Does it give you a sense of accomplishment?
- Are you handy with tools?
- Is it easy for you to learn how to use a tool you've never used before?

Automobile mechanics sometimes must search for the cause of car trouble. They have to solve mechanical puzzles.

- Do you like to work on written mathematics problems?
- Do you like to do three-dimensional puzzles?
- Do you try to solve problems in an orderly and logical way?
- Are you persistent? Will you work on a problem until you solve it?

Automobile mechanics use technical books such as repair manuals.

- How well do you understand technical reading? Your science and mathematics textbooks are examples. Do you enjoy this sort of reading?
- Can you use charts, graphs, and diagrams?
- Can you look at a drawing and picture the three-dimensional object in your mind?

Automobile mechanics usually work alone. They must have confidence in themselves.

- Do you like to work by yourself?
- Do you do your homework by yourself?
- Do you like to make decisions?

Automobile mechanics do strenuous work.

- Do you enjoy activities such as sports, hiking, dancing, or gardening?
- Do you like to be active most of the time?

Mechanics set their own work pace. A rushed job could cause more trouble later.

Exploring Careers

Computer Service Technician

"I've always been curious about how things work," says Jackie.

Mechanics and Repairers

"Cunningham, call Mr. Arnold, Commerce National Bank," crackled the radio's speaker.

"Not again," groaned Jackie. She had left Commerce National only a half hour before. After she turned the car around, Jackie looked at her watch. Almost noon. Jackie wondered whether there would be time for lunch today. She already had worked through lunch twice this week.

At one of the busy intersections traffic slowed to a crawl.

"Why are there so many cars on the road on the busy days?" she thought. Jackie drummed her fingers on the steering wheel and looked about. She caught sight of the pile of papers, tools, and trash from fast food restaurants on the back seat of the car. "What a mess," she thought. "Almost time for the semiannual cleaning. I hate to use this car for anything but work, it's so sloppy."

A car horn blared. Another horn sounded impatiently behind her and Jackie stepped on the accelerator. Soon she was pulling into a parking lot near the Benton Building, where Commerce National had its offices.

Jackie grabbed her jacket and picked up the briefcase that held her tools, reports, and repair manuals. She didn't have to take much with her because supplies were stored right at the bank. Data Products, the company Jackie worked for, saw to that. The company also sent spare parts and repair instructions directly to the bank's computer center. That way Jackie and the other service technicians didn't have to carry a lot of supplies around or transport spare parts from Data Products' regional office.

In fact, Jackie sometimes worked for several weeks without going to the regional office at all. As she saw it, her job was taking care of the computer equipment at her three "accounts"—the Commerce National Bank, the County Hospital, and the Wilson Manufacturing Company. So naturally she spent most of her time in those places, not at the Data Products office.

As she rushed through the parking lot, Jackie put on her jacket. "It couldn't be much hotter," she thought as she hurried into the air-conditioned building. Data Products expected the service technicians to dress up for work and fortunately Jackie liked to. But a suit, even this cotton one, certainly could be uncomfortable during the summer.

Jackie pulled out her Data Products' identification card as she passed the bank's security guard and headed for the computer center. When she entered the center, Jackie quickly spotted Mr. Arnold, who ran the office.

"Is it the sorter again, Tom?" she called from across the room.

"Right," replied Mr. Arnold.

"I wish you could have arranged to have it break down when I was here a little while ago instead of making me drive back."

"That would be too easy," joked Mr. Arnold.

Jackie went to the side room where the sorter was located. The room also was used to store supplies and it was cramped. However, Jackie did not have to move the machine as she did in some offices.

The sorter was used to group bank documents in several ways. Checking accounts, for example, could be grouped by the amount of money in them. Twice during the past 5 days the sorter had failed to separate the papers correctly. From Mr. Arnold's description of what had happened, Jackie got an idea of what the problem might be. By listening to the machine she decided that the rubber belts and metal rollers that moved papers through the sorter needed adjustment. Although she already had fixed several of the belts, Jackie was sure that they were the cause of the trouble. She knew that it was not unusual for complex equipment to require several adjustments. She was used to visiting an office several times to fix a machine.

Jackie raised the metal cover on the front of the sorter and turned on the machine. She listened to the hum from the rollers and belts. In a few seconds she located a belt that seemed to need adjustment.

From a cabinet in the room Jackie took a can of oil and a rag. After pouring some lubricant on the rag, she held it against the moving belt for a few minutes. She turned off the machine and tightened a screw at the end of the roller that the belt wound around. This made the belt tighter. Jackie then let the sorter run while she watched and listened to the belt.

"I've got you this time," she murmured to the machine. She had begun to think the sorter had a grudge against her. From the very first time she had worked with electrical equipment—as a hobby when she was a junior high school student—Jackie had noticed that some machines seemed to have personalities. She'd had a lot of experience with data processing equipment since then, and it only confirmed her impression that machines could be as different as people. Yes, quite a bit of experience, now that she thought about it. She'd taken electronics courses in high school. Then the training classes at basic school when she'd first started working at Data Products. And 2 years on the job.

In a way Jackie preferred mechanical problems to the electronic ones, because they were easier to explain to the customers. She could show them a worn or loose belt. Most electronic problems were caused by burnt-out circuit boards. Jackie could locate a bad board with a voltmeter and she could replace it with a new one. However, a burnt-out board looked exactly like a new one. It was sometimes hard to convince customers who knew little about computers that those innocent-looking boards caused their expensive computers to go haywire.

Jackie closed the machine cover and put away her tools. From her briefcase she took a repair report form. She filled in the date, the machine model, the account's name, and the code letters for the type of breakdown and repair.

She made out a repair report for every service call. Data Products used the information on the forms to determine what kinds of problems there were with the equipment the company made. Engineers used the information to design machines that broke down less often and could be serviced more easily.

Returning to the main computer room, Jackie wrote the date and a brief description of the work she had done in the record book that was kept with the equipment itself. The information in the book would be used by other computer technicians who might work on the machine. Jackie also used the records to keep track of the maintenance that she had done on the machines.

After putting the record book away, Jackie walked to Mr. Arnold's office.

"I think I've fixed it for good this time. But I'd like to be here the next time you use it, just to make sure that everything's okay. Will you be using it soon?"

"Not until tomorrow," said Mr. Arnold.

"Hmm, I'm scheduled for training the rest of the week—well, my backup can handle any problem."

"Training again! I thought you'd already learned everything you needed to know in Data Products' basic school. And aren't you going to night school now?" said Mr. Arnold.

"At basic school I learned how to keep wise guys like you happy and machines like your sorter working," replied Jackie. "The training this week is for your new 360 printer, and night school is part of my plan for the future. I want to be an engineer one day. Then I'll be designing these computers instead of fixing them.

"Well, I'd better run," Jackie continued as she picked up her briefcase. "We've been really busy the last 2 days and I'm supposed to do some maintenance at Wilson Manufacturing this afternoon. If I don't get it done Ken Marcus will have problems and he can be awfully disagreeable when his machines act up."

"Well, not everyone can be a nice guy like me," teased Mr. Arnold.

"True," replied Jackie. "See you next week."

"Take care," called Mr. Arnold, as Jackie rushed out the door.

Jackie called the office dispatcher from the security guard's desk to say that she had answered the Commerce National call. To her surprise there were no other repair calls. Jackie looked at her watch. There was plenty of time to get to the Wilson account. Suddenly she felt relaxed. "I guess I get to have lunch after all," she thought as she headed for her car.

"It's amazing how some computers seem to be personalities," remarks Jackie. "Machines can be as different as people."

Mechanics and Repairers

Exploring

Computer service technicians repair and service keypunch machines, computer terminals, and other computer equipment.

- Do you enjoy fixing things?
- Do you like to work with your hands?
- Are you interested in electronics and computers?
- Have you ever wondered how computers work? Have you ever tried to find out how other kinds of electronic equipment work—television sets, stereos, tape recorders, or calculators?
- Do you read the owner's manual for calculators, television sets, stereos or radios? Are you interested in finding out about the machines' specifications?
- Have you ever tried to fix a radio or a pocket calculator?

Computer service technicians must find and correct the cause of computer breakdowns quickly. They work under pressure all the time.

- Do you like to solve problems? Do you like to do written mathematics problems?
- Do you like to do puzzles or brain teasers?
- Can you usually understand instructions the first time?
- Can you do manual work quickly without making mistakes?
- How well do you work under pressure? Do you have trouble taking tests?

Computer service technicians must get along easily with their customers.

- Do you usually get along with people?
- Are you outgoing?
- Do you enjoy doing things with people?
- How good are you at calming someone down when he or she is angry with you?
- Can you talk your way out of trouble?
- How well can you explain things? Can you give directions?

Computer service technicians spend a lot of time in their clients' offices. They must dress neatly and act professionally.

- Do you like to dress well?
- Do you try to make a good appearance?

Jackie's ambition is to be an engineer. "Then I'll be designing computers instead of fixing them."

Jeweler

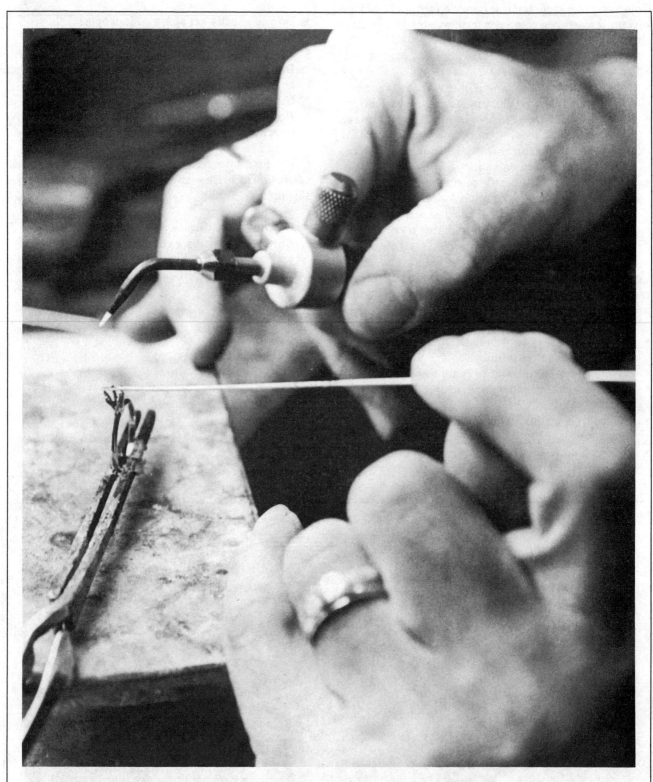

Mr. Anthony is a perfectionist. ''I would rather lose money than do a job that I'm not satisfied with.''

Mechanics and Repairers

The jewelry store was dark except for a single bright light in the back, where Mr. Anthony sat at his repair bench. Scattered on top of the bench were some tweezers and pliers, small brown envelopes, eyeglasses, wooden blocks, and gold wire.

Mr. Anthony straightened his back and stretched his arms over his head to loosen up before starting the next job. His eyes were tired from working under the bright light. He placed the bracelet that he had just finished in a small case lined with velvet.

Glancing at his watch he thought, "Less than an hour till the store opens. I'd better not start making Mrs. Blue's earrings. Once the customers begin coming in it'll be too hard to concentrate."

As Mr. Anthony placed the gold wire in one of the drawers, he looked at the brown envelopes on the top of the bench. One was marked, "Repair ring setting". Mr. Anthony picked up the envelope and removed the ring. Then he slipped on his magnifying glasses and examined it.

The ring was made of gold and had an emerald in the center. Two small loops of gold held the stone in place, but one of the loops had broken at the bottom. To fix the ring, Mr. Anthony would have to remove the stone and then solder the loop to the top of the ring. The work would be delicate (a slip of the pliers and the valuable stone could be chipped and ruined). However, Mr. Anthony had fixed many rings in the years he had worked as a jeweler. He knew that interruptions wouldn't bother him.

Using a pair of pliers, Mr. Anthony bent back both the loops of wire. He worked the stone loose from the small gold plate on which it was mounted.

The opening of the store's front door startled him. "Mr. Anthony, is that you?" It was Ms. Rothstein, the salesclerk.

"Yes, it's me, Deb."

"Have you been here long?"

"Only a few hours."

"Honestly, this is the third time this week that you've come in early. If you don't slow down, your ulcer will act up again."

"Well, with the holidays coming up, there's a lot of work to do and with so many customers coming in I can't work undisturbed during the day."

"I know, but you really should take it easy or..."

"Okay, okay! Let's get some work done," snapped Mr. Anthony. "Set the jewelry in the display cases and get ready to open the store."

Ms. Rothstein quickly returned to the front of the store. Her feelings were hurt, and it showed. He appreciated her concern, but he was tired and irritable. In a few moments Mr. Anthony was sorry that he had been rude. He made up his mind to smooth things over as soon as he could. After all, Deb was a first class salesperson...and a good friend. Funny how people you work with every day can become like members of your family, he thought. He put on his magnifying glasses and returned to work.

Before he could solder the wire, it had to be filed so it would lie flat on the top of the ring. With a few swift movements the filing was done. Using the pliers, Mr. Anthony bent the wire down so it touched the top of the ring. He examined the ring to be sure it was ready and stepped to the table where he kept his soldering equipment.

Holding the ring with tweezers, he dipped it in an acid solution that would keep the metal from turning black under the torch's flame. Placing the ring in a soldering clamp, he took a pack of gold solder from a drawer in the table.

"Excuse me," called Ms. Rothstein from the sales floor. "Did the gift boxes come in yesterday?"

"No, and I hope we get them today. We're almost out. If there's one thing we don't need now it's customers complaining about boxes. If they don't come in by noon, let's call Schmit's," he added.

Mr. Anthony took a piece of solder from a drawer in his bench. From this piece he clipped a speck of solder smaller than a grain of sand. Taking the torch from its stand, he lit it and adjusted the flame to a fine line. With the tip of an old file, he held the speck of solder to the break in the ring, then carefully but quickly applied the torch. In seconds the solder had melted in place. Mr. Anthony made sure he turned off the torch and replaced it in the stand. Once he had burned his hand because he had not turned off the flame completely. Mr. Anthony removed the ring from its stand and looked closely at the soldered joint. Everything was all right.

Mr. Anthony went into the back room where he kept his polishing machine. He took a wheel with bristles from a set on the table. After slipping the wheel onto the machine and turning it on, he touched the edge of the spinning bristles with a lump of abrasive clay called "tripoli." The tripoli quickly covered the end of the bristles. Holding the ring in his fingers he ran the soldered joint under the bristles. When he pulled the ring back from the wheel, the lump of solder was smooth with the joint. Mr. Anthony stopped the polishing machine and slipped on a different wheel. To the bristles on this wheel he applied jeweler's rouge (a red clay made of iron oxide). This time he polished the entire ring. Mr. Anthony then placed the ring in an ultrasonic cleaner. The cleaner used air bubbles to remove tiny particles of dirt. After a few minutes he removed the ring from the machine and examined it under a lamp. The gold sparkled under the light and there was hardly a trace of the soldered joint. But a jeweler could see that the solder was a different color than the gold.

"One more step," thought Mr. Anthony. Although many jewelers might reset the stone at this point, Mr. Anthony was a perfectionist. He would rather lose money than do a job that didn't satisfy him. To "do it right" he would goldplate the ring to hide the soldered joint. Mr. Anthony quickly set up the equipment to goldplate the ring. The process would take several minutes, so he leaned against the wall and relaxed.

"Do it right" had been Mr. Konczynski's motto, thought Mr. Anthony, suddenly remembering the days when he was first learning his trade. He had gone to Mr. Konczynski's jewelry repair shop as an apprentice when he was just 16 and stayed there 4 years. The apprenticeship had been hard. The pay was low and Mr. Konczynski was a demanding boss. Nothing less than perfect work would suit him. However, Mr. Anthony never regretted the years he had spent learning his trade. He had learned all types of jewelry work—stone setting, watch repair, jewelry making and repair, and modelmaking. These days, only a few shop or store owners hire apprentices. Most jewelers learn their trade in jewelry factories. But factory work is so specialized that a person usually can learn only one or two skills.

The buzz of the timer interrupted Mr. Anthony's thoughts. The goldplating was done. The ring had been covered by a new layer of gold. No one would be able to see it was soldered.

All that remained of this job was to reset the stone, but this was no simple task. The stone had to be set exactly right. If it tilted even a little, the ring would look lopsided. Further, when he was setting the prongs over the stone, a slip of his hand could easily chip or scratch the emerald.

As Mr. Anthony returned to his bench, Ms. Rothstein called from the sales floor.

"Mr. Anthony, could you step out here for a moment? This gentleman has a problem." She was standing behind a display case, across from a customer. Mr. Anthony straightened his tie, glanced in the mirror by his bench to see that his hair was neat, and went to the counter.

"How can I help you?" he asked the man on the other side of the counter.

"You can help me by giving me my wife's necklace," snapped the man.

"Mr. Johnson brought a necklace in to have the clasp fixed yesterday," explained Ms. Rothstein. "You weren't here at the time, so I put it on your table."

"If you could wait a few minutes, I can fix the necklace right now," he said.

"Well, I don't have a few minutes to waste," com-plained Mr. Johnson. "I have things to do and my wife wants to wear that necklace to a party tonight."

"It won't take long at all," said Mr. Anthony, reassuringly.

"I should hope not. After all the business I've given this store, I think I have a right to expect decent service."

Mr. Anthony did not wait for him to continue. He stepped back to his bench, took the necklace out of a brown envelope, and quickly replaced the clasp.

When he stepped back to the counter, Mr. Johnson said, "Well, it's about time." He was taking out his billfold when Mr. Anthony said, "No charge, to make up for the inconvenience."

"Oh! Well . . . thank you," said Mr. Johnson as he left the store.

"He is a good customer but he's hard to handle when he's rushed," said Ms. Rothstein.

"I know," sighed Mr. Anthony. "But I guess everyone gets a little touchy before the holidays. I'm sorry I snapped at you before."

"That's okay."

The door opened and Ms. Wang entered.

"Good morning, Ms. Wang. You've come for the ring?" said Mr. Anthony.

A slip of the hand could chip or scratch a valuable gem.

Mechanics and Repairers

"Yes, I'm anxious to see it."

"It's in the safe in the back room. I'll get it."

Mr. Anthony returned to the sales floor holding a black ring box. He held the box under a fluorescent lamp on the counter and opened it. The ring in the box sparkled as the lamp light was reflected from the three diamonds which surrounded a ruby on the top of the ring.

Ms. Wang stared at the ring and murmured, "Beautiful, truly beautiful."

"I'm glad you like it," said Mr. Anthony.

Mr. Anthony had made the ring by hand following a design Ms. Wang had given him. He had used pliers to shape the ring from gold wire. He had made the settings for the stone from platinum in a similar fashion. It had been a long and difficult job but worth the effort. To Mr. Anthony the ring was a work of art in metal and stones.

"Ms. Rothstein will wrap the ring and make out your receipt," said Mr. Anthony.

"Fine," replied Ms. Wang. "Thank you again. You've done a magnificent job."

Mr. Anthony smiled broadly, then hurried back to his bench.

Mr. Anthony designs jewelry to suit the customer.

Exploring

Jewelers make and repair jewelry. They work with precious stones and metals.

- Does jewelry interest you?
- Do you like to look at jewelry displays in stores or in museums?
- Do you like to look at exhibits of precious stones and metals?
- Have you ever wondered how jewelry is made?
- Have you ever watched a jeweler or watch repairer at work in a store?
- Did you ever try to make or design a piece of jewelry or some other ornament?

Working from drawings or sketches, jewelers shape metal into pins, earrings, rings, and other jewelry. Their work must be attractive.

- Do you like to make or build things?
- Do you like to work with tools?
- Can you look at a drawing and picture a three-dimensional object?
- Are you interested in art?
- Can you explain why a piece of jewelry appeals to you?
- Do you select jewelry to match your clothing?

Jewelers must be able to do very delicate work with their hands. They often work with small, valuable objects, such as gold ring settings and diamonds.

- Do you enjoy doing detailed work such as embroidering or building models from kits?
- Do you have nimble fingers? Can you thread a needle quickly?

Jewelers work without supervision. They must be responsible and take pride in their work.

- Do you usually complete your homework assignments on time?
- Are you one of the "workers" when you are on a school committee?
- Do you work on a project for one of your classes in school until it's just right?
- Do you stick with an activity such as building a model until it's done as well as you can do it?

Job Facts

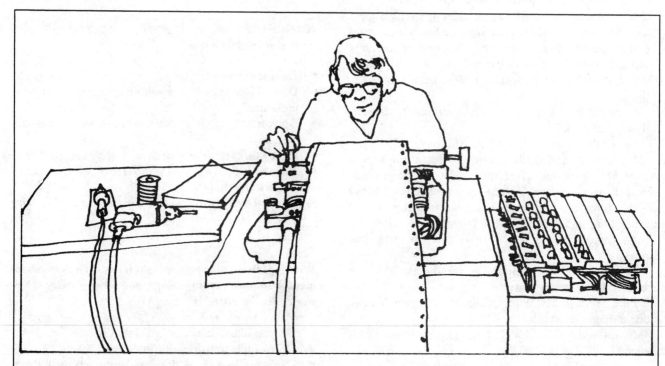

There isn't room in this book for a story about every kind of mechanic and repair occupation. However, you'll find some important facts about 28 of these occupations in the following section. If you want additional information about any of them, you might begin by consulting the *Occupational Outlook Handbook,* a publication of the Department of Labor which should be available in your school or public library.

Occupation	Nature and Places of Work	Training and Qualifications	Other Information
TELEPHONE CRAFT OCCUPATIONS			
Central Office Craft Occupations	Central office craftworkers work for telephone companies throughout the country. Most central offices are in or near large cities.	Central office craftworkers usually begin working for the telephone company in other jobs. To become craftworkers they take classes at company schools and receive on-the-job training from experienced workers. Some craftworkers learn their skills in vocational schools or apprenticeships.	Central office craftworkers may have to work evenings, weekends, and holidays. They often work in teams.
Central Office Equipment Installers	Most installers work for companies that make central office equipment. Some work for telephone companies. Most central offices are in or near large cities.	Central office equipment installers are trained by the companies they work for. Usually they receive on-the-job training plus classroom instruction. Classes may be held at the factory where the equipment is made.	Some installers do a lot of travelling. They may be assigned to areas that include several States. Installers often work in teams.

Mechanics and Repairers

Occupation	Nature and Places of Work	Training and Qualifications	Other Information
Line Installers and Cable Splicers	Line installers and cable splicers work for telephone companies throughout the country.	Telephone companies usually provide both on-the-job training and classroom instruction. Some line installers and cable splicers learn their skills in vocational schools or apprenticeships.	Some line and cable work is strenuous. Workers have to climb poles and lift heavy cables and equipment.
Telephone and PBX Installers and Repairers	Telephone and PBX installers and repairers work for telephone companies throughout the country.	Installers and repairers usually begin working for the telephone company in other jobs. To become installers and repairers, they take classes at company schools and receive on-the-job training from experienced workers. Some installers and repairers learn their skills in vocational schools or apprenticeships.	PBX stands for Private Branch Exchange. Telephone and PBX installers and repairers do much of their work in customers' homes and offices. They travel in trucks equipped with tools and supplies. Sometimes they work outdoors, often making repairs in bad weather.

TECHNICIANS

Occupation	Nature and Places of Work	Training and Qualifications	Other Information
Air-Conditioning Refrigeration, and Heating Mechanics	Most air-conditioning, refrigeration, and heating mechanics work for companies that sell and install cooling and heating equipment.	Most of these mechanics start as helpers and learn their skills by working with experienced mechanics for several years. Some learn through apprenticeships. Employers prefer to hire people with a high school education.	Air conditioning, refrigeration, and heating mechanics often working, irregular hours during peak seasons in the summer and winter.
Aircraft Mechanics	Over one-half of all aircraft mechanics work for the airlines. About one-third are employed by the Federal Government. The rest work for small repair shops or companies with their own planes.	Most aircraft mechanics learn their trade in the Armed Forces or in trade schools certified by the Federal Aviation Administration (FAA). A high school diploma is preferred by employers. The majority of mechanics have FAA licenses. Applicants for licenses must have work experience and pass written and oral tests.	Aircraft mechanics often work in high places, such as on top of wings and fuselages of large jet planes.
Appliance Repairers	Most appliance repairers work for appliance stores and repair shops. Others work for appliance manufacturers, department stores, wholesalers, and utility companies.	Most appliance repairers start as helpers and learn their trade on the job. A high school education is preferred by employers.	Appliance repairers usually work with little or no direct supervision. Some spend several hours a day driving to job sites.
Automobile Body Repairers	Most automobile body repairers work for repair shops or for automobile and truck dealers. Some work for trucking companies, buslines, and motor vehicle manufacturers.	Most automobile body repairers start as helpers and learn their trade by working with experienced repairers for several years. Some learn through apprenticeships or in vocational school programs.	Automobile body repairers usually work with little or no direct supervision. The work often is dirty and strenuous. Repairers usually buy their own handtools.

Exploring Careers

Occupation	Nature and Places of Work	Training and Qualifications	Other Information
Automobile Mechanics	Most automobile mechanics work for automobile dealers, automobile repair shops, or gasoline service stations. Some mechanics work for government agencies and businesses that have their own automobile repair departments. Still others work for automobile manufacturers.	Automobile mechanics usually learn their skills on the job. Some mechanics learn through apprenticeships that combine classroom instruction and on-the-job training. Courses in automobile repair are helpful in getting a job. Vocational or technical courses in mechanics may give some applicants an advantage. Mechanics must have a driver's license.	After they have worked for a while and mastered their skills, some automobile mechanics open their own repair shops or gasoline service stations. Mechanics often work over 40 hours a week. They usually buy their own handtools.
Boat-Engine Mechanics	Most boat-engine mechanics work for boat dealers or marinas. Some work for companies that manufacture boats.	Boat-engine mechanics usually learn on the job. They start as helpers and work under the supervision of experienced mechanics. Employers prefer to hire high school graduates. Vocational and technical courses in mechanics may give some applicants an advantage.	Boat-engine mechanics often work overtime during the spring and summer. Mechanics may repair minibikes, motorcycles, snowmobiles, and lawnmowers.
Bowling-Pin-Machine Mechanics	Almost all bowling-pin-machine mechanics work in bowling centers. A few work for companies that manufacture automatic pin-setters.	Bowling-pin-machine mechanics learn on the job under the supervision of experienced workers.	In some bowling centers, mechanics do all the maintenance work such as polishing lanes and reconditioning pins.
Business Machine Repairers	Most business machine repairers work for companies that make such business machines as typewriters, postage meters, and photocopiers. Some repairers work directly for companies that use the machines.	Business machine repairers usually attend schools run by their employers. They learn on the job under the supervision of experienced workers. Employers require a high school diploma and prefer people who have had some technical training in machine repair.	Business machine repairers must keep customers satisfied. They have to be pleasant and cooperative and dress neatly. Training in electronics is becoming more important.
Computer Service Technicians	Most computer service technicians work for companies that repair computer equipment or for companies that make the equipment. Some technicians work for organizations that have large computer centers.	Computer service technicians usually attend company schools for several months and study computer theory, math, electronics, and other subjects. They also learn on the job under the supervision of experienced workers. Employers look for people with some post-high school technical training.	Computer service technicians cannot count on a 9-to-5 workday. They often are on call 24 hours a day or work shifts. They must dress neatly, be pleasant, and know how to deal with people.
Diesel Mechanics	Most diesel mechanics work for distributors and dealers of diesel equipment. Some work for trucking firms, buslines, independent repair shops, or diesel engine manufacturers.	Diesel mechanics usually train on the job under the supervision of experienced workers. Some mechanics learn their skills through apprenticeships or in vocational schools. Most employers prefer high school graduates.	Most jobs in the field are filled by mechanics who have experience repairing gasoline engines.

Mechanics and Repairers

Occupation	Nature and Places of Work	Training and Qualifications	Other Information
Electric Sign Repairers	Most electric sign repairers work in small shops that manufacture, install, and service electric signs.	Electric sign repairers usually start as helpers and learn their skills by working with experienced repairers. Some train through apprenticeships. A high school diploma is preferred by most employers and required for apprenticeships.	Electric sign repairers cannot be afraid of heights. They often work in ladders or in the baskets of boom trucks.
Farm Equipment Mechanics	Most farm equipment mechanics work in the service department of farm equipment dealers. Some work in independent repair shops or for large farms. They usually work in small towns or rural areas.	Farm equipment mechanics usually start as helpers and learn their trade by working with experienced repairers. Some train through apprenticeships or vocational schools. Most employers prefer high school graduates. Vocational or technical courses in mechanics may give some applicants an advantage.	Farm equipment mechanics work long hours during planting and harvesting season—as much as 10 to 12 hours a day, 7 days a week. They often travel to the fields to repair broken equipment.
Industrial Machinery Repairers	Industrial machinery repairers work in manufacturing plants. They maintain and repair the machines used to make food products, chemicals, paper, and thousands of other products.	Most industrial machinery mechanics start as helpers and learn their trade by working with experienced repairers. Some train through apprenticeships. Most employers prefer high school graduates.	Industrial machinery mechanics may work nights and weekends. They have to be agile and in good physical condition in order to work with large machines.
Instrument Repairers	Most instrument repairers work for industrial firms or power companies. They maintain and repair the instruments used in producing chemicals or petroleum, for example. Some repairers work for companies that manufacture instruments. Some work for repair companies or for the Federal Government.	There are several ways of training for a job in this occupation. Instrument repairers often start work as production workers, then train on the job. Some train through apprenticeships. Technical schools, community or junior colleges, and the military also teach the skills needed to become an instrument repairer. A high school diploma is required.	Technical training following high school is increasingly important. Instrument repairers may work nights and weekends.
Jewelers	Most jewelers work in precious jewelry factories or jewelry repair shops. Some work in stores that sell jewelry. Most precious jewelry factories are in New York City.	Jewelers usually learn their skills by working under the supervision of experienced jewelers. Some train through apprenticeships or in vocational schools. Most employers prefer a high school education.	Once they have mastered the trade, many jewelers open their own jewelry repair shops.
Locksmiths	Most locksmiths work for locksmith shops or operate their own shops. Some work in hardware and department stores or in large industrial plants.	Beginners usually learn their trade by working with experienced locksmiths. Some train in vocational schools. A high school education is preferred by most employers. Many states and cities have licensing requirements.	Locksmiths may be on call and work nights and weekends. They spend several hours a day driving to job sites.

Exploring Careers

Occupation	Nature and Places of Work	Training and Qualifications	Other Information
Maintenance Electricians	More than half of all maintenance electricians work for manufacturing industries. Some are employed by public utilities, mines, railroads, and Federal, State, and local governments.	Most maintenance electricians learn their trade on the job as helpers or through apprenticeship. Some learn the trade in the Armed Forces. A high school diploma is required for an apprenticeship. Many local governments have licensing requirements.	Following safety principles is very important, because maintenance electricians work near high-voltage industrial equipment.
Motorcycle Mechanics	Most mechanics work for motorcycle dealers. Some are employed by city governments to repair police motorcycles.	Motorcycle mechanics usually start as helpers and learn their skills by working with experienced mechanics. Most employers prefer high school graduates. Vocational or technical courses in mechanics may give some applicants an advantage. Mechanics must have a motorcycle driver's license.	Motorcycle mechanics often work overtime during the summer. Mechanics must buy their own handtools.
Piano and Organ Tuners and Repairers	Most work for repair shops or operate their own shops. Some repairers are employed by piano and organ dealers and manufacturers.	Piano and organ tuners and repairers usually start as helpers and learn their skills by working with experienced repairers. A small number of technical schools and colleges have courses in piano repair. Most employers prefer high school graduates.	Piano and organ tuners and repairers often work evenings and weekends. They are busiest during the fall and winter because people spend more time inside.
Shoe Repairers	Most shoe repairers work in repair shops. About half own their own shops. Some repairers are employed in shoe stores, department stores, and dry-cleaning shops.	Shoe repairers usually start as helpers and learn the trade by working with experienced repairers. Some train at vocational schools.	Self-employed shoe repairers work long hours—sometimes as much as 10 hours a day, 6 days a week.
Radio and Television Service Technicians	Most radio and television service technicians work in shops and stores that sell or service radios, television sets, and other electronic products.	Up to 2 years of technical training in electronics and 2 to 4 years of on-the-job experience usually are required to become a service technician. Technical training is available from high schools, vocational schools, and the Armed Forces. Many states require service technicians to have licenses.	Many radio and television service technicians open their own repair shops.

Mechanics and Repairers

Occupation	Nature and Places of Work	Training and Qualifications	Other Information
Truck Mechanics and Bus Mechanics	Most truck mechanics work for companies that own fleets of trucks. Others are employed by truck dealers, truck manufacturers, or Federal, State, and local governments. Most bus mechanics work for local transit companies or intercity buslines.	Most truck and bus mechanics start as helpers and learn the trade by working with experienced mechanics. Some mechanics train through apprenticeships. A high school education is preferred by most employers. Vocational or technical courses in mechanics may give some applicants an advantage. Truck and bus mechanics may need a state chauffeur's license.	Truck and bus mechanics may work evenings, nights, and weekends. They occasionally make emergency repairs on the road.
Vending Machine Mechanics	Most vending machine mechanics work for companies that install and service vending machines. Some work for companies that own beverage machines, juke boxes, pinball machines, and laundry and dry-cleaning machines.	Vending machine mechanics usually start as helpers or route drivers. They learn their trade by working with experienced mechanics. A high school education is desirable. A driver's license is required.	Vending machine mechanics frequently work at night and on weekends and holidays.
Watch Repairers	Most watch repairers work in jewelry stores or repair shops. A small number work in watch factories.	Most watch repairers learn their skills in watch repair schools. Courses last from 1 to 3 years. Some watch repairers train through apprenticeship or on the job. A high school education is preferred by most employers and schools. Some states require watch repairers to have a license.	Many watch repairers open their own shops.

An electrician may be needed to work odd hours in order to correct problems that can arise at any time of day or night.

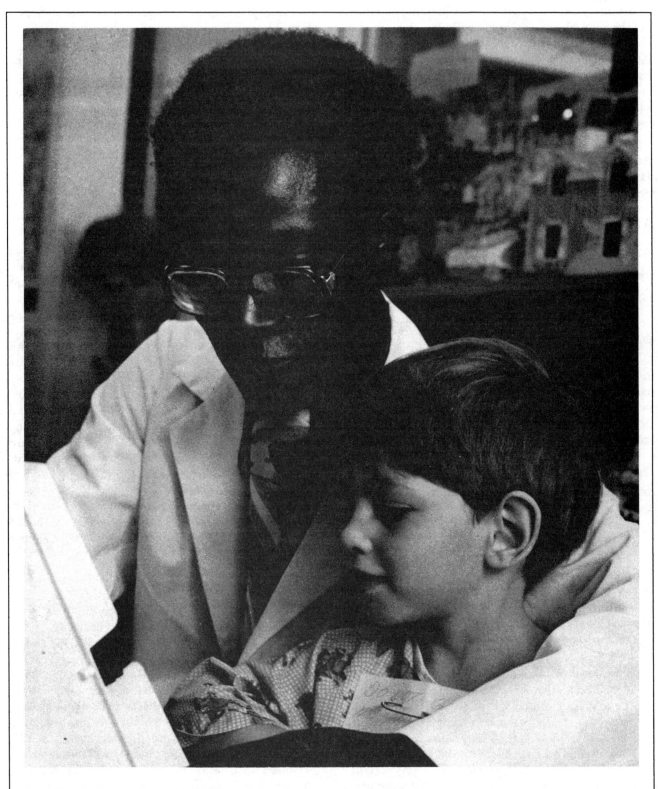

In addition to his work at a children's hospital, this pediatrician teaches at a medical school.

Exploring Careers

Luther Knight was nervous. The clock read 9:57, almost time for science class. That by itself didn't bother him; he enjoyed science. Occasionally Ms. Dombrowski talked too much and the students got fidgety. But Luther liked Ms. Dombrowski's course in general science, and the unit in biology they were doing now fascinated him. He planned to study biology in high school and then in college. And someday he would be a famous biologist. Every day he looked forward to science class.

Every day, that is, except today. Today Luther was nervous. Today he was scheduled to give a report to the class and very soon he would be standing at the front of the room and talking while 30 pairs of eyes watched him. Luther had prepared his report; he knew what to say. But the thought of all those eyes on him sent shivers up his spine.

Luther and his classmates sat down as the bell rang. A minute later, a woman entered the room. She moved quickly and gave an impression of barely contained energy. After dropping some papers on her desk, she went straight to the chalkboard and picked up a piece of chalk.

"Good morning, everyone," she began, getting straight to the point. "Monday, as you remember, we started talking about the science of health. Yesterday we got into the history of health care, and today we have individual reports on health occupations..." Ms. Dombrowski looked up. "I'm sure everyone is ready," she added with a wide smile.

Luther moved nervously in his seat as the teacher continued. "Before we hear the reports, though, let's review yesterday's discussion. What did we say about health care?"

Allison spoke up. "Caring for the sick is one of the world's oldest occupations. People have been doing it for thousands of years. But ways of taking care of the sick have changed a great deal. In the old days, health care was all mixed up with magic and superstition. Today, medicine is a science and medical researchers keep looking for better ways of treating illness and keeping people healthy.

"Many medical procedures, and many of the rules about good health that we take for granted, were discovered quite recently—after lots of scientific observation and research. Anesthetics to keep people from feeling pain and shots to protect them against diseases like smallpox or polio are such discoveries. *We* all know how important it is to keep wounds clean to prevent infection, but doctors didn't always know that. Centuries ago, operations took place in dirty surroundings; doctors didn't realize that the germs on a dirty scalpel might make a sick person even sicker.

"And," continued Allison, "new medical discoveries are taking place all the time. Some medicines and operations that are used today were unknown just 5 or 10 years ago!"

"Although the field of health care is very old," she said, speaking rapidly, "it's also very new. And advances in medical science are taking place so fast that the field is changing all the time."

"That's an excellent summary, Allison," said the teacher. "Now, what else can we say about health care? Why should we bother to learn about health occupations?"

Hesitating at first, Luis finally raised his hand. "Because some of us may want to become doctors and nurses when we're older," he said.

"Yes, of course, Luis," answered Ms. Dombrowski. "We've already learned that several million people in this country work in the health field, and that there are health careers of all kinds for people with different interests and abilities.

"Many of these jobs were created by the rapid developments in medicine that Allison just mentioned. Remember that many of the things that people in the health field do today would have been unimaginable 100 years ago. The health occupations as we know them today were "created" by such things as the invention of a new machine, the discovery of a new way of diagnosing illness, or the introduction of a better way of helping people take care of themselves. New occupations are emerging all the time, and quite possibly the health occupations of the future won't resemble the jobs we're going to hear about now."

Glancing at her paper again, the teacher continued. "We have eight reports to hear today, so let's go ahead with them. First is Toni Crowley, who will tell us about medical practitioners."

Medical Practitioners

Note cards in hand, Toni walked to the front of the room, faced the class, and began to speak.

"Medical practitioners, whom we usually refer to as doctors, are called that because they "practice" the profession of medicine. When they treat patients, their hardest and most important job is making a diagnosis—figuring out what's wrong and what to do about it. They usually start by taking a medical history and doing a physical examination, plus ordering whatever tests or X-rays seem appropriate. The results give them the clues they need to determine how sick someone really is. Coming up with the correct diagnosis can be hard if the patient is a baby who can't explain what hurts. Or if the disease is very rare, the kind doctors read about in textbooks but never expect to see. At any rate, diagnosing

Health Occupations

illness and prescribing the proper treatment take so much knowledge and skill that medical practitioners spend years and years going to school.

"Most medical practitioners are *physicians* and have a degree called a Doctor of Medicine, or M.D. Some physicians are *general practitioners,* doctors who see patients of all ages and treat all kinds of illnesses. But most physicians specialize. We're all familiar with some of these experts. On television we've seen *surgeons* operate. When our mothers were expecting us, they probably visited *gynecologists* or *obstetricians*. These doctors took care of problems related to the pregnancy, and delivered us when we were born. And many of us have visited *pediatricians,* doctors who treat children and youngsters. There are other specialists whom you may not have heard of. *Cardiologists,* for example, concentrate on diseases of the heart. *Neurologists* treat problems of the brain and nervous system. *Radiologists* specialize in using X-rays to find or treat illnesses. The list goes on and on. In fact, there are more than 30 fields of medicine in which doctors can take graduate training after they earn the M.D.

"There are other kinds of medical practitioners you've probably heard about. *Osteopathic physicians* help patients who have problems involving muscles and bones.

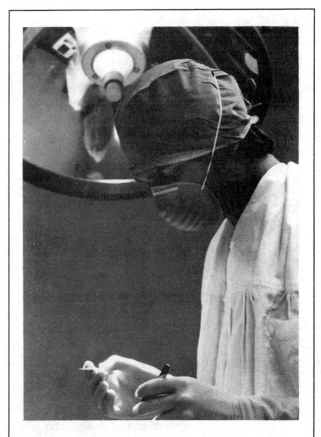

Surgeons must be able to make decisions in emergencies.

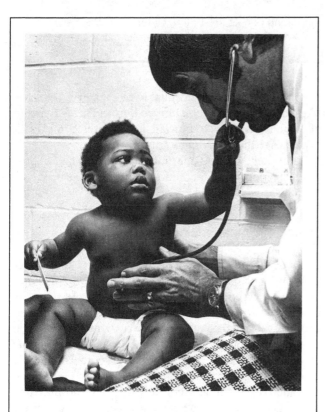

The diagnosis can be difficult if the patient can't explain what's wrong.

They use hand manipulation as a form of treatment in addition to surgery, drugs, and other conventional medical treatments. *Chiropractors* deal with the nervous system, and treat patients by manipulating the spine. And *podiatrists* treat foot disease and deformities such as corns or bunions. They also take care of problems with the arch, or curve of the foot."

Toni looked up from her paper. "There are other kinds of health practitioners that I haven't mentioned," she said. "But they will be covered in other reports. Any questions?"

When no hands appeared, Toni returned to her seat. "That was very good, Toni," commented Ms. Dombrowski. "And now let's hear about another kind of health practitioner, the dental practitioner, or dentist. Sharon Dailey's report on dental occupations is next. Then Pilar Chavez will tell us about optical occupations. Sharon?"

As Sharon walked to the front of the room, Luther shifted in his seat. His ordeal was at least 10 minutes away. Maybe, if he was lucky, the other reports would take the whole hour and he'd be saved for today. But that was too much to hope for....

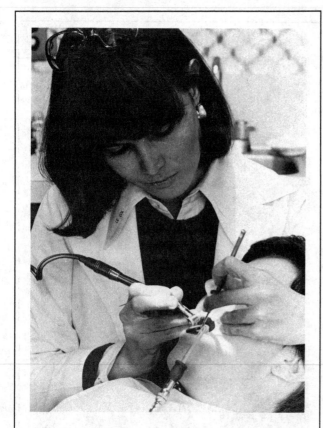

Dentists need talented hands as well as scientific ability.

Helping people select frames for their eyeglasses takes courtesy and tact.

Dental Occupations

"Dental workers," began Sharon, "are concerned with the teeth and gums. Many of us have gone to the *dentist* to have a cavity filled. But dentists do much more than that. They give us advice on taking proper care of our teeth. They examine teeth and gums for signs of disease. Depending on the problem, they take X-rays, straighten teeth, and treat gum disease. When necessary, they pull teeth and substitute false teeth, called dentures. Some of us have visited an *orthodontist*—a dentist who specializes in straightening teeth.

"When you visit a dentist's office to have your teeth cleaned, it may not be the dentist who does the cleaning. Dentists often employ *dental hygienists* to clean and polish teeth, take X-rays, and tell patients how to care for their teeth properly. Many dentists also have a *dental assistant* who makes the patient comfortable in the dental chair and helps the dentist by handing instruments and keeping the patient's mouth clean.

"There is one other kind of dental worker whom we rarely see, the *dental laboratory technician.* This is the person who makes braces, dentures, crowns, and bridges.

If you wear braces, you probably remember what it was like when the dentist took impressions and measurements of your teeth. The technician used these to make the braces. Are there any questions?"

Since there were no questions this time, either, Sharon gave the floor to Pilar and sat down. Luther couldn't keep his eyes off the clock on the wall.

Optical Occupations

"Look around the room," began Pilar, "and notice how many people wear glasses. Quite a few. And some of you wear contact lenses. Who told you that you needed glasses? An *optometrist,* probably. Optometrists are medical practitioners and have extensive training, as do the other doctors Toni just told us about. But instead of being Doctors of Medicine they go to colleges of optometry and earn the degree of Doctor of Optometry. Optometrists examine their patients' eyes and may prescribe glasses or contact lenses to correct poor vision. When necessary, they can suggest other treatments, such as eye drops, that don't involve drugs or surgery.

Health Occupations

"Many optometrists employ an *optometric assistant* who helps them the way a dental assistant helps a dentist. Optometric assistants keep patients' records, make appointments, and do other office work. They also prepare a patient for an eye examination and help the optometrist perform it.

"When I was in fifth grade, the optometrist tested my vision and told me that I needed glasses. At the time, I never wondered where those glasses came from. But in doing the research for this report, I learned that an *ophthalmic laboratory technician* was the person who actually made my glasses. Sometimes these workers are called *optical mechanics*. Anyway, they start with a standard piece of glass, called a lens blank. Using precision tools, they grind and polish the blank until it fits the prescription. Then they mark and cut the lens to fit the frame.

"I remember the day my father and I picked up the glasses at the office of the *dispensing optician*. We had already been there once, to bring the optometrist's prescription and choose the frames. When the glasses were ready, they didn't fit comfortably. They felt funny on my

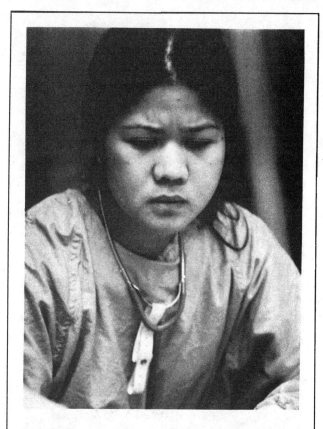

This surgical intensive care nurse has had to find her own way of dealing with serious illness and death.

nose and I didn't want to wear them. So the optician adjusted them for me. Besides fitting glasses, opticians help patients select frames. And they write up work orders that the technicians use to make glasses.

"But what if you need more than just glasses? Fortunately, I don't. But many people have serious eye diseases that require medicine or surgery. These people go to an *ophthalmologist*. Also know as *oculists*, ophthalmologists are physicians—medical doctors who specialize in problems of the eye. Like other physicians, they are licensed to prescribe drugs or surgery to correct a problem."

Pilar looked around the room and asked for questions. Someone in the back had one. Luther didn't pay any attention; he was busy reading his report to himself, afraid he might be called next. His report was as good as the others, he told himself. There was nothing to be afraid of.... But everyone would be looking at him! What if he tripped as he walked to the front of the room?

"Thank you, Pilar," Ms. Dombrowski was saying. "Let's see, who's next?"

Luther crossed his fingers and held his breath.

"Greg Tanimoto has a report on nursing occupations," continued the teacher.

Luther relaxed. Greg was sure to give a long report; he always did.

Nursing Occupations

Standing confidently at the front of the room, Greg paused to get everyone's attention and then began to read from his note cards.

"When we think of health care," he said, "we think of nurses as well as doctors. We all know that nurses play a very important role in caring for the sick. However, there's more to nursing than that.

"Just think about Ms. O'Hare, the school nurse. Like many nurses, she devotes a lot of her time to health education—teaching us things about our eating, sleeping, and living habits that can make us healthier. She also gives us tips on how to keep from hurting ourselves."

"That's right! She talked to our gym class last week about the dangers of skateboarding," broke in Charlie.

"Yes," agreed Greg, a little startled by the interruption. Regaining his composure, he continued. "You may not know that people in several different jobs provide nursing care: Registered nurses, practical nurses, nursing aides, attendants, and orderlies. The differences among these workers boil down to training and responsibility. The more training you have, the more responsibility you can assume and the more decisions you can make about what kind of care the patient should have.

"In a hospital or nursing home, *registered nurses* supervise nursing care. They keep track of the patients' progress. They must know enough to be able to judge a patient's condition and tell if it is getting worse. If so, they must know exactly what action to take. Nurses see to it that the physician's orders are carried out and consult the physician when problems occur. But when emergencies arise, they may have to take charge and rely on their own training and experience to do the best thing for the patient.

"Training for this profession takes from 2 to 5 years, depending on the program. That's considerably more training than people in other nursing occupations have, so registered nurses often act as team leaders in providing patient care. With their extra training they have greater responsibility for the patient's health. They not only give shots, for example, but know what the medicine is for and what side effects it might have.

"*Practical nurses* help physicians and registered nurses by handling routine aspects of patient care. They take temperatures and blood pressures, change bandages or dressings, and give cetain medicines. Their training usually takes 1 year. Practical nurses must pass a special exam in order to use the title "licensed practical nurse" or LPN.

"*Nursing aides* also help with the daily routine in a hospital or a nursing home. They answer patients' bell calls, deliver messages, carry food trays into patients' rooms, and feed patients who are too sick to feed themselves. *Orderlies* and *attendants* escort patients to operating and examining rooms. These nursing occupations require the least training—from a few days to a few months—and that usually is provided on the job."

Greg looked up from his note cards. "That's it. Are there any questions?"

Somebody *please* ask a question, thought Luther as he counted the minutes remaining in this class period.

"I have a question," said Lisa. "You mentioned the school nurse and talked about nurses who work in hospitals. I have a cousin who works in the health unit at Consolidated Petroleum, so I know that nurses also work in business and industry. Do they work in other places, too?"

"Sure they do," said Charlie before Greg had a chance to reply. "They work in doctors' offices!"

"Right," agreed Greg. "And nurses work in other places that are a little less obvious. Many nurses and nursing aides work in nursing homes, rehabilitation centers, psychiatric hospitals, and mental health clincs. The atmosphere is different from that in general hospitals, which usually are pretty hectic places where the patients are extremely sick, but stay for only a short time. Patients in nursing homes and mental hospitals may stay for months or years. Progress can be very slow, and that

requires a great deal of patience and encouragement from the nursing staff. These nurses must be good at dealing with people during a difficult period in their lives. They must be able to reach out and encourage people who feel sad and hopeless. In institutions where the patients need rehabilitation or long-term care, the human side of nursing is especially important. Sometimes a nurse is the patient's only friend.

"Community health nursing is something else you should know about," Greg continued. "*Public health nurses* run clinics that deal with health care needs in neighborhoods where people live—housing projects in rundown parts of the city, migrant labor camps, remote communities in the mountains or the desert. *Visiting nurses* care for people in their homes; often, their patients are elderly people who are too sick or weak to manage all by themselves. Visiting nurses usually travel by car and see many patients in the course of a day. They're on the go all the time, and no two days are alike. Community health nurses do other things, too. They organize neighborhood health programs and try to educate people about good health and sensible living habits. They may,

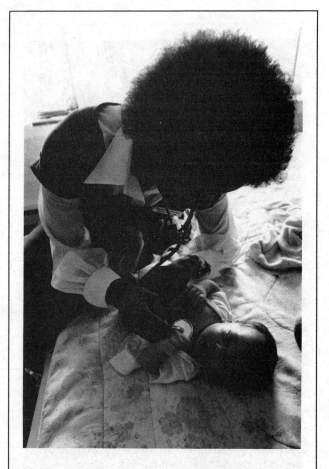

Visiting nurses are on the go all the time.

for example, help start a campaign to wipe out rats; bring in speakers to teach shoppers about the nutritional value of the food they buy; or teach youngsters about drug abuse."

Toni raised her hand. "When I was preparing my report, I came across the term "nurse practitioner." Can you explain that?"

Excellent, thought Luther. The more questions the better. Greg certainly was wound up about nursing!

"*Nurse practitioners,*" began Greg, "are registered nurses who have gone back to nursing school for advanced training that lasts 1 year or more. The additional skills they learn enable them to provide basic health care on their own. For example, some nurse practitioners run maternal health clinics—clinics for mothers and babies. They know all about common childhood complaints, and can handle ordinary illnesses so well that the mother doesn't have to take her baby to a physician. A few nurse practitioners have private practices—just as doctors and dentists do—and treat patients with routine health problems such as colds, sore throats, sprains, and broken bones. Nurse practitioners are trained to substitute for a physician in specific situations."

"Good job, Greg," said Ms. Dombrowski. "Now let's hear from Kevin about medical record occupations."

Medical Record Personnel

"Medical records are an important part of health care," Kevin began. "Medical records are nothing more than written information about patients, including their "medical histories"—what illnesses they have had and when, what doctors they visited, what treatment or drugs they've had, and so on. The records also contain X-ray reports, results of laboratory tests, and notes from doctors and nurses.

"Many people use this information. Of course, a doctor usually needs to know your medical history in order to treat you. But medical records serve other purposes, too. Researchers use them in looking for cures for diseases. National and State health agencies use them in developing public health programs. And insurance companies use them in setting rates for their policies.

"Medical recordkeeping is a complicated process because the information is so technical. To handle the job, hospitals and clinics employ several kinds of workers. *Medical record clerks* do the more routine tasks. They translate age and sex information into codes, for example, so that this information can be stored and easily retrieved when necessary. They also answer routine requests for files. *Medical record technicians* handle tasks that require more technical knowledge, such as reviewing records for internal consistency and cross-indexing med-

ical information. In most hospitals, a *medical record administrator* directs the records department and trains the technicians and clerks. These workers don't take care of sick people the way doctors and nurses do, but they're health workers all the same. Are there any questions?"

Luther looked around the room hoping to see hands go up, but none did. He became nervous again as Kevin went back to his seat and Ms. Dombrowski looked at her list. Luther glanced at the clock. He was counting on the hour running out before his turn. Or would it be better just to get it over with and not worry anymore? No, giving the report tomorrow would be better than giving it today . . . .

"Ramon Ramirez, let's hear your report on therapy and rehabilitation occupations," the teacher said suddenly.

So far, so good, thought Luther.

Therapy and Rehabilitation Occupations

"Think about the handicapped students in our school," began Ramon. "Some have obvious disabilities, such as blindness or a withered arm. Others have problems that aren't noticeable right away, such as hearing difficulty. But whatever the problem, many of these students learned to cope with their handicap through therapy.

"Therapists and rehabilitation workers help people with handicaps learn to move around, communicate, and go through everyday activities as normally as possible. With therapists' help, more handicapped people than ever before are managing very well in schools just like this one, in college, and in the world of work.

A speech pathologist is helping this little girl overcome her hearing problems.

Exploring Careers

"The largest group of therapists includes *speech pathologists,* who treat speaking problems, and *audiologists,* who work with hearing problems. Speech and hearing are very closely related, so a specialist in one field must know the other pretty well.

"I chose this topic for my report because of my cousin Maria," explained Ramon. "She was in a motorcycle accident last year and hurt her leg very badly. When she got out of the hospital, she couldn't use her leg at all—couldn't stand on it, or walk, or run. It was awful. But the *physical therapist* she saw every day helped Maria learn to use the muscles in her leg again. During her treatment sessions, she did exercises with special equipment and practiced "ordinary" things like climbing stairs. That wasn't an ordinary thing for her, I can tell you! It took a lot of determination on her part, and a lot of encouragement from the therapist, for her to get back the use of that leg. The therapist really inspired her when her spirits were low; I guess that's a very important part of the job.

"*Occupational therapists* also work with people who have trouble using their muscles. The difference is, while physical therapists help you use your muscles again, occupational therapists teach practical skills that make your life easier or make you feel good about yourself.

"I'll give you another example. When my grandmother had a stroke, she was paralyzed on one side and couldn't dress herself or eat without help. She even had trouble using the telephone. She was very upset about her condition because she hates to ask anybody to do things for her. But she's in a nursing home that has occupational therapy classes every day, and she is gradually learning to do simple things for herself again.

"Occupational therapists do a lot of their work with patients like my grandmother, people who need to relearn everyday skills because their muscles were damaged by illness or an accident. Some occupational therapists work with retarded or emotionally disturbed patients in mental hospitals. By teaching these patients simple skills like gardening or weaving, for example, they hope to give them self-confidence and help pave the way for emotional stability. And occupational therapists help mentally or physically handicapped persons prepare for a job by teaching them skills like typing or the use of power tools."

Ramon looked around for questions, but there were none. He took his seat while Ms. Dombrowski looked at her list.

"We have two reports left," said the teacher, "Which shall we hear first?"

Luther looked at the clock—only a few minutes left. If he wasn't called now, the hour would run out. He'd be saved until tomorrow.

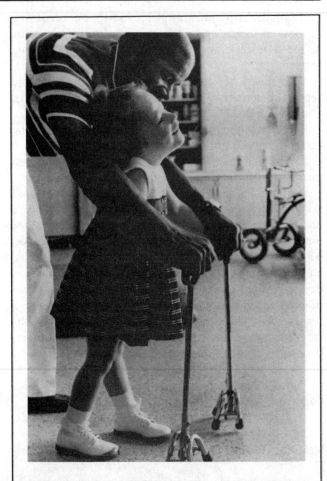

Physical therapists encourage their patients to keep trying, even when progress is slow.

This occupational therapist knows that putting a mosaic together is good exercise for stiff fingers.

This technician operates machinery that records the electrical impulses in our brains.

"Cathy Chan will tell us about medical technologists, technicians, and assistants," said Ms. Dombrowski finally. "And Luther Knight will be last with a report on other health occupations."

Bingo, said a voice in Luther's mind.

Medical Technologists, Technicians, and Assistants

Cathy quickly took her place at the front of the room. After getting the attention of the class she started to read.

"There are many people besides doctors and nurses who help run a hospital or clinic. Among them are the technologists, technicians, and assistants. Some operate special kinds of equipment. The electrocardiograph, or EKG, for example, measures the rate and strength of a patient's heartbeat. It takes a specially trained *EKG technician* to operate it. Similarly, an *electroencephalographic technician* or *technologist* is needed to operate an electroencephalograph, or EEG. This machine records electrical impulses from a person's brain.

"For obvious reasons," Cathy said with a smile, "these workers usually are called *EEG technicians*. And next we come to the *radiologic technologist* who operates X-ray equipment."

Cathy paused to turn the page. At the same moment, a young man walked into the classroom. Luther thought he recognized him; he worked in the school office. Moving quietly along the wall so as not to disturb the class, he went up to Ms. Dombrowski and handed her a note. A minute later he was gone.

Cathy continued reading. "Other workers help in different ways. *Medical laboratory workers,* for example,

Medical laboratory technicians perform tests that help physicians arrive at a correct diagnosis.

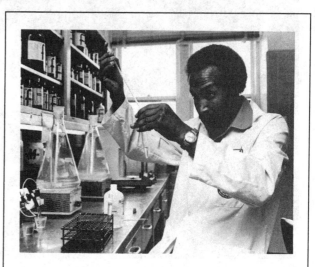

A patient's life might depend on this medical technologist's ability to work under pressure.

Exploring Careers

perform tests that help doctors understand and treat diseases. With microscopes and other equipment, the laboratory workers analyze samples of blood, tissue, and fluids from the human body.

"Surgeons receive important help from *operating room technicians* before, during, and after surgery. Technicians help set up the operating room with instruments, equipment, and linens. They also prepare patients for surgery by washing, shaving, and disinfecting the parts of the body where the surgeon will operate. During surgery they hand the surgeon instruments, sterile pads, and whatever else is needed. And after the operation they move the patient to the recovery room and help clean up.

"Other medical assistants, *respiratory therapy workers,* treat patients who have breathing problems. Also known as *inhalation therapy workers,* they give emergency treatment in cases of heart failure, stroke, drowning, and shock. This treatment is very important to prevent brain damage when a patient stops breathing. Generally, damage to a person's brain occurs if the person has stopped breathing for 3 to 5 minutes. And after 9 minutes without oxygen, a person usually dies. It's no wonder that respiratory therapy workers are among the first medical specialists called for in an emergency.

"And speaking of emergencies, *emergency medical technicians,* or EMT's, specialize in handling them. They

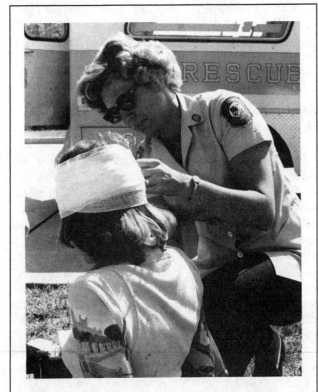

Emergency medical technicians must act quickly when they arrive at the scene of an accident.

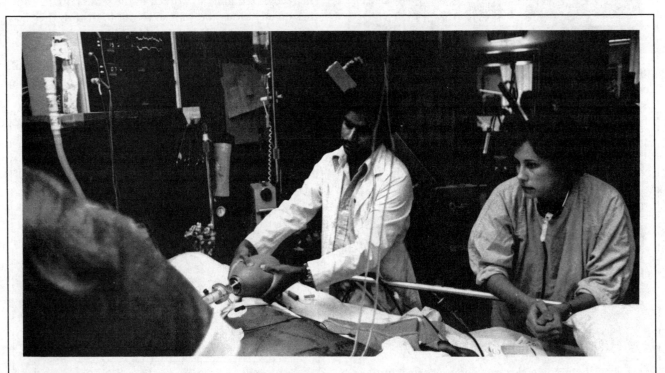

Members of a health team are oblivious to the outside world when they are fighting to save a life.

Health Occupations

are called when someone has an automobile accident or a heart attack. They determine how bad the victim's illness or injury is and what emergency medical care is needed. Depending on the case, the EMT's may have to restore a victim's breathing, stop a wound from bleeding, give first aid for poison, or help deliver a baby. Whatever the situation, though, EMT's must work quickly. Their emergency care often means the difference between life and death."

Cathy looked around the room. "Any questions about what I've said?" she asked. No hands appeared, but this time Luther didn't care. There was only a minute left in the period, not enough time for him to give his report. He smiled to himself.

"Very good, Cathy," said the teacher, walking to the front of the room. "That leaves us with Luther's report. Normally we wouldn't have time for it, but your schedule has been changed today. The school office tells me that your next-period teacher, Mr. Borden, suddenly got sick and went home. They don't have a substitute, so for the next period you'll be with me. We'll hear Luther's report, then take a break. After the break we'll discuss the reports. Luther?"

Luther groaned and stood up. Trying to avoid the others' eyes he walked stiffly to the front of the room. There he turned around, looked down, and began to read. His eyes never left the page.

This student nurse volunteers her time to teach senior citizens about nutrition.

Other Health Occupations

"There are several health occupations that don't fit into any of the other groups," he began nervously. "But they are important, too. Take *pharmacists,* for example. If you are sick, your doctor may suggest you take a certain drug. The doctor writes an order, or prescription, for the drug. When you go to the drugstore, a pharmacist fills that prescription by giving you the exact drug the doctor ordered. But pharmacists do more than just putting pills in a bottle. They test each drug to see how strong and fresh it is. They must know what goes into each drug, how it is used, and what effect it has. And they give doctors advice on choosing and using drugs properly.

"Another important person is the *dietitian.* As you can tell from the word itself, dietitians are experts in diet or nutrition. They help plan meals for patients in hospitals and clinics. Since doctors sometimes prescribe certain foods for their patients, dietitians in a hospital may have to plan hundreds of individualized meals every day. Of course, not all dietitians work in hospitals. Many work in nursing homes, large companies, and schools like ours. And some work in neighborhood health centers, organizing programs to teach people about nutrition, meal planning, and the importance of good eating habits."

Luther turned the page without looking up. "But let's go back to the hospital for a moment," he continued. "We've heard about many of the people who work there: Nurses, doctors, laboratory workers, technicians, dietitians, and so on. It's clear that a hospital needs some people to coordinate the activities of all the others and make everything run smoothly. This is the job of *health administrators.* They supervise the operations of hospitals, nursing homes, and other health facilities. This job requires a great deal of business and organizational skill—the top administrator, after all, is responsible for keeping costs within a budget, hiring and training staff, and purchasing all the supplies. But health care is a very technical field. Moreover, it's one that's in the public eye and subject to lots of regulations. Administrators need to know about all the different aspects of providing and paying for health care in this country.

"There are many other important health occupations. Let me tell you about just a few of them. *Physician assistants,* sometimes called physician associates, perform many patient care tasks traditionally handled by doctors. They may do physical examinations, prescribe certain drugs, and advise patients about their health problems—all under the direct supervision of a physician. Their work frees doctors to devote their time to more complex diagnoses and treatments.

"*Health sciences librarians* do things that are done in

any library. They order library materials and organize them as conveniently as possible for use by readers. But these librarians are different. They have a very specialized knowledge of books, journals, and reports in the field of medicine and health. Medical researchers, students, physicians and nurses, and many other health workers use their services.

"*Medical illustrators* are people with artistic talent as well as a strong science background. They create drawings, sculptures, and other art forms to illustrate medical and surgical procedures. Their work appears in books, films, exhibits, and on television, and is important for research and for teaching purposes.

"*Biomedical engineers* use their knowledge of chemistry, physics, engineering, and other fields to design medical equipment such as cardiac pacemakers, heart-lung machines, artificial kidneys, and electroencephalograph machines. *Biomedical equipment technicians* install and repair such equipment.

"There's one last occupation I want to mention. All along we've talked about health care for people. But if your dog or cat got sick, what kind of doctor would you visit? A *veterinarian,* of course. Many veterinarians treat only small animals and pets. Others specialize in farm animals. Still others inspect meat for public health agencies or do research. Whatever they do, though, their

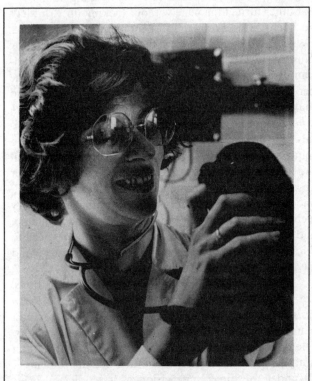

Experience working with animals can help you decide about a career as a veterinarian.

work is very important because animal diseases can spread to people—and because animals have value in themselves."

There was nothing more on the page to read, so Luther looked up. Everyone was staring at him. After a nervous silence, he remembered what came next. "Are there any questions?" he asked.

Nobody moved. Finally, the teacher ended the uncomfortable silence. "Thank you, Luther. That was very good. You may sit down now.

"All right, class, let's take a 5-minute break," continued Ms. Dombrowski. "Then we'll talk about these occupations some more."

What Makes a Good Health Worker?

After the break, Ms. Dombrowski led the class discussion. "We've just heard about dozens of different health careers," she began. "We were told what each worker does. Now let's see if we can figure out what kind of person is best suited for a job in this field. Does anyone have any ideas?"

Greg raised his hand. "It seems to me," he said, "that the health field is so broad there is room for people with all kinds of interests."

"That's a very important point, Greg," said Ms. Dombrowski. "Jobs in this field aren't all alike. There are careers in health for people who enjoy running machines and handling equipment; for people who like to work with numbers or scientific data; for people who like to work with others; for people who are interested in business; and for people who are interested in consumer and public interest issues."

Toni spoke up. "But people in many of the health occupations *do* have something in common. They're working in scientific surroundings: Collecting specimens of blood or tissue, for example; analyzing them; interpreting laboratory results; and making decisions on the basis of scientific data and research. It seems to me that you'd have to like science to observe very strict procedures, as a laboratory technician has to. Or to understand how the muscles in our body work, as a physical therapist must."

"Good point, Toni," said Ms. Dombrowski. "*Science and math* are important," she wrote on the chalkboard. "And the way you feel about your science courses in school may be a sign of whether or not you'd like a health career. Now what else?"

Luis had something to say. "The main thing about these occupations is liking people. That's what health care is really all about. If I'm a doctor, nurse, or whatever, I want to help my patients. That means more than examining them or giving them medicine. It also means putting them at ease and making them confident that I can help them. That confidence might make the difference in their recovery."

"Health workers should be *good at working with people*," Ms. Dombrowski wrote. "We often call that "having a good bedside manner." That's good, Luis. Does anyone have more to say about that?"

Saul had a comment. "Getting along with people is more than just being nice. Look at speech pathologists, for example. Often their patients are retarded or emotionally disturbed. Progress often comes slowly or not at all. These workers must have a *positive outlook* and be able to inspire their patients to keep trying."

"You're right, Saul," said the teacher. "What else?"

The next hand in the air was Kevin's. "Liking people is important in some of the occupations," he said, "but not in all of them. Look at the medical record personnel, for example. They work with the patients' files. Or the laboratory workers, who test blood and tissue samples. Or the dental lab technicians, who make dentures. These workers never see the patients. So while many workers must have a good bedside manner, not all of them do."

"That's a good point, Kevin," said the teacher. "You don't have to be warm and outgoing for all of these jobs. And just because you can't stand the sight of blood doesn't mean you should rule out the health field either! Now what other qualities are important?"

Jessica spoke up. "My cousin is a physician, and she talks about how much *motivation* the job takes. It's more than just patience or compassion; it's the ability to keep yourself going when you want to give up. My cousin had years of hard training that left her little time for other things. And even now, as a doctor, her work still cuts into her private life. She never would have made it if practicing medicine hadn't been so important to her." Jessica paused and thought about it. Then she added, "I guess nurses, emergency medical technicians, and many other health workers need the same kind of motivation. They have to get through difficult training, or work long hours, or do some work that is very unappealing. It helps if they consider their work important."

"I think that's true, Jessica," answered the teacher. "Feeling that their work is important may not be the only reason they do what they do, but it is a big part. Does anyone else have a suggestion?"

This time no hands appeared. "Well, let me make a couple," continued Ms. Dombrowski. "Health practitioners, dental workers, nurses, technicians, and others perform many detailed tasks with their hands. These workers must have *good manual dexterity*, which means the ability to work well with their hands. Not everyone has that quality.

"One other characteristic we should mention is the *ability to work under pressure.* Surgeons and emergency medical technicians, to name only two, often have to think and act quickly to save a patient. They can't let the pressure make them upset or careless.

"Does anyone have anything to add to the list? No? Well, I think we've covered the most important qualities of good health workers. And since you've all contributed

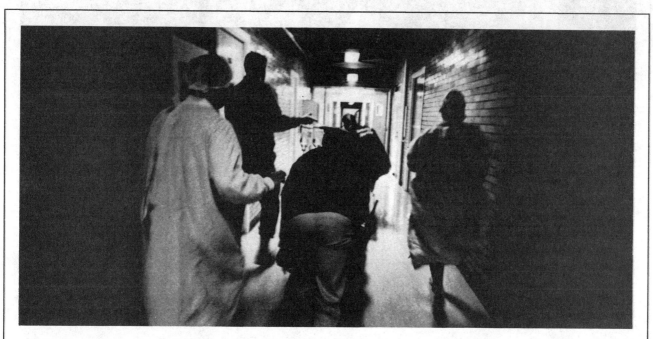

Emergencies require expert medical teamwork.

so much today, you deserve a rest. You may use the remainder of the period as you wish."

Training

No matter how much or how little time you're willing to put into training after high school, there may be a health career for you. You could start working as a hospital orderly without finishing high school; you'd receive your training on the job. Before becoming a physician, however, you'd have to train for 10 years or more after high school graduation. Those are the extremes. The training required for each of 32 health occupations is described in the Job Facts at the end of this chapter.

While formal training for a health career may be several years away, there are things you can do now to explore your interest in the field.

Science is very important in many of these occupations, and high school courses in biology, chemistry, physics, and mathematics provide the foundation you'll need for the science courses you'll take later on. Science fairs give you an opportunity to do projects on medicine and health.

Join a Health Careers Club if there is one in your school. The school nurse or science teacher often is the sponsor, and club activities may feature films, speakers, hospital tours, and other ways of providing information about health careers.

Volunteer to work in a health setting. Many hospitals have "candy striper" programs open to both boys and girls. The American National Red Cross provides a variety of volunteer opportunities for youngsters. Positions for Red Cross youth volunteers are available in nursing homes, day care centers, day camps, bloodmobiles, and in programs for the handicapped. Organizations concerned with diseases or health problems such as heart disease or cancer use volunteers to assist in their public education efforts. Working in such volunteer positions will acquaint you with what goes on in a health care setting.

It takes years of rigorous training to become a physician.

Health Occupations

Registered Nurse

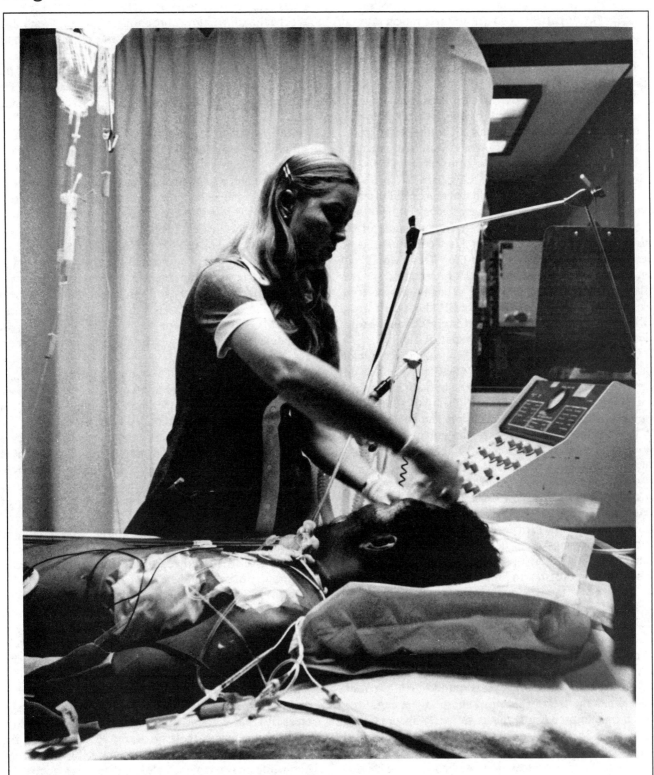

Kathy Wright works in an intensive care unit where she takes care of patients who are in serious condition following surgery.

Exploring Careers

Kathy Wright is a nurse at Leeds Memorial Hospital. She works in the surgical intensive care unit and takes care of patients who are in serious condition following surgery. Most patients go back to their rooms after an operation. But not all of them. Kathy's patients are in such critical condition that they are in a special unit where they can be watched every minute for changes that could mean life or death.

To provide the 24-hour care so necessary for these patients, the nurses at Leeds Memorial work day, evening, or night shifts of 8 hours each. The shifts rotate, so that Kathy and the other nurses in surgical intensive care take turns on each of the three shifts. This week Kathy is working from 7 a.m. to 3 p.m.

Kathy grew up in a household where medical research and hospital gossip were ordinary topics of dinner table conversation. Her father is a sales representative for a drug company, and her mother is a pediatrician. As a girl, she heard enough about the "real world" of medicine and nursing to dispel any romantic notions that she might have picked up from novels or from television. Listening to the adults talk about their work, Kathy soon came to realize that a professional health career means lots of work and responsibility.

To become a registered nurse (RN), Kathy completed a 5-year program at a university that led to a B.S. degree in nursing. As a student nurse, she had a heavy dose of science courses, including chemistry, anatomy, microbiology, physiology, nutrition, and public health. Clinical practice—working in the university hospital under the close supervision of the nursing instructor—was another important part of her training.

After graduation, Kathy took the state board examination for licensure. In New York, as in all states, nurses must have a license. Just as a driver's license is proof that you know how to drive, the license required to practice nursing, medicine, dentistry, dental hygiene, or pharmacy, for example, shows that you know enough about your profession to provide safe and proper care.

Kathy chose the B.S. program in nursing because she wanted to keep her options open. She knew, from her talks with her mother, that advancement opportunities for nurses were best for those with a bachelor's degree. And she felt that, after several years of bedside nursing, she might want to move into another kind of job.

At this point, just a few years out of nursing school, she thinks she'll probably stay in hospital nursing. Still, from time to time Kathy thinks seriously about making a change. She wonders what it would be like to fulfill her youthful dream of nursing needy people abroad as a Peace Corps volunteer or a Medico nurse. She also thinks about returning to nursing school for the master's degree or Ph.D. she would need to teach or do research.

The bachelor's degree program that Kathy completed isn't the only way to become a nurse. Hospitals offer 3-year diploma programs and community and junior colleges offer 2-year associate degree programs. However, the bachelor's degree program in nursing generally opens more doors than either of the other two. Some states now require a 4 year B.S. degree for all RNs and efforts are under way to require a bachelor's degree for all registered nurses. It's important to consider all of the different kinds of training programs before choosing one.

Kathy gets off the elevator at the third floor, walks through the heavy double doors, and stops at the nurses' station. There she spends a few minutes with Mr. Cochrane and Ms. Wall, the two nurses who have been on duty to give a general report to the incoming nurses. The group is joined by Ms. Rubel, the nurse who will be on the day shift with Kathy this week.

Ms. Wall begins talking to Kathy about the patients they share. "Mr. Young needed medication for pain at 2 o'clock," she explains, "and Ms. Lance's temperature rose to 102 degrees around midnight, but went down shortly thereafter. Otherwise, their vital signs were normal. Ms. Vaughn slept very well. Ms. Lance is scheduled to be discharged from intensive care tomorrow."

"Fine," replies Kathy. "See you tomorrow."

The nurses in the surgical intensive care unit at Leeds Memorial practice primary nursing. This means that each nurse is responsible on a 24-hour-a-day basis for the continuity, planning, and evaluation of nursing care for one to three patients. Currently, Kathy is responsible for Mr. Young, Ms. Lance, and Ms. Vaughn, while Ms. Rubel is responsible for two other patients. Nurses may act as associate nurses to patients during the absence of their primary nurse.

Kathy enters Mr. Young's room. Mr. Young is recovering from open heart surgery. She checks his vital signs: Blood pressure, pulse, temperature, and respiratory rate. All appear normal. Then she checks his skin color, and afterwards, sees to it that he is comfortable. Kathy records the information on his chart for the doctors who will be by later on. She looks carefully at the tube inserted in his chest to drain blood and restore pressure around the lung after the open heart surgery. Everything is as it should be.

She also checks a tube inserted into the bladder to drain urine into a plastic bag. Kathy removes the bag, measures the amount drained, records this measurement, and replaces the bag. Kathy then examines the tubing inserted in a vein in Mr. Young's left arm to feed him while he is unable to eat. Kathy makes sure that the fluid is flowing smoothly into his blood stream, then looks to see if there is enough fluid in the bottle suspended from a floor stand next to the bed.

Health Occupations

Kathy checks patients' vital signs regularly. Sometimes she must change dressings. When he was first admitted to the intensive care unit, Mr. Young was so weak he couldn't even breathe without help. He needed a respirator—a machine that breathed for him mechanically. Now that he's breathing on his own again—a good sign—Kathy checks often to make sure that Mr. Young is coughing and doing deep breathing to help clear his lungs.

Next, Kathy goes to see Ms. Lance, a young woman who underwent surgery a few days ago. Her doctors had ordered surgery because they suspected lung cancer, but when they tested the tissue they removed during the operation, they found that the tumor in her lung was not cancerous after all. Mr. Lance was overjoyed to learn

"I observe every little thing about my patient's condition—and I have to understand what I see," emphasizes Kathy.

his wife didn't have cancer; her children are too young to understand what all the fuss is about. Kathy bends over to listen to Ms. Lance's chest and lungs, checks for signs of infection, and changes her dressing. Everything is satisfactory. Since Ms. Lance is scheduled to be transferred to another part of the hospital tomorrow, Kathy discusses the details of her transfer with her and tells her what to expect.

Kathy visits her third primary patient, Ms. Vaughn, who is recovering from surgery to repair a large aneurysm in her abdomen. An aneurysm is an expansion in one of the arteries caused by a weakening in the arterial wall. If the artery were to burst, the patient could die from internal bleeding. Fortunately, the surgeon repaired Ms. Vaughn's aneurysm in time. Ms. Vaughn is dozing but wakes up as she hears Kathy approaching her bed.

"Hello, Ms. Vaughn, how do you feel today?"

Ms. Vaughn doesn't reply, just points to her stomach to show that she is in great pain. Kathy gives her some medication and tells her to wait until the pain eases to do her coughing and deep breathing exercises. While Kathy is bathing Ms. Vaughn and making her comfortable in bed, Dr. Church enters the room. Kathy tells him about the severe pain. She also shows that Ms. Vaughn's lungs sound clear and that she has bowel sounds, and suggests that Ms. Vaughn might be fed orally instead of intravenously. After further examination, Dr. Church agrees, orders the intravenous tube removed, and writes a prescription for a stronger medication for pain.

The remainder of the day goes smoothly. Just before lunch, Kathy receives a message to call Mrs. Young, the worried wife of her open heart patient. Kathy makes the phone call and reassures Mrs. Young. "Your husband is getting along nicely. He needed medication for pain last night, but he rested well and is making good progress. I looked in on him early this morning."

Mrs. Young thanks Kathy and adds, "I'll be around to see my husband this afternoon after work." In intensive care, only family members may visit and only for short periods of time.

At 3 o'clock, Kathy and Ms. Rubel meet the incoming nurses and give their report. "No emergencies, no unusual circumstances," comments Kathy.

"This is the first time in weeks that there have been no major problems in the unit," puts in Ms. Rubel. "I can't quite believe it."

Kathy can't believe it, either. She can, however, recall the many times when she has placed an emergency call to the resident or intern on duty. Emergencies always take a lot out of her, although it doesn't show. Kathy responds cooly to the tense, highly charged atmosphere of a crisis in the intensive care unit; she moves quickly and does what has to be done. She likes being part of an efficient health care team and she also likes being in a large hospital that has very sophisticated medical equipment and technology. In an emergency, Kathy handles her share of the work as smoothly as if she were a machine herself. Her years of training show. But afterwards, when the crisis is past, she unwinds.

Sometimes, despite the efforts of the doctors and nurses, a patient dies. That's hard on everyone. And Kathy, like everyone else in the unit, has had to find her own way of coming to grips with the sorrow of serious illness and the reality of death.

"I will remain in medical-surgical nursing, muses Kathy as she walks through the parking lot toward her car. "After all," she continues, "although quiet days like this one are nice for a change, I really like the pressure of working in the intensive care unit. And I like the fact that the job is so exacting and precise. We really zero in on the patient's problem. I constantly observe every little thing about my patient's condition—and I have to understand what I see. If the patient's breathing or heart rhythm changes, it's up to me to know what that might mean and to make a decision about what to do next... Yes, hospital nursing seems right for me."

Exploring

Nurses must be concerned about good health.

- Do you eat a well-balanced diet?
- Do you get enough sleep?
- Do you see the dentist regularly?
- Do you pay attention to warnings about alcohol, drug, or tobacco abuse?
- When you ask someone how he or she is feeling, are you really concerned or do you merely consider it a social custom?

Nurses must have an interest in science.

- Do you like science?
- Do you enjoy doing projects for a science class or science fair?
- Do you read articles about science in magazines or the newspaper?
- Do you like to visit museum exhibits on science and technology?
- Do you enjoy watching medical programs on television?

Nurses must be able to tolerate unpleasant sights and sounds.

- Does the sight of blood upset you?
- Do you look the other way when you pass the scene of an automobile accident?
- Does it bother you to change a diaper?
- Do you feel uneasy about going with an injured friend to the emergency room of a hospital?
- Do the signs and smells bother you when you visit people in a hospital or nursing home?
- Dose the idea of dissecting a frog in a science class bother you?

Nurses must be very observant. They must recognize danger signals right away.

- Can you tell when your pet isn't feeling well?
- Can you tell when you have had too much sun?
- Can you tell when you should take a break from a

After a crisis, Kathy takes time to unwind.

baseball game or other athletic activity?

- Can you tell when a car needs a tune-up?
- Do you notice minor changes in television or radio reception?
- Do you notice it when a movie reel is changed?
- Can you tell when something is missing from your room?

Nurses must carry out instructions precisely. There's no room for error when they give measured doses of medicine to patients.

- Are you good at following written instructions for assembling things?
- Can you remember road directions when someone gives them to you over the phone?
- Do you remember jokes and funny stories?
- Can you memorize plays and coaches' instructions in football, basketball, and other sports?
- Can you remember a teacher's exact instructions for a homework assignment or a test?

Nurses should care about people. They deal with patients who often are at their worst during an illness or accident.

- Do you put up with friends even when they are grouchy?
- Do you mind hearing people complain?
- Do you visit relatives or neighbors when they are sick?
- Are you patient with your younger brothers or sisters when they are tired or irritable?

Nurses must stay calm during emergencies. A nurse might have to set up an oxygen tent, administer artificial respiration, or treat a patient having a heart attack.

- Could you keep calm and get help right away if your kitchen caught fire?
- Would you know what to do if an infant got hurt or stopped breathing while you were baby-sitting?
- Would you act sensibly if a pet were injured?
- Would you know what to do if a friend injured himself or herself on the playground?

As a member of a health team, nurses must be good at giving an taking instructions and also must understand the limits of their authority.

- Can you give orders to your younger brothers and sisters?
- Do people do what you ask without getting angry?
- Do you recognize the need for laws, even those dealing with relatively minor offenses such as littering or jaywalking?

- Can you judge how far you can go when arguing with a teacher over a grade?

Nurses must have stamina. They spend a lot of time on their feet.

- Do you like to be active most of the time?
- Do you enjoy activities such as sports, hiking, backpacking, dancing, or gardening?

Nurses must keep accurate records of patients' medication, blood pressure, temperature, and so forth.

- Do you keep good records when you're a club treasurer or secretary?
- Do people ask you to keep score in bowling and other activities?
- Are you good at taking the minutes at meetings?
- Are you conscientious when you take notes in class?

Nurses must have manual dexterity to handle patients and medical equipment.

- Do you like working with your hands?
- Are you accustomed to using tools for work around the house?
- Are you good at setting up displays for class projects or school exhibits?

Nurses cannot afford to become emotionally involved with their patients.

- Can you remain calm when a friend or relative tells you about a serious problem?
- Does it upset you to visit someone who is very sick?
- Can you comfort a friend or family member during a time of sorrow?
- Can you argue a point calmly in a heated discussion?

Nurses keep up with the field by reading professional literature and attending lectures and conferences.

- Do you like to read for pleasure?
- Do you like to read popular science magazines?
- Do you show initiative in doing research on subjects of personal interest?
- When you are curious about something, do you go to an encyclopedia or library to learn more about it?
- Do you look up words you don't understand in the dictionary?
- Do you like to browse in the "new books" section of your library?

Medical Technologist

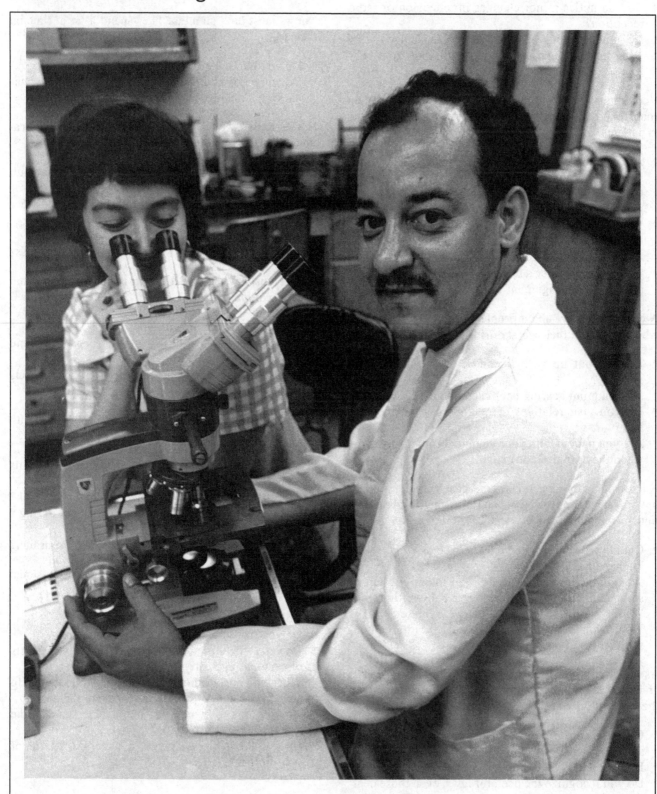

Roberto Torres' interest in science led to a career as a medical technologist.

Health Occupations

I'm Roberto Torres, a medical technologist at St. John's Hospital. In the medical laboratory where I work, we do tests to find out exactly what's wrong with people who are sick. Doctors need to know what the problem is in order to take care of it.

Our medical laboratory is divided into four departments: Clinical chemistry, bacteriology, hematology, and the blood bank. I'm in bacteriology, or microbiology—have been ever since I started work here at St. John's. My training covered the other areas, though, and chances are that sooner or later I'll be in hematology or one of the other departments of the lab.

I became interested in chemistry during my freshman year in college. I did so well in it that Professor Reiber encouraged me to consider a career in science. Following his suggestion, I visited the Kroner Laboratories and talked to some of the people who worked there. One thing led to another and I decided to become a medical technologist. My college offered a B.S. in medical technology and that's the degree I have.

During my senior year in college, I worked at City Hospital, rotating among the various departments of the medical laboratory. Clinical rotations give you a chance to put your classroom knowledge to work in a real life situation. They're part of the training for just about every health occupation, I guess. After I graduated, I took a special exam and when I passed I was officially "registered" as a medical technologist. Exams, certification, registration—it's a way of protecting the public and you find it in most health careers. But from my point of view, registration helps in getting a job and, sometimes, a higher salary. All the medical technologists at St. John's are registered.

A pathologist is in charge of the medical laboratory here. He's a physician, of course, one who has spent years studying the ways in which disease shows up in the tissues and fluids of our bodies. More people work in a medical laboratory than you might think. St. John's isn't a huge hospital, yet there are about 70 people working in the medical laboratory here. In addition to medical technologists like myself, there are technicians and assistants who take care of the more routine kinds of lab work. They didn't have to take as much training as I did, just 1 or 2 years in most cases.

Yesterday was a fairly typical day in the bacteriology department. We had the usual sorts of things to test: Samples of urine, spinal fluid, throat cultures, material from wounds, and blood. Physicians have samples sent to bacteriology when they suspect an infection or a disease. I'll give you an example. One of the patients we're trying to help is a woman who's worried and upset because she's gradually losing the strength in her legs, and the doctors don't know why. They've tried lots of different tests, and yesterday she had an extremely painful one: The doctor used a long hypodermic needle to remove some fluid from her spinal canal. Now we're testing that fluid to see what it can "tell" us. If some of the cells are abnormal, we'll know she has a nerve disease, which could explain her weakness.

This morning, a throat culture came in to the lab. The doctor who sent it suspects an infection and wants to find out which antibiotic to prescribe for the patient's sore throat. An antibiotic is a chemical substance that destroys bacteria. But since there are so many kinds of bacteria that make people sick, and so many different antibiotics to combat them, the first step is to find out exactly what we're dealing with. That's where the lab comes in.

The culture arrived on a swab in a sterile tube. I placed some of it in a special dish containing nutrients that make bacteria grow, then put the dish in an incubator—a warm place where the bacteria probably will grow overnight. Tomorrow morning I'll try to identify the bacteria, using chemicals. I'll also make slides and examine them under a microscope. Then I'll experiment to find out which antibiotic works against the strain of bacteria I have identified.

When I finish all the tests the doctor has asked for, I'll record the results and notify her. We come up with

A technologist must do accurate testing. "A patient's life could depend on it," says Roberto.

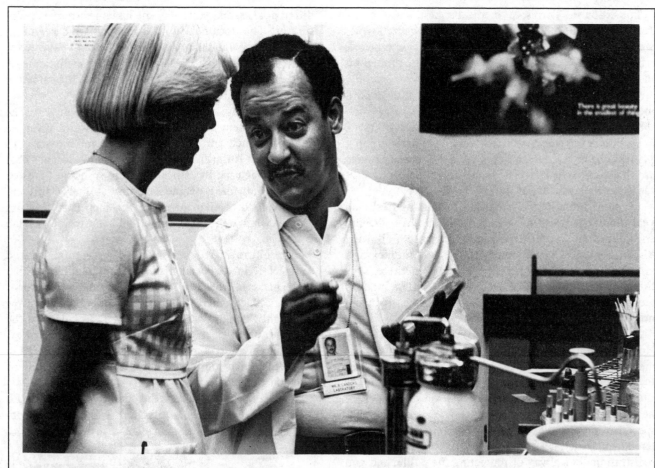

Roberto confers with a coworker. "The hospital staff is a team," notes Roberto, "so you have to depend on each other."

results quickly, I'd say. I usually have something to report in 48 to 72 hours. Once in a while, when test results don't make sense to the patient's physician, we run tests on another specimen just to make sure. You can't be too careful in a medical lab. But mistakes sometimes happen, and our test results can be wrong. That's why the human factor—judgment—is so important.

Jessica just started working in the lab last week. She's in the clinical chemistry department and operates machinery that tests blood for sugar, salt, fat, and protein content, and for disease. She's testing for sugar content right now. She begins by placing tubes of blood in a machine that spins very fast, so fast that the blood cells fall to the bottom of each tube. The material that remains on top is the serum. It looks like water and contains the sugar; chemicals in the machine make the sugar turn blue. Knowing whether or not a patient has the proper amount of sugar in his blood helps a physician treat him properly. Many of the machines Jessica works with are

linked up with a computer, enabling her to run literally thousands of different tests in a very short period of time. Computers have made a big difference in medicine, and you really appreciate that in a lab.

I ate lunch with Fritz today, as usual. Fritz has worked at St. John's nearly as long as I have, and we're good friends. He's in hematology, where they specialize in testing blood. Fritz does blood counts much of the time; he's concerned with the number of red cells and white cells in the blood. I guess you know already that red cells carry oxygen and white cells fight infection. Fritz operates machinery that places drops of a blood sample on a slide, stains the sample with colored dyes to help identify the cells, and smears the blood across the slide. Then he sets the slide under a microscope and looks closely at the white blood cells. Red cells all look alike, but white cells don't. Fritz can differentiate among white cells, and his count of the various kinds of white cells in the patient's blood will give the physician a good idea of whether or not something is wrong.

Another friend of mine, Wanda, works in the blood bank. Wanda and I talk about our jobs a lot. One of the things we both like is that our jobs rarely intrude on our personal time. In short, we leave our work in the laboratory. Wanda and the other technologists in the lab draw blood from blood donors—healthy people who donate blood to the blood bank. This blood is refrigerated in plastic bags and usually stays healthy for 21 days. The laboratory receives patients' blood samples in tubes from other parts of the hospital or from private physicians. These patients often are scheduled to undergo surgery, and doctors need to have blood available for transfusions. Medical technologists in the blood bank must find donors' blood that is compatible with patients' blood samples sent to the lab.

Technologists perform chemical tests to determine the type of blood in the sample. Blood may be typed A, B, AB, or O. In addition, technologists must determine the Rh factor as Rh positive or Rh negative, referring to the presence or absence of certain inherited substances in the red blood cells. The technologists then find stored blood that matches the blood in the patient's sample, and retest it as a precautionary measure. To be usable, the stored blood must be exactly like the patient's blood. In the event that no compatible blood is in storage, the technologists would contact the Red Cross to obtain the appropriate type.

Accuracy is essential in the blood bank and the workers here are under great pressure to avoid mistakes. A mistake by a laboratory technologist can kill a patient. Take the case of someone in an automobile accident who needs emergency surgery. If the lab made an error in testing and the patient received the wrong blood during the operation, he or she could die. That's an awesome responsibility.

Last fall I was invited to supervise some medical technology students who were doing their senior year clinical rotation in the biochemistry department here. I was surprised to discover how much I enjoyed teaching! I'm thinking of going back to school for a master's or Ph. D. so that I can teach full time in a college or university program in medical technology. But that's a pretty big step, after all.

Although my job can be routine at times, I know enough science to understand what the tests really mean. Once I've run some tests, I usually have an idea of what's going on inside the body of a patient with this or that disease. That makes the work interesting, and I don't know whether I want to give it up to teach.

And another thing. If I went into teaching, I might miss the day-to-day contact with the hospital staff. I like being part of the team effort here to help sick people. Well, I guess I'll have to give it a lot more thought . . . .

Exploring

Medical technologists must have a strong interest in science.

- Do you like science? Are you interested in biology and chemistry?
- Do you like to do laboratory experiments in class or on your own?
- Do you pursue science projects independently?
- Have you ever entered a science fair?
- Are you curious about the unknown?
- Do you like to study things under a microscope?
- Do you like to experiment with chemistry sets?

Medical technologists must be very accurate. Sometimes they are under pressure to work quickly, but they must be precise just the same. A patient's life might depend on it.

- Do you check your homework for errors?
- Do you check your answers on a test before handing it in?
- Do you do things in a methodical way?

Medical technologists must have an eye for detail. They have to detect even the slightest variations in the samples they examine.

- Do you enjoy identifying trees, leaves, or birds?
- Do you collect and identify sea shells?
- Can you tell that something is missing from your room?
- Can you find a place on a road map quickly?
- Do you like to do word-finds and other games where you must find hidden objects in pictures?

Medical technologists need manual dexterity to handle medical equipment such as test tubes, slides, and microscopes.

- Do you like working with your hands?
- Do you enjoy building models, setting up electric trains, framing pictures, making ceramics, making electronic equipment from a kit, or working with photographic equipment?
- Are you accustomed to using tools for work around the house?
- Are you good at setting up displays for class projects or school exhibits?

Exploring Careers

Medical technologists don't spend much time with patients. They work with laboratory equipment instead.

- Do you like building things?
- Do you like collecting things?
- Do you enjoy class assignments that involve working with scientific equipment?

Medical technologists must be able to follow strict laboratory procedures.

- Do you pay attention to instructions when you're taking a test or doing a homework assignment?
- Are you good at following a recipe?
- Do you use patterns for sewing, knitting, or needlework?
- Do you follow the instructions carefully when you mix chemicals from your chemistry set, build a model, or assemble electronic equipment from a kit?

Medical technologists are members of a health care team. They must work well with others.

- Do you enjoy working with other people on class projects? Do you accept your share of the responsibility?
- Do you like working with others on school clubs or committees?
- Do you like team sports?
- Do you like to organize group activities such as parties, sports events, picnics, and dances?

Medical technologists must be concerned about good health.

- Do you eat a well-balanced diet?
- Do you see the dentist regularly?
- Do you get enough sleep?
- Do you pay attention to warnings about alcohol, drug, or tobacco abuse?
- When you ask someone how he or she is feeling, are you really concerned or do you consider it a social custom?

Medical technologists keep up with the field by reading professional literature and attending lectures and conferences.

- Do you like to read for pleasure?
- Do you like to read popular science magazines? Do you read articles on medicine and health in magazines and newspapers?

- Do you show initiative in doing research on subjects of personal interest?
- When you are curious about something, do you go to an encyclopedia or library to learn more about it?
- Do you look up words you don't understand in a dictionary?
- Do you like to browse in the "new books" section of your library?

Health Occupations

Physical Therapist

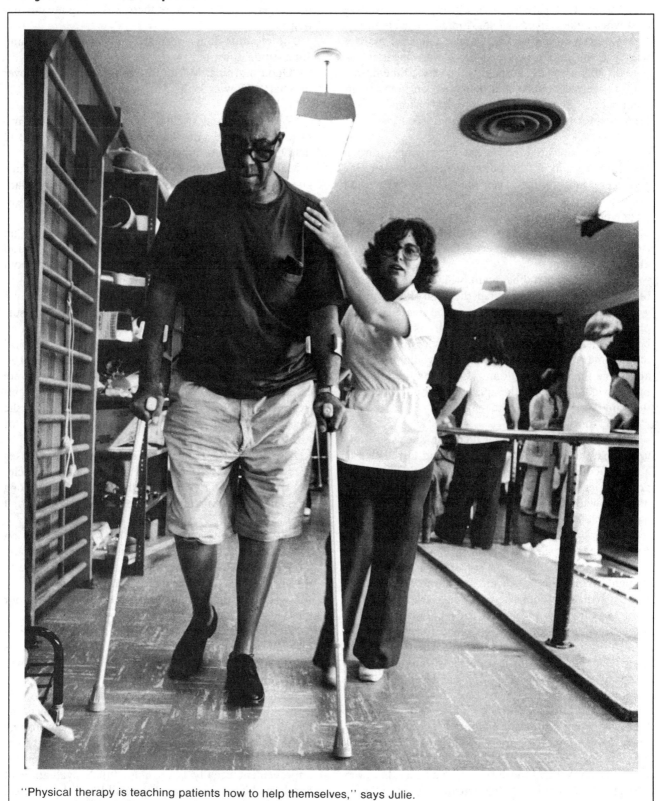

"Physical therapy is teaching patients how to help themselves," says Julie.

Doctors Hospital, with 500 beds, always seems busy, and the physical therapy department isn't immune from that hustle. Two patients were already in the waiting area when Julie arrived at 7:45. A middle-aged man was sitting quietly in a wheelchair and a fellow in his 20's was lying on a transport bed. Both were inpatients—patients staying at the hospital. Julie greeted them, said hello to the receptionist, and then went on to the treatment rooms. There, two other physical therapists were preparing for the patients in the waiting room.

"Hi, Tom."

Tom Harmon was adjusting the water temperature in the Hubbard tank for his burn patient, Joe Power. Joe had been badly burned when the gasoline can he had been holding had exploded. He had second and third degree burns on his legs and arms and first degree burns on his face. Joe had been using gasoline to restart the fire in a pile of smoldering weeds. He prefers not to talk about the accident.

The water in the Hubbard tank will make bending the burned limbs easier and soften the dead skin tissue so Tom can remove it. This was one of the treatments that physical therapists like Tom and Julie liked the least, because the patient usually is in so much pain. Without the treatment, though, the burned skin would tighten up and leave the patient with much less mobility after the burn healed. It gives the therapists some comfort to know the pain is worthwhile in the long run.

"Good morning, Nicki."

Nicki Bathista was the other therapist. She was setting up the parallel bars. Her first patient had lost his leg in a construction accident. He had just been fitted with an artificial leg and Nicki would help him learn to walk normally with it.

Julie was bound for room 514 and a patient she had seen several times in the last 2 days. After collecting the patient's records, she headed for the elevators.

"I hope the swelling in his leg is down today," Julie thought. While she waited for the elevator and on the ride up to the fifth floor, she reviewed Mark's case. Mark is an 18-year-old gas station attendant. Two nights ago, he was riding his motorcycle on the freeway when a drunken driver swerved into his lane, knocking him to the pavement. Mark's helmet prevented any head injuries and probably saved his life, but he didn't escape unharmed. He wound up with a cracked forearm, a fractured hip, and a badly fractured femur or thigh bone that was giving him a lot of trouble. The fracture had severed some important arteries in his leg. The surgeons had reconnected the arteries, but the swelling in his leg was considerable and the doctors weren't sure there was enough blood circulation. Inadequate circulation could mean that Mark would lose his leg. Before the fractured

leg could be set and Mark wrapped in a cast to immobilize his hip and leg, the swelling had to be reduced and the surgeons had to be sure there was adequate circulation.

The elevator doors opened onto the fifth floor and Julie strode down to 514.

"Good morning, Mark," she said as she looked over his chart. "How is the leg?"

"It hurts a lot."

"Well, when the swelling goes down, that will improve," Julie told him. The exercises she was about to help him with were supposed to reduce the swelling.

Mark looked unhappy. Although she didn't ask, Julie guessed that no one had visited him yet. Yesterday, Mark had told her that no one had come to see him. He was sure no one cared.

"Come on, Mark. Let's get to it! We'll have you up and out in no time!" Julie tried to encourage Mark and boost his morale. Realizing that she was concerned about him would, she hoped, ease his loneliness.

The exercises Mark performed were prescribed by a physician. After she had performed the emergency surgery on Mark's injured leg, the surgeon had written an "order" or prescription for Mark to receive physical therapy. Ordinarily, Julie would know exactly what to do after reading the order, but Mark's injuries were extensive and Julie wanted no chance for an error in his treatment. So, before she even visited with Mark, she consulted with the physician and discussed her goals for Mark's treatment.

The surgeon wanted her to exercise Mark's injured leg to promote improved circulation and prevent the muscles from withering away. Mark would be hospitalized a long time and where muscle tone is concerned, "If you don't use it, you lose it."

"We'll start out slowly, Mark. Just wiggle the toes on this injured leg." The exertion caused Mark some pain, but Julie explained how necessary the exercises were to the leg's recovery, so Mark didn't complain.

"O.K. Now tighten your thigh muscles to move your knee caps."

"He's doing pretty well," Julie thought. "In spite of his depression, he's trying hard at his therapy, so, as his physical condition improves, his spirits probably will improve too."

Julie's next patient was a special one. Sarah was a 5-year-old with cerebral palsy. Cerebral palsy affects the brain so that the patient has great difficulty controlling the muscles used for moving about. Physical coordination is greatly hampered, but with the proper therapy, improvement usually is possible. Julie's evaluation of Sarah at this time indicated the child had the physical coordination of an 8-month-old baby. Sarah was still

Health Occupations

"The best part of my job is sharing the joy of patients who are making progress."

improving, though, so she may eventually learn to walk. The damage from cerebral palsy is difficult to identify. The therapist doesn't know the limits of a patient's abilities until he or she reaches them. When the patient stops improving, then the therapist knows the extent of the damage.

"Good morning, Sarah. Let's practice our rolling."

She and Sarah then rolled around on the floor mats of the treatment room. First, Julie rolled over—demonstrating the move with considerable enthusiasm. Then, with Julie's help, Sarah took her turn.

"She almost has the knack of rolling over," thought Julie. "Maybe next week I can start teaching her to crawl."

After crawling, Julie would try to teach Sarah to sit, then kneel, then stand, and, she hoped, walk.

As Sarah and her mother were leaving, Toby Pappas walked in. Toby, a high school junior, is a volunteer aide here in the P.T. department. Two months ago, when he first started working here, he transported patients to and from their rooms. Since then, he has gradually been learning how to assist with the treatments. His friendly, easygoing manner has won him quick acceptance from the patients. Toby obviously enjoys helping Julie, and she takes extra time to explain the equipment and procedures to him. Toby is a bright student and Julie hopes to interest him in physical therapy as a career.

"Hi, Toby. Want to help with a stroke patient?"

"Sure, Julie, but I haven't had experience with a stroke victim."

Julie explained that a stroke occurs when the flow of blood is cut off to some part of the brain. "Without the lifegiving oxygen supplied by fresh blood from the lungs,

brain cells will be damaged after only a few minutes. If the interruption is complete enough, the brain cells will die in less than 10 minutes. The effects of the stroke depend on the area of the brain involved.

"The first job of the therapist, Toby, is to evaluate the patient. Every stroke patient is different. Some patients can't use their legs. With others, only the arms are affected. Many can't talk. So you have to isolate the muscle groups that are affected and then work to reeducate those muscles and raise the patient's level of functioning to his or her full potential.

"Mr. Davis' stroke left him with his right side paralyzed. At first, he wasn't even aware of the position of his right arm or leg. We first moved the arms and legs for him to maintain the capability for motion in his joints. Then we helped him roll from side to side on his bed. After he could do that by himself, we taught him to sit up in bed. Now we are going to work on teaching him to kneel, to stand, and to walk.

"Of course, all that will take time. And, if the stroke completely killed the brain cells that control those functions, Mr. Davis won't make any more progress."

"What can I do to help today?" asked Toby.

"I'll be teaching Mr. Davis how to move his body from a sitting position to a kneeling one. He won't be able to master that today, though, and that may discourage him. You can help boost his spirits by encouraging him and giving him praise."

"I'll do my best."

"Oh, Toby. One more thing. Mr. Davis' speech was affected by his stroke. A speech therapist is working with him, but he still can't talk. Don't worry, though. He understands every word that is said."

Toby went to the waiting room and brought Mr. Davis to the treatment area while Julie reviewed his treatment record.

After Mr. Davis had completed his routine, Toby took him in his wheelchair back to his room.

It was lunchtime for Julie, and she had been looking forward to it. A quick lunch at the El Sombrero, a restaurant across the street. "Come on, Toby, I can't wait for those tacos and tamales."

At night the El Sombrero was a posh dining spot with mariachi singers and substantial prices. At noon, however, it offered a quick and reasonable lunch.

After they were seated, Toby asked Julie how she first became interested in physical therapy.

"Doing volunteer work, just like you," replied Julie. "I volunteered to help at St. John's Hospital and was assigned to the P.T. department. I liked the work so much that I majored in physical therapy when I went to college."

"What was the course work like in college?"

Exploring Careers

"A lot of science. I had courses in chemistry, biology, physics, neurology, physiology, and anatomy. Psychology was required, too, and that proved to be very helpful. A course in psychology of the handicapped really opened my eyes to the way handicapped persons view the world and helped me understand some of their hopes and fears."

Julie went on to explain the "rotating" assignments she had had during the last half of her senior year in college. "That was a valuable experience. It gave me a taste of the day-to-day work in most of the specialty areas as well as the general practice of physical therapy. I spent 1 week in Children's Hospital, 6 weeks in the Wheaton Rehabilitation Center, 2 weeks at Pleasant View Nursing Home, and 5 weeks here at Doctors Hospital.

"It was during my rotation that I discovered I really preferred working with a variety of patient problems— the sort of variety you're most likely to find in a hospital like this. After I passed the State board examination and got my license to practice physical therapy, I applied here at Doctors.

"Since then," she said with a smile, "I've had to take up swimming just to keep my weight down and still eat lunches here at El Sombrero."

Exploring

Physical therapists must be concerned about good health.

- Do you eat a well-balanced diet?
- Do you get enough sleep?
- Do you see the dentist regularly?
- Do you pay attention to warnings about alcohol, drugs, or tobacco abuse?
- When you ask someone how he or she is feeling, are you really concerned or do you consider it a social custom?

Physical therapists must be interested in science.

- Do you like science courses?
- Do you enjoy doing projects for a science class or a science fair?
- Do you read articles about science in magazines or the newspaper?
- Do you like to visit museum exhibits of science and technology?

Physical therapists must teach patients special exercises.

- Do you like to help your friends with homework?

- Are you good at teaching children sports or directing them in arts and crafts?
- Are you good at teaching a child to swim or ride a bicycle?
- Have you ever tutored elementary school children?
- Do you help your younger brothers or sisters with reading, writing, or arithmetic?

Physical therapists don't see the results of their work right away. They must remain supportive and hopeful even when progress is slow.

- Do you appreciate small gains or progress?
- Do you have the patience to grow a garden?
- Can you stick with a diet or exercise program?
- Do you appreciate the eventual benefit of having braces on your teeth right now?
- Do you have the patience to practice a musical instrument faithfully?

Physical therapists must believe that one can succeed if he or she really tries.

- Are you an optimistic, upbeat person?
- Can you make people believe in themselves?
- Do you look at the bright side of things?
- Can you talk someone into a good mood?
- Are you able to comfort a younger brother or sister when his or her feelings have been hurt?
- Are you good at boosting a friend's confidence when he or she is nervous about an exam, a tryout, or asking someone for a date?
- Would you be good at coaching a team that's on a losing streak?

Physical therapists who are physically fit are more effective on the job. They serve as models for their patients.

- Are you in good physical condition?
- Do you enjoy strenuous activities such as sports, hiking, backpacking, climbing, track and field, dancing, and gardening?
- Do you like to be active most of the time?
- Do you consider physical exercise and development as important as mental development?

Physical therapists need manual dexterity. They must be good with their hands to help patients perform exercises and to handle equipment.

- Do you like working with your hands?

328

Health Occupations

- Do you enjoy building models, setting up electric trains, framing pictures, making ceramics, weaving, or doing macrame?
- Are you accustomed to using tools for work around the house?
- Are you good at setting up displays for class projects or school exhibits?
- Have you ever helped build the props for a school theatrical production?

Physical therapists keep up with the field by reading professional literature and attending lectures and conferences.

- Do you like to read for pleasure?
- Do you like to read popular science magazines?
- Do you show initiative in doing research on subjects of personal interest?
- When you are curious about something, do you go to an encyclopedia or library to learn more about it?
- Do you look up words you don't understand in the dictionary?
- Do you like to browse in the "new books" section of your library?

Physical therapists are part of a health team. They work with physicians, psychologists, nurses, and social workers in planning patient care.

- Do you enjoy working with other people on class projects?
- Do you like working with others on school clubs or committees?
- Do you like taking part in recycling campaigns or scrap paper drives?
- Do you like to help organize trips, parties, sports events, picnics, and dances?

Job Facts

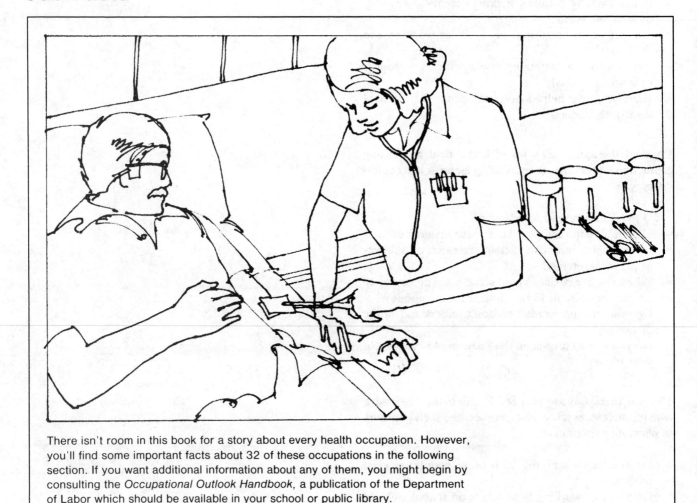

There isn't room in this book for a story about every health occupation. However, you'll find some important facts about 32 of these occupations in the following section. If you want additional information about any of them, you might begin by consulting the *Occupational Outlook Handbook,* a publication of the Department of Labor which should be available in your school or public library.

Occupation	*Nature and Places of Work*	*Training and Qualifications*	*Other Information*

MEDICAL PRACTITIONERS

Chiropractors	Chiropractors treat patients primarily by using their hands to manipulate parts of the body, especially the spinal column. Their practice is based on the principle that one's health is determined largely by the nervous system. Most are in private practice. Some are salaried assistants of established practitioners or work for chiropractic clinics. Others teach or do research at chiropractic colleges. Chiropractors often set up their practices in small communities—about half work in cities of 50,000 people or less.	It takes many years of schooling to become a chiropractor. To qualify for the license required to practice, applicants must graduate from a chiropractic college and pass a State board examination. Most States require 2 years of study in a college or university before entering the 4-year program in a chiropractic college. Chiropractors licensed in one State often may obtain a license in another State without further examination. High school students interested in becoming chiropractors should take as many science courses as possible.	Most newly licensed chiropractors either set up a new practice or purchase an established one. A moderate financial investment usually is necessary to open and equip an office. Most states require chiropractors to earn a certain number of continuing education credits each year in order to maintain their license.

Health Occupations

Occupation	Nature and Places of Work	Training and Qualifications	Other Information
Optometrists	Optometrists examine people's eyes. They prescribe lenses, corrective eye exercises, and other treatment not requiring drugs or surgery. Some optometrists specialize in working with special groups such as the elderly, children, and industrial workers. Most are in solo practice. Others are in partnership or group practice. Some treat patients in hospitals and eye clinics, or teach. Others work for insurance companies, act as consultants to engineers specializing in safety or lighting, or to educators in remedial reading. Some serve on health advisory committees.	It takes many years of training to become an optometrist. To qualify for the required license, applicants must complete a 4-year program in a college of optometry and pass a State board examination. This is preceded by at least 2 years of study in a college or university. Several States allow applicants to be licensed without lengthy examination if they have a license in another State. Optometrists wishing to advance in a specialized field may study for a master's or doctor's degree in physiological optics, neurophysiology, public health administration, health information and communication, or health education. High school students interested in becoming optometrists should take as many science courses as possible.	Optometrists should not be confused with ophthalmologists or dispensing opticians. Ophthalmologists are physicians who specialize in eye care, perform eye surgery, and prescribe drugs or other treatment, as well as lenses. Dispensing opticians fit and adjust eyeglasses according to prescriptions written by optometrists or ophthalmologists. Independent practitioners may work over 40 hours a week including weekends. Because the work is not strenuous, they often can continue to practice after normal retirement age. Most states require optometrists to earn a certain number of continuing education credits each year in order to maintain their license.
Osteopathic Physicians	Osteopathic physicians diagnose and treat medical problems involving the muscles and bones. Manipulation with their hands is a basic form of treatment. They also use surgery, drugs, and other methods of medical care. Most osteopaths are in private practice. A small number work in osteopathic colleges and hospitals, private industry, or government agencies.	It takes many years of schooling to become an osteopathic physician. To qualify for the required license, candidates must graduate from an osteopathic college and pass a State board examination. Candidates must complete at least 3 years of college (although most earn a bachelor's degree) before entering the 3–4 year program in an osteopathic college. Nearly all serve a 1-year internship after graduation. Specialists complete 2–5 years of additional training. Nearly all States grant licenses without further examination to those already licensed in another State. High school students interested in becoming osteopathic physicians should take as many science courses as possible.	Newly qualified doctors of osteopathic medicine usually establish their own practice, although a growing number are entering group practice. Many work over 50 or 60 hours a week. Those in general practice work longer, more irregular hours than specialists.

Exploring Careers

Occupation	Nature and Places of Work	Training and Qualifications	Other Information
Physicians	Physicians perform medical examinations, diagnose disease, treat people who are suffering from injury or disease, and advise patients on self-care to prevent illness. A decreasing percentage of physicians are general practitioners; most specialize in one of many fields for which there is graduate training.

Nine out of 10 physicians provide patient care. Most of these have office practices although some work as residents or full-time staff in hospitals. Other physicians teach or perform administrative or research duties. | It takes many years of schooling to become a physician. To qualify for the required license, candidates usually must complete at least 3 years of college (although most earn a bachelor's degree) and 4 years of medical school, pass a licensing examination, and, in most States, serve a 1- or 2-year residency after graduation.

Those planning to work in general practice often spend an additional year in a hospital residency. Those seeking certification in a specialty spend from 2 to 4 years in advanced residency training, followed by 2 years or more of practice in the specialty. They then must pass specialty exams.

Some physicians who want to teach or do research earn a master's or Ph. D. degree in a field such as biochemistry or microbiology.

Although physicians licensed in one State usually can get a license in another State without further examination, some States limit the reciprocity.

High school students interested in becoming physicians should take as many science courses as possible. | Competition is very stiff for acceptance to medical schools. Students must have an excellent academic record along with good scores on the Medical College Admission Test to be accepted. Personal interviews, letters of recommendation, and extracurricular activities which demonstrate leadership are also important.

Many physicians have long work days and irregular hours. Most specialists work fewer hours than general practitioners. Most physicians also are "on call" and may be called for emergencies at unusual hours, including weekends and holidays.

Persons who wish to become physicians must be self-motivated and competitive to survive the pressures of medical school and the demanding schedules during internship and residency. They must read and study a great deal throughout their career to keep up with developments in research and medical science.

It is also important for physicians to have a sincere and pleasant personality to deal with the sick and injured and their families. Emotional stability is also important to deal with the pressue of the profession and be able to make decisions in emergencies.

Newly qualified physicians who establish their own practice must make a sizeable financial investment to equip a modern office. |

Health Occupations

Occupation	Nature and Places of Work	Training and Qualifications	Other Information
Podiatrists	Podiatrists diagnose and treat corns, bunions, calluses, ingrown toenails and other foot problems. They perform surgery, fit corrective devices, and prescribe drugs, physical therapy, and proper shoes. Some specialize in foot care for the elderly or for children, or in foot surgery. But most podiatrists provide all types of foot care. Most podiatrists are in private practice. Some, however, are employed by hospitals, podiatric medical colleges, and public health departments.	It takes many years of schooling to become a podiatrist. To qualify for the required license, candidates usually must complete at least 3 years of college (although most earn at least a bachelor's degree) and 4 years in a podiatry school, and pass a State board examination. Additional education and experience are necessary to practice in a specialty. Several States require a 1-year residency after graduation. Most States grant licenses without further examination to those licensed by another State. High school students interested in becoming podiatrists should take as many science courses as possible.	Most newly licensed podiatrists set up their own practices. Some obtain salaried positions to gain the experience and money needed to begin their own practice.
Veterinarians	Veterinarians deal with diseases and injuries among animals. They perform surgery and prescribe and administer drugs, medicines, and vaccines to animals. Over one-third of veterinarians treat small animals exclusively. About another third treat both large and small animals. Many specialize in the health and breeding of cattle, poultry, sheep, swine, or horses. Some inspect foods as part of public health programs, teach, or do research. Most veterinarians are in private practice. Some work for government health agencies, colleges of veterinary medicine, research laboratories, large livestock farms, animal food companies, and pharmaceutical firms.	It takes many years of schooling to become a veterinarian. To qualify for the required license, candidates usually must complete at least 2 years of college (although most complete more) and 4 years in a college of veterinary medicine, and pass a State board examination. Positions in research and teaching often require an additional master's or Ph. D. degree. Some States issue licenses to veterinarians already licensed by another State without further examination. High school students interested in becoming veterinarians should take as many science courses as possible.	Due to overcrowding in veterinary schools, acceptance to these programs is highly competitive. Serious applicants usually need excellent academic records and a good score on the Veterinary Aptitude Test, Medical College Admission Test, or Graduate Record Exam. Experience in part-time or summer jobs working with animals is advantageous. The type of practice varies according to the geographic setting. Veterinarians in rural areas mainly treat farm animals; those in small towns usually engage in general practice; those in cities and suburban areas often limit their practice to pets. Most begin as employees or partners in established practices. The job may involve long and irregular hours, traveling and outdoor work, and danger of injury, disease, or infection. Those in private practice usually work well beyond normal retirement age.

Exploring Careers

Occupation	Nature and Places of Work	Training and Qualifications	Other Information
DENTAL OCCUPATIONS			
Dentists	Dentists examine and treat patients for oral diseases and abnormalities, such as decayed and impacted teeth. Most dentists are general practitioners, but some specialize. Orthodontists are the largest group of specialists; they straighten teeth. The next largest group, oral surgeons, operate on the mouth and jaws. About 9 out of 10 dentists are in private practice. Some dentists teach in dental schools, do research, or administer dental health programs.	It takes many years of schooling to become a dentist. To qualify for the license to practice dentistry, applicants must graduate from dental school and pass written and practical examinations. Dental school training generally lasts 4 years following 2 to 4 years of study in a college or university. Most people have a bachelor's or master's degree before they begin their dental training. Specialists need 2 to 3 years of formal training after graduation from dental school; they may also have to pass a special exam. Dentists who want to teach or do research also spend additional years in advanced training. In order to practice in another State, dentists usually must pass the State's exam. High school students who want to become dentists should take as many science courses as possible.	Dentists usually work between 40 and 45 hours per week, although many spend over 50 hours a week in their offices. Many continue part-time practice well beyond usual retirement age.
Dental Assistants	These workers help dentists while they are working with patients. They do such things as obtain dental records, hand the dentist the necessary instruments, keep the patient's mouth clear, and prepare materials for impressions of teeth. Most dental assistants work in private dental offices. Some work in dental schools, hospital dental departments, State and local public health departments, or private clinics.	Most learn their skills on the job. However, an increasing number of dental assistants complete 1- or 2-year post-high school programs, primarily in junior or community colleges and vocational or technical schools. Graduates of accredited programs who complete an exam may be certified. Certification is an acknowledgment of one's qualifications, but is not generally required for employment. High school students interested in this work should take courses in biology, chemistry, health, typing, and office practices.	The work of the dental assistant should not be confused with that of the dental hygienist, who must be licensed to scale and polish teeth. Dental assistants must be careful in handling radiographic and other equipment.

Health Occupations

Occupation	Nature and Places of Work	Training and Qualifications	Other Information
Dental Hygienists	Dental hygienists scale, clean, and polish teeth, expose X-rays, and instruct patients in proper oral hygiene. Most work in private dental offices. Others work in public health agencies, school systems, industrial plants, clinics, hospitals, dental hygiene schools, and the Federal Government. Some who are graduates of bachelor's degree programs are commissioned officers in the Armed Forces.	Dental hygienists must have a license. Candidates for licensure in most States must be graduates of an accredited dental hygiene school and pass both a written and a clinical exam. Most schools of dental hygiene grant an associate degree; some programs lead to a bachelor's degree. A few schools offer master's degree programs in dental hygiene or related fields. Among the courses recommended for high school students interested in this occupation are biology, health, chemistry, and mathematics.	Many hygienists work part time. Hours may include weekends and evenings. Some work for more than one dentist.
Dental Laboratory Technicians	These workers make dentures, braces, crowns, and other dental and orthodontal appliances. All work is done following the dentist's written instructions. Most technicians work in commercial laboratories. Others work in dentists' offices, hospitals, and for the Federal Government.	Many dental laboratory technicians learn their skills on the job, although more and more are taking formal training programs before starting work. On-the-job training generally takes 4 to 5 years. Some schools offer 2-year programs for high school graduates. About 3 years of practical experience are needed after that, however. Technicians may become certified by passing written and practical exams. Certification is becoming increasingly important as evidence of a technician's competence. High school students interested in this occupation should take courses in art, crafts, metal shop, and sciences.	Salaried technicians usually work 40 hours a week while self-employed technicians often work longer hours. Experienced technicians may advance to jobs as supervisors or managers in dental laboratories, teachers in dental lab training programs, or sales representatives for companies that manufacture dental materials and equipment.

335

Exploring Careers

Occupation	Nature and Places of Work	Training and Qualifications	Other Information

NURSING OCCUPATIONS

Occupation	Nature and Places of Work	Training and Qualifications	Other Information
Registered Nurses	Registered nurses provide care for the sick and help healthy people stay well. The setting in which they work usually determines the scope of their responsibilities. They observe their patients' progress; administer medications; assist in rehabilitation of patients; teach people about good health; and do research. Most nurses work in hospitals, nursing homes, and other institutional health facilities. Others work in public health departments, home health agencies, clinics, and private industry. Some work in offices of physicians or are private duty nurses hired directly by patients. Some nurses teach, do research, or are staff members of professional organizations.	A license is required. A nurse must be a graduate of an approved school of nursing and pass a State exam. Training programs include 2-year associate degree programs in junior and community colleges; 3-year diploma programs in hospitals and independent schools; and 4 or 5-year bachelor's degree programs in colleges and universities. A minimum of a bachelor's degree, and often a master's or doctoral degree, is preferred for administrative or management, teaching, research, or consulting jobs, and for clinical specialization. High school students interested in becoming registered nurses should take as many science courses as possible.	About one-third work part-time. Most hospital and nursing home nurses receive extra pay for work on evening and night shifts. Proposals are under consideration to increase the educational requirements for nurses. Persons considering nursing careers should carefully investigate the regulations in their state to select an appropriate education program.
Licensed Practical Nurses	Licensed practical nurses provide much of the bedside care needed by hospital patients. They take temperature and blood pressure, change dressings, and bathe patients. They perform many other nursing functions such as making patients comfortable in their homes and preparing patients for examination in doctors' offices. Three out of 5 work in hospitals. Most of the others work in nursing homes, clinics, doctors' offices, sanitariums, and long-term care facilities. Some work for public health agencies and welfare and religious organizations. Self-employed nurses work in hospitals or in the homes of their patients.	A license is required. Applicants must complete an approved practical nursing course, generally 1 year long, and pass an exam. Although requirements for enrollment in training programs range from eighth or ninth grade to high school graduation, high school graduates are preferred. State-approved programs are offered in trade, technical, and vocational schools, junior colleges, local hospitals, health agencies, and private educational institutions. High school students interested in becoming licensed practical nurses should take as many science courses as possible.	In California and Texas, these nurses are called licensed vocational nurses. In hospitals, hours may include nights, weekends, and holidays. In private homes, LPN's often work 8 to 12 hours a day but can arrange their own hours and vacations. Advancement is limited without additional training or education. In-service educational programs prepare LPNs for work in specialized areas such as intensive care units or post-surgery recovery rooms. Proposals are under consideration to increase the educational requirements for nurses. Persons considering nursing careers should carefully investigate the regulations in their state to select an appropriate education program.

Health Occupations

Occupation	Nature and Places of Work	Training and Qualifications	Other Information
Nursing Aides, Orderlies, and Attendants	These workers handle many of the routine aspects of patient care in hospitals, nursing homes, and other health facilities. They answer patients' bell calls, assist patients in walking, transport and set up heavy equipment, and clean patients' rooms.	Nursing aides, orderlies, and attendants train on the job from several days to a few months, sometimes combined with classroom instruction. Some employers prefer high school graduates while many do not. Courses in home nursing and first aid, offered by many public school systems and community agencies, provide a useful background. Volunteer work and temporary summer jobs in hospitals and similar institutions also are helpful.	Other job titles include hospital attendant, nursing assistant, auxiliary nursing worker, geriatric aide, and psychiatric aide. Similar work is done in patients' homes by homemaker-home health aides, who provide personal care plus some cooking and light housework. Hours may include nights, weekends, and holidays.

THERAPY AND REHABILITATION OCCUPATIONS

Occupational Therapists	Occupational therapists organize educational, vocational, and recreational activities to help mentally or physically disabled persons become self-sufficient. Therapy programs are tailored to the clients' needs, and often are part of an overall treatment plan developed by a health team. Therapists teach skills such as weaving, leather working, typing, and the use of power tools; they also help patients relearn daily routines such as eating and dressing. Almost half work in hospitals. Most of the rest work in rehabilitation centers, nursing homes, schools, clinics, community mental health centers, and research centers. Some work in sanitariums or camps for handicapped children, public health departments, or for home health agencies.	A bachelor's degree in occupational therapy usually is required. Certificate programs are available to those with a bachelor's degree in another field. A graduate degree is often required for teaching, research, or administrative work. Graduates of accredited programs who pass an exam become registered occupational therapists. High School students interested in becoming occupational therapists should take courses in health, biology, chemistry, and crafts. Acceptance to educational programs is very competitive and applicants are screened carefully. Applicants should have above average grades in the sicences. Preference is often given to persons with previous part-time or volunteer experience in a health care setting. Acceptance to a program as a transfer from another major after freshman year is often difficult.	Newly graduated occupational therapists begin as staff therapists. Advancement is chiefly to supervisory or administrative positions. Many part-time jobs are available. Many work for more than one employer and travel between locations.

Exploring Careers

Occupation	Nature and Places of Work	Training and Qualifications	Other Information
Occupational Therapy Assistants and Aides	Assistants work directly with physically or mentally disabled patients under the supervision of occupational therapists. They help patients with their exercises and teach them simple skills. About half work in hospitals. The rest work in nursing homes, clinics, schools for handicapped or mentally retarded children, and rehabilitation centers. Aides handle the more routine tasks, including clerical duties. They prepare work materials, keep patients' records, and prepare clinical notes.	Assistants usually complete a 2-year associate degree program in a junior college or a 1-year vocational or technical school program after high school. Aides train on the job. The length and content of training vary. Among the subjects recommended for high school students interested in the occupational therapy field are health, biology, and crafts.	Some work evenings, weekends, and part-time.
Physical Therapists	Physical therapists help people with muscle, nerve, joint, and bone disease and injuries to regain some of their strength and ability to move. Therapy consists of exercise massage, and the use of heat and cold, light, water, or electricity to relieve pain or improve the condition of muscles and skin. Some therapists work in hospitals. Others work in nursing homes, rehabilitation centers, schools for handicapped children, and clinics. Some work for public health departments or home health agencies. Others teach or serve as consultants.	A license is required. Candidates must either earn a bachelor's degree in physical therapy, or for those who have a bachelor's degree in another field, earn a second bachelor's degree or certification through a special 12- to 16-month program. They must pass a State board exam. A graduate degree may be important for teaching, research, and administrative positions. Health, biology, mathematics, and physical education are useful high school courses.	Many physical therapists work part-time.

Health Occupations

Occupation	Nature and Places of Work	Training and Qualifications	Other Information
Physical Therapist Assistants and Aides	Assistants work directly with patients under the supervision of a physical therapist. They help patients do their exercises and instruct them in the proper use of artificial limbs, braces, and splints. Aides handle more routine tasks, including clerical duties. They help patients prepare for treatment, assemble equipment, and keep records. Most assistants and aides work in hospitals. Some work for physical therapists who are in private practice. Still others work in clinics, rehabilitation centers, nursing homes, community health agencies, and schools for handicapped or mentally retarded children.	Training requirements for assistants are not uniform throughout the country. Some states require a license calling for graduation from an approved 2-year associate degree program from a junior college and passing an exam. In states not requiring a license, aides may advance to assistants through on-the-job training, but graduates of approved programs often are preferred. Aides train on the job. The length and content of programs vary widely, but high school graduation generally is required. Recommended high school courses include health, biology, physical education, and mathematics.	In some small health care institutions, the assistant or aide may assume most of the duties of the physical therapists, within the limits of his or her training.
Speech Pathologists and Audiologists	Speech pathologists and audiologists work with children and adults who have speech or hearing disorders. After testing to find out the cause of the problem, they provide treatment. While most work directly with patients, some teach, do research, or perform administrative duties. Over half work in schools. Others work in speech and hearing clinics, research centers, government agencies, and industry. Some speech pathologists and audiologists are in private practice.	The master's degree, offered by several hundred colleges and universities is the usual requirement for entry into the field. Some states require speech pathologists and audiologists who work in public schools to have a teaching certificate, too. Many states require licenses of those who practice outside of schools. Certification by the American Speech and Hearing Association requires a master's degree, a 1-year internship, and an exam, and usually is necessary to advance. High school students interested in becoming speech pathologists and audiologists should take as many courses in science and language as possible.	Many work over 40 hours a week. Many, particularly those in colleges and universities, supplement their salaries through consulting, research, and writing books or articles.

Exploring Careers

Occupation	Nature and Places of Work	Training and Qualifications	Other Information

MEDICAL TECHNOLOGIST, TECHNICIAN, AND ASSISTANT OCCUPATIONS

Occupation	Nature and Places of Work	Training and Qualifications	Other Information
Electrocardiograph (EKG) Technicians	These workers operate machines that record electrical changes that occur during a heartbeat. This machine is used to help diagnose heart disease and record the progress of patients with heart conditions. Most work in hospitals. Some work in clinics and doctors' offices.	EKG technicians generally train on the job for several months to 1 year. High school graduation generally is required. Vocational school or college courses in cardiology technology and anatomy are helpful. Large hospitals sometimes promote EKG technicians to supervisors. Advancement to cardiovascular technician, cardiopulmonary technician, and cardiology technologist also is possible. Among high school courses recommended for students interested in the field are health and biology.	Mechanical aptitude, the ability to follow detailed instructions, and presence of mind in emergencies are important qualities. Hours may include weekends.
Electroencephalographic (EEG) Technologists and Technicians	These workers operate machinery that records electrical activity of the brain. This machinery is used to help diagnose disease and determine how it is affecting the brain. Technologists, as a result of their more thorough understanding of electroencephalography, supervise technicians. Although most work in hospitals, many have jobs with private physicians who specialize in brain and nervous system disorders—neurologists and neurosurgeons.	Although many are trained on the job, formal training programs are increasingly important, as a way of learning to operate the sophisticated equipment these workers use. Training programs in colleges, junior colleges, medical schools, hospitals, and vocational and technical schools generally last 1 to 2 years. Some workers advance to chief electroencephalographic technologist. Chief technologists are supervised by an electroencephalographer, or by a neurologist or neurosurgeon. High school students considering this occupation should take courses in biology, health, and electronics.	Manual dexterity, good vision, and an aptitude for working with electronic equipment are important qualities. Some hospitals require standby emergency service after hours and on weekends and holidays.

Health Occupations

Occupation	Nature and Places of Work	Training and Qualifications	Other Information
Emergency Medical Technicians	These workers provide immediate medical care in such emergencies as an automobile accident, heart attack, near-drowning, unscheduled childbirth, poisoning, or gunshot wound. They must quickly determine the nature of the emergency and establish priorities for medical care. About half are volunteers on rescue squads. Paid technicians work for police and fire departments, private ambulance companies, funeral homes, and hospital-based ambulance squads.	Good eyesight, dexterity, and physical coordination are necessary. Because they work under trying conditions, good judgment under stress, leadership ability, and emotional stability are important. Emergency medical technicians must complete a 110-hour training course developed by the U.S. Department of Transportation. Other training courses are available, too. Applicants must be 18 years old and have a high school diploma and a driver's license.	There are two other types of emergency medical technicians: Paramedics and dispatchers. Paramedics, working under the direction of physicians by radio communication, administer drugs and use more complex equipment than basic emergency medical technicians. Dispatchers, by means of telephone and radio, serve as a communications link between the medical facility and those who are sent to attend the emergency patients. Those in fire departments often work 56 hours a week. Volunteers work 8 to 12 hours a week. Those in ambulance services often work nights and weekends.
Medical Laboratory Workers	People in this occupation are either medical technologists, technicians, or assistants. These workers analyze the blood, fluids, and tissues in the human body, using precision instruments such as microscopes and automatic analyzers. Laboratory tests help in the detection, diagnosis, and treatment of disease. Workers with more training can handle the more complex jobs in the laboratory. Most work in hospitals. Others work in independent laboratories, physicians' offices, clinics, public health agencies, pharmaceutical firms, and research institutions.	Medical technologists are the most highly trained. They are college graduates with a major in medical technology. Technicians get their training in 2-year programs in community and junior colleges, trade schools, technical institutes, or in the Armed Forces. Assistants learn their skills on the job or take 1-year programs in hospitals, trade schools, or technical institutes. Some community and junior colleges offer programs in cooperation with hospitals. In some States, technologists and technicians must be licensed. This may require a written examination. High school courses in science and mathematics are recommended for students interested in this field.	Technologists may advance to supervisory positions or to administrative medical technologist in a large hospital. With additional education and experience, technicians can advance to technologists and assistants to technicians. Accuracy, the ability to work under pressure, manual dexterity, and normal color vision are important. In hospitals, workers can expect night and weekend duty.

Exploring Careers

Occupation	Nature and Places of Work	Training and Qualifications	Other Information
Medical Record Technicians and Clerks	These workers maintain medical records, reports, disease indexes, and statistics. Medical records are indispensable for diagnosis and treatment and also are used for verifying legal claims, charting health trends, and medical research. In large hospitals, the medical records department is supervised by a medical record administrator; in smaller hospitals, experienced medical record technicians have this responsibility. Clerks perform more routine tasks that require a minimum of specialized knowledge. Although most work in hospitals, some work in clinics, nursing homes, community health centers, government agencies, consulting firms, and health maintenance organizations. Others work for insurance companies, public health departments, and manufacturers of medical record systems and equipment.	Employers prefer graduates of approved 2-year associate degree programs as technicians. Clerks generally are high school graduates and complete 1 month or more of on-the-job training. Correspondence courses offered by the American Medical Record Association are available to those wishing to become clerks and to clerks seeking advancement to technicians. Those who pass an examination become accredited record technicians and often can look forward to more responsible positions. High school courses in science, health, typing, mathematics, and office practice are recommended to students interested in this field.	Medical record personnel must be accurate and pay attention to detail.
Operating Room Technicians	Operating room technicians, also called surgical technicians, assist surgeons and anesthesiologists before, during, and after surgery. Operating room technicians work in hospitals or other institutions that have operating room, delivery room, and emergency room facilities, and in the Armed Forces.	Most train for 9 months to 2 years in trade schools or technical institutes, hospitals, or community and junior colleges. Some train on the job for 6 weeks to 1 year. High school graduation generally is required. Some train in the Armed Forces. Operating room technicians may advance to assistant operating room administrator and assistant operating room supervisor. High school students interested in this field should take courses in health and biology.	Manual dexterity is important for handling instruments quickly. They may be required to work "on call" shifts, staying available to work on short notice.

Health Occupations

Occupation	Nature and Places of Work	Training and Qualifications	Other Information
Optometric Assistants	Optometric assistants perform routine eye care duties when optometrists test patients' eyes in order to prescribe corrective glasses. In a large office, assistants specialize; some handle visual training and others provide chairside assistance or administer the office. In a smaller practice, one person would do all these things. Most optometric assistants work for optometrists in private practice. Others work for health clinics and some serve in the Armed Forces.	Although most train on the job, employers prefer to hire graduates of 1- or 2-year training programs. High school graduation, including courses in mathematics and office procedures, is a preferred background for admission to a formal training program or on-the-job training. In addition, the U.S. Air Force offers accelerated 16-week training programs.	Because optometric assistants deal with instruments, manual dexterity and accuracy are important. Courtesy and tact are important in their dealings with patients. Hours may include weekend duty. Many opportunities for part-time jobs are available.
Radiologic (X-ray) Technologists	These workers operate X-ray equipment and take X-ray pictures (known as radiographs), usually under the supervision of a radiologist. Three specialties in this field include X-ray technology, the use of pictures of bones and inner organs of the body to detect abnormalities; nuclear medicine technology, the application of radioactive material to help diagnose or treat illness; and radiation therapy, the use of radiation-producing machines to give therapeutic treatments. Most work in hospitals. The remainder work in medical laboratories, physicians' and dentists' offices or clinics, Federal and State health agencies, and public school systems.	Completion of a 2- to 4-year post-high school program is required. Graduates of approved programs who pass an exam become registered with the American Registry of Radiologic Technologists, an asset in obtaining skilled positions. They then may be certified in radiation therapy or nuclear medicine by completing an additional year of training. Some technologists in large X-ray departments may qualify as instructors in X-ray techniques or advance to supervisory X-ray technologists. High school courses in mathematics, physics, chemistry, and biology are recommended to students interested in this field.	Full-time workers may be "on call" for emergency weekend or night duty. Most part-time jobs are in physicians' offices and clinics. Safety devices are used to avoid radiation hazards.

Exploring Careers

Occupation	Nature and Places of Work	Training and Qualifications	Other Information
Respiratory Therapy Workers	These workers, sometimes called inhalation therapists, use special equiment such as respirators and positive-pressure breathing machines to treat patients who need temporary or emergency respiratory assistance. There are three levels of workers within the field: Therapists, technicians, and assistants. Therapists and technicians perform essentially the same duties, although therapists may teach and supervise. Assistants have little contact with patients and spend most of their time taking care of the equipment. Most work in hospitals. Others work for oxygen equipment rental companies, ambulance services, nursing homes, and universities.	Although a few train on the job, most workers complete post-high school programs ranging from 18 months to 4 years. A bachelor's degree is awarded for completion of a 4-year program and an associate degree for shorter courses. Respiratory therapists can advance to assistant chief, chief therapist, or, with graduate education, to college instructor. Technicians and assistants can advance to the therapist level by taking appropriate training courses. High school students interested in this field should take courses in health, biology, physics, and mathematics.	Mechanical ability, manual dexterity, and the ability to follow instructions and work as part of a team are important. After-hours and weekend duty generally is required. Adherence to safety procedures and regular testing of equipment minimize the fire hazard.

OTHER HEALTH OCCUPATIONS

Occupation	Nature and Places of Work	Training and Qualifications	Other Information
Dietitians	Dietitians plan and manage food service programs and advise on good eating habits. Over half work in health facilities of various kinds, including hospitals, nursing homes, and clinics. Others work in colleges and universities, schools, restaurants, cafeterias, large companies, and the Armed Forces. An increasing number work as consultants to hospitals, health-related facilities, and commercial enterprises including food processors and equipment manufacturers.	A bachelor's degree in foods and nutrition or institution management usually is required. The American Dietetic Association recommends completion of a 6- to 12-month internship or 1- to 2-year traineeship. Some undergraduate programs combine the educational and clinical experience in 4 years. Experienced dietitians may advance to assistant or associate director of a dietetic department. Advancement to higher levels in teaching, research, and other areas usually requires a graduate degree. High school students interested in this field should take courses in home economics, business, biology, health, mathematics, and chemistry.	Those in hospitals may work weekends while those in commercial food service have irregular hours. Some dieticians work for more than one institution, dividing their time between different locations.

Health Occupations

Occupation	Nature and Places of Work	Training and Qualifications	Other Information
Medical Record Administrators	These workers manage medical record departments and develop systems for documenting, storing, and retrieving medical information. They supervise and train medical record technicians and clerks, compile medical statistics, and help evaluate patient care and research studies. Most work in hospitals. Others work in clinics, nursing homes, State and local public health departments, medical research centers, and health insurance companies. Some work for firms that develop and print health insurance and medical forms, and manufacture equipment to record and process medical data. Some are consultants to small health care facilities.	A bachelor's degree in medical record administration usually is required. Those who have a bachelor's degree in another field and the required courses in the liberal arts and biological sciences may complete a 1-year certificate program. Medical record administrators with experience in smaller health facilities may advance to positions as department heads in large hospitals or to higher level positions in hospital administration. Some coordinate the medical record departments of several small hospitals; others take positions in health agencies; many teach in the expanding 2- and 4-year college programs for medical record personnel. High school students interested in this field should take courses in health, business, mathematics, and biology.	Part-time jobs are available in teaching, research, and consulting. However, a 36- to 40-hour week is usual.
Pharmacists	Pharmacists dispense drugs and medicines prescribed by medical and dental practitioners, and supply and advise people on the use of many non-prescription medicines. An increasing number of pharmacists serve as consultants to physicians, nurses, and other health professionals in matters relating to daily patient care. Most work in pharmacies. The rest work for hospitals, drug companies, government agencies, colleges of pharmacy, pharmaceutical and other professional associations, and the Armed Forces.	To qualify for the license required to practice pharmacy, one must graduate from an accredited college of pharmacy, pass a State board exam, and have a specified amount of experience or internship under the supervision of a registered pharmacist. At least 5 years of study beyond high school are required to become a pharmacist. One generally must complete at least 1 to 2 years of prepharmacy education and 3 to 4 years in a college of pharmacy. Teaching, research, or administrative jobs may require additional education. Pharmacists often begin as employees in community pharmacies. As they gain experience and the necessary funds, they may become owners or part-owners of pharmacies. Others may gain executive positions with chain drugstores, become directors of pharmacy service in hospitals, or advance in management, sales, and other areas in industry. High school students interested in this field should gain a strong background in the sciences.	Hours may include evenings and weekends. Pharmacists in community settings generally work longer hours than those in institutional settings, and self-employed pharmacists often work more hours than those in salaried positions.

Exploring Careers

Occupation	Nature and Places of Work	Training and Qualifications	Other Information
Dispensing Opticians	Dispensing opticians, also called ophthalmic dispensers, accept prescriptions for eyeglasses. They determine the size and style of the customer's eyeglasses, write work orders for the technicians who actually grind the lenses, and adjust the finished glasses to fit the customer. Some specialize in fitting cosmetic shells to cover blemished eyes or in fitting artificial eyes. Most work for optical shops or department stores that sell prescription lenses. Others work for optometrists and ophthalmologists, in hospitals and eye clinics, or schools of ophthalmic dispensing.	Most learn through several years of on-the-job training. Formal training is available at community and junior colleges, and through 3- to 4-year formal apprenticeships. Some States have licensing requirements that generally include education and training standards and a written and/or practical examination. High school students interested in this field should take courses in physics, algebra, geometry, and mechanical drawing. The ability to do precision work is very important.	Many dispensing opticians go into business for themselves. Others advance by becoming managers of retail optical stores or sales representatives for wholesalers or manufacturers of eyeglasses or lenses. Those in retail shops generally work a 5½- to 6-day week.
Health Services Administrators	Health services administrators manage hospitals, nursing homes, clinics, and other kinds of health facilities. About half work in hospitals. The rest work in nursing homes, home health agencies, public health departments, and the Armed Forces. Some work in health planning agencies, or for management firms.	Educational requirements for this occupation vary widely. Entry jobs may require a 2-year associate degree, a bachelor's degree, or a master's degree. A Ph. D. usually is needed for teaching or research, and is an asset for more prestigious administrative jobs. Administrators of nursing homes must be licensed. Requirements are not uniform, but generally specify education and experience.	Health services administrators should be able to motivate people, direct large-scale activities, and enjoy public speaking. They advance by taking increasingly more responsible jobs. The ultimate goal in hospitals or nursing homes is the job of chief administrative officer. They often work long hours and may be called at any time in emergencies. Some travel may be required to attend meetings or inspect facilities.

Margaret Mead's field work in Samoa established her reputation as one of the world's foremost anthropologists.

Cleaning a specimen from a tar pit is painstaking work for this archeology student.

"Brian, come here! I found some coins!"

Shirley Margolis looked up delightedly from the long shallow trench she was digging in the desert. She was very hot and dusty but that was forgotten in her excitement over her find.

"That's great, Shirley," called Brian O'Shea, who was working in another trench a few yards away. "What a sight after all this time! I'll tell Dr. Berenson."

"Congratulations, Shirley," said the archeology professor a few minutes later. "I knew our perseverance would pay off. Before removing the coins, let's update our records and note the exact location of the find on our maps."

Dr. Berenson supervises an archeological team that has spent several months excavating a site in the Middle East, a fruitful area for archeological finds. Before beginning this excavation, the team from Western State University had a lot of background work to do. They wanted to select a site that would be likely to yield artifacts of earlier civilizations, and this took careful preparation. The team spent weeks examining the area, talking to local residents, poring over maps and aerial photographs, and digging test pits to sample the depth and contents of the soil. They also used electronic devices to help them determine what was underground.

Dr. Berenson's team of archeology students was searching for the remains of a civilization that had flourished in the area thousands of years ago. By studying what was left of these people's homes, tools, and clothing, the archeologists hoped to find out how they lived.

The work of archeologists on a dig involves slow, painstaking digging, scraping, and sifting. They examine every handful of dirt and use trowels, whiskbrooms, kitchen spoons, even toothbrushes to avoid damaging or destroying the evidence. There is an element of detective work in the conclusions archeologists draw from the artifacts they uncover. Pottery fragments may have to be fitted together to form a dish, for example. By comparing the size and shape and decorations on different dishes from the same site, archeologists can determine what these dishes were used for.

Careful recordkeeping and laboratory work are important, too. The coins that Shirley discovered must be cleaned, assigned a code number, and recorded in the excavation log. The exact place they were found must be noted. When the team finishes this dig, their records should be complete enough to enable them to reconstruct the site on paper. The examinations and tests they do here in the field laboratory—and back at the university a few months from now—will enable them to classify every object, determine how old it is, and decide what it was used for. The classification and dating techniques they use were developed through years of scientific research.

In their work, archeologists use the scientific method to study the past. Unlike historians, who work with documents and other written records, archeologists uncover and analyze physical evidence of cultures that existed long ago. They typically study such things as burial mounds, tools, weapons, ornaments, and home furnishings. Their purpose in reconstructing cultures that existed hundreds or even thousands of years ago is to find out how human culture changes over time.

Cultural change is of interest not just to archeologists but to all social scientists. Social scientists do research, teach, consult, and administer programs in a number of different fields: Anthropology, economics, geography, history, political science, psychology, and sociology. What all of them have in common is a professional interest in people and society. Social scientists study and describe human behavior and social institutions. You're already aware that the work of astronomers and physicists tells us a great deal about the universe and the planet earth. The work of biologists tells us about the

Social Scientists

Conducting a nationwide survey takes organizational ability as well as a knowledge of statistics.

plants and animals with which we share this earth. In much the same way, the work of social scientists tells us about ourselves.

Social scientists study our behavior in order to understand what makes us live the way we do. Such an understanding is essential for government leaders and others trying to develop policies and plan programs that meet our needs. Such dominant concerns of our time as equality of opportunity and the threat of a nuclear war, for example, require a better understanding of how our society works. As we learn more about the underlying causes of our problems, we are in a better position to do something about them.

Research is a basic tool of social science. Like other scientists, social scientists seek to establish a body of fact and theory that contributes to human knowledge and enables us to manage our affairs more rationally. Field work such as the archeological dig that Dr. Berenson is leading is a traditional method of gathering information or "data"—not only in archeology and anthropology, but in history and sociology as well.

Surveys are widely used to collect facts or opinions. Indeed, surveys are conducted by so many organizations for so many purposes, they are a familiar part of our daily lives. Literally thousands of polls, questionnaires, and surveys are going on here and abroad at any given moment. Political scientists use surveys to assess voting behavior; market researchers use them to determine what brand of toothpaste we prefer; economists use them to measure employment, unemployment, wages, and prices; demographers use them to detect changes in population patterns; educators use them to measure students' progress and see how well different teaching methods work.

Probably the greatest single change in the social sciences in recent times has been the widespread introduction of mathematical and other quantitative research methods. Calculus, for example, is used in economics, and algebra is used in anthropology and linguistics. Mathematics also provides the basis for the formal mathematical models used widely in economics and political science. We already have noted that surveys are used extensively to gather social science data. Survey methods rely heavily on statistical concepts, and statistics has become an essential part of the training for most social science careers.

The computer is a staple of social science research and the ability to use computers for research purposes is a "must" for many social scientists. Because computers can handle vast amounts of data very quickly, social scientists are able to work with tremendous amounts of very detailed information about every conceivable aspect of human behavior. Researchers have at their fingertips an astonishing amount of information about our beliefs, opinions, attitudes, and lifestyles. Such information assists those concerned with finding solutions to our social problems.

Now let's take a closer look at the kinds of work that social scientists do.

Anthropologists study the differences among people—differences in their physical characteristics as well as in their customs, behavior, and attitudes. They usually specialize in one of the four subfields of anthropology: Physical anthropology, archeology, cultural anthropology, and linguistics. *Physical anthropologists* are concerned with humans as biological beings. They study the evolution of the human body and look for the earliest evidences of human life. They also do research on racial groups and may, for example, explore the effect of heredity and environment on different races. Because of their knowledge of body structure, physical anthropologists are consulted on such practical matters as the sizing of clothing and the design of cockpits for airplanes and spacecraft. *Archeologists* like Dr. Berenson usually study cultures that no longer exist by digging out and examining tools, clothing, and other evidences of human life. *Cultural anthropologists* study the customs, culture, and social life of living peoples. Traditionally, they have been concerned with primitive tribes and peasant societies, but increasingly cultural anthropologists are turning their attention to social patterns in modern settings and studying the behavior of drug addicts or corporate executives, for example. *Linguists* study the role of language in various cultures. Their research tells us, for example, that the way people use language influences the way they think about things. Thus language itself helps explain some of the differences among groups.

Economists study the way we use our resources to produce goods and services. They compile and analyze data that help us understand the costs and benefits of making, distributing, and using things the way we do. Some economists are primarily theoreticians. They may develop theories to explain the causes of inflation, for example, through the use of mathematical models. Others deal with practical matters such as business cycles, tariff policies, tax policies, farm prices, or unemploy-

The ability to use computers for research purposes is important for many social scientists.

An authority on the corrections system, this psychologist is testifying on prison conditions.

Social Scientists

Business economists like this one use math to forecast future sales.

These geographers are working up suggestions for supermarket locations in and around a large city.

ment. They use their understanding of the way the economy works to advise government officials, business firms, insurance companies, banks, industry associations, labor unions, and others. The work that economists do affects us directly, too. Government economists in the Bureau of Labor Statistics, for example, issue monthly figures showing how much the prices of goods and services have changed over time. On the basis of these figures, known as consumer price indexes, cost-of-living increases are granted to social security recipients. Business firms and labor unions use these indexes in negotiating wages.

Economics is such a large and complex field that nearly all economists specialize. *Business economists* analyze and interpret government policies and actions that are likely to affect the firm they work for. They commonly prepare economic forecasts and then explain how their forecast applies to various aspects of the business, such as marketing, purchasing, industrial relations, and finance. They also advise on the internal operations of the firm, applying their knowledge of economic principles to such practical problems as inventory levels and pricing policies. Other kinds of economists include *agricultural economists, financial economists, industry economists, labor economists, international trade economists,* and *tax economists.*

Geographers are primarily concerned with space and the way we use it. They try to understand and explain why people, things, and activities are located where they are. Their studies help to explain changing patterns of human settlement—where people live, why they live there, and how they earn a living. Because geographers are concerned with why people settle where they do, their work touches upon economics, politics, culture, health, and other aspects of society. Their work has numerous practical applications. A geographer doing flood plain research might advise inhabitants of the probability of a flood and tell them how urgent it was to take precautions. Another geographer might advise a supermarket chain on store locations. Still another might consult with officials of a foreign government concerning the need for an irrigation project.

Like other social scientists, geographers apply their knowledge in a variety of areas. *Economic geographers* study proposed locations for business or industrial firms and make recommendations. *Urban geographers* study cities and make suggestions concerning transportation, housing, parks, and sites for industrial plants. *Cartographers* compile and interpret data on the physical environment and make maps and charts. *Medical geographers* study the effect of the natural environment on health and take into account such factors as climate, vegetation, mineral traces in water, and air pollution.

Exploring Careers

Historians study past events, institutions, ideas, and people. Some historians specialize in a particular period of time—18th century history, for example. Others explore the history of a subject such as economics, philosophy, science, religion, art, or military affairs. Although many specialize in the social or political history of the United States or Europe, a growing number are concerned with the history of Africa, Latin America, Asia, or the Middle East—areas of great importance in our lives. By putting international issues in proper historical perspective, historians can be instrumental in increasing understanding and respect among the nations of the world. Because of historians' insights into what happened in the past—and why—the President and Congress sometimes consult them when they formulate domestic or foreign policy.

Traditionally, most historians have taught and done research in colleges and universities. Publishing is very important in the academic world, and historians spend much of their time doing research and writing scholarly books and articles, textbooks, and publications on historical subjects for the general public. Depending on their specialization, their research might take them to records kept in a county courthouse, an old church, a State legislature, or the National Archives.

Historians do many things besides teach, however. They administer historical activities in archives, museums, historical societies, and places such as Mount Vernon and Independence Hall. This involves helping scholars to use manuscripts and artifacts and educating the public through exhibits and publications. Many historians preserve, identify, and classify historical documents, treasures, and other materials. A growing number are concerned with the restoration of historic buildings and sites. Their goal is to preserve and interpret our historical heritage, which consists of historic houses, churches, forts, public markets, battlefields, and other places. Historians are employed to manage, interpret, and write about such places as the Manassas National Battlefield Park in Virginia and Old Sturbridge Village in Massachusetts. Historic preservationists also work to save city neighborhoods and maintain their unique historic and architectural features. This usually means joining forces with architects, lawyers, planners, business and community leaders, and city officials.

Political scientists study the objectives, organization, and actual operations of government in the United States and abroad. They explore such areas as public opinion; the nature of political parties; the influence of special interest groups; the workings of the Presidency, Con-

Volunteers are helping an archeological team expose the foundations of a canal.

Social Scientists

gress, and the judicial system; political decisionmaking at the State and local levels; the role of the United States in world affairs; mass movements, revolution, and ideology; community organization and urban politics; and policy studies.

Most political scientists teach or do research at colleges and universities. Very often, they do consulting work as well. Some political scientists are employed by public interest groups, survey research institutes, and foreign affairs organizations; they do research, prepare publications, and consult. Others work as aides to elected officials, serve on the staff of committees of Congress and State legislatures, and work for legislative bodies in cities and counties. Still others administer government programs.

Because of their understanding of the political process and how it really works, political scientists are often asked to give advice and make recommendations. Busi-

ness firms, labor unions, citizens' groups, political candidates, and government agencies themselves all seek the advice of political scientists from time to time. Political scientists, like other social scientists, provide opinions only after a careful study of the matter at hand—which might be anything from "Which party will win the election in the 8th precinct?" to "What effect will this treaty have on our position in the United Nations?" To find the answers, political scientists begin by gathering information. They may examine documents, conduct a survey, or interview people to get the information they need. Then they carefully weigh all the facts and arrive at a conclusion.

Psychologists study people in order to understand and explain their actions. Psychologists' insights into human behavior enable them to help people who are mentally or emotionally disturbed or deeply unhappy. *Clinical psychologists* work with people who have mental or emotional disorders. They learn more about their pa-

Volunteer campaign work is a good way to launch a career in politics.

Many social scientists have teaching or research positions with colleges and universities.

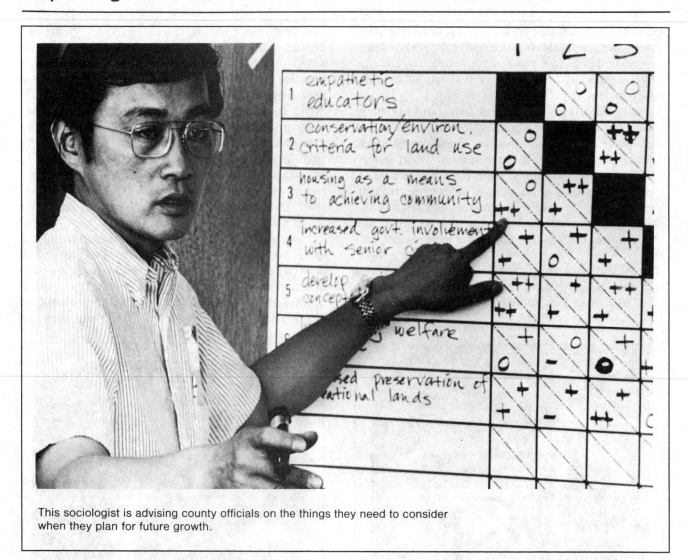

This sociologist is advising county officials on the things they need to consider when they plan for future growth.

tient's frame of mind by giving standardized tests and taking a personal history, but mostly they help by talking to the patient and listening. They counsel their patients, individually and in groups, and try to help them deal with their problems.

Some psychologists specialize in the behavior of people in a particular place. *School psychologists* help with learning and social problems in schools. *Industrial psychologists* might study the reasons a company's employees are absent from work so much. They would also work with the company's personnel department on selection and training procedures, and might counsel employees who were unhappy or depressed.

Social psychologists usually do research, administer programs, or teach. They examine such issues as leadership and group behavior. Sometimes their research is designed to find out how well government programs are working. This is called evaluation research, and is an important field of social science research. There are other

kinds of psychologists, too, including *developmental psychologists, educational psychologists, experimental psychologists,* and *comparative psychologists.*

Sociologists analyze society and human behavior by studying people in groups. They are interested in human interaction as such, and explore such social processes as competition and cooperation. In their research, sociologists may work with groups as different as families, tribes, communities, and governments. Or they may work with social, political, religious, ethnic, business, or professional groups. For example, a sociologist might study families to discover the causes of social problems such as crime, juvenile delinquency, alcoholism, and poverty. Sociologists apply their knowledge of people's behavior in groups in many areas including family counseling, public opinion analysis, education, law, religion, public relations, and planning.

Most sociologists teach and do research in colleges and universities. Others, however, are employed by research organizations to conduct studies and prepare reports. Still other sociologists administer programs in such fields as corrections, mental health, social welfare, and education.

Areas of specialization in sociology include *social organization,* which deals with the origin, development, activities, and interaction of social groups; *urban sociology,* which deals with life in cities and highly populated areas; *criminology* and *penology,* which deal with the causes of juvenile deliquency and crime and the life of inmates in penal institutions; and *demography,* which deals with the composition, growth, and movement of populations.

Personal Characteristics

What makes a good social scientist? They are scientists, after all, who seek knowledge and apply it to a variety of social needs and situations. Therefore, two fundamental traits needed by all social scientists are *intellectual curiosity* and *creativity.* Social scientists must constantly seek new information about people, things, and ideas. Their curiosity inspires them to devote their lives to understanding the causes of social problems. History, geography, and economics can all be taught, but creativity cannot be. Successful social scientists have it, however, and use their creativity to attack social problems in new ways. Although social scientists study the work of others before them, they constantly face problems that require original solutions.

Social scientists must be willing to spend considerable time and effort in study and research. This requires a number of personal traits. For example, an economist who is studying tax reform needs the *ability to analyze data* on the proportion of total taxes paid by people at different income levels. A political scientist who is studying the differences between democratic forms of government and dictatorships must have the *ability to think logically and methodically* about what influences the actions of government leaders. A psychologist who is studying the behavior of mice over a period of months must have *systematic work habits* if he or she expects to reach valid conclusions. *Objectivity* and *open-mindedness* are important in all kinds of social science research. An economist must be able to make an unemotional and detached analysis of the issues when reviewing a proposal to amend a city's rent-control legislation. *Perseverance* is essential for an anthropologist who might spend years accumulating and piecing together artifacts from an ancient civilization.

Social scientists must apply their research findings to practical situations. This requires other traits. For ex-

Economists develop the Consumer Price Index, a measure of inflation.

ample, a sociologist who is preparing a report on the causes of juvenile delinquency needs *intellectual creativity* to approach the problem from a new perspective. A historian who is delivering a lecture on regional differences in American social customs needs the *ability to communicate effectively.* This historian must be good at public speaking, of course. The ability to handle written material is just as important. Because communicating their findings and analyses to other people is such an important part of the job, social scientists must be able to speak and write clearly, concisely, and effectively. The written report is the standard form of communication in the social sciences, and the ability to prepare a well-organized, well-documented, and well-written report is a "must."

For some social scientists, *emotional stability* is important. A clinical psychologist who is working with a group of mental patients must understand other people and be sensitive to their moods. The manner in which he or she conducts himself is important, because psychologists often serve as models for their patients.

For other social scientists, *physical stamina* is important. An anthropologist or geographer doing field work may have to lift equipment, walk considerable distances, or spend a long time in uncomfortable surroundings.

Some social scientists *work alone*. An economist who studies imports and exports may spend most of his or her time behind a desk, with only a calculator for company. The job involves analyzing statistics and preparing tables and charts.

Other social scientists *work as part of a team*. The archeological team led by Dr. Berenson is learning how important it is to work together. Teamwork is important, too, because studies of social problems often require the skills of people from several disciplines. Thus a sociologist might head a study group on prison conditions consisting of a lawyer, a social worker, and a corrections official.

Training

Formal training requirements for seven social science occupations are described in the Job Facts at the end of this chapter.

High school offers you a good opportunity to get the background you'll need for further training. History, geography, economics, and other social studies courses are, of course, very important. You also should take as much mathematics as possible. Social science research increasingly requires knowledge of mathematics, statistics, and computer science, and a strong mathematics background will prepare you for more advanced courses in these fields later on. English courses are valuable, too, since communications skills are so important to social scientists. Your high school probably offers other courses that would relate to some of the social science occupations. For example, biology, physics, and other sciences are very important for some geographers, anthropologists, and psychologists. Drawing and design are important for cartographers.

Most of your training would occur after high school. Social scientists generally earn a bachelor's degree after 4 years' study in college, and then go on to graduate school. Teaching or research in a college or university almost always requires a Ph. D. degree. The Ph. D. is important for many nonacademic positions as well. And it is essential for recognition as a scholar in your chosen field.

Nevertheless, many persons with a bachelor's or master's degree in economics, geography, and other social sciences are working successfully in their chosen field.

It's important to remember that a college degree in one of the social sciences can prepare you for graduate or professional education in law, business, journalism, and a number of other fields. Moreover, it gives you the background you'd need for many kinds of jobs in business, industry, and government.

Training does not end when you earn a college or graduate degree. New theories and new research findings emerge so often that what you learn in college soon will become outdated—though not useless. Just as you can expect to learn new words your whole life, social scientists continue to learn new theories and applications their entire lives. They learn by reading books and magazines, going to conferences, and attending seminars from time to time. Careers in this cluster are for people who like to learn outside as well as in school.

A Final Word

If you have a strong interest in social issues, don't stop here! Other chapters of *Exploring Careers* describe several more occupations that are worth looking into.

Urban planners share the historic preservationist's concern with preserving the interesting and distinctive qualities of buildings and neighborhoods. In fact, planners and historians often work together to preserve historic sites and communities. A story about a planner appears in the chapter on Office Occupations.

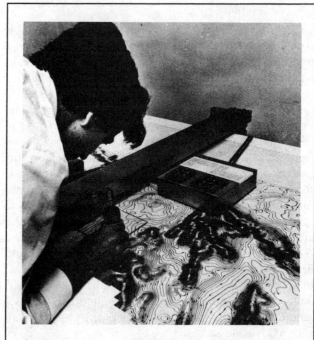

Cartographers can use data from satellite sensors to make maps.

Social Scientists

Are you caught up in current events? Do you think you would like to be one of the people investigating local or national issues and informing the public of what's really going on? There's a story about a newspaper reporter in the chapter on Performing Arts, Design, and Communications Occupations.

Social workers devote their lives to helping people. Some do research to identify community needs. They work with health, housing, transportation, and other planners to suggest ways of making our communities better places to live. A story about a social worker appears in the chapter on Social Service Occupations.

Are you fascinated by the workings of the financial world? Bank officers and securities sales workers handle their clients' money and are just as concerned with understanding why the economy works as it does as economists are. Training in economics is important for these workers. A story about a bank officer appears in the chapter on Office Occupations. A day in the life of a securities sales worker is described in the chapter on Sales Occupations.

The level of education in any society is one indicator of the standard of living. Teachers devote their lives to educating people to fulfill their own potential and become productive members of society. Many people with training in history, geography, and other social sciences become teachers. A story about a secondary school teacher appears in the chapter on Education Occupations.

You've learned that computers are an important research tool for social scientists. If the field of computer science fascinates you, learn more about computer occupations by reading the story of the programmer/systems analyst in the chapter on Office Occupations.

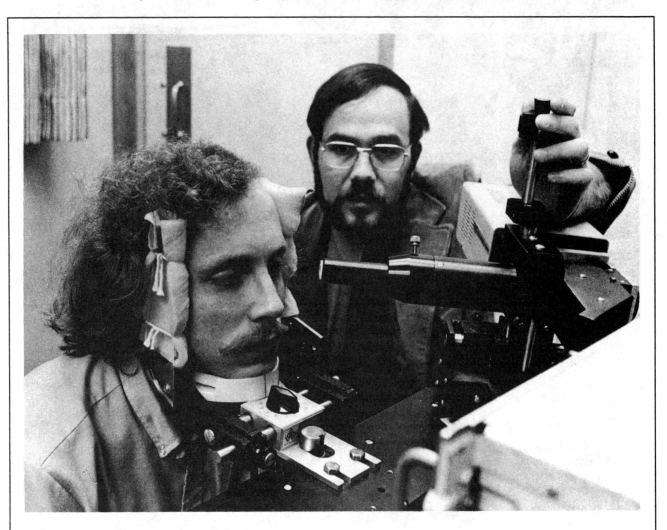

This psychologist is doing research on eye movements.

Museum Curator

Jill's love of history inspired her to look for a job as a museum curator.

Social Scientists

Jill rounded the corner sharply, the gravel from the dirt road flying in all directions as her sports car sped by. She was on her way to a country antique show and wanted to get there before dark.

Jill Winitsky is the curator of engineering at the Wood Museum. She considers herself lucky to be working at a large museum such as the Wood, where she can concentrate on engineering history—her area of expertise. Curators at the Wood Museum generally specialize; their subject may be agriculture, textiles, mining, atomic energy, or political, cultural, or military history.

Jill had come across the notice of the antique show in the morning newspaper and thought it seemed worth looking into. Not that she was counting on finding anything at the show. Jill had gone to a number of antique shows in the 5 years she had worked at the Wood Museum but she rarely found anything worth acquiring. Generally the museum relies upon gifts—of historical objects and of the money to purchase them.

"It's a nice drive," thought Jill as she spotted the turnoff to the grange hall where the antique show was being held. "And you never know, of course. Maybe I'll be lucky for once and find something worth adding to the museum's collection."

Only a few people were there when Jill walked into the hall where the antiques were being shown for sale. She paused for a moment to get an idea of the layout. Then she moved purposefully into the exhibit area, carefully noting each object on display. Something in the center of the room made her stop in her tracks. It was an old rotary printing press, the kind consisting of a large cylinder bearing columns of type and several small cylinders. The black metal press was somewhat worn; a number of cracks were visible. But otherwise it was in fair condition.

Jill estimated that the press was about 70 years old. Considering that the rotary printing press had only been invented in the mid-19th century, this press was well worth acquiring. Of course the museum had several other printing presses in its collection, but Jill was excited at the prospect of getting this particular press, which probably had been made shortly before the manufacturer went out of business.

Jill didn't lose any time locating the manager of the antique show.

"Mr. Williams, I am Jill Winitsky, curator of engineering at the Wood Museum," she said by way of introduction. "I am interested in acquiring that old printing press for the museum. Can you put me in touch with the owner?"

"Mrs. Cortland owns the press," Mr. Williams replied. "You could probably reach her tomorrow morning." He handed Jill a business card that read: Mrs. Virginia Cortland, 544 West Lorch Street, Telephone 345-6111.

Jill called Mrs. Cortland right after she arrived at work the following morning. She explained her interest in the press and suggested that she and Mrs. Cortland get together to talk about it some more. Mrs. Cortland agreed, but reluctantly. She made it clear that she really wanted to sell the press.

"The press is something my late husband acquired a long time ago out west," Mrs. Cortland explained. "We kept it in the basement. But now I am moving to an apartment and I don't want to take it with me. It seemed like a good idea to sell it."

"I see," said Jill. "However, I'd really like the chance to talk with you about the press. How about coming to the museum tomorrow? We could have lunch here and talk about it then."

After lunch the following day, Jill gave Mrs. Cortland a tour of the engineering section and gave her a brief but lively history of the printing press. She explained the historical significance of the press that had been in the Cortland basement all these years. Mrs. Cortland's resistance began to fade. Nevertheless, it took several more conversations before she agreed—enthusiastically, at last—to donate the press to the museum.

Now, every time Jill walks through the exhibit on printing technology, she remembers the antique show at the end of a country road and innumerable conversations with Mrs. Cortland.

Jill was born and raised in the oldest house in Macon County, Georgia, and has been interested in history since she was a girl. Genealogy in particular fascinated her when she was growing up, and she thought nothing of spending hours and hours poring over records of her family's history in the county courthouse. She also developed an extensive correspondence with other genealogy buffs.

Much as she loves her job, Jill hadn't planned to become a museum curator when she was in school. Nonetheless, her background suits her for the job very well. She finished college with a double major in history and engineering. That is, she completed the college work for a bachelor's degree in both history and engineering. She also has a master's degree in history. Curatorial jobs are relatively few and far between, Jill knows, and she considers herself lucky to be in a job that she likes so much. She realizes, too, that she'd probably need a Ph. D. to be hired at the Wood Museum today.

Jill spends much of her workday dealing with letters and telephone calls. One recent letter began, "I am writing a book to be called *Tunneling Through Solid Rock*, and I need photographs of several different kinds of tunnels for the book. Can you supply them?" Jill usually can help with this kind of request; she checks the museum's extensive photograph file and selects those that will fit the author's needs.

Just a few days ago, she received a letter from the director of a historic preservation society. The society plans to restore an old grist mill and wanted to know if Jill could give them some advice. Restoration work is something Jill particularly enjoys, and she's even had some experience with grist mills. She'd like to take on this project, but the mill is nearly 100 miles away. The trips back and forth would keep her away from the museum too much. Jill wrote back, referring the society to several books on the subject and giving them the name of another authority who might be willing to help.

The grist mill restoration had been tempting. But it really was out of the question since Jill had been away so much on that steel plant project. That request had come through several months ago. The mayor of a nearby city had written, "We have an old steel plant that has not been in operation for many years. The city council joins me in believing that the structure might have some historical value and they are considering allocating funds to restore the plant and make it a historic site. We would appreciate it if you would examine the structure and give us your opinion. May we expect to hear from you soon?" That request had led to an inspection trip, and then several return trips, as Jill was called upon to testify before the city council and then speak at a town meeting to explain the plant's historic significance.

Today's paperwork taken care of, Jill turns to the exhibit on industry in 19th-century America that she's been working on for nearly a year. The exhibit will open next summer in a newly renovated wing of the museum. It will include early industrial machinery, handtools, company records, and many other items. Putting together an exhibit is a big job, one that involves an almost overwhelming amount of detail. Jill has acquired items from literally hundreds of sources: Other museums, historical societies, archives, private collectors, antique dealers, and manufacturing firms. Much of her time has gone into the search for historically significant items and negotiations with the owners for their acquisition. Documenting every item has been a tedious, time-consuming task. Now she's busy preparing the catalog that will be published when the exhibit opens.

As a curator, Jill is concerned with educating and informing the public. She contributes articles on her section of the museum to *Wood Light,* a monthly newsletter that is sent to members of the museum. The new printing press, for example, will make a good subject for a short article. From time to time, she conducts special tours for dignitaries, reporters, students, and other special groups. Normally, of course, museum tours are con-

"I consider myself very lucky," says Jill. "Museum jobs are hard to find."

ducted by the Wood's volunteer guides. Jill is one of the curators who help train the volunteers. Not long ago, Jill gave a talk on the history of textile manufacturing in New England during the intermission of a weekly concert sponsored by the museum and broadcast over a local radio station.

Doing research and keeping up with recent developments in her profession are important parts of Jill's job. Last year, she devoted quite a bit of her free time to research on textile mill restoration. That was the subject of a paper she presented at the annual meeting of State historians.

Jill enjoys her work. She particularly enjoys seeing the way some people become totally absorbed in one of her exhibits and lose all track of their surroundings. Jill is proud, too, of being able to maintain and restore structures that are part of the region's historic heritage. Nevertheless, she feels the pressure when she faces the deadline for opening an exhibit, completing a research report, or making a speech. The job has built-in frustrations, too. Just recently, for example, she lost a chance to buy a very old drill press because the museum didn't have the funds.

Social Scientists

Jill's job demands a commitment. She is expected to complete original research projects that require night and weekend work. She must be "constructively aggressive" in always being on the lookout for objects of historic value. She often attends auctions and flea markets in this never-ending search. Even while she's on vacation, Jill takes time to investigate leads for new exhibit items. She knows that casual conversations can lead to major acquisitions. Because Jill finds her job so interesting, she doesn't mind giving so much of her time to it. As a curator, she's doing something that she very much wants to do.

Exploring

Curators must have a strong interest in history.

- Do you look forward to history class?
- Do you do extra reading on historical topics?
- Do you enjoy visiting historical sites?
- Are you interested in genealogy—learning about your family history?
- Are you interested in historic preservation projects in your community?
- Are you interested in the history of your part of the country?

Curators need to do careful research and think logically and analytically in order to explain the origins and uses of the objects in their collections.

- Do you check the facts before deciding whether something is so?
- Do you ask questions in class? If you don't understand the answer, do you keep asking until you're sure it's clear?
- Do you look up words you don't know in the dictionary?
- Do you use the encyclopedia?
- Do you do research on subjects of personal interest?
- Do you check your answers before you turn in a test paper?
- Do you like to solve puzzles, riddles, and brain teasers?

Curators must be objective and exercise good judgment in selecting items for the museum's collection.

- When preparing a report for school, do you include all relevant information regardless of your own point of view?
- Are you interested in hearing all sides of an issue?

- Can you tell when someone has a biased viewpoint?

Curators must have an aesthetic sense to arrange exhibits in an appealing manner.

- Do you notice your surroundings?
- Can you name some of the things that make a room, a building, or a neighborhood pleasant to look at? Can you name things that make it unpleasant or even ugly?
- Do you have a flair for decorating?
- Do you have good taste in selecting clothes?
- Can you fit a great deal into a relatively small area without having things look cluttered?

Curators must set priorities because museums have limited budgets.

- Are you good at getting all the facts and weighing them carefully when you make a big purchase—a bicycle, camping gear, or stereo equipment, for example?
- Are you aware of making choices about the way you use your time when you decide to go to a party instead of studying for a test?

Curators must be persuasive in order to convince potential donors to contribute time and money to the museum.

- Are you good at getting your point of view across?
- Are you persuasive?
- Is it easy for you to persuade your friends to work on school or extracurricular projects with you?
- Are you good at collecting contributions for school or community benefits?

Curators must be effective communicators. They write letters and reports, give speeches, and spend a great deal of time on the telephone.

- Are you good at writing term papers and compositions for school?
- Are you good at doing essay questions on tests?
- Do you enjoy writing letters to friends?
- Do you write poetry or short stories in your spare time?
- Are you good at crossword puzzles, Scrabble, Password, and other word games?
- Are you good at giving oral reports?
- Do your friends ever ask you to speak on behalf of a group—at a club meeting or going-away party, for example?

Political Aide

"Working on the Hill pays reasonably well and I make important contacts," says Bruce, "but I am tied hand and foot to the job."

Social Scientists

Bruce Yamasaki usually arrives on Capitol Hill in Washington, D.C., well before 8 o'clock in the morning. As administrative assistant to Pearson Boyne, a U.S. Senator, Bruce must be on the job whenever Senator Boyne is. When Congress is in session, about two-thirds of each year, Bruce works well into the evening—until 8:00 or later. Senator Boyne, the senior Senator from his State and a member of the Foreign Relations and Governmental Affairs Committees, often attends committee meetings in the morning and participates in business on the floor of the Senate in the afternoon.

When Congress is not in session, Bruce meets with representatives of political and business groups and with the Senator's staff. He frequently visits Senator Boyne's home State to get closer to the Senator's constituents—to learn their needs and their sentiments on bills being considered by the Congress. If the issue is a particularly sensitive one, Bruce may decide to poll the Senator's constituents, using questionnaires mailed to every voter in the State.

Bruce lives and breathes politics; he always has. Political campaigns and elections have interested him since he was a youngster. Bruce has an excellent background for this position. His credentials include a bachelor's degree in political science, followed by several years' experience as a journalist covering local politics for a big city daily. Perhaps most important of all, Bruce has practical experience in government and politics. As a teenager, he worked on local political campaigns. The heady, hectic months of campaigning meant stuffing envelopes, putting up posters, delivering messages, anything at all that needed to be done. Bruce became so wrapped up in politics that he stayed on as a volunteer party worker in the much quieter period between election campaigns. He did some grass roots organizing and learned what kinds of things citizens complain to local politicians about.

Bruce's understanding of the way local politics actually works continued to stand him in good stead when he left the newspaper to work on his State's model cities program. From there, he moved to a job with a political consulting firm in Washington, D.C., where he planned the advertising for Senator Boyne's reelection campaign. After the Senator's victory at the polls, the next step for Bruce was the top job on Senator Boyne's staff.

Last night, Senator Boyne had told Bruce to come in early this morning and meet him in the Senate Caucus Room. It is 7:20 a.m. as Bruce enters the Senate Office Building. The place is alive with journalists and camera crews because several Senate committees are about to meet early to discuss parts of the Federal budget. As Bruce walks down a corridor, he is collared by a reporter, Barbara Weld.

"Bruce, how does the Senator feel about the changes that are due to be introduced today in the education bill? As you know, the leading teachers' groups are split. What position is Boyne going to take?"

"The Senator is all for the changes," replies Bruce without breaking stride. "Two weeks ago," he continues, "the Senator made a major speech on the education bill back home. He's a strong supporter of the changes that will be brought up on the floor today. Sorry, but I'm in a hurry. See you later."

Bruce continues on his way to the Senate Caucus Room, where a political strategy meeting of all the Senators from Boyne's party is about to begin. Entering the room, Bruce immediately spots a familiar, craggy face. It's Senator Boyne, deep in conversation with the junior Senator from North Carolina.

"Good morning, Bruce," says Senator Boyne, moving aside for a private conversation with his aide. "The meeting is about to begin," the Senator continues. "I've spoken with a few of my colleagues about the Middle East situation. It looks like we are going to support the administration's proposal in that area. We'll also be discussing the vacancy on the Supreme Court. We are backing Ambassador John Farmer for the appointment. Have my press secretary write a news release about the Middle East proposal and arrange a news conference for noon tomorrow. But don't answer any questions. We can review the statement tonight."

"Yes, sir, I'll take care of everything right away," says Bruce. Then he races back to his office to work out a news release with a press aide. He calls several prominent reporters about the news conference and tells his secretary to notify the Senate Press Gallery.

The office is bustling, as always, There are other Capitol Hill staffers who want copies of Boyne's statement on the START (Strategic Arms Reduction) talks, several lobbyists who want to express their clients' point of view to the Senator, and a few tourists.

Several of the Senator's staff aides are busy replying to the hundreds of letters that pour into the office every week. Recently, there have been a number of letters asking what Senator Boyne's position is on national health insurance. The administration's farm bill has generated an outpouring of letters from the Senator's constituents, most of whom oppose it. The Senator's constituents write every day to express strongly held feelings on inflation, housing, transportation, tax relief, governmental waste and corruption—virtually every subject under the sun. Senator Boyne sees to it that every letter is answered.

Bruce usually holds a staff meeting every morning between 9 and 10 to go over proposed speeches, pending legislation, and staff problems. Today, Bruce's meeting

Exploring Careers

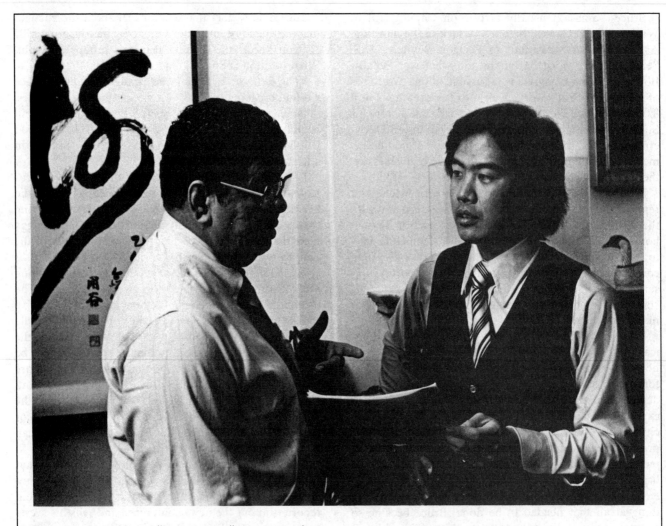

Bruce confers with a colleague regarding a news release.

with the staff will take place a little later than usual because of the news release. While the Senator is at committee meetings or on the floor of the Senate, it is Bruce who oversees everything that goes on in the office. Senator Boyne's staff consists of 25 people—legislative aides who do research on proposed legislation and answer letters; press aides who write speeches, floor statements, and press releases; a receptionist; secretaries and typists; and clerks who operate the computerized filing system. Senator Boyne also has a staff of eight in his home State.

As soon as the news release is taken care of, Bruce calls the staff together and announces, "Senator Boyne is going to Japan next month with some other members of the Foreign Relations Committee. I am getting a fact sheet together for you that will have the details. I'll include a few standard paragraphs that you can use in answering correspondence."

After several minutes of discussion of the Japanese trip, Bruce says, "We'll have to cut the meeting short because the office is so busy today. Thank you."

As head of the office, Bruce sets the working hours for all staff members. His own hours depend upon circumstances and generally are longer when the Senator has a bill pending before the Senate or one of its committees. Bruce sometimes works at home. And his job involves travel to the Senator's home State. Several months ago, for example, Bruce was informed by the Army that it planned to sell some surplus land in the Senator's home State. After consulting with the Senator, Bruce arranged meetings with the Governor and with community and business groups to discuss ways of attracting purchasers who would use the land in a way that matched State residents' own interests and needs. Bruce outlined the results of the meeting to Senator Boyne when he returned to Washington.

364

Social Scientists

Bruce reviews all outgoing letters before presenting them to his boss, Senator Boyne, for approval.

"Senator, Governor Johnson was pleased to learn about the sale of Army land, but she was angry because the military had failed to advise her in advance. We discussed ways of ensuring that most of the land is reserved for community purposes such as low-income housing and park and recreation areas. Several developers have expressed an interest in building a shopping center, a proposal that's meeting a favorable response. All in all, everyone is enthusiastic, and I've arranged some follow-up meetings later in the year."

"Great work, Bruce. Keep me informed. I may want to attend one of those meetings."

"Fine, Senator, I can arrange a dinner and invite some of your top campaign contributors, local business and community leaders, and government officials. You and the Governor might both want to address the group."

Bruce gets together with Senator Boyne every evening. Often, they have dinner together and discuss the day's events. At this evening's dinner session, Bruce hands the Senator the news release on the Middle East proposal that will be distributed at tomorrow's press conference. There also are a few letters that require the Senator's approval; he makes a few changes and returns them to Bruce.

It is close to 9 o'clock when Senator Boyne and Bruce are ready to go home. Bruce stops to buy the evening newspaper and arrives home just before 10. Bruce's job is interesting and challenging, but it is very demanding as well. He flops down on the sofa and wonders, not for the first time, what he's doing with his life.

"The job pays well and I make many important contacts. But I'm tied hand and foot to the job. I don't have enough time for myself. All those dates I had to cancel and the skiing trips I could never go on . . . . But if I were married, it might be even more difficult to hold down this job."

Exploring Careers

Bruce's thoughts stray to the future. "I wonder what I'll do next. After all, Senator Boyne won't be in office forever! I'll probably return to the political consulting firm for a while, but I'd really like to run for office some day. I have some great experience for that."

Bruce is too tired to continue with that train of thought. Tomorrow is another day, and so to bed.

Exploring

Political aides must understand our system of government, especially the legislative process.

- Do you enjoy social studies and civics courses?
- Do you do outside reading about politics and government?
- Do you read the editorial section of the newspaper?
- Do you like to discuss current events?
- Have you ever taken part in campaigns for school or local elections?
- Do you understand how the President is elected? Do you understand how laws are made?

Political aides must have leadership and organizational abilities to coordinate the work of the politician's staff.

- Are you a good leader? Do other people go along with your ideas when you're in charge of a group? Do they follow your suggestions?
- Do you enjoy organizing trips, parties, sports events, picnics, or dances?
- Have you ever organized a fund-raising event or a recycling campaign?
- Do you enjoy working with other people on class projects?
- Do you like working with others on school clubs or committees?

Political aides work long, irregular hours and must be able to handle problems on a moment's notice. They must adapt their personal lives to the needs of the job.

- Can you work under pressure?
- Can you do a good job when you're given something to do at the last minute?
- Do you perform well on pop quizzes?
- Are you a member of the school debate team?
- Are you able to stick to schedules? Do you usually get your school assignments in on time?
- Can you sacrifice leisure activities such as a movie or a baseball game when you have school work to do?

Political aides must be good at getting along with people of widely different backgrounds and points of view.

- Do you get along well with classmates and others you may meet?
- Do you make friends easily?
- Can you put other people at ease?

Political aides must be effective communicators. They need writing and public relations skills to present an appropriate image of the politician in speeches, letters, and press releases.

- Are you good at writing compositions and term papers for school?
- Are you good at doing essay questions on tests?
- Do you enjoy writing letters to your friends?
- Have you ever written a letter to the editor of your school or local newspaper?
- Are you good at getting your point across when you speak or write?

Social Scientists

Job Facts

There isn't room in this book for a story about every social science occupation. However, you'll find some important facts about seven of these occupations in the following section. If you want additional information about any of them, you might begin by consulting the *Occupational Outlook Handbook*, a publication of the Department of Labor which should be available in your school or public library.

Occupation	Nature and Places of Work	Training and Qualifications	Other Information
Anthropologists	Anthropologists study the human race. They examine people's traditions, beliefs, customs, languages, religions, art, law, and social systems. Most teach and do research in colleges and universities. Some work for museums, National Parks, foundations, and in private industry. Others are consultants for development organizations both here and abroad.	Anthropologists usually need a Ph. D. degree in anthropology. This requires 7 or 8 years of study, or more, beyond high school. High school students interested in becoming anthropologists should take courses in the social and physical sciences as well as mathematics.	Anthropologists generally specialize. That is, they do most of their work in one branch of anthropology—cultural anthropology (also called ethnology), archeology, linguistics, or physical anthropology. Traveling to remote areas, working in an uncomfortable climate, and living in primitive housing are sometimes necessary to do field work.

Exploring Careers

Occupation	Nature and Places of Work	Training and Qualifications	Other Information
Economists	Economists study the way our society uses natural resources, labor, and capital to produce goods and services. They compile and analyze data that help them understand the costs and benefits of making, distributing, and using things the way we do. Most economists work in research organizations and private industry, including manufacturing firms, banks, insurance companies, securities and investment companies, and management consulting firms. Others work in colleges and universities and for government agencies. Some run their own consulting firms. Many economists work in the New York City and Washington, D.C. areas.	A bachelor's degree in economics, requiring 4 years of college, is sufficient for many beginning positions. However, a master's degree or Ph. D. is important for advancement. Economists who teach at colleges and universities usually need a Ph. D., which takes 7 or 8 years of study after high school. Since economists spend much time analyzing data, the ability to work with numbers is important. Familiarity with the computer as a research tool also is important in this field. High school students interested in becoming economists should take courses in social studies and mathematics.	Economists generally specialize. They do most of their work in one field, such as money and banking, economic theory, economic history, or in business, labor, agricultural, industrial, health, regional, urban, or international economics.
Geographers	Geographers study the physical characteristics of the earth in order to understand why people live where they do. Their research helps explain how the environment affects our health, our way of earning a living, and the kind of society we develop. Some geographers collect data for maps. Most geographers teach and do research in colleges and universities. A number work for the Federal Government, primarily for mapping and intelligence agencies. Those in private industry work for textbook and map publishers, travel agencies, manufacturing firms, real estate development corporations, insurance companies, communications and transportation firms, or chain stores. Others work for scientific foundations and research organizations or run their own research or consulting businesses.	A bachelor's degree in geography, usually requiring 4 years of college, is the minimum requirement for beginning positions. However, a master's degree or Ph. D. is required for advancement. Geographers who teach in colleges and universities generally need a Ph. D., which takes 7 or 8 years of study after high school. High school students interested in becoming geographers should take courses in the social and physical sciences and mathematics.	Some geographers do field work in regions of the world where living conditions and social customs are quite different from ours. Geographers often specialize. They do most of their work in a particular field such as cartography (mapmaking) or economic, urban, political, regional, physical, or medical geography.

Social Scientists

Occupation	Nature and Places of Work	Training and Qualifications	Other Information
Historians	Historians study the past. They examine things that happened in the past, the ideas people had, and the ways in which they lived and earned a living. Historians study these things to help us understand the present and predict the future. Most historians teach and do research in colleges and universities. Others work in archives, libraries, museums, research organizations, historical societies, publishing firms, and large corporations.	Historians usually need a Ph. D. degree in history or a related field. This takes 7 or 8 years of study, or more, beyond high school. High school students interested in becoming historians should take social studies and English courses to develop research and writing skills. Mathematics also is important.	Historians usually specialize. Some do all their research on the history of a particular country, region, or era. The American Civil War is an example of such a specialization. Others specialize in the history of a field such as religion, art, architecture, philosophy, science, medicine, women, black peoples, or military affairs. Others specialties are historic preservation and archival management.
Political Scientists	Political scientists study government. They examine the ways in which political power takes shape and is used, how government operates, and how it affects us. Most political scientists teach and do research in colleges and universities. The rest work in government, management consulting firms, political organizations, research organizations, civic and taxpayers' associations, and business firms.	Political scientists generally need a Ph. D. This takes 7 or 8 years, or more, beyond high school. Familiarity with quantitative research methods, including mathematics, statistics, and research uses of computers, is important in political science. High school students interested in becoming political scientists should take courses in social studies, English, and mathematics.	Political scientists usually specialize. They do most of their work in a particular field such as political theory, political behavior, public policy, State and local government, international relations, or comparative political systems—government in other countries.
Sociologists	Sociologists study people in groups. They learn about human society and social behavior by studying families, tribes, gangs, communities, and governments. Sociologists apply their knowledge in family counseling, public opinion analysis, law, education, regional planning, and many other areas. Most sociologists teach and do research in colleges and universities. A number work for government agencies in such fields as poverty, welfare, health, rehabilitation, population studies, community development, and environmental impact. Some work for private industry, research firms, or consulting firms. Others have their own consulting firms.	A Ph. D. in sociology often is required. This takes 7 or 8 years, or more, beyond high school. Because sociologists, like other social scientists, apply statistical and computer techniques in their research, an ability to work with numbers and solid grounding in mathematics are important. High school students interested in becoming sociologists should take courses in social studies and mathematics.	Among the many specialties are social organization, social pathology, rural or urban sociology, industrial sociology, medical sociology, criminology, and demography—the study of the size and characteristics of human populations, and how they change.

Exploring Careers

Occupation	Nature and Places of Work	Training and Qualifications	Other Information
Psychologists	Psychologists study the behavior of individuals and groups in order to understand and explain their actions. Many psychologists work directly with people who are mentally or emotionally disturbed or deeply unhappy. They conduct interviews, administer tests, and counsel clients in order to help them deal with everyday life. Others teach, do research, plan and conduct training programs for employees, design surveys, and help industrial designers improve products by explaining the interaction between people and machines. Many psychologists work in colleges and universities as teachers, researchers, administrators, or counselors. Others work in hospitals, clinics, rehabilitation centers, other health facilities, and government agencies. Some work in correctional institutions, research organizations, and business firms, while others are in independent practice or work as consultants.	A doctoral degree in psychology is usually required. This takes 7 to 8 years of study, or more, beyond high school. Psychologists in private practice must meet certification or licensing requirements. Although these vary by State, they generally include a doctorate in psychology, 2 years of professional experience, and an examination. Emotional stability, maturity, and the ability to deal effectively with people are important qualities in this field. Sensitivity, patience, and a genuine interest in others are particularly important for work in clinical and counseling psychology. High school students interested in becoming psychologists should take courses in the social, biological, and physical sciences as well as mathematics.	Evening work is common, particularly for clinical and counseling psychologists, since patients often are unable to leave their jobs or school during the day. Among the many specialties in this field are clinical, counseling, industrial and organizational, experimental, developmental, social, and comparative psychology.

In colleges and universities, counselors help students prepare for the job hunt after graduation.

Brrringgg! Brrringgg! Brrringgg! The phone rang persistently.

"Hello. This is Teen Hotline. My name is Gary. Can I help you?"

"I don't know," replied the caller defiantly.

"Tell me what's on your mind. I'm here to listen," responded Gary in a pleasant, easygoing voice.

"My parents are impossible—I can't stand living with them any longer. I'm going to run away!"

"You're going to run away?" repeated Gary. His matter-of-fact tone let the caller know he was with him.

The caller continued. "I just don't know what to do anymore. I'm being treated like a child and I'm not going to take it any more!"

"When did all this start?" Gary's manner encouraged the caller to open up. He seemed interested in hearing the details.

"Oh, I don't know. They're down on me all the time. Always picking on me to mow the lawn, to do my homework, to get home early. Nag, nag, nag. And nothing I do is ever good enough for them! They criticize my grades, tell me my friends are no good, bug me about playing my stereo too loud. They keep saying I'll never make anything of myself ... I don't know what they want."

The caller paused for a breath. Then he burst out, "I'm just sick and tired of being treated like a little kid!"

"Sounds like your parents have a lot of rules."

"I'll say," exploded the caller. "Rules, rules, rules, that's all my parents ever think of. And do you know the worst rule of all? I can't use the car!"

"Sounds like you're pretty upset about that. How did that come about?"

"Oh, well, there was an accident. Last year. I sideswiped a truck when I was driving my mom's car."

"Bad news."

"Right. My mom was pretty mad about it. It was a new car, you know? She had to get a new door and a new fender, and then she didn't like the paint job."

"You say your mom was pretty mad?"

"You're not kidding! Both my parents yelled and carried on about it. They kept after me and after me about it. Really made me feel bad."

"What I hear you saying is that you felt badly enough about the accident as it was ..."

"Yes, that's right, I felt terrible, that's what my parents don't understand," said the caller excitedly. "To hear them tell it, you'd think I didn't care at all about those accidents."

"Accidents?"

"Well, yes, as a matter of fact something else happened. I have crummy luck."

"Tell me about it."

"About a month after I banged up my mom's car, I was driving my dad's car. That one wasn't a new car, you understand, just an old tin can he used to drive to work. Anyway, I swerved, lost control of the car, and totalled it. The police said I was going too fast."

"Too fast?"

"I guess so, I really was moving along. No one was hurt. The car was smashed up, though. To hear my dad tell it, I'm the rottenest kid in the neighborhood. Totally irresponsible."

"And that's when they took your driving privileges away?"

"Right. That's when they lowered the boom on me."

"How did you feel about that?"

"Well, at first I felt so bad about the cars that I felt I deserved it. But those accidents took place 10 months ago! I feel I've paid for my mistakes. It's time for my parents to let up a little. I want them to let me have the car this summer. But they won't hear of it."

"Are they planning to let you drive again when the year is up?"

"Yes. Or so they say. But that's 2 months from now!"

"You don't believe them?"

"Oh, yes, I believe them. But I need the car now. It's summertime. Two months from now I'll be in school again and I won't need the car as much." The caller grew more agitated. "Tonight we had a big blow-up over it. I told them I was going to leave! What do you think I should do?"

"I take it you're not sure whether you want to leave or not?"

"Well—it could be the only way out of this. As I said before—I can't stand being treated like a little kid. Besides, some of my friends think I should leave."

"How is it that you've gone along with this for 10 months without running away?"

"Well, it's not as though I haven't thought about it!"

"What are some of the things that make you hesitate?"

"I guess I feel it will mess things up between me and my parents even more than they are right now. What do you think?"

"Well, I'm wondering what else makes you uneasy about trying it ..."

"I guess I think it would be a chicken way out. To run away from something instead of seeing it through," said the caller, interrupting Gary.

"Is that important to you ... to see things through?"

"Yes, I guess so. I can usually stick in there until the very end. I guess I'd better sit tight and wait another 2 months."

"Sounds like you've made a decision."

"Yes. Thanks for listening ...."

Social Service Occupations

To do their jobs well, those in the helping professions must be genuinely interested in other people.

Gary's call was one of many that came into Teen Hotline that day. Gary is a college student majoring in psychology; he volunteers at the Hotline one afternoon a week. Himself just a few years older than the would-be runaway, he sensed that the youth just needed to talk through his family problems.

And that was what the hotline was for: Volunteers like Gary were trained to listen and help callers sort out their feelings. In this case, Gary had relieved the youngster's panic and had, by listening, given him the feeling that he counted. The youth seemed able to take it from there.

Family disputes like this one were behind many of the calls. So were dating problems. But calls on any subject were welcome, and youngsters called the hotline every day because they were lonely or depressed. They called with questions about sex, drugs, jobs, medical help, shelter for runaways, you name it.

Not all of Gary's calls go as smoothly as this one.

Sometimes a caller gets angry and upset and hangs up abruptly. Sometimes Gary can tell that the situation is too serious for him to handle by himself. He suggests that the caller come in to talk with one of the counselors at the community center where Teen Hotline has its headquarters.

No matter what hour of the day it is, there usually are a few youngsters at Teen Hotline's drop-in center—just sitting around and talking things over among themselves. A trained counselor is on hand most of the time to talk out serious problems and direct youngsters to other sources of help in the community: Doctors, lawyers, psychologists, social workers.

The Helping Professions

The counselors and volunteer listeners at Teen Hotline are in the business of helping others. In fact, helping

Exploring Careers

This psychologist needed years of training to learn how to help people deal with their emotions.

people is such an important part of the job that social workers, counselors, and clergy are called members of the "helping professions." To do their jobs well, they have to be people-oriented. They must like people, be interested in all kinds of people, and have a genuine desire to help others.

Caring about people and wanting to help them is not enough, though. People in these occupations must be good at dealing with people and relating to them. They must have a manner that inspires trust and confidence. Nearly all of them have had training in how to deal with people and their problems.

Gary had been taught to handle phone calls like the one from the youngster who was having trouble with his parents. When he was first accepted as a peer counselor at Teen Hotline, Gary went through a course that taught him when to speak and when to listen. He had learned how to phrase probing questions. He had attended lectures, practiced role-plays with other volunteers, used audio tapes of crisis situations, and listened in on actual phone calls handled by experienced volunteers. Only then was he permitted to take his first call.

People who have professional jobs in this field need considerably more training than a hotline volunteer does. You probably know that doctors must study for years to learn enough to take care of people's bodies safely and wisely. Similarly, it takes years of training for a psychologist or a counselor to learn enough to help people deal with their feelings, emotions, fears, and worries. It also takes time to learn how to help people with their practical problems.

Supervision and backup are very important in this field, where people with different backgrounds and skills often work together as members of a team. Some have years of professional training; others are aides and volunteers like Gary. Their joint efforts help people who are troubled or unhappy. Gary knows that he can count on backup from the counselors and youth workers at Teen Hotline. That way, he handles telephone calls more confidently than he would if he were all on his own. He knows his limits, and has learned which calls to refer to other members of the staff. If a caller threatens suicide, for example, Gary knows what to do.

Now let's take a closer look at these occupations.

Social Service Occupations

Social Work Occupations

Social workers help people cope with crises that threaten to disrupt their lives. They help their clients understand what is happening to them and why, so that they can find their own solutions.

Social workers assist families that are being torn apart by poverty, alcoholism, drug abuse, behavior problems, or illness. They help children in many ways: They find families to adopt or provide foster care for children whose parents can't take care of them; they see to it that needy families are able to give their children proper food, health care, and schooling; they step in when there is evidence of parental neglect or abuse. *School social workers* help students who have such severe personal or family problems that they can't concentrate on learning. Social workers such as those at Teen Hotline give young people guidance and support so that they will learn to deal with their changing lives and develop into responsible adults. Some social workers do corrections work—they counsel juvenile delinquents and serve as *probation officers* or *parole officers*.

Sometimes, the problems that families and individuals face are so complicated that it takes people with several kinds of training to suggest a solution. This is one important reason why social workers have teamed up with members of other professions: Medicine, nursing, therapy, psychology, education, law, and religion, among them. A *medical social worker*, for example, may counsel a hospital patient who is feeling hopeless about his illness and advise the family as well—perhaps suggesting ways of caring for the patient at home that won't totally disrupt the family's normal routine.

Growing attention is being given within the social work profession to directing and influencing social change. Social workers whose specialty is social planning work with health, housing, transportation, and other planners to suggest ways of making our communities more wholesome places to live. Social workers use various forms of direct action to help people deal with some of the basic forces that shape their lives. They may, for example, do research to identify community needs; publicize their findings; draft legislation; or comment on government proposals in such areas as housing, health, and social and welfare services.

Counseling Occupations

Counselors help people understand themselves. They help them come to terms with their lives. And they give them the support and encouragement they need to make the most of their opportunities. Counselors usually specialize.

Family and child welfare is an important social work specialty.

Rehabilitation counselors help people with physical, mental, or social disabilities. They help them deal with the tremendous psychological adjustments they may have to make in order to cope with a handicap. They encourage their clients to learn new skills and to live as normally as possible. Some of their clients have been retarded or handicapped since birth. Others face the shock of blindness, or deafness, or an amputation when they are already grown. Such is the case, for example, with veterans who were badly injured or disfigured in the line of duty.

School counselors help elementary and secondary school students plan their courses and decide what they will do after they graduate. They spend a lot of time helping students with personal problems—behavior problems, family disputes, emotional upsets.

College career planning and placement counselors help college students choose a career and advise them on the kind of training or experience that will best help them find a job. They usually help students set up job interviews and give them ideas on how to prepare for these interviews.

Employment counselors help people of all ages plan careers and find jobs. Their advice helps people figure out what kind of work they're best suited for, and then prepare for it. They also give their clients tips on the best way of looking for a job.

Clergy

A career in the clergy is unlike any other. Members of the clergy counsel people of their faith and provide spiritual leadership within their communities. They enable people to worship according to the dictates of their consciences. As spiritual leaders, members of the clergy are widely regarded as models for moral and ethical conduct.

They frequently counsel people who have problems in their jobs, homes, schools, or social relationships; often, these are emotional problems. In fact, they deal in such delicate personal and emotional areas that the law provides that they need not disclose the nature of their communications with their congregants.

Members of the clergy help people in their commun-

Straight talk about adjusting to life "outside" can help a prisoner after he is released.

ities in many other ways. They may set up programs that feed the poor, care for the sick, provide companionship for the lonely, and involve children and adults in educational and recreational activities.

The three major religions in the United States are the Protestant, Roman Catholic, and Jewish faiths. But there are quite a few other religions in this country, too. How many can you name? In each of these, the clergy lead and counsel members of their congregation, conduct services, and represent their faith within the community.

Other Social Service Occupations

Other occupations involve helping people, too. *Cooperative extension service workers* work with people who live in rural areas. They teach and provide technical assistance in agriculture and home economics. Encouraging youth activities is another important part of the job.

Home economists provide training and technical assistance in areas that make everyday life more comfortable and livable—consumer economics, housing, home management, home furnishings and equipment, food and nutrition, clothing and textiles, and family development and relations.

Park, recreation, and leisure service workers plan, organize, and direct activities that help people enjoy themselves, learn something new, or find a way of getting closer to nature and the environment.

Personal Characteristics

People in social service occupations become closely involved with other people's lives and their advice can have far-reaching effects. A social worker's advice may lead an individual to change the course of his or her life. That's a big responsibility. For this reason, a genuine *concern for people* and a *desire to help them* are essential for anyone considering a career in this field.

In order to make a difference in others' lives, however, you must be *good at dealing with people*. You need the sort of personality that puts other people at ease and encourages them to open up. The ability to achieve a warm relationship with others is important in all of these occupations. Your effectiveness will depend on your ability to listen, understand, explain, and persuade.

You should be *sensitive* and *tactful* and have a keen sense of what words or actions might offend others. Anyone who comes in contact with people's deepest feelings and beliefs—as members of the clergy and counselors often do–needs *empathy*, the ability to sense others' feelings. *Patience*, too, is required, for you may be dealing

Social Service Occupations

with people who are confused, hesitant, fearful, angry, and hard to talk to. Often, they aren't clear themselves about what the problem is—or how it should be dealt with.

Imagination and *resourcefulness* are necessary. People in these occupations may have to call on all their mental resources to find a solution. And sometimes just as much ingenuity is required to get a client to accept a suggestion.

Speaking and *writing skills* are important. In some of these jobs, workers have to keep a lot of notes and records. They must be able to present all the important points about a client's situation clearly and quickly. Verbal skills are also necessary. Counselors and social workers must be able to communicate on a one-to-one basis, and to work easily with groups. There also are occasions when they must speak before large audiences. Members of the clergy, of course, do this regularly.

Finally, workers in the social service occupations should know themselves—their own strengths, weaknesses, and goals. *Emotional stability* is important because people in this field are so often in touch with situations that are worrisome or depressing. There are "occupational hazards" in this work. There is danger of being overwhelmed by others' misery, the danger of expecting too much of yourself, the danger of "burning

out" and losing the sensitivity that brought you to the field in the first place. The inner strength that comes with emotional stability will help you remain levelheaded and objective so that you can in fact *help* people—not just sympathize with them.

Training

Training for a social service career ranges from just a few weeks for an aide to many years for a professional. If you were a hotline volunteer, for example, you'd be given a 1- or 2-week course right after you began work. Training for homemaker-home health aides is handled much the same way. Many other social service aides—those doing valuable work in reaching out to their neighbors and others in need—have little formal training. They don't even have to be high school graduates, for that matter. What counts in getting their jobs and doing them well is their understanding of their community . . . and their ability to deal with people.

For professional occupations such as social worker and counselor, however, 6 to 8 years of study after high

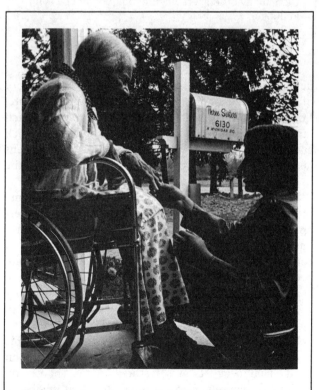

Some social workers specialize in serving the elderly.

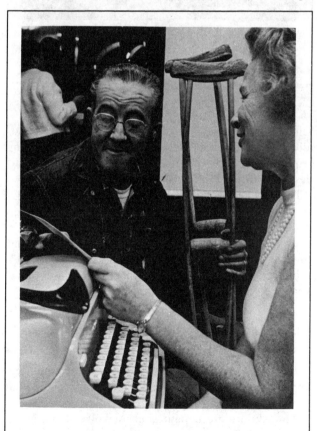

The staff at this center for the handicapped help clients believe in themselves.

Exploring Careers

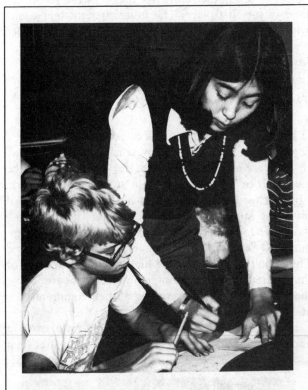

School counselors give tests to get a clearer picture of students' interests and abilities.

Community organizers need to be good at speaking in public.

school are necessary. Rabbis, priests, and ministers usually have even more training than this. The training required for each of 13 social service occupations is described in the Job Facts at the end of the chapter.

To see whether this field really is for you, try doing volunteer work in your spare time. There are many things you can do as a volunteer. Your teacher or counselor can provide you with suggestions. Bear in mind, however, that your duties as a volunteer are not likely to be the same as those of a social service professional, whose job requires years of formal training.

A Final Word

If the idea of working with people and helping them appeals to you, there are other chapters of this book that you might want to read.

The education occupations also involve reaching out to people—advising, suggesting, persuading, motivating, and teaching. A story about a school counselor is one of several in the chapter on Education Occupations.

Cooperative extension service work is another way of helping people by teaching and advising them. The story of a county agent appears in the chapter on Agriculture, Forestry, and Fishery Occupations. These workers teach farmers about new methods of raising crops and livestock and help homeowners keep their lawns and gardens healthy. Their work is considered an "extension" of the State agricultural university's teaching and research.

Health workers and social service workers need some of the same personal traits. Physicians, nurses, and therapists who deal with sick or handicapped people on a one-to-one basis must be objective, resourceful—and compassionate. The ability to encourage and inspire people, so important in the rehabilitation counselor's job, is just as important for the physical therapist. The story of a physical therapist appears in the chapter on Health Occupations.

Planners, like social workers, often work with people in their neighborhoods and communities for the common good. That occupation is featured in the chapter on Office Occupations. Another occupation that involves a sensitivity to public concerns and an understanding of people's behavior in groups is political aide, described in the chapter on Social Scientists.

Protestant Minister

"I work hard preparing a sermon," emphasizes Reverend Spencer, "because it's my opportunity to reach many people at one time."

Exploring Careers

The phone rang in the Reverend William Spencer's bedroom just before dawn one September morning. Mrs. Wilson, a member of his congregation, was sobbing uncontrollably at the other end of the line. "Reverend Spencer," she finally managed to say, "my husband died in his sleep last night and I don't know what to do."

The clergyman came awake immediately. He calmed Mrs. Wilson, then said, "I'll be at your house in 20 minutes." Dressing quickly, he rushed down the stairs and out the front door, started his car, and drove through the silent streets to the Wilsons' house. There he found his parishioner crying soundlessly. He spoke gently, preparing her to cope with the immediate situation. After a while, Rev. Spencer reported the death to the police and placed a call to a local funeral home. Then he phoned a neighbor and asked her to stay with Mrs. Wilson that day, until her son and daughter-in-law arrived from out of town. It was nearly 9 o'clock by the time Rev. Spencer left, confident that Mrs. Wilson had the help she'd need to get through the rest of this tragic day.

As he drove back toward his church, he thought about how helpless he sometimes felt in the face of a parishioner's grief. It still wasn't easy to find the right words, although he'd helped people deal with pain and sorrow many times during his years in the ministry.

He hadn't originally intended to enter the clergy. In college, he had been deeply concerned about social justice, the morality of war, and fundamental issues of right and wrong. He found himself translating his concern into social action—organizing programs to help the poor and taking part in demonstrations—and by his junior year Bill Spencer decided that he had a "calling." The ministry, he believed, offered him a meaningful way to spend his life.

After he graduated from college, he entered the seminary and spent the next 3 years studying there. In the seminary, he had learned a great deal about religion. He had learned about himself. And he had learned about working with people. During his first year as a seminarian, he served as chaplain in a local hospital. There he had learned to understand grief and to help people deal with the shock of sudden loss, just as he had helped Mrs. Wilson today. After he completed his training in the seminary, he was ordained as minister.

His first church was in a suburb of Columbus, Ohio. The bishop arranged for him to serve there for 1 year. After that, he was on his own. He remembered the day a classmate from the seminary had told him about the job opening here at St. Andrew's. He had applied along with 75 other ministers and was fortunate enough to be chosen for an interview. Finally, after several interviews, he was invited to serve this congregation. He remembered feeling a great sense of joy—and relief! The competition had been tough but somehow it seemed as though this church had been his destiny. He hoped so, anyway.

Rev. Spencer pulled into the church parking lot just in time for the 9:30 meeting with the vestry—members of the congregation who serve as a board of directors. Today they would be discussing a proposal to build a new wing for the church school.

Jim Atwood began by saying, "I like the idea, but we just don't have the money for the new wing. Why don't we wait a couple of years and then perhaps we will be able to afford it." Several other board members agreed.

Then Rev. Spencer spoke up. "First," he said, "I have to point out that we desperately need the additional classroom space. As you all know, we're overcrowded now—mainly because our program is such a success. Take our activities for teens, as just one example. We have teenagers here several nights a week. They have a Bible study group; they run the youth hotline; and they come for folk dancing and other strictly social gatherings. There's just as much demand for meeting room space from our adult groups. Not to speak of the children who use the rooms in the daytime!"

"Second," Rev. Spencer continued, "I believe that we can raise the money for the building expansion if we try hard enough. Remember last year we felt we couldn't afford to hire an additional minister to help with our youth program, but we took on an assistant anyway? The church activities and projects she's planned have helped us reach many more young people than we did before. I think you'd agree that we're making a real difference in their lives. Our youth progam is so important to us that, as you know, we've managed to find a way to pay for it. I believe we can be just as successful in finding the money to expand our school.

"Let's not give up on the new wing," the minister concluded. "Let's explore ways of raising the funds we need."

After the meeting with the vestry, Rev. Spencer spent a few minutes with the church music director. They were doing lots of exciting things with music at the church these days. One of the services Sunday would feature folk music, and the guitarists would need rehearsal space at least one night this week. The organist and the church choir would be rehearsing on Tuesday, as usual; they were preparing some new hymns for the other two services on Sunday. Later in the year, the church musicians hoped to produce their own version of a medieval mystery play—a religious drama with music and dance. One of the parishioners was already working on the choreography. Opportunities like these for artistic and

Social Service Occupations

Reverend Spencer's job involves a lot of time away from the pulpit.

intellectual creativity made Rev. Spencer feel he was lucky indeed in his life's work. He also was glad he had this particular congregation.

Just before lunch there was a brief meeting with other members of the church staff—the sexton, the church school director, and the assistant ministers. Together, they reviewed some of the many programs that the church sponsored in the community. At today's session, they concentrated on the Saturday field trips the church ran during the school year for children from all parts of the city. Very few Spanish-speaking children participated, although the city had a large Hispanic community. Various suggestions for reaching out to these children were discussed, but the meeting came to an end before anything was decided. "That's often the way," thought Rev. Spencer, who felt too much of his time was spent in meetings.

Rev. Spencer did not have any appointments scheduled for early afternoon, which meant he had a good stretch of time to work on his sermon for next Sunday.

And, before the afternoon was over, he hoped to be able to spend some time visiting members of the congregation who were sick or lonely or in need of spiritual counsel. There were many people—too many—who needed comfort that day. A young woman who had attempted suicide was still in the hospital. A widower was having so much trouble adjusting to life without his wife that it was clear to Rev. Spencer that some special effort would have to be made to help him. And several families, he knew, had more than their share of pain right now. It bothered Rev. Spencer a great deal to realize that he wouldn't be able to visit all the people who needed consolation that day. The conflicting demands on his time weren't easy to resolve, and he prayed for guidance when he had to make difficult decisions such as these.

As he glanced at his appointment calender, Rev. Spencer saw that he was scheduled to see Bob Dudney and Gretchen Moser that evening to discuss their forthcoming marriage. Helping two young people get a good start in marriage was the sort of thing he most liked to do. It was a joyous task, one that lifted his spirits even at the end of a long day.

Bob and Gretchen were waiting nervously in the comfortable, book-lined study when Rev. Spencer walked in shortly after 8 o'clock. "Sorry to keep you waiting," he said. "Now let's get to the matter at hand. I'm amazed at how much it takes to keep a marriage together today. I was reading in the *Journal of Applied Psychology* that one theorist believes that the stress some marriages cause is equal to that experienced by a soldier in combat."

"Does that mean I'm liable to get shot?" asked Bob as he nervously shifted in his chair.

"No, no," replied the minister, chuckling. "But it does mean that many married people believe it is easier to go AWOL—absent without leave—than to stay in there and keep trying. What I think we need to discuss tonight is how to make marriage work. I don't have all the answers. But I have a good sense of the kinds of things that cause trouble in a marriage. What do you think the most common marital problems are, Gretchen?"

"Well, let's see. Money and not getting along with each other?"

"Two very common ones," Rev. Spencer assured her. "What are your guesses, Bob?"

"I guess I'd say sex problems and poor communication."

"Both of you are on the right track, but you left out a very common problem."

"Tell us what it is!" said Bob quickly.

"In-laws. Believe it or not, in-laws can be the source of a lot of marital difficulties. Almost without realizing it, and certainly without meaning it, your parents can cause tension in your marriage."

"I should have thought of that myself," groaned Gretchen. "Particularly with your mother, Bob!" she said, half teasingly.

"Is your mother a problem, Bob?" probed the minister.

"Oh, no real problem. She's just having a hard time accepting the fact that I'm actually getting married. I think she'd like to have me around the house for a few more years. But she'll get used to all of this in time!"

"Not without your help, Bob," Rev. Spencer said sternly.

"What do you mean by that?"

"It is important that you both begin presenting yourselves as a team to your families. Get in the habit of saying things like, "I'll have to discuss that with Gretchen," or "I'll have to ask Bob what he thinks about that." As the Bible says, "Leave thy mother and thy father and cleave unto thy wife." There is a world of truth in that verse. It doesn't mean that you stop loving your mother and father—it just means that you love one another more. Nothing should supersede the importance of the marital relationship. Am I getting through to you?"

"Yes, I think so," said Bob slowly. "Do you mean that before my mom can respect Gretchen as my wife, she'll have to see that I do?"

"That's exactly what I mean," said Rev. Spencer with a glow in his eyes. "You have a commitment to each other as life partners."

"Sounds like good advice," said Gretchen seriously. "How about discussing some of the other problems, Reverend? Or don't we have time tonight?"

"Let's save them for our next session, okay?" said the minister warmly.

Exploring

A member of the clergy must have a compelling sense that serving God and working for the betterment of humanity should be his or her life's work.

- Do you feel strongly about your faith and your religion?
- Are you active in your church?
- Are you interested in and concerned about problems in your community and in the world? Are you aware of such problems as poverty, hunger, poor housing, unemployment, injustice, and illiteracy in your own community?

The clergy must set an example of high moral and ethical conduct.

- Do questions and discussions about right and wrong interest you?
- Can you hold firmly to what you believe is right even when your friends don't agree?
- Do you treat others as you wish to be treated?
- Are you comfortable with the idea of people looking to you as an example?
- Would you mind having your life subject to public scrutiny?
- Are you conscious of your public responsibility when you are elected to the student council, chosen to be yearbook or newspaper editor, or asked to chair a church or school club?

The clergy must be approachable and warm since personal counseling is one of their prime responsibilities.

- Can you make a friend feel better about a problem such as failing a test or being turned down for a date?

Social Service Occupations

- Do people come to you for advice?
- Are you able to keep a secret?
- Are your friends able to talk to you about "anything?"
- Are you able to put house guests at ease?
- Are you able to talk to people you don't know very well?

The clergy must have the ability to inspire others.

- Have you ever changed a friend's viewpoint?
- Can you argue your point persuasively?
- Do your friends ask your opinion on things?
- Are you able to get your way without seeming bossy?
- Do you understand the importance of praising a child when he or she behaves very well, does a lesson correctly, or masters a skill?
- Can you see that such praise "works" with grownups too?
- Can you help people to help themselves?

A member of the clergy must be able to command the attention of a group.

- Are you good at making class presentations?
- Is it easy for you to "get the floor" at club meetings or parties?
- Do your friends ever ask you to be the spokesperson for a group? At a friend's going-away party? At a victory celebration? At a birthday party?

In order to help others, clergy must be able to regulate their own reactions to the crises in people's lives.

- Can you remain calm when a friend or relative faces a very serious problem?
- Can you remain calm when a parent is upset?
- Can you think and act quickly in a crisis situation?
- Does it upset you to visit people who are very sick?
- Can you comfort a friend or family member during a time of sorrow?
- Can you overcome your anger and keep from holding a grudge when someone hurts you?
- Can you maintain some sense of proportion about school rivalries?

The clergy must perform ceremonies and conform to traditional rituals.

- Do you enjoy initiation ceremonies?
- Do you understand the importance of such ceremonies as confirmation, marriage, or graduation?
- Do you understand the importance of school and community awards for scholarship, athletic ability, bravery, or public spiritedness?

The clergy must be creative in communicating their ideas.

- Are you good at writing compositions or short stories?
- Can you write an interesting letter to a friend?
- Do you like thinking of ways to interest children in their school work? In crafts or sports? In Bible verses?

Teaching children the rituals of their faith is one of the many ways this rabbi serves his congregation.

Social Worker

Mary Rogers is a social worker at a senior center.

Social Service Occupations

Mary Rogers is a social worker. Her office is in a senior center in one of the poorer sections of the city. Her job there is to find places to live for elderly people who have no home of their own. Some of Mary's clients are former mental patients. Having lived for years in institutions where other people made all the decisions, they do not find it easy to manage on their own. Some of them are too confused or afraid to talk to a landlord or landlady about renting a room. Others are illiterate. Since they can't read, they can't use the newspaper want ads to find a place to live. All of Mary's clients are poor.

The program she runs was Mary's idea in the first place. Basically, she does three things: She finds sponsors willing to take elderly people into their homes, interviews clients who need homes, and keeps up with any problems that might develop. So many problems *do* come up that Mary spends most of her time talking with people, listening, and sorting things out.

Mary never knows what to expect when she sits down to talk with one of her clients. She's found that some of these conversations enrich her life and brighten her day—much as her talks with her grandmother did when she was growing up.

Mary's grandmother was a good friend. The two of them found a lot to talk about, for they shared an enthusiasm for living. Mary never tired of listening to her grandmother's stories about the years she worked as a union organizer in a mill town. The girl had listened, spellbound, to tales of the hardship and heartbreak endured by workers' families in those difficult days. The older woman's insights into human nature and compassion for people in trouble had made a strong impression on Mary.

She began considering ways in which she, too, could work with people and help them. That eventually had led to a master's degree in social work and the important decision to specialize in work with the elderly.

Mr. Adams is one of Mary's clients at the senior center. He's one of her most exasperating clients, for Mr. Adams has a drinking problem. His bouts with the bottle are causing sleepless nights for the Youngs, his home sponsors. Today, there was a note on Mary's desk from Mrs. Young. She wanted to talk with Mary right away; she couldn't stand to have Mr. Adams in her house one day longer.

"I can't take it any more," Mrs. Young greeted Mary as the social worker came up the front steps. "Last night he got so drunk that he sang until 4 o'clock in the morning! It's just too much for me to handle."

Mary managed to patch things up for the time being. There was a promise of one last try from Mrs. Young and a pledge to keep sober from Mr. Adams. She knew, however, that in just a few days she was likely to have

another desperate message from Mrs. Young. She'd have to start planning ahead for Mr. Adams.

Mary returned to her office just as a busload of the center's members was returning from a trip to the zoo. She could hear the excitement in their voices as they came inside. "It's amazing how a change of scene can lift people's spirits," Mary thought.

Just then she caught sight of Mrs. Hodge in the hallway. Mrs. Hodge hadn't gone on the outing to the zoo, and Mary knew she'd welcome some special attention.

"Mrs. Hodge, let's go back to my office so we can talk."

Mrs. Hodge was a gentle, rather timid woman who had taken a bad fall the winter before and was still suffering from the pain in her hip. "I've just been to the doctor," she said with a sigh as she painfully lowered herself in the chair across from Mary.

"It hurts right now, doesn't it, Mrs. Hodge?" Mary inquired in a sympathetic tone.

"Oh yes, dear, it does hurt. I just wish the doctor would visit with me a little longer. I saw him this morning, you know. It's so hard for me to get to the clinic and then I have to wait at least an hour to see him and, well, I think he should extend me the courtesy of a little talk. Don't you, Mary?"

"Absolutely, Mrs. Hodge, that's entirely reasonable. We all need some time to discuss our problems, physical or otherwise."

"Well, anyway, he gave me another prescription for the pain. I have to get over to the drug store before it closes."

"Why don't I pick up the medicine and drop it by your house tonight on my way home from work?"

"Oh, would you, Mary? Thank you. That's so kind of you." The older woman's eyes filled with tears.

Emotional moments like these punctuated Mary's day. But, she reminded herself, they happened only if you really cared about people. That, she knew, was what social work was all about—caring for people enough to help them make their own decisions about their problems.

Right after lunch, a sandwich at her desk, Mary called a meeting of the social workers she supervised. Together, Mary and the others reviewed the caseload for the center's home placement program, concentrating on cases that were causing problems. One of the workers wanted ideas for dealing with a client who spent all of her money early in the month and then had nothing to live on until the next check came. After discussing a number of possibilities, Mary suggested that the social worker arrange for the client to get her money a little at a time throughout the month instead of receiving everything at once.

Mary spent the rest of the afternoon making final arrangements for tomorrow's forum on the needs of the city's elderly. The forum was sponsored by We Care, a coalition of local organizations including senior centers, churches, legal aid programs, and citizens' groups. Mary was one of the founders of the coalition. She and the others who had started the group just 3 years ago wanted to educate the public—and influence city officials—about the problems faced by elderly people in their city. They arranged for newspaper and television coverage, made speeches, testified before the city council, and sponsored public forums such as the one that would take place tomorrow.

We Care already had focused attention on proposed cutbacks in Medicaid payments and improper procedures in assigning apartments in the city's public housing project for the elderly. By now, local politicians took the coalition seriously. The mayor herself had agreed to attend tomorrow's forum.

As Mary walked through the double doors of the municipal auditorium the next day, she noticed that a busload of people from her senior center already had arrived. More elderly people were coming in every minute. They looked purposeful; many compared notes.

"I hope the mayor is prepared for this one," Mary thought. "The audience certainly is prepared for her."

After several minutes, the mayor arrived. She walked briskly to the podium, apologized for being late, and asked for questions. Soon they were coming thick and fast—questions on property taxes, housing, crime, transportation, red tape. Most of the questioners were older people—some retired, some still working, all concerned about the inconveniences and hardships they faced because of diminished incomes and diminishing strength. A tall, elegant, white-haired woman moved slowly through the hall to the speaker's podium. She lived in a nursing home, and the plastic identification band around her wrist clashed incongruously with her beautifully tailored suit. She spoke movingly of the need for transportation services for people who, like herself, were infirm. And for people who were handicapped.

As the mayor spelled out the details of a tax relief proposal she had just put before the city council, Mary's attention wandered. The meeting appeared to be a success. Elected officials were listening to citizens' concerns. She found herself thinking how important that was ... and how much she liked being one of the people who made such a meeting possible.

Yes, she was pleased with her job. She enjoyed finding ways to help people take charge of their lives. And she knew that in helping older people now, she was helping the older person she would be herself one day.

Still, what *would* she do about Mr. Adams?

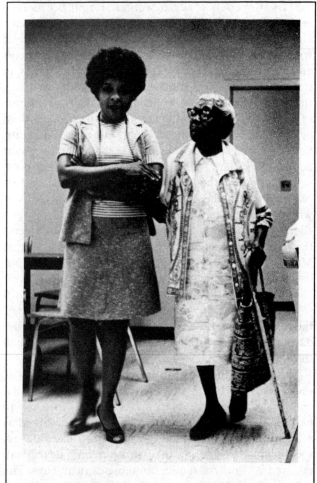

"By helping older people now," says Mary, "I am helping the older person that I will be."

Exploring

In order to give people the confidence to deal with their problems, social workers must value the dignity and worth of the individual.

- Do you believe that you can learn something from everyone?
- Do you feel badly when a classmate is embarrassed?
- Do you think it's important that all people enjoy equal rights?
- Do you want to be personally involved in working for social justice? Do you want to do something about poverty, hunger, or hatred?
- Are you open-minded about other people's right to think, feel, and act in ways that may seem strange, even wrong, to you?
- Do you think people who are unhappy or mixed up or in trouble can be helped?

Social Service Occupations

Mary finds that conversations with clients frequently enrich her life and brighten her day.

Social workers must show their concern for people through a manner that is sympathetic yet objective.

- Are you able to see both sides of an argument?
- When something goes wrong, what do you do first? Look for a solution or place the blame?
- Are you happy for your friends when they meet with good fortune?
- Do you feel a genuine concern for your friends' and relatives' welfare?
- Do you like most people?
- Are you aware and considerate of the feelings of others?

Social workers must build a basis for trust.

- Are you able to maintain friendships over long periods of time?
- Do your friends confide in you?
- Do people often ask your advice or opinion?
- Are you able to keep a secret?
- Do you make friends easily?
- Are you able to make your house guests feel welcome?
- Are you able to put people at ease?

- Can you work closely with others and be flexible enough to do things someone else's way?

Social workers must understand human behavior.

- Do you know your own strengths and weaknesses?
- Do you understand why you do the things you do?
- Do you understand why your parents do the things they do?
- Do you know when to speak and when to listen?
- Are you able to get your friends to do things your way without seeming bossy?
- Are you able to feel what kind of mood a friend is in just by observing his or her facial and body expression or tone of voice?
- Are you more apt to judge people by their good points than by their faults?

Social workers must be able to speak the client's language. They must be good at communicating effectively in different kinds of situations.

- Can you talk to all kinds of people?
- Are you able to carry on a conversation with a child?
- Are you able to express your feelings to most adults?
- Are you good at speaking in front of a group?
- Are you ever asked to be the spokesperson for a group?

Social workers must be able to express themselves clearly in the written record of their work.

- Are you good at organizing your thoughts for a school assignment or an essay question on an exam?
- Are you good at writing compositions?
- Do you enjoy writing to your friends?

Social workers don't always see the results of their work immediately. Often they must remain supportive and helpful during times of slow progress.

- Do you appreciate small gains or progress?
- Do you have the patience to grow a garden?
- Do you have the patience to pursue projects such as needle work or modelbuilding?
- Are you able to stick with a diet or exercise program?
- Can you be patient with people whose pace is slower than yours?
- Can you persist in the face of setbacks?
- Can you cope with failure?
- Are you realistic in your expectations even though you may be idealistic in your goals?

Exploring Careers

Job Facts

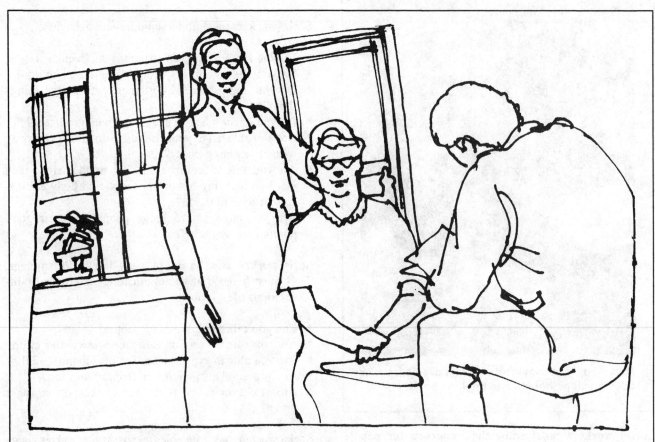

There isn't room in this book for a story about every social service occupation. However, you'll find some important facts about 13 of these occupations in the following section. If you want additional information about any of them, you might begin by consulting the *Occupational Outlook Handbook*, a publication of the Department of Labor which should be available in your school or public library.

Occupation	Nature and Places of Work	Training and Qualifications	Other Information
COUNSELING OCCUPATIONS			
School Counselors	School counselors help students understand themselves and resolve their problems. They give aptitude, interest, and ability tests. They hold individual and group sessions so that students can "talk through" their concerns. They may teach classes in occupations and careers or other special subjects. Most counselors work in elementary or secondary schools.	A master's degree in counseling and some teaching experience usually are necessary. Most States require school counselors to have counseling and teaching certificates. The education and experience requirements for these certificates vary among States. School counselors must be able to deal with all types of people. They work with students, parents, teachers, and school administrators.	Some counselors work part time as consultants for private or public counseling centers, government agencies, or private businesses.

Social Service Occupations

Occupation	Nature and Places of Work	Training and Qualifications	Other Information
College Career Planning and Placement Counselors	These workers help college students and graduates examine their career goals and find jobs. Sometimes they arrange for job recruiters to visit the campus and set up interviews with students. They work for colleges and universities and for community and junior colleges.	A bachelor's degree in psychology or sociology is customary for a job in this field. A master's degree in clinical or counseling psychology is helpful. People in this field should be energetic and able to work under pressure because they must organize and administer a wide variety of activities. They must have an interest in people and be able to get along with them easily.	These workers also are known as college placement officers. These workers frequently work more than 40 hours a week. The workload is especially heavy during the recruiting season.
Employment Counselors	Employment counselors help people who are looking for jobs. They interview job seekers to find out about their interests, training, work experience, and personal traits. Then they may suggest specific jobs and how to apply for them, or recommend job training. They also contact employers to find out what kinds of workers they need. Over half work in public employment service offices located everywhere in the country. Many work for private employment agencies. Some work for community agencies concerned with finding jobs for teenagers, ex-offenders, handicapped persons, older workers, and other people in special need of counseling.	Training requirements vary depending on the employer. A bachelor's degree generally is the minimum educational requirement, and many jobs require graduate courses in counseling plus counseling experience. Many agencies prefer to hire people with a master's degree in counseling or in a related field such as psychology or personnel administration. Persons who want to be employment counselors should have a strong interest in helping others make vocational plans and carry them out. They should be able to work independently and to keep detailed records.	Well-qualified counselors with experience may advance to supervisory or administrative positions in their own or other organizations. Some may become directors of agencies, or area supervisors of guidance programs; some may become consultants; and others may become professors in the counseling field.
Rehabilitation Counselors	Rehabilitation counselors help people who are mentally or physically disabled or emotionally disturbed. They give them the support and encouragement they need to live with a disability, learn a job skill, or adjust to a new way of life. Counselors may find jobs for disabled persons and follow their progress. Many counselors specialize. They may work exclusively with blind people, alcoholics, drug addicts, the mentally ill, or retarded persons. They work in rehabilitation centers, sheltered workshops, hospitals, and special schools and training institutions.	A bachelor's degree is the minimum educational requirement. The master's degree in rehabilitation counseling or vocational counseling often is preferred. A master's degree in psychology, education, or social work also provides a good background. Work experience in related fields is also an asset. Because they deal with the welfare of individuals, the ability to accept responsibility is important. Patience, the ability to motivate others, and emotional stability are important in dealing with severely disabled people.	Rehabilitation counselors generally work a 40-hour week or less, with some overtime work required to attend community and civic meetings in the evening.

389

Exploring Careers

Occupation	Nature and Places of Work	Training and Qualifications	Other Information
CLERGY			
Protestant Ministers	Protestant ministers lead their congregations in worship services and administer the rites of baptism, confirmation, and Holy Communion. They prepare and deliver sermons and instruct persons who wish to join the church. They counsel church members, visit the sick, comfort the bereaved, and serve church members in many other ways. Most ministers serve individual congregations in churches throughout the country. Some work as chaplains in hospitals, prisons, and the Armed Forces. Still others work in social service agencies or community organizations that serve youth or families.	Educational requirements vary greatly among the various Protestant denominations. Many require a 3-year course of study in a theological school or seminary following college graduation. All ministers must be ordained by their denomination.	Persons who are interested in entering the Protestant ministry should seek the counsel of a minister of church guidance worker. In some denominations, ministers are assigned to their jobs, which may mean moving to a new area, possibly every few years.
Rabbis	Rabbis are spiritual leaders for their congregations and teachers and interpreters of Jewish law and tradition. They conduct religious services, deliver sermons, visit the sick, help the poor, comfort the bereaved, supervise religious education, and involve themselves in community affairs. Rabbis serve congregations in all parts of the country. Some serve as chaplains; others work in Jewish community service agencies; still others teach Jewish studies in colleges and universities.	To become eligible for ordination as a rabbi, a student must complete a prescribed course of study in a seminary. Entrance requirements and curriculum depend upon the branch of Judaism with which the seminary is associated. Courses studied in Jewish seminaries generally provide students with knowledge of the Bible, Talmud, Rabbinic literature, Jewish history, and theology, and courses in education, pastoral psychology, and public speaking.	Nearly all rabbis serve Orthodox, Conservative, or Reform congregations. Persons who are interested in becoming rabbis should discuss their plans for a vocation with a practicing rabbi.

Social Service Occupations

Occupation	Nature and Places of Work	Training and Qualifications	Other Information
Roman Catholic Priests	Roman Catholic priests attend to the spiritual, pastoral, moral, and educational needs of members of their church. They conduct religious services, administer the Sacraments, give sermons, visit the sick, comfort the bereaved, help the poor, and work on behalf of the community in many ways. Most priests serve Catholic congregations in all parts of the country. Some, however, teach or do administrative work instead. They work in Catholic seminaries, colleges and universities, and high schools; in Catholic social service and welfare agencies; and in missionary organizations.	Preparation for the priesthood generally requires 8 years of study beyond high school. Over 450 seminaries offer this training. The Roman Catholic priesthood is open only to unmarried males.	There are two types of priests: Diocesan and religious. Diocesan priests work individually within a parish, while religious priests work as part of a religious order. Young men interested in entering the priesthood should seek the guidance and counsel of their parish priest. Priests are assigned to their jobs by the superiors in their religious order. They are usually transferred to new assignments every few years, which often requires moving.

OTHER SOCIAL SERVICE OCCUPATIONS

Occupation	Nature and Places of Work	Training and Qualifications	Other Information
Cooperative Extension Service Workers	These workers conduct educational programs for rural residents. They give farmers technical advice; help farm families learn about home economics and home management; organize activities for youth; and help community leaders plan economic development. Extension workers usually specialize. They may deal primarily with farmers; with community leaders; or with youth.	Extension workers must have at least a bachelor's degree in their subject field. They often receive additional training on the job. They should like working with people and have a genuine desire to help them. A farm background is almost a requirement for agricultural extension workers. High school courses in English, public speaking, science, and math are helpful.	Most extension service offices are located in small towns. People who are good at teaching and getting ideas across, and who wish to live outside the city, may find extension work the ideal career.
Home Economists	Home economists work to improve products, services, and practices that affect the comfort and well-being of the family. Most home economists teach. Others do research or test products for business firms and trade associations. Still others do research or serve as consultants for agricultural experiment stations, colleges, universities, and private organizations. Some advise and counsel the public on home management, consumer issues, and family budgeting.	A bachelor's degree in home economics qualifies graduates for most entry positions in the field. A master's or doctor's degree is required for college teaching, certain research and supervisory positions, work as an extension specialist, and for some jobs in nutrition. The ability to write and speak well is important. High school courses in home economics, speech, English, health, mathematics, chemistry, and the social sciences are helpful.	Employment of home economists is affected by growing public awareness of the contributions that can be made by home economists in child care, nutrition, housing and furnishings design, clothing and textiles, consumer education, and ecology.

Exploring Careers

Occupation	Nature and Places of Work	Training and Qualifications	Other Information
Homemaker-Home Health Aides	These workers come to people's homes and help with routine health care, shopping, cooking, cleaning, and many other every-day chores. Usually, their help is needed because the client is sick or disabled and has no family or friends to take care of these things. Sometimes, the client is a parent whose small children require care. Homemaker-home health aides are employed by public health and welfare departments, private health care agencies, and non-profit community health or welfare organizations, such as visiting nurse associations. Some work for hospitals and nursing homes that have home care programs.	A high school education is recommended, but not required. Aides are trained on the job. A sense of responsibility, the desire to help people, and a willingness to perform hard work are important to this job.	Nursing students or college students in appropriate fields such as home economics or social work can often find summer work as aides.
Park, Recreation, and Leisure Service Workers	These workers plan, organize, and direct individual and group activities that help people enjoy their leisure hours. Most work for city and county park and recreation departments and State park systems. Others work for National Parks, the Peace Corps, Vista, Boys' and Girls' Clubs, senior centers, hospitals, private amusement parks, and apartment complexes.	A college degree in recreation and leisure services is an asset. Creativity, the ability to motivate people, and good health are useful personal attributes for potential recreation workers.	There are numerous opportunities for volunteer work in this field.

Social Service Occupations

Occupation	Nature and Places of Work	Training and Qualifications	Other Information
Social Service Aides	These workers serve as a link between professional social workers or rehabilitation counselors and people who need help. They explain the services the agency provides, help clients fill out forms, and keep records. Aides often specialize. Their job titles reflect the kind of work they do: Income maintenance worker, casework aide, neighborhood worker, employment aide, chore worker, and homemaker-home health aide. Almost all work for social service agencies run by local health or welfare departments or by voluntary or religious organizations. Some work in hospitals, clinics, community health programs, schools, and public housing projects.	A high school education is recommended, but not required. Persons seeking jobs in this field should get along well with people and be able to work as part of a team. They should be tactful, courteous, and want to help others.	Opportunities for part-time work are very good.
Social Workers	Social workers help individuals, families, groups, and communities understand and deal with their problems. Most social workers are employed by social service agencies run by State and local governments; voluntary organizations such as the Salvation Army; and by religious organizations such as Catholic Charities. Some are college teachers, researchers, or consultants. Others are in private practice and provide counseling services to individuals and groups.	For many jobs, a master's degree in social work is required or preferred. This takes 2 years of study after college and includes a "field placement" that provides actual job experience. For other jobs, a bachelor's degree—in social work, psychology, sociology, education, or a related field—is sufficient. Many States require that social workers be licensed.	Students should get as much related work experience as possible during high school and college to see whether they are interested and able to do the work. Working part time as a social service aide is a good way to obtain this experience.

Exploring Careers

Employment counselors can show people where to find career information and get a better job.

It takes creativity to dance in a manner that moves an audience.

Exploring Careers

"Bravo!" The applause was thunderous. The curtain opened once more and the performers took a final bow. As the curtains swung closed again, the auditorium lights came on.

Backstage, Sally and Betsy hugged each other in delight. Jake, Kevin, and John laughed and talked excitedly. They had good reason to be elated: The play had been a huge success.

"You were terrific!" John told Sally. "You really had the audience in the palm of your hand."

"I knew they were with me," Sally agreed. "I could feel their support. And they loved you too!"

Liz Swoyer, the drama teacher who had directed the play, rushed over to the students. "You were marvelous!" she said happily, embracing each one in turn.

"I guess we've learned the secret of success in performing," John said, looking over at Ms. Swoyer. "You have to win the audience over—get them on your side."

"Well, that's true," Ms. Swoyer agreed. "But it's easier said than done. Getting the audience to sympathize and identify with you takes talent and hard work. You know

yourselves how much practice you had to put in to get your lines just right and learn the action too. Each of you spent weeks trying to become the character you portrayed."

"Right," responded Kevin emphatically. "After a while I felt as though I could say my lines in my sleep."

"Me too," joined in Betsy, "I became so familiar with the character I was playing that I thought I knew how she would react in any situation."

Ms. Swoyer smiled and continued, "Of course, you're all talented and creative; that's important."

"It certainly is," laughed Jake as he looked at John. "You were pretty creative when you forgot your lines in the second act and had to ad lib. That was quick thinking—I'm sure nobody noticed."

"That's right," Ms. Swoyer joined in. "That was creative. So were the gestures you all incorporated into your roles. Betsy, when you started crying in the last scene I saw tears in the eyes of several people in the first row. It takes a great deal of creativity to interpret drama, music, or dance in a manner that moves an audience."

Getting the audience to identify with you takes talent and hard work.

Performing Arts, Design, and Communications Occupations

"You know," said Kevin, "I really was nervous before the show. I was sure my voice would crack, or I'd trip and fall, or my mind would go blank. I'm surprised at how quickly I lost my nervousness once I started saying my lines. I completely forgot my fears once the play began."

"You all handled yourselves very well," Ms. Swoyer said warmly. "Stage fright has ruined many a performance. Luckily, none of you seems to have a big problem with that. Stage presence is probably one of the most important qualities you need for success as a performer. As you probably know by now, stage presence is largely a matter of self-confidence. For some performers, it takes a long, long time to develop that self-confidence, and the jitters never really go away."

Jake spoke up. "Even though talent and creativity are very important, they're not enough to guarantee success. A good performance also requires practice and hard work. And even those aren't enough if the performers don't have that special magic called stage presence."

"You put that very well, Jake," replied Ms. Swoyer.

"But if you're already considering a career as an actor on the basis of tonight's triumph, there's one more thing to remember. Success in the performing arts often is a matter of sheer luck. No matter how good you are, there's no guarantee of success."

"Well," said John, "I'm so happy with the way things went tonight that I don't really care about finding the key to success. We can worry about that when we start rehearsing our next production. After we take off our stage makeup, why don't we all go over to my house for some music and food?"

Performing Arts Occupations

John, Betsy, and the other students so happily enjoying their moment of glory are amateur performers. Whether amateurs at Middlesex Junior High or professionals on Broadway, people in the performing arts are involved in creating and communicating ideas and emotions. Through their art, they're trying to say something about what it's like to be alive. Sometimes the message is

A good performance also requires many hours of practice.

Stage presence is one of the most important qualities for success as a performer.

Exploring Careers

Performers communicate feelings and emotions.

All kinds of performers use their talents to entertain people.

thoughtful, serious, profound; other times, it's joyful, lighthearted, even silly. In any event, when performers share their talents with an audience, they express themselves in a highly creative and personal manner. Indeed, for people with the personality, the talent, and the drive, the performing arts offer outstanding opportunities for self-expression.

We've already met some *actors and actresses.* What other performers come to mind? *Musicians,* perhaps—jazz musicians, folk musicians, rock musicians, members of symphony orchestras or chamber music ensembles, solo guitarists, violinists, pianists, and organists. Then there are the *singers*—opera singers, folk singers, pop singers, country and western singers, choral singers. And *dancers*—tap dancers, modern dancers, ballet dancers, chorus dancers, nightclub dancers. *Comedians* tell jokes to amuse people. *Magicians* perform sleight-of-hand to amaze and delight their audiences. *Mimes* act out scenes or imitate objects or animals using gestures but no words. *Television* or *movie stunt people* substitute for regular actors in scenes that require daredevil feats. Circus performers such as *lion tamers, tightrope walkers,* and *trapeze artists* thrill their audiences with daring deeds. *Clowns* make people laugh. *Gymnasts* and *figure skaters* fill crowds with admiration at their grace and skill.

What does it take for a career in the performing arts? *Talent* is probably the most essential quality for a performer. Without talent, all the years of study and practice may be wasted.

The performing arts are different from other arts in that the performer is an essential part of the product that he or she produces. That's why *stage presence* and the ability to communicate with an audience are so important. Performers must like expressing themselves in front of an audience in order to develop an exciting give-and-take with all those people on the other side of the footlights.

Other traits are needed, too. *Ambition* and *persistence* are necessary for success in this highly competitive field. Performers usually have to audition before they are hired—they have to "sell themselves" to critical producers, directors, or conductors. They may be in a show that folds because of empty houses and unfavorable reviews. There are, in fact, hundreds of reasons why performers need a temperament that urges them to keep going in spite of failures, a spirit that drives them to try, try again.

As Ms. Swoyer reminded the students, there's no guarantee of success if you decide to try a career in the performing arts. There is little financial security, working

Artists spend countless hours mastering new techniques.

hours are odd, and there sometimes is so much travel that it's hard to put down roots in a community. Yet many performers find the desire to express themselves so important that they take part-time jobs in other fields in order to earn enough money to live.

Design Occupations

People in design occupations use visual means to convey ideas and emotions. They use their hands as well as their minds to create things. Some create objects whose sole purpose is to be appreciated for their beauty. Others design objects that are meant to serve a useful purpose; the designer's aim is to make these objects attractive as well as useful. Let's explore some of the design occupations.

The works of art you see as you wander through a museum or an art gallery are examples of objects produced by people called "fine artists." The fine arts are concerned with beauty for its own sake. People who devote their lives to creating works of fine art include *painters* who paint landscapes, portraits, scenes of daily life, or abstract works. The fine arts also include the works of *sculptors*, who carve or model objects out of

This Pueblo artist uses traditional designs in his work.

399

Designing the layout of a book calls for a sense of balance and proportion.

clay, stone, metal, wood, and other materials, and the works of *printmakers*, who transfer images to paper, canvas, or cloth to reproduce a design they have already created.

Not many people are able to make a living solely in the fine arts. Many with an artistic flair work at jobs that have a more regular income, putting their talents to use designing the products we use every day and making our surroundings pleasant to look at. An *architect*, for example, designs the buildings you see around you. A *commercial artist* creates the artwork in the newspapers and magazines you read, on the packages and containers you pick up, and on the billboards or television commercials you see. A *display worker* designs and installs the displays in stores and store windows that attract you and other customers and encourage you to buy. A *floral designer* arranges flowers and greenery into the corsage or boutonniere you wear to a school dance. An *industrial designer* designs typewriters, telephone receivers, and other everyday industrial products—trying to make them as useful and attractive as possible. An *interior designer* decides what colors to use in a new office, how to arrange the space, and what furniture to buy. A *landscape architect* designs the lawns and shrubbery for a golf course or public garden. A *photographer* takes pictures of people, places, and things to convey an idea or tell a story.

These industrial designers are working on a full size model of a new car.

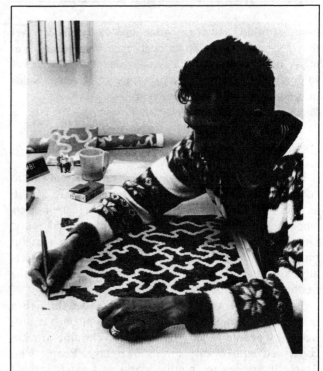

The ability to work on your own is important for people in the design field.

Performing Arts, Design, and Communications Occupations

Exhibit designers set up displays in museums, art galleries, and exhibitions; they figure out what objects to display and how to show them most effectively. *Costume designers* plan performers' wardrobes for theatrical productions, operas, ballets, movies, and television shows. *Clothing designers* develop ideas and patterns for the clothing we wear—everything from jackets to jeans. *Furniture designers* make sketches of new designs for the furniture in our homes, schools, and public buildings.

What does it take for a design career? *Artistic talent* is crucial. People in this field need a strong color sense, an eye for detail, and a sense of balance and proportion. An aesthetic sense, or *sensitivity to beauty*, is essential, since people in design must be aware of what is artistically good and what is not before they can produce works that are appealing to others.

Styles and tastes in art and fashion change with almost breathtaking speed, and people who work in this field need to be able to keep up. Much of the challenge of a design career lies in the opportunity to rely on your own creativity, to trust your own artistic instincts—all the while remaining open to new ideas and methods. Creativity does not always mean thinking up completely new ideas. Rather, creative expression may involve picking and choosing from ideas around you, and then bringing

A photographer must know what will make a good picture.

Floral design is taught in trade schools and community colleges.

English courses helped this woman prepare for her editorial job.

everything together to form something quite new. *Flexibility*, the ability to adjust to change, is important.

The persistence that comes from a *belief in your own artistic vision* is, at the same time, an important trait for someone in the design field. Creative work can be frustrating, even discouraging, during periods when new ideas don't come—or when your ideas clash with those of a client. There will be times when you'll have to change a concept or layout to accommodate your client. Handling this sort of situation requires flexibility, of course, and the ability to "sell" your ideas to other people. But it also takes a sure sense of your own artistic integrity. Only with a belief in your own ideas will you know when to change a design—and when not to.

Problem-solving ability is sometimes quite important, too, for often it is the designer's job to come up with a solution to a client's design problem that is both aesthetic and practical.

Self-discipline, motivation, the ability to work independently—all are important traits for people in the design field. These workers must be willing to assume responsibility for the final product. And since they often work on tight deadlines, they need the initiative to start projects on their own, to budget their time, and to complete everything as scheduled.

A feeling for language enables a writer to breathe life and meaning into the ordinary happenings of everyday life.

Performing Arts, Design, and Communications Occupations

Communications Occupations

People in communications occupations deal with mental images created by words. For these workers, language is a "tool of the trade." They use the written or spoken word to inform, persuade, or entertain others and they need to be able to express themselves clearly, accurately, and in an interesting manner. Some talented people use language to express their ideas and emotions in a highly creative fashion. A *poet*, for example, captures a feeling or an event through words much as a photographer uses film. You probably are familiar with *novelists, playwrights, essayists,* and *short story writers* from your English classes.

There are many other kinds of writers, too. *Reporters* gather information on current events and use it to write stories for publication in newspapers and magazines and for broadcast. *Advertising copywriters* write the text, or "copy", for advertisements that appear in newspapers and magazines, or on radio or television. *Educational writers* write textbooks and scripts for filmstrips. *Technical writers* write service manuals, catalogs, and instructions for users of all kinds of machinery and equipment—from dishwashers to missile launching systems. *Political speechwriters* write the speeches that are given by public officials and candidates running for political office. *Joke writers* write the jokes and gags told by comedians and the skits acted out in situation comedies on television. *Script writers* write original scripts for movies and television shows, or rework books or short stories into suitable scripts. *Business and financial writers* write newspaper columns and magazine articles on economic issues. *Medical writers* write for newsletters, scientific journals, and professional and trade publications on topics in medicine and health care. *Editors* revise and coordinate the work of other writers.

People in some communications occupations do relatively little writing. *Proofreaders* read and correct copy that others have written. *Literary agents* read and appraise clients' manuscripts, and then market them to editors, publishers, and others. *Radio and television announcers* comment on music, news, weather, and sports and sometimes deliver commercials. *Interpreters* help people overcome language barriers by translating what is being said in one language into a language that the listener can understand. *Translators*, who also work with foreign languages, prepare written translations of material in another language. Many translators specialize in a particular subject, such as poetry, chemistry, medicine, or politics.

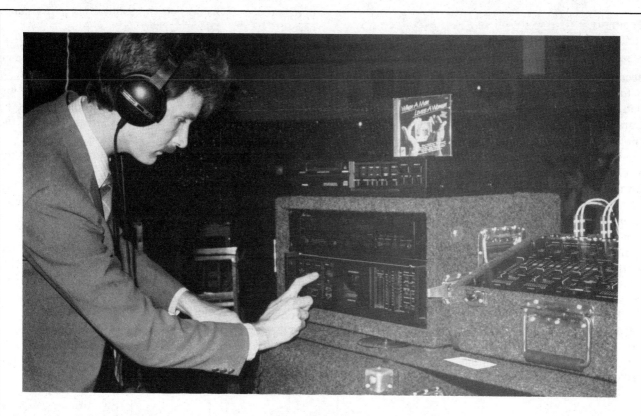

Professional Disc Jockeys sometimes work on location away from the radio station.

Exploring Careers

What does it take for a communications career? People in the communications occupations need an excellent *command of language*. It is through the right choice of words or phrases that interpreters and translators, for example, succeed in expressing the thought behind the factual information they convey. A feeling for language enables a poet or short story writer to breathe life and meaning into the ordinary happenings of everyday life.

Self-discipline is important in these occupations, where so many people face deadlines. Getting an article or report written by a certain date is almost entirely the author's responsibility. *Persistence* is important, too. The first effort of almost every writer—even those whose books are best-sellers—can be terrible. Professional writers can't let themselves be discouraged by this—they continue to "polish" the piece by revising, reorganizing, and rewriting it. If necessary, they tear it up and start all over.

For people in many communications occupations, acute *powers of observation* and the *ability to think clearly and logically* are necessary traits. A broadcast journalist covering a turbulent political convention, for example, needs a probing, analytical mind to discern shifting patterns of support for contending candidates and come up with a good story.

Training

People in performing arts, design, or communications occupations often put in years of practice and hard work before they achieve a reputation for excellence. But they had to start out somewhere. Let's take a look now at the training needed to launch a career in one of these fields. More detailed information is given in the Job Facts at the end of this chapter.

The performing arts are noteworthy for the absence of formal educational requirements. What counts is ability or talent, not the schooling you have had. Of course, talent has to be developed through practice and guidance from skilled artists, and lessons can be quite important. Many ballet dancers, for example, begin taking lessons at the age of 7 or 8, and professional ballet dancers continue practicing for hours each day throughout their careers.

There are different ways of preparing for a career in music, drama, or dance. Many colleges and universities offer degrees in these fields, as do music and drama conservatories and schools of dance. And of course you can take private lessons with an accomplished artist.

Newspaper reporters need insatiable curiosity to get all the details for a story.

Experience in amateur productions is very important for developing one's innate talent and stage presence. Previous performing experiences can also serve as valuable credentials which may help in landing other performance work.

The design occupations vary greatly in training requirements. On-the-job training is sufficient for some jobs. Many design occupations, however, require at least a bachelor's degree. For other design careers, a combination of formal training and practical experience is the best preparation. Bear in mind that artistic ability is the basic requirement for all design careers.

How much schooling do you need to start out in the communications field? You will find that a high school diploma is essential. Beyond that, the amount of formal education you need depends on the type of work you do. The basic requirement for all these occupations is an exceptional command of the English language. You need to be able to speak and write fluently, imaginatively, and gramatically. Community and junior colleges and 4-year colleges and universities offer programs in English, journalism, creative writing, languages, linguistics, or communications. Many universities offer advanced degrees in these subjects. Practical experience working for a school or community newspaper, or for a radio or television station, is a good background for a career in this field.

Performing Arts, Design, and Communications Occupations

Architect

Jack Myers says, "The best part of being an architect is seeing my ideas turn into buildings that are real."

Exploring Careers

Jack Myers takes out his key as he approaches the door with "J. Myers, Architect" stenciled in neat black letters. Unlocking the door and turning on the lights in one swift motion, he hurries into the attractive office. It is a large, cheerful room, full of light and color. But Jack is in a hurry this morning; he scarcely notices. Hanging baskets overflowing with plants fill the windows. The bright orange sofa where clients usually sit looks inviting. Across the room is Jack's desk, a broad expanse of while formica. On the walls are photographs and architectural drawings, all carefully matted and framed.

Jack notices none of this. He heads for a table in the corner, picks up some floor plans from the pile of papers and drawings there, and then settles down at his CAD terminal and turns the system on. He glances at the clock as the system warms up: 6:45 a.m. "Two hours of design time before I have to take care of other things," he thinks. "I should be able to make these changes in the Wrights' house plans...maybe even spend some time on the plans for the library."

Jack has been coming in to the office very early ever since he opened his own business about 2 years ago. That had been a big step, one he had taken only after gaining experience working with other architects in a large firm. Jack had gone to work for Jarvis Associates right after completing the 5-year college program that resulted in a bachelor's degree in architecture.

At Jarvis, Jack had started out with simple tasks such as tracing details from a book of standard architectural forms onto otherwise completed plans. Sometimes he would put dimensions or other notations on plans.

Later he advanced to drafting. He did the "working drawings" that the builder followed in constructing the building. Drafting was enjoyable and taught him a lot, but Jack knew almost from the start that he wouldn't be completely satisfied until he could design an entire building from start to finish. He stayed with Jarvis for about 6 years before deciding to open his own firm.

Now, because he hasn't been in business for himself long enough to develop a large clientele, he operates his office alone. That means long hours almost every day, because Jack does all of the office work as well as the architectural design and drafting. He goes to the post

An architect has to understand what clients want.

office to mail finished plans to clients, answers the telephone, makes appointments with clients, and sends out the bills. He's working much harder now than he did when he was with Jarvis Associates. But he doesn't expect to work such long hours forever! He knows that the more projects he designs, the more people will hear about him and see his work. And that, after all, is the way architects create names for themselves...and build up a clientele.

The plans Jack has just spread out on the worktable are for a new home he's designing for Neal and Ellen Wright. The plans include marks and notations for some changes that the Wrights requested. "These changes would have meant a lot more work before I installed this computer aided design system," Jack thinks as he loads the Wrights' house plans into the system and brings the first drawing to the screen.

As he works on the changes, Jack thinks about how well he's come to know the Wrights over the last few months. Knowing the client is an important part of the architect's job, for it's up to the architect to understand how a client wants to use the space that's being designed. It's the architect who translates the client's needs into something real and practical—as real and practical as a kitchen with lowered counter tops and appliances for a wheelchair user.

In fact it's hard to believe it's been only 6 months since that first phone call, when Ellen had asked whether Jack Myers, Architect, would be interested in designing the new house she and her husband were about to build. A friend had recommended Jack, she explained. Jack depends on recommendations like that from former clients to bring in new assignments; that's why it's so important that his clients be pleased with his work.

At their first meeting, in Jack's office, the Wrights had explained what kind of house they were interested in and had told him how much money they were prepared to spend. Jack had known right away that he wanted to design the Wright house. It was bound to be an interesting and worthwhile project.

After signing a contract with the people, Jack had gone into the zoning commission office to make sure that such a project was in accordance with zoning regulations for the area where the Wrights owned land.

Later, Jack had spent some time with the entire family in order to learn how they lived—and how they wanted to use the space he was designing for them. He had asked questions about how and where they spent their time at home. He had asked about their hobbies, and had learned that Ellen had a "green thumb." She was delighted when Jack said it would be fairly easy to put in a greenhouse for her. The Wrights had definite ideas about some things. Mr. Wright wanted high ceilings, so

that the house would seem as spacious as possible. Lee, their 10-year-old daughter, wanted lots of windows, especially in her bedroom. In addition to indoor growing space for plants, Mrs. Wright wanted a library or reading room. And she insisted on lots of closet space. Dani, the 8-year-old, wanted a game room for the ping-pong table the family was planning to get. Jack took notes throughout the session.

Feeling that he understood the Wrights' preferences and needs, Jack had turned to the next step—designing preliminary floor plans. The Wrights were excited with the plans when Jack brought them over for their approval. Like all clients, they had suggested some changes, so Jack had gone back to the computer to alter the original set of plans. That had been almost 5 months ago.

Since then, while Jack had been drawing up more detailed plans, there have been even more changes for him to bring into his design. The Wrights, just like his other clients, seem to change their minds every week. That meant a lot more work in "the old days" when all of the changes meant work at the drafting table to create new drawings. The CAD system was a big financial investment, but it has made it much easier to incorporate changes. It saves so much time, that it has allowed Jack to take on more projects.

Being able to get along with clients is important in Jack's job. He has to treat his clients with tact and respect and consider their needs and desires. At the same time, he must gain *their* trust and respect so that they will value his opinions and suggestions and have faith in his work.

The plans on Jack's drafting table include several site plans, which show from different viewpoints how the Wright house will fit on the property. There also are floor plans, which show the layout of the rooms in the house and include such details as the sizes of the doors, the thickness of the windows, and the width of the stairway. Jack has still other kinds of plans to draw. Plans called "sections" show different vertical slices of the house and illustrate such things as insulation in the walls and roof. And he must also prepare plans that show the plumbing and electrical systems with their code markings. On these plans, Jack will indicate where to put all the plumbing fixtures and pipes, as well as the electrical wiring system, outlets, and light fixtures.

Jack has always been proud of the neatness and accuracy of his drawings, even when he drew them by hand. The computer assures that the drawings are always neat. But it is still essential for Jack to know the proper design principles and to make accurate calculations of dimensions. He must also be creative, and have a sense of beauty and harmony so that the buildings will be pleasant to look at and fit naturally into the environment. The CAD system makes a lot of the routine work simpler. However, it just manipulates the information about a design which Jack puts into the system. He must know a great deal about building materials, since it's the architect's job to indicate which materials will be used. It means some knowledge of structural engineering concepts—in order to know how much weight a foundation can hold, for example.

Jack is eager to get the revised plans to the Wrights for their approval this week so that he can get in touch with some contractors and open bidding for the project. Contractors supply the materials and skilled workers needed to construct a building. Contractors such as plumbing and electrical contractors, painters, carpenters, and bricklayers handle different phases of the job. The contractors figure out how much time, labor, and materials will be involved, and then make their cost estimate. They do this carefully, knowing that they'll have to stick to the agreed-on estimate if they get the job. Usually Jack acts as general contractor himself, coordinating the work of all the other contractors. He generally tries to get more than one estimate of cost for each construction job in order to be sure that he gets a good price.

The sound of a fire engine racing down the street breaks Jack's concentration. He looks at his watch: 8:30 a.m. "Time passes so quickly when you're absorbed in your work," he thinks. Jack rolls up the revised set of plans for the Wrights' house, which he has just taken from the printer. These new copies include the changes they had requested. "With any luck," Jack thinks, "this will be the last of the changes and we can start building soon."

Just then, the telephone rings. "J. Myers, Architect," says Jack. The voice at the other end of the line identifies itself as Arthur Sullivan.

"I'm interested in renovating some rowhouses. They're about 50 years old, and could use some changes in the plumbing and electrical systems. I guess they need general modernizing, and I'd like to see some of them enlarged if possible. A friend of mine told me you're the right architect for the job."

The prospect of a renovation job appeals to Jack. In fact, when he first started out on his own, he did practically nothing else. In some ways, Jack finds renovation work even more challenging than designing a new building from scratch, because renovation so often involves dealing with the unknowns—unknown building materials and construction techniques, to start with. And there's the satisfaction of finding solutions to structural and design problems. How do you create more space, or more light, without tearing down the whole building and starting all over again?

Jack agrees to meet Mr. Sullivan the next afternoon

to look at the rowhouses and discuss the type of work that should be done and the cost involved.

After stopping at the Post Office to mail the Wright plans, Jack drives across town to the site of a garden apartment complex he has designed. Construction is supposed to be completed by September 1. Jack tries to visit the construction site at least two or three times a week to see how things are going. With so many people handling different parts of the job, problems seem to crop up frequently. Just last week the glass supplier had cut the window glass to the wrong size. Every delay creates a problems for Jack, whose responsibility it is to make sure the apartments are completed on time.

Today things seem to be running smoothly. Jack catches sight of the contractor and walks over to him.

"Hi, Lou," says Jack. "How are things going today?"

"Everything's running like clockwork. If things continue at this pace we'll have these apartments completed next month."

"That's a relief," Jack thinks to himself as he goes inside one of the buildings to see what progress has been made since his last visit. After asking the contractor a few questions about touch-up work that needs to be

Jack knows many building contractors. "I shop around to see who will give me the best price on the job."

done, he walks outside for another look at the exterior of the building.

Looking up at the six buildings that make up the complex, Jack feels a surge of pride and satisfaction. "The best part of being an architect," he thinks to himself, "is seeing my ideas take shape in brick and glass and steel."

Jack decides he has just enough time to look inside some of the other apartment buildings before lunch. Afterwards, he'll head back to his office to spend the rest of the afternoon drawing—this time, working on the plans for a small library. He turns with a quick step and heads for the next apartment building.

Exploring

Architects are concerned with the relationship between people and their environment. They must have an aesthetic sense as well as a practical understanding of people's needs.

- Do you notice your surroundings?
- Can you name some of the things that make your neighborhood or community pleasant to look at? Can you name things that make it unpleasant or even ugly?
- Do you notice different styles of architecture?
- Do buildings that are aesthetically pleasing or displeasing make a strong impression on you?
- Have you ever thought about the design of your school? Is it attractive? Is it functional? Can you explain why? Are the design and layout of your school similar or dissimilar to those of other schools in your community?

Architects use drawings and sketches to express their ideas. They must sketch quickly, neatly, and accurately.

- Do you like to draw?
- Do you draw landscapes? Portraits?
- Do you draw illustrations or cartoons for the school newspaper?
- Do you like to draw posters for school and community events?
- Do you draw signs and illustrations for exhibit areas in your school?
- Is the written work for your school projects neat and accurate?
- Is your homework easy to read?
- Is your handwriting neat?

Architects have to understand how things are put together.

- Do you like to take things apart just to see how they are put together?
- Do you take apart radios, clocks, toys, household appliances, or engines?
- Are you good at doing jigsaw puzzles, crossword puzzles, mathematical puzzles, or brain teasers?
- Do you enjoy putting things together by following diagrams or written instructions?
- Do you like to sew clothes, build models, or assemble radios from kits?

Architects are responsible for many of the details involved in putting up a building. They must be good at organizing work and getting along with people.

- Are you a good leader? Do other people go along with your ideas when you're in charge of a group?
- Do they follow your suggestions?
- Do you like working with others on school clubs or committees?
- Do you like to coordinate cookie sales, calendar sales, car washes, greeting card sales, or other fund-raising projects?

Architects must meet deadlines. They often work under pressure, so they must be self-motivated and good at working independently.

- Are you able to stick to schedules? Do you usually get your school assignments in on time?
- Can you sacrifice leisure activities such as a movie or a baseball game when you have school work to be done?
- Do you take pride in completing projects by yourself?

Newspaper Reporter

''The investigative side of reporting is the most challenging part of my job.''

Performing Arts, Design, and Communications Occupations

Linda picked up the phone on the second ring.

"The Messenger. Good morning. May I help you?" she said in rapid-fire fashion. She was in a hurry that morning, had already taken five phone calls, and wasn't really in the mood for a sixth. But you never knew. Any call might be "the" call, the one leading to the story of the century. Or the story of the week, at any rate.

At the other end of the line, a tiny voice announced that his name was Joey, that he was 9 years old, and that he thought he had a story for her. A tree in his backyard had been knocked down during the weekend rainstorm, he explained, and two baby squirrels had been orphaned and left homeless.

Well, that wasn't Linda's idea of a big story. It might do for filler in a small-town newspaper, but it didn't have the right appeal for a weekly paper that served 35,000 suburbanites. Linda had learned from 6 months on the job that a news reporter had to know her audience in order to select suitable topics for articles. Since the paper came out only once a week, every story had to count.

Besides, it was Tuesday, and *The Messenger* came out on Thursday. Linda was busy enough with last minute follow-ups for stories she already had begun. Not that it was too late to start looking into a new story, but it would have to be something special. Soon she'd have to starting writing up her articles for Thursday's edition. She had been doing research and making notes all week. She would spend most of today actually writing her articles for Thursday's edition. Linda thanked Joey and told him she was afraid she wouldn't be able to use his story.

The Messenger was a small weekly community newspaper. Like other weeklies, it operated with a small staff: Two news reporters, one photographer, and four editors altogether. Fortunately, the two reporters weren't responsible for all the articles that went into each edition. The newspaper bought some syndicated articles and columns that also appeared in other newspapers around the country. These articles came from a syndicate, or organization, that sold them to a number of different newspapers for publication at the same time. In addition, the newspaper used a number of "stringers," freelance writers who covered specific topics such as church and garden club activities and community meetings. Juan Rodriquez was one of the best stringers. Juan was a junior at Central High, and he reported on the school's basketball games. For each of his stories that was published, Juan received $10. Another source of material for the newspaper was the press releases sent in by local government agencies, political figures, local firms, and community groups.

The door opened and Bill, *The Messenger's* other reporter, walked quietly into the office. He had just returned from interviewing one of the candidates running for an at-large seat on the school board. He dropped his note pad on his desk and fell wearily into his seat. "Boy, I can hardly wait until Thursday so I can get some sleep!" he said. Both reporters had been working long hours this week, and no rest was in sight until after the paper was completely put together.

Bill sat down at his desk, turned on his computer terminal, and began typing from his notes. It had taken a while to get used to the new word processing system at first, but now he couldn't imagine how they ever got along without it! Linda looked around the room at the other four desks which, together with hers and Bill's, filled the large office. The room gave the impression of careless activity, with papers scattered on all the desks, keyboards clicking, and phones ringing continuously. Once she had trained herself to ignore all the background noises, Linda found that working in this busy environment was a spur to her own activity. The energy in this room seemed to be contagious. And working so closely with others on the staff kept her aware of every aspect of producing the newspaper.

As far as the news was concerned, Linda was at the center of activity. Her workweek began on Thursday morning and didn't end until Wednesday night when the newspaper staff "put the paper to bed."

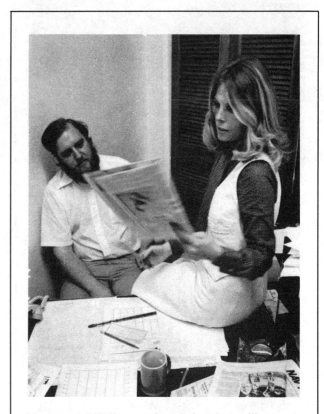

Linda and Bill discuss the stories they will cover this week.

411

The Thursday before, Linda and Bill and the managing editor, Craig, had met as they did every Thursday to put together the story lists—the list of stories each reporter would cover for the week. Stories were assigned to each reporter according to his or her beat. Linda's beat was broad; she was responsible for covering the State General Assembly, the City Council, transportation, the fire and police departments, and parks and recreation. Covering so many different areas was one of the things that Linda liked best about working on *The Messenger.* The job required a broad knowledge of the community. If she were working on a city paper, she probably would cover just one small area of news—business and finance, perhaps, or education. She might be so busy covering the news that she wouldn't even have time to write the stories herself. In that case she would just call in her stories to another writer. Linda thought she got a much wider range of experience on *The Messenger.*

Linda liked to uncover the inside story, to find out what was really going on in the community. The inves-

"I spend a large part of my time checking out leads for stories."

tigative side of reporting was the most interesting and challenging part of her job. At the same time, it probably was the most difficult part, and something she had not been fully prepared to handle when she first started work. Even with a degree in journalism! Only through experience had she learned how much research was involved in reporting, and how vital it was for a reporter to know where to go for information. Reporting for a weekly newspaper often involved more research than reporting for a daily paper would. Because Linda and Bill didn't always have the advantage of publishing a big story as soon as it broke, they compensated by spending more time on their articles. They'd do extra research into the subject or present a new slant on a story. Many times they'd take a more personal human interest approach than a reporter on a big city daily would.

To keep up to date on what was happening on her beat, Linda often had to work nights as well as days, attending meetings of the City Council, the Parks and Recreation Commission, and citizens' groups. Covering meetings, Linda discovered, was not easy, and the proper techniques were not always taught in school. Interviewing 1 or 2 people at a meeting was not enough; she often had to speak to 20 different people. And she found that she had to do research before the meeting began to find out what was scheduled on the agenda, and to explore the different sides of each issue.

Attending meetings was just one way of gathering information for stories. Linda also used leads furnished by people who were in a position to know something useful. Developing these sources or contacts in the right places was another part of Linda's job. Of course, leads didn't always come from regular sources; often they came from total strangers who called in with questions or complaints or information they thought might be of general interest. Like Joey.

Linda spent a large part of her time checking out these leads for stories, but not all of her research was fruitful. Out of a dozen or so tips, only a few would result in articles. Sometimes she did research at the local library. Other times she had to examine police records or go to the County Clerk's office at the courthouse to look through records on file there. Most of the time, though, she used the telephone to check out leads.

A few days before, someone had called in to ask why construction work was beginning on parkland owned by the county. Linda quickly found the right people to talk to: The director and the public information representative of the county park department, then the county's lawyers, then the land developer and his attorney, and finally back to the park authorities. Just yesterday Linda learned that the county had decided to take the developer to court. That was one lead that had developed into an interesting article, and Linda felt the satisfaction of having done something worthwhile for the community as well. Knowing that people depended on her for news also gave Linda a sense of responsibility.

Linda began gathering her notes from the stories she had followed during the past week. Most of her articles had yet to be composed from the fragments of notes she had hurriedly scribbled during telephone conversations or interviews. She usually ended up doing most of her composing at the keyboard. The word processor made it much easier to re-arrange things and re-word an article. But it was still important to be able to think clearly, accurately, and creatively under pressure of an approaching deadline. With experience, Linda had improved her first drafts of articles so that she didn't have to waste very much time with re-writes.

Linda decided she'd better take advantage of the lull in activity and start typing her articles. She knew there were likely to be many interruptions throughout the afternoon. The typed articles had to be ready by tomorrow morning so they could be edited, revised, and then entered into the composing machine that would set them in columns of type.

Some part-time members of the staff would spend most of Wednesday arranging and pasting up the "flats." The "flats" were large sheets of cardboard on which were pasted the photographs and typeset articles that would appear in that week's edition of *The Messenger*. In pasting up the flats, the artists followed the layout design for each page that showed placement of articles and photographs. The layout designs, called "dummy sheets," were drawn up beforehand by the editors. The pasted flats would later be photographed and metal plates made from negatives. The metal plates would then be used to print actual copies of the newspaper. Linda turned to her terminal and opened a new file. She began typing the opening paragraph of her lead article. "The next day and a half will be hectic," she thought to herself, "but by Thursday morning the paper will be out on the street." Then there would be some time to relax, at least until the new stories were assigned and the cycle started all over again....

Linda watches as her articles are pasted up on the flats.

Exploring Careers

Exploring

Newspaper reporters communicate ideas. They must be good at expressing themselves in writing.

- Do you enjoy writing letters to friends?
- Do you write poetry or short stories in your spare time?
- Do you keep a diary or journal?
- Is English one of your favorite classes?
- Are you good at writing term papers?
- Are you good at doing essay questions on tests?
- Are you good at crossword puzzles, Scrabble, Password, and other word games?

Newspaper reporters need an insatiable curiosity to get all the details for a story.

- Do you enjoy talking to people?
- Are you interested in hearing many different points of view?
- Are you skeptical about things you read or hear?
- Do you check the facts before deciding whether something is so?
- Do you ask questions in class?
- If you don't understand an answer, do you ask again? Do you keep asking until you're sure you understand what a teacher or classmate is trying to say? Can you do this without rubbing people the wrong way?
- Do you use the encyclopedia?
- Do you use the dictionary to look up words you don't know?
- Do you follow current events? Do you read newspapers and magazines? Do you watch the television news?

Getting information is not always easy. Many times newspaper reporters run into obstacles when they're after a story. They need to be aggressive and confident.

- Are you outgoing?
- Are you comfortable talking to strangers?
- Do you enjoy selling tickets to dances or athletic events? Do you enjoy selling magazine subscriptions? Girl Scout cookies?
- Do you like collecting for charity drives?
- Are you confident in trying out for school activities?
- Do you strive for leadership positions in organizations?

Newspaper reporters have to rewrite their stories until they're just right.

- Do you rewrite your English papers several times before turning them in?
- Do you rewrite letters to friends?

- Do you check over your math homework before turning it in?
- Do you ever use a thesaurus when you're writing in order to find just the right word?

Newspaper reporters face deadlines all the time. They must be able to work under pressure.

- Do you get your homework assignments in on time?
- Are you able to take tests without panicking? Do you organize your time on tests to have time for all the parts?
- If a pressing deadline for a school project comes up, are you willing to spend extra time on it until it's finished, even if it means staying late after school or taking it home and working on it at night?
- Do you enjoy being busy and "on the go" all the time?

Newspaper reporters need to be flexible. Their assignments change often, and sometimes they have no advance notice at all.

- Can you work on more than one task at a time? Do you get everything done?
- Is it easy for you to go from one subject to another in your homework?
- Do you read several books at a time?
- Do you like variety and change in your weekly or daily schedule?

Newspaper reporters have to be able to think and write objectively. They should be honest, idealistic, and interested in the truth.

- Are you interested in many different points of view?
- Can you tell when someone has a biased viewpoint?
- Are you good at settling arguments with rational thinking?
- Do you believe in telling the truth even if it hurts someone?

414

Musician

"I'm lucky to be able to support myself making music."

Exploring Careers

Ever since he was a child, Bob has enjoyed playing musical instruments. In high school, he learned to play in front of an audience and to use his musical skills to entertain others. He now teaches music in a Junior college during the school year. Two years ago, the city hired him to perform outside to small groups during their lunch hour. Bob enjoyed this so much that he continues to do it whenever his teaching schedule allows him to.

Bob looks the crowd over with a practiced eye as he stride up to the busy corner in the heart of the business district. "Mostly office workers out for lunch, as usual, but there seem to be some tourists today too. Quite a mixture, in fact. They have the makings of a good audience," he thinks to himself as he begins to set up his gear.

He removes the backpack that holds his guitar and a folding stool, then sets up his speaker system and hooks the microphone into it. After removing his guitar and leaning it upright against the stool, he unpacks a large cymbal and places it on the ground. He takes several cassettes out of the pack and stacks them in front of the speaker. Next he pulls his harmonica out of a side pocket of the pack and attaches it to a brace around his neck. Finally he places a very small cardboard box a few feet in front of the stool.

"Hello, folds. How are you today?" he says into the mike as he sits down and beings tuning his guitar. A few people stop to watch, but most just continue on their way. Bob blows into the harmonica a few times, strums a chord, and then, assured that his guitar is in tune, begins to play.

"Bob Devlin's my name, and I'm going to start off today with an old ballad that you may know." With that, Bob starts to sing. More people stop to watch. As he begins the second verse, he can feel himself warming up to the song. About a dozen people have gathered around him, although most of the sidewalk traffic is still moving. As he finishes his song, a distinguished-looking man in a pin-striped suit walks over and drops some coins into the box. Bob acknowledges the contribution with a nod and a smile, then moves right into another tune. A faster one, this time. His right foot moves in time to the music, tapping the brass cymbal.

He's feeling fine. It is a beautiful summer day, sunny and warm, and Bob knows from experience what a difference the weather makes to a street musician. A balmy day like this is perfect. Bob moves quickly from one song into another, pausing between songs only now and then to talk to people gathered around him.

He is recognized by a number of people, including some former music students from school, and called by name. Bob has played on this corner before, and many of the people who work in nearby office buildings are familiar with his music. They make a point of coming when they find out that he's giving a lunchtime concert here. Bob is pleased with the audience he's developing in this part of the city.

That audience gives him the exposure he needs, and the $100 he can make for a few hours' work adds to his teacher's salary. More people hear him play on this corner sidewalk than would hear him play at a coffeehouse or club. In fact, most of the club dates he's gotten lately have come about because someone from a nightclub heard him on the sidewalk, liked his music, and offered him the job. Playing on the street has actually saved him the trouble of having to go and audition for additional work.

Right now, Bob's musical goal is to become better known, and more easily recognized by the people he plays for on street corners and in the parks. He hopes more and more people will make an effort to catch his performances wherever he happens to be playing. Then, as his reputation grows, there will be more demand for

Although Bob has made a record album, most of his income comes from his position as a music professor at the local junior college.

416

him to perform. In the future, Bob would like to go on tour with an established singer or group.

Bob already has made one album, and he expects to make more. He cut the album last fall, thinking he could make some extra money even in the winter months when playing on the street is impossible because of the cold weather. He sold them wherever he played, in nightclubs, coffeehouses, and private parties.

Like all musicians who are just starting out, Bob had to cover the cost of cutting the record himself. He used his savings, around $700, and borrowed the rest from friends. He made the recording, or master tape, during a session when he was playing on the street. That saved him the expense, which can be quite substantial, of having to rent a recording studio. Later he took the master tape to a production plant that would copy the master tape, duplicate the cassettes, and insert them into plastic cases along with the cover insert. Having the cover insert designed had been expensive, but it was necessary to give the tapes a professional look and to list Bob's name along with credits for the other people

who had helped produce the album. The $2000 that Bob had available allowed him to produce 500 tapes in the first batch.

Selling his tapes for $8 each, Bob was able to regain his initial investment after selling half of the first printing. From then on, everything he sold was pure profit. He'd sold the initial 500 in just 6 months and when people kept asking where they could buy the copies, he decided to order 1,000 more! With the master tape and the cover insert already done, the second batch was much less expensive. He was able to pay from them with the profits that had been left from earlier sales after he'd re-paid the loans from his friends.

A few college and underground FM radio stations have given his music air time, but he's found it difficult to get his music played on most of the commercial AM stations. "I'm lucky to have the opportunities like this to advertise my record," he thinks as a teen-ager in faded jeans picks up one of the cassettes and then pulls a wallet from her pocket.

The music Bob plays is easy to listen to and appeals to a large audience.

As Bob finishes another song, a few people begin to clap. Soon the entire crowd is applauding. He pauses for a moment, then starts into a well-known folk tune. "You probably all know this one," he says, "so sing along if you like." The music Bob plays is easy to listen to and appeals to a large audience. That's part of the reason for his success. It would be harder for Bob to be successful at his part-time profession of street musician if he had a classical repertoire. His rapport with his audience is another reason for Bob's popularity. He talks and jokes with the people gathered around him in a relaxed, easygoing way. At the same time, Bob attributes some of his success to downright practical considerations—picking the right time of day and the right places to play.

The crowd around Bob grows larger, and people start walking up and dropping money into his box. He continues playing, responding to the encouragement and appreciation of his audience.

Bob's interest in music began in the 8th grade, when he learned how to play the guitar by ear and by picking up what his friends knew. When he was in college study-ing to be a music teacher, he played occasionally in coffeehouses to earn extra money.

Not long after he was hired as music professor, he realized how much he missed performing in front of people. When the city asked him to perform for downtown workers on their lunch hours, he knew it was the perfect opportunity for him to make a little extra money and make people feel good with his music he is so willing to share.

Exploring

Musicians have to be devoted to their music.

- Do you love listening to music? Do you often get involved in, excited by, or caught up with the music you hear?
- Would you rather go to a concert than to a movie or play?

Bob knows that performing is a very competitive field, and he doesn't expect to become famous over night.

Performing Arts, Design, and Communications Occupations

- Would you rather play your musical instrument or sing than take part in a sports event or read a book?
- Do you ever think of songs that express your feelings?
- Do you ever write songs?
- Do you relate easily to characters in stories or movies who are musicians?
- Do you ever daydream about playing in front of an audience?

Musicians must be good at recognizing and reproducing sound differences. They need a "good ear" for music and rhythm.

- Can you tell when someone is singing off key? Can you tell when someone plays a flat note on a musical instrument?
- Can you pick up the beat after hearing just a few bars of music? Can you remember the beat to a song the next day? Do you like to tap out rhythms on desk tops or chair arms?
- Can you pick out a tune you know on a piano or guitar without reading the music.

Musical ability is only partly a mater of talent; practice is responsible for the rest. Musicians spend many hours practicing.

- Can you stick with a task to perfect it? Do you rewrite your English compositions or rework your math homework?
- How willing are you to practice the skills you have now? Do you practice the piano, typing, your foul shots for basketball, your tennis serve, or your cheerleading cheers?

Musicians, like all performing artists, have to be comfortable in front of an audience.

- Do you like being the center of attention?
- Can you speak in front of the class without getting embarrassed?
- Are you good at telling jokes?

Musicians need to be good at memorizing the words or music they perform.

- Is it easy for you to memorize words and tunes to popular songs?
- Do you have a good memory for names, phone numbers, and addresses?
- Can you remember the right keys to hit when you're typing?
- Are you good at memorizing poetry?

Musicians sometimes have to perform when they don't want to, or perform pieces they've grown tired of.

- Can you put your own wishes aside in order to please other people?
- Can you hid your feelings from your friends when you're tired, upset, or bored?

Job Facts

There isn't room in this book for a story about every performing arts, design, and communications occupation. However, you'll find some important facts about 19 of these occupations in the following section. If you want additional information about any of them, you might begin by consulting the Department of Labor's *Occupational Outlook Handbook*, which should be available in your school or public library.

Occupation	Nature and Places of Work	Training and Qualifications	Other Information

PERFORMING ARTISTS

Occupation	Nature and Places of Work	Training and Qualifications	Other Information
Actors and Actresses	Actors and actresses perform in stage plays, motion pictures, radio and television programs, and commercials. In the winter, most employment opportunities on the stage are in New York and other large cities. In the summer, stock companies in surburban and resort areas provide jobs, too. Acting jobs in "little theaters", repertory companies, and dinner theaters are available year round. Employment in motion pictures and film television is centered in Hollywood and New York City. In television, most opportunities for actors are in New York, Los Angeles, and Chicago, at the headquarters of the major networks. However, some local television stations employ actors, too.	Talent is the most important qualification for a career in acting. Creativity and imagination, expressive ability, a clear, well-trained voice, poise and stage presence, and the ability to memorize are essential ingredients. Perseverance and the ambition to succeed are also important. Previous experience, including amateur productions, is very helpful in getting a professional acting job. Formal training in acting is also important. Colleges, universities, and dramatic arts schools offer courses and degrees in drama. Training and practice continue throughout an actor's career, however.	More actors and actresses than there are jobs makes this a competitive field. Many actors and actresses cannot obtain year-round work in acting, and must work at other jobs to make a living.

Performing Arts, Design, and Communications Occupations

Occupation	Nature and Places of Work	Training and Qualifications	Other Information
Dancers	Professional dancers perform in classical ballet, modern dance, and musical shows. They may perform on stage, screen, or television. However, relatively few dancers are full-time performers. Many dancers teach in colleges and universities, and at dance schools and studios. Teachers trained in dance therapy work in mental hospitals, nursing homes, and other facilities. Dance teachers are located chiefly in large cities, but many smaller cities have dance schools as well. New York City is the hub for performing dancers.	Talent, in the form of agility, grace, a feeling for music, and the creative ability to express oneself through dance are the most important qualifications. Average body height and build, good feet with normal arches, and a well-formed body with good muscle control are also important. In addition, dancers need a strong desire to become good dancers, determination, physical stamina, and perseverance. Serious training at a dance school or with a private teacher should begin at an early age, particularly for ballet. Training and practice are part of the daily routine and must continue throughout a dancer's career.	More dancers than there are jobs makes this a competitive field. Many dancers cannot obtain year-round work as performers, and must work at other jobs to make a living.
Musicians	Nearly all musicians play in musical groups, including symphony orchestras, dance bands, rock groups, and jazz combos. Popular musicians play in nightclubs, restaurants, and at special concerts and parties. Classical musicians play in symphony, opera, ballet, and theater orchestras, and in chamber music groups. Many pianists accompany soloists or choral groups, or provide background music in restaurants or bars. Most organists play in churches; often they direct the choir. In addition to performing, many musicians teach music in schools and colleges, or give private lessons in their own studios or in pupils' homes. Others combine careers as performers with work as arrangers, composers, or conductors. Musicians who have taken additional training work as music librarians or music therapists.	Musical talent, versatility, creativity, poise, and stage presence are important qualifications for musicians. Self-discipline, perseverance, and physical stamina are also necessary. Training on a musical instrument should begin at an early age. Music lessons can begin at school or with a private teacher. More advanced training can be acquired through further private study with an accomplished musician, in a college or university with a strong music program, or in a music conservatory. Training and practice generally continue through a musician's life, however.	Musicians often work at night and on weekends, and they must spend a great deal of time practicing and rehearsing. Performing engagements usually require some travel. More musicians than there are jobs makes this a competitive field. Many musicians cannot obtain year-round work as musicians and must work at other jobs to make a living.

Exploring Careers

Occupation	Nature and Places of Work	Training and Qualifications	Other Information
Singers	Popular music singers perform in the movies, on the stage, on radio and television, in concerts, and in nightclubs and other places. Other professional singers are members of opera and musical comedy choruses. Outstanding singers may obtain leading or supporting roles in operas, popular music shows, or choral performances such as oratorios. Singing stars make recordings or go on concert tours in the United States and abroad. Some singers combine their work as performers with jobs teaching voice or directing choral groups. They give private voice lessons and direct choruses in schools, music conservatories, colleges, and universities. Many singers work part time as church singers and choirmasters. Opportunities for singing engagements are concentrated mainly in New York City, Los Angeles, Las Vegas, San Francisco, Dallas, and Chicago—the Nation's chief entertainment centers. Nashville is one of the most important places for employment of country and western singers for both "live" performances and recordings.	Musical ability, an attractive appearance, poise, and stage presence are important qualifications for a career as a singer. Perseverance and physical stamina are also necessary to adapt to frequent traveling and long and irregular working hours. Voice training is an asset for singers of all types of music. As a rule, voice training should not begin until after the individual has matured physically. Training can be obtained through private voice lessons or in a music conservatory or department of music in a college or university. In addition to voice, singers also should study music theory and composition. In general, training and practice continue throughout a singer's career.	Singers usually work at night and on weekends, and most spend considerable time in practice and rehearsal. Performing engagements often require some travel. More singers than there are jobs makes this a competitive field. Many singers cannot obtain year-round work singing and must work at other jobs to make a living.

Performing Arts, Design, and Communications Occupations

Occupation	Nature and Places of Work	Training and Qualifications	Other Information

DESIGN OCCUPATIONS

Occupation	Nature and Places of Work	Training and Qualifications	Other Information
Architects	Most architects work in architectural firms, for builders, for real estate firms, or for other businesses that have large construction programs. Some work for government agencies, often in city and community planning or urban development. Most architects work in large cities where the major architectural firms are located.	Architects must be able both to work independently and to cooperate with others. They should be artistic as well as have a capacity for solving technical problems. A 5-year college program resulting in a Bachelor of Architecture degree is the usual way of entering this profession. All States require architects to be licensed for independent private practice. Unlicensed architectural school graduates work under the supervision of licensed architects. Admission to the licensing exam usually requires a Bachelor of Architecture degree followed by 3 years of experience, or a Master of Architecture degree followed by 2 years of experience.	An architect may have to work overtime and under pressure when necessary to meet deadlines.
Commercial Artists	Most commercial artists work for advertising departments of large companies, advertising agencies, printing and publishing firms, textile companies, photographic studios, television and motion picture studios, and department stores. Others are self-employed or freelance artists. Some salaried artists do freelance work in their spare time. Some artists teach in art schools. Although there are jobs for commercial artists in nearly every city, the majority work in large cities, such as New York, Los Angeles, Boston, Washington, D.C., and Chicago, where the largest users of commercial art are located.	Artistic ability, imagination, neatness, and a capacity to visualize ideas on paper are important qualifications for success in this field. People can prepare for a career in this field by attending a school that offers a program in commercial art. These include trade schools and technical institutes, community and junior colleges, and colleges and universities. Training in commercial art also may be obtained through high school vocational programs and practical experience on the job. Formal training beyond high school usually is needed for advancement, however.	Most commercial artists advance by specializing either in the mechanical elements of producing an ad (letterers and mechanical and layout artists) or in pictorial elements (sketch artists and illustrators).

Exploring Careers

Occupation	Nature and Places of Work	Training and Qualifications	Other Information
Display Workers	Most display workers work for large stores: Department stores, clothing stores, home furnishing stores, variety stores, drugstores, shoe stores, book stores, and gift shops. Freelance or self-employed display workers have accounts with small stores that need professional window dressing but cannot afford a full-time display worker.	Display workers need imagination and knowledge of color harmony, composition, and other fundamentals of art. Most display workers are trained on the job. A beginner can usually become skilled in 1 to 2 years. Employers usually require a high school diploma.	Constructing and installing props means standing, bending, stooping, and working in awkward positions. During busy seasons, such as Christmas and Easter, display workers may have to work overtime, nights, and weekends to prepare special displays.
Floral Designers	Nearly all floral designers work in retail flower shops, and these are found almost everywhere in large cities, suburban shopping centers, and small towns.	Manual dexterity and a good sense of color, balance, and proportion are important qualifications for floral design. Many floral designers are trained on the job by the manager or an experienced floral designer. Usually a trainee can become a fully qualified floral designer after 2 years of on-the-job training. Courses in floral design offered by community colleges and floral design schools also prepare people for careers in this field.	Most retail flower shops are small and employ only one or two floral designers; many designers manage their own stores. In small shops, floral designers often work 8 hours a day, Monday through Saturday. Designers generally work long hours around certain holidays, such as Easter and Valentine's Day, when the demand for flowers is great.
Industrial Designers	Most industrial designers work for large manufacturing firms or for design consulting firms. Some do freelance work or are on the staffs of architectural and interior design firms. The jobs of all these designers have one thing in common: They design products for consumer or industrial use. Some industrial designers teach in colleges, universities, and art schools. Industrial design consultants work mainly in large cities such as New York, Chicago, Los Angeles, and San Francisco. Industrial designers with industrial firms usually work in or near the manufacturing plants of their companies, which often are located in small and medium-sized cities.	Industrial designers need creative talent, drawing skills, and the ability to see familiar objects in new ways. They should be able to work and communicate well with others. To become an industrial designer, it's usually necessary to complete a 4-or-5 year program in industrial design. Such programs are offered by art schools and by the design or art departments of colleges and universities. Persons with degrees in engineering, architecture, and fine arts may qualify as industrial designers if they have appropriate experience and artistic talent. Many industrial designers use computer aided design (CAD) systems and familiarity with their use is becoming increasingly important.	Although most industrial designers are product designers, others develop trademarks or symbols that appear on products, advertising, stationery, and brochures. Some design containers and packages, while others design display exhibits. Industrial designers use both sketches and 3-dimensional models to convey their ideas.

Performing Arts, Design, and Communications Occupations

Occupation	Nature and Places of Work	Training and Qualifications	Other Information
Interior Designers	Most interior designers work for design firms or have their own firms. Some work in department or furniture stores, or for hotel and restaurant chains. Other designers work for architects, furniture suppliers, antique dealers, furniture and textile manufacturers, or other manufacturers in the interior furnishings field. Interior designers also have jobs with magazines that feature articles on home furnishings. Interior designers are employed primarily in large cities.	Interior designers should be creative, have good color sense and good taste, and be able to work well with people. Training in interior design is becoming more and more important. The types of training available include 3-year programs in a professional school of interior design, 4-year college or university programs that grant a bachelor's degree, or post-graduate programs leading to a master's degree or Ph. D. People starting in interior design usually serve a training period with a design firm, department store, or furniture store.	Interior designers' work hours are sometimes long and irregular. Designers usually adjust their workday to suit the needs of their clients, meeting with them during the evenings or on weekends when necessary. Some interior designers are paid straight salaries, some receive salaries plus commissions based on the value of their sales, and others work entirely on commissions.
Landscape Architects	Most landscape architects are self-employed or work for architectural, landscape architectural, or engineering firms. Government agencies concerned with land management, forests, water, housing, planning, highways, and parks and recreation also employ landscape architects. Some landscape architects work for landscape contractors and others teach in colleges and universities.	Drawing talent, a creative imagination, and an appreciation for nature are important qualifications for landscape architects. A bachelor's degree in landscape architecture takes 4 or 5 years and is usually the minimum for entrance to the profession. A master's degree is becoming increasingly important. Thirty-nine states require a license for independent practice of landscape architecture. Admission to the licensing examination usually requires 2 to 4 years of experience in addition to a degree in landscape architecture.	Some landscape architects specialize in certain types of projects such as parks and playgrounds, hotels and resorts, shopping centers, or public housing. Others specialize in services and resource management, feasibility and cost studies, or site construction.

Exploring Careers

Occupation	Nature and Places of Work	Training and Qualifications	Other Information
Photographers	Most photographers work in commercial studios; many others work for newspapers and magazines. Government agencies, photographic equipment suppliers and dealers, and industrial firms also employ photographers. In addition, some photographers teach in colleges and universities, or make films. Still others work freelance, taking pictures to sell to advertising agencies, magazines, and other customers.	Photographers need good eyesight and color vision, artistic ability, and manual dexterity. They also should be patient and accurate and enjoy working with detail. There are no set requirements for becoming a photographer. However, the training a prospective photographer has determines the type of work for which he or she qualifies. People may prepare for work as photographers in a commercial studio through 2 or 3 years of on-the-job training as a photographer's assistant. Training in photography can also be acquired in colleges and art schools. Post-high school education and training usually are needed for industrial, medical, or scientific photography, where it is necessary to have some knowledge of the field in which the photography is used.	Many photographers specialize in a particular type of photography, such as portrait, commercial, newspaper, industrial or medical photography. About one-third of all photographers are self-employed.
Planners	Planners prepare programs for the future development of communities. They take into account population trends, land use, public facilities, economic factors, and civic goals. Most planners work for city, county, or regional planning agencies. Some work for government agencies that deal with housing, transportation, or environmental protection. Others work for architectual, engineering, or construction companies. Planners also work for public interest organizations concerned with environmental protection and community development. Many planners do consulting work, either part time in addition to a regular job or as employees or owners of consulting firms.	Planners need analytical and abstract reasoning abilities above all. They need to be creative and resourceful in developing possible solutions to complex problems, and must have drive, tact, and persuasive and administrative skills in order to get their ideas across. A master's degree in urban or regional planning is usually required for a job in this field. However, people with bachelor's degrees in city planning, architecture, or engineering may qualify for beginning positions. Most graduate programs in urban planning require 2 or 3 years of study in addition to the 4-year undergraduate college degree. Graduate students gain practical experience through workshops, laboratories, and summer or part-time employment in a planning office.	In large organizations, planners specialize in areas such as housing or economics, while in small offices they must work in several different areas.

Performing Arts, Design, and Communications Occupations

Occupation	Nature and Places of Work	Training and Qualifications	Other Information

COMMUNICATIONS OCCUPATIONS

Occupation	Nature and Places of Work	Training and Qualifications	Other Information
Advertising Workers	There are both creative and sales jobs in advertising. Creative workers such as writers, artists, and designers develop and produce advertisements, while business and salesworkers handle the arrangements for broadcasting advertisements on radio and TV, publishing them in magazines or newspapers, mailing them directly, or posting them on billboards. Advertising workers are employed by different kinds of firms. Primarily, they work for advertising agencies. But they also work in the advertising departments of manufacturing firms, retail stores, and banks. Some work for printers, art studios, letter shops, and similar businesses. Most of those employed by advertising agencies work in New York City, Chicago, or Los Angeles.	Advertising copywriters must have a flair for writing, imagination, salesmanship, and an understanding of people. A sense of the dramatic and the vision to see the effect of ideas are also important qualities. Account executives, whose job it is to create ad campaigns for clients, need writing skills and imagination too. In addition, they must be friendly, outgoing, and very good at communicating with others and selling their ideas. Most employers prefer to hire college graduates. A liberal arts degree usually provides good preparation for a job in this field, but work experience and creativity may be more important than educational background. Experience selling ads for school publications or radio stations can be a help in looking for a job.	Among the jobs in this field are those of advertising manager, account executive, research director, advertising copywriter, artist, layout worker, media director, and production manager. People in advertising work under great pressure to do the best job in the shortest period of time. Often they work long or odd hours to meet deadlines.
Interpreters	The largest concentration of full-time interpreters in the United States is at the United Nations in New York. Other international organizations that employ regular staff interpreters include the Organization of American States, the International Monetary Fund, the Pan American Health Organization, and the World Bank. All are situated in Washington, D.C. There also are jobs for freelance interpreters, many of whom serve as escort interpreters for foreign visitors to the United States. Other freelance interpreters work at international conferences, or work for business firms.	People interested in becoming interpreters should be articulate speakers and have good hearing. The exacting nature of this profession requires quickness, alertness, and a constant attention to accuracy. Good sense, honesty, tact, and discretion are also important. A university education usually is essential. A complete command of at least 2 languages generally is required. Interpreters who work at the United Nations must know at least 3 of the 6 official U.N. languages.	Interpreters make up a very small occupational group in the United States, and competition for interpreting jobs is great.

Exploring Careers

Occupation	Nature and Places of Work	Training and Qualifications	Other Information
Newspaper Reporters	Reporters work for big city daily newspapers, for suburban community or small town weekly papers, and for press services. Reporters work in cities and towns of all sizes.	Important personal characteristics for newspaper reporters include curiosity, persistence, a "nose for news," initiative, resourcefulness, an accurate memory, and physical stamina. Most newspapers consider only applicants who have a college education, preferably with a degree in journalism or some other liberal arts area. Graduate work is increasingly important.	Although the majority of newspapers are in medium-sized towns, most reporters work in cities, since big city dailies employ many reporters whereas a small town paper generally employs only a few. Newspaper reporters generally have a busy daily schedule and may often have to work under pressure to meet deadlines.
Public Relations Workers	Public relations workers plan activities and create programs to promote a favorable public image of their client. Writing is an important aspect of the work. They write and edit articles, speeches, reports, pamphlets, and press releases.	Public relations workers need writing ability, imagination, an outgoing personality, initiative, and drive. They must be fluent in conversation, effective public speakers, and persuasive. They should have the enthusiasm to motivate others.	Public relations workers often have to work overtime on a project. Occasionally they travel on business.
	Public relations workers have jobs with business and industrial firms, insurance companies, transportation companies, public utilities, hospitals, colleges and universities, nonprofit organizations, and government agencies. Many work for public relations firms, which are most numerous in New York City, Los Angeles, Chicago, and Washington, D.C.	A college education with public relations experience is excellent preparation. Appropriate majors include public relations, journalism, liberal arts, and business. Experience writing for a school publication or for a radio or TV station can be helpful.	

Performing Arts, Design, and Communications Occupations

Occupation	Nature and Places of Work	Training and Qualifications	Other Information
Radio and Television Announcers	Radio and television broadcasting stations all over the country employ announcers. The average commercial radio or television station employs 4 to 6 announcers, although larger stations employ 10 or more. In addition to staff announcers, several thousand freelance announcers sell their services for individual assignments to networks and stations, or to advertising agencies and other independent producers.	Announcers must have a pleasant and well-controlled voice, a good sense of timing, correct English usage, and excellent pronunciation as well as an attractive personality. There are no fixed requirements for entering this field. A college liberal arts education provides an excellent background for an announcer, and many universities offer courses in the broadcasting field. A number of private broadcasting schools offer training in announcing also.	Most radio announcers act as disc jockeys. Announcers employed by television stations and large radio stations usually specialize in particular kinds of announcing, such as sports, news, or weather. Announcers frequently participate in community activities.
Technical Writers	Many technical writers work for electronics, aviation, aerospace, ordnance, chemical, pharmaceutical, and computer firms. Others work for energy or communications firms. Research laboratories also employ technical writers. Some technical writers hold writing and editing jobs with business and trade publications, professional journals in engineering, medicine, physics, chemistry, and other sciences; and publishers of textbooks and scientific and technical literature. Established technical writers sometimes work on a freelance basis or open their own agencies or consulting firms.	Technical writers need writing skills and technical expertise above all. They also should be intellectually curious and able to think logically. They must be accurate in their work. They should be able to work well with others as part of a team. A college degree is important, and should include courses in a technical area such as science, engineering, medicine, business, or agriculture as well as writing, editing, and publication production.	Technical writers sometimes work under considerable pressure, working overtime to meet publication deadlines. Employers often promote technicians or research assistants to writing and editing jobs. Technical writers have a place in the information industry. Commercial firms employ technical information specialists to collect, process, and manage the information stored in computerized data bases. Technical information centers run by major industrial firms and research laboratories employ information specialists for the same purpose.

Newspaper reporters must be able to work under pressure.

Soil research helps farmers grow better crops.

"Sue, would you drive me downtown today?" Larry Cohen asked his older sister. "I've got to do some shopping. Tryouts for the basketball team start tomorrow, and I need some new gym shoes."

Sue, who was taking a day off from her job as nutritionist in a local hospital, couldn't think of an excuse for not taking Larry. So they went downtown to buy Larry some shoes.

After they finished shopping, Sue and Larry decided to stop in a fast-food store and grab a bite to eat. Once they had gotten their food and sat down at a table, Sue noticed that Larry was staring into space with a worried look on his face.

"What's bothering you, Larry?" Sue asked. "Are you that worried about making the team?"

"I wish it was that simple," answered Larry. "I have to give a report tomorrow on the kinds of jobs in agriculture, and I don't know where to start."

Sue thought for a minute and then said, "How about starting with what's in your right hand?"

"Do you mean this fish sandwich?" Larry asked in an unbelieving tone.

"Sure," Sue replied. "Did you ever stop to think about how many different ingredients there are in that sandwich and where they all came from?"

"No, but it doesn't seem that complicated," Larry answered. "Let's see, the roll came from a bakery, the fish came from the ocean, and the sauce ..."

"Very cute, Larry," snapped Sue. "I'm sure you'll make an A with such a comprehensive report. Now, do you want me to help you or not?"

"Sure I do," Larry answered contritely. "I just don't see what my fish sandwich has to do with agriculture."

"Take the bun, for example," responded Sue. "The wheat for the flour in it probably came from a grain farm in the Midwest. And quite possibly that particular variety of wheat was developed by an agricultural scientist. Can you think of any other ingredients in the roll?"

"I'm not sure," Larry replied. "Does the roll have milk or sugar in it?"

"Yes, dried milk and probably corn syrup also," replied Sue. "The milk may be from a dairy farm in Wisconsin, which is one of the big dairy States, and the corn syrup, from Iowa. Probably many more agricultural products are in the roll, but I'll leave them for you to investigate later. You might start by reading the ingredients listed on the wrapping of a loaf of bread. Now, to keep this conversation rolling, could you tell me where the fish in your sandwich came from?"

"I guess somebody caught it in the ocean," Larry replied, "but I'm not sure."

"You're probably right, Larry," answered Sue. "If the fish is a hake, haddock, or pollack, then it was probably caught by a fisher in the North Atlantic. But if it is catfish, it probably was raised on a fish farm."

"A fish farm?" asked Larry. "Now I think you're putting me on."

"No, aquaculture, or fish farming, is a rapidly growing area of agriculture that is still far from reaching its full potential," said Sue. "If you think I'm just telling you a fish story, then check it out in your school library."

"I think I will," said Larry. "That sounds like it might make a good topic for my report."

"Good," said Sue with a smile. "Now, can you tell me where that napkin you're wiping your face with came from?"

"Sure, that's easy," answered Larry with a grin. "It came from a napkin farm."

"Believe it or not, you're almost right," said Sue. "Most paper products come from pulp made from trees. And many trees come from tree farms. Now can you see what your fish sandwich has to do with agriculture?"

"Yes," said Larry, "the sandwich and everything in it are products of agriculture and the many different types of agricultural workers. I just didn't realize that a fish sandwich could be so complex."

"Good thinking, Larry," said Sue, "but remember that we've just scratched the surface of the wide variety and complexity found in modern agriculture. I think, however, that you've made a good start now on thinking about your report."

Workers in agriculture, forestry, and fishery produce many of the products we use every day. The following sections will tell you about their jobs.

Agricultural Production Occupations

First, of course, there are the workers who are engaged directly in agricultural production. This broad group includes producers of plant products, such as corn, wheat, and vegetables, and producers of animals, such as chickens, cattle, and sheep. Most *farmers* and *ranchers,* however, now specialize in particular varieties of crops and animals. As a result, specialized types of workers are now needed for these various types of farm products. Many of these specialized workers are discussed in the following sections on occupations in *plant farming* and *animal farming*.

Accompanying this trend toward crop specialization is a trend toward larger sized farms—farms that are often too big for one person, or even one family, to take care of alone. Because of this, there are some opportunities for farm laborers and farm labor supervisors to help run the farms. These occupations also provide opportunities

Agriculture, Forestry, and Fishery Occupations

Texas cantaloupes are shipped throughout the world.

for workers who want to farm but who don't yet have enough money to buy the necessary land and equipment.

Many large corporations, and some wealthy individuals also, are engaged in what is now called agribusiness. A corporation, for example, may hold large amounts of land on which grain is grown to be fed to cattle kept in pens or feedlots also owned by the corporation. Farm operations of this size are very complex and create jobs for *farm managers*.

The competition caused by agribusiness, and increasing consumer and environmental demands make it important for many farm workers to be more knowledgeable about technology and business. Many farmers, ranchers, and farm managers in all specialities must be familiar with the latest scientific studies about pesticides, fertilizers, animal feed additives, breeding techniques, etc. They may use computers to keep track of the type and amount of seed and chemicals used in each field, or the type and amount of feed given to each animal, and their costs and revenue. They must also be very familiar with business practices to calculate costs and profits and to plan ways to cope with changes in the economy and financial losses from bad weather.

Let's take a closer look at the types of workers needed in agriculture.

Plant Farming Occupations. Most farmers and farm workers are employed in plant farming.

The grain farming occupations include *cash grain farmers*, who are responsible for raising the various grains we use for food. Often these farmers' job titles refer to the specific type of grain they grow, such as *corn grower, rice farmer, soybean grower,* and *wheat grower*. Cash grain farmers cannot handle all the different jobs associated with raising large quantities of grain by themselves. *Grain farm workers* operate the farm machinery used in planting and harvesting grain and perform other duties, such as checking irrigation ditches and carrying supplies. *Farm labor supervisors* direct activities of farm workers. *Detasseling crew supervisors*, for example, direct the activities of workers who break and pull tassels from corn plants on hybrid seed-corn farms.

Other workers grow and harvest vegetable crops. *Vegetable farmers'* job titles often refer to the vegetable they specialize in growing, such as *onion farmer* or *lettuce grower*. Farmers who grow a variety of different vegetables are sometimes called *truck farmers*. *Vegetable farm workers* do much of the labor required in raising and harvesting vegetables. Some farm workers called *vegetable harvest workers* pick, bunch, and wash vegetables. Supervisors oversee the vegetable farm workers.

Fruit and nut farming also requires workers with specialized skills. Farmers in this field usually are named by the type of crop they grow, such as *apple grower*, cherry grower, orange grower, pecan grower, grape grower, blueberry grower, and strawberry grower. In addition to laborers and supervisors, this kind of plant raising requires some highly specialized workers. Fig caprifiers, for example, attach figs containing wasps to fig trees in order to help ensure pollination. Vine pruners cut back berry vines so they will produce more fruit.

Field crops, such as cotton, peanuts, potatoes, sugar beets, sugarcane, and tobacco, also require specialized workers. Seed-potato arrangers and cutters, for example, are needed to attend the machines that cut potatoes into sections for use as seed. Field crop supervisors, farmers, and other types of farm laborers are also needed. Shed worker supervisors, another type of specialized worker, direct the activities of the workers who cure tobacco leaves in sheds on farms.

Animal Farming Occupations. The largest group of occupations in animal farming are the domestic animal farming occupations. Among these are livestock ranchers, such as cattle ranchers, dairy farmers, and sheep farmers, who breed and raise livestock for sale. Livestock farm workers, or ranch hands as they are more commonly called, assist ranchers by performing a wide variety of chores around the ranch, such as feeding and vaccinating animals and repairing fences. Many types of animal farming require specialized workers. Top screws, or ramrods, for example, supervise and coordinate the activities of cowpunchers in cattle ranching. Lambers assist ewes during lambing, while sheep-shearers clip the wool from live sheep in sheep ranching. Fur farmers breed and raise animals such as mink, fox, or chinchilla, and are assisted by pelters who skin the animals for their fur.

Poultry farming also requires many different types of workers. Poultry farmers, for example, raise improved strains of poultry developed by poultry breeders to produce eggs and meat. Many other specialized workers assist in poultry farming. Poultry tenders care for poultry used in experimental tests to develop better feeding systems. Poultry farm workers do many of the day-to-day jobs involved in poultry raising. Poultry vaccinators vaccinate poultry against diseases such as pox and bronchitis. Chicken graders grade baby chicks according to appearance and separate healthy from deformed or diseased chicks. Chicken sexers determine the sex of young chickens and separate them by sex.

Game animals, such as deer, pheasant, and quail, also are raised under controlled conditions. Game farm supervisors oversee and plan the activities of workers involved in breeding, raising, and protecting game on private or State game farms. Game farm helpers do most of the physical work associated with game farming. And game-

Assisting with the birth of a calf is part of a rancher's job.

Agriculture, Forestry, and Fishery Occupations

Modern poultry farms have automatic feeding and watering systems.

Science has made significant contributions to modern agriculture.

bird farmers raise birds such as pheasant, quail, or partridge for sale to gun clubs, game preserves, or poultry houses.

Mammals and birds are not the only types of animals raised commercially. *Beekeepers* raise bees to produce honey and pollinate crops. *Reptile farmers* breed and raise reptiles such as rattlesnakes for their meat, venom, and skins. *Worm growers* assisted by *worm farm laborers* breed and raise earthworms for sale as fishing bait, garden soil conditioners, and food for exotic fish and animals.

Agricultural Support Occupations

Modern agriculture is a complex undertaking that requires many thousands of workers who are not directly involved in agricultural production. These workers are needed to help support agriculture in a number of areas, such as agricultural business, education, food processing, and science. Now let's take a quick look at some of these occupations.

Most types of farming, for example, require the use of large amounts of machinery, equipment, and other farm supplies, such as chemicals and pesticides. As a result there are some jobs for workers who sell, maintain, and explain how to use machinery and supplies. *Farm equipment sales workers* are needed to sell the tractors, combines, plows, planters, and other farm equipment used in agriculture. These workers also help farmers choose the equipment that best suits their particular farming needs. *Farm equipment mechanics* maintain and repair tractors and a wide variety of other farm equipment.

Agricultural engineers help improve efficiency in agriculture by designing new types of farm equipment or improving existing model lines. *Agricultural chemical sales workers* sell and explain the use of the different types of pesticides, herbicides, and fertilizers that have greatly increased agricultural production in this country. *Agricultural pilots* spray chemicals on crops from airplanes and helicopters.

Workers in agricultural production also need considerable assistance with the financial and technical aspects of farming. *Bankers* in rural areas, for example, help support agriculture by providing loans for farmers to buy land, equipment, and other supplies needed in raising crops. *Agricultural economists* deal with problems related to production, financing, pricing, and marketing of farm products. *Agricultural cooperative extension service workers* provide information on agricultural research to farmers and encourage its use to increase the amount of agricultural products that farms can produce. *Veterinarians* provide valuable technical assistance to livestock

435

producers by keeping animals healthy and productive. Farmers also, of course, need markets for their farm products once they are harvested. *Buyers and shippers* help fill this role. Keeping accurate financial records is also an important part of agriculture. *Agricultural accountants* prepare and analyze financial reports for farm managers. *Agricultural commodity graders,* such as grain inspectors, also help support agriculture by assuring that farm products are of uniform quality and fit for consumption.

Science has made significant contributions to modern farming and is expected to produce even greater benefits in the years ahead. As a result, there are many jobs for scientists and other professionals who concentrate on agriculture. *Agronomists,* for example, conduct experiments and develop better methods of growing crops. *Plant pathologists* study the causes of plant diseases and develop ways to control weeds, insects, and plant diseases. *Plant physiologists* study the structure of plants and devise ways to improve their growth and storage life. *Geneticists* try to develop breeds of plants and animals that are better suited for the production of food and fiber. *Microbiologists* study bacteria and other tiny organisms to understand better their relation to human, plant, and animal health. *Animal physiologists* study the functions of the various parts of animals. *Animal scientists* develop improved methods of housing, sanitation, and parasite and disease control for livestock. *Animal nutritionists* specialize in finding feed requirements that will maximize production and in developing new livestock and poultry feeds. *Entomologists* study insects to try to find ways to control harmful insects and manage beneficial ones. *Seed analysts* conduct tests on samples of seeds to determine their rate of germination, purity, and weed content. *Agricultural chemists* develop chemical compounds for controlling insects, weeds, fungi, and rodents. They also perform experiments to determine how to use fertilizers properly and investigate problems of nitrogen fixation in soils. *Food scientists* develop new foods, food preservatives, and similar products. *Soil scientists* and *soil conservationists* study ways to improve the use of soils upon which agriculture is based.

Becoming a farmer can be very expensive. This tractor, for example, costs over $50,000.

Agriculture, Forestry, and Fishery Occupations

Scientists and technicians help assure a plentiful supply of clean water for fish and wildlife.

Forestry Occupations

Forests are a vital natural resource that can be used repeatedly if they are properly managed. They provide habitats for conserving our wildlife as well as recreational facilities for ourselves. Forests also provide the raw materials for lumber and paper. Workers in the forestry occupations are concerned with the management and proper utilization of our forests.

Foresters, who often specialize in one area of work, such as timber management or outdoor recreation, are key workers in this field. Foresters plan and supervise the cutting and planting of trees and also protect the trees from fire, harmful insects, and disease. They may be responsible for other duties ranging from wildlife protection and watershed management to the development and supervision of camps, parks, and grazing lands. *Forestry technicians* assist foresters in many of their tasks, such as mapmaking, selecting and marking timber to be harvested, and planting seedlings.

Fires are one of the major dangers facing our forest resources. Thus *fire lookouts* and *fire rangers* are stationed in remote areas to spot and then put out or report forest fires. If a fire is reported in an inaccessible area, then *smoke jumpers,* under the direction of *smoke jumper*

A skilled logger can drop a tree exactly where he wants it.

Some college students work during summer vacation as fire fighters for the U.S. Forest Service.

Exploring Careers

supervisors, parachute into the area and put out the fire. *Forest-fire fighters,* sometimes called *smoke eaters,* also help control forest fires.

Harvesting forest products, or logging, is an important part of managing our forest resources. Before a stand of timber is cut, foresters, with the assistance of *forestry aides* and *timber cruisers,* decide what trees should be harvested and estimate the amount of wood in these trees. *Heavy equipment operators* then build access roads and trails to the cutting and loading areas.

Fallers, working singly or in pairs, then cut down the large trees marked by the forester. Expert fallers can usually drop a tree in the exact spot where they want it, without injuring nearby trees. Once the tree is down, *buckers* saw the limbs off and saw the trunk into logs. Sometimes small trees are felled with tree harvesters, machines mounted on a tractor and operated by *logging-tractor operators.*

Next, the logs must be removed from the cutting area. One method is called skidding. In this method, a choker (steel cable) is noosed around the log by *choker setters* and then attached to a tractor which drags or skids the log to the landing. A *rigging slinger* supervises and assists choker setters and tractor drivers.

After the logs reach the landing, they are loaded on a truck trailer and hauled to the mill. A *loader engineer* operates a machine that picks up logs and places them on the trailer. A *second loader* directs the positioning of logs on the trailer.

Forest nursery supervisors oversee and coordinate the activities of workers who raise tree seedlings for reforestation. Some of these workers are *seedling sorters,* who sort seedlings according to size and quality, and *seedling pullers,* who harvest tree seedlings in forest nurseries.

Millions of hardy seedlings are grown on tree farm nurseries. They get a good start at the nursery, then are transplanted.

Agriculture, Forestry, and Fishery Occupations

Fishery Occupations

Fish provide an important source of protein for both humans and animals around the world. There are two major ways of obtaining fish. The oldest is simply to harvest the fish that are found in our oceans, rivers, and lakes. In recent years, however, another method, called aquaculture, or fish farming, has been growing in importance. Let's take a look at some of the workers in these two broad areas of fishery.

Fishers harvest aquatic animal life from our oceans, rivers, and lakes in a number of ways, depending on the location and the type of fish being sought. *Net fishers,* for example, catch finfish, shellfish, and other marine life using seines, trawl nets, gill nets, and a wide variety of other types of nets. These workers are often named according to the type of net they use, such as *dip net fisher, beach seine fisher,* or *purse seine fisher. Pot fishers* use pots (cages with funnel-shaped openings) to harvest marine life including crabs, eels, or lobsters. These fishers

These workers are checking salmon to see if they are ready to lay their eggs.

Fishing is one of the oldest ways of getting food.

Exploring Careers

Some oysters are raised for pearls.

Fish farming, or aquaculture, is a rapidly growing area of agriculture. These workers are harvesting catfish.

also may use dredges (rake scoops with bag attached) during certain times of the year. Pot fishers are usually named according to the type of marine life they fish for, such as *crab fishers, eel fishers,* or *lobster fishers. Line fishers* catch fish using hooks and lines. *Hand line fishers* simply use a line they hold in their hand, while *trawl line fishers* may use long lines that extend for over a mile with thousands of hooks hung at intervals on the line. *Diving fishers* gather marine life such as sponges, abalones, and pearl oysters from the sea bottom. *Fishing vessel deckhands* do a wide variety of jobs that assist fishers aboard ship. *Net repairers* assemble and repair nets on shore and aboard ship.

Aquaculture, or fish farming, is a rapidly growing field that offers many employment opportunities. *Fish farmers,* such as *trout farmers* or *catfish farmers,* spawn and raise fish for sale to supermarkets and other commercial interests. *Fish hatchery workers,* under the direction of *fish hatchery supervisors,* trap and spawn fish, incubate fish eggs, and rear young fish in hatcheries. Some of

these fish, such as trout, are then stocked in streams to be caught by sport fishers, while others are used for commercial purposes. Shellfish, such as oysters, clams, and scallops, can also be raised commercially. *Shellfish-bed workers,* under the direction of *shellfish farming supervisors,* plant, cultivate, and harvest these various types of shellfish. These workers are usually named according to the types of shellfish they work with and the type of duties they perform, such as *clam-bed worker, oyster unloader, scallop dredger, oyster picker,* or *clam digger. Aquatic life laborers* perform a number of routine tasks involved in raising marine life. *Shrimp pond laborers* may, for example, patrol shrimp ponds looking for predators. They also may help in feeding and harvesting fish or in preparing shellfish beds.

Fishery also offers numerous opportunities for professional workers. *Fishery biologists,* for example, collect and analyze data on the physiology of fish, transplanting methods, fish raising techniques, and management of fish and shellfish stocks.

440

Agriculture, Forestry, and Fishery Occupations

Personal Characteristics

The basis for the work done by people in each of these fields lies in nature. Agriculture, forestry, and fishery would not be possible were it not for the sun and the clouds, the soil and the seas, rivers and lakes, and forests and fields. It is not surprising, therefore, that successful workers in these fields have been actively interested since childhood in hunting and fishing or in observing birds, insects, wildlife, trees, and flowers. They have a strong *interest in nature* and the environment around them.

Not surprisingly, people in many of these occupations *enjoy working outdoors.* Working outdoors, however, can often be physically demanding; these workers are exposed to all types of weather conditions and often must lift heavy objects or perform hard physical labor for extended periods. Forestry workers, for example, may have to hike many miles to reach fires or when "cruising" timber stands. As a result, *physical strength* and *stamina* are assets.

Agriculture, forestry, and fishery have become highly mechanized and machines do much of the work that used to be done by hand: Planting and harvesting crops, hauling in fishing nets, and harvesting trees. But these machines must be maintained and repaired. A belt may snap on a farmer's combine during the critical harvest time, for example. Or a winch used for hauling in nets

Carrying 50-pound sacks of feed is hard work.

may break down while a fisher is far out at sea. If the farmer and fisher can't fix these problems by themselves, they may experience costly delays. Because of this, *mechanical ability* and the *ability to work with your hands* are extremely important.

Work schedules in agriculture often are set by elements beyond human control. A farmer, for example, may have only a few days when conditions are just right for planting or harvesting crops. If the farmer is not fully prepared when this time arrives, there will simply be no crop and thus no farm income that growing season. Consequently, being *well organized* is essential.

Agriculture, forestry, and fishery workers often must choose the best way to spend their time and money from among a wide variety of options. A forester, for example, may be given a limited budget for managing a section of woodland and must decide how best to use the money. Should part of the money be spent on firefighting equipment or on fertilizer, for example? Workers in these fields must be *able to set priorities.*

Many people in agriculture, forestry, and fishery are their own bosses or work with little or no supervision. This takes *initiative* or the *ability to be a self-starter.*

Crops, animals, trees, and other agricultural products do not grow overnight. Some years you may see little or no income or other visible results for your work. Because of this, *patience* and the ability to withstand bad years and save during good years are important qualities.

Much of the work in agriculture, forestry, and fishery is based on the ability to apply science on the job. Do you have a strong *interest in science?* Are you curious about life and living things? Are you a good observer? Do you examine things critically and analyze what you have seen? These traits are essential for such workers as fishery biologists, plant breeders, poultry scientists, and botanists who must understand science and use it in their work.

Many agriculture, forestry, and fishery occupations involve *working with people.* Frequent, if not daily, exchanges with other people are an important part of the job for cooperative extension service workers, feed sales workers, and farm credit managers, among others.

Finally, a *sense of responsibility* is very important for workers in agriculture, forestry, and fishery. You should care not only for this season's crops or animals, but also for the long-range protection and improvement of the environment. If you don't, then surely you are not meeting your responsibilities toward future generations.

Training

Training requirements vary widely. Farm laborers, fishers, and smoke jumpers, on the one hand, may find jobs without finishing high school; they learn on the job. On the other hand, cooperative extension service workers, fish biologists, and many others need college degrees in agriculture or a science. The training requirements for 18 selected occupations are listed in the Job Facts section at the end of this chapter.

Since there is a wide variety of training paths for such a broad field as the agriculture, forestry, and fishery occupations, no one path is the best for all of them. There are, however, some things you can do now to explore your interest.

Science is very important in many of these occupations. High school courses in biology, chemistry, physics, and mathematics provide the foundation you'll need for the science courses you'll take later on. Science fairs give you the opportunity to do projects in agriculture, forestry, and fishery. High school courses in vocational agriculture, although not essential, are useful for testing your interests and seeing if you have the skills needed by workers in agricultural production.

As a general rule, growing up on a farm or having some agriculture background or experience is helpful. One reason for this is that the day-to-day tasks involved in many of these occupations are best learned through experience. In addition, working at a job is one of the best ways to find out if you like the work and are able to meet the demands of the job. Even if you do not live on a farm, you can gain useful experience by working part time or summers on a farm or for a summer camp.

You also might participate in farming programs for young people, such as the Future Farmers of America or the 4-H Clubs. These organizations are important sources of training for young farmers and provide practical experience in agriculture along with awards and other forms of recognition. Members also are active in fairs, agricultural contests, horse shows, and a wide variety of other activities.

Farm experience, however, is not essential for many of the scientific, technical, and business careers in agriculture, forestry, and fishery. In fact, many of the students enrolled in State schools of agriculture are from urban areas. Even if you live in a city, however, you should learn as much about the environment and the natural world as you possibly can. Taking nature walks and observing wildlife, trees, and flowers as well as hunting and fishing are activities you might consider.

The Boy Scouts, Girl Scouts, Campfire Girls, and similar organizations offer good opportunities for getting outdoors and learning about your environment. Youth organizations offer numerous programs and proficiency badges that are directly related to the fields of agriculture, forestry, and fishery.

Farmers need to know how to repair machinery.

Agriculture, Forestry, and Fishery Occupations

Farmer

John O'Quinn samples the crop. "The harvest is the best part of farming," he explains, "because it's everything you've been working for."

The sun had not yet risen over the Eastern Shore of Maryland when John O'Quinn climbed into his pickup truck to drive to his farm for another day's work. Getting up before dawn was nothing new to John, though; he had worked on the farm since he was a very young boy. Even while he was studying agriculture at the University of Maryland, he had come home almost every weekend to help his father run the family's 500-acre farming operation. Then, about 2 years ago, his father had retired, and John, along with his sister Alice, had taken over the operation of the farm.

As he was driving to the farm, John felt a sense of excitement because today was a very special day, the beginning of the watermelon harvest. Work had begun on preparing about 100 acres of land for watermelons back in September with the planting of a rye cover crop to strengthen the soil and also to prevent soil erosion from occurring over the course of the winter. As soon as winter had passed, John plowed up the rye cover crop and began preparing a seedbed for the melons. Then, around the middle of April, after most of the danger of frost had passed and after a good rain, John had planted the watermelon seeds. During the planting process, he also had worked hundreds of tons of fertilizer into the soil. The seeds had sprouted quickly, and it looked as though there would be a good crop if only it would rain a little.

But the rains had stayed away. Every day for over a month John had checked the weather reports and scanned the sky for clouds. As the plants began to wither and die, John regretted the fact that he hadn't installed the expensive irrigation system he had considered buying the year before. Then, in late June when the crop seemed almost lost, the rains came and the field sprang to life.

Now it was August, and John would soon be checking on how the first day of the harvest was progressing. But first he had to feed a few hungry animals.

Upon arriving at the farm, John stopped by the barn where Pete Ward was waiting. Pete was a farmhand who had worked with John's family for over 20 years.

Pete was standing beside some large sacks of grain that he had brought out of the barn. Together he and John loaded the grain into the back of the pickup and drove to a nearby pen where John kept about 100 hogs. As the truck stopped by the pen, the pigs ran toward it squealing and grunting in obvious expectation of a good meal.

Pete began mixing the feed grains while John climbed into the pen to check the pigs. As soon as he entered the pen, John was surrounded by a crush of squealing pigs. He scratched the backs of a few, which the pigs loved. While he was doing that, John was checking for signs of disease or other problems. In addition, and to the pigs' misfortune, John was estimating the time required before they would be ready for market, which he determined to be about 2 more weeks.

After John and Pete finished feeding the pigs, they drove back to the barn, where they picked up a couple of salt licks, 50 gallons of molasses, and about 10 bales of hay. They then drove to a nearby field where John was grazing about 75 head of cattle. As John and Pete approached the field, the cattle began moving towards the gate, just as the pigs had done earlier. John drove the pickup slowly into the field, while Pete pulled bales of hay off the back of the truck and kicked them open for the cattle. When they finished putting out the hay, John and Pete drove across the field to some large boxes that had about a quarter of a wheel showing above each of their tops. These were molasses feeders that John used to help the cattle put on weight more quickly. When the cattle licked the wheel on top, the wheel turned, bringing up molasses from the bottom of the box. John and Pete quickly checked the molasses level in the boxes and filled up those that needed it. John was a little disappointed by the fact that the cattle didn't seem to be eating much of the molasses, but he knew that this wouldn't keep him from trying more experiments in the future. If he didn't keep improving his farm's efficiency, John knew he would not be able to compete with other farmers and would have to go out of business.

By now the sun was getting fairly high in the sky and the temperature was approaching 90 degrees, but John and Pete still had a lot to do. First, John wanted to see how the watermelon harvest was progressing. Then, if all was going well there, he and Pete would drive to another field and begin preparing the land for next year's crop.

When he arrived at the watermelon field, John felt elated, as he always did at harvest time, because for John, as for all farmers, harvesting crops or sending livestock to market provides tremendous rewards. These rewards come not only from the money gained, which sometimes isn't much, but also from a sense of pride and satisfaction at seeing the results of many months of long, hard work.

Alice, John's sister, was overseeing the harvest, so John drove over to her as soon as he got to the field. Alice was standing near a machine like a conveyor belt that was feeding melons into the backs of three large trucks. The machine also automatically separated the melons according to size. Thus small melons were going into one truck, average size melons into a truck from a large supermarket chain, and large melons into a truck from a processing plant.

Agriculture, Forestry, and Fishery Occupations

"How are things going?" asked John as he got out of his pickup. "Are there any problems?"

"Nothing major," answered Alice, "but I sure could use another skilled cutter or two. We've already had one truck come back because there were too many green melons in it." Cutters are usually the most experienced and skilled field laborers in harvesting watermelons. They usually go down the rows in front of the other laborers and determine, almost by instinct, which melons are ripe. They then cut the ripe melons from the vines and stand them on end to be loaded on wagons by other laborers following behind. If the cutter selects too many unripe melons, the truck will be sent back by the agricultural broker who acts as a middleman between the farmer and the crop's buyers.

John groaned in response to Alice's request for more cutters, because he knew what she was asking. Everyone in the area was harvesting melons right now, and there wasn't an extra laborer to be found anywhere, especially a skilled cutter.

"It looks like you and I have just been drafted as cutters, Pete," said John with a grin as he looked at Pete who was pretending to hide behind the pickup.

John went home very tired that night and awoke early the next morning with very sore muscles from the constant lifting and stooping required in cutting watermelons. Nevertheless, he felt the sense of satisfaction and accomplishment that only a hard day of physical labor can bring.

There was, however, one thing that bothered him. He hadn't been able to prepare the grain field for planting as he and Pete had planned, and there were still a lot of watermelons to be harvested. John couldn't help smiling, though, when he thought of the conversation he and Pete would have while feeding the stock that morning about who would get to sit on a tractor all day and who would have to work another day as a cutter.

John hires vacationing students for the melon harvest. Following the cutters through the fields, they pick up the ripe melons and load them on wagons.

Exploring Careers

Exploring

Farmers spend much of their time outdoors in all kinds of weather.

- Do you enjoy working outdoors, or would you prefer to work in a controlled environment such as an office building?
- Do you like outdoor activities such as swimming, hiking, fishing, camping, and hunting?
- Do you mind working in the garden or mowing your family's lawn?
- Do extremes of heat and cold bother you?

Because they are their own bosses, farmers must have initiative and be self-starters.

- Do you get up in the morning by yourself?
- Do you do your homework and household chores without being prodded by your parents?
- Do you stick with projects until they are finished?
- Do you take responsibility for your family's pets?
- Do you get to class on time everyday?

As farming methods grow more complex, farmers must take on more planning and managerial duties.

- Do you always finish your homework on time?

- Do you keep a diary?
- Do you use a calendar to organize your time?
- Do you make lists of things to do?
- Are you good at long-range projects, such as gardening, that require a good deal of organization?
- When you are in control of a project, can you get people to work without resenting you?

Farmers must respect the environment.

- Do you throw trash in the trash can?
- Does it bother you when you see a polluted river?
- Do you save cans for recycling?

Farmers must work with machinery and often maintain and repair their own equipment.

- Do you like to build things?
- Do you like to work with your hands?
- Do you repair your own bicycle?
- Do you like to learn how machines work?
- Are you handy with tools?
- Before you start working on something, do you think about how you will go about it?

John sells some of his crop to the local auction. "It gives me a chance to socialize with other farmers while I do business."

Agriculture, Forestry, and Fishery Occupations

Cooperative Extension Service Worker

Bev Williams has a master's degree in dairy science. "I grew up on a farm," says Bev, "so it seemed natural to make agriculture my career."

It was a cold winter night on a dairy farm in northern Maryland. Jack and Anne Medgar, the owners, were relaxing before the fire after a hard day's work. Jack was reading a farm trade journal, *Modern Dairy Farmer.*

"Listen to this, Anne," he said with a laugh. "Dairy farmers in Ohio are feeding their cattle cement and getting increased milk production. Can you believe that crazy idea?"

"I'm not sure it's such a crazy idea, Jack," said his wife. "Agricultural science is continually coming up with new ideas. Some of the things you do now on the farm wouldn't have been possible 20 years ago. Why don't you call Bev Williams and see if she's heard of it? Who knows, using cement might increase milk production on this farm."

A few days later, Jack called Bev, the county extension service agent. He asked her about cement in cattle feed.

"I have read about it," Bev assured him, "but it is still in the experimental stage. In fact, the university is now testing it. The idea is to use cement dust as a dairy cattle feed supplement. Apparently the idea has been tried a few times and has resulted in higher milk production. But it hasn't been done under controlled conditions, and we're not sure if there is a connection between the cement and the milk production. Possibly the high calcium content of the cement dust is a factor. I'll try to keep abreast of the research, though, and see if it might work in your farming operation."

As she put down the phone, Bev made a mental note to call the scientist at the university who was in charge of that research project and find out how the experiment was going.

"I might even mention this in my monthly newsletter," she thought.

Bev doesn't get calls about feeding cement to cattle every day. But she has to be prepared for calls like Jack's. Keeping track of current agricultural research, making it known to farmers, and encouraging them to use the results of this research—that's what a county extension service agent's job is all about.

Farmers have to be convinced that new ways of doing things are worth trying. They won't listen to just anyone who comes along with advice. Bev and other extension agents need years of training to develop the expertise that will make listening to their advice worthwhile. Extension agents usually know a lot about agriculture from growing up on a farm—or at least having a farm background.

Bev grew up on a dairy farm right in the area. After high school, where she was active in 4-H, she attended the State agricultural university. There she earned a bachelor's degree and then went on to earn a master's degree in dairy science. After graduation, she worked for a farm supply company for about 5 years before getting the job she has now.

Now let's look at one of her workdays. There's no such thing as a "typical" day for Bev. There's so much variety in her job that every day is different. That's one of the things she likes best about the job.

Today, Bev will be spending most of the morning in her office. As soon as she gets there, Bev goes through her mail. She notices some soil test results from the university and sets them aside. She'll go over them later. When she examines the soil results, she'll decide on fertilizer and crop recommendations. Later on, she'll discuss these with the farmers who submitted samples of their soil.

As she continues to go through the pile of mail, she finds circulars from farm supply companies promoting new machines, seeds, feeds, and chemicals. She looks these over carefully since farmers often ask her opinion on new developments in farm supplies.

Bev then turns to the rest of her paperwork. She puts together her notes for the report she has to submit to the university four times a year. In this report, Bev will list the farmers she has been in touch with, describe the advice she has given them, and explain how her suggestions are working out.

Bev also works on her monthly newsletter for the farmers in the county. In the newsletter she discusses new research developments, such as the cement dust in cattle feed. She also reports on regulations and government policies affecting farmers and on agricultural prices and farm management.

Around 11 o'clock, Bev leaves her office and drives to the local radio station to tape her weekly farm report. She usually chooses a topic that will interest most farmers in the county. This week, for example, she discusses some of the methods for controlling Johnson Grass, a weed that infests many farms. After lunch, Bev drives to a dairy farm to go over a suggested feeding program for the farmer's herd. The farmer had noticed a decline in his herd's milk production and about 2 weeks ago asked Bev if she had any suggestions. Bev had told the farmer to bring some forage samples of his hay and silage into the extension office. She sent the samples to the State agricultural university for analysis. When the results came back, Bev studied them carefully, noting among other things the protein and water levels of the forage. Now, she and the farmer are working together on a feeding plan that would be economical but still ensure good milk production. After a few hours of work, they finally arrive at what they both think will be a good combination of roughage and grain for the farmer's herd.

Bev's next stop is at a farm whose owner has asked for help concerning a sensitive financial question. The

Agriculture, Forestry, and Fishery Occupations

farmer is nearing retirement and would like to see his son take over the farm. The son has the knowledge and ambition to take over the farm, but he doesn't have the money to buy the farm. Bev and the farmer and his son sit down and discuss the situation from all angles. Finally, the farmer reaches a decision that would give him a retirement income and still enable the son to enter the farming business. He decides to sell the cows and machinery to his son and keep the land. The son would then rent the land from his father. While Bev does not make this decision for the farmer, she does help present him with a wide range of options from which to choose. Helping the farmer make a wise decision gives Bev a real feeling of satisfaction.

By now it is after dark, so Bev does not return to her office. But her workday is still not over. She drives home to have supper and get ready for a meeting she is to attend that night. The meeting is being conducted by a farmers' organization, and Bev wants to be there for two reasons. First, she will have the opportunity to speak with a number of farmers and thus keep informed of their latest concerns. Second, she knows the subject matter of the meeting will be of interest to a number of farmers who cannot attend. By attending, Bev can later answer any questions they have about the meeting. Perhaps one of her answers to a farmer's question will help the farmer run a more productive and profitable operation.

Exploring

Extension agents must be able to work with and gain the respect of other people.

- Do you listen to what your friends have to say?
- Do you enjoy participating in group activities?
- Are you a leader in these activities?
- Do you enjoy speaking in front of your class?
- Are you good at giving directions?
- Do you organize activities?
- Do people ever ask you for your opinion?

Extension agents advise farmers on methods chosen from a wide variety of alternatives.

- Are you able to plan your time effectively?
- Can you set priorities?
- Do you like looking into all of the various aspects of a subject?

- Do you have trouble making decisions when given a wide range of choices?
- When buying clothes, do you buy the first ones you see, or do you shop around for something better?

Extension agents must be able to express themselves well both orally and in writing.

- Do you keep a diary?
- Do you write many letters?
- Do you enjoy explaining things to people?
- Do you like writing themes in English class?

Even after they complete school, extension agents must keep abreast of new developments in agricultural science and farming methods.

- Do you enjoy reading on your own?
- When you see something that interests you, do you enjoy learning more about the subject?
- Do you enjoy school subjects such as science?
- Do you like reading about your hobbies?
- Are you interested in how things work?

When farmers seek help from extension agents, they depend on getting help quickly and efficiently.

- Can people depend on you?
- Do you do the things you promise to do?
- Do you get to class on time everyday?
- Do you ever volunteer to help around the house?

Forester

Paul Ivy manages over 60,000 acres of timberland. With this tool, he can find out how fast his trees are growing.

Agriculture, Forestry, and Fishery Occupations

Paul Ivy works as a forester for a medium-sized forest products company based in the Middle Atlantic region of the United States. Although he has been working for only a few years, Paul's job is an important one. He is responsible for managing over 60,000 acres of company timberland that is scattered over a 10-county area. Managing this land encompasses a wide range of duties including budgeting, planning, mapmaking, and overseeing the planting, clearing, harvesting, and selling of the trees. The variety makes Paul's work even more interesting.

Paul didn't just suddenly decide to become a forester. As a youngster, he was active in Scouting and enlarged his interest in and knowledge of the outdoors. Then he attended a college with a forestry curriculum and obtained a bachelor's degree in forestry. While in college, Paul participated in a work-study program 6 months out of each year. In this program, Paul acquired practical experience working as a forestry technician in the National Parks in Montana. Then, during the final summer before his graduation, Paul got a job with a private company. They liked his work and hired him full time when he graduated from college.

There is really no such thing as a typical workday for Paul. His job has variety. In the summer, for example, he may have to direct firefighting activities, while in the winter he may have to check on the company's logging roads to be sure they are passable.

Today, however, is a beautiful March day, and he has neither of these problems. But he does have a full day ahead.

After breakfast, Paul gets in his pickup truck and drives about 30 miles to a section of land being "cruised" by forestry aides. The aides are trying to determine how much marketable wood there is in this particular forest stand. To do this, they have to find out a number of things, including how many trees there are and how much wood each tree contains. Obviously, they cannot count and measure every tree in the stand. Instead, they mark off a typical sample area of the stand and carefully count and measure the trees in the sample area. They also use a tool called an increment borer to determine the age of the trees in the stand. This tool, without harming the tree, can take a pencil-thin sample from the tree's core. To determine the tree's age, the aides simply count the number of rings present from the center to the

Paul has been interested in the outdoors since he was a youngster. "I started thinking about a forestry career when I was working on Scout merit badges," he recalls.

edge of the tree. They can also tell how fast the tree is growing by looking at the distance between the rings.

By the time Paul arrives, the aides have almost finished "cruising" this timber stand. He helps them finish and then carefully records the data they have obtained. When Paul returns to his office, he will enter the data into a computer and onto detailed maps of the tract he has prepared. Then he can determine if the tract is ready to be harvested and, if so, how to harvest the timber in a way that will not harm the environment.

Paul's next stop is at another tract nearby that has just been harvested. Now the site is being prepared for replanting. Paul wants to be sure that the work is going well and according to plan. Much of Paul's work on this tract was completed long ago. Even before the trees were cut, for example, he decided which trees should be left to provide windbreaks and cover for wild game and protection from erosion. These remaining trees are called a leave strip.

Today, huge bulldozers and other pieces of earthmoving equipment are making windrows on the bare land. This is similar to the contour plowing done by farmers and serves the same purpose. Windrowing helps protect the land from erosion. Paul is pleased with the work and compliments the workers on a job well done. Before leaving, he checks to see if they need any more equipment or supplies.

By now it is almost time for lunch, so Paul drives into a nearby town to buy a sandwich. He eats in the truck while driving to a site about 20 miles away.

This site has already been prepared for planting but is on very uneven land. Because the land is so uneven, it is impossible to use the automatic tree-planting machine that can plant up to 8,000 trees in a day. Instead, the company has hired inexperienced laborers who can at best hand plant only about 1,000 trees per day. Paul wants to check to see that the work is going well and is being done properly.

When he arrives at the site, Paul is not at all happy with what he sees. The laborers have begun planting, but Paul knows many of the trees cannot possibly survive, as they have been improperly planted. Some seedlings, for example, have been planted too deep in the ground, while others don't have enough soil around them. One worker has even planted some seedlings upside down! Paul doesn't lose his temper, though, as he knows it

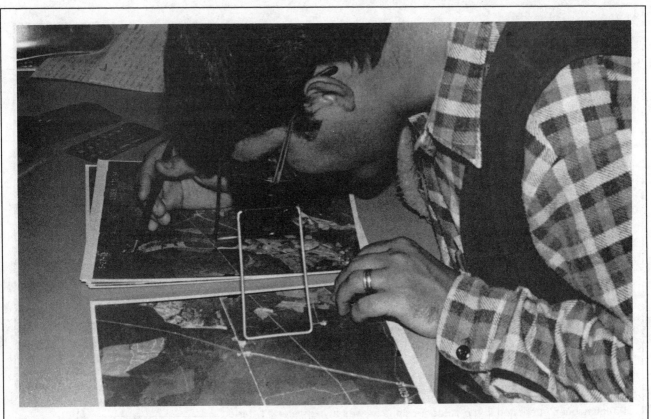

Paul can estimate the number of trees in an area by studying an aerial photograph.

would do no good and, in fact, might really alienate the workers. Instead, he patiently and clearly explains how the job should be done. He also talks a little about the business in general and answers any questions the workers have. Paul then works with the men for a couple of hours, planting trees himself and just talking with the workers. Once he is sure the job is going properly, he gets into his pickup truck for the drive back to the office.

The next item on Paul's schedule for today is a short budget meeting at his office. During the meeting, Paul and his supervisory employees discuss how much money can be spent on the various timber operations under his control. This requires some difficult decisions since there is only a certain amount of money available to divide among a number of forestry operations. Should they spend operating money to purchase some new fire-fighting equipment, or would the money be better spent on additional fertilizer for the growing trees?

After the budget meeting, Paul speaks individually with a few of the people around the office before going into his office to do paperwork for about an hour. During this time, he makes notes on some of the items discussed in the budget meeting and also works for a while on the map of the area he helped cruise this morning.

Then Paul decides to call it a day and gets in his pickup to drive home. On the way home, however, he receives a call over his two-way radio about a complaint from Jan Wiley, who owns land nearby. Apparently, the heavy equipment of one of the company loggers is tearing up a road on her land. The farm is nearby, so Paul decides to stop by and speak with Ms. Wiley. After visiting with her and looking at the damage to the road, Paul promises to get the road fixed. This calms Ms. Wiley, and Paul finally goes home.

But his day is not quite over. After supper tonight, Paul is scheduled to speak to a high school science club on forestry and the economic and environmental roles of his company. This is a part of his job that Paul really enjoys. In fact, he has even developed a slide show to help make his talks more interesting and meaningful to the students.

Exploring

Foresters must be well organized and able to set priorities.

- Are you able to plan your time efficiently?
- Do you keep lists of things to do?
- Do you find yourself able both to finish your homework and have time left for recreation?
- Do you keep a diary?

- Do you have trouble deciding between different things to do?
- Do you take part in extracurricular activities at your school?

Foresters must be patient to see the end results of their work.

- Do you enjoy long-term projects, such as gardening?
- Do you ever think about or plan what you will be doing 5 years from now?
- Can you save your money for something you want?

Foresters often must work with other people. There's a lot more to the job than just being out in the woods.

- Do you like to speak in front of your class?
- Do you enjoy working with other people on class projects?
- Do you join organizations and take an active part in them?
- Do you like to help organize activities such as trips, parties, sports events, picnics, and dances?

Foresters must have a genuine love of the outdoors and respect for the environment.

- Do you enjoy outdoor activities such as camping, fishing, hunting, gardening, and hiking?
- Does it bother you when you see a polluted river?
- Do you ever try to think of ways to make the river clean again?
- Do you throw your trash in the trash can?

Job Facts

There isn't room in this book for a story about every agriculture, forestry, and fishery occupation. However, you'll find some important facts about 18 of these occupations in the following section. You can find additional information about some of them in the Department of Labor's *Occupational Outlook Handbook*, which should be available in your school or public library.

Occupation	Nature and Places of Work	Training and Qualifications	Other Information

AGRICULTURAL PRODUCTION OCCUPATIONS

Farmers	Farmers plan, till, plant, fertilize, cultivate, and harvest crops. Those who raise livestock must feed and care for their animals, and keep barns, pens, milking parlors, and other farm buildings clean. The size of the farm determines how many of these tasks farmers do themselves. On most farms, the farmer does the work with the help of one or two family members or hired hands. Large farms, however, have 100 employees or more.	Experience gained growing up on a farm is very important. A college degree in agriculture is important, too. It is almost essential for people who haven't grown up on a farm. Most colleges of agriculture offer programs in dairy science, crop science, agricultural economics, horticulture, and animal science. Physical stamina and strength are important. Initiative, resourcefulness, and a sense of responsibility are essential. High school courses in mathematics, accounting, shop, and science are helpful, as are courses in vocational agriculture.	Most farmers own or rent the land they farm. Farmers are usually their own bosses. However, land and equipment costs are very high, and many young farmers start out as hired hands or tenant farmers.

Agriculture, Forestry, and Fishery Occupations

Occupation	Nature and Places of Work	Training and Qualifications	Other Information
Farm Managers	These workers perform much of the same duties as farmers. They usually work for others, however, unlike farmers, who are generally self-employed. Farm managers usually work on large farms or for corporations engaged in agribusiness.	A farm background is helpful, and a college degree in agriculture is important. Farm managers should be good at planning work and supervising people. High school courses in math, accounting, shop, and science are helpful, as are courses in vocational agriculture.	Beginning farmers who cannot afford to purchase their own land, buildings, and equipment may find opportunities in this field. Farm managers who have extensive training have an advantage over other workers due to an increase in the average size of farms and the complexity of farming and agricultural technology.
Farm Laborers	Farm laborers, also known as farm hands, help do all kinds of work. They may, for example, operate farm equipment, feed and care for livestock, and help in harvesting crops. Job duties usually vary according to season and type of farm products. Most laborers are employed on the larger farms.	Farm laborers should be in excellent physical condition. Stamina and strength are important since they must often work long days on their feet or stooped over under the hot sun and may have to carry heavy objects such as bales of hay. High school courses in vocational agriculture are helpful.	A job as a farm laborer is a good way of gaining farm experience. Some of these workers are members of unions.
Farm Labor Supervisors	These workers oversee farm laborers and are responsible for seeing that assigned tasks are done properly and on time. They coordinate work activities, such as planting, cultivating, and harvesting. They schedule the work of crews and may hire additional hands, especially during harvesting season. They work under the general direction of farmers or farm managers.	A sense of responsibility and the ability to direct and work well with others are essential. A farm background is an asset. High school courses in vocational agriculture are helpful.	Most jobs are on large farms that employ farm laborers.

AGRICULTURE SUPPORT OCCUPATIONS

Occupation	Nature and Places of Work	Training and Qualifications	Other Information
Cooperative Extensive Service Workers	These workers conduct educational programs for rural residents. They give farmers technical advice, help farm families learn about home economics and home management, organize activities for youth, and help community leaders plan economic development. Extension workers usually specialize. They may deal primarily with farmers, with community leaders or with youth.	Extension workers must have at least a bachelor's degree in their subject field. They often receive additional training on the job. They should like working with people and have a genuine desire to help them. A farm background is almost a requirement for agricultural extension workers. High school courses in English, public speaking, science, and math are helpful, as are courses in vocational agriculture.	Most extension service offices are located in small towns. People who are good at teaching and getting ideas across, and who wish to live outside the city, may find extension work the ideal career.

Exploring Careers

Occupation	Nature and Places of Work	Training and Qualifications	Other Information
Soil Conservationists	These workers provide technical assistance to farmers, ranchers, and others concerned with the conservation of soil and water. They help develop programs that make the most productive use of the land without damaging it. Most work for the Federal Government. Others work for State and local governments or teach at colleges and universities. Some work for rural banks that make loans for agricultural lands and for lumber and paper companies that have large holdings of forested land.	Only a few colleges and universities offer a degree in soil conservation, and most soil conservationists have college degrees in agronomy. High school courses in math, science, English, and public speaking are helpful. They should be able to get along easily with others and get their ideas across, since their job is one of educating farmers and ranchers about sound conservation practices.	Soil conservationists do most of their work in the field.
Soil Scientists	These workers study the characteristics of soils to help us use our soil resources wisely. Some study the chemical and biological properties of soils to determine their uses in farming. Most, however, prepare maps showing different kinds of soils that are used by builders, land developers, and planners. More than half work for the Soil Conservation Service of the U.S. Department of Agriculture.	A bachelor's degree with a major in soil science or a closely related field, such as agronomy or agriculture, is the minimum requirement.	Soil scientists generally spend much of their time doing field work, which requires travel.
Range Managers	Range managers manage, improve, and protect range resources to maximize their use without causing damage to the environment. They may, for example, determine the number of animals that can be grazed on a given area of range. The majority work for the Federal Government. State game and fish departments also employ range managers, and private industry is hiring increasing numbers. Range managers also work in such closely related fields as wildlife and watershed management, forest management, and recreation.	A bachelor's degree in range management, range science, or a closely related field, such as agronomy or forestry, is the usual minimum educational requirement. Besides having a love for the outdoors, range managers should be able to speak and write effectively and work with others. High school courses in biology, chemistry, physics, and mathematics are helpful.	These workers also are known as range scientists, range ecologists, or range conservationists. Range managers may spend considerable time away from home working outdoors in remote parts of the range.

Agriculture, Forestry, and Fishery Occupations

Occupation	Nature and Places of Work	Training and Qualifications	Other Information
Agricultural Engineers	These workers are concerned with improving efficiency in agriculture. To do this, they design machinery and equipment and develop new methods used in the production, processing, and distribution of food and other agricultural products. Most work for manufacturers of farm equipment, electric utility companies, and distributors of farm equipment and supplies. Many do farm consulting work independently or for consulting firms. Others work for the U.S. Department of Agriculture, for colleges and universities, and for State and local government agencies.	A bachelor's degree in engineering is required for most beginning jobs. Some engineering jobs are filled by people trained in the appropriate natural science or in mathematics. Graduate study is increasingly important for advancement. Engineers should be able to work as part of a team and should have creativity, an analytical mind, and an ability to deal with details. They should be able to express their ideas well orally and in writing. High school courses in mathematics, physics, chemistry, and English are helpful.	Agricultural engineers may work in research and development, production, sales, or management.
Food Scientists	Most of these workers do research on the chemical, physical, and biological nature of various foods. They then apply this knowledge to come up with new food products, improved processing and packaging techniques, and better ways of storing an adequate, wholesome, and economical food supply. Others work in quality control in laboratories or in production areas of food processing plants. Food scientists work in all sectors of the food industry and in every State. Some do research for Federal agencies, such as the Food and Drug Administration. A few work for private consulting firms or agencies, such as the United Nations. Others teach or do research in colleges and universities.	A bachelor's degree in food science, biology, or chemistry is the minimum requirement for beginning positions. Many jobs, especially teaching and research, require a graduate degree. Food scientists with a bachelor's degree might start work as quality assurance chemists or as assistant production managers. After gaining experience, they can advance to more responsible management jobs. A food scientist might also begin as a junior food chemist in a research and development laboratory of a food company and be promoted to section head or another research management position. People who have master's degrees may begin as senior food chemists in a research and development laboratory. Those who have doctor's degrees usually begin their careers doing basic research or teaching. High school courses in biology, chemistry, physics, mathematics, home economics, and English are helpful.	Food scientists work with different products, depending upon the part of the country where they are employed. In Maine and Idaho, for example, they work with potato processing; in the Midwest, with cereal products and meat-packing; and in Florida and California, with citrus fruits and vegetables.

Exploring Careers

Occupation	Nature and Places of Work	Training and Qualifications	Other Information
Farm Equipment Mechanics	These workers maintain and repair the wide variety of agricultural equipment used in modern agriculture. Most work in service departments of farm equipment dealers. Others work in independent repair shops, in shops on large farms, and for wholesalers and manufacturers.	Most are hired as helpers and learn the trade on the job. Employers prefer applicants who have an aptitude for mechanical work. A farm background is an advantage. High school or vocational school courses in repairing diesel or gasoline engines, blueprint reading, the maintenance and repair of hydraulics, and welding are helpful, as are basic math and science courses.	Mechanics often have to travel miles to repair equipment in the field, especially during busy harvest and planting times.
Buyers and Shippers, Farm Products	These workers perform a variety of duties, depending on the type of commodity they deal in. Most buy commodities from producers and then sell and ship them to retail or wholesale outlets. Many buyers work for themselves. Others work for supermarket chains and other large purchasers of farm products.	A farm background is helpful since buyers are responsible for the quality of the products they deal in. They also should possess many of the traits of successful sales workers, such as aggressiveness and the ability to deal with people. Some States require that buyers be licensed.	The job provides numerous opportunities for travel, working outdoors, and dealing with other people.
Veterinarians	Veterinarians deal with diseases and injuries among animals. They perform surgery and prescribe and administer drugs, medicines, and vaccines. Some inspect foods as part of public health programs, teach, or do research. Most veterinarians are in private practice. The type of practice varies according to the geographic setting. Veterinarians in rural areas mainly treat farm animals; those in small towns usually engage in general practice; those in cities and suburban areas often limit their practice to pets. Some work for government health agencies, colleges of veterinary medicine, research laboratories, large livestock farms, animal food companies, and pharmaceutical firms.	It takes many years of schooling to become a veterinarian. To qualify for the required license, candidates usually must complete at least 2 years of college (although most complete more) and 4 years in a college of veterinary medicine and pass a State Board examination. Positions in research and teaching often require an additional master's or Ph. D. degree. Some States issue licenses to veterinarians already licensed by another State without further examination. High school students interested in becoming veterinarians should take as many science courses as possible.	Most veterinarians begin as employees or partners in established practices. The job may involve long and irregular hours, traveling and outdoor work, and danger of injury, disease, or infection. Due to overcrowding in veterinary schools, acceptance to these programs is highly competitive. Serious applicants usually need excellent academic records and a good score on the Veterinary Aptitude Test, Medical College Admission Test, or Graduate Record Exam. Experience in part-time or summer jobs working with animals is advantageous.

Agriculture, Forestry, and Fishery Occupations

Occupation	Nature and Places of Work	Training and Qualifications	Other Information

FORESTRY OCCUPATIONS

Occupation	Nature and Places of Work	Training and Qualifications	Other Information
Foresters	Foresters manage, develop, and protect forest resources, including timber, water, wildlife, forage, and recreational areas. They plan and supervise the cutting and planting of trees and have other duties ranging from wildlife protection and watershed management to the development and supervision of camps, parks, and grazing lands. Not quite half work in private industry. About one-fourth work for the Federal Government, primarily in the Forest Service. The remainder work for State and local governments, colleges and universities, or consulting firms.	A bachelor's degree with a major in forestry is the minimum requirement. Advanced degrees, however, are becoming increasingly important. Foresters must enjoy working outdoors, be able to work well with people, express themselves clearly, and be willing to move to remote places. High school courses in English, public speaking, math, and science are helpful.	Foresters often specialize in one area of work, such as timber management, outdoor recreation, or forest economics.
Forestry Technicians	These workers help foresters care for and manage forest lands and their resources. They may help estimate timber production for a certain area; inspect trees for disease and other problems; help prevent and control fires; and maintain forest areas for hunting, camping, and other activities. About half work in private industry, mainly for logging, lumber, and paper companies. Federal and State governments employ the rest, with the Forest Service employing the majority.	Enthusiasm for outdoor work, physical stamina, and the ability to work without direct supervision are essential. Formal training after high school is becoming increasingly important, although some people get jobs based on work experience on firefighting crews, in tree nurseries, or in park and recreation work. One and two-year programs in forestry technology are offered by technical institutes, community and junior colleges, and universities. High school courses in English, math, and science are helpful.	Opportunities for summer and part-time work are good. Working summers provides experience that can later help in getting a job. Forestry technicians spend considerable time outdoors in all kinds of weather, sometimes in remote areas. They work many extra hours in emergencies, such as fighting fires and controlling floods.
Loggers	These workers harvest trees. Their specific job titles usually indicate the part of the harvesting process with which they are involved. *Fallers*, for example, use power saws to cut down large trees. As soon as the tree is down, *buckers* saw the limbs off and cut the trunks into logs. *Choker setters* then attach steel cables (chokers) to the logs which are then skidded out of the woods by *logging-tractor operators*. A *rigging slinger* supervises and assists choker setters and tractor drivers.	Most loggers get their first jobs without previous training. Entry level jobs usually can be learned in a few weeks by observing and helping experienced workers. Because the jobs involve some heavy labor, loggers should be in good physical condition and have stamina and agility. Because of the dangers involved in the work, loggers should be alert and well coordinated. Loggers usually start by helping choker setters or buckers. As they become more experienced, they may advance to more highly skilled jobs as vacancies occur.	Loggers often must do their jobs under unpleasant working conditions. Most jobs are outdoors and the weather can be very hot and humid or extremely cold. The forest may be very wet and muddy, with many annoying insects during the summer. Sometimes, working time and pay may be lost because of bad weather. Also, the work is more hazardous than most jobs. For many persons, however, the opportunity to work and live in forest regions, away from crowded cities, more than offsets these disadvantages. Many loggers are members of unions.

Exploring Careers

Occupation	Nature and Places of Work	Training and Qualifications	Other Information
FISHERY OCCUPATIONS			
Fishers	These workers harvest fish, shell-fish, and other aquatic animal life using a variety of methods. Usually, the methods depend on where they are fishing and the type of fish they are trying to catch. Tuna fishers on the West Coast, for example, may use huge nets that encircle an entire school of tuna fish, while lobster fishers in Maine use wooden traps to catch their quarry.	Commercial fishing is not easy work. Fishers should be willing to work long hours and should be in good physical condition. Good eyesight is also essential for fishers involved with operating fishing vessels. High school courses in mathematics, chemistry, and physics are helpful.	Many fishers must spend considerable time at sea. Earnings fluctuate greatly in this field, since they often depend on the number and type of fish caught.
Fish Farmers	These workers, also called fish culturists, raise fish for stocking streams and for the live-bait industry. They also raise fish for food. They work mainly in fish hatcheries and are responsible for providing a suitable environment for the type of fish being raised. To do this, they adjust the volume, depth, velocity, and temperature of the water. They also plan feeding programs and check fish for signs of disease. They also may make arrangements with buyers for the sale of the fish they raise.	These workers usually need a minimum of 4 years in college leading to the bachelor's degree in an aquatic biology curriculum. Experience gained working part time or summers in a fish hatchery is also useful. High school courses in physics, chemistry, biology, English, communications, and mathematics are helpful.	Aquaculture is an area offering increasing opportunities for employment with private enterprises.

Acknowledgements

This edition of *Exploring Careers* is a revision of a book originally developed by the U.S. Department of Labor. That project was conducted by the Bureau's Division of Occupational Outlook under the supervision of Russell B. Flanders and Neal Rosenthal.

Exploring Careers was prepared in the Bureau's Division of Occupational Outlook under the supervision of Russell B. Flanders and Neal H. Rosenthal. Max L. Carey provided general direction. Anne Kahl supervised the planning and preparation of the publication. Members of the Division's staff who contributed sections were Lisa S. Dillich, David B. Herst, H. Philip Howard, Chester Curtis Levine, Thomas Nardone, Debra E. Rothstein, and Kathy Wilson. Gloria D. Blue, Brenda Marshall, and Beverly A. Williams assisted.

The Bureau interviewed and photographed many workers, teachers, counselors and students in preparation of the original work and each contributed their ideas and support.

Although much of the content is based on actual interviews with workers, the occupational narratives are largely fictitious. Their real names and identities have not been used.

Photograph Credits

Original Edition

Many of the photographs that appear in the Bureau's original work have been replaced in the revision, but some of the original photographs remain. The origins of these photographs can not be easily determined so the photograph credits, as they appeared in the Bureau's original work, is included here:

Photography for the original edition of *Exploring Careers* was directed by Max L. Carey of the Bureau of Labor Statistics, Division of Occupational Outlook. Members of the Division's staff who assisted with obtaining and editing photographs were Anne Kahl, Kathy Wilson, Chester Curtis Levine, and Gloria D. Blue. Contributing photographers were Al Whitley of Whitley Associates, and Harrison E. Allen, Robert Donaldson, and Fleming P. Rose of the U.S. Department of Labor, Division of Graphic Services. The Bureau gratefully acknowledges the cooperation of the many government and private sources that either contributed photographs or made their facilities available to photographers. Depiction of company or trade names in no way constitutes endorsement by the Department of Labor. Some photographs may not be free of every possible safety or health hazard.

Government Sources
Federal. Armed Forces Radiobiology Institute; Board of Governors of the Federal Reserve System; Bureau of Prisons; Department of Agriculture; Department of Health Education and Welfare; Department of the Interior; Federal Aviation Administration; Government Printing Office; National Aeronautics and Space Administration; National Institute of Mental Health; National Park Service; Smithsonian Institution; Tennessee Valley Authority; and U.S. Postal Service.

State and local. City of San Antonio; City of San Diego; District of Columbia—Department of Human Resources, Police Department; Fairfax County (Va.)—Public Schools, Public Libraries; Maryland National Capital Park and Planning Commission; Montgomery County Public Schools (Md.); University of Texas Health Science Center at San Antonio; and Washington Metropolitan Area Transit Authority.

Private Sources
Individuals. Robert Devlin; Robert Miller; The Honorable Eligio de la Garza; The Honorable Henry B. Gonzalez; The Honorable Daniel K. Inouye; and David Weitzer.

Membership groups. Air Transportation Association of America; American Iron and Steel Institute; American Petroleum Institute; Associated General Contractors of America; Association of American Railroads; Chamber of Commerce of the U.S.A.; International Association of Machinists and Aerospace Workers; Motor Vehicle Manufacturers Association of the U.S., Inc.; National Education Association; and United Brotherhood of Carpenters and Joiners of America.

Industry and business. Allen-Mitchell and Co.; American Telephone and Telegraph Co.; Arlington Hobby Crafters; Babcock and Wilcox Co.; Badger America Inc.; The Big Cheese; Blake Construction Co; Bob Peck Chevrolet; Carl T. Jones Associates; Chase Manhattan Bank; Chessie System; Cycles Inc.; Del Mercado Shell Service Center; Everhart Jewelers; General Truck Sales; The Hecht Co.; Hyatt Regency of Washington; Heritage

Acknowledgements

Exxon Sevicenter; International Business Machines Corp.; Mayflower Hotel; Merrill Lynch Pierce Fenner and Smith, Inc.; Navy Marshall and Gordon; Nike of Georgetown; Riggs National Bank; Southeast Auto Supply; State Farm Insurance Companies; Texaco Inc.; WGMS Broadcasting Co.; Westinghouse Electric Corp.; and Westvaco Corp.

Publications. Arlington News; Co-ed Magazine; Law Enforcement Communications; The New Prince George's Post, and *The Washington Post.*

Other. Alexandria Archaeology Research Center (Va.); American National Red Cross; Catholic Charities of the Archdiocese of Washington; Floger Shakespeare Library; Forsyth County Heart Association (N.C.); George Washington University Hospital; Model Cities Senior Center (D.C.); St. Columba's Episcopal Church (D.C.); St. Thomas Apostle Catholic Church (D.C.); United Way of America; Visiting Nurse Association of Washington, D.C.; and Washington Hospital Center (D.C.).

Revised Edition

Private Sources

Individuals. Tom Abeel, Michael R. Adams, Jack Barkley, Kim A. Barnett, Don Baum, Carol Black, Georgia Brandlein, Robin R. Brown, Dave Collar, John Davis, Robert Davis, Fred Douglass, Thomas R. Draper, Gary W. Gabbard, Eddie C. Hall, William H. Hunt, Anthony W. Inman, Debra Knuteson, Amber P. Love, Eric L. Mahone, Betsy Merrill, Mark A. Paschal, Karen Rau, Bert I. Reader, Pamela J. Reed, Julie Roney, Barbart Stoots, Sidney Taylor, Matt Thrine, Vicki E. Vitatoe, Joyce Wade, Don White, Jil Wilkins, Sally Williams, Judy Yancey.

Industry and business. Bash's Seed Store; D. Everett Alan Construction Management, Inc.; Ermco Electrical Contractors & Engineers; The Hilton Hotel; *The Indianapolis Recorder,* Jack's Barber Shop; Jack's Vending; McCarter-Paschal Enterprises Inc.; NACLO; Ohio Valley Contractors; Printing Resources; Ray & Schumaker Tool & Engineering; The Reef.; Thomson McKinnon Securities, Inc.

JIST Order Form

Please copy this form if you need more lines for your order.

Purchase Order #: _____

Billing Information
Organization Name: _____
Accounting Contact: _____
Street Address: _____
_____
_____
City, State, Zip: _____
Phone Number: ( ) _____

Phone: 1-800-547-8872
1-800-JIST-USA
Fax: 1-800-547-8329

Shipping Information (if different from above)
Organization Name: _____
Contact: _____
Street Address: (we canNOT ship to P.O. boxes) _____
_____
_____
City, State, Zip: _____
Phone Number: ( ) _____

Credit Card Purchases: VISA____ MC____ AMEX____
Card Number: _____
Exp. Date: _____
Name as on Card: _____
Signature: _____

Quantity	Product Code	Product Title	Unit Price	Total
			Subtotal	
			+Sales Tax _Indiana Residents add 5% Sales Tax._	
			+Shipping / Handling _Add $3.00 for the first item and an additional $.50 for each item thereafter._	
			TOTAL	

JIST Works, Inc.
720 North Park Avenue
Indianapolis, IN 46202

JIST thanks you for your order!